# AMNESTY IN THE AGE OF HUMAN RIGHTS ACCOUNTABILITY

This edited volume brings together well-established and emerging scholars of transitional justice to discuss the persistence of amnesty in the age of human rights accountability. The volume attempts to reframe debates, moving beyond the limited approaches of truth versus justice or stability versus accountability in which many of these issues have been cast in the existing scholarship. The theoretical and empirical contributions in this edited book offer new ways of understanding and tackling the enduring persistence of amnesty in the age of accountability. Authors use social movement, ideational, legal, path-dependent, qualitative case study, statistical, and cross-national approaches in their chapters. In addition to cross-national studies, the volume encompasses eleven country cases of amnesty for past human rights violations, some well-known and others with little scholarly or advocacy exposure: Argentina, Brazil, Cambodia, El Salvador, Guatemala, Indonesia, Rwanda, South Africa, Spain, Uganda, and Uruguay. The volume goes beyond describing these case studies and considers what we learn from them in terms of overcoming impunity and promoting accountability to contribute to improvements in human rights and democracy.

Francesca Lessa is a postdoctoral research assistant at the Latin American Centre and a junior research Fellow at St. Anne's College, University of Oxford, where she works on "The Impact of Transitional Justice on Human Rights and Democracy," a project funded by the National Science Foundation (U.S.) and the Arts and Humanities Research Council (U.K.). Before joining the University of Oxford, she was a research associate for the Latin America International Affairs Programme, IDEAS Centre, at the London School of Economics, and also a visiting lecturer on transitional justice and human rights in the Faculty of Psychology, University of the Republic, Montevideo, Uruguay. Lessa is co-editor (with Vincent Druliolle) of *The Memory of State Terrorism in the Southern Cone: Argentina, Chile, and Uruguay* (2011) and (with Gabriela Fried) of *Luchas contra la impunidad: Uruguay, 1985–2011* (2011).

Leigh A. Payne is a professor of sociology and Latin America at the University of Oxford and a St. Antony's College Fellow. She also holds a senior research Fellow post in human rights at the University of Minnesota. She is the recipient of numerous research awards including one, most recently, from the National Science Foundation (U.S.) and the Arts and Humanities Research Council (U.K.) for a collaborative research project titled "The Impact of Transitional Justice on Human Rights and Democracy." Her recent publications include (with Ksenija Bilbija) *Accounting for Memory: Marketing Memory in Latin America* (2011); (with Tricia D. Olsen and Andrew G. Reiter) *Transitional Justice in Balance: Comparing Processes, Weighing Efficacy* (2010); and *Unsettling Accounts: Neither Truth nor Reconciliation in Confessions of State Violence* (2008).

# Amnesty in the Age of Human Rights Accountability

## COMPARATIVE AND INTERNATIONAL PERSPECTIVES

Edited by

**FRANCESCA LESSA**

University of Oxford

**LEIGH A. PAYNE**

University of Oxford

Arts & Humanities
Research Council

CAMBRIDGE
UNIVERSITY PRESS

CAMBRIDGE UNIVERSITY PRESS
Cambridge, New York, Melbourne, Madrid, Cape Town,
Singapore, São Paulo, Delhi, Mexico City

Cambridge University Press
32 Avenue of the Americas, New York, NY 10013-2473, USA

www.cambridge.org
Information on this title: www.cambridge.org/9781107617339

First published 2012

Printed in the United States of America

A catalog record for this publication is available from the British Library.

Library of Congress Cataloging in Publication data
Lessa, Francesca.
    Amnesty in the age of human rights accountability : comparative
and international perspectives / Francesca Lessa, Leigh A. Payne.
        p.   cm.
    Includes bibliographical references and index.
    ISBN 978-1-107-02500-4 (hardback) – ISBN 978-1-107-61733-9 (pbk.)
    1. Amnesty.   2. Human rights.   3. Liability (Law)   I. Payne, Leigh A.   II. Title.
    K5132.L47   2012
    345'.077–dc23         2012005154

ISBN 978-1-107-02500-4 Hardback
ISBN 978-1-107-61733-9 Paperback

# Contents

# Contributors

**Paulo Abrão** (PhD Law, Rio de Janeiro Pontifical Catholic University) is the Brazilian national secretary of justice and president of the Amnesty Commission. He holds a doctorate in law from the Pontifical Catholic University of Rio de Janeiro, a master's degree in law from the Universidade do Vale do Rio dos Sinos (Unisinos), and a diploma degree in human rights and democratization processes from the University of Chile. He is a faculty member at the Pontifical Catholic University of Rio Grande do Sul and a visiting professor in the Masters of Law course of the Catholic University of Brasília. He works as an advisor to the "Revealed Memories" Reference Center of the Brazilian National Archive and is also a former member of the working group that prepared the draft project for the Brazilian Truth Commission (Law 12,528/2011). Since 2009, he has worked as a judge for the International Tribunal for Restorative Justice in El Salvador. He is also a former member of the Brazilian Mission on the amnesty law at the Organization of American States and the international mission for the implementation of Cape Verde University. In 2010, he edited the book *Repressão e memória política no contexto Ibero-Brasileiro* (*Repression and Political Memory in the Ibero-Brazilian Context*, Brazilian Ministry of Justice/Coimbra University) with Boaventura de Sousa Santos, Cecília MacDowell, and Marcelo D. Torelly, and in 2011, together with Leigh A. Payne and Marcelo D. Torelly, the book *A anistia na era da responsabilização: O Brasil em perspectiva internacional e comparada* (*Amnesty in the Age of Accountability: Brazil in International and Comparative Perspective*, Brazilian Ministry of Justice). His recent work can also be found in the journal *Anistia Política e Justiça de Transição* (*Political Amnesty and Transitional Justice*) and the *Journal of the Brazilian Bar Association of Rio de Janeiro* (*Revista OABRJ*).

**Paloma Aguilar** (PhD Political Science, UNED) teaches political science at the Universidad Nacional de Educación a Distancia in Madrid. She was Tinker Professor in the political science department of the University of Wisconsin,

Madison (2001–2). She has published *Políticas de la memoria y memorias de la política* (Madrid: Alianza Editorial, 2008) and *Memory and Amnesia: The Role of the Spanish Civil War in the Transition to Democracy* (Oxford and New York: Berghan Books, 2001). She has co-edited with Alexandra Barahona de Brito and Carmen González-Enríquez the volume *The Politics of Memory: Transitional Justice in Democratizing Societies* (Oxford: Oxford University Press, 2001). She has published in journals such as *Comparative Political Studies, Politics & Society, West European Politics, South European Society & Politics, Democratization, Revista Española de Investigaciones Sociológicas, Matériaux pour l'histoire de notre temps, History and Memory, Ricerche di Storia Politica, Revista Internacional de Sociología, Claves de Razón Práctica,* and *Revista Internacional de Filosofía Política.* Her main research fields are transitions to democracy, memories of violence and repression, legacies of authoritarian regimes, transitional justice mechanisms, political violence, the duration of dictatorships, and nationalism.

**Emily Braid** (MPhil Development Studies, University of Oxford) is a research assistant at the department of sociology, University of Oxford, currently working on a project with Amnesty International and funded by the Oak Foundation titled "The Access to Justice Project: Overcoming Amnesty in the Age of Accountability." Braid is also the events manager for the Oxford Transitional Justice Research (OTJR) group and coordinates a termly seminar series focused on transitional justice and human rights issues. Braid's research interests include the relationship between formal and informal forms of truth telling in postconflict settings in Latin America, comparative studies on truth commissions and how they represent victim-survivor narratives, and the impact of amnesty on prevailing cultures of impunity in Central America.

**Patrick Burgess** (LLB, LLM, University of New South Wales) is the president of Asia Justice and Rights (AJAR). He is an Australian barrister who has served as a senior member of the Australian Refugee Tribunal, the director of human rights for two UN missions in Timor Leste, and a team leader for a number of emergency aid programs in postgenocide Rwanda, DRC, Yemen, Indonesia, and Timor Leste. Formerly, he was the Asia director for the International Center for Transitional Justice, managing transitional justice programs in Afghanistan, Nepal, the Solomon Islands, Thailand, Indonesia, Timor Leste, and Bangladesh. Relevant publications include "A New Approach to Restorative Justice: East Timor's Community Reconciliation Processes" in *Transitional Justice in the Twenty-First Century: Beyond Truth versus Justice* edited by Naomi Roht-Arriaza and Javier Mariezcurrena (Cambridge and New York: Cambridge University Press, 2006), and "Justice and Reconciliation in East Timor: The Relationship Between the Commission for Reception, Truth and Reconciliation and the Courts," *Criminal Law Forum*, 15, no.1 (2004): 135–58.

**Phil Clark** (DPhil Politics, University of Oxford, Rhodes Scholar) is a lecturer in comparative and international politics at the School of Oriental and African Studies, University of London, and was the founder and convenor of Oxford Transitional Justice Research (OTJR) at the University of Oxford between 2007 and 2011. Dr. Clark's research addresses the history and politics of the African Great Lakes, focusing on causes of and responses to mass violence. His work also explores the theory and practice of transitional justice, with particular emphasis on community-based approaches to accountability and reconciliation and the law and politics of the International Criminal Court. Dr. Clark's latest book is *The Gacaca Courts, Post-Genocide Justice and Reconciliation in Rwanda: Justice without Lawyers* (Cambridge and New York: Cambridge University Press, 2010). He is currently completing another book, *Doing Justice during Conflict: The International Criminal Court in Uganda and the Democratic Republic of Congo.* He has advised a wide range of government and nongovernmental organizations on conflict issues in Africa.

**Antje du Bois-Pedain** (Dr. Jur., Humboldt University) is a university senior lecturer in the faculty of law at the University of Cambridge; a Fellow of Magdalene College, Cambridge; and convenor of the Cambridge Transitional Justice Research Network (CTJRN). Her main research interests consist of transitional justice, criminal law, and legal theory. Her publications include *Transitional Amnesty in South Africa* (Cambridge and New York: Cambridge University Press, 2007, paperback edition 2011) and, co-edited with François du Bois, *Justice and Reconciliation in Post-Apartheid South Africa* (Cambridge and New York: Cambridge University Press, 2008).

**Par Engstrom** (DPhil International Relations, University of Oxford) is a lecturer in human rights at the Human Rights Consortium, School of Advanced Study, University of London. He teaches human rights at the Institute for the Study of the Americas and the Institute of Commonwealth Studies. He is also co-chair of the London Transitional Justice Network. His current research interests focus on regional human rights institutions both comparatively and with a particular reference to the inter-American human rights system. Further research interests include the relationship between human rights and democratization; judicialization of politics; transitional justice; the international relations of the Americas; human rights, humanitarianism, and foreign policy; theories of international relations, particularly relating to international law and institutions; and interdisciplinary approaches to the study of human rights. Recent publications include, as co-editor, *Critical Perspectives in Transitional Justice*, edited by Oxford Transitional Justice Research (Cambridge: Intersentia, 2012); "Brasil: los derechos humanos en la política exterior de una potencia emergente," edited by Ana Covarrubias and Natalia Saltalamacchia,

*Los derechos humanos y la política exterior de los países de América Latina* (México D.F.: ITAM & Editorial Porrúa, 2011); and "Human Rights: Effectiveness of International and Regional Mechanisms" in *The International Studies Encyclopedia*, edited by Robert A. Denemark (Oxford: Blackwell Publishing, 2010); and, with Andrew Hurrell, "Why the Human Rights Regime in the Americas Matters," in *Human Rights Regimes in the Americas*, edited by Monica Serrano and Ramesh Thakur (Tokyo: United Nations University Press, 2010).

**Mark Freeman** (JD, Ottawa) is an international lawyer and leading expert in the field of transitional justice. During the last fifteen years, he has worked extensively with societies in transition and has published several leading texts in the field. His most recent book is *Necessary Evils: Amnesties and the Search for Justice* (Cambridge and New York: Cambridge University Press, 2009). Currently he is directing the startup phase for a new organization called the Institute for Integrated Transitions. Previously, he served as the chief of external relations at the International Crisis Group and as the director of international affairs at the International Crisis Group.

**Francesca Lessa** (PhD International Relations, London School of Economics) is a postdoctoral research assistant at the Latin American Centre, University of Oxford, working on the project funded by the National Science Foundation (U.S.) and the Arts and Humanities Research Council (UK) titled "The Impact of Transitional Justice on Human Rights and Democracy." Dr. Lessa's research interests include questions of transitional justice in the Southern Cone, particularly Argentina and Uruguay; the policies and politics of memory of state terrorism in the Southern Cone; and the question of impunity and continuing human rights violations in Argentina and Uruguay. Dr. Lessa is co-editor with Vincent Druliolle of *The Memory of State Terrorism in the Southern Cone: Argentina, Chile, and Uruguay* (New York: Palgrave Macmillan, 2011) and with Gabriela Fried of *Luchas contra la impunidad: Uruguay, 1985–2011* (Montevideo: Trilce, 2011). Dr. Lessa is also author of "Beyond Transitional Justice: Exploring Continuities in Human Rights Abuses in Argentina between 1976 and 2010," *Journal of Human Rights Practice* 3, no.1 (2011): 25–48.

**Louise Mallinder** (PhD Law, Queen's University Belfast) is a lecturer in international law and human rights at the Transitional Justice Institute, University of Ulster, and the Institute's "Dealing with the Past" research coordinator. She previously worked as a research Fellow at Queen's University Belfast on a two-year, AHRC-funded research project titled "Beyond Legalism: Amnesties, Transition and Conflict Transformation." This was an interdisciplinary, comparative study of the impact of amnesty laws in Argentina, Bosnia-Herzegovina, South Africa, Uganda, and Uruguay, and the project team conducted fieldwork in these jurisdictions. Dr. Mallinder's research interests include amnesty laws, transitional justice, international criminal justice, international humanitarian law, international human rights law, and conflict transformation. Dr. Mallinder is the author of *Amnesty, Human Rights and Political Transitions: Bridging the Peace and Justice Divide* (Oxford: Hart Publishing, 2008), which was awarded the 2009 Hart SLSA Early Career Award and the 2009 British Society of Criminology Book Prize. She is also the author of several book chapters and articles, including "Rethinking Amnesties: Atrocity, Accountability and Impunity in Post-Conflict Societies," in *Contemporary Social Science: The Journal of the Academy of Social Science* 6, no.1 (2011): 107–28 (with Kieran McEvoy) and "Amnesties in the Pursuit of Reconciliation, Peacebuilding and Restorative Justice," in *Restorative Justice, Reconciliation and Peacebuilding*, edited by Daniel Philpott and Jennifer Llewellyn (Oxford: Oxford University Press, forthcoming).

**Juan E. Méndez** (JD, Stella Maris University) is a visiting professor of law at the American University Washington College of Law and the UN special rapporteur on torture and other cruel, inhuman, and degrading treatment or punishment since November 2010. Mr. Méndez has dedicated his legal career to the defense of human rights and has a long and distinguished record of advocacy throughout the Americas. He has been an advisor on crime prevention to the prosecutor at the International Criminal Court. He was co-chair of the Human Rights Institute of the International Bar Association and the author (with Marjorie Wentworth) of *Taking a Stand* (New York: Palgrave MacMillan, 2011). Until May 2009 he served as the president of the International Center for Transitional Justice (ICTJ) and in the summer of 2009 he was a scholar in residence at the Ford Foundation in New York. Concurrent with his duties at ICTJ, he was Kofi Annan's special advisor on the prevention of genocide (2004 to 2007). From 1996 to 1999, Mr. Méndez was the executive director of the Inter-American Institute of Human Rights in Costa Rica, and between October 1999 and May 2004 he was professor of law and the director of the Centre for Civil and Human Rights at the University of Notre Dame, Indiana. Between 2000 and 2003 he was a member of the Inter-American Commission on Human Rights of the Organization of American States and served as its president in 2002.

**Tricia D. Olsen** (PhD Political Science, University of Wisconsin, Madison) is an assistant professor of business ethics and legal studies at the University of Denver Daniels College of Business. Olsen studies and teaches about the political economy of development with a focus on business ethics, human rights, and sustainability in emerging and developing countries. Her current research focuses on the development of microfinance across countries. Dr. Olsen is also involved in a collaborative project with Leigh A. Payne and Andrew G. Reiter that explores the determinants and effects of transitional justice mechanisms. This work has been published in a co-authored book, *Transitional Justice in Balance: Comparing Processes, Weighing Efficacy* (Washington, DC: United States Institute of Peace, 2010) and in articles in

*Human Rights Quarterly, International Studies Review, Journal of Human Rights, Journal of Peace Research*, and *Taiwan Journal of Democracy*. Olsen has received support from Fulbright-Hays, NSF-AHRC, United States Institute of Peace, FLAS, the PEO Foundation, the Latin American Public Opinion Project, and Zennström Philanthropies, among others.

**Leigh A. Payne** (PhD Political Science, Yale University) is a professor of sociology and Latin America at the University of Oxford and a senior research Fellow in human rights at the University of Minnesota. Her most recent book is a co-edited volume with Ksenija Bilbija titled *Accounting for Violence: Marketing Memory in Latin America* (Durham: Duke University Press, 2011). In 2010, she co-authored, with Tricia D. Olsen and Andrew G. Reiter, *Transitional Justice in Balance: Comparing Processes, Weighing Efficacy* (Washington, DC: United States Institute of Peace, 2010), and they have published various articles related to that work in *Human Rights Quarterly, Journal of Peace Research*, and elsewhere. Prior to these projects she published *Unsettling Accounts: Neither Truth nor Reconciliation in Confessions of State Violence* (Durham: Duke University Press, 2008), which explores the politics of perpetrators' public confessional performances in Argentina, Brazil, Chile, and South Africa. She published a Spanish translation with an additional chapter on Colombia as *Testimonios perturbadores: ni verdad ni reconciliación en las confesiones de violencia de estado* (Bogotá: Universidad de los Andes, 2009, translated by Julio Paredes).

**Max Pensky** (PhD Philosophy, Boston College) is professor of philosophy and chair of the department of philosophy at Binghamton University, the State University of New York. He publishes in critical social theory, contemporary democratic theory, transitional justice, and the philosophy of international law. He has held fellowships at Johann Wolfgang Goethe University in Frankfurt, the University of East Anglia, Cornell University, and most recently the University of Oxford where he was Oliver Smithies Fellow at Balliol College and a senior visiting research Fellow at the Institute for the Study of Social Justice, Department of Politics and International Relations, from 2006 to 2007. He is the author or editor of eight books including *Globalizing Critical Theory* (Lanham: Rowman & Littlefield Publishers, 2005) and *The Ends of Solidarity: Discourse Theory in Ethics and Politics* (Albany: State University of New York Press, 2008). His essay "Amnesty on Trial: Impunity, Accountability, and the Norms of International Law" appeared in *Ethics & Global Politics* 1, no.1–2 (2008).

**Gabriel Pereira** (MSc Democracy and Democratization, University College London) is a DPhil candidate in the department of politics and international relations of the University of Oxford. He is a research assistant in the department of sociology, University of Oxford, working on the project funded by the John Fell OUP Research Fund titled "Accounting for Amnesty: Justice for Past Atrocity." As a Chevening Scholar funded by the British Council, he obtained his MSc at the School of Public Policy, University College London. He was also a visiting scholar at the Social Justice Initiative of Columbia University (U.S.) and the University of Palermo (Argentina). He has worked for national and international human rights organizations, including the Center for Justice and International Law (CEJIL) and the *Asociación por los Derechos Civiles*, and was a founding member and executive director of *Abogados y Abogadas del Noroeste Argentino en Derechos Humanos y Estudios Sociales* (ANDHES) in Argentina. His publications include "Participación Política y Grupos Desaventajados" in *La Constitución Argentina del 2020* edited by Roberto Gargarella (Buenos Aires: Siglo XXI, 2011) and, co-edited with Josefina Doz Costa and Patricio Rovira, *Transparencia y Accountability en los Poderes Judiciales Provinciales* (Tucumán: El Graduado, 2007).

**Andrew G. Reiter** (PhD Political Science, University of Wisconsin, Madison) is an assistant professor of politics at Mount Holyoke College in South Hadley, Massachusetts. His research interests include transitional justice, democratization, violence, and civil war. In particular, he is interested in the challenges societies face as they make the difficult transition from periods of war and violence to peace. Reiter is a cofounder of the Transitional Justice Data Base Project, which has developed a comprehensive, global dataset of trials, truth commissions, amnesties, reparations, and lustration programs used by states over the past four decades to confront past human rights violations. The project has received funding from the National Science Foundation and the United States Institute of Peace, among others. As part of the project, he has co-authored a book with Tricia D. Olsen and Leigh A. Payne, titled *Transitional Justice in Balance: Comparing Processes, Weighing Efficacy* (Washington, DC: United States Institute of Peace Press, 2010), as well as numerous articles and book chapters in such venues as *Human Rights Quarterly* and *Journal of Peace Research*.

**Naomi Roht-Arriaza** (JD University of California, Boalt Hall) is a professor of law at the University of California, Hastings College of the Law. Her research interests include accountability of states and private entities for human rights violations, transitional or postconflict justice, universal jurisdiction, indigenous rights, and the human rights implications of climate change. She is the author of *The Pinochet Effect: Transnational Justice in the Age of Human Rights* (University of Pennsylvania Press, 2005); *Transitional Justice in the Twenty-First Century: Beyond Truth versus Justice* with Javier Mariezcurrena (Cambridge and New York: Cambridge University Press, 2006); and a casebook with Mary Ellen O'Connell and Richard Scott, *The International Legal System*, Sixth Edition (New York: Foundation Press, 2010). She has also written dozens of articles on these and related topics. She is a member of the legal team working on the Guatemala genocide case before the Spanish courts.

She was a senior advisor to the U.S. Agency for International Development during 2011 and a senior Fulbright scholar in Botswana in 2012.

**Kathryn Sikkink** (PhD Political Science, Columbia University) is a Regents professor and the McKnight Presidential Chair in Political Science at the University of Minnesota. Her publications include *Mixed Signals: U.S. Human Rights Policy and Latin America* (Ithaca and London: Cornell University Press, 2004); with Margaret Keck, *Activists Beyond Borders: Advocacy Networks in International Politics* (Ithaca and London: Cornell University Press, 1998, awarded the Grawemeyer Award for Ideas for Improving World Order and the ISA Chadwick Alger Award for Best Book in the area of International Organizations); and *The Power of Human Rights: International Norms and Domestic Change*, co-edited with Thomas Risse and Stephen Ropp (Cambridge and New York: Cambridge University Press, 1999). Her most recent book is *The Justice Cascade: How Human Rights Prosecutions Are Changing World Politics* (New York: W.W. Norton, 2011). Sikkink has been a Fulbright scholar in Argentina and a Guggenheim Fellow. She is a Fellow of the Council on Foreign Relations and the American Association for Arts and Sciences and a member of the editorial boards of *International Studies Quarterly* and *International Organization*.

**Ronald C. Slye** (JD, Yale Law School) is currently a commissioner with the Kenyan Truth, Justice and Reconciliation Commission. He is a professor of law at the Seattle University School of Law, where he teaches in the areas of international law, human rights, and international criminal law. He is also an honorary professor at the University of the Witwatersrand School of Law. He is the author or co-author of numerous articles and books in the areas of international human rights law, international criminal law, transitional justice, poverty law, and environmental law. He is co-author with Beth van Schaack of the casebook *International Criminal Law and Its Enforcement, Cases and Materials*, Second Edition (New York: Foundation Press, 2010). His current research interests center on international criminal law and transitional justice, including a detailed study of the South African amnesty process.

**Marcelo D. Torelly** (MSc Law, Brasília University) is the general coordinator of historical memory at the Brazilian Ministry of Justice/Amnesty Commission and teaches theory of law at the Brasília Catholic University Law School. He is a PhD candidate and holds a master's degree in law, state, and constitution from the University of Brasília; diplomas in human rights and democratization processes from the University of Chile and human rights and development from the Pablo de Olavide University (Spain); and a bachelor's degree in law from the Pontifical Catholic University of Rio Grande do Sul. He is currently the national director of the joint program between the Brazilian Ministry of Justice and the United Nations

Development Program for international exchange on transitional justice issues and the editor of the journal *Revista Anistia Política e Justiça de Transição (Political Amnesty and Transitional Justice)*. He is a former member of the working group that proposed the new Brazilian legislation on archives and access to information (Law 12,527/2011) and integrated several international missions from the Brazilian federal government to countries such as Argentina, Colombia, France, Portugal, Spain, the United Kingdom, and Venezuela. In 2010, he edited the book *Repressão e memória política no contexto Ibero-Brasileiro (Repression and Political Memory in the Ibero-Brazilian Context)* with Boaventura de Sousa Santos, Paulo Abrão, and Cecília MacDowell (Brazilian Ministry of Justice/Coimbra University, 2010) and in 2011, together with Leigh A. Payne and Paulo Abrão, the book *A anistia na era da responsabilização: O Brasil em perspectiva internacional e comparada (Amnesty in the Age of Accountability: Brazil in International and Comparative Perspective)* (Brazilian Ministry of Justice, 2011). His recent work can also be found in the journal *Anistia Política e Justiça de Transição (Political Amnesty and Transitional Justice)*, the *Journal of the Brazilian Bar Association of Rio de Janeiro (Revista OABRJ)*, and the *Revista Sistema Penal & Violência (Penal System and Violence)*.

# Foreword

## Juan E. Méndez

I am immensely grateful for the opportunity the editors of this book have given me to contribute this foreword. More than that, I am proud to be part of an effort to bring about an honest and thoughtful conversation about peace, justice, and reconciliation, a conversation that in the past has been marked by useless recrimination and accusation. Just as peace should not be pursued at the cost of forcing victims to abandon all hope of seeing justice done, human rights activists also have the responsibility to reckon with the fact that war itself is the ultimate violation of human dignity and the occasion for more and more tragic abuses. This book elevates the discussion well above where it has been until now.

The body of international law on amnesties has evolved significantly over the last quarter century. First, the era of complete and absolute deference to the state as it reckons with how to deal with serious human rights violations and international crimes has come to a close.[1] Second, a state is no longer entitled to exercise absolute discretion regarding the manner in which it chooses to address the legacies of its past when these amount to grave human rights violations and international crimes.[2] Newly formed democratic governments looking to implement clemency and reconciliation measures can no longer do so through amnesties that prevent victims from enjoying certain fundamental rights or that further a state of impunity.[3] Instead, in recent decades, countries have implemented transitional justice mechanisms to address massive and systematic violations of fundamental rights, including criminal prosecutions, truth commissions, reparations programs, and institutional reform.[4]

---

[1] Garth Meintjes and Juan E. Méndez, "Reconciling Amnesties with Universal Jurisdiction," *International Law FORUM du Droit International* 2 (2000): 76.

[2] Ibid., 76.

[3] Ibid.

[4] "What Is Transitional Justice?" The International Center for Transitional Justice, accessed September 11, 2011, http://ictj.org/about/transitional-justice.

The author wishes to acknowledge the invaluable research and writing support of Ms. Catherine Cone.

These innovative state practices amount to a paradigmatic shift in the way societies reckon with legacies of human rights violations.

The evolution of international law and policy on amnesties is grounded in recent history; it shows that blanket amnesties exempting those responsible for atrocious crimes are not a necessary condition for achieving peace.[5] If experience has taught the international community a valuable lesson, it is that these types of amnesties often fail to secure peace and at times embolden their beneficiaries to commit further crimes.[6] Moreover, international experience and international human rights law have served to reinforce each other in supporting the thesis that amnesty is not a necessary prerequisite for peace.[7] Countries have repeatedly relied on international human rights principles in choosing to restore justice rather than to leave unsettled accounts following the commission of atrocities in their territories.[8] At the same time, the varied country approaches seeking to meet the demands of truth and justice further enriched and developed the practices and experiences of international human rights law.[9] Perhaps the most significant change in many schools of thought regarding amnesties is that when properly pursued, justice and accountability measures can help ensure a sustainable peace.

Amnesties are now regulated by a substantial body of international law that sets limits on their permissible scope.[10] "Most importantly, amnesties that prevent the prosecution of individuals who may be legally responsible for war crimes, genocide, crimes against humanity and other gross violations of human rights are inconsistent with States' obligations under various sources of international law as well as with United Nations policy."[11] Amnesties are now deemed contrary to international law when they restrict the rights of victims of violations of human rights or of war crimes to an effective remedy and reparations, and the right of victims and society to know the truth about the circumstances surrounding such abuses.[12]

The sweeping changes in the law applicable to amnesties are due largely in part to the principles of accountability that have emerged in international human rights law. In the new "age of accountability," explained quite adeptly by Kathryn Sikkink in her chapter in this book, international human rights law recognized as an

---

[5] United Nations Office of the High Commissioner for Human Rights (OHCHR), *Rule-of-Law Tools for Post-Conflict States, Amnesties*, United Nations, HR/PUB/09/1 (New York and Geneva: OHCHR, 2009), accessed September 8, 2011, http://www.ohchr.org/Documents/Publications/Amnesties_en.pdf.

[6] Ibid.

[7] Meintjes and Méndez, "Reconciling Amnesties with Universal Jurisdiction," 77.

[8] OHCHR, *Rule-of-Law Tools.*

[9] Ibid.

[10] Ibid.

[11] Ibid.

[12] Ibid.

international norm what was once viewed only as an emerging principle – namely, that states have an affirmative duty to investigate and punish perpetrators.[13] The state's obligation to investigate, prosecute, and punish arises in cases of grave breaches of humanitarian law or human rights violations and following the commission of international crimes against a narrow class of fundamental rights.[14] International crimes include war crimes, crimes against humanity, enforced disappearances, genocide, and torture.[15] Within the transitional justice framework, these state obligations coexist with even more specific duties to prosecute and punish international crimes; uncover the truth and disclose any information to families and society pertaining to these crimes; provide redress and reparations to victims, including guarantees of nonrepetition; and implement comprehensive institutional reforms, which in some cases requires removing known perpetrators from their institutional ranks.[16]

As relates to grave breaches in international armed conflict, the duty of the state to investigate and prosecute was set forth early in the 1949 Geneva Conventions.[17] Two other treaties, the Convention on the Prevention and Punishment of the Crime of Genocide[18] and the Convention against Torture and Other Cruel, Inhuman or Degrading Treatment or Punishment,[19] entail additional obligations for state parties to prosecute the crimes of torture and genocide. Most recently, the 2006 International Convention on Enforced Disappearances[20] declared that states are required to criminalize enforced disappearances and to take necessary measures

---

[13] Kathryn Sikkink's chapter references the rise of international treaties providing for these state obligations, including the Convention against Torture and Other Cruel, Inhuman or Degrading Treatment or Punishment (CAT) and the Genocide Convention of 1948. Sikkink also discusses the influential role played by various international courts in interpreting and declaring what is required by states in these cases. Those findings are more thoroughly developed in Kathryn Sikkink, *The Justice Cascade: How Human Rights Prosecutions Are Changing World Politics* (New York: Norton, 2011).

[14] Meintjes and Méndez, "Reconciling Amnesties with Universal Jurisdiction," 81.

[15] Inter-American Court of Human Rights, Case of *Anzualdo Castro v. Perú*, Merits, Judgment of September 22, 2009, Ser. C, No. 202, para.59. See also Meintjes and Méndez, "Reconciling Amnesties with Universal Jurisdiction," 79–81; Antonio Cassese, *International Law* (New York: Oxford University Press, 2005), 436.

[16] Meintjes and Méndez, "Reconciling Amnesties with Universal Jurisdiction," 82.

[17] See Geneva Convention for the Amelioration of the Condition of the Wounded and Sick in Armed Forces in the Field, August 12, 1949, 75 U.N.T.S. 31, art. 49; Geneva Convention for the Amelioration of the Condition of Wounded, Sick and Shipwrecked Members of Armed Forces at Sea, August 12, 1949, 75 U.N.T.S. 85, art. 50; Geneva Convention Relative to the Treatment of Prisoners of War opened for signature, August 12, 1949, 75 U.N.T.S. 135, art. 129; Geneva Convention Relative to the Protection of Civilian Persons in Time of War, August 12, 1949, 75 U.N.T.S. 287, art. 146.

[18] Convention on the Prevention and Punishment of the Crime of Genocide, General Assembly Resolution 260 A (III), adopted December 9, 1948, 78 U.N.T.S. 277, arts. 1–3.

[19] The Convention against Torture and Other Cruel, Inhuman or Degrading Treatment or Punishment, UN Doc. A/39/51 (1984), entered into force June 26, 1987, arts. 2, 4, 6.

[20] The International Convention for the Protection of All Persons from Enforced Disappearances, December 20, 2006, UN Doc. A/RES/61/177; 14 IHRR 582 (2007), arts. 4, 7.

to extradite or prosecute – including a thorough and effective investigation of the crime – any person responsible for committing, ordering, soliciting, inducing, or participating in an enforced disappearance. A number of human rights treaties also obligate states to ensure enumerated rights set forth in these treaties and to provide an effective remedy to individuals whose rights were violated under the treaty in question.[21]

The international community universally recognizes that states fail to meet their obligations to investigate, prosecute, and punish when they grant certain types of amnesties. For this reason, blanket amnesties, unconditional amnesties that have the effect of precluding investigation of international crimes, are a violation of a state's obligations under international law.[22] In *Gomes Lund v. Brazil*, as Paulo Abrão and Marcelo Torelly discuss in their chapter on Brazil in this volume, the Inter-American Court of Human Rights (IACtHR) defined the state's obligations in cases of enforced disappearances as a duty to investigate without delay and to do so in a serious, impartial, and effective manner.[23] To be effective, the "[S]tate must establish an appropriate normative framework to develop the investigation … [It] must guarantee that no normative or other type of obstacles prevent the investigation of said acts…."[24] Because Brazil had applied a broad amnesty law, the Court found that the state had failed to investigate and punish serious human rights violations, ultimately preventing the next of kin of the disappeared from being heard before a judge and knowing the truth.[25] According to the Court, the state has a responsibility to remove any law or similar measure serving as a legal roadblock, including amnesty laws.[26] Otherwise, the state would effectively prevent the investigation of serious human rights violations, leading to the perpetuation of impunity, the defenselessness of victims, and the inability of the next of kin from knowing the truth.[27] The chapter by

---

[21] International Covenant on Civil and Political Rights (ICERD), General Assembly Res. 2200 A (XXI), adopted December 16, 1966, UN GAOR, 21st sess., Supp. No. 16, UN Doc. A/6316 (1967), 171; the American Convention on Human Rights, 1144 U.N.T.S. 123, entered into force July 18, 1978; the European Convention for the Protection of Human Rights and Fundamental Freedom, November 4, 1950, CETS No.: 005.

[22] See OHCHR, *Rule-of-Law Tools*, 8–9 (noting that both blanket amnesties and pseudo amnesties, laws that when enacted have the same legal effect as amnesties despite not being directly labeled amnesties, are prohibited under international law).

[23] Inter-American Court of Human Rights, *Gomes Lund v. Brazil*, Merits, Judgment of November 24, 2010, Ser. C, No. 219, 45, para. 108. See also Inter-American Court of Human Rights, *Manuel Cepeda Vargas v. Colombia*, Merits, Judgment of May 26, 2010, Ser. C, No. 213, paras. 117–19 (explaining that the duty to investigate extra-judicial execution implies determining patterns of collaborative action and all individuals who participated together with corresponding responsibilities).

[24] *Gomes Lund v. Brazil*, 45, para. 109.

[25] Ibid., 69, para. 172.

[26] Ibid., 69–70, para. 173. See also Inter-American Court of Human Rights, *Almonacid-Arellano et al. v. Chile*, Merits, Judgment of September 26, 2006, Ser. C, No. 154, 52, para.114.

[27] *Gomes Lund v. Brazil*, 69–70, para. 173.

Par Engstrom and Gabriel Pereira on Argentina and Francesca Lessa's chapter on Uruguay in this volume further discuss the impact of Inter-American Court rulings in those countries' cases.

Since states can no longer unilaterally decide that they will abdicate their roles in effectively investigating and prosecuting international crimes, other states may meet these obligations under the principle of universal jurisdiction.[28] Universal jurisdiction has gained valuable ground as a means of allowing the international community to intervene and prevent impunity for international crimes. Paloma Aguilar shows in her chapter in this volume how Spain has played a key role in advancing universal jurisdiction, even while failing to fulfill its own responsibilities to address impunity. The principle of universal jurisdiction empowers any state "to bring to trial persons accused of international crimes regardless of the place of commission of the crime, or the nationality of the author or of the victim."[29] Universal jurisdiction can be implemented in one of two ways: (1) a state can prosecute the perpetrator so long as the accused is in that state's custody; or (2) a state may prosecute the perpetrator regardless of the perpetrator's nationality, the location of the commission of the crime, or whether the state has custody over the perpetrator.[30] The interest of the international community in breaking the cycle of impunity is a recognition of the inseparability of justice and peace. This recognition is also at the heart of the creation of ad hoc war crimes tribunals for the former Yugoslavia and Rwanda and the adoption of the Rome Statute for an International Criminal Court (ICC).[31]

However, some countries stand out for a middle ground approach whereby the state chooses neither to bury its past nor to imprison all perpetrators, but makes a good faith effort to confront its past.[32] Inevitably, the effort includes truth telling and reparations but also a promise of immunity from prosecutions to those who contribute to the knowledge of the past and to reconciliation. The extent to which such middle ground complies with international standards depends largely on whether, both as conceived and as applied, measures of clemency have the effect of crystallizing impunity for international crimes.[33] It follows, therefore, that not all amnesties violate international law. The persistence of amnesties, documented cross-nationally in studies by Louise Mallinder and by Tricia Olsen, Leigh Payne, and Andrew Reiter

---

[28] See Cassese, *International Law*, 451–2.

[29] Ibid., 451.

[30] Ibid., 452.

[31] See S.C. Res. 827, para. 5, UN Doc. S/RES/827 (May 25, 1993); S.C. Res. 955, para. 6, UN Doc. S/RES/955 (Nov. 8, 1994); Rome Statute of the International Criminal Court, Preamble, July 17, 1998, 2187 U.N.T.S. 3 [hereinafter Rome Statute].

[32] Meintjes and Méndez, "Reconciling Amnesties with Universal Jurisdiction," 77.

[33] Garth Meintjes and Juan E. Méndez, "Reconciling Amnesties with Universal Jurisdiction – A Reply to Mr. Phenyo Keiseng Rakate," *International Law FORUM du Droit International* 3 (2001): 47–9.

in this volume, may reflect the ways countries have found legal loopholes through which to employ amnesties for past violations.

Amnesties are sanctioned and often called for directly under international law. As Mark Freeman and Max Pensky discuss in their chapter in this volume, Protocol II of 1977 states that those in power following a noninternational armed conflict can and should provide a broad amnesty to persons who participated in the armed conflict as well as those otherwise deprived of their freedom of movement because of the armed conflict.[34] This language has been authoritatively interpreted to mean that the states may grant amnesties for participating in the conflict but may not condone violations of international law in cases of international crimes or grave breaches of human rights and humanitarian law.[35]

South Africa presents one of the most well-known examples of a carefully crafted amnesty that falls into a middle ground, described by Antje du Bois-Pedain in this volume. The new government under the African National Congress (ANC) struck a balance between responding to the former government's security force's insistence on amnesty as a precondition for transition and rejecting the choice to bury South Africa's past.[36] Rather than adopt a blanket amnesty, the ANC chose to implement a different kind of amnesty that offered conditional clemency ("immunity") but only on a much narrower set of criteria.[37] The Truth and Reconciliation Commission's Amnesty Committee specifically assessed individual eligibility for amnesty based on two factors: first, whether the criminal act was associated with a political objective committed in the course of the conflicts of the past; and second, whether the applicant made a full disclosure of all relevant facts.[38] In this way, the Truth and Reconciliation Commission lived up to its mandate by considering the perspectives of the victims and the motives and views of the perpetrators.[39] The downsides to the amnesty, however, included granting immunity to civil liability; a lack of credible threat of prosecution reinforced by an overly reconciliatory rhetoric; an inability of ANC officials to delve deeply into the past particularly as related to torture in training camps; and, most important, the utter lack of sincere

---

[34] Protocol Additional to the Geneva Conventions of August 12, 1949, and relating to the Protection of Victims of Non-International Armed Conflicts, June 8, 1977, 1125 U.N.T.S. 609, art. 6 (5).

[35] Afghanistan Independent Human Rights Commission, "The Legality of Amnesties" (discussion paper, International Centre for Transitional Justice, Afghanistan Human Rights Commission, February 21, 2010), accessed January 3, 2012, http://www.unhcr.org/refworld/publisher,AIHRC,,,4bb31a5e2,0.html.
See also Letter by Toni Pfanner, Legal Director, ICRC, to Cassel, dated April 15, 1997: quoted in Douglass Cassel, "Lessons from the Americas: Guidelines for International Response to Amnesties for Atrocities," *Law and Contemporary Problems* 59 (1996): 218.

[36] Meintjes and Méndez, "Reconciling Amnesties with Universal Jurisdiction," 88.

[37] Ibid., 78.

[38] Ibid., 93.

[39] Ibid., 89.

remorse displayed by most of the former government officials, even those few who actually applied for amnesty.[40]

Interesting, too, although the South African–style "conditional amnesty" was regarded in 1994 as compliant with international law, the rapid evolution of international law since then suggests that today, even a *conditional* amnesty would be inconsistent with international law if it covered war crimes, crimes against humanity (including disappearances), or torture.[41] It may be for this reason that despite the important precedent set by the South African TRC experience, its example has been followed by other states with respect to truth telling, but not with respect to limited or conditional amnesty.

As the South Africa case illustrates, varying interpretations on the legality of amnesties arise when amnesties do not amount to a full pardon for the most serious crimes but instead are offered on a more limited scope. In assessing the legality of such amnesties, the international community should focus on two factors: (1) the criteria by which the amnesties were granted, and (2) the manner in which the criteria were applied in each case.[42] For example, amnesties provided to perpetrators of political crimes like sedition are valid under international law because the criteria for eligibility would be narrowly tailored to a kind of offense much lesser in degree than international crimes.[43] The international community, however, would still have to conduct a second inquiry into the manner in which such an amnesty is applied. In the example previously mentioned, if a state grants the benefits of an amnesty for political crimes to a large group of demobilized individuals in a haphazard manner, the amnesty would be void because it was applied indiscriminately. Thus a government seeking to apply a limited amnesty would also need to devise a set of mechanisms providing for thorough investigations into who deserves the benefits of the law based on how these actors conducted themselves. Such procedures go a long way in weeding out perpetrators who might confess to committing political crimes for the sake of receiving a pardon even when they transgressed beyond the limits of such crimes.

The two-step inquiry required to assess the validity of a limited amnesty under international law often involves complicated exercises in line drawing. In devising suitable criteria for eligibility, states may also take into account the levels of complicity or degree to which an actor played a decisive role in a crime. International

[40] Ibid., 90–2.

[41] See John Dugard, "Reconciliation and Justice: The South African Experience," *Transnational Law & Contemporary Problems* 8 (Fall 1998): 301 (highlighting the international community's support and approval of the South African TRC). See also OHCHR, *Rule-of-Law Tools*, 11.

[42] Meintjes and Méndez, "Reconciling Amnesties with Universal Jurisdiction," 93.

[43] In this context, political crimes include nonviolent offenses of political opposition as well as rebellion or sedition as crimes in domestic law consisting of rising up in arms against the state, as long as the rebels have not also committed violations of the laws of war.

judgments on a particular amnesty's validity often diverge here. However, certain baselines of amnesty-worthy conduct should be drawn to ensure that perpetrators do not receive benefits for actions that crossed the line from lesser to more serious crimes. For example, a guard who was a lookout at a prison where torture was known to occur cannot be said to have played a direct role in torturing. Thus, this actor could be considered for a limited amnesty. However, a low-level guard who did directly torture victims but who claims in his defense that he merely followed orders should not receive an amnesty.

The ICC adds yet another layer of complexity by drawing its own line at cases focused on the perpetrators who bear the highest level of responsibility for international crimes. In the fight to end impunity, the ICC operates under a two-tiered approach.[44] On the one side, the Court focuses its limited resources on prosecuting leaders who bear the most responsibility for the crimes. On the other, the Court "encourage[s] national prosecution for lower-ranking perpetrators and works with the international community to ensure that the offenders are brought to justice by some other means."[45] Therefore, that the ICC focuses its efforts on individuals bearing the highest responsibility does not mean countries themselves are released from their duty to investigate and prosecute. Moreover, the jurisdiction of the ICC is based on the principle of complementarity whereby the Court complements the investigations and prosecutions of the state over the most serious crimes, asserting sole jurisdiction over these crimes only when the state is unwilling or unable to prosecute and investigate.[46] The Rome Statute does not directly mention the effect of domestic amnesties. However, the Rome Statute permits a reasonable inference that the ICC's jurisdiction is not barred by these measures unless such amnesties conform to international expectations.[47] Depending on how they are drawn and actually applied, amnesties can be indicative of a state's willingness or ability to investigate and prosecute, which in turn can influence the ICC's discretion on whether or not to exercise its own jurisdiction.[48] Even though the Rome Statute does not by its terms prohibit amnesties, it is clear that the ICC panel will be guided by international law and will not be bound by domestic decisions on amnesty when it makes a judgment under the complementarity principle.

[44] International Criminal Court, "Paper on Some Policy Issues before the Office of the Prosecutor," International Criminal Court, page 3, accessed January 3, 2012, http://amicc.org/docs/OcampoPolicyPaper9_03.pdf.

[45] Ibid.

[46] See Rome Statute, arts. 1, 17 (indicating that investigating and prosecuting crimes outside of those of the most serious international concern continue to rest under each state's international law obligations regardless of how or whether the state proceeds with investigations and prosecutions of the most serious crimes).

[47] Meintjes and Méndez, "Reconciling Amnesties with Universal Jurisdiction," 83–4.

[48] Ibid., 84.

Though international law provides clear boundaries prohibiting broad amnesties, this does not foreclose the possibility of using limited amnesties as a mechanism for resolving international and internal conflicts. Limited amnesties are not only consistent with international law; they are also an important tool in the conflict resolution process. It is for this reason that the international community should not only accept them but actively promote them, so long as these amnesties do not serve as a disguise for impunity for international crimes. For example, northern Uganda enacted the Uganda Amnesty Act, which applied to those who voluntarily left the Lord's Resistance Army (LRA).[49] This is the kind of amnesty the international community should support because for the most part LRA soldiers were forcibly recruited as children, which makes these soldiers victims as well as perpetrators.[50] However, Uganda and the international community should implement appropriate screenings to ensure no impunity is granted for major crimes committed when these soldiers were already adults and not acting under coercion.

Besides the move toward limited amnesties, evolving amnesty law has also contributed to the ongoing development of the justice and peace debate. On the one hand, the new international paradigm under which general amnesties are banned and limited amnesties are considered and promoted, but only after undergoing careful scrutiny, makes conflict resolution more difficult. On the other hand, it forces the parties and the mediators to search for solutions that consult the legitimate interests of victims and not just those of the perpetrators of abuse. A first step is to recognize that the terms of a peace agreement cannot be dictated only by the parties to an armed conflict. Although in the end those armed actors will have to agree to lay down their arms, the innocent victims of the conflict must also be given a voice in the process. Civilian populations have borne the brunt of the fighting and its excesses and will have to live with the consequences of an unfair and unjust peace. An unjust peace, by definition, is one that leaves innocent victims without any recourse to obtain redress for what they have suffered. Peace achieved in a manner that consults the legitimate interests of all actors in peace but also the equally legitimate interests of victims in justice may have a better chance of lasting. If anything, the changing stance toward amnesty can further the idea that conflict resolution should be about reaching terms that make justice and peace reinforce each other within a particular conflict. Amnesties as part of a peace deal require an approach that mirrors the larger pattern of addressing the nature of each conflict on a case-by-case basis when attempting to reconcile and promote the demands of both justice and of peace.

---

[49] OHCHR, *Rights of the Child*, UN H.C.H.R. *Report on Mission to Assess the Situation on the Ground with Regard to the Abduction of Children from Northern Uganda*, U.N. Doc. E/CN.4/2002/86 (OHCHR: November 9, 2001), para. 33 [hereinafter *Rights of the Child Uganda Report*].

[50] Ibid., para. 15.

Within many of these case-by-case approaches, reconciliation is often described as an end goal of conflict resolution. Properly understood, reconciliation is a worthy objective of transitional justice and conflict resolution. This, however, depends on how reconciliation is understood and implemented. When reconciliation is understood as intercommunal talks about property restitution, return to villages, water rights, or grazing rights, it should be part of the peace-making process. These kinds of processes help separate the perpetrators of crimes from the communities they claim to represent, thereby avoiding the cycle of vengeance that can foster new deadly conflict even generations later. It follows that reconciliation in this sense is most appropriate to the resolution of conflicts marked by a distinctive ethnic, religious, or racial character, a discussion Phil Clark pursues in his chapter on Rwanda and Uganda in this volume. However, even in those cases reconciliation cannot be a code word for impunity. In fact, actual reconciliation (between communities) cannot proceed while impunity reigns because it promotes distrust and vindictiveness.

Moreover, as stated originally, amnesties should not be construed as prerequisites for peace. In several instances peace has been achieved without blanket amnesties, including the Dayton accords, Cote d'Ivoire, and Colombia. Yet conversely, even agreements with blanket amnesties have held as in the case of Mozambique. Other amnesties did not result in an end to fighting or an end to mass violations like in Sierra Leone and Angola.[51] Today, however, given the clear demarcation of what constitutes an amnesty against international law, the tougher questions focus on whether other types of legislation, implementing peace agreements or peace enforcement mechanisms, serve as the current and functional equivalents of amnesty, a discussion that Emily Braid and Naomi Roht-Arriaza engage in this volume with regard to Central America.

The obligation to prosecute international crimes cannot be separated from the obligation to conduct such trials with absolute respect for the internationally recognized standards of due process and fair trial. It follows, therefore, that in order to prosecute such crimes a state must have a functioning independent and impartial judiciary. Countries emerging from deadly conflict are seldom equipped with such institutions, and time is needed to rebuild them or create them from scratch. For that reason, immediate prosecutions are not to be expected and may be a bad idea. In that context, transitional justice mechanisms can serve the valuable purpose of sequencing the various measures to be implemented. For example, a truth telling exercise can provide an accurate picture of the universe of crimes and of victims

---

[51]  OHCHR, *Rule-of-Law Tools*, 3 (citing the amnesty provision of the 1999 Lomé Peace Agreement as an example of an amnesty that failed to end the armed conflict in Sierra Leone and did not serve to deter further atrocities).

while the state builds courts and prosecutorial offices eventually able to turn those findings into evidence for proper prosecutions.

In some peace accords, sequencing has been discussed in the context of amnesties and in recognition that some amnesties are impermissible under international law. If, however, the final peace accord is not clear on the issue of sequencing, the resulting ambiguity can pose interesting challenges for the international community. On the one hand, sequencing can be interpreted as a future commitment on the part of the state to prosecute when appropriate conditions are achieved; on the other hand, the silence regarding amnesty, or rather the lack of specific endorsement of amnesty, when coupled with a lack of or delay in action, will be understood (especially by perpetrators) to function like a broad implicit amnesty, as Patrick Burgess discusses in relationship to Indonesia in this volume.

Also, a distinction between how sequencing operates in domestic prosecutions as opposed to ICC prosecutions may be necessary.[52] If the ICC has jurisdiction to act in the specific scenario, there is no justification for sequencing because the ICC is already an impartial and independent court that can render fair trials. Sequencing can be fatal to ICC jurisdiction because of the difficulties involved in investigating crimes and the risk of loss of evidence during a suspension of ICC activities. In addition, sequencing affects the independence and impartiality of the ICC because it subjects it to decisions of political organs and for that reason, political decisions affecting ICC jurisdiction should be kept to a minimum. With respect to domestic prosecutions, on the other hand, some reasonable sequencing can be helpful because the state needs time to restore the credibility and legitimacy of its judiciary, and a period of truth telling can lay the groundwork for later prosecutions.

In addition to sequencing, some countries, like Colombia, have chosen to implement a transitional justice framework that operates as an alternative sentencing law. The framework, known as the Justice and Peace Law (Ley 975),[53] provides reduced sentences – five years to eight years – to demobilized paramilitaries bearing the highest responsibility for grave crimes committed in the course of the internal armed conflict in exchange for the beneficiary's "contribution to the attainment of national peace, collaboration with the justice system (including a full confession exposing the truth of the events), reparation for the victims,

---

[52] Art. 16 of the Rome Statute for an International Criminal Court allows the Security Council, in exercise of its powers to ensure peace and security of nations under Chapter VII of the UN Charter, to suspend ICC activities in a given conflict for renewable periods of one year at a time. In suggesting such a measure for the conflict in northern Uganda, for example, it has been argued that it would allow the peace process to go forward, thereby sequencing peace and justice.

[53] Ley 975 of 2005, Diario Oficial No. 45.980 (julio 25, 2005), accessed on January 3, 2012, http://www .fiscalia.gov.co/justiciapaz/Documentos/LEY_975_concordada.pdf. An unofficial English translation of Law 975 is available at http://www.mediosparalapaz.org/downloads/Law_975_HRW_and_AI.rtf.

and adequate re-socialization."[54] This kind of reduced sentencing framework for serious international crimes does not on its face conflict with international law or equate to an amnesty contrary to international law because the law takes into account the interests of victims and society. Whether the law is proportional to the severity of the crimes committed is an issue that the IACtHR left open.[55] So long as these kinds of frameworks are carefully monitored to ensure that their benefits are afforded properly, meaning only to those perpetrators who genuinely contribute to truth building, reparation, and peace efforts, then these laws can avoid perpetuating impunity.

The Colombian model was made to comply with international law mainly by a decision of the country's Constitutional Court that amended some key features in the law passed by the congress.[56] As applied until now, however, the Colombian scheme has been an utter disappointment to most victims of paramilitary violence and those interested in reconciling demobilization with justice. The main perpetrators have been extradited to the United States on drug charges and have thereby lost any incentive to contribute to truth, justice, or reparations in Colombia. The process by which the prosecutors and courts decide whether to apply the benefits of the law (a process that should allow for active participation by victims) has been mired in interminable bureaucratic complications, leaving most demobilized paramilitaries outside of the framework of the Justice and Peace Law. These paramilitaries who do not fall under the Justice and Peace Law should be tried under ordinary criminal jurisdiction for their crimes or otherwise risk perpetuating a cycle of impunity. In addition, many perpetrators of egregious violence against civilians have spent years in comfortable internal exile on lands that they confiscated by force while others enjoy house arrest rather than face time in prison. The most notorious paramilitary groups have indeed demobilized, but some have rearmed and new armed groups of a similar kind have emerged.[57] Ultimately, a lasting peace in Colombia is far from accomplished.

---

[54] Ibid., art. 1.

[55] See Inter-American Court of Human Rights, *Case of the Rochela Massacre v. Colombia*, Merits, Judgment of May 11, 2007. Ser. C, No. 59, para. 196 (highlighting that punishment imposed by the state is intended to be proportional to the rights recognized by law and the level of culpability of the perpetrator. Culpability turns on the nature and gravity of the acts committed. In choosing the appropriate punishment, the state needs to determine specific reasons for the punishment and "every element which determines the severity of the punishment should correspond to a clearly identifiable objective and be compatible with the Convention").

[56] Corte Constitucional [C.C.] [Constitutional Court], mayo 18, 2006, Sentencia C-370/06 (Colom.), accessed January 3, 2012, http://www.fiscalia.gov.co/justiciapaz/Documentos/SentenciaC-370.pdf.

[57] Tadeo Martínez, "La dura guerra contra las bacrim," *Semana*, April 20, 2011, accessed January 3, 2012, http://www.semana.com/nacion/dura-guerra-contra-bacrim/155461-3.aspx (referring to the newly emerged armed group phenomenon known as *bacrim* – criminal gangs – that surfaced following the demobilization of the AUC, the former umbrella paramilitary group).

The evolution of international law has made great strides in recent decades. Today, certain types of amnesties are entirely prohibited while others that are more limited in scope are touted as valuable contributions to peace building efforts. Limited amnesties, as Ronald C. Slye mentions in his chapter in this book, can serve as valuable conflict resolution tools. In those cases, it is the duty of conflict resolution specialists and of human rights activists alike to promote and advocate solutions that harmonize the aspirations of the civilian population to peace and justice. It should be clear, however, that some countries suffered mass atrocities without an underlying armed conflict and often arrive at a transition to democracy without the need to put an end to an armed internal rebellion. In those cases, amnesties are unnecessary for purposes of peace and are also a grave injustice to victims. Still other country contexts have illustrated that peace and justice can simultaneously be achieved without affording amnesty measures to perpetrators at all. The peace paradigm may now be more complex because the tools available in the conflict and postconflict context have changed. Clemency measures have become more targeted and limited but the panoply of transitional justice mechanisms that have surfaced instead, when implemented seriously and earnestly, are more likely to yield better results because these mechanisms do not leave behind a legacy of unheard victims, victims who on top of suffering at the hand of war would normally be left to endure a cycle of impunity and unjust peace. Instead, the harmful rhetoric of winners and losers has been replaced by a candid discussion on how best to represent and create just solutions for all of the parties' interests to a conflict.

The essays in this volume thoughtfully and carefully explore these difficult issues. They consider the costs of amnesties and the desire for justice. Special mention must be made of the editors, Francesca Lessa and Leigh A. Payne; not only have they assembled an impressive lineup of contributors, but they have also made sure that all the various legitimate points of view on these matters are represented. The result is a collection of chapters that constitute the state of the art on the matter of peace and justice and their enduring and ever-present dilemmas. Through their contributions, authors who have amassed an impressive array of diverse experiences reflect on these struggles from the past and their persistence in the age of accountability.

# Acknowledgments

This volume is the first of its kind. No other project analyzes theoretically and empirically, through cross-national and qualitative country case studies around the world and using a range of disciplinary approaches, the processes of amnesty in the age of accountability. Indeed, the volume fills a void in transitional justice scholarship by addressing in detail the question of amnesty. While some scholarship on amnesty exists, this volume draws together the foremost authorities on these amnesty processes and the countries in which they unfold. It also introduces new researchers who have begun to make a mark in the study of transitional justice. This book also contributes to the literature by raising and beginning to answer particular questions about amnesty processes and their impact on accountability.

Such a volume would not be possible without support from a wide range of sources. Most of the chapters included in this volume were initially presented as papers at a conference on "Amnesty in the Age of Accountability: Brazil in Comparative and International Perspective" held at the University of Oxford on October 22–23, 2010, and organized with the generous assistance of the Latin American Centre, the Brazilian Studies Program, St. Antony's College, Oxford Transitional Justice Research (OTJR), and the School of Interdisciplinary Area Studies. Each of those Oxford units included dedicated staff who managed the maddening day-to-day tasks with aplomb and efficiency. In particular, we would like to thank David Robinson for his careful attention to every single detail before, during, and after the conference. We also thank St. Antony's College for providing the Nissan Theatre as the venue for the conference. The delightful tea breaks, receptions, and High Table stimulated the creative environment in which our work evolved.

The John Fell OUP Research Fund of Oxford University Press and the Brazilian Ministry of Justice generously provided the funding for the conference and the subsequent book publication. Paulo Abrão and Marcelo Torelly from the ministry not only secured funding for all of the Brazilian participants at the conference, as well as most of the translation and interpreting, they also followed up on that conference with a Portuguese version of the conference proceedings: Leigh A. Payne, Paulo Abrão, and Marcelo D. Torelly, eds. *A anistia na era da responsabilização: O Brasil em perspectiva internacional e comparada* (Brazilian Ministry of Justice, 2011). In addition to thanking Marcelo Torelly for the translation work he spearheaded, we thank Anna Mackin for working on the final translations into English. For the conference funding and the publications that emerged from them, we are particularly indebted to Paulo Abrão and Marcelo Torelly, as well as Joe Foweraker, David Robinson, and Andreas Schmidt. They contributed at every stage, from the initial proposal to the successful funding outcome, and now the two book publications.

Funding for the research in Chapters 4, 5, 7, the introduction, and the conclusion to this volume are partially based on research supported by the National Science Foundation (Grant No. 0961226) and the Arts and Humanities Research Council (Grant No. AH/I500030/1) relating to the project titled "The Impact of Transitional Justice on Human Rights and Democracy." Any opinions, findings, and conclusions or recommendations expressed in this material are those of the authors and do not necessarily reflect the views of the National Science Foundation.

Oxford Transitional Justice Research (OTJR) provided invaluable logistical support. We particularly thank Nicola Palmer, who took on a major role of coordinating OTJR volunteers, welcoming presenters, and contributing with her characteristic wit and intelligence to the intellectual value of the conference. Emily Braid, Caitlin Goss, Cheah Wui Ling, and Laura Pereira, as OTJR volunteers, remained on their toes to deal with the inevitable problems that arose during the two days of the conference.

The substantive outcome of the conference, and therefore the intellectual mission behind this volume, emerged in the fruitful presentations and discussions during the two days of the conference and its aftermath. We would particularly like to acknowledge the significant intellectual contributions made by participants in the conference, ideas that have surely made their way in some form into this book. For their insights into these contentious issues, we thank Beatriz Affonso, Roberta Camineiro Baggio, Leslie Bethell, Jo-Marie Burt, Cath Collins, Geoff Dancy, Luciana Garcia, Viviana Krsticevic, Fiona Macaulay, José Carlos Moreira de Silva Filho, Timothy Power, Elin Skaar, Ruti Teitel, Deisy Ventura, Jessie Jane Vieira de Souza, and Leslie Vinajmuri.

Although they did not participate in the conference, Lisa Hilbink and Stephen Meili played key roles at various points in helping us find legal terminology in English to fit practices in non-English-speaking countries. Our colleagues at Amnesty International's international justice team, particularly Christopher Hall, Francesca Pizzutelli, Hugo Relva, and Diana Florez refined our understanding of amnesty processes around the world.

The volume has relied on additional support at crucial moments. Emily Braid became our editorial assistant extraordinaire, acting nearly like a ghostwriter in attempting to transform and merge conference papers into single new chapters. She also carefully checked each chapter for consistency and tracked down elusive foot-notes. And she did all of this while co-authoring her own chapter. Pierre Le Goff and Diana Florez provided research support, the latter working particularly on the back-ground research for the case of El Salvador. John Berger of Cambridge University Press with great humor and efficiency saw the project through from its original idea to its completion. We also thank David Jou, Ami Naramor, and Deborah Patton for their assistance in the book's production, copyediting, and index.

We have dedicated this book to two human rights advocate-academics who fought tirelessly against impunity and who recently passed away: Carlos Ivan Degregori and Ellen Lutz. They will always be for us the inspiration behind engaged scholarship.

# Introduction

*Francesca Lessa and Leigh A. Payne*

Is amnesty an appropriate response to past human rights atrocities? Scholars and practitioners promoting transitional justice around the world have argued, in general, that it is not. They contend that legal, moral, and political duties compel governments emerging from authoritarian rule to hold perpetrators of human rights violence accountable.[1] Beginning with the post-World War II Nuremberg and Tokyo Trials and continuing with the creation of the ICC, the international human rights system has attempted to replace the traditional practice of amnesty with a new norm of accountability for human rights violations. International conventions – adopted in the second half of the twentieth century – now obligate state parties to provide redress for victims of torture and genocide. The UN international criminal tribunals for the former Yugoslavia and Rwanda, set up in the early 1990s, underscore the international duty to hold perpetrators accountable. The notion of universal jurisdiction, and its use in the effort to extradite former Chilean dictator General Augusto Pinochet from the United Kingdom to stand trial in Spain in the late 1990s, claims that courts in one country can hold foreign perpetrators accountable for crimes against humanity committed in another country.

An accountability norm has spread throughout the world, producing dramatic and unprecedented results. Although General Pinochet did not stand trial in Spain, he did face charges in his own country before he died. Other heads of state responsible for human rights abuses have also faced trials, convictions, and prison sentences

---

[1] See for example: M. Cherif Bassiouni, "Searching for Peace and Achieving Justice: The Need for Accountability," *Law and Contemporary Problems* 59, no. 4 (1996); Juan E. Méndez, "Accountability for Past Abuses," *Human Rights Quarterly* 19, no. 2 (1997); Diane F. Orentlicher, "Settling Accounts: The Duty to Prosecute Human Rights Violations of a Prior Regime," *The Yale Law Journal* 100 (1991); Jon M. Van Dyke and Gerald W. Berkley, "Redressing Human Rights Abuses," *Denver Journal of International Law and Policy* 20, no. 2 (1992).

Many thanks to Paulo Abrão and Marcelo D. Torelly for permission to use in this chapter parts of the introduction to the volume *A anistia na era da responsabilização: O Brasil em perspectiva internacional e comparada* (Brazilian Ministry of Justice, 2011) (co-written with Leigh A. Payne).

in Latin America, including former Peruvian and Uruguayan presidents Alberto
Fujimori and Juan María Bordaberry.[2] In December 2011, former military dictator
Manuel Noriega was extradited from France to his native Panama to serve his prison
sentence for human rights violations for which he had already been convicted *in
absentia*.[3] No region of the world has been exempt from accountability efforts.
In Europe, one landmark case is the UN International Criminal Tribunal for the
Former Yugoslavia efforts to convict former President Slobodan Milošević for grave
human rights violations, including genocide, torture, and extermination committed
in Bosnia and Herzegovina, Croatia, and Kosovo; Milošević died in 2006 while the
trial was still ongoing.[4] In Africa, former Liberian President Charles Taylor faces prosecution before the Special Court for Sierra Leone for eleven counts of war crimes,
crimes against humanity, and other serious violations of international humanitarian
law perpetrated in Sierra Leone.[5] In Asia, the Extraordinary Chambers in the Courts
of Cambodia began in 2011 the ongoing trials of four high-ranking former Khmer
Rouge officials – including Ieng Sary, the former deputy prime minister for foreign
affairs, and Khieu Samphan, the former head of state – on charges of crimes against
humanity, grave breaches of the Geneva Conventions of 1949, and genocide.[6] In the
Middle East, former Egyptian President Hosni Mubarak is currently standing trial
for the premeditated murder of protesters during the 2011 revolution.

This age of accountability has meant that amnesty laws around the world have
faced challenges from domestic, regional, and international courts, as well as from
mobilized local and international victims, survivors, and human rights organizations. This tremendous and unprecedented global progress suggests that we now
live in an age of accountability in which governments and international institutions
are expected to hold perpetrators of atrocities legally responsible for their acts. The
impressive list of court cases against human rights violators in Chile, for example,
seemed to erode the power of the amnesty law there without annulling it outright.
Lawyers representing victims have found ways to circumvent amnesty laws in many
countries, but have not yet succeeded in removing those laws from the statute books.

---

[2]   See on the Fujimori case: Ellen L. Lutz and Caitlin Reiger, *Prosecuting Heads of State* (Cambridge:
      Cambridge University Press, 2009); Jo-Marie Burt, "Guilty as Charged: The Trial of Former Peruvian
      President Alberto Fujimori for Human Rights Violations," *International Journal of Transitional Justice*
      3, no. 3 (2009). On the Bordaberry case: Gabriela Fried and Francesca Lessa, eds., *Luchas contra la
      impunidad: Uruguay 1985–2011* (Montevideo: Trilce, 2011).
[3]   "Manuel Noriega Extradited to Panama to Serve Jail Terms," *BBC News*, December 11, 2011, accessed
      January 2, 2012, http://www.bbc.co.uk/news/world-latin-america-16129630.
[4]   "Kosovo, Croatia & Bosnia" (It-02–54) Slobodan Milošević, accessed January 18, 2012, http://www.icty.
      org/x/cases/slobodan_milosevic/cis/en/cis_milosevic_slobodan_en.pdf.
[5]   The Prosecutor vs. Charles Ghankay Taylor, "The Indictment," accessed January 18, 2012, http://www.
      sc-sl.org/LinkClick.aspx?fileticket=lrnobAAMvYM%3d&tabid=107.
[6]   The Extraordinary Chambers in the Courts of Cambodia, "Case 002," accessed January 18, 2012,
      http://www.eccc.gov.kh/en/case/topic/2.

In Guatemala, for instance, the 1996 National Reconciliation Law is not applicable to the crimes of genocide, torture, and forced disappearance as stipulated in international conventions, but nonetheless advancement in prosecuting those responsible for atrocious human rights violations has been slow. Progress in law, in other words, has not always translated into progress in legal practice. Indeed, despite this remarkable shift toward accountability, little evidence supports the view that amnesty processes have declined in number and impact as a result; on the contrary, as Louise Mallinder shows in Chapter 3 in this volume, and Tricia Olsen, Leigh Payne, and Andrew Reiter demonstrate in their book, the rate of amnesty laws introduced has remained constant despite the age of accountability.[7] The continued adoption of amnesty laws seems to suggest that some governments and judiciaries still disregard the accountability norm and that cultures of impunity persist even during the age of accountability.

## AMNESTY IN THE AGE OF ACCOUNTABILITY

States have adopted amnesties to promote political settlements, reconciliation, and stability since times immemorial. The word *amnesty* comes from ancient Greek, the word ἀμνηστία (*amnestia*) meaning forgetfulness or oblivion.[8] These acts of political forgiveness have been used since ancient times, such as in the Code of Hammurabi (1700 B.C.), the aftermath of the Athenian Civil War in 404–3 B.C., and the Byzantine Empire.[9] In one of the earliest studies on amnesties, UN special rapporteur Louis Joinet traces the historical origins of amnesties as "an outgrowth of the right of pardon, an act of individual clemency of theocratic origin."[10] Amnesties and pardons are closely related to powers of clemency initially associated with the king and, subsequently, the state. The "true ancestor of the modern amnesty," Joinet claims, is "collective pardon," which developed concurrently with individual ones.

In the aftermath of the birth of modern nation states, with the 1648 peace treaties of Westphalia, amnesties were often adopted in international peace agreements and their use has persisted up to the present in different forms and contexts.[11] When

---

[7]  Tricia D. Olsen, Leigh A. Payne, and Andrew G. Reiter, *Transitional Justice in Balance: Comparing Processes, Weighing Efficacy* (Washington, DC: United States Institute of Peace, 2010).

[8]  The Greek root connotes oblivion and forgetfulness rather than forgiveness of a crime. See OHCHR, *Rule-of-Law Tools*.

[9]  See Ruti G. Teitel, *Transitional Justice* (Oxford: Oxford University Press, 2000); Jon Elster, *Closing the Books: Transitional Justice in Historical Perspective* (Cambridge: Cambridge University Press, 2004); Louise Mallinder, *Amnesty, Human Rights and Political Transitions: Bridging the Peace and Justice Divide* (Oxford: Hart, 2008).

[10]  Louis Joinet, *Study on Amnesty Laws and Their Role in the Safeguard and Promotion of Human Rights*, June 21, 1985, ECOSOC, E/CN.4/Sub.2/1985/16, para 9, page 5.

[11]  Mallinder, *Amnesty, Human Rights and Political Transitions*.

looking at state practice, we indeed see different types of amnesty contexts, structures, effects, and functions; these range from amnesties adopted after/during conflict, in nonconflict situations, or as part of negotiated transitions; amnesties can serve to encourage demobilization of combatants, to extinguish liability for serious human rights offenses, or to release political prisoners. Further, amnesties can be enacted by parliaments or presidents, or form component parts of peace accords; benefit state or nonstate agents, or both; and finally, they can be accompanied by other measures of transitional justice or stand alone, be unconditional, or impose preconditions for their potential beneficiaries.[12] Despite this wide variety, all amnesties share the following characteristics: they are ad hoc, sanctioned to extinguish liability for specific crimes committed by particular individuals and/or groups; they are retroactive, applying to acts perpetrated before their enactment; finally, they are extraordinary measures, enacted beyond existing legislation.[13]

While amnesties have been granted in many diverse circumstances (i.e., to raise revenues, deal with issues of immigration, or release nonviolent political prisoners), in this volume we use the term *amnesty* to refer specifically to legal measures adopted by states that have the effect of prospectively barring criminal prosecution against certain individuals accused of committing human rights violations. These individuals may be agents of the state (members of the armed forces, security forces, or paramilitary groups) or nonstate actors (rebel groups, guerrillas, or members of the opposition). Different types of amnesties are discussed in this book, such as: self-amnesties, "amnesties adopted by those responsible for human rights violations to shield themselves from accountability,"[14] such as Argentina's 22.924 Law of National Pacification enacted by the outgoing military junta in September 1983 discussed in Chapter 4; pseudo-amnesties, "designed to have the same effect as amnesty laws [...] while avoiding the damning name of amnesty,"[15] such as Uruguay's 15,848 Law on the Expiry of the Punitive Claims of the State of December 1986 analyzed in Chapter 5; blanket amnesties, which apply "across the board without requiring any application on the part of the beneficiary or even an initial inquiry into the facts to determine if they fit the law's scope of application,"[16] such as El Salvador's 486 Decree examined in Chapter 7; and conditional amnesties that exempt "an individual from prosecution if he or she applies for amnesty and satisfies several conditions,"[17] such as the

---

[12] Mark Freeman, *Necessary Evils: Amnesties and the Search for Justice* (Cambridge: Cambridge University Press, 2009).

[13] Freeman, *Necessary Evils*; Joinet, *Study on Amnesty Laws*; Mallinder, *Amnesty, Human Rights and Political Transitions*.

[14] OHCHR, *Rule-of-Law Tools*, 43.

[15] Garth Meintjes and Juan E. Méndez, "Reconciling Amnesties with Universal Jurisdiction," *International Law FORUM Du Droit International* 2, no.2 (2000): 85 n. 26.

[16] Ibid., 84.

[17] OHCHR, *Rule-of-Law Tools*, 43.

truth finding process in South Africa that linked the amnesty provision to the Truth and Reconciliation Commission discussed in Chapter 9. The volume also discusses cases of pardons, which "are similar to, yet quite distinct from, amnesties."[18] Pardons exempt convicted individuals from serving their sentences without expunging the underlying convictions. They differ from amnesties in that pardons tend to be issued after an individual has been found liable for a wrongful act and perhaps even begun serving a criminal sentence.[19] Chapter 11 discusses, for instance, the 1996 pardon granted in Cambodia to the former deputy prime minister of the Khmer Rouge government, Ieng Sary, for his conviction *in absentia* for gross violations of human rights committed while he was deputy prime minister for foreign affairs from 1975 to 1979. Finally, this volume also considers cases of de facto amnesty, a term referring to "legal measures such as State laws, decrees or regulations that effectively foreclose prosecutions;"[20] while these may not explicitly rule out criminal prosecution or civil remedies, they have the same effect as an explicit amnesty law – as examined in Chapter 10 on Indonesia.

## THE AMNESTY DEBATE

While for centuries the international community had little hope of bringing to justice perpetrators of human rights violations, since state leaders "acted with impunity, wielding the shield of state sovereignty,"[21] developments in human rights account-ability have accelerated in the twentieth century. In a century that witnessed unprec-edented horrors and conflicts, such as the Holocaust, the killing fields of Cambodia, and the Rwandan genocide, resulting in an "estimated 75 to 170 million persons killed,"[22] amnesty is no longer accepted as the only way to transition from civil con-flict or authoritarian repression. Instead, many scholars today consider prosecutions "the preferred choice."[23] We might even go so far as to claim that the "prosecution preference,"[24] or at least a focus on accountability for human rights violations, domi-nates transitional justice scholarship. The diffusion of the accountability norm and

---

[18] Ronald C. Slye, "The Legitimacy of Amnesties Under International Law and General Principles of Anglo-American Law: Is a Legitimate Amnesty Possible?" *Virginia Journal of International Law Association* 43 (2002): 235

[19] Ibid., and also OHCHR, *Rule-of-Law Tools*, 43.

[20] OHCHR, *Rule-of-Law Tools*, 43.

[21] Charles P. IV Trumbull, "Giving Amnesties a Second Chance," *Berkeley Journal of International Law* 25, no. 2 (2007): 284.

[22] M.Cherif Bassiouni, "Combating Impunity for International Crimes," *University of Colorado Law Review* 71, no. 2 (2000): 409.

[23] John Dugard, "Dealing With Crimes of a Past Regime. Is Amnesty Still an Option?" *Leiden Journal of International Law* 12, no. 4 (1999): 1001.

[24] Miriam J. Aukerman, "Extraordinary Evil, Ordinary Crime: A Framework for Understanding Transitional Justice," *Harvard Human Rights Journal* 15 (2002): 39–40.

its impact on international and local courts has in fact attracted substantial attention, leading scholars to label this process a "justice cascade" or "a revolution in accountability."[25] These academics contend that governments have little alternative to promoting accountability owing to international pressure and domestic mobilization. As a result of this trend in the literature, amnesties are often overlooked by transitional justice scholars.

International pressure for accountability has emerged in parallel to shifts in international law and in the enforcement of human rights protections since World War II and the Holocaust. International human rights law obligations, moreover, emerge from states' moral duty to victims of atrocity. States emerging from conflict or authoritarian spells also have a political duty to attempt to deter future violations by holding perpetrators accountable and restoring trust in legal institutions and rule of law.[26] These moral, legal, and political duties appear in the literature as the impetus behind the shift away from amnesties in the aftermath of atrocities and toward punishing perpetrators. International pressure and demand from victims and survivors converge, reducing the likelihood that transitional governments will select the amnesty option.

Not all scholarship, however, concurs with these assumptions regarding the duty to prosecute. Recent literature contends that international law does not compel states to prosecute, providing legitimacy for some types of amnesties. International law on amnesties, as legal scholars and others contend, remains "unsettled,"[27] and the status of "an outright prohibition on amnesty remains unclear,"[28] an argument developed by Mark Freeman and Max Pensky in Chapter 2 in this volume.[29] Other scholars, such as Jack Snyder and Leslie Vinjamuri, have found that amnesties may better serve the processes of peace building, deterring human rights violations, and establishing rule of law by appeasing potential "spoilers" of these processes.[30] Corresponding to the legal and philosophical discussion of the compatibility of amnesty laws in the age of accountability is the continued practice of the adoption of

[25] See Ellen L. Lutz and Kathryn Sikkink, "The Justice Cascade: The Evolution and Impact of Foreign Human Rights Trials in Latin America," *Chicago Journal of International Law* 2, no. 1 (2001); Chandra Lekha Sriram, *Globalizing Justice for Mass Atrocities: A Revolution in Accountability* (London: Routledge, 2005).

[26] Juan E. Méndez, "Accountability for Past Abuses," *Human Rights Quarterly* 19, no. 2 (1997); Naomi Roht-Arriaza, "State Responsibility to Investigate and Prosecute Grave Human Rights Violations in International Law," *California Law Review* 78, no. 2 (1990).

[27] Dugard, "Dealing with Crimes," 1015.

[28] Lisa J. Laplante, "Outlawing Amnesty: The Return of Criminal Justice in Transitional Justice Schemes," *Virginia Journal of International Law* 49, no. 4 (2009): 943.

[29] See for instance: Max Pensky, "Amnesty on Trial: Impunity, Accountability, and the Norms of International Law," *Ethics and Global Politics* 1 (2008); Trumbull, "Giving Amnesties a Second Chance."

[30] Jack Snyder and Leslie Vinjamuri, "Trials and Errors," *International Security* 28, no. 3 (2003/2004).

amnesty laws. At least two recent studies have shown that amnesties have increased in number or persisted at the same rate during this same era marked by an increase in prosecutions and domestic and international pressure for prosecutions.[31] The study by Louise Mallinder suggests that amnesty laws may have increased as security forces around the world seek to protect themselves from the ever more likely threat of prosecution.[32] The other, by Tricia Olsen et al., suggests that amnesties have continued at the same rate as before, but appear to have increased given the higher number of transitions.[33] Neither argument supports the view that prosecutions have replaced amnesties. Instead, it appears that the accountability mechanisms of trials and truth commissions have accompanied amnesties.[34]

The literature has also generated different claims about the success of amnesties in promoting human rights and democracy. Cross-national statistical analysis that shows a positive impact on human rights in countries that adopt trials would logically lead to the conclusion that the use of amnesties without trials would have a detrimental impact on human rights.[35] Findings by other researchers challenge that view, suggesting that trials alone do not have a statistically significant relationship on human rights or democracy measures, and neither do amnesties used alone.[36] Tricia Olsen et al. find, however, that trials and amnesties, with or without truth commissions, increase the likelihood of improvement on human rights and democracy scores.[37] Still other scholars consider amnesties to be "necessary evils," essential and unavoidable in countries emerging from mass atrocity.[38] A group of scholars working on postconflict justice acknowledges the value of amnesties in negotiating peace after civil conflict, but they raise doubts about amnesties or trials sustaining peace.[39]

## BOOK OUTLINE

The debate over amnesty processes, legality, and outcomes would seem to suggest that scholars have engaged with one another over these issues. Yet this is not the case.

---

[31] See Mallinder, *Amnesty, Human Rights and Political Transitions* and Olsen, Payne, and Reiter, *Transitional Justice in Balance.*

[32] Mallinder, *Amnesty, Human Rights and Political Transitions.*

[33] Olsen, Payne, and Reiter, *Transitional Justice in Balance.*

[34] Ibid.

[35] Hunjoon Kim and Kathryn Sikkink, "Explaining the Deterrence Effect of Human Rights Prosecutions for Transitional Countries," *International Studies Quarterly* 54, no. 4 (2010).

[36] Olsen, Payne, and Reiter, *Transitional Justice in Balance.*

[37] Tricia D. Olsen, Leigh A. Payne, and Andrew G. Reiter, "The Justice Balance: When Transitional Justice Improves Human Rights and Democracy," *Human Rights Quarterly* 32, no. 4 (2010).

[38] Freeman, *Necessary Evils.*

[39] Tove Grete Lie, Helga Malmin Binningsbø, and Scott Gates, *Post-Conflict Justice and Sustainable Peace* (Oslo: PRIO, 2007).

Debates exist over tradeoffs, such as amnesty and truth versus justice or amnesty and peace versus justice. Nonetheless, few scholars focus specifically on amnesty.[40] This edited volume, in contrast, brings established, as well as emerging scholars, together to discuss a number of important aspects of amnesty: comparative and empirical cases; political, legal, moral, and philosophical debates in international and domestic human rights law; and effectiveness in terms of the goals of democracy, human rights protections, and peace.

This volume ponders the role of amnesties in the age of accountability. Through theoretical and empirical chapters, the volume attempts to provide answers to two main questions: what explains the persistence of amnesties in the age of accountability; and what impact do persistent amnesties have on the prospects for accountability? Authors use a range of approaches – social movement, ideational, legal, philosophical, path dependent, qualitative case study, statistical, and cross-national – in addressing these questions in their chapters.

In the "Theoretical Framework," Part I of this volume, chapters by Kathryn Sikkink and by Mark Freeman and Max Pensky set out perspectives on amnesty in the age of accountability. The authors examine historical, international, and domestic legal processes and philosophies to explain the relationship of amnesties to the age of accountability. The chapters consider amnesties from an ideational and human rights activist perspective, as well as seeing them as practical responses by governments to a range of different political contexts and challenges.

Kathryn Sikkink, in Chapter 1, explains the emergence of the age of accountability in the twentieth century. She examines the forces and streams – norms and norm diffusion, international actors and institutions, and domestic and foreign actors and institutions – that have converged to establish the age of accountability. She shows that the age of accountability has had global reach, compelling governments around the world to succumb to international and domestic pressure to hold perpetrators accountable. Kathryn Sikkink argues that this process constitutes "a dramatic shift in the legitimacy of the norms of individual criminal accountability for human rights violations and an increase in actions (prosecutions) on behalf of those norms," a process Kathryn Sikkink and Ellen Lutz have defined elsewhere as the "justice cascade."[41] Kathryn Sikkink argues that the continued use of amnesty is not evidence of the failure of the age of accountability or the justice cascade. Rather, she claims, it might be seen as a response to the increasing threat of prosecution. Previously, during the era of impunity, governments did not have to protect perpetrators from prosecution; prosecution was not even imaginable.

---

[40]  Notable exceptions include Mallinder, *Amnesty, Human Rights and Political Transitions*; Freeman, *Necessary Evils*; Pensky, "Amnesty on Trial"; Slye, "The Legitimacy of Amnesties Under International Law"; and, Trumbull, "Giving Amnesties a Second Chance."

[41]  Lutz and Sikkink, "The Justice Cascade."

The era initiated by the Nuremberg Trials and involving the third wave of democratization, of UN ad hoc tribunals, the ICC, and universal jurisdiction does not allow governments to completely ignore accountability pressures. On the other hand, they may not necessarily annul existing amnesty laws or fail to adopt new ones. The desire by states to protect certain perpetrators from prosecution, even while hoping to retain international legitimacy, would likely lead to an increase in amnesties. These amnesties, however, might look different from earlier ones, with greater compliance to international human rights standards. The theoretical contribution of the chapter, however, is not about explaining the persistence or impact of amnesties; rather it describes the age of accountability and the factors that have contributed to an increase in individual criminal accountability around the world in local, foreign, and international courts.

Chapter 2 by Mark Freeman and Max Pensky employs legal philosophy and positivist legal approaches to assess the degree to which the age of accountability has produced exaggerated claims about the invalidity of amnesties. While recognizing that amnesties constitute potentially serious failures of justice, the authors nonetheless suggest that the anti-impunity assertion that amnesties are in every instance contrary to international law rests on weak legal arguments. They contend that the status of amnesty under international law remains unsettled, given the silence of international treaties on the question and the existence of an only slightly stronger argument against the use of amnesty in customary international law regarding states' obligations to outlaw *jus cogens* crimes. A central goal of this chapter is to offer a critical reconstruction of the relevant international legal sources in order to chart more clearly what states' obligations are in respect to amnesties. It suggests that there may be more room for transitional and posttransitional governments to adopt internationally legitimate amnesties than the age of accountability might expect.

The "Comparative Case Studies" in Part II include ten chapters written by country experts and transitional justice specialists. These constitute the empirical portion of the volume, offering a comprehensive assessment and discussion of amnesties across the globe. The authors examine emblematic case studies from eleven countries in the Americas, Africa, Asia, and Europe. With the exception of Argentina and Uruguay's success stories, the chapters explore the continued persistence, as well as appeal, of amnesties in the age of accountability in countries as varied as Brazil, Cambodia, El Salvador, Guatemala, Indonesia, Rwanda, South Africa, Spain, and Uganda. They include single case studies, paired comparisons, clustered comparisons of several countries, as well as cross-national comparisons of amnesties in the age of accountability.

Louise Mallinder's cross-national study of amnesty laws in Chapter 3 begins the empirical exploration of amnesties in the age of accountability. Drawing on the data compiled in her "Amnesty Law Database," she documents and explains the unrelenting practice of amnesty laws around the world in the period from 1979 to 2011. Louise Mallinder describes regional and global trends in amnesty law enactment and interprets the existence of a global accountability norm in light of these trends. She argues that, although there has been a surge in the number of prosecutions for perpetrators of mass atrocities over the past thirty years, amnesty laws have also continued to be enacted at a steady pace. Thus, she concludes that, despite significant developments in international criminal law and transitional justice, the use of amnesty laws to address past atrocity has not lessened in the age of accountability. Rather, she suggests, the threat of prosecution may have prompted more, not fewer, amnesty laws.

Chapter 4 by Par Engstrom and Gabriel Pereira offers a detailed discussion of Argentina's success in overcoming a series of amnesty processes. Argentina represents the first case in Latin America where past amnesty laws and pardons were effectively overturned, resulting in a dramatic justice cascade in which hundreds of perpetrators are currently held individually and criminally accountable for human rights crimes. The chapter focuses particularly on the ways in which amnesty laws and pardons, relating to human rights crimes committed by state agents and their associates during the military regime of the 1970s and 1980s, have been challenged and successfully bypassed. The authors argue that the process of accountability in Argentina has not been linear; rather, three different transitional justice phases can be observed: the first is characterized by a move from full to restricted accountability; the second moves from a situation of complete impunity to restricted accountability; and the third constitutes a stage of outright accountability. In 1985, Argentina's first democratic government surprisingly held legally accountable the members of the military junta (1976–83) responsible for an estimated nine thousand to thirty thousand disappearances, imposing life sentences on some of the military commanders. The subsequent enactment of amnesty laws and pardons in the late 1980s and early 1990s did not deter innovative mechanisms to continue to promote accountability. In the mid- and late 1990s, human rights lawyers, defending victims and their relatives, circumvented amnesty laws and used international human rights provisions to investigate and subsequently prosecute perpetrators. This sustained domestic pressure, accompanied by international reverberations, challenged the ironclad amnesty laws. Political will, not only on the part of the early Alfonsín government (1983–9) but picked up again under the Kirchner governments (2003–11), has made Argentina a model for annulling amnesty laws. The chapter argues that variations among and within these phases can be explained with reference to the interaction of three factors: the role and relations of key actors (government, civil society, and the armed forces); the type of amnesties and pardons enacted; and the challenges against them (exceptions to the amnesty laws, recourse to the Inter-American system, or foreign courts). Is the Argentine success replicable? The chapter ends with an evaluation of the extent of Argentina's uniqueness and the degree to which other countries in the region might follow a similar pathway in challenging their own amnesty laws.

Francesca Lessa offers an analysis of the frequently overlooked case of Uruguay and its amnesty law, the Ley de Caducidad, in Chapter 5. She argues that, until the October 2011 derogation of the amnesty, justice in Uruguay was only achieved on a few occasions involving crimes outside the amnesty law's scope. Since 2005, important sentences were rendered, mainly owing to the continued mobilization of civil society and relentless denunciations of past crimes by victims and human rights lawyers. Until recently, these were exceptional circumstances in which the amnesty was bypassed. As a consequence, victims of human rights violations lacked for almost twenty-five years access to justice and the amnesty undermined the separation of powers, resulting in judicial courts being dependent on the executive. Francesca Lessa further suggests that some of the reasons behind the endurance of the amnesty law were specific to the Uruguayan context, including a negotiated transition in 1984, the predominance of traditional and conservative presidents until 2005, the particular mechanisms set up by the Ley de Caducidad, the nature and features of the Uruguayan judiciary, and the implications of the 1989 referendum and 2009 plebiscite on the legitimacy enjoyed by the amnesty. The Uruguayan case reflects at different junctures the different theoretical perspectives on amnesties outlined in this volume. There are elements of the justice cascade in Uruguay, particularly the continued activism against impunity and the recourse to regional and international courts and committees while simultaneously attempting to achieve accountability at home. Despite the existence of justice streams that could fill a justice cascade, the amnesty was also frequently defended as a necessary evil for peace and democracy, most notably by Presidents Sanguinetti and Lacalle in the aftermath of the 1989 referendum, as well as in recent debates in 2010 and 2011. Finally, between 2005 and October 2011, elements of the justice balance argument existed in Uruguay; the Ley de Caducidad coexisted in an environment characterized by sustained efforts for accountability, with approximately 60 cases of human rights crimes under judicial investigation.

In Chapter 6, Paulo Abrão and Marcelo Torelly offer a discussion of the enduring appeal of amnesty in Brazil. Brazil's nearly unchallenged 1979 amnesty law potentially questions the power of the accountability norm. It suggests that the norm and its embodiment in international and domestic institutions and activism have not necessarily shifted states' behavior. Brazil's amnesty law, however, cannot be viewed as a necessary evil designed to address ongoing or massive violence. Neither is it consistent with international conventions' tolerance of amnesties to secure peace and protect democracy. Among its South American neighbors, Brazil may have had the lowest numbers of dead and disappeared, but human rights violations in general

reached similar levels to those seen in Argentina and Chile. The authors argue
that the Brazilian amnesty law must be viewed as an ambiguous mechanism of the
transition. The law provided a mechanism for the regime to extricate itself from
power while controlling the transition process and retaining protection from prosecution for human rights violations. Despite protecting the authoritarian regime
and its security forces, it also provided amnesty to political prisoners and exiles. The
opposition to the authoritarian regime embraced the amnesty process – indeed, it
provided the impetus behind the law – as a step toward democracy and not a retreat
from that process. Amnesty thus has positive and negative connotations in Brazilian
society today. It is distinct from the reaction to amnesty laws in Argentina and Chile
where they are viewed as a way to guarantee impunity to members of the repressive
regimes and the security forces in those countries. Efforts to erode the impunity
dimension of the amnesty law have so far failed in Brazil. The IACtHR's recent
condemnation of the law in December 2010 (the *Gomes Lund* case) has not yet produced any behavior shift in Brazil; neither have criminal and appeals processes in
Brazilian courts. Civil suits have also failed to catalyze a national rejection of the
amnesty laws. At most, a truth commission process might hold the authoritarian
regime symbolically culpable, while it is likely to protect perpetrators from individual responsibility. The Brazilian case thus far represents a case in which new forms
of symbolic accountability, such as truth gathering mechanisms and reparations,
seem to have replaced, rather than complemented, the individual criminal responsibility considered fundamental to the age of accountability.

In Chapter 7, Emily Braid and Naomi Roht-Arriaza examine whether accountability mechanisms in certain contexts act as mere window dressing, disguising
underlying cultures of impunity. They consider the amnesties adopted after authoritarian rule and civil conflict in the Central American countries of El Salvador and
Guatemala. Most of the streams identified by Kathryn Sikkink in her justice cascade
analysis exist: domestic and international pressure from governments, legal entities,
and victims' and human rights movements. Such pressure has resulted, however,
in only a limited number of successful, case-specific challenges to these amnesty
laws. The propitious context and the disappointing results in terms of prosecution
lead Emily Braid and Naomi Roht-Arriaza to use the Central American countries as
examples of the difficulty, in practice, of holding perpetrators individually responsible for human rights violations. The very few cases of accountability represent the
exception and not the rule. Emily Braid and Naomi Roht-Arriaza explore the factors that pose obstacles to accountability, even when all of the streams that should
feed the justice cascade have begun to flow. These barriers include lack of political
will, weak and corrupt judicial systems, and the persistent absence of respect for the
rule of law. The chapter poses the question of whether most countries will enjoy

individual criminal responsibility in the age of accountability, or if it will remain elusive to most countries except those few with exceptional circumstances.

Phil Clark questions the assumption that the international promotion of individual criminal responsibility is universally positive. In Chapter 8, he examines the cases of Rwanda and Uganda. His extensive fieldwork in both countries suggests that the international community has failed to agree on the appropriate form that justice should take in these two cases. The result is a lack of support for local forms of traditional justice, especially in the case of Rwanda's *gacaca* courts; most in the international community instead favor a perceived ideal of individual criminal responsibility. Phil Clark argues that the preference for prosecutions championed by the international community has resulted in the overlooking of the specific context and dynamics of Rwanda and Uganda, particularly the absence of the legal procedures, institutions, and capacity that would render such judicial processes ideal. Furthermore, the international community has failed to provide support for innovative approaches that might constitute more appropriate ways to achieve accountability in the contexts of weak rule of law, ongoing violence, and widespread culpability for massive levels of violence that characterize the transitional context in Rwanda and Uganda. His analysis thus questions whether the model of criminal prosecutions is appropriate, feasible, or desirable in all contexts if the goal is accountability for past atrocity. Phil Clark's chapter strongly challenges the assumptions of one size fits all and the inevitable and linear positive progress to accountability. He calls on international scholars and activists to pay more attention to the local and specific contexts that make each case of violence and transition unique and to support appropriate and effective forms of local justice in those contexts.

In Chapter 9, Antje du Bois-Pedain discusses the South African Truth and Reconciliation Commission (TRC) and its unique amnesty process that received praise throughout the world. The chapter reviews the history and implementation of South Africa's conditional amnesty law and its longer term domestic impact. The chapter suggests that South Africa's conditional amnesty arguably offers an enduring example of an ethically justifiable and politically effective transitional amnesty law that could serve as a blueprint for a credible accountability process in other transitions. Nonetheless, a conditional amnesty process is not an easy way out for a polity incapable or unwilling to conduct successful prosecutions. In order to reap its benefits, it needs to be embedded in a broader truth finding effort and supported by a real threat of prosecution against those who fail to participate. As this study of the South African model of conditional amnesty reveals, it is possible to mold an amnesty arrangement into a building block for an accountability process capable of reaching the fundamental objectives of truth, justice, and social healing that any given set of transitional policies seeks to achieve.

Not all amnesty processes involve laws. In Chapter 10 Patrick Burgess discusses the protection of perpetrators of mass crimes in Indonesia where no amnesty law for serious crimes has been passed. This protection is not achieved through a failure to pass laws, establish mechanisms, or bring perpetrators to trial. On the contrary, Indonesia has passed a national law on crimes against humanity and genocide, established a range of commissions of inquiry, included TRCs in a number of national laws, and brought a total of thirty-four prosecutions before the special human rights courts. Despite all of these efforts, the results include failure to make public the findings of many important inquiries, refusal to implement the laws establishing regional TRCs, and a reversal of all eighteen convictions from the thirty-four human rights court trials. The net result is that not one senior commander or official has been brought to account for any of the seven major instances of mass violations that resulted in more than a thousand deaths or a number of other lesser examples of international crimes. While recognizing that no definitive answer is available, Patrick Burgess raises the question of whether, in such a context, overcoming the complex, hidden web of contributing factors that serve to conceal the nature of de facto amnesty may be even more challenging than struggling against a clearly visible amnesty law.

Ronald Slye's Chapter 11, rather than discussing what international law and morality require with respect to accountability for gross atrocities, uses the example of the Cambodian amnesties and the Extraordinary Criminal Court for Cambodia (ECCC) to discuss two important choices facing drafters of laws with implications for an amnesty's legitimacy: *who* should be protected by an amnesty and *how long* such an amnesty should last. Furthermore, a new form of amnesty that may to be attractive to its beneficiaries while at the same time providing some possibility of accountability is suggested, a form of limited amnesty. This type of amnesty would see a period of time during which accountability is initially barred and then lifted so that some form of accountability – sometimes a criminal trial – can take place. Such an amnesty would provide an incentive for its beneficiaries to contribute in a meaningful way to truth, accountability, and reconciliation. These limited amnesties are unlike the Cambodian amnesties discussed in the chapter which, as promulgated, are amnesic; their primary purpose is to conceal and forget rather than reveal and account. They provide no accountability, no benefits to victims, and no revelations concerning the violations of the amnesty's beneficiaries. If allowed to survive in their present form through enforcement before the ECCC, they will continue to be illegitimate.

Chapter 12 by Paloma Aguilar, in looking at the Spanish case in comparison with the cases of Chile and Argentina, discusses the reasons for the survival of long-standing amnesties and the challenges these have to face during the age of accountability. The Spanish 1977 amnesty law was adopted to deal with crimes committed during the Francoist dictatorship. The general benefits of the law (e.g., in terms of annulment of criminal records and pensions) were available to the victims of the civil war and their relatives. The amnesty, not unlike the Brazilian law, included atrocities committed on both sides (the Francoist authorities and the anti-Francoist groups). While Paloma Aguilar's analysis of the Spanish case does not equate the Francoist and anti-Francoist atrocities during the war – and, in particular, after-ward – she recognizes that the law's appeal may result in part from those who do not want to fight new battles over the legitimacy or lack of legitimacy of that violence. When Franco died, more than thirty-five years after the civil war, the call for "Never Again" in Spain did not include a demand for justice, in contrast to Latin America. It instead reflected a near nationwide unwillingness to look back, a fear of resur-recting old animosities, and a rejection of returning the country to violent conflict. Paloma Aguilar suggests that the national perception of a fragile peace did not rely solely on the memories of the civil war era, but was also influenced by the political violence occurring during the transition, particularly that committed by Basque ter-rorists. The idea of peace at any cost pervaded national consciousness and led to an almost universal tolerance of amnesty as the price of stability. Also, the existence of a very conservative judiciary in Spain, unwilling to search for loopholes in the leg-islation in order to hold perpetrators accountable or at least to publicly expose the truth about the dictatorial repression, helps to partly account for the lack of transi-tional justice measures in Spain. In addition, when, many years later, Judge Baltasar Garzón threatened that foundational pact of the transition by initiating efforts to investigate the executions carried out by Francoist forces, he faced substantial oppo-sition by the judiciary and the most conservative sectors of public opinion. Rather than undermining the amnesty law, the response to Garzón's efforts seemed instead a warning to those who might wish to challenge the foundational pact of the Spanish democracy.

In the conclusion, Tricia Olsen, Leigh Payne, and Andrew Reiter use their own quantitative and qualitative analysis of amnesty laws and processes in ninety transi-tions since 1970 to consider the questions raised theoretically and empirically in the volume. They suggest that the literature has made a stark contrast between amnesty processes and prosecutions, when these processes are often compatible in one form or another. They thus offer a middle ground, or third way, between the seemingly incompatible theoretical stands that have characterized the debate on amnesty in the transitional justice literature thus far. The chapter suggests that scholars and practitioners do not want to promote amnesties in the age of accountability or to condemn all forms of amnesty. Instead, these authors call on an accountability driven approach to amnesties that analyzes when they block individual criminal responsibility and when they may pave the way to the right to redress. Drawing on the theoretical and empirical chapters in this book, as well as additional processes and explanations beyond the scope of this volume, they develop a set of scenarios that countries have pursued to make amnesties and trials compatible. These scenarios, as the chapters in this book show, do not always lead to more justice. In some cases, they may lead to less justice. Nonetheless, some ideal models emerge that suggest new directions for activism that accepts the prevalence of, and desire for, amnesty while refusing to succumb to impunity or to avoid accountability.

## CONCLUDING REMARKS

This volume attempts to reframe debates on the topic of amnesty and accountability in a new light, moving beyond the limited framing of truth versus justice or stability versus accountability in which many of these issues have been cast in the existing transitional justice scholarship. The theoretical and empirical contributions in this edited book offer new ways of reading and tackling the enduring persistence of amnesty in the age of accountability. In particular, several of the empirical chapters outline the trickling in of the accountability norm from the international sphere to domestic contexts and the continued obstacles still standing in the way of justice in many countries. Further, the chapters call attention to the unique dynamics and specificities of each case when trying to illuminate the sustained appeal and endurance of amnesties. Finally, in addition to the success cases of Argentina and Uruguay, many other significant inroads against impunity have been obtained, such as the recent sentence (August 2011) in the Guatemalan *Las Dos Erres* case, in which four former soldiers have been sentenced to life in prison for the massacre of more than 200 people.

Based on analyses of the case studies included in this volume, scholars, human rights practitioners, and policy makers cannot assume that the age of accountability has brought an inexorable or linear process toward individual criminal justice for human rights violations. Neither can they assume, however, that the persistence of amnesties has blocked progress toward accountability. Instead, this volume shows that the struggle against impunity exists despite the age of accountability. That struggle includes victories and setbacks. An easy or obvious solution to avoid impunity does not exist, but this volume offers scenarios to make accountability more likely even when amnesty prevails.

# PART I

# Theoretical Framework

# 1

# The Age of Accountability

## The Global Rise of Individual Criminal Accountability

### Kathryn Sikkink

What do we mean by an age of accountability? In the fifteen years from 1975 to 1990, the first prosecutions of individual state officials for human rights violations (after the post-World War II Nuremberg and Tokyo Trials) were carried out in the domestic judicial systems of Greece, Portugal, Argentina, Bolivia, and Guatemala. These prosecutions often moved slowly and were contested, uncertain, and perceived as dangerous and reversible. Indeed, prior to the early 1980s, accountability was often unimaginable.[1] In the period from 1990 to 2010, individual criminal accountability would gain momentum and, eventually, would be permanently embodied in international law, international and domestic institutions, and in the global consciousness. This momentum prompted UN Secretary General Ban Ki-moon to say in May 2010 that a "new age of accountability" was replacing an "old era of impunity."[2]

Together, these prosecutions comprise an interrelated, new trend in world politics toward holding individual state officials, some of whom are heads of state, criminally accountable for human rights violations.[3] Elsewhere I have referred to this trend as "the justice cascade," a dramatic shift in the legitimacy of the norms of individual criminal accountability for human rights violations and an increase in actions (prosecutions) on behalf of those norms.[4] The justice norm is nested in a larger movement for accountability for human rights violations. Since the 1980s, states

---

[1]  For example, as Paloma Aguilar's chapter on Spain in this volume points out, Francoist forces did not even consider the possibility that they might be held accountable.
[2]  "At ICC Review Conference, Ban Declares End to 'Era of Impunity,'" UN News Centre, *UN News Service*, accessed July 8, 2011, http://www.un.org/apps/news/story.asp?NewsID=34866.
[3]  See, for example, Lutz and Reiger, *Prosecuting Heads of State*.
[4]  Sikkink, *The Justice Cascade*. Originally, this term served as the title of an article that I co-wrote with my colleague, Ellen Lutz, "The Justice Cascade."

This chapter draws extensively on material from chapter four of my book, *The Justice Cascade: How Human Rights Prosecutions Are Changing World Politics* (New York: W.W. Norton, 2011). I wish to thank Geoff Dancy for research assistance and for verbally presenting an earlier draft of this chapter at a workshop in Oxford in October 2010 which I could not attend.

have not only initiated prosecutions, but have increasingly used multiple alternative transitional justice mechanisms, including truth commissions, reparations, partial amnesties, lustration, museums and other memory sites, archives, and oral history projects to address past human rights violations.[5] The escalating use of these practices attests to a broader movement for human rights accountability in critical times of political transition, of which the justice norm is only one part. We might think of this broader trend as the global rise of the age of accountability. The rise of accountability has been much more prominent in some regions, especially Latin America, Europe, and Africa, than in others, but it is not entirely absent from any region of the world, as we are seeing most recently in the many demands for accountability during the revolts of the Arab Spring.

Although there is an ample debate, including in this volume, about the superiority of one form of transitional justice over another, in case studies and in databases on the topic, most notable is that multiple transitional justice mechanisms tend to be used together rather than in isolation from one another.[6] Nor is there strong evidence that the use or advocacy of one form of transitional justice crowds out others. Phil Clark's chapter on Rwanda and Uganda in this volume expresses concern that advocates for trials may stand in the way of justice by promoting only one type of accountability. Looking at global trends, those fears may be misplaced, since equally eloquent norm entrepreneurs for restorative forms of justice have led to an increase, not a decrease, in the range of accountability options available to transitional countries, including traditional forms of justice. Indeed from Latin America to the Asia Pacific, those countries that have made the greatest use of prosecutions also have used amnesties and other transitional justice mechanisms most actively. In this sense, the notion of a justice cascade does not imply a linear process in which states move inexorably from employing amnesties to prosecutions, as Phil Clark suggests in his chapter in this volume. Rather, increasing numbers of prosecutions have been accompanied by high levels of amnesties as well as other forms of transitional justice. The combination of amnesty and prosecutions was possible, first, because each amnesty law was different and some exempted certain actors or actions. These partial amnesty laws can and have coexisted with prosecutions, and thus are consistent with individual criminal accountability. Second, blanket amnesty laws often faced challenges in courts that led to their later erosion or reversal in practice, if not on the books. As Tricia Olsen, Leigh Payne, and Andrew Reiter discuss in the

---

[5] Elizabeth Jelin, *State Repression and the Labors of Memory* (Minneapolis: University of Minnesota Press, 2003).

[6] Olsen, Payne, and Reiter, *Transitional Justice in Balance*, and Kathryn Sikkink and Carrie Booth Walling, "The Impact of Human Rights Trials in Latin America," *Journal of Peace Research* 44, no. 4 (2007): 427–45.

conclusion to this volume, multiple pathways exist around amnesty in the age of accountability.

In this chapter, I will focus on the history of the rise of individual criminal prosecutions. In the next chapter, Mark Freeman and Max Pensky provide a corresponding history and legal analysis of the use of amnesties. Other chapters in this volume document the rise and persistence of amnesties in the context of increasing demands for accountability. Some scholars, such as Louise Mallinder in her chapter in this volume, have argued that the persistence of amnesties casts doubt on the notion of a justice cascade.[7] I suspect that the adoption of amnesties may sometimes act as a *response* to the justice cascade; it is not evidence against its existence.[8] As perpetrators of human rights violations observe the increasing use of trials for individual criminal accountability, they may pressure governments to provide more guarantees against prosecution in the form of amnesties. In Chapter 2 of this volume, Freeman and Pensky refer to a related argument, made by Ronald Slye, that the increased use of amnesties is a result of "the growing influence of international criminal law, which now represents a credible threat that perpetrators of the most serious of international crimes will face indictment and prosecution."[9] In short, I would suggest, and most of the chapters in this volume seem to agree, that amnesties are part and parcel of the age of accountability, not an opposing historical trend. Trials and amnesties coexist in the age of accountability. We would not expect an increase in trials to necessarily lead to a decrease in amnesties.

The accountability trend occurred simultaneously at multiple levels. At one level, individual states, especially in Latin America but increasingly in other parts of the world as well, prosecuted human rights violations in domestic courts. At another level, states drafted new international human rights law and eventually international criminal law that fortified the legal underpinnings of the cascade. Existing institutions, such as the Inter-American Court of Human Rights (IACtHR), began to interpret state obligations under existing human rights law as including a responsibility to investigate and punish perpetrators. Next, states created specific ad hoc international institutions – the UN International Criminal Tribunal for the Former Yugoslavia (ICTY) and the ICTR – that put into practice and furthered the doctrine and jurisprudence of individual criminal accountability. Responding to demands from nongovernmental organizations and victims' groups, some domestic courts began to hold accountable foreign perpetrators of human rights violations in their own countries.

---

[7] See also, for example, Olsen, Payne, and Reiter, *Transitional Justice in Balance*, 104.
[8] I am indebted to Louise Mallinder, Leslie Vinjamuri, and Jack Snyder for helping me articulate this point.
[9] See Chapter 2, 56.

The culminating point of the justice cascade was the creation of the ICC, a legal development opposed initially by all five powerful permanent members of the Security Council. The ICC was eventually created through a campaign led by the pro-change coalition of a small "like-minded group" of states and NGOs, many in Europe, but including states and NGOs from around the world, with important leadership from former authoritarian countries such as Argentina and South Africa.

Some of these developments appeared quite separate from one another. We can think of various streams from different sources flowing in to create the justice cascade, streams that began to merge in the Rome Statute. The stories behind these developments have been told in a series of excellent books and articles,[10] but rarely do all the pieces of this global trend come together in one place.[11] Some suggest that all of the action happened in Rome in 1998, when the delegates gathered to draft the Statute of the ICC. But Rome was an outgrowth of processes that started in Nuremberg and continued in Athens, Buenos Aires, Madrid, London, and Geneva – accelerating in the last thirty years. When the delegates met in Rome, an important backstory made the ICC possible but not inevitable. This chapter describes and explains the course and the origins of the various streams of political and legal doctrines and practices that flowed into the justice cascade.

## HUMAN RIGHTS ACCOUNTABILITY: THREE MODELS

What do we mean by *accountability*? Accountability means that "some actors have the right to hold other actors to a set of standards … and to impose sanctions if they determine these responsibilities have not been met."[12] In the area of human rights, states are held accountable in two main ways: through legal prosecution in courts or quasi-judicial arenas like some of the human rights bodies of the United Nations, and by reputational accountability. The trend I am describing here toward individual criminal accountability is a pure form of legal accountability.[13] But most human

---

[10] See, for example, Ann Marie Clark, *Diplomacy of Conscience: Amnesty International and Changing Human Rights Norms* (Princeton: Princeton University Press, 2001); Michael J. Struett, *The Politics of Constructing the International Criminal Court* (New York: Palgrave Macmillan 2008); Naomi Roht-Arriaza, *The Pinochet Effect: Transnational Justice in the Age of Human Rights* (Philadelphia: University of Pennsylvania Press, 2005); Gary Bass, *Stay the Hand of Vengeance: The Politics of War Crimes Tribunals* (Princeton: Princeton University Press, 2000); Samantha Power, *A Problem from Hell: America and the Age of Genocide* (New York: Basic Books, 2002); Benjamin Schiff, *Building the International Criminal Court* (New York: Cambridge University Press, 2008); Olsen, Payne, and Reiter, *Transitional Justice in Balance*.

[11] For an exception, see Ruti G. Teitel, "Transitional Justice Genealogy," *Harvard Human Rights Journal* 16 (2003): 69–94. See also Lutz and Reiger, eds., *Prosecuting Heads of States*.

[12] Ruth Grant and Robert O. Keohane, "Accountability and Abuses of Power in World Politics," *American Political Science Review* 99, no. 1 (February 2005): 29–43.

[13] *Legal accountability* is the requirement that "agents abide by formal rules and be prepared to justify their action in those terms, in courts or quasi-judicial arenas." Grant and Keohane, "Accountability and Abuses of Power in World Politics," 36.

rights work has relied on reputational accountability, where NGOs and states try to stigmatize other states by documenting and denouncing their violations. This was the so-called name and shame strategy long adhered to by the human rights movement.

Historically, states have used three different models of accountability for past human rights violations: (1) the immunity or "impunity" model; (2) the state accountability model; and (3) the individual criminal accountability model. By far the most common historically is the impunity model, where no one is held accountable for human rights violations. Under a state accountability model the state is held accountable and it provides remedies and pays damages, while under a criminal model individuals are prosecuted, and if convicted, they go to prison.

Prior to World War II, the reigning orthodoxy was the impunity model, dictating that neither states nor state officials should or could be held accountable for human rights violations.[14] There were isolated examples of accountability in ancient Greece and in revolutionary France, but no sustained attempts at domestic human rights prosecutions emerged until after the Second World War.[15] At the international level, various pre-WWII attempts at accountability for war crimes and mass atrocities fell short of establishing the necessary institutions.[16] The impunity model relied on a doctrine wherein the state itself and officials of the state should remain indefinitely immune from prosecution, both in domestic courts and, particularly, in foreign courts.

The immunity model began to erode shortly after World War II. The Holocaust revealed the deep moral and political flaws of the reigning orthodoxy. States and nonstate actors saw the complete lack of international standards and accountability for massive human rights violations aimed at populations. To address this problem, they initiated action through the newly formed United Nations, first by drafting a set of standards in the Universal Declaration of Human Rights in 1948, and later in a series of more detailed human rights treaties. In these treaties, states proposed a new model of accountability in which the state as a whole was held accountable for human rights violations and was expected to take action to remedy the situation. But the state accountability model went hand in hand with the idea that state officials themselves remained immune from prosecution for human rights violations. So, for example, when a state violated rights under the International Covenant on Civil and Political Rights, in some cases individuals could bring petitions before the UN Human Rights Committee (UNHRC). But these petitions were against the state itself, not a particular state official.

---

[14]  I borrow the term *reigning orthodoxy* from Jeffrey Legro to describe old ideas that are later replaced by new ones. Jeffrey Legro, *Rethinking the World: Great Power Strategies and International Order* (Ithaca: Cornell University Press, 2005).

[15]  See Elster, *Closing the Books*.

[16]  Bass, *Stay the Hand of Vengeance*.

States negotiated and produced dozens of human rights treaties in the second half of the twentieth century, most of which incorporate this state accountability model. It began to be the new orthodoxy for accountability. It continues to be the model used by virtually the entire human rights apparatus in the United Nations, including almost all of the treaty bodies. It is also the model employed by regional human rights institutions – the European Court of Human Rights, the IACtHR, and the new African Court on Human Rights and Peoples' Rights.

In the 1980s and 1990s, after decades of drafting and ratifying human rights treaties, it appeared that human rights violations were getting worse, not better. In this context, some activists argued that as long as no individuals were held personally responsible for human rights violations, there would be no strong incentives for changing behavior. They suggested that holding individual state officials criminally accountable could supplement state accountability and add a new way to enforce human rights law. But the reigning orthodoxy, the impunity model, did not disappear; it continues to coexist with the new criminal accountability model. Although impunity was ever more called into question, the increasing use of amnesty laws around the world shows the model is still alive and well. Changing ideas about the desirability and possibility of some form of accountability for human rights violations, however, made it more difficult to advocate a pure impunity model. Those who advocate immunity from prosecutions today are more likely to also encourage some form of restorative justice. Nor did the state accountability model disappear. It continues to be the main model used by the UN system and the regional human rights courts, and often complements criminal accountability. So what we have at present is *not* replacement of one model by another, but a layering of multiple models.

This new individual criminal accountability model (ICA) does not apply to the whole range of civil and political rights but, rather, to a small subset of rights sometimes referred to as *physical integrity rights*, the "rights of the person" or "core crimes." These include prohibitions on torture, summary execution, and genocide, as well as on war crimes and crimes against humanity. This ICA regulatory model involves an important convergence of international law (human rights, humanitarian, and international criminal law) and domestic criminal law.[17]

## THE RISE OF THE INDIVIDUAL ACCOUNTABILITY MODEL

The age of accountability was in part a result of key changes in the area of international law, which helped make the individual a subject of international human rights

[17] Steven Ratner and Jason Abrams refer to four interrelated bodies of law that underpin the move toward individual accountability for human rights violations: international human rights law, international humanitarian law, international criminal law, and domestic law. Steven Ratner and Jason Abrams, *Accountability for Human Rights Atrocities in International Law: Beyond the Nuremberg Legacy* (Oxford: Oxford University Press, 2001), 9–14.

law alongside the state. A key step in the process was the drafting of the Convention against Torture and Other Cruel, Inhuman or Degrading Treatment or Punishment (CAT). The idea of the international criminalization of torture started with Amnesty International (AI) when it launched its first worldwide campaign, the "Campaign for the Abolition of Torture" in December 1972. As part of that campaign, AI issued a series of recommendations it believed would contribute to its efforts against torture, including a recommendation for international tribunals to investigate torture. Eight months after AI launched its campaign, the Chilean military overthrew the democratically elected government of Salvador Allende. When the Chilean military's widespread use of torture was publicized, the outrage it provoked added more fuel to AI's campaign. In turn, stimulated by AI's campaign against torture and by the situation in Chile, the Swedish and Dutch governments brought the question of torture before the UN General Assembly through a resolution in the autumn of 1973. This resolution initiated a long process of UN involvement in the quest to abolish torture.

Two years later, Greek domestic trials of military officials for torture in 1975 gave a boost to the emerging norm of accountability. The Greek trials showed that it was possible to hold human rights prosecutions that respected due process without endangering the stability of democracy. Just a few months after the main torture trials in Athens, on December 9, 1975, the countries in the UN General Assembly adopted the Declaration on the Protection of All Persons from Being Subjected to Torture and Other Cruel, Inhuman or Degrading Treatment or Punishment (the "Torture Declaration").

The Declaration was the starting point for individual criminal accountability for torture specifically and for core human rights violations more generally. But the Declaration only mentioned criminal proceedings under *national* law and made no reference to the possibility of foreign or international accountability. The Greek delegate from the new democratic government worked hard to include language about international implementation because, as he explained, during the dictatorship in Greece "domestic legislation did not suffice," and international condemnation was essential to stop torture.[18] But states, ever jealous of their sovereignty, had cut even the modest language within the draft declaration about international assistance, fearing such language could encourage international intervention in their affairs. After approving the Declaration, delegates passed a resolution proposed by Greece, the Netherlands, and Sweden calling on the UN to promote further international efforts against torture.[19] They wanted a more binding treaty against torture.

---

[18]  Nigel Rodley, *The Treatment of Prisoners Under International Law* (Oxford: Clarendon Press, 1999).
[19]  J. Herman Burgers and Hans Danelius, *The United Nations Convention Against Torture: A Handbook on the Convention against Torture and Other Cruel, Inhuman or Degrading Treatment or Punishment* (Dordrecht, Netherlands: Martinus Nijhoff, 1988), 13–18.

A committee of experts, organized by the International Association of Penal Law (AIDP), met in Syracuse in December of 1977 to prepare a Draft Convention for the Prevention and Suppression of Torture. The experts included Cherif Bassiouni, secretary general of the AIDP; Nigel Rodley, legal counsel for AI; and Niall MacDermot, head of the International Commission of Jurists; together with twenty-seven other experts, mainly law professors from Western countries, although some experts also came from Brazil, Egypt, India, Nigeria, and Japan. They explicitly chose to use an international criminal law approach to establish an obligation on states to prosecute or punish offenders or to extradite them to another state willing to do so.[20] Once they had completed the draft convention, the AIDP, under Bassiouni's leadership, presented the draft of the Torture Convention to the subcommission. This draft was the starting point for the drafting of the CAT. It showed how international NGOs worked directly to influence the content of international law. The fact that an association of criminal law scholars was involved in the draft helps explain why this was the first major human rights treaty that put the individual at the center of the treaty as the perpetrator of torture and provided for individual criminal accountability for torture. The draft speaks throughout of "a person," or a state official, as responsible for committing or instigating torture or failing to prevent it. This draft clearly states that persons believed responsible for torture should be prosecuted, and it leaves open the possibility of domestic, foreign, and international prosecutions. An unobtrusive clause making universal jurisdiction possible appears here for the first time. Sweden later submitted this draft to the Human Rights Commission, since formal drafts must be submitted by governments, and it was the starting point for negotiations on the CAT.

Sweden and the Netherlands were among the primary instigators of the Declaration against Torture and the Convention against Torture, following up their earlier work on the Greek case at the European Commission on Human Rights. The efforts of Swedish diplomat Hans Danelius, assisted by Dutch diplomat Jan Herman Burgers, were particularly important. Burgers became a member of Amnesty International in the early 1970s, and he stressed that in the Netherlands and Sweden, the influence of local human rights groups like Amnesty International had been very important in stimulating the governments to work against torture.[21]

Danelius and the Swedish government submitted the AIDP draft that served as a basis for the treaty's negotiation. The final version of the Convention called for state accountability and individual criminal accountability. The Convention requires states to ensure that acts of torture are offenses under domestic criminal law, to

---

[20] Committee of Experts on Torture, "Committee of Experts on Torture, Syracuse, Italy, December 16–17, 1977," *Revue Internationale de Droit Pénal* 48 (1977).

[21] J. Herman Burgers, Interview with the author, November 13, 1993, The Hague.

investigate alleged cases of torture, and to either extradite or prosecute the accused. Most significant, the Convention granted universal jurisdiction for torture, which simply meant that each state party shall take measures to establish its jurisdiction over torture if the alleged offender is present in its territory. In other words, a torturer can be prosecuted by any state that has ratified the Convention if the offender is in that country. Universal jurisdiction provided for a system of decentralized enforcement in any national judicial system against individuals who committed or instigated torture. Sweden considered this provision the cornerstone of the Convention because it was intended to make it hard for torturers to evade domestic prosecution by finding a safe haven in a foreign country. Many countries, including the United States, supported the inclusion of universal jurisdiction in the treaty.[22] Legal experts from AI were highly involved in proposing and supporting the language about individual criminal accountability and universal jurisdiction in the Convention.[23]

Universal jurisdiction simply complements rather than replaces domestic prosecution. If the accused travels to or lives in another country, the judicial officials of that country may prosecute him or her, extradite him or her home, or send him or her to a third country for legal action. Universal jurisdiction is only one part, and not the most important part, of the justice cascade. "[S]uch jurisdiction will by its nature always be a supplementary jurisdiction, of last resort, and it will often not be feasible to exercise it."[24]

As the negotiations for the treaty drew to an end, countries such as Argentina, Uruguay, and Brazil, which had originally opposed the treaty, experienced transitions to democracy. The democratization in Argentina contributed fundamentally to the passage of the CAT, when the new Alfonsín government instructed its representatives to work for the passage of the Convention. This helped shift the balance in the negotiations in favor of the Convention, contributing to its passage by the UN General Assembly in December 1984.[25] The Convention was opened for signatures in February 1985 and it went into effect in 1987 after ratification by twenty states. Among the first twenty states to sign the CAT (though not necessarily the first to ratify it), were not only well-established Western democracies, but also a number of the states where early human rights prosecutions were used, including Argentina, Bolivia, Greece, Portugal, and Panama.

---

[22] Burgers and Danelius, *The United Nations Convention against Torture*, 78–9. See also 58, 62–3.

[23] See Nigel Rodley and Jayne Huckerby, "Outlawing Torture: The Story of Amnesty International's Efforts to Shape the UN Convention against Torture," in *Human Rights Advocacy Stories*, ed., Deena Hurwitz, Margaret L. Satterthwaite, and Douglas B. Ford (New York, NY: Foundation Press: Thomson/West, 2009).

[24] Bruce Broomhall, *International Justice and the International Criminal Court: Between Sovereignty and the Rule of Law* (Oxford: Oxford University Press, 2003).

[25] Chris Ingelse, *The U.N. Committee against Torture: An Assessment* (The Hague: Martinus Nijhoff Publishers, 2001).

At the same time states were redrafting the Convention against Torture, they were working on two regional treaties, the Inter-American Convention to Prevent and Punish Torture and the European Convention for the Prevention of Torture and Inhuman or Degrading Treatment or Punishment.

All three treaties entered into force between 1987 and 1989, with the Inter-American Convention going first in February 1987. Latin American countries recently returned to democracy took the lead in drafting the Inter-American Convention. It contains very similar language to the CAT: torture is an offense under national criminal law and also a crime subject to universal jurisdiction.

## THE ANTI-APARTHEID CONVENTION

At the same time as these states were negotiating the Torture Convention in the mid-1970s, African states took the leadership in drafting one of the most progressive treaties with a very strong criminal law component: the International Convention on the Suppression and Punishment of the Crime of Apartheid (hereinafter the Apartheid Convention). The Apartheid Convention begins with the statement that apartheid is a crime against humanity, referring directly to criminal law language from the Nuremburg tribunal. A Senegalese colleague in the AIDP asked Egyptian legal scholar Cherif Bassiouni to draft the statute for the establishment of an international criminal court to prosecute apartheid. In 1980 and 1981, Bassiouni drafted a statute for such a court, one never put into effect to prosecute apartheid. But almost twenty years later, when state delegations at the UN started talking again about an international criminal court, Bassiouni's draft statute was one of the drafts used in the discussion and drafting process.

## DISAPPEARANCES AND A NEW GOVERNMENT OBLIGATION TO PUNISH

After the passage of the Apartheid Convention and the Torture Convention, an informal coalition of NGOs – mainly in Latin America, the United States, and Europe – started working on another human rights treaty that would enhance legal support for individual criminal accountability. These groups were working on drafting a declaration and then a treaty to prohibit and punish the use of disappearances – when governments detain their opponents, imprison them in clandestine prisons, or kill them and deny responsibility. The most important international court case on disappearances was decided before the norm against disappearances had been fully developed in international law. The Inter-American Commission on Human Rights (IACHR) and the IACtHR played a very early role in pushing for individual criminal accountability, this time with regard to disappearances. In April 1986, the

IACHR submitted to the IACtHR three cases alleging disappearances in Honduras between 1981 and 1984.

Since disappearances are not mentioned specifically in the American Convention on Human Rights, the IACHR asked the IACtHR to determine that Honduras had violated those parts of the American Convention that guarantee the rights to life, humane treatment, personal liberty, and security. The IACtHR handed down its decisions in the three Honduran cases in 1988 and 1989. These cases established important precedents, especially as regards the international responsibility of the state for human rights violations. In its decision on the merits in the *Velásquez Rodríguez* case, for example, the IACtHR concluded that the American Convention establishes that governments have the obligation to respect the human rights of individuals and to guarantee the enjoyment of these rights. As a consequence of this obligation, the IACtHR found that "states must prevent, investigate and *punish* any violation of the rights recognized by the Convention ..."[26] (emphasis added). In this groundbreaking decision, a regional human rights court found for the first time that states had a "duty to punish."

Activists and their state allies drafted a Declaration on the Protection of All Persons from Enforced Disappearance, adopted in 1992, and a regional treaty, the Inter-American Convention on Forced Disappearance of Persons, which entered into force in 1996. The Inter-American Convention contains virtually identical language on universal jurisdiction as the CAT and thus underscores a move toward individual criminal accountability for issues beyond torture.

The Inter-American Convention on Forced Disappearance of Persons included other legal innovations with important implications for individual criminal accountability and for the amnesties that are the topic of this volume. First, as in the Apartheid Convention, it used the term "crimes against humanity" to describe the crime of disappearance. Such a description is important because it was generally understood that crimes against humanity were not subject to statutes of limitations. The Inter-American Convention defined disappearance as a "continuous" or permanent offense "as long as the fate or whereabouts of the victim has not been determined." These provisions improve the chances of prosecution against individuals actively participating in disappearance. Countries generally block human rights prosecutions through amnesty laws and statutes of limitations. A statute of limitations sets a time limit within which legal action must be brought. These statutes are designed to prevent stale claims from arising after the facts of the case have become obscure through the passage of time. But in the case of human rights violations, a statute of limitations can block many human rights prosecutions. Likewise, the definition of disappearance as a continuous crime means that disappearances will normally not

---

[26] Inter-American Court of Human Rights, *Velásquez Rodríguez* case, Judgment, (ser. C) No. 4 (1988).

be covered by amnesty laws because amnesty applies to already completed crimes, not to ongoing ones. Thus, by defining disappearances as crimes against humanity or as continuous crimes, these treaties gave tools to activist lawyers and judges to bypass the main legal blocks to prosecutions.

## INDIVIDUAL CRIMINAL ACCOUNTABILITY FOR WAR CRIMES

Humanitarian law and human rights law had been analytically separate up to this point. Humanitarian law, also known as "the laws of war," was governed by the four Geneva Conventions and three additional protocols and monitored by the Red Cross. Traditionally, the laws of war only governed crimes committed between combatant groups in war, whereas human rights law applied to state repression of civilians. Early in the 1980s, lawyers started to blur these lines, especially given that many human rights abuses were perpetrated by states and armed groups in the context of civil war. Because the Geneva Conventions established individual criminal accountability for war crimes, applying it to actions in the domestic sphere offered another way to deepen the justice cascade.

A new organization at the time, Human Rights Watch (HRW), took the initiative in integrating humanitarian law into the work of human rights organizations. The director, Aryeh Neier, and the head of Americas Watch, Juan Méndez, a former Argentine lawyer and political prisoner, played a particularly important role in helping HRW become a foremost opponent of impunity internationally.[27] In 1982, Neier and his staff hit upon the idea of monitoring the laws of war as well as human rights law, which permitted them to talk about violations committed by insurgents as well as by governments. For example, Human Rights Watch criticized violations of humanitarian law by the El Salvadoran government, by the Farabundo Martí National Liberation Front (FMLN) guerrillas in El Salvador, and by the United States-supported insurgent group, the Contras, fighting against the Sandinista government in Nicaragua.[28]

The effort by HRW to incorporate humanitarian law in its work was a prescient move that foreshadowed the merging of elements of human rights law and humanitarian law in the ICTY and the ICC. At the time, for insiders, it was a novel move, although outsiders, including many governments and the general public, had never clearly understood the division between human rights law and humanitarian law to begin with. This embrace of humanitarian law later put HRW in a place to take leadership in calling for an international war crimes tribunal in the former Yugoslavia.

---

[27] Aryeh Neier, *Taking Liberties: Four Decades in the Struggle for Rights* (New York: Public Affairs, 2003), 194, 195, 224.

[28] Aryeh Neier, Interview with the author, March 19, 1992, New York City.

## DOMESTIC HUMAN RIGHTS PROSECUTIONS ACCELERATE

As the CAT was being drafted and ratified, legal developments continued in domestic polities around the world – developments that began to reinforce the idea of individual criminal accountability for state officials. Before the ICTY began working in 1993, prosecutions had taken place in court settings scattered across twenty-three different states, and universal jurisdiction had been exercised by concerned states at least three times. Many of the countries that carried out these prosecutions were from Latin America, but after the end of the Cold War and the process of transition in the Soviet Bloc, they also included countries from Eastern Europe and eventually from Africa. Courts in each of these countries used different legal reasoning to justify the prosecutions, but what is important is that they began to implement an individual criminal accountability model for human rights violations.

## THE INTERNATIONAL CRIMINAL TRIBUNAL FOR THE FORMER YUGOSLAVIA

On February 22, 1993, without dissent, the UN Security Council approved a plan submitted by Secretary General Boutros Boutros-Ghali to establish an international criminal tribunal, the ICTY, to try individuals accused of war crimes in the former Yugoslavia. The combination of the end of the Cold War, the reemergence of genocide on the soil of Europe, and the inability of the world to gather the political will to stop that genocide gave impetus to the creation of the first international war crimes tribunal since World War II, the ICTY. But as the first half of this chapter makes clear, by the time the Security Council created the ICTY, the members of the United Nations had been working for twenty years, since the Torture Declaration in 1973, to establish in international law the obligation to prosecute and punish state officials for human rights violations. In this sense, the creation of the ICTY was not quite as unprecedented as some of its creators would suggest.

The first person to advocate publicly for an international war crimes tribunal in the former Yugoslavia was a Yugoslav journalist who issued an appeal that appeared in May 1991 as a newspaper article titled "Nuremberg Now!"[29] Shortly after, in July 1992, HRW called for the establishment of a tribunal to prosecute human rights violations and war crimes in the former Yugoslavia, among the earliest recommendations for individual criminal accountability in the Balkans. Although Bassiouni and the AIDP had campaigned for many years for an international criminal court, neither HRW nor any other prominent human rights group had ever before campaigned to establish an international war crimes tribunal. Researchers from HRW and other human rights organizations were on the ground in the former Yugoslavia,

---

[29] Power, *A Problem from Hell*, 18.

and their reports revealed that the situation continued to worsen: the scope and type of violations in the war in Bosnia-Herzegovina after 1992 made it appropriate not only to use the phrase *crimes against humanity*, but also to use "the name for the ultimate crime: genocide."[30]

Only a few days after the appeal by HRW, the media carried the first exposé of concentration camps in the Balkans, with photos of emaciated prisoners in camps that looked frighteningly similar to those seen during the Holocaust.[31] On the back of these new images and this new information, the appeal for a tribunal resonated with the global public. On August 13, 1992, states took the first step toward a tribunal when the UN Security Council set up a Commission of Experts to Investigate Grave Breaches of the Geneva Conventions and appointed Bassiouni as chair. The Security Council requested that states and international humanitarian organizations submit to the Commission substantiated information concerning Balkan war crimes. In this first step, decision makers consciously echoed the Nuremberg precedent; the Nuremburg Trials had begun with a request for states to submit evidence of war crimes.

An important turning point came after the Clinton administration took office in January 1993 and appointed Madeline Albright as the ambassador to the UN. Born in Czechoslovakia, Albright had a strong interest in Central and Eastern Europe and a commitment to human rights. She became "one of the most tireless supporters of the Court."[32]

After the UN authorized the creation of the ICTY in February 1993, the Security Council appointed South African jurist Richard Goldstone as the chief prosecutor of the ICTY. Goldstone, like others involved in the tribunal, saw the Nuremberg precedent as the primary source for the work on the ICTY. But Goldstone recognized that, because it was a path breaking decision to create the new tribunal, all the conditions had to be in place, and all these factors converged in the case of the former Yugoslavia. The conditions included the end of the Cold War, the media images of ethnic cleansing that evoked the Holocaust, and the fact that the national and international NGOs campaigning for the tribunal had "recently acquired the power to influence public opinion."[33]

Once the ICTY was established, it became possible to set up other international tribunals. The creation of the ICTY in 1993 was a turning point in the campaign against impunity. The ICTY sparked the establishment of the ICTR in 1994 to

---

[30] Aryeh Neier, *War Crimes. Brutality, Genocide, Terror, and the Struggle for Justice* (New York: Times Books, 1998), 120.

[31] Bass, *Stay the Hand of Vengeance.*

[32] Powers, *A Problem from Hell*, 326.

[33] Richard J. Goldstone, *For Humanity: Reflections of a War Crimes Investigator* (New Haven: Yale University Press, 2000), 79–80.

prosecute perpetrators of the genocide in Rwanda, fueled efforts to bring justice to the Khmer Rouge in Cambodia, and eventually mobilized states to support the creation of the ICC.

## THE CREATION OF THE ICC

The end of the Cold War and the institutionalization of the two ad hoc tribunals reinvigorated international interest in establishing a permanent international criminal court. The work on an international criminal tribunal had first begun after World War II, but few countries were deeply committed to the project, and the Cold War and its attendant stalemate at the UN disrupted serious efforts in this regard. The International Law Commission of the UN suspended further discussion of the issue in 1953 after it was unable to arrive at a definition of aggression as one of the key crimes that the new tribunal would address.

Renewal of these efforts in the early 1990s was spearheaded by a coalition of actors, including international members of the AIDP who had worked for a permanent international criminal court. They were now joined by human rights NGOs, such as HRW, the Lawyers Committee for Human Rights, and AI, which had long pushed for prosecutions of perpetrators and other forms of accountability in the wake of gross violations of human rights. Governments also joined, particularly those from Europe and Latin America that had internalized the international justice ethic.

In 1990, an NGO committee of experts, chaired by Bassiouni, prepared a draft statute for an ICC that would have jurisdiction over all international crimes. The draft was modeled after the 1981 text Bassiouni had prepared for the implementation of the Apartheid Convention. Germany helped the process gain momentum when the German foreign minister, Hans-Dietrick Genscher, also an advocate of the ICTY, called on the UN General Assembly to create an international court "where crimes against humanity, crimes against peace, genocide, war crimes, and environmental criminality can be prosecuted and punished."[34] His proposal eventually received strong support from the group of like-minded states and from the coalition of human rights NGOs.

Although the United States would later be an opponent of the ICC, in the early period, the U.S. government under the Clinton administration was favorable to the idea of the creation of an international criminal court. Historically, the United States "had been the leading proponent of international institutions based on principled rules" and, for a brief moment in the mid 1990s, "the U.S. seemed willing

[34] Michael J. Struett, *The Politics of Constructing the International Criminal Court* (New York: Palgrave Macmillan, 2008), 71.

and able to play this role again."[35] Michael Scharf, a lawyer in the U.S. Department of State from 1989 to 1993 who crafted the U.S. government's position on the ICC, said that in 1993 the United States significantly changed its stance on the ICC. Previously, the policy had been "to prolong without progressing the debate." In 1993, the United States "committed itself actively to work towards resolving the remaining political and legal issues" involved with the creation of the ICC.[36] The most important factor for the change in the U.S. position on the ICC, Scharf argued, was the establishment of the ICTY. In its work on the ICTY, the United States had successfully tackled the "same complex legal and political issues that it had identified as obstacles" to the ICC.[37] This made it harder for the United States to justify its future opposition to the ICC. In this context, the United States changed its position, and this made it easier for the General Assembly to decide to move ahead with an ICC treaty conference. Of course, the Clinton administration expected the negotiations to produce a court the United States could support, that is, a court over which the United States would have more control. Without U.S. acquiescence in the early stages, it is unlikely that the negotiations for the court would have gotten off the ground.[38] By the time the negotiations gained momentum around proposals that the United States would not support, it was too late to stop the process. This shows the strength of the idea of individual responsibility for human rights violations. It was not just too late for the United States to stop the ICC; it was too late to stop the idea of individual criminal accountability.

The International Law Commission (ILC) of the UN took up the issue of the ICC again and produced a conservative draft statute in 1994 that envisioned a less powerful and independent court than the one eventually created. Even the firmest supporters of the idea of an ICC, like Professor Bassiouni, did not imagine in their writings at the time that a strong court with compulsory jurisdiction and an independent prosecutor would emerge.

These conservative expectations changed in the four years between the ILC draft and the signing of the Rome Statute in 1998. An Argentine diplomat, Silvia Fernández de Gurmendi, was intimately involved with the process leading up to the ratification of the Rome Statute. In 1994, Fernández was assigned to be the legal advisor to the Argentine mission to the UN in New York. She soon became part of a small group of government officials from Canada, the "Nordics," and Italy, who called themselves the coalition of friends of the international criminal court. At

[35]  Struett, *The Politics of Constructing the International Criminal Court*, 70.
[36]  Michael Scharf, "Getting Serious about an International Criminal Court," *Pace International Law Review* 6 (1994): 103.
[37]  Scharf, "Getting Serious About an International Criminal Court," 106–7.
[38]  Struett, *The Politics of Constructing the International Criminal Court*.

this time, Fernández recalls, there was a kind of "parting of the waters," between countries that wanted to support the creation of a criminal court and others that did not accept the proposals. Among those who opposed the idea of an independent court, she pointed out, were all the permanent members of the Security Council (the United States, the United Kingdom, France, China, and Russia), as well as a number of developing countries, including Mexico and India. The supporters were able to convince the UN to create two different preparatory committees for the ICC, and Fernández and Bassiouni were named as the two vice presidents of these committees. Fernández became one of the founders of the like-minded group of states in support of the Court. Particularly important was the parallel NGO group that worked in partnership with the like-minded group of states, the Coalition for the ICC, a global network of over 2,000 NGOs advocating for the ICC and ratification of the Rome Statute.

Throughout the process of creating the ICC, whenever the negotiations got difficult, Bassiouni organized informal intercessional meetings at the Siracusa Institute in Sicily. The Siracusa meetings were not only for the like-minded, but also for opponents of the Court. Meetings became increasingly open over time; the last was open to all states. The like-minded group continued to expand and it reached sixty by the time of the Rome conference. In Latin America, it came to include Uruguay, Chile, Brazil, and Venezuela. South Africa was also an important member, persuading other African states to join. A crucial turning point was the election of the Labour government of Tony Blair, and the United Kingdom switched sides and joined the like-minded. The wall of opposition from the permanent five members of the Security Council to the ICC was finally broken.

In the summer of 1998, the UN diplomatic conference in Rome finalized the statute for the ICC. A big effort was made to encourage smaller and poorer countries to come to the conference and a special fund supported the participation of developing countries at Rome and to provide technical assistance to their delegations.

In Rome the group of like-minded states and hundreds of NGOs propelled the process and achieved consensus or compromise to produce a comprehensive 128-article statute, the Rome Statute. The Rome Statute is the clearest statement of the new doctrine of individual criminal accountability. The Rome Statute is explicit: the fact that an individual has been a head of state or a member of government "shall in no case exempt a person from criminal responsibility" nor lead to a reduction of sentence.[39] The ICC, as the clearest distillation of new rules, came relatively late in the regulatory process and drew upon the experience of other efforts at individual criminal accountability, especially the ad hoc tribunals but also the experiences of individual nations.

[39]  Rome Statute, art. 27.

The alliance of like-minded states and human rights NGOs promoted the ICC and eventually persuaded a large number of states to sign and ratify the Rome Statute, despite strong U.S. opposition to the final draft. The Rome Statute opened for signature in 1998; by 2011, 116 states had ratified it. The ICC statute underscored international commitment to the principle that certain crimes are crimes not only against individuals but against the entire world. In consequence, jurisdiction lies with any state, or the international community as a whole, to prosecute those who engage in them.

But those who focus on the ICC do not fully appreciate how the dramatic success of the ICC was not only the result of specific moves in the negotiations leading up to the Rome Statute, but rather was the culmination of decades of work in favor of accountability. The ICC creation was not an isolated event. It built off not only the obvious international precedents like the ICTY and the ICTR, but also the dozens of countries with domestic experience with human rights prosecutions. Some of the states and NGOs present at the Rome Conference had advocated accountability since the Greek trials in 1975. Many had been involved in drafting the Convention against Torture, with its provisions for individual criminal accountability. The ICC was the culmination of almost twenty-five years of legal and political work. These states and NGOs had learned about the possibility of accountability from watching domestic human rights prosecutions. But some had become pessimistic about the possibility of accountability if it was limited to domestic courts. Amnesties everywhere blocked domestic prosecutions. Accountability needed international support, and the ICC seemed to be the institution for the job.

## FOREIGN HUMAN RIGHTS PROSECUTIONS BEGIN AND ACCELERATE

When delegates completed the Rome Statute in July 1998, it was still only a great promise. Despite the euphoria of having drafted a statute far stronger than any imagined possible, originally no one was sure how many states would ratify the Statute, or how soon the new court would come into being. The idea of international justice was still hypothetical, a proposition, an idea not yet realized in practice.

Only a few months later, an event occurred that would embody the idea of international justice. It is difficult to recreate the electricity produced when British police arrested former Chilean dictator General Augusto Pinochet in a London hospital on a Spanish extradition warrant for torture and other human rights crimes. Even the most ardent advocates of accountability did not really believe such an arrest was realistic. International lawyers knew it was legally possible, but no one believed it was politically possible. Opponents of international justice were outraged. The Pinochet case was so prominent because General Pinochet epitomized the modern authoritarian dictator. As opposed to other countries with faceless juntas or rotating presidencies, Pinochet had kept all the power to himself and maintained himself as chief executive for seventeen years. He had controlled the transition to democracy to maintain his position as commander in chief of the armed forces, and eventually become a senator for life. Pinochet, through his own efforts and those of his opponents, was a global symbol. Thus, his arrest personified and embodied the struggle over global justice. People around the globe watched, transfixed, over the next two years as the British justice system and the streets of London and Santiago played out the drama of his detention and trial.

The British courts assiduously confronted the jurisdictional questions posed by the Spanish request, eventually determining that the Spanish courts had jurisdiction to try Pinochet for crimes committed in Chile over a decade before. The ruling was based primarily on the positive law of the Torture Convention and the extradition treaties signed by Spain and the U.K. Although the CAT granted universal jurisdiction in the case of torture, this provision was not enforced until the Pinochet case, over ten years after the CAT went into effect. The Law Lords (the British Supreme Court) determined that a Chilean politician was not immune from extradition to Spain for torture committed while he was head of state since both countries had ratified the Torture Convention recognizing international jurisdiction for the crime of torture. The Law Lords limited their decision only to the Torture Convention because the letter of treaty law ratified by all parties clearly stated that universal jurisdiction existed for torture.

Although British authorities ultimately allowed Pinochet to return to Chile after finding him too incapacitated to stand trial, the events in Europe had important political repercussions in Chile that rippled across South America and the rest of the world. Once frozen, an unprecedented number of human rights cases started moving ahead in Chile's courts. The Chilean Supreme Court punched holes in Pinochet's self-awarded shield of immunity from prosecution. After Pinochet's arrest, an upsurge of other foreign prosecutions began, generated by what Naomi Roht-Arriaza has called "the Pinochet Effect."[40] The Pinochet case galvanized lawyers around the world, as it made them aware of the possibilities of prosecutions. A human rights lawyer in Germany, Wolfgang Kaleck, who handled foreign Argentine cases in German courts and who brought a case against Donald Rumsfeld for torture, recalled, "The 1998 Pinochet case: that was the trigger moment. From now on they have to be aware that this is serious, not just raising public awareness."[41]

Since that time, a number of high-profile convictions of state officials for human rights violations have occurred. In 1999, President Slobodan Milošević of Yugoslavia

---

[40] Roht-Arriaza, *The Pinochet Effect.*
[41] Interview with Wolfgang Kaleck, Berlin, Germany, June 6, 2010.

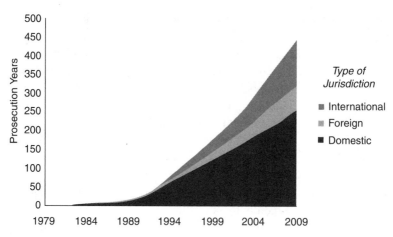

FIGURE 1.1. The justice cascade (stacked area chart of cumulated prosecution years by type).

became the first *sitting* head of state to be indicted for war crimes. Facing intense pressure from the United States and the European Union, the government of the new Federal Republic of Yugoslavia extradited Milošević to The Hague to stand trial, where he died before he could be convicted for his crimes. In March 2003, a second sitting president was charged for war crimes, when the Special Court for Sierra Leone (SCSL) indicted Charles Taylor, the warlord president of Liberia. Taylor went into exile in Nigeria in August of 2003 after a rebel group defeated his forces. In 2006, he was turned over to the Special Court, where he is currently on trial for human rights violations and war crimes. In 2009, the ICC indicted a third sitting President, Omar al-Bashir, for war crimes and crimes against humanity in the Darfur region of Sudan. In 2009, a domestic Peruvian court sentenced Alberto Fujimori, the former president of Peru, to twenty-five years in prison for human rights violations; the former authoritarian presidents of Uruguay, Gregorio Álvarez and Juan María Bordaberry, were convicted and sentenced to prison terms of twenty-five years and thirty years in domestic courts; and General Ríos Montt of Guatemala is the subject of ongoing trials in Spain and Guatemala. Finally, of the two most notorious Bosnian Serbian fugitives from justice, Radovan Karadžić is currently being prosecuted by the ICTY in The Hague, and Ratko Mladić has recently been extradited to The Hague.

Figure 1.1 summarizes the global trend in individual criminal accountability.[42] When one counts by country the number of years that prosecutions were held and then adds these figures together over time, one sees an unprecedented spike in

---

[42]  Sikkink, *The Justice Cascade*, 21.

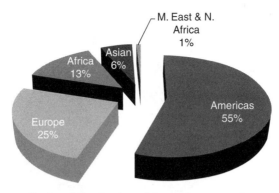

FIGURE 1.2. Regional distribution of domestic prosecutions 1979–2009.

worldwide efforts to address past human rights abuses by focusing on individual criminal responsibility.[43]

Significant variation occurs in the frequency of human rights prosecutions in different regions of the world. As the pie chart above (Figure 1.2) indicates, the trend toward domestic human rights prosecutions has been most pronounced in Latin America and in Central and Eastern Europe. Prosecutions are underway in Asia, Africa, and the Middle East, but to a lesser extent than in Europe and the Americas. International and foreign prosecutions are also unevenly distributed across different regions in ways that do not simply reflect where the worst human rights violations in the world have occurred (see Figure 1.3). Figure 1.3 records the regions of the countries whose nationals have been subject to outside efforts to achieve justice, not the countries where the prosecution occurred. Europe is heavily represented, in large part because of the prosecutions of the ICTY of individuals from what are now six different European states. There is a common perception that international and foreign prosecutions are used by countries in the global north to try individuals from the global south. Instead, currently the bulk of international prosecutions are held in Europe for human rights violations committed in Europe.

## CONCLUSIONS

In this chapter I have described the transnational spread of the norm of individual criminal accountability. I have tried to show that there is not a single historical

---

[43] The definition of prosecutions used in the database involves the entire judicial process of prosecution, including indictment, arrest, detention of a suspect (whether in house or in prison), or extradition that is being actively pursued, the initiation of a trial, or the continuance of a trial so long as there is active progress being made in the case, or a ruling in a trial. Therefore this is not a record of prosecutions necessarily resulting in convictions. Civil prosecutions, the granting of reparations, apologies, or purely administrative inquiries, investigations, or punishments do not count as human rights prosecutions for our purposes.

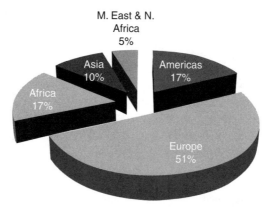

FIGURE 1.3. Regional distribution of foreign and international prosecutions 1979–2009.

process but rather separate streams that eventually flow into and converge into the justice cascade. These include a strong accountability stream from Latin America, focused on domestic prosecutions for accountability for past human rights violations, but instigated in some cases and reinforced in others by regional human rights institutions and by the work of international and domestic human rights NGOs.

A second stream comes from global efforts to provide for the international implementation of human rights norms, starting with the Genocide Convention in 1948, the Geneva Conventions in 1949, and the Torture Convention in 1984. But these provisions for implementation were still inert; increasingly, they were legal possibilities, but these possibilities had not been translated into political action. They were, however, necessary for later legal action, as the Law Lords would make quite clear in their Pinochet decision. The evolution of human rights law and humanitarian law, the proliferation of new treaties with increasingly precise language about individual criminal accountability, and widespread ratification of those treaties were all necessary conditions for the justice cascade. But it was not in any sense sufficient.

The third stream was the creation and practice of international criminal tribunals, beginning with Nuremberg and continuing today in the ICTY, the ICTR, and the new hybrid tribunals in Sierra Leone, East Timor, and Cambodia. Creation of these tribunals required specific exercises of political will that drew on existing human rights and humanitarian law and contributed dramatically to its development through their sentences.

By the time of the turn of the twenty-first century, however, a backlash had already emerged against the justice cascade. Scholars like Jack Snyder and Leslie Vinjamuri claimed that the idealists advocating prosecutions had not considered political realities and that those advocating prosecutions actually create more abuse than they prevent.[44] Other scholars like Luc Reydams wrote articles with titles like "The Rise and Fall of Universal Jurisdiction," in which he concluded that "universal jurisdiction was essentially a post-Cold War discourse and self-feeding hype generated by NGOs, activist lawyers and judges, academic conferences and papers, and mass media."[45] The ICC's first three cases involved crimes against humanity in Africa. Two of these cases, one against an insurgent group in Uganda and one in the DRC, had been referred to the ICC by the governments of Uganda and the DRC. The third, relating to Sudan, was referred to the Court by the UN Security Council. The final case, involving Kenya, was the only one that prosecutor Luis Moreno Ocampo brought to the Court using his independent powers as prosecutor, the very powers that the United States had worked so hard to limit. But now the euphoria had worn off and the Court born of such high expectations in 1998 had come to be seen by some as a court created by the north to prosecute crimes of the south.

The narrative told in this chapter calls into question this ex post facto interpretation of the rise of the age of accountability. The idea of individual criminal accountability arose and was supported by a coalition of individuals, NGOs, and like-minded states from semi-peripheral and small European states, with the support of key INGOs like AI and HRW, as well as domestic NGOs in countries around the world. Since its initiation, the trend is increasingly based on a hard law foundation of treaties drafted and ratified by a wide variety of states. Only nineteen countries have not ratified at least one of the three treaties that underpin the move toward individual criminal accountability. Even more states have ratified the core human rights treaties that call on them to ensure rights and provide remedies, phrases increasingly interpreted as implying an obligation to investigate and prosecute. The fact that the justice cascade is embodied in both domestic and international law and in domestic and international institutions makes it unlikely that the trend will be reversed.

---

[44] Snyder and Vinjamuri, "Trials and Errors."

[45] Luc Reydams, "The Rise and Fall of Universal Jurisdiction" (unpublished paper, Leuven Center for Global Governance Studies), accessed September 4, 2011, http://ghum.kuleuven.be/ggs/publications/opinions/opinions3_luc_reydams.pdf P. 3.

**2**

# The Amnesty Controversy in International Law

*Mark Freeman and Max Pensky*

Amnesty provisions offered by states as components of peacemaking or of longer term transitional processes are surely among the most controversial aspects of contemporary transitional justice. The offer of immunity from criminal prosecution to perpetrators of the most heinous of crimes is undeniably at odds with the demand for retribution, an affront to victims and survivors, and potentially a blow to the longer term prospects of establishing and strengthening legal institutions and the rule of law in transitional states. And yet amnesties have also undeniably proven themselves important components of negotiations that have resolved protracted conflicts or restored democracy after periods of authoritarian rule.

Arguments for and against domestic amnesties for serious crimes under international law are many and complex, in keeping with the remarkable number and diversity of amnesty policies and measures that have emerged in transitional contexts around the world over the past several decades. However, since the 1990s at least, an anti-impunity position has taken hold across a wide spectrum of international legal and political bodies such as the United Nations Secretariat and the IACHR, as well as international NGOs and academics. According to this position, as Kathryn Sikkink discusses in her chapter in this volume, individual criminal accountability for serious crimes under international law is a cornerstone of a global human rights community. Domestic amnesties that waive prosecution of individuals for designated acts are thus at odds with the basic values of such a community, and for this reason should be interpreted as contrary to states' commitments under international

This chapter draws directly from longer works by the authors, namely: Freeman, *Necessary Evils*; and Max Pensky, "The Status of Domestic Amnesties for International Crimes in International Law: Beyond the Crystallization Thesis" (paper presented at the "Amnesty in the Age of Accountability: Brazil in Comparative and International Perspective" Conference, University of Oxford, United Kingdom, October 22–23, 2010). Please consult those texts for more comprehensive analysis of the issues covered in this chapter, which were necessarily treated in a condensed form for purposes of this publication.

law. The position, in other words, entails the project of removing amnesties, especially in relation to international crimes such as genocide, war crimes, and crimes against humanity, from the political and legal tool kits of transitional states.

The anti-impunity position has very serious implications for the conduct of international peace negotiations, for the comportment of regional and international courts, and for the judicial interpretation of the obligations of states. In this chapter, we examine the legal claims on which the anti-amnesty position rests. Specifically, we review some of the most relevant aspects of public international law, both treaty-based and customary, as a way of assessing the strength and cogency of the claim that general amnesties violate states' international legal obligations.

This chapter does not offer a defense of amnesties, whether on principled or on pragmatic grounds. We regard amnesties as potentially serious failures of justice whose legitimacy and prospects for contributing to a more just and lasting peace rest upon a complex and contextual evaluation of a myriad of factors that will vary from place to place. We do suggest, however, that the assertion that such amnesties are in every instance contrary to international law rests on legal arguments considerably weaker than the advocates of the position acknowledge.

By reviewing the most significant sources of public international law, relevant texts, and rulings on the permissibility of domestic amnesties for international crimes, we argue that treaty law has little directly to say about the permissibility of amnesties, though it does offer numerous arguments for a state's duty to prosecute and punish from which the incompatibility of amnesties can be, and has frequently been, inferred. Customary international law has also been appealed to as evincing a "crystallizing" norm against impunity, from which a corresponding crystallizing anti-amnesty position has once again been inferred. However, this inference is seriously compromised by the inconsistency of established state practice regarding the use of amnesty in the context of transitional justice schemes, a necessary condition for the crystallization thesis to be convincing. Finally, recent rulings of international criminal tribunals and the conduct of the ICC offer some interesting, though not entirely consistent, subsidiary sources of international criminal law regarding amnesties. In the case of the ICC in particular, serious questions persist regarding what sort of postconflict amnesty arrangements would be acceptable.

By the end of the discussion, we hope to make clear why the debate on amnesty continues to raise controversy. The subject is one on which it always will be difficult to remain neutral – especially when, as is so often the case, the interests of peace and justice must compete for priority. Precisely for that reason, a central goal of this chapter is to offer a critical reconstruction of the relevant international legal sources in order to chart more clearly just what states' obligations amount to with respect to amnesties.

## TREATIES AND CONVENTIONS

International treaties represent the obvious first place to look for a definitive state-ment of the legality of domestic amnesties for international crimes. Yet in this area, what stands out the most is the *absence* of an explicit prohibition of amnesty in any human rights, humanitarian, or criminal treaty. There is not a single multilateral treaty that, in an explicit way, discourages any kind of amnesty. This remarkable fact about amnesties and international law should cause us to question any thesis about widespread state antagonism to amnesties for human rights crimes.

Examining this lacuna from the perspective of international relations rather than international law makes it less mysterious. In the diplomatic realm, states are jealous of their sovereignty. When negotiating the terms of international treaties, states unsurpris-ingly have been extremely reluctant to bind themselves to treaties that explicitly remove a powerful tool in any diplomatic tool kit. Further, we should be careful to understand amnesties not just as pragmatic tools for tough negotiations with perpetrators, but also as powerful, more general expressions of state sovereignty, useful in foreign and domes-tic policy spheres. Amnesties for any crime under domestic law, let alone those crimes the gravity of which rises to meet the definition of an international crime, are acts whereby the normal operation of a domestic law system is suspended. The power to dic-tate the normal and extraordinary function of domestic law – as German legal theorist Carl Schmitt would put it, the power to declare the exception to the law – is an integral and highly symbolically visible dimension of state sovereignty.

Thus on pragmatic and what we can call symbolic grounds, states have shown extreme reluctance to commit to treaty language that disavows the power to grant amnesties, and this may be particularly apposite for postconflict democratizing states, for whom the expressive dimension of sovereignty, internally and externally, may well be very significant.

The silence of international treaty law on the notion of amnesties does have one exception, though it is an unexpected one. The 1977 Protocol II to the Geneva Conventions, which governs the protection of victims in noninternational conflicts, provides that "[a]t the end of hostilities, the authorities in power shall endeavor to grant the broadest possible amnesty to persons who have participated in the armed conflict, or those deprived of their liberty for reasons related to the armed conflict, whether they are interned or detained."[1] The majority of national courts that have applied Article 6(5) have used it as a legal basis to validate or uphold amnesties covering serious crimes, including war crimes that would violate Protocol II to the Geneva Conventions.[2]

---

[1] Protocol Additional to the Geneva Conventions of August 12, 1949, and relating to the Protection of Victims of Non-International Armed Conflicts, June 8, 1977, 1125 U.N.T.S. 609, art. 6 (5).

[2] Naomi Roht-Arriaza and Lauren Gibson, "The Developing Jurisprudence on Amnesty," *Human Rights Quarterly* 20 (1998): 862–6; Mallinder, *Amnesty, Human Rights and Political Transitions*, chapter 5.

Perhaps the most well-known analysis to date is the judgment of the South African Constitutional Court in the AZAPO case, in which it held that the amnesty provisions of the 1995 Promotion of Unity and Reconciliation Act (which established the country's TRC) were consistent with both the national constitution and international law.[3] Though its analysis of Article 6(5) is made *in obiter* (i.e., as a judicial aside), the Court offered a compelling explanation of why the article appears specifically in Protocol II and not in humanitarian law treaties that concern international armed conflicts:

> It is one thing to allow the officers of a hostile power which has invaded a foreign state to remain unpunished for gross violations of human rights perpetrated against others during the course of such conflict. It is another thing to compel such punishment in circumstances where such violations have substantially occurred in consequence of conflict between different formations within the same state in respect of the permissible political direction which that state should take with regard to the structures of the state and the parameters of its political policies and where it becomes necessary after the cessation of such conflict for the society traumatized by such a conflict to reconstruct itself. That is a difficult exercise which the nation within such a state has to perform by having regard to its own peculiar history, its complexities, even its contradictions and its emotional and institutional traditions. What role punishment should play in respect of erstwhile acts of criminality in such a situation is part of the complexity.[4]

Despite the (near) absence of any explicit reference to amnesties in the language of international treaties, many courts and legal scholars have nevertheless argued that international treaty obligations entail states' duties to prosecute and punish the prohibited acts of genocide and crimes against humanity.[5] This of course establishes an inference that amnesties, precisely insofar as they may bar prosecutions for such acts, are contrary to, or in violation of, a state's treaty obligations, and in this sense, contrary to international law.[6]

This inference from international treaties can be drawn in several ways, all of which involve treaty sources implicitly related to amnesty: 1) in some cases, international treaties can be interpreted to establish a binding legal obligation on states to *prosecute*; 2) in others, treaties imply a variety of rights of *legal remedy* on the part of victims and survivors that are at least in principle incompatible with amnesties; 3) certain treaties contain prohibitions on *statutory limitations* for certain

---

[3] *Azanian Peoples Organization (AZAPO) and Others v. President of the Republic of South Africa and Others*, Constitutional Court of South Africa, Case No. CCT17/96, July 25, 1996.

[4] Ibid., para. 31.

[5] For a recent nuanced view see Michael Scharf, "From the eXile Files: An Essay on Trading Justice for Peace," *Washington & Lee Review* 63 (2006): 339–78.

[6] For a classic statement see Orentlicher, "Settling Accounts."

international crimes, which a general amnesty would effectively erase by eliminating the possibility of prosecution; and 4) state parties may have the duty to "respect and ensure" certain *nonderogable rights*, entailing policies of prevention of international crimes that could preclude amnesties. Though the legal issues here are complex and have generated a large interpretive literature, no unambiguous reading of treaty law exists that definitively rules out domestic amnesties, since every attempt to infer such a ban is subject to alternative interpretations that establish at least the possibility of plausible arguments for the compatibility of amnesties. Let us now examine each of these distinct inferential paths.

### Prosecutorial Obligations

The first and perhaps most frequently used argument against amnesties centers on the significant number of multilateral treaties that explicitly require criminal prosecution of individuals responsible for specific crimes.[7] The precise nature and scope of the obligation varies from one treaty to the next, but the general obligation to ensure individual criminal accountability is clear.[8] Examples include the following:

**Genocide:** Article I of the Genocide Convention provides: "The Contracting Parties confirm that genocide, whether committed in time of peace or in time of war, is a crime under international law which they undertake to prevent and to punish."[9] This seems to imply that states offering amnesties to potential *genocidaires* are in breach of their treaty obligations, but this would be a matter for adjudication since it is not immediately obvious whether punishment could only entail the kind of investigation, prosecution, trial, conviction, and sentencing normally envisioned as the suite of legal procedures that amnesties foreclose.

**Grave Breaches of the Geneva Conventions and Protocol I:** All states are parties to the four Geneva Conventions.[10] Each convention creates state duties concerning "grave breaches," which include willful killing, torture, or inhuman treatment, willfully causing great suffering or serious injury to body or health, and unlawful

---

7   Andreas O'Shea, *Amnesty for Crime in International Law and Practice* (The Hague: Kluwer Law International, 2002), chapter 7.

8   Darryl Robinson, "Serving the Interests of Justice: Amnesties, Truth Commissions and the International Criminal Court," *European Journal of International Law* 14 (2003): 491.

9   Convention on the Prevention and Punishment of the Crime of Genocide, General Assembly Resolution 260 A (III), adopted December 9, 1948, 78 U.N.T.S. 277.

10  Geneva Convention for the Amelioration of the Condition of the Wounded and Sick in Armed Forces in the Field, August 12, 1949, 75 U.N.T.S. 31; Geneva Convention for the Amelioration of the Condition of Wounded, Sick and Shipwrecked Members of Armed Forces at Sea, August 12, 1949, 75 U.N.T.S. 85; Geneva Convention Relative to the Treatment of Prisoners of War, August 12, 1949, 75 U.N.T.S. 135; Geneva Convention Relative to the Protection of Civilian Persons in Time of War, August 12, 1949, 75 U.N.T.S. 287.

confinement of civilians committed in the context of international, but not internal, armed conflicts. State parties are also obligated to search for, prosecute, and punish perpetrators of grave breaches, unless they extradite them for purposes of trial by another state party. It has been asserted that the official commentary to the Geneva Conventions indicates that the obligation to prosecute grave breaches is absolute.[11] This implies that an amnesty or any similar impediment to prosecution of grave breaches would violate a state's obligations under the treaty.

But whether the "grave breaches" provisions of the Geneva Conventions unambiguously determines a state's legal duty to eschew amnesties for its own nationals is, in practical terms, of limited relevance. The ultimate purview of all the Conventions, international warfare, is now actually a rather small subset of all global conflicts in which international crimes are committed, as many commentators have noted. Therefore, insofar as we can interpret the Geneva Conventions to declare amnesties as violations of states' legal obligations to investigate and prosecute grave breaches, this would apply only to the small minority of domestic amnesties granted for involvement in an interstate, as opposed to an internal, conflict.

**Torture:** Article 7 of the UN Convention against Torture and Other Cruel, Inhuman or Degrading Treatment or Punishment (CAT) declares an obligation on the part of state parties to prosecute or extradite persons alleged to have committed torture.[12] Yet the precise wording implies something less than an absolute obligation. The convention requires any state party in which an alleged torturer is present to investigate the facts, and, if appropriate, "submit the case to its competent authorities for the purpose of prosecution" or extradite the suspect.[13] This wording is more ambiguous than the explicit obligations outlined in the Genocide Convention, and consequently has caused many commentators to argue that there is a degree of permissiveness regarding the manner in which a state must carry out its duties under the CAT. It seems, instead, to leave the decision whether to prosecute alleged torturers to the prosecutorial authorities.[14]

Therefore, while the requirement to prosecute torture is explicit, it is not mandatory, and the ambiguity of the language gives states considerable discretion on what kind of investigation or prosecution they must conduct. Moreover, the treaty covers only allegations of torture committed by public officials or those acting under

[11]   Michael Scharf, "The Letter of the Law: The Scope of the International Legal Obligation to Prosecute Human Rights Crimes," *Law and Contemporary Problems* 59 (1996): 43.

[12]   Convention against Torture and Other Cruel, Inhuman or Degrading Treatment or Punishment, UN Doc. A/39/51 (1984), entered into force June 26, 1987.

[13]   CAT, art. 7(1): "The State Party in territory under whose jurisdiction a person alleged to have committed any offence referred to in article 4 is found, shall in the cases contemplated in article 5, if it does not extradite him, submit the case to its competent authorities for the purpose of prosecution."

[14]   Mallinder, *Amnesty, Human Rights and Political Transitions*, 127–8.

some sort of authorization of public officials, effectively excluding members of rebel groups from the relevant provisions.

**Enforced Disappearance:** Article 6 of the International Convention for the Protection of All Persons from Enforced Disappearance requires state parties to hold criminally responsible those directly and indirectly responsible for the commission of enforced disappearance.[15] Article 11(1) further provides: "The State Party in the territory under whose jurisdiction a person alleged to have committed an offense of enforced disappearance is found shall, if it does not extradite that person or surrender him or her to another State in accordance with its international obligations or surrender him or her to an international criminal tribunal whose jurisdiction it has recognized, submit the case to its competent authorities for the purpose of prosecution." The Inter-American Convention on the Forced Disappearances of Persons uses a similar formulation.[16] However, like the definition of torture, the definition of forced (and enforced) disappearance is applicable only to state actions. There is no treaty-based concept of enforced disappearance applicable to acts committed outside of the state's direction and control.

## Right to Remedy

A second treaty-based justification used to oppose the legality of certain amnesties concerns the right to remedy provisions established in various human rights treaties. The obligation to ensure an effective remedy in the event of a human rights violation appeared as early as the adoption of the Universal Declaration on Human Rights.[17] Other prominent examples include Article 2(3) of the International Covenant on Civil and Political Rights (ICCPR) and Article 6 of the International Convention on the Elimination of All Forms of Racial Discrimination (ICERD).[18] Broadly understood, the right to remedy obligation encompasses, inter alia, state responsibility and authority to ensure the punishment of human rights violators. In that respect, it could arguably be in direct conflict with the primary function of amnesties, namely to remove the prospect and consequences of domestic criminal judgment.

Yet the right to an effective remedy is not as broad as it may appear. For example, it does not provide private persons with a right to force the state to prosecute a

---

[15] International Convention for the Protection of All Persons from Enforced Disappearance, December 20, 2006, UN Doc. A/RES/61/177; 14 IHRR 582 (2007).

[16] Inter-American Convention on the Forced Disappearances of Persons (adopted June 9, 1994, entered into force March 28, 1996) 33 I.L.M. 1429 (A-60), art. 3.

[17] Universal Declaration on Human Rights (adopted December 10, 1948), UN Doc. A/810, art. 8

[18] International Covenant on Civil and Political Rights (ICERD), General Assembly Res. 2200 A (XXI), adopted December 16, 1966, UN GAOR, 21st sess., Supp. No. 16, UN Doc. A/6316 (1967), 52.

specific person.[19] The decision to prosecute an individual – or to decline to do so – is for the state to make. In addition, the right to remedy merely places an obligation on the state to make a good faith effort to conduct "a thorough and effective investigation capable of leading to the identification and punishment of those responsible, including effective access for the complainant to the investigatory procedure."[20] The primary function of right to remedy provisions is to ensure the right of victims of human rights violations to compensation through a judicial, or possibly nonjudicial, proceeding. There is therefore leeway in the type of "thorough and effective investigation" required. For example, Louise Mallinder emphasizes that amnesties from criminal proceedings do not necessarily impede the right of victims to compensation, since there may be acceptable nonjudicial recourses that fulfill this right. A prominent example of this is the introduction of community-based justice processes in Uganda. Traditional Acholi justice practices such as *mato oput*, in combination with conditional amnesties, have been offered as reconciliation mechanisms and as a potential replacement for standard trials.[21]

## Prohibitions on Statutory Limitations

A third treaty-based justification advanced for opposing the legality of certain amnesties is related to prohibitions on statutory limitations for certain international crimes. The Convention on the Non-applicability of Statutory Limitations to War Crimes and Crimes against Humanity is the best-known treaty on the subject.[22] Article 1 of the convention provides that no statutory limitations shall apply to war crimes and crimes against humanity. Article 4 provides that state parties to the convention must ensure that statutory "or other limitations" shall not apply to the prosecution and punishment of war crimes and crimes against humanity, and "shall be abolished." Article 29 of the Rome Statute similarly provides that genocide, crimes against humanity, and war crimes "shall not be subject to any statute of limitations."[23]

The statutory limitations argument against amnesties is straightforward. By putting an immediate end to prosecutions for specific crimes, an amnesty effectively erases

---

[19] See, for example, UN Human Rights Committee, General Comment No. 31 (adopted on March 29, 2004), CCPR/C/21/Rev.1/Add.13, para. 18. See also *Prosecutor v. Kondewa*, Decision on Lack of Jurisdiction/Abuse of Process: Amnesty provided by the Lomé Accord (Special Court for Sierra Leone, Appeals Chamber), Case No. SCSL-2004–14-AR72 (E), May 25, 2004, para. 40.

[20] *Abdülsamet Yaman v. Turkey*, European Court of Human Rights, November 2, 2004, App. No. 32446/96, para. 53.

[21] Louise Mallinder, "Can Amnesties and International Justice be Reconciled?" *The International Journal of Transitional Justice* 1 (2007): 208–30.

[22] G.A. Res. 2391 (XXIII), annex 23 UN GAOR Supp. (No. 18) at 40, UN Doc. A/7218 (1968), entered into force November 11, 1970. See also Joinet, "Study on Amnesty Laws."

[23] Rome Statute, art. 29.

the protection afforded by statutes of limitation, whose primary function is to pre-serve the possibility of prosecutions during a designated time frame. The argument, in short, is that it would be logically inconsistent to forbid statutory limitations for specific crimes yet allow amnesties for the same crimes. This argument is initially appealing, but ultimately unconvincing. The main purpose of treaty provisions pro-hibiting statutory limitations for specific crimes is to prevent states from creating a general or standing law that would restrict, ad infinitum, the timing for prosecution of certain international crimes. The main purpose of amnesty, by contrast, is to put an immediate end to prosecutions and punishment for specific crimes, not as a gen-eral rule, but as an ad hoc, extraordinary legal measure.[24] In other words, the effect of an amnesty would not be to undermine the benefit of the statutory limitation prohi-bition in any general and prospective sense. It would apply once, and not generally, and would have effect retrospectively, not prospectively.

Another significant weakness in the statutory limitations argument against amnes-ties is the lack of evidence that states view or treat such prohibitions as limits on their discretion to promulgate amnesties. This fact was underscored most recently in the context of the negotiations of the Rome Statute, where the discussions of statutory limitations and amnesties were conducted and concluded separately. There is no evi-dence that any government viewed Rome Statute Article 29, which prohibits statutory limitations for ICC crimes, as having legal consequences for the issue of amnesty.

## Nonderogable State Obligations

The nonderogability of state obligations in the realm of human rights has been used as an argument against the legality of amnesties. In times of genuine public emergency threatening the life of a state, governments may temporarily suspend or derogate from certain rights pursuant to certain treaties that contain explicit dero-gation clauses.[25] However, most derogation clauses provide that certain core rights – including the right to life and the prohibitions against torture and slavery – cannot be the subject of derogation.[26] On this basis, it has been asserted, for example, that an amnesty that includes torture would, *ipso facto*, violate international law.[27]

---

[24] See, for example, European Commission on Human Rights, *Dujardin and Others v. France* (September 2, 1991), App. No. 16734/90, 72 D.R. 236.

[25] See, for example, ICCPR, art. 4(1); ECHR, art. 15; ACHR, art. 27(2). These derogation clauses stipu-late that the derogating states may not adopt measures inconsistent with their other international legal obligations or that would involve discrimination.

[26] See, for example, ICCPR, art. 4(2). Moreover, certain human rights treaties do not permit deroga-tions at all. For example, derogations are not permitted under the ICERD; the CAT; the International Covenant on Economic, Social and Cultural Rights G.A. res. 2200A (XXI), 21 UN GAOR Supp. (No. 16) at 49, UN Doc. A/6316 (1966), 993 U.N.T.S. 3, entered into force Jan. 3, 1976.

[27] See *Prosecutor v. Anto Furundzija*, International Criminal Tribunal for the former Yugoslavia, Case No. IT-95–17/1-T (December 10, 1998), para. 155, accessed September 4, 2011, http://www.icty.org/case/furundzija/4).

However, the argument is mistaken. The fact that the freedoms from state-sponsored torture, murder, or slavery are nonderogable state obligations only establishes a hierarchy of violations. That is to say, it establishes only that certain duties are nonderogable (e.g., ensuring the right not to be tortured) whereas others are not (e.g., ensuring the right of peaceful assembly). Nowhere do treaties state, for example, that the duty to investigate and punish torture or slavery is paramount to the duty to halt or prevent their commission.

Instead, there is simply the right to be free from such acts. Indeed, in considering the relevant articles of the ICCPR in this context, they provide only that individuals shall not be subjected to state-sponsored torture or slavery.[28] In other words, it is the negative duty to refrain from the carrying out of violations such as torture or slavery, and not the positive duty to ensure legal remedies for such violations, which is explicitly nonderogable during a national emergency. Therefore, it does not necessarily follow that amnesties, which remove criminal liability for previously committed offenses, would violate these obligations.

In sum, while it is certainly true that states are under a number of general obligations to do, or refrain from doing, certain acts as parties to selected international treaties, it is far less clear whether any treaty requires a state party to refrain from a specific act of national amnesty. The chain of inferences leading from states' obligations via the paths of prosecutorial duties, rights of remedy, or obligations regarding statutes of limitations or nonderogation entails a number of steps between the general legal duties of states and the specific amnesty positions that states may take. In most cases, these intermediate steps require quite extensive interpretations and the weighing of competing and equally important obligations. And while such interpretations may well resolve that a specific amnesty does indeed comprise a breach of a state's legal obligations, others may well not.

## CUSTOMARY INTERNATIONAL LAW

Public international law claims among its sources not just the text of international treaties (most of which, in any case, have less than universal ratification among the community of nations) but also customary international law, which, as its name implies, refers to firmly established legal principles reflecting a widespread and consistent practice of states.[29] Under the relevant definitions as laid out in Article 38 of the Statute of the International Court of Justice, custom is equally valid as a source of law as international treaties.

---

[28]  ICCPR, arts. 7 and 8.
[29]  The traditional source for the definition of customary international law is the Charter of the International Court of Justice Art. 38.1.b., which defines custom as "evidence of a general practice accepted as law."

Two conditions must be met in order for a law or legal principle to meet the requirements of customary international law. First, the legal principle must be factually observed to be a general state practice – in layperson's terms, one must show convincingly that the principle is actually applied by the vast majority of states. Second, such practice must in each case reflect an *opinio juris*; that is, it must be demonstrable that states conform to the principle in question because they recognize that they are legally obligated to do so, rather than, say, because they believe conformity may be in their temporary interest or because it is expedient to do so.

While customary international law provides a much richer and more promising resource for answering the question of the legal status of domestic amnesties, that richness comes with its own price, since customary international law, in its vagueness and curiously self-validating quality, can be remarkably open ended, leaving all too much room for interpretation.

The questions for us are now the following: first, whether established customary norms of international law prohibit domestic amnesties; second, if we cannot answer this question affirmatively, whether there is nevertheless growing evidence that an explicit anti-amnesty norm is in the process of emerging as custom, or as legal scholars occasionally put it, "crystallizing" as a customary norm.

The first question deals with the specific relevance of customary international law in its determination of *jus cogens*, literally "compelling" or higher law. The 1969 Vienna Convention on the Law of Treaties defines *jus cogens* as "a norm accepted and recognized by the international community of States as a whole as a norm from which no derogation is permitted and which can be modified only by a subsequent norm of general international law having the same character."[30]

As it is commonly used in the language of international criminal law, *jus cogens* refers to a set of acts that all domestic criminal law systems are obligated to treat as illegal, even in the absence of specific treaty obligations. Such *jus cogens* crimes establish a set of corresponding norms that are considered peremptory; that is, they are universally binding on states without exception or derogation. This special status of *jus cogens* crimes, in turn, can be used to ground an inference to a universal or peremptory obligation on the part of states to prevent, investigate, prosecute, and punish such crimes. And in the terminology of international law, insofar as a state accepts that certain acts are violations of *jus cogens*, they also thereby assume a duty *erga omnes*, that is, a duty of adherence owed to everyone, universally and independently of any particular jurisdiction or any treaty obligations a state may or may not have.[31]

---

[30] Vienna Convention on the Law of Treaties, 1155 U.N.T.S. 331, art. 53.

[31] In the "Barcelona Traction Case," the International Court of Justice defined *erga omnes* obligations as those that "derive, for example, in contemporary international law, from the outlawing of acts of aggression, and of genocide, as also from the principles and rules concerning the basic rights of the

Such an *erga omnes* obligation certainly entails that states cannot adopt laws that permit *jus cogens* offenses. An argument can therefore be mounted that amnesties covering such offenses would deviate from this obligation, and indeed much of the legal opinion that holds domestic amnesties as contrary to *customary* international law infers such a status from these peremptory universal obligations to outlaw and punish.

*Jus cogens* originated in the universal and exceptionless ban on crimes such as high seas piracy and state-sanctioned slavery. The expansion of the catalog of *jus cogens* crimes to genocide, crimes against humanity, torture, rape, and other grave violations of international treaty law was among the less spectacular but most influential developments in the post-Nuremberg regime of international criminal law. If, therefore, customary law has in fact generated a coherent set of legal norms, under which are included most if not all of the acts usually proscribed as grave violations of human rights under international treaties, then a number of conclusions may follow that bear directly on our question.

First, identifying crimes such as genocide and crimes against humanity as *jus cogens* violations, which in turn implies *erga omnes* duties to prosecute, circumvents the obvious limitations of treaty law: the absence of explicit references to amnesties, and the patchwork nature of treaties. Not all states are parties to all international treaties, after all. Many states are signatories of treaties without having ratified them; some states may ratify treaties but subsequently fail to incorporate the treaty provisions into their domestic law systems, and so on. The strongest treaty-based duty, the "grave breaches" regime of the Geneva Conventions, governs international conflicts only.

But a duty to prosecute derived from customary international law would be binding on all states irrespective of their treaty commitments or lack of them, covering both international and internal conflicts. This commitment is to some degree evident in experiments in universal jurisdiction, in which sovereign states investigate and prosecute non-nationals outside of their own territory. While the most famous of these experiments were the legal proceedings against former Chilean dictator Augusto Pinochet, arrested in London on a Spanish warrant, other (West European) countries, most notably Belgium, also made concerted attempts to transform international criminal law by asserting their duty and jurisdiction to prosecute *jus cogens* crimes.[33] On the surface at least, customary international law's

human person, including protection from slavery and racial discrimination." 91, Barcelona Traction Case, (1970) ICJ Reports 3 at page 32.

[33] For a balanced and not uncritical account of the ICTR in Rwanda, see Payam Akhavan, "Justice and Reconciliation in the Great Lakes Region of Africa: The Contribution of the International Criminal Tribunal for Rwanda," *Duke Journal of Comparative and International Law* 7 (1997): 325–48.

exceptionless character presents a more tempting basis to infer a proscription of amnesties than treaty law.

However, the use of customary international law as a resource for mounting this kind of argument against amnesties comes at a high price. The process by which a legal norm is granted customary status is not merely and perhaps not even predominantly legal but ultimately political in nature. State practices, in other words, are frequently said to crystallize into a new legal norm, a metaphor suggesting a great deal of causal complexity. As a new legal norm crystallizes, what begins as a fluid and dynamic process of political activity gradually solidifies into hard law as states, looking to other states, accept that a given norm is not just one policy option among others to be followed or rejected according to the calculation of national interest, but indeed a generally acknowledged legal obligation that constrains the freedom of states' political action. And once crystallized, so the metaphor implies, cold hard law will remain a durable barrier to state practice indefinitely (modifiable only by a subsequent norm of general international law having the same character).

The widespread use of the crystallization metaphor certainly has the advantage that it describes the deep mutual dependence of the development of new international law norms and the dynamic process of political and moral norms in the context of international politics and international relations. States' adoption of norms as binding on their practice obviously has both a political dimension where in the course of a justice cascade[34] a norm reaches a tipping point where it is accepted as valid, rather than conformed to strategically, and a legal dimension that corresponds to the concept of *opinio juris*, the second necessary condition for custom together with consistent state practice.

But like any controlling metaphor, crystallization also has the potential for producing a range of interpretive problems, both generally and in the particular context of the question of the legality of national amnesties.

Crystallization is, crucially, in the eye of the beholder: both established state practices and *opinio juris* are liable to subjective judgments, and those doing the judging are often interested parties. When it comes to amnesty, in particular, even disinterested parties looking at the same facts can come to opposite conclusions. For example, one party may view the widespread resistance to a purported anti-amnesty norm as evidence of an absence of *opinio juris* on the subject, whereas another may view such resistance as an implicit recognition of the existence of the norm. Although the latter account is more circular in its reasoning, because it means that resistance or endorsement of the norm constitutes evidence of its existence, both views have merit. Yet there should be little tolerance of failure to examine actual amnesty practice, including what amnesty laws actually say, how the enacting parties actually

---

[34] See Sikkink's chapter in this volume.

explain and defend them, and how the external community of states actually reacts. On the latter aspect, a review of the outcomes of the UN Human Rights Council's Universal Periodic Review process is telling for its near total lack of peer criticism of states that recently adopted amnesties covering human rights crimes, such as Algeria and Afghanistan.[35]

Thus, declaring a customary norm to be crystallized or crystallizing can raise the suspicion of wishful thinking, bootstrapping, or the hope of a self-fulfilling prophecy dressed up as an objective claim of fact. The very idea of customary international law labors under the suspicion of enacting what philosophers call a naturalistic fallacy, an unjustified inference from facts about what is the case to normative claims about what ought to be.

Naturalistic fallacies, however, run in two directions, and claims about a given norm having already crystallized in custom, or about norms that are in the crystallization process, can easily appear as unjustified inferences from what the commentator wishes to be so, to what she or he claims is already so. Indeed the peculiarities of the emergence conditions for new legal norms lie at the heart of multiple criticisms of custom as a valid source of international law on a par with treaty law.[36]

On the question of the legality of amnesties for international crimes, appealing to customary international law to argue for a crystallizing or crystallized norm that such amnesties are contrary to states' legal obligations to prosecute, and are therefore contrary to international law, presents us with an enormous problem. On the one hand, there can be no doubt whatsoever that the category of *jus cogens* crimes, and their *erga omnes* character, has in fact crystallized, incorporating the Nuremburg era schedule of fundamental human rights and the corresponding set of international crimes as the expression of a set of peremptory legal norms. This crystallization accelerated dramatically in the late 1980s and throughout the 1990s in the wake of democratization processes in Latin America, the former Soviet Union, and parts of East Asia and sub-Saharan Africa. With all obvious caveats, it is settled practice among the community of sovereign states to bar such acts as torture, genocide, ethnic cleansing, and mass atrocity; and one can certainly argue that these bars are not mere expediency but express *opinio juris*; that states may not legally torture or murder their way toward their national interest.

---

[35] See, for example, OHCHR, *Report of the Working Group on the Universal Periodic Review – Algeria*, UN Doc. A/HRC/8/29 (OHCHR: May 23, 2008), accessed September 14, 2011, http://www.ohchr.org/en/hrbodies/upr/pages/dzsession1.aspx, in which only Canada appears to have raised concerns about the impunity created by Algeria's 2006 general amnesty. According to the draft *Report of the Working Group on the Universal Periodic Review – Afghanistan*, UN Doc. A/HRC/WG.6/5/L.8, May 11, 2009, no state appears to have mentioned, let alone criticized, Afghanistan's 2007 general amnesty.

[36] See, for example, J. Patrick Kelly, "The Twilight of Customary International Law," *Virginia Journal of International Law* 40 (2000): 449–544. Also N. C. H. Dunbar, "The Myth of Customary International Law," *Austin Yearbook for International Law* 1 (1983): 1–19.

And yet on the other hand, Louise Mallinder's amnesty database, collecting and analyzing amnesty policies internationally, offers strong empirical confirmation for the claim that, in the period subsequent to the rise of a far stronger anti-impunity sentiment over the last ten years, far from reducing the number of domestic amnesties for suspects of international crimes, states have in fact *increased* the number of such amnesties.[37]

One explanation for this apparent paradox is simply a product of realism in international relations: given the overall lack of effective sanctions in the enforcement of international law, the fact that international legal norms crystallize does not mean that states are prepared to apply or practice those norms. However, Louise Mallinder cites another explanation, originally offered by Ronald Slye, that opposes this realist view.[38] The increased use of amnesties since the early 1990s may actually reflect the growing influence of international criminal law, which now represents a credible threat that perpetrators of the most serious of international crimes will face indictment and prosecution. Rather than take impunity for granted, then, state agents issue amnesties to guard against prosecutions that previously would have been unlikely, whether at the domestic or the international level. Hence in a classic example of the blowback of unintended consequences, the rise of international law has actually served if not to raise the value of domestic amnesties, then to raise at least the perception of this value to relevant state agents, and quite possibly for expressivist reasons (the expression and solidification of the sovereignty claims of a particular administration) that are distinct from the immediate pragmatic goals of the amnesty policy itself.

This casts arguments for a customary anti-amnesty norm under a certain cloud of suspicion – of attempting to promote (on scant evidence), rather than report, the crystallization of such a norm: as Michael Scharf puts the matter, "[T]hose who argue that customary international law precludes amnesty/exile for crimes against humanity base their position on nonbinding General Assembly resolutions, hortative declarations of international conferences, and international conventions that are not widely ratified, rather than on any extensive state practice consistent with such a rule."[39]

One should note, however, that some legal scholars take the view that customary international law is forming in such a way that *opinio juris* is ahead of state practice in its development. Applied to amnesty, the argument is that despite the inconvenient realities of amnesty practice (i.e., amnesties are still extensively used, accepted,

---

[37] Mallinder, *Amnesties, Human Rights, and Political Transitions*, chapter 3.
[38] Ibid., See also Slye, "The Legitimacy of Amnesties." See also Trumbull, "Giving Amnesties a Second Chance," 295.
[39] Scharf, "From the eXile Files," 360–1.

and unlike the practice of torture, openly defended by practicing states), one could still assert the existence of an emerging customary norm on the basis that states increasingly believe themselves forbidden from amnestying certain international crimes. If this were the case, such state beliefs could indeed constitute evidence of an embryonic customary norm. However, a bolder claim of crystallization would be untenable in light of contradictory state practice and the absence of discouraging or prohibitive wording about amnesties in treaty law.

In conclusion, even based on a selective and partial account of amnesty practice, the most that one can proclaim is the existence of an emerging customary norm against amnesties that purports to cover international crimes. Whether such a norm ultimately crystallizes, or whether a reinterpretation arises on the basis of a more complete consideration of amnesty practice, is a matter of speculation for the time being. But this discussion should suffice to show that the most promising source of a univocal voice in international law on the status of amnesties, a purportedly crystallizing norm in customary international law, cannot be said to exist.

## INTERNATIONAL COURT RULINGS

State practice can be expressed not just by national legislation but also by national adjudication; that is, how domestic law systems operate, what kind of judicial rulings they produce, and whether these rulings become definitive precedent for subsequent state practices. But beyond such national sources, transnational and international courts play a crucial role in the production of customary law. Indeed the remarkable rise of the profile and influence of public international law over the course of the past years consists largely in the case law of important international tribunals such as the European Court of Human Rights (ECHR), the IACtHR, ICTR, ICTY, the Special Court for Sierra Leone, and, since 2002, the ICC. Some of these judicial bodies are well-established, permanent courts with a lengthy history of rulings; for example, the ECHR dates to 1959 and the IACtHR to 1979. Others, such as the ICTY and the Special Court for Sierra Leone, are extraordinary criminal tribunals with limited temporal and geographical jurisdiction.

All of these courts in varying degrees have had to deal with the amnesty controversy, even if the case law as a whole is limited in number and scope. For the most part, they have been consistent in their position that domestic amnesties for international crimes are incompatible with international legal norms and represent failures of states to fulfill various international legal obligations. Moreover, international courts frequently appeal to one another's rulings, reinforcing and consolidating a network of case law. Therefore one might be inclined to see the development of jurisprudence from the constellation of supernational courts as making a significant contribution to the crystallization of a customary anti-amnesty norm.

This conclusion would be difficult to justify, however. The customary impact of such judicial rulings is strongly limited. Custom in international law arises by statute from a combination of established state practice and *opinio juris*. The rulings of international courts are only directly relevant as secondary resources that may indicate the broad outlines of developing international law. While such courts can offer observations on perceived trends in customary law or on its perceived content, they cannot "make" customary law. In that respect, any trend in amnesty jurisprudence, as such, bears no direct relation to the formation of custom.

Furthermore, it is worth noting that state practice and international jurisprudence can move in contrary directions, as evidenced by the continuous and apparently increasing use of amnesties at the domestic level. Nevertheless, the amnesty-relevant rulings of international criminal courts have been frequently appealed to by commentators arguing for the crystallization of an anti-amnesty principle, and for this reason it is important to discuss some of the most significant and influential of international courts' more recent decisions regarding the status of amnesties.

But before doing so it is necessary to acknowledge the amnesty jurisprudence of the IACtHR in particular, which has developed a substantial record in battling impunity in the Americas and has long played a lead role in the effort to compel regional states to enforce human rights; to make public information about the fate of disappeared victims of state repression; and to prevent, investigate, prosecute, and punish serious human rights violations. The chapter by Par Engstrom and Gabriel Pereira in this volume discusses the Court's case law in detail. We focus on one clearly germane recent ruling to indicate the Court's posture and influence.

In its ruling in *Gomes Lund v. Brazil* (2010), examined by Paulo Abrão and Marcelo Torelly in this volume, the IACtHR took up the case of members of the "guerrillas of Araguaia," a small group of students and workers, over sixty of whom were disappeared (in fact, brutally tortured, murdered, and tossed in local rivers) by elements of the Brazilian army and state police in the mid-1970s. Brazil's 1979 Amnesty Law[40] has prevented the release of definitive information on the fates of the victims and the investigation and prosecution of those responsible for their disappearance. In its decision, the IACtHR found that the many transitional justice efforts of the post-1982 Brazilian government – including extensive efforts to locate the bodies of the missing and monetary reparations – did not meet its obligations under the American Convention, which requires states to guarantee their citizens recourse to fair legal procedures in cases where the citizens' fundamental rights have been violated. Indeed, the IACtHR held, "the investigation and punishment of those responsible for the enforced disappearance of the victims [...] is impossible due to the Amnesty Law.[...] The application of amnesty laws to perpetrators

---

[40]  Lei n. 6.683 de 28 de agosto de 1979. Also see Chapter 6 in this volume on the case of Brazil.

of serious human rights violations is contrary to the obligations established in the Convention and in the Inter-American Court's jurisprudence."[41]

By inferring Brazil's inability to discharge its obligations under the American Convention because of its domestic amnesty legislation, the IACtHR's ruling in *Gomes Lund v. Brazil* asserted not only the "non-compatibility of amnesties related to serious human rights violations with international law," but indeed such amnesties' "illegality."[42] Citing Article 2 of the American Convention, which requires state parties to take measures to ensure that human rights are protected and enforced in their own domestic legal systems, the IACtHR found that "the provisions of the Brazilian Amnesty Law that impedes the investigation and punishment of serious human rights violations lack legal effect."[43]

Given the Brazilian Supreme Court's affirmation of the Amnesty Law only six months before the IACtHR's ruling, this is a remarkably forceful expression. Moreover, the IACtHR was explicit in its cataloguing of parallel transnational courts' rulings on amnesties in other contexts that it was attempting to crystallize and consolidate an international law norm. However, despite such a muscular ruling, the IACtHR is of course limited in its jurisdiction to its regional state parties. More substantially, however, its decision in *Gomes Lund v. Brazil*, while affirming that such "soft" justice mechanisms as monetary reparations for next of kin do not meet states' obligations to investigate and punish human rights abuses, does not resolve whether criminal prosecution, at the domestic or international level, is the sole avenue for discharging such obligations or whether other accountability and sanction mechanisms might also satisfy them.

We now turn briefly to emblematic rulings in two other cases judged by international criminal tribunals. First, in *Prosecutor v. Furundzija*, the trial chamber of the ICTY ruled that, insofar as torture is a *jus cogens* violation implying a legal obligation to prosecute, any amnesty for such an act would be "generally incompatible with the duty of states to investigate" torture.[44] Insofar as the discussion of amnesties was not central to the facts or the legal issues of the case, however, the ICTY's assertion was *obiter dictum*; that is, a comment not essential to any legal principles at stake in the resolution of the case. Nevertheless, many commentators cite the assertion as proof of the state of international law in relation to amnesties. The ICTY's logic, however, is seriously open to question. To the extent that the torture prohibition may be considered a *jus cogens* norm, this fact would establish only that states are precluded from engaging in torture. To determine whether, when, or how

[41] Inter-American Court of Human Rights, *Case of Gomes Lund v. Brazil*, Judgment of November 24, 2010, 47.

[42] Ibid.

[43] Ibid.

[44] *Prosecutor v. Anto Furundzija*, Judgement, Case No., IT-95–17/1-T, para. 155.

acts of torture may be the subject of an amnesty involves more legal analysis than the ICTY provided. The ICTY did not even undertake the prior step of adducing existence of widespread state practice or *opinio juris* in support of its legal assertion concerning amnesty, without which it does not attain customary status, let alone the supercustomary status of *jus cogens*.

In the more significant case of the Special Court for Sierra Leone, among the Court's most pressing initial tasks was to confront the general amnesty granted to Foday Sankoh and his rebel movement in the 1999 Lomé Accord, which brought a temporary stop to the ongoing violence in Sierra Leone's civil war. Already at the time of the signing of the Lomé Accord, the official UN representative present had registered a last-minute reservation to the amnesty's nonexclusion of crimes against humanity and war crimes and explained that the UN, for its part, would not recognize any amnesty that encompassed such crimes.

The eventual statute of the Special Court for Sierra Leone incorporated the same principle: an amnesty for crimes against humanity and war crimes could not bar prosecution for these crimes before the Court. This statute and its implications were subsequently challenged. In its ruling in *Prosecutor v. Kallon and Kamara*, the Court rejected the claim that its refusal to recognize the Lomé amnesty violated valid international treaties. Supporting its ruling, the Court wrote "that there is a crystallizing international norm that a government cannot grant amnesty for serious violations of crimes under international law is amply supported by materials placed before the Court [but the view] that it has crystallized may not be entirely correct ... it is accepted that such a norm is developing under international law."[45] The Court's judgment, however, has been criticized on a number of grounds. These include the confusing claim to be a court possessing universal jurisdiction instead of transferred territorial jurisdiction, the failure to classify the Lomé amnesty according to the specific terms and circumstances of its adoption, and the cursory analysis of the link between an obligation to prosecute and the validity of an amnesty.[46] The Court's approach and conclusions are especially unconvincing when put side by side with the research and findings of Louise Mallinder, confirmed by Tricia Olsen, Leigh Payne, and Andrew Reiter, whose research shows the ongoing and extensive state practice of adopting broad amnesties and the lack of criticism by other states of such practice.[47] It is also worth remarking that the Court's views contrasted with

[45] *Prosecutor v. Morris Kallon, Brima Bazzy Kamara*, SCSL-2004–15-AR72(E) & SCSL-2004–16-AR72(E), Decision of March 13, 2004, para 71; *Prosecutor v Augustine Gbao*, SCSL-2003–01-I, Decision of May 31, 2004, para 9. For a complete account of the Lomé process and its subsequent legal effect on the Special Court for Sierra Leone see Priscilla Hayner, *Negotiating Peace in Sierra Leone: Confronting the Justice Challenge*, (Geneva: Centre for Humanitarian Dialogue, 2007), 1–40.

[46] Sarah Williams, "Amnesties in International Law: The Experience of the Special Court of Sierra Leone," *Human Rights Law Review* 5 (2005): 307–8.

[47] Olsen, Payne, and Reiter, *Transitional Justice in Balance*.

those of Sierra Leone's Truth and Reconciliation Commission, another product of the Lomé Accord, which endorsed the terms of the accord's amnesty as a necessary last recourse to avoid continued mass violence.

While international tribunals such as the Special Court for Sierra Leone and the ICTY are sharply limited in their territorial jurisdiction and their duration, the ICC is meant to be a permanent, global court of international criminal law. Like other international treaties, the Rome Statute of the ICC makes no explicit reference to amnesty. Like other treaties, this omission expresses the reluctance of the negotiating state parties to commit to such language. It is therefore an awkward compromise that attempts to define the ICC's core value of complementarity of prosecution in such a way that amnesties are at least indirectly discouraged. The ICC's self-defined role is as a "backstop" criminal venue, and the principle of complementarity holds that preference will always be given to domestic prosecutions for the crimes of genocide, crimes against humanity, war crimes, and (potentially as of 2017) crimes of aggression, the four categories of international crime that the Rome Statute determines to be under the ICC's jurisdiction. Given the obvious relevance of domestic amnesties for the principle of complementarity, the Rome Statute's silence on the topic can be spun as a kind of creative ambiguity[48] that consciously refrains from tying the hands of the ICC's Office of the Prosecutor and that ensures tough cases regarding domestic amnesties will be the subject of accumulated case law as the ICC receives referrals and initiates prosecutions of its own.[49]

More realistically, however, the status of amnesties under international criminal law is such an immediate and pressing concern for the most basic prosecutorial functions of the ICC that the Statute's subtlety has deprived the ICC and its member states of a minimally requisite degree of legal clarity, and the ICC's work, from its very first referral, has reflected this absence. The very complex role played by the ICC's arrest warrant against Joseph Kony, leader of the Lord's Resistance Army in Uganda, is a demonstration of the challenges arising when a domestic amnesty has no *domestic* effect according to an international prosecutor.[50]

---

[48]  Scharf attributes this term to Phillipe Kirsch, chairman of the Rome Diplomatic Conference. Scharf also cites the comments of Kofi Annan that it would be "inconceivable" for the ICC to "undermine an amnesty-for-peace arrangement by pursuing prosecution in a situation like South Africa." Kofi Annan, Speech at the Witwatersrand University Graduation Ceremony, September 1, 1998, quoted in Robinson, "Serving the Interests of Justice," 12; quoted here in Scharf, "From the eXile Files," 367.

[49]  See Antonio Cassese et al., ed., *The Rome Statute for an International Criminal Court: A Commentary* (Oxford: Oxford University Press 2002), 1910.

[50]  See Max Pensky, "Amnesty on Trial: Impunity, Accountability, and the Norms of International Law," *Ethics and Global Politics* 1(2008). Also Louise Mallinder, "Uganda at the Crossroads: Narrowing the Amnesty?" (working paper 1 from *Beyond Legalism: Amnesties, Transition and Conflict Transformation*, Institute of Criminology and Criminal Justice, Queen's University Belfast, March 2009).

Article 17 of the Rome Statute expresses the principle of complementarity by determining the admissibility of cases before the ICC; specifically the article stipulates that such cases are inadmissible where "[t]he case is being investigated or prosecuted by a State which has jurisdiction over it, unless the State is unwilling or unable genuinely to carry out the investigation or prosecution."[51] Hence the question arises of what attitude the ICC, in particular the Office of the Prosecutor, will take in cases in which a domestic amnesty can be interpreted as an expression or documentation of a state's unwillingness or inability to prosecute. The introduction of the word "genuinely" in the language of the article bears all the marks of a cumbersome negotiated compromise, at once granting room for maneuver for international negotiators, but also creating a legal gray area.

Thus, the ICC has the discretion to call off a prosecution if the case would be inadmissible under Article 17. This could arguably include a situation in which a state party adopts an amnesty covering ICC crimes. Most experts have in fact concluded that Article 17 is the provision of the Rome Statute that offers the most plausible basis to allow for the types of amnesties under examination in this chapter. For example, it is an open question "whether intense military pressure not to prosecute falls within the category of inability or whether an unwillingness to jeopardize a democratic transition constitutes unwillingness within the terms of the Statute."[52] Be that as it may, the ICC is independent. Thus, even where an amnesty has been adopted in good faith under extreme exigency, the ICC's judges might decide to ignore the amnesty and proceed with the case based on a strict interpretation of unwillingness or inability.

There is no question that the ICC does not and should not regard itself as bound in any way by a domestic amnesty for a person who has been investigated and indicted in the course of its own procedures. Such a person – for example, Joseph Kony in Uganda – could not expect a national amnesty to have any extraterritorial effect, but could also not expect the ICC to recognize the amnesty as valid for its own purposes even within Ugandan national territory (though the question of the execution of an arrest warrant, or more likely the impossibility of such an execution, raises questions about the practical meaning of the ICC's position). In reference to Uganda, it was, and continues to be, impossible for the government to guarantee that the ICC would respect any amnesty it wishes to offer to the Lord's Resistance Army (LRA). Once the ICC is operating in a country – whether through state referral, Security Council referral, or prosecutorial initiation of an investigation in respect of such a crime in accordance with Article 15 – control over the solutions necessarily becomes

---

[51]  Rome Statute, art. 17.

[52]  Jessica Gavron, "Amnesties in the Light of Developments in International Law and the Establishment of the International Criminal Court," *International and Comparative Law Quarterly* 51 (2002): 111–12.

a shared burden, and all concerned parties enter a realm of uncertainty in which politics inevitably compete with law.

A more pertinent question is whether the ICC in general, and the Office of the Prosecutor in particular, would be prepared to accept as legally appropriate a domestic transitional justice approach that replicated the relevant quasi-juridical accountability mechanism of the South African TRC. That is, would a domestic transitional justice approach that integrated conditional, individualized amnesties for perpetrators of international crimes meet Article 17's definition of a "genuine unwillingness" to prosecute?

Of course, the South African amnesty model was inseparable from the mechanism of prosecution. There were prosecutions under way during the TRC's operations that, in addition to constituting genuine efforts to ensure criminal accountability, also served to create a threat credible enough to motivate perpetrators to come forward to the TRC with their criminal confessions and amnesty applications. In addition, as Antje du Bois-Pedain explains in her chapter in this volume, those perpetrators unwilling to satisfy the numerous requirements for the amnesty application – including a criminal confession and exhaustive testimony – remained liable to prosecution, as did those whose applications were refused by the courtlike Amnesty Committee. Yet even in cases where such conditional, individualized amnesties were approved – where selective amnesties in exchange for demanding conditions could be documented to contribute to larger goals of justice and to conditions of relative peace and security – many commentators find it difficult to imagine that an international court would attempt to block such a policy, which in any event would require a politically unlikely constellation of events, including the prosecutor's decision to initiate investigation and prosecution under his or her own initiative (the *proprio motu* provision of the Rome Statute), and referral or at least noninterference by the UN Security Council. Pragmatically, such a unilateral initiative could demonstrate that the ICC's willingness to intrude in the course of domestic transitional justice processes well in hand would be too high a price for its role as a "backstop" source of criminal justice.

In light of the challenges that the ICC has already faced and will continue to face, in which it risks being seen as the spoiler of sincere nonjudicial and quasi-judicial efforts at transitional justice, we may see the ICC begin to redefine its mission. Rather than framing its role as a provider of individual accountability, the focus may turn to the direct and indirect benefits of the Rome Statute framework as a whole in the realm of international justice. Signs of this rebranding already are apparent to some degree. The ICC is increasingly emphasizing, for example, how the threat of ICC prosecution can lead to more principled peace deals,[53] increase the

---

[53] Presentation by Luis Moreno-Ocampo, December 7, 2008, The Hague, "Conference on 60 Years of the Genocide Convention."

international criminal law component of military training,[54] and encourage changes in domestic legislation and practice through what the prosecutor's office terms positive complementarity.[55] These signs reflect awareness that in the court of public opinion, the ICC will lose if it is primarily perceived as a court, whereas it will win if it is perceived primarily as a lynchpin in a new global system of justice. As the prosecutor emphasized from an early stage, a lack of ICC trials would, paradoxically, constitute the best evidence of an effective ICC, as that would imply state parties are able and willing to deal with Rome Statute crimes on their own.[56]

## CONCLUSION

In the current geopolitical constellation, international criminal law cannot offer clear guidance regarding the legality of domestic amnesties for international crimes. The language of international treaties, silent on such amnesties, can be only indirectly interpreted as banning such amnesties, by asserting the paramounce of a nonderogable duty to prosecute such crimes. This indirect route has enough areas of ambiguity and loopholes to make treaty-based arguments relatively weak. Likewise, arguments against the use of amnesty based on claims of customary international law – specifically the crystallization of a norm of states' obligations to outlaw *jus cogens* crimes – fail to convince. A key requirement for such a crystallized norm, established state practice, cannot be proven. On the contrary, the rise of international criminal law is associated with an increase in such amnesties, not a decrease.

As for the rulings of the international criminal tribunals for Sierra Leone and the former Yugoslavia, these have offered instances in which amnesties were regarded as contrary to international law and indicate an emerging trend in international criminal case law. But the weakness of the courts' legal arguments and the rarity of international case law in general when it comes to amnesty – including the lack of any definitive position on the part of the ICC – preclude any serious claim of a solidified anti-amnesty norm in international law.

In brief, the status of amnesty under international law is truly unsettled. Indeed, if there is such a thing as an emergent legal position, it may be an accountability norm that moves beyond a narrow and retributivist conception of legal punishment: given a pyramid of accountability, processes of demilitarization, disarmament, and reintegration of low-level combatants may be linked to conditional, individualized

---

[54] Ibid.

[55] Office of the Prosecutor, *Report on Prosecutorial Strategy* (Office of the Prosecutor: September 14, 2006), 4–5, accessed September 3, 2011, http://www.icc-cpi.int/library/organs/otp/OTP Prosecutorial-Strategy-20060914 English.pdf.

[56] Upon his election, Prosecutor Ocampo declared that an absence of ICC trials "would be its major success." See Statement by Luis Moreno Campo to Assembly of States Parties, April 22, 2003.

amnesties, maximizing the effectiveness of other mechanisms to reconcile the goals of security and criminal accountability. However, even an accountability norm calling for a combination of low-level conditional amnesties and high-level mandatory prosecutions does not answer the core question of the legal status of amnesties, and in fact raises significant new questions of its own (not least, the status in such an approach of the mid-level of criminal responsibility, where arguably many of those most appropriately prosecuted would be found). It also highlights a central challenge facing international criminal justice, which can serve as a provisional conclusion to this chapter.

As the global experiment with new and energized institutions of international criminal justice approaches its twentieth birthday, lingering questions remain concerning the fit, or the lack of fit, between the paradigmatic commitments of criminal justice – the deontological approach – and the characteristic challenges of postconflict and postauthoritarian transitions. The former is based on a retributivist claim that punishment of perpetrators is such a powerful intrinsic good that it is a duty urgent enough to trump other considerations. The latter involves a broad, socialized, and diverse set of events, persons, and processes in which individual criminal acts can certainly always be identified, but only at the potential cost of a loss of perspective and context.

Within this wider framework, the question surrounding amnesty is what one can do about it to limit the concessions to impunity. There are actually dozens of significant choices in the design and negotiation of an amnesty that can, and should, affect our evaluation of any individual amnesty. Such choices make the difference between what one might characterize as a principled versus an unprincipled amnesty. At the same time, it is important to recognize that even a principled amnesty cannot guarantee accountability in practice. Amnesties are merely legal instruments, and no more or less likely to be honored in the breach than other laws. We should judge states not merely by their adoption of good laws but also, and to a much greater extent, by their implementation of both the letter and the spirit of such laws.

# PART II

# Comparative Case Studies

# 3

## Amnesties' Challenge to the Global Accountability Norm?

### Interpreting Regional and International Trends in Amnesty Enactment

*Louise Mallinder*

It is widely acknowledged that during the last decades of the twentieth century, the engagement of states with international human rights norms underwent a significant transformation.[1] Evidence for this can be seen in states' involvement in the creation of new human rights institutions and international treaties. For example, with the entry into force of human rights instruments such as Optional Protocol to the International Covenant on Civil and Political Rights (in 1976)[2] and the American Convention on Human Rights (in 1978),[3] participating nation states empowered human rights monitoring institutions to investigate individual complaints of state responsibility for human rights violations, even when the complaints were made by the states' own citizens. In addition, through the enactment of treaties such as the Convention against Torture,[4] states created new transnational offenses that state parties were obliged to prevent and punish. Furthermore, in addition to submitting themselves to greater scrutiny on their adherence to human rights, states have also increasingly sought to promote human rights overseas through rule-of-law programs[5]

---

[1] See Chandra Lekha Sriram, "Revolutions in Accountability: New Approaches to Past Abuses," *American University International Law Review* 19, no. 2 (2003): 301–429.

[2] Optional Protocol to the International Covenant on Civil and Political Rights, G.A. res. 2200A (XXI), 999 U.N.T.S. 302, entered into force March 23, 1976.

[3] American Convention on Human Rights, 1144 U.N.T.S. 123, entered into force July 18, 1978.

[4] Convention against Torture and Other Cruel, Inhuman or Degrading Treatment or Punishment, UN Doc. A/39/51 (1984), entered into force June 26, 1987.

[5] See Vera Gowlland-Debbas and Vassilis Pergantis, "Rule of Law," in *Post-Conflict Peacebuilding: A Lexicon*, ed. Vincent Chetail (Oxford: Oxford University Press, 2009); Giovanni Bassu, "Law Overruled: Strengthening the Rule of Law in Postconflict States," *Global Governance* 14 (2008): 22–38.

An earlier version of this chapter was presented at the "Amnesty in the Age of Accountability: Brazil in Comparative and International Perspective" Conference, University of Oxford, October 22–23, 2010. The author thanks the conference participants for their valuable feedback.

and cooperation with an ever-increasing range of international and hybrid criminal courts that hold individual perpetrators accountable for serious violations of human rights and humanitarian law.[6] These forms of state behavior were mirrored by an increased emphasis on human rights and the rule of law among international policymakers following the end of the Cold War.[7] In a groundbreaking article in 2001, Ellen Lutz and Kathryn Sikkink labeled these developments a "justice cascade."[8]

In developing the justice cascade theory, Lutz and Sikkink relied primarily on developments in Latin America from the late 1970s to the late 1990s. They argued that during this period the region underwent "a rapid shift toward recognizing the legitimacy of the human rights norms and an increase in international and regional action to effect compliance with these norms."[9] Furthermore, pointing to the creation of the ICC in 1998 and increasing acceptance by domestic judges in several countries of the principle of universal jurisdiction for serious human rights violations, the authors argued that the justice cascade was "not limited to Latin America," but was also "reverberating internationally."[10] These findings have been supported by other scholars who refer to the existence of "revolutions in accountability"[11] or an "age of accountability."[12]

In relation to amnesty laws, the justice cascade theory appears to suggest that, as the relevant human rights norms spread around the world, fewer amnesty laws that violate these norms will be enacted and where preexisting amnesty laws come into conflict with evolving norms, they will be eroded or annulled.[13] However, the data collected to support the justice cascade focuses on the growth in trials to hold human rights violators to account.[14] It does not document or explain the continued international

---

[6]   See Sarah Williams, *Hybrid and Internationalised Criminal Tribunals* (Oxford: Hart Publishing, 2011).

[7]   See Stephen Humphreys, *Theatre of the Rule of Law: Transnational Legal Intervention in Theory and Practice* (Cambridge: Cambridge University Press, 2010).

[8]   Lutz and Sikkink, "The Justice Cascade."

[9]   Ibid., 4.

[10]  Ibid.

[11]  See Sriram, *Revolutions in Accountability*.

[12]  See Tricia D. Olsen, Leigh A. Payne, and Andrew G. Reiter. "Amnesty in the Age of Accountability" (paper presented at the Annual Meeting of the Law and Society Association, Chicago, 2010).

[13]  Drawing on literature on customary international law, the investigation of the existence of a global accountability norm could entail investigating a broad range of issues relating to amnesty laws, such as the existence or absence of relevant domestic legislation (either granting amnesties or requiring prosecutions); the derogation, annulment, or reinterpretation of amnesties; state practice in relation to mediating peace agreements that include or exclude amnesty provisions or to financial and diplomatic support for amnesty processes; state willingness to include provisions prohibiting amnesty in international conventions; voting patterns in UN General Assembly resolutions; or judgments of domestic courts. However, such a broad analysis is beyond the scope of this chapter, which will instead focus on rates of the introduction of amnesty laws, the contexts that give rise to amnesties, and the resulting scopes of the amnesty legislation.

[14]  Hunjoon Kim and Kathryn Sikkink, "Explaining the Deterrence Effect for Human Rights Prosecutions for Transitional Countries," *International Studies Quarterly* 54 (2010): 939–63.

use of amnesty laws highlighted by this author and other scholars.[15] Drawing on the data compiled by the author in the Amnesty Law Database, this chapter will seek to address this gap by describing regional and global trends in amnesty law enactment and interpreting the existence of a global accountability norm in light of these trends. It will begin by discussing how "mapping" amnesty laws through a large-N comparative study can contribute to transitional justice knowledge. It will then briefly outline how the concept of amnesties has been defined within the Amnesty Law Database and describe the data categorization and collection processes used to construct this database. In the following section, the findings from the database will be used to present an overview of regional and international trends in amnesty law enactment from 1979 to 2011. This section will focus in particular on the period since the Rome Statute in 1998,[16] often pointed to as a watershed event in the development of a global accountability norm. It is beyond the scope of this chapter to highlight trends in relation to all aspects of amnesty law scope and legal effects. Instead, it will focus on whether contemporary amnesties are more likely to exclude or include crimes under international law from their scope, which is a central issue to understandings of the justice cascade. In the final section, the chapter will interpret the implications of these trends on the existence of such a cascade.

## WHY "MAP" AMNESTY LAWS?

Amnesty laws have played a central role in addressing political crises and violent conflicts for millennia.[17] However, they have rarely been subjected to extensive comparative study. Instead, the literature has focused predominantly on in-depth studies of particular amnesty processes,[18] or since the 1990s, on the relationship between amnesty laws and states' duties to investigate and prosecute under international law.[19] These studies have provided significant insights into how distinct forms of amnesties have operated in particular countries and on the parameters of the international legal framework relating to amnesties. However, they left considerable gaps in transitional justice knowledge on the causes, scope, legal effects, and impact of amnesty laws.

---

[15] See Mallinder, *Amnesty, Human Rights and Political Transitions*; Freeman, *Necessary Evils*; Trumbull, "Giving Amnesties a Second Chance"; Olsen, Payne, and Reiter, *Transitional Justice in Balance.*

[16] Rome Statute, 2187 U.N.T.S. 3

[17] See Robert Parker, "Fighting the Siren's Song: The Problem of Amnesty in Historical and Contemporary Perspective," *Acta Juridica Hungaria* 42, no. 1/2 (2001): 69–89.

[18] See Jeremy Sarkin, *Carrots and Sticks: The TRC and the South African Amnesty Process* (Antwerp: Intersentia, 2004); Helena Cobban, *Amnesty After Atrocity? Healing Nations After Genocide and War Crimes* (Boulder, CO: Paradigm Publishers, 2007).

[19] See O'Shea, *Amnesty for Crime in International Law and Practice*; Faustin Z. Ntoubandi, *Amnesty for Crimes against Humanity under International Law* (Leiden: Brill, 2007).

For example, as is common to transitional justice literature in general, the majority of in-depth country studies on amnesty laws focused on a handful of countries, notably Argentina and South Africa. As a result, these high-profile cases shaped much of the scholarly and practitioner debate on the nature of acceptable amnesties and on their impact on victims and societies. However, focusing on such single cases or small sets of cases can provide data with limited global applicability.[20] For example, the amnesties in Argentina and South Africa were enacted following democratic elections, which creates different political dynamics and legitimacy than amnesties proclaimed in the midst of warfare. Furthermore, in both countries, even though the former regimes had severely corroded the rule of law, formal legal processes were nonetheless familiar to wide sections of the populations, whereas in other transitional contexts, traditional or community-based forms of justice may have greater resonance for affected peoples.[21] In addition, Argentina and South Africa experienced distinctive forms of human rights violations in the policy of widespread enforced disappearances and the repressive apartheid regime. These experiences differ from the crimes committed in other transitional contexts. The focus on individual cases in the Americas and sub-Saharan Africa has also meant that the literature has neglected the role of amnesties in other regions, notably Asia and the Middle East. This gap is particularly significant because both regions currently have higher rates of new amnesty law enactment than the Americas.

The gaps created by the relative absence of large-N comparative studies on the scope of amnesty laws are also problematic since knowledge of trends in the scope of amnesty laws is crucial to understanding whether customary international law is evolving to prohibit certain forms of amnesty laws. In recent years, international jurists and scholars have increasingly made proclamations on the status of amnesty laws under customary international law, but few have based their assertions on extensive comparative studies of state practice.[22] Indeed, by relying on a small number of cases, many of these analyses have overlooked the continued prevalence and endurance of amnesties around the world.

Of the few large-N comparative studies of amnesty laws conducted to date, the first was a United Nations report prepared by Louis Joinet in 1985. This influential report

---

[20] Oskar N. T. Thoms, James Ron, and Roland Paris, "State-Level Effects of Transitional Justice: What do we Know?" *International Journal of Transitional Justice* 4 (2010): 336.

[21] See Rosalind Shaw and Lars Waldorf, eds., *Localizing Transitional Justice: Interventions and Priorities after Mass Violence* (Palo Alto: Stanford University Press, 2010); Luc Huyse and Mark Salter, eds., *Traditional Justice and Reconciliation after Violent Conflict: Learning from African Experiences* (Stockholm: International IDEA, 2008).

[22] For a more detailed discussion of this argument, see Louise Mallinder, "Peacebuilding, the Rule of Law and the Duty to Prosecute: What Role Remains for Amnesties?" in *Building Peace in Post-Conflict Situations*, ed. Faria Medjouba (London: British Institute of International and Comparative Law, 2012).

sought to "set out the practices followed by states dealing with amnesties," with the understanding that such comparative research could contribute to "deducing a number of rules or constants which might serve as a framework for authorities proposing to initiate an amnesty, as well as to the jurists responsible for drafting legislation."[23] The report further stated that "[t]his frame of reference might also be of use to the experts of the various specialized international supervisory bodies, in order to enable them to better assess the impact – positive, negative or nil – of an amnesty law" and for nongovernmental organizations (NGOs).[24] As explored later in this chapter, this technical analysis of the nature of amnesty laws is similar to the approach pursued in the Amnesty Law Database because, rather than treating amnesty laws as a homogenous group, it distills consideration of amnesty laws into distinct factors such as how and why amnesties are enacted, the crimes and categories of individuals covered, and the legal effects of amnesties.

It is interesting to note that, although Lutz and Sikkink date the origins of the justice cascade to the early 1980s when the UN Sub-Commission on Prevention of Discrimination and Protection of Minorities commissioned the Joinet report in 1983, the sub-commission stated that it had become aware of the importance the promulgation of amnesty laws "could have for the safeguard and promotion of human rights and fundamental freedoms."[25] In the final report, the positive role was described as including not just releasing all political prisoners,[26] but also encouraging "national consensus in the wake of political change brought about in a democratic framework;" the "first act in the initiation of a democratic process;" and blocking "an internal crisis" or marking "the end of an international armed conflict."[27]

In the years following the Joinet report, amnesty laws became increasingly controversial and this contributed to the UN publicly changing its position on amnesties at the signing of the 1999 Lomé Accord which sought to end the conflict in Sierra Leone.[28] Despite this controversy, no further large-N studies of amnesties were conducted until the mid-2000s, at which point academics and conflict resolution practitioners commissioned a few such studies. However, these studies only provided a partial picture of the use of amnesty laws around the world. For example,

---

[23] Joinet, *Study on Amnesty Laws*, para 85.

[24] Ibid., para 86.

[25] UN Sub-Commission on Prevention of Discrimination and Protection of Minorities, Resolution 1983/34. The administration of justice and the human rights of detainees. UN Doc E/CN.4/Sub.2/RES/1983/34, September 6, 1983.

[26] Joinet, *Study on Amnesty Laws*, para 81.

[27] Ibid., para 7.

[28] See William A. Schabas, "Amnesty, the Sierra Leone Truth and Reconciliation Commission and the Special Court for Sierra Leone," *U.C. Davis Journal of International Law & Policy* 11 (2004): 145–69.

the comparative studies of peace agreements conducted by Christine Bell[29] and by Leslie Vinjamuri and Aaron Boesenecker[30] highlight state practice in relation to amnesties only within peace agreements. In addition, neither these studies, nor the Transitional Justice Data Base Project, which compiles quantitative data on a range of transitional mechanisms enacted globally between 1970 and 2009, differentiate between different forms of amnesty laws.[31] Instead, these projects adopt a universal operating definition of amnesties that can be applied across all contexts under investigation, but does not take into account the different forms of amnesty and the impact these differences can have on the law's impact in a transition.

The Amnesty Law Database can be distinguished from the other comparative studies on amnesties in relation to its research purposes and design. In particular, it was not developed with the aim of testing hypotheses regarding the causes or impacts of amnesty laws. Instead, it sought to address the gaps in transitional justice knowledge of amnesty laws by developing thicker descriptions of the forms that these laws take, where they are enacted, and their legal effects. In this way, the purpose of the Amnesty Law Database is primarily to "map" or to provide a descriptive foundation on which future evaluation and assessment of amnesty laws can be based. This mapping can provide data that is geographical in the sense that it reveals trends in amnesty law enactment within countries and across continents. However, it can also describe the terrain and contours of amnesty laws themselves, in their internal characteristics and external boundaries. To do this, as will be explored in this chapter, rather than treating amnesty laws as a homogenous group, the Amnesty Law Database breaks down individual amnesty laws into constituent elements, which are then classified and systematically analyzed in order to identify patterns, correlations, and anomalies in the different characteristics of these laws. As this chapter will explore, this more fine-grained analysis is useful inter alia when determining whether amnesty laws are evolving in response to the justice cascade since it reveals the extent to which contemporary amnesty laws grant or withhold amnesty for serious human rights violations.

## DEFINING AMNESTIES

For all large-N comparative studies of amnesty laws, a central challenge is to define the concept of amnesty laws and then develop an operational definition of this

---

[29] See Christine Bell, *On the Law of Peace: Peace Agreements and the Lex Pacificatoria* (Oxford: Oxford University Press, 2008).

[30] Leslie Vinjamuri and Aaron Boesenecker, *Accountability and Peace Agreements: Mapping Trends from 1980 to 2006* (Geneva: Centre for Humanitarian Dialogue 2007).

[31] Olsen, Payne, and Reiter, *Transitional Justice in Balance*. This team is currently investigating distinctions among amnesty laws and practices.

concept. As has been noted for other transitional justice mechanisms,[32] there is a lack of conceptual clarity on the nature of amnesty laws. This problem arises for several reasons. First, within national legal systems, the term *amnesty* may be defined differently and different bodies may be empowered to grant amnesties.[33] Second, because amnesty laws have traditionally fallen within the domain of state sovereignty, no accepted international definition has developed. As a result of these conditions, the scope and legal effects of amnesty laws around the world can look very different, ranging from amnesty laws that aim to provide a form of reparations to persons arbitrarily detained by a repressive state to self-amnesty laws enacted by dictatorial rulers or war criminals eager to avoid penal sanctions. Indeed, Mark Freeman has suggested that "the difference between certain amnesties is so vast ... that it is almost nonsensical to compare them."[34]

Developing a clear definition of amnesty is further complicated because, although international law seeks to differentiate between amnesties and other leniency measures such as pardons and use immunity, domestic law can blur these distinctions. For example, the American constitution empowers the president "to grant Reprieves and Pardons for Offenses against the United States, except in Cases of Impeachment,"[35] but makes no explicit reference to amnesties. However, in practice, the U.S. Supreme Court has interpreted this provision to include the power to grant amnesties[36] and has proclaimed that the president can exercise this power for offenders who have been convicted and for persons who have yet to be investigated or stand trial.[37] In addition, many amnesty laws seek to distinguish between categories of offenders with the result that one law may offer a range of different forms of leniency such as amnesty, probation, and sentence reductions, which are allocated to distinct categories of offenders.[38]

To accommodate these conceptual difficulties, the Amnesty Law Database has taken a broad, inclusive approach. Unlike quantitative databases, which before beginning to collect and code data develop tightly defined and measureable definitions of amnesties drawn deductively from theoretical literature, the Amnesty Law Database takes a more inductive, grounded approach. As a result, a working definition was initially drawn from the theoretical and legal literature on amnesties, but during the process of data collection this definition was developed and redefined

---

[32] See Geoff Dancy, Hunjoon Kim, and Eric Wiebelhaus, "The Turn to Truth: Trends in Truth Commission Experimentation," *Journal of Human Rights* 9, no. 1 (2010): 45–64.

[33] See René Lévy, "Pardons and Amnesties as Policy Instruments in Contemporary France," *Crime and Justice* 36 (2007): 551.

[34] Freeman, *Necessary Evils*, 13.

[35] U.S. Constitution, art. II, § 2.I

[36] *United States v. Klein*, 80 U.S. 128, 147 (1871).

[37] *Ex Parte Garland*, 71 U.S. 333 (1866).

[38] See *Loi Relative Au Rétablissement De La Concorde Civile*, Loi no 98–08, (1999).

in response to the identification of common features of amnesty laws. This process has resulted in the adoption of an operational definition, which requires that to be included in the database, an amnesty process must be:

- A de jure measure[39]
- Enacted by state authorities[40] through promulgated laws, peace agreements, or executive policies[41]
- Related to political offenses (this can range from nonviolent dissident activities to the perpetration of crimes under international law)[42]
- Designed to remove criminal and/or civil sanctions – this primarily entails amnesties that apply preconviction, but postconviction measures are included where (1) they are granted in conjunction with preconviction amnesties; or (2) they eliminate not just the penalty, but also the criminal record for political prisoners
- Formally implemented and/or taken advantage of by some of the targeted individuals.

As a result of this broad definition, the Amnesty Law Database contains great disparity in the types of amnesties included. However, because each of these amnesties is then broken down into distinct categories, researchers can develop more narrowly focused comparisons by, for example, looking only at amnesties granted for members of nonstate armed groups or only at amnesties for crimes under international law.

## DATABASE DESIGN: TABLES AND VARIABLES

As the Amnesty Law Database was intended primarily to describe amnesty processes, it was not created using spreadsheets or statistical software. Instead, the database was developed using relational tables in Microsoft Access since this facilitated the inclusion of extensive descriptive text rather than coded data, although the database does nonetheless facilitate some limited counting to identify patterns. In the initial design phase, key issues relating to the causes, scope, and legal effects of amnesty laws were identified from the theoretical literature, an initial survey of amnesty legislation, and national and international case law. These issues included why and how the amnesty was introduced, what crimes it covered, who benefited from the

---

[39] Amnesty Law Database does not contain data on de facto amnesties, a term that describes failures to prosecute for whatever reason, rather than enacted policies to prevent prosecution.

[40] Amnesty Law Database excludes amnesties proclaimed by nonstate actors.

[41] The inclusion of executive policies means that for some amnesty processes no formal law was enacted.

[42] Amnesty Law Database excludes amnesties granted for common crimes or for economic crimes (e.g., the National Reconciliation Ordinance 2007, Pakistan).

amnesty, whether conditions were attached, what legal effects the amnesty had, how the amnesty was implemented, how it related to other transitional justice mechanisms, and how courts and other stakeholders responded to the amnesty process. The relational tables in the database correspond to these issues.

After the relational tables had been identified, each of these issues was broken down into specific variables based deductively upon the international legal standards and on issues that arose from the secondary analyses of amnesties, and inductively from frequently occurring elements within amnesty legislation. For example, the table relating to the crimes covered by the amnesty contained variables on whether crimes under international law, political crimes, economic crimes, or other crimes against individuals were included or excluded from the amnesty.[43] It also included variables on temporal or geographic restrictions relating to the commission of these crimes. For each of these variables, where appropriate, the database contains text detailing the scope of the amnesty law drawn from the law itself and other sources. Only a small sample of this data will be explored here since the majority of the variables are beyond the scope of this chapter.

Once the data has been compiled for a number of amnesty processes, the database is used to identify patterns by running queries to view the total number of amnesties with data for a particular variable, to examine patterns for a particular variable over time or across regions, and to identify relationships between different variables, such as whether amnesties for crimes under international law are more likely to be granted to nonstate actors. In addition, by entering the descriptive text rather than numerical codes for each variable, the exact provision of the amnesty law can be easily retrieved.

## DATA COLLECTION: CONTEXTS, SCOPE, AND SOURCES

Following the model outlined in the Joinet report, the Amnesty Law Database does not restrict itself solely to amnesties enacted during political transitions, but gathers data on amnesties emanating from all forms of political crises including civil unrest, military coups, international or internal conflict, authoritarian government, or states transitioning from such crises. Pursuing this broader approach is significant for several reasons. First, it includes analyses of amnesty laws introduced in contexts where crimes under international law may not have been committed, or where the amnesty laws are designed to remedy human rights violations such as arbitrary detention or forced displacement rather than promote impunity. By including these forms of amnesties, the research casts light on how amnesty laws can be used in ways that

---

[43]  Data is only collected on amnesties for economic crimes or common crimes where they are part of a broader amnesty for political offenses.

do not conflict with international law. Second, in many transitional contexts, questions of whether international crimes were committed are often highly contested. For example, in Northern Ireland during the Troubles, the British government resisted efforts to characterize the violence as a conflict, which would fall under the international humanitarian law framework, and instead preferred to apply domestic criminal law. By extending the scope of the database beyond situations in which international crimes have been widely recognized, the Amnesty Law Database can incorporate such contested contexts. Third, by including amnesty laws introduced in pretransition periods, the database can capture information on amnesties used as counterinsurgency tools or to facilitate peace negotiations. Although such contexts are not transitions strictly speaking, where amnesties are granted prior to a transition, they can influence the choice of transitional justice policies adopted by constraining the extent of accountability that can be pursued.

Although political amnesties have been used for millennia, the temporal scope of the Amnesty Law Database is restricted to amnesties introduced after the end of the Second World War. This cut-off date was selected since 1945 marks the initiation of international human rights law and international criminal law developments. For amnesties occurring after this date, the database, rather than sampling, includes all amnesty laws that meet the operational definition.[44]

In compiling data on individual amnesty processes, a range of documentary sources was employed including domestic legislation; international treaties and peace agreements; scholarly writings; jurisprudence from national and international courts and opinions given by treaty monitoring bodies; statements and reports by intergovernmental organizations (particularly the UN institutions); reports by states (particularly Country Reports on Human Rights Practices from the U.S. Department of State); reports by NGOs (particularly Amnesty International, Human Rights Watch, and International Crisis Group); and newspaper articles.[45] Challenges to data collection were similar to those faced by other comparative social science scholars and included language difficulties, the time that had elapsed since the amnesty was introduced, the lack of transparency in the state concerned, bias within the available sources, or a relative lack of academic research on the relevant transitional state. To try to combat these problems, as well as often obfuscatory language within amnesty laws, efforts were made to base the description of each amnesty on as wide a variety of sources as possible.

---

[44] However, due to the difficulties in identifying and compiling information on amnesty laws, it will be impossible to determine whether the database will ever provide a fully comprehensive survey of amnesty laws for this period.

[45] For each amnesty profile in the database, the range of sources used to compile the information is listed at the end of the profile.

At the time of this writing, the Amnesty Law Database contains information on 537 amnesty laws in 129 countries that were introduced between 1945 and June 2011. Because the start of the justice cascade or the global accountability norm is commonly dated to the late 1970s, this chapter will limit its analysis to amnesties introduced between 1979 and 2011. This means that global and regional trends will be explored for a total of 398 amnesties laws enacted in 115 countries.

## GLOBAL AND REGIONAL TRENDS IN AMNESTY ADOPTION, 1979–2011

With the expansion of international criminal law and transitional justice, scholars and practitioners have frequently proclaimed "the impending demise of amnesty."[46] This section will explore whether these assertions are premature by analyzing global and regional trends in amnesty adoption over the past thirty years. In particular, it will assess whether the growth of the justice cascade has contributed to a fall in the number of amnesty laws enacted for crimes under international law.

### Amnesty Trends by Year

In the midst of the Cold War, many countries experienced dictatorship or conflict. For example, according to Freedom House, forty-one percent of the world's countries were "not free" and thirty-one percent were only "partially free" in 1978.[47] In addition, the Uppsala Conflict Data Program has found that the number of active conflicts around the world increased during the 1970s.[48] As a result of these dynamics, the number of amnesty laws also increased sharply during that decade.[49] Because the focus of this chapter is on the period from 1979 to 2011, the global trend in the enactment of political amnesties in each of the following years is shown in Figure 3.1.

Between January 1979 and December 2010, an average of 12.25 amnesty laws was enacted each year, and from January 2011 to June 2011 a further six amnesties were introduced. However, as Figure 3.1 illustrates, between 1979 and 2010 the global rate of amnesty law enactment went through a number of peaks and troughs. For example, following the end of the Cold War in 1989, the number of amnesty laws rose sharply. This increase can be attributed to, first, the political transitions that took place in the former communist states in Eastern Europe, which resulted in a

---

[46] See Laplante, "Outlawing Amnesty," 932.

[47] Freedom House, "Freedom in the World Country Ratings," accessed July 11, 2011, http://www.freedom-house.org/uploads/fiw09/CompHistData/CountryStatus&RatingsOverview1973–2009.pdf.

[48] Uppsala Conflict Data Program, "Active Conflicts by Region," accessed July 26, 2011, http://www.pcr.uu.se/research/UCDP/graphs/conflict_region_2008.pdf.

[49] See Mallinder, *Amnesty, Human Rights and Political Transitions*, 19.

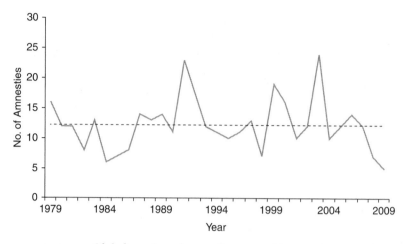

FIGURE 3.1. Global number of amnesties enacted by year (1979–2010).

series of amnesty laws enacted predominantly to benefit dissidents whose actions had been criminalized by the former regimes. The end of the Cold War also meant that the superpowers stopped propping up dictatorial regimes or intervening in civil wars to prolong the violence. The end of these interventions meant that many countries moved toward negotiated peace agreements or pacted transitions that included amnesties. Conversely, the collapse of the Soviet Union and the former Yugoslavia caused newly independent states to spiral into civil war as ethnic tensions that had previously been suppressed came to the fore. These conflicts contributed to a series of amnesties in the late 1990s. The impact of the end of the Cold War on amnesty rates has been noted by other comparative studies. For example, in 2005 Helga Binningsbø et al. wrote that "the probability of amnesty after the Cold War is … higher than the probability that a conflict was followed by amnesty in the decades after the Second World War."[50] Although the frequency with which amnesties were enacted varied considerably during these three decades, the global trend, as shown by the dotted line, indicates that the rate of amnesty laws introduced has remained constant. This trend has also been found by Tricia Olsen et al., who argue that their Transitional Justice Data Base illustrates "a steady persistence of amnesties."[51] Similarly, Freeman has argued that "amnesties are as prevalent today as at any time in modern history … we are no more at the end of amnesties than we are at the 'end of history.'"[52]

[50]  Helga Malmin Binningsbø, Malmin, Jon Elster, and Scott Gates, "Civil War and Transitional Justice, 1946–2003: A Dataset" (paper presented at the "Transitional Justice and Civil War Settlements" workshop in Bogotá, Colombia, October 18–19, 2005), 17–18.
[51]  Olsen, Payne, and Reiter, *Transitional Justice in Balance*.
[52]  Freeman, *Necessary Evils*, 4.

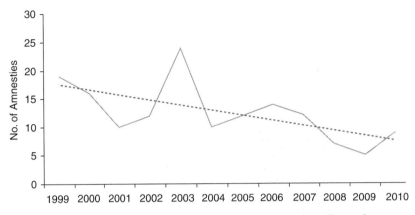

FIGURE 3.2. Global amnesty enactment trends, January 1999 – December 2010.

The past decade has seen many developments in international criminal law, including the creation of the ICC, universal jurisdiction proceedings for human rights violations in several countries, and the UN's decision in 1999 to refrain from recognizing amnesty laws for serious crimes under international law. The expectation among human rights campaigners has been that these developments would make amnesty laws less attractive for perpetrators and would gradually lead to a reduction in their use. To explore whether such a decline has begun to develop, Figure 3.2 isolates global trends in amnesty enactment from January 1, 1999.

From January 1999 to December 2010, an average of 12.5 amnesty laws was enacted annually, but as with the longer time period, Figure 3.2 indicates that the past decade has seen considerable variation in the total number of amnesties introduced each year. For example, in 2003, the year following the creation of the ICC, the number of amnesty laws enacted was almost double the average annual enactment rate and amounted to the largest annual total enacted in any year. During 2003, amnesty laws were enacted in every region of the world, although to differing frequencies[53] and in diverse political contexts.[54] In contrast to 2003, in 2009 only half the annual average of new amnesty laws was enacted. Overall, however, although the average number of amnesty laws enacted annually since 1999 is slightly higher than for the period from 1979 to 2010, the global trend as illustrated by the dotted lines indicates a fall in the rate of amnesty enactment since 1999. As the rate of amnesty law enactment frequently goes through sizeable peaks and troughs, it is too early to determine whether this reflects an emerging trend in state practice or a temporary fall in the numbers.

---

[53] For example, over a third of the total was enacted within sub-Saharan Africa, whereas only one was enacted in the Americas.

[54] For example, thirty-five percent emanated from repressive regimes and forty-three percent from ongoing conflicts or transitions from conflict.

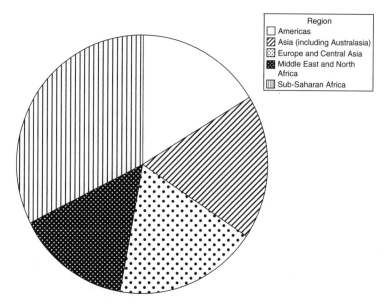

FIGURE 3.3. Amnesty laws by region, 1979–2010.

Indeed, beginning in January 2010, the number of amnesty laws introduced seems to be climbing again, a change which in 2011 can be partially attributed to the amnesties proclaimed in the "Arab Spring." It seems caution is warranted when looking at these contemporary trends, particularly since the rates of change have not occurred uniformly across all regions.

### Amnesty Laws by Region

Within the Amnesty Law Database, countries are allocated to one of the five following regions: the Americas, Asia, Europe and Central Asia, the Middle East and North Africa, and sub-Saharan Africa. As shown in Figure 3.3, amnesties were enacted in all regions of the world after 1979.

It is perhaps unsurprising that the greatest proportion of amnesty laws enacted from 1979 to 2010 was introduced in sub-Saharan Africa (thirty-three percent) due to that region's large number of states and high incidence of conflict.[55] However, it is quite striking that there is very little difference between the proportions of amnesty laws enacted in the Americas (sixteen percent), Asia (eighteen percent), and Europe and Central Asia (nineteen percent) during this period. This is particularly remarkable considering Europe and the Americas have more developed regional human

---

[55] Uppsala Conflict Data Program, "Active Conflicts by Region."

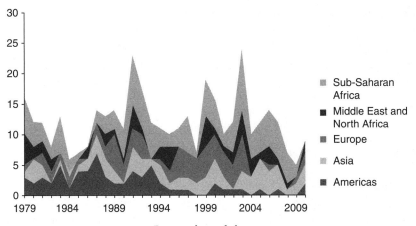

FIGURE 3.4. Regional trends by year, 1979–2011.

rights monitoring mechanisms than Asia. However, among these regions there are considerable variations over time, as shown in Figure 3.4.

When looking at the regional trends over time, interesting patterns emerge. For example, during the 1980s, the Americas had the highest rate of amnesty law enactment, which can be attributed to the military dictatorships and civil wars that occurred in the region during this decade. However, the region's rate of amnesty enactment declined sharply beginning in the mid-1990s, from which point it has had the lowest rate of new amnesty laws (although most of its preexisting amnesty laws have remained in effect). The overall trend for the Americas between 1979 and 2010 is one of declining numbers of new amnesty laws. This finding reflects the changing political conditions in the region since the late 1980s, particularly the establishment of democratic governments in many countries.[56] The rate of amnesty law enactment in the Middle East and North Africa remained constant. However, four amnesties were introduced in this region between January 2011 and June 2011, which could mark the start of a change in this trend, particularly since the rate of amnesties in this region has historically been low.[57] In contrast, the amnesty trends for the remaining three regions showed an increased reliance on new amnesties between 1979 and 2010. The sharpest increase in the rate of amnesty law enactment occurred in Asia, although the numbers of new amnesties in this region remain fewer than in sub-Saharan Africa. If the regional trends are analyzed for the years from 1999 to 2010, unsurprising given the global trends for the decade, an increasing number of regions have witnessed declining amnesty law enactment rates. Asia remains the

---

[56] Sikkink and Walling, "The Impact of Human Rights Trials in Latin America."

[57] Between 1979 and 2010, only fifty-three amnesties were introduced in the Middle East and North Africa, which gives an average of 1.65 amnesty laws per year.

only region where the rate of new amnesty law enactment has remained constant, while Europe and Central Asia have witnessed the steepest decline. The constant rate in Asia could perhaps reflect that during the past decade, this region has had the highest rates of ongoing conflict.[58] The impact of the different political crises on the rates of amnesty law introduction will be explored later in this chapter.

## Amnesty Laws by Political Crises

As noted previously, the Amnesty Law Database compiles data on amnesty laws introduced in response to a range of political crises. Within the database, these crises have been broken down into seven fields[59]: conflicted democracy,[60] coup attempt, ongoing conflict, ongoing repression, transition from dictatorship, transition from internal conflict, and transition from international conflict.[61] The distribution for each of these transition types for the years from 1979 to 2011 can be seen in Figure 3.5.

This chart illustrates that over the past thirty years almost half of all amnesties enacted were related to conflicts; many were enacted when the conflict was ongoing or during peace negotiations. If the data is restricted to the years from 1999 to 2011, the proportion of amnesties related to conflict rises to slightly over fifty percent. The relationship of amnesties to conflict resolution has been explored in comparative large-N studies on peace agreements, which have found that peace accords are more likely to include amnesty laws than other forms of transitional justice. For example, in a survey of peace agreements made between 1980 and 2006, Leslie Vinjamuri and Aaron Boesenecker found that while "provisions for prosecutions and truth commissions are rare in peace agreements … the use of amnesty is comparatively common."[62] They further found that the rates of amnesties in the agreements remained "relatively stable over the time period analyzed,"[63] even though

---

[58] Uppsala Conflict Data Program, "Active Conflicts by Region."

[59] There is overlap between some of these categories, for example, a country could be in transition from dictatorship but the military could still exercise considerable influence resulting in repression. Furthermore, distinguishing between internal and international conflicts can be problematic. In addition, these categorizations simplify what in many states could be multiple transitions, for example, from conflict to peace, but also from authoritarian rule to democracy. Finally, the transitions are classified according to the moment when the amnesty was introduced. For example, the term *transition from conflict* is used if elections have been held or peace agreement signed, even where violence later reignites.

[60] Within this study, *conflicted democracy* denotes various contexts including widespread antigovernment protests, violence erupting from elections, or terrorist violence within democratic states. See Fionnuala Ní Aoláin and Colm Campbell, "The Paradox of Transition in Conflicted Democracies," *Human Rights Quarterly* 27, no. 1 (2005): 172–213.

[61] As noted earlier, this is a much broader range of contexts than that included in other datasets on amnesty laws that focus solely on amnesties enacted as part of a transition or negotiated peace agreements.

[62] Vinjamuri and Boesenecker, *Accountability and Peace Agreements*, 5.

[63] Ibid., 9.

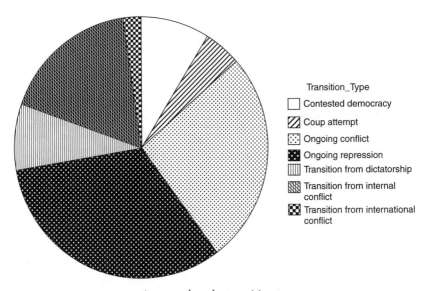

FIGURE 3.5. Amnesty laws by transition type, 1979–2011.

beginning in 2000 the number of peace agreements concluded declined.[64] Among the amnesty provisions identified by Leslie Vinjamuri and Aaron Boesenecker, they found that twenty-one percent of the agreements contained "no justice mechanism, amnesty provision, or IHL/HR law reference whatsoever."[65] This finding has been interpreted by the Center for Humanitarian Dialogue as illustrating that:

> the most active proponents and perpetrators of war are relatively unchallenged by law in most peace agreements. When justice mechanisms are adopted, the overwhelming trend is towards strategies of co-existence, forgiveness and reconciliation instead of legal accountability.[66]

The prevalence of amnesty laws in peace agreements perhaps reflects that within much of the literature, amnesties introduced to bring mass violence to an end are viewed as more acceptable than self-amnesties introduced by dictatorial rulers or amnesties enacted by democratic politicians after a transfer of power. The role of amnesty in facilitating the peaceful resolution of violent conflict has been recognized by state parties to the Additional Protocol II to the Geneva Conventions. This is the only treaty to mention amnesty laws explicitly and it encourages state

---

[64] Ibid., 13.
[65] Ibid., 9.
[66] Centre for Humanitarian Dialogue, "Charting the Roads to Peace: Facts, Figures and Trends in Conflict Resolution," *Mediation Data Trends Report* (Geneva: Centre for Humanitarian Dialogue, Geneva 2007), 15.

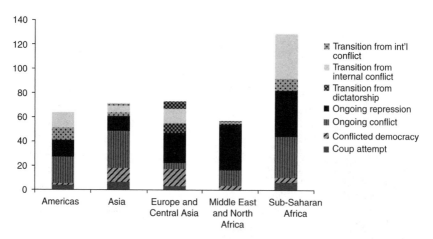

FIGURE 3.6. Regional trends by political crisis, 1979–2011.

parties to enact the "broadest possible amnesty to persons who have participated" in noninternational armed conflicts.[67]

In addition to conflict-related amnesties, forty percent of amnesties resulted from dictatorial rule, either introduced by the repressive regime itself (thirty-eight percent) or by its successors (eight percent). The number of repressive regimes in the world has declined since 1979 and consequently the number of amnesties that result from such contexts has declined over the past three decades.

If these global trends on political crisis are analyzed by region considerable divergences are apparent, as illustrated in Figure 3.6.

This chart illustrates that, during the past thirty years, amnesties resulting from ongoing conflicts featured most heavily in sub-Saharan Africa, followed by Asia and the Americas. If the data is analyzed just for the past decade, ongoing conflicts remain a significant factor in Africa and Asia, and in particular, amnesties as part of transitions from internal conflict are most prevalent in sub-Saharan Africa. In contrast, since 1979 amnesties relating to dictatorial regimes were introduced most often in the Middle East and North Africa. Despite the differences in the type of political crisis that can trigger the enactment of amnesty laws, in many of these contexts serious human rights violations were committed by government forces and nonstate actors alike.

### Amnesties and Crimes under International Law

Unlike other datasets that focus only on amnesty laws for human rights abuses, the Amnesty Law Database includes amnesties enacted for a wide range of political

---

[67] Protocol Additional to the Geneva Conventions of August 12, 1949, and relating to the Protection of Victims of Non-International Armed Conflicts, June 8, 1977, 1125 U.N.T.S. 609, art. 6 (5).

offenses. As a result, serious human abuses are not a factor for all amnesties in the Amnesty Law Database. Furthermore, due to the differences in states' ratifications of human rights treaties and the existence of human rights institutions in different regions, the Amnesty Law Database does not focus on gathering data on human rights abuses broadly defined. Instead, it isolates amnesties for international crimes, namely genocide, war crimes, crimes against humanity, disappearances, and torture. Where the text of amnesty laws does not explicitly state which crimes are included or excluded in an amnesty, determining whether international crimes are a factor is problematic, particularly when states for political reasons decline to acknowledge the inclusion of international crimes in the amnesty legislation, preferring instead to frame them as domestic crimes. In addition, some individual amnesty processes include and exclude crimes under international law, by for example, excluding crimes against humanity from the amnesty but allowing torturers to escape prosecution. In constructing the Amnesty Law Database, the author has taken a cautious approach and entered data relating to international crimes only when (1) the following crimes were explicitly mentioned in the text of the amnesty: war crimes, genocide, crimes against humanity, torture, and disappearances; (2) when case law indicated that the amnesty included or excluded these crimes; and/ or (3) when there is substantial evidence in reports by UN or regional human rights institutions or by respected human rights organizations, such as Amnesty International or Human Rights Watch, that crimes under international law took place. As a result, it is probable that the Amnesty Law Database underrepresents the number of amnesty processes granting impunity for crimes under international law. Nonetheless, Figure 3.7 illustrates trends in the relationship between amnesties and international crimes.

The trends illustrated in Figure 3.7 relate only to amnesty laws clearly stating that crimes under international law have been included or excluded. When examining the patterns of the past thirty years, it becomes apparent that both approaches have been a feature of amnesty laws around the world. The rates of amnesties including crimes under international law have increased over the past thirty years, but for most years since the early 1990s, more amnesties have excluded crimes under international law. However, it is interesting to note that after a peak around 1999, the number of amnesties explicitly excluding crimes under international law has fallen.

The past decade is perhaps the most significant period in the relationship between crimes under international law and amnesties due to the creation of the ICC and the change in the UN's stance toward amnesties for serious human rights violations. The yearly trends for this decade are illustrated in Figure 3.8.

This chart shows that, as the rate of amnesty law enactment has fallen since 1999, the number of amnesties including and excluding crimes under international law has also fallen. However, where states still chose to enact amnesty laws, this chart

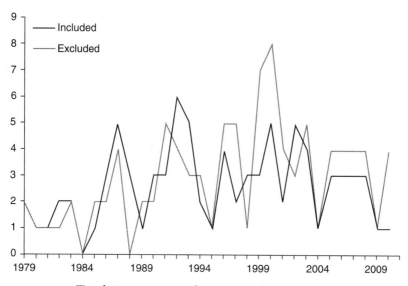

FIGURE 3.7. Trends in amnesties and international crimes by year, 1979–2010.

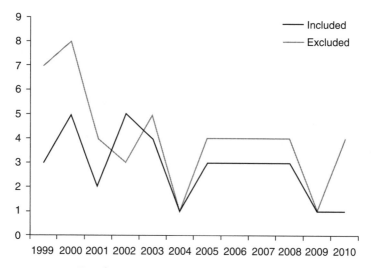

FIGURE 3.8. Trends in amnesties and international crimes, 1999–2010.

indicates that states are only slightly more likely to exclude serious human rights violations from the amnesty law than to include them.

During the period from 1979 to 2010, regional differences were found in approaches to granting amnesties for crimes under international law as illustrated in Figure 3.9.

From Figure 3.9, we can see that the only regions where the number of amnesties excluding crimes under international law exceeded the number of amnesties that

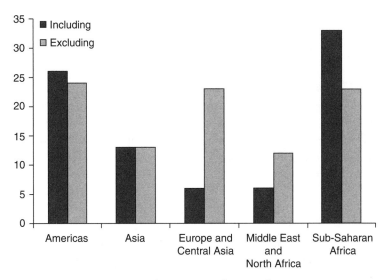

FIGURE 3.9. Amnesties and international crimes by region, 1979–2011.

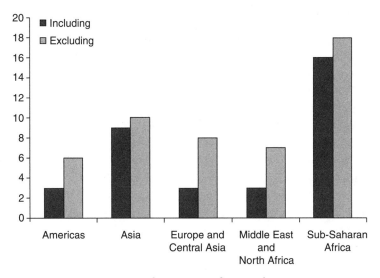

FIGURE 3.10. Amnesties and international crimes by region, 1999–2010.

included such crimes are Europe and Central Asia and the Middle East and North Africa. In all other regions during the past thirty years, states have been more likely to include crimes under international law in new amnesties than to exclude them. These trends have changed during the past decade, particularly in relation to the Americas, as shown in Figure 3.10.

From this chart, we can see that Europe and Central Asia is now the region least likely to grant new amnesties for crimes under international law. Furthermore, in all regions of the world in the past decade, newly enacted amnesty laws have been more likely to exclude crimes under international law than to include them. However, in Asia and sub-Saharan Africa, the likelihood is less pronounced.

This section has illustrated a range of trends relating to when, where, and in what context new amnesty laws have been enacted and the extent to which these laws apply to crimes under international law. The implications of these global and regional trends for the theory of the justice cascade will be explored later in this chapter.

### Amnesty Trends and the Global Accountability Norm

The emergence of a global accountability norm under which prosecutions would replace impunity as the presumptive response to atrocity has been subject to extensive debate among scholars, jurists, and human rights activists.[68] Proponents of this norm highlight multiple "norm-affirming events"[69] to support its existence. These events include the enactment of international conventions such as the 1998 Rome Statute, the judgments of international and hybrid tribunals on customary international law relating to international crimes, the speeches of officials of national governments and intergovernmental bodies acknowledging the norm, and the enactment of domestic legislation.[70] Since the end of the Cold War, there is ample evidence of these types of events supporting the development of a global accountability norm. However, as the data in the previous section indicates, states facing political crises continue to pass amnesty laws. This suggests that the global accountability norm has not yet reached the point where it has "become so widely accepted" that it is "internalized by actors" and has achieved "a 'taken-for granted' quality that makes conformance with [it] almost automatic."[71] Nonetheless, its emergence may be shaping amnesty trends.

When global trends in amnesty law enactment were analyzed for the years from 1979 to 2011, the data indicated that the rate of amnesty laws had remained steady throughout the period despite developments in accountability. At face value, these

---

[68] See Decision on challenge to jurisdiction: Lomé Accord Amnesty in *Prosecutor v. Morris Kallon, Brima Bazzy Kamara*, SCSL-2004–15-PT-060-I, SCSL-2004–15-PT-060-II, Appeal (March 13, 2004), para 73; *Prosecutor v. Anto Furundzija*, Case No. IT-95–17/1-T, Judgement (December 10, 1998).

[69] Ellen L. Lutz and Kathryn Sikkink, "International Human Rights Law and Practice in Latin America," *International Organizations* 54, no. 3 (Summer 2000, 2000): 633–59; Lutz and Sikkink, "The Justice Cascade," 1–34.

[70] Lutz and Sikkink, "International Human Rights Law and Practice in Latin America," 655–6.

[71] Martha Finnemore and Kathryn Sikkink, "International Norm Dynamics and Political Change," *International Organizations* 52, no. 4 (1998): 904.

findings appear to undermine the existence of a justice cascade in which, according to Cass Sunstein, "societies are presented with rapid shifts towards new norms."[72] However, as Sikkink notes in her chapter in this volume, amnesties may increase as a response to increased demand for accountability. This suggestion has also been made by the author elsewhere[73] when contending that the sharp increase in the rate of amnesty laws during the 1970s and their endurance over the past thirty years may indicate a move away from lawlessness and de facto impunity, where states simply failed to prosecute, toward an increasingly legalistic approach in which states use law in the form of amnesty legislation to address legacies of past crimes. Arguably, these changes could indicate increasing recognition of international legal obligations relating to the duty to investigate and prosecute, both among human rights abusers causing them to seek amnesties and among transitional governments. If this is the case, we could then expect it to eventually cause a decline in the number of amnesty laws.

When the global trends in amnesty introduction were analyzed just for the past decade, this research found that, in contrast to the longer time period, the rate of amnesty laws has in fact decreased. In addition, where amnesty laws are proposed or enacted today they are often met by social disapproval from international civil society,[74] intergovernmental human rights bodies,[75] and governments of other states.[76] This disapproval can be expressed in written or oral statements or in some cases by threats to withhold support for transitional justice projects. For example, the UN refused to cooperate with the Commission for Truth and Friendship jointly established by Indonesia and Timor Leste because the commission was empowered to "recommend amnesty for those involved in human rights violations who cooperate fully in revealing the truth."[77] Cass Sunstein has argued that the production of social disapproval indicates that a "tipping point" has been reached and that the costs of expressing new norms have become lower than adherence to the old norm.[78]

[72] Cass R. Sunstein, *Free Markets and Social Justice* (Oxford: Oxford University Press, 1997), 38.

[73] Mallinder, *Amnesty, Human Rights and Political Transitions.*

[74] Amnesty International, *Uganda: Agreement and Annex on Accountability and Reconciliation Falls Short of a Comprehensive Plan to End Impunity* (Amnesty International: London 2008); Amnesty International, *Kenya: Concerns about the Truth, Justice and Reconciliation Commission Bill* (Amnesty International: London 2008); Sara Darehshori, *Selling Justice Short: Why Accountability Matters for Peace* (New York, NY: Human Rights Watch, 2009).

[75] OHCHR, *Report from OHCHR Fact-finding Mission to Kenya,* (Geneva: OHCHR, February 6–28, 2008); OHCHR, *Rule-of-Law Tools.*

[76] Mallinder, *Amnesty, Human Rights and Political Transitions,* ch. 8.

[77] Commission of Truth and Friendship, "Terms of Reference," March 9, 2005, para 14, accessed September 3, 2011, http://www.kbri-canberra.org.au/special/TOR_CTF.pdf. See, for example, "Indonesia, East Timor Seal Deal on Atrocities Despite UN Opposition," *Agence France Presse,* March 9, 2005; "UN Demands Indonesia Re-Try Military Officers East Timor Killings," *ABC Radio Australian,* June 30, 2005.

[78] Sunstein, *Free Markets and Social Justice,* 38.

There are, however, several reasons for caution when pronouncing that the global accountability norm's "tipping point" has arrived.

First, although the rate of amnesty laws has declined in last decade, this is due primarily to a drop in the number of amnesty laws in 2008 and 2009. If only the years from 1999 to 2007 are considered the decline does not appear to be pronounced. In addition, the increase in the number of amnesty laws enacted between January 2010 and June 2011 suggests that the recent decline was an anomaly rather than a sustained trend. Overall, the data reveals that amnesty laws continue to be enacted by states facing political crises, and as a result, it is too early to determine whether the decline in the rate of amnesty law enactment over the past decade represents a lasting change in norm adherence among states.

Second, since the global accountability norm should encourage an increase in support for trials for serious violations of human rights, its existence should result in these crimes' increased exclusion from amnesty legislation. As the data indicated, since 1979 the rate of amnesty laws excluding these crimes has indeed increased, but so too has the rate of amnesties including serious human rights violations. Overall, there is little difference between the rates for including or excluding these crimes.

Third, social disapproval of amnesty laws expressed by governments and intergovernmental bodies does not represent condemnation of all forms of amnesty in political transitions. For example, amnesty laws for political prisoners or to facilitate the return of refugees still have strong international support.[79] Social disapproval is triggered primarily in relation to amnesties for serious human rights violations. However, even this disapproval is rarely consistent. For example, some transitional states, such as Kenya and Nepal, have been subject to substantial international pressure to investigate and prosecute, whereas amnesties enacted in other states have been largely overlooked even where they were granted for serious crimes.[80] Furthermore, donor states that admonish developing countries for proposing amnesty legislation for serious human rights violations generally do so without applying the same condemnation to their own preexisting amnesty legislation.[81]

---

[79] See UN High Commissioner for Refugees, Legal Safety Issues in the Context of Voluntary Repatriation, UN Doc EC/54/SC/CRP.12 (UNHCR: Geneva June 7, 2004), para 12.

[80] For example, an amnesty measure contained in paragraph 445 of the constitution of the Republic of the Union of Myanmar of 2008 preventing any legal proceedings against "any member of the Government, in respect of any act done in the execution of their respective duties," attracted little international condemnation despite the regime's appalling human rights record.

[81] For example, in UN Security Council debates on postconflict justice, countries such as France, Spain, and Algeria emphasized the importance of prosecutions for serious human rights violations. Yet France and Spain have amnesty laws relating to past serious human rights violations, which remain in effect, and Algeria has introduced two amnesty laws within the past decade, albeit with some limited restrictions on the crimes to which they apply. UNSC, "In Presidential Statement, Security Council Reaffirms 'Vital Importance' of United Nations' Role in Post-conflict Reconciliation," January 27, 2004. Press release SC/7990.

Recent years have also seen cases of strong international support for amnesty processes. For example, during the final stages of the conflict between the Tamil Tigers and the Sri Lankan government in 2009, international actors made statements endorsing an amnesty for surrendering insurgents.[82] These statements of support did not refer to the need to prosecute serious human rights violations committed during the conflict. In addition to statements of support, some amnesty processes receive financial backing. For example, the 2000 Ugandan Amnesty Act, which grants amnesty for all conflict-related crimes committed by insurgents fighting against the government, including the atrocities committed by the Lord's Resistance Army, has consistently received financial support from international donors for its implementation.[83] These endorsements of amnesties for serious crimes appear not to have been motivated by a desire for impunity, but rather a recognition of the role that amnesty can play in encouraging combatants to surrender and disarm.

Fourth, states have consistently failed to prohibit amnesty laws in international conventions. For example, during the Rome Conference delegates debated a range of proposals relating to amnesty laws, but were ultimately unable to reach a consensus on prohibiting them in the ICC Statute. As a result, the ICC Statute contains no reference to amnesty legislation.[84] Indeed, to date, the only convention to discuss amnesty laws explicitly is Additional Protocol II to the Geneva Conventions, which in Article 6(5) encourages state parties to enact the "broadest possible amnesty to persons who have participated" in noninternational armed conflicts.[85] The Commentary on the Additional Protocol asserts that this provision is "to encourage gestures of reconciliation which can contribute to re-establishing normal relations in the life of a nation which has been divided."[86]

Finally, where there is international pressure in favor of prosecutions, it can result in serious human rights violations being excluded from the scope of amnesty

---

[82] For example, "Co-Chairs Of Sri Lanka Peace Process Urge Tamil Tigers To End Hostilities," *RTT News*, February 3, 2009; "Lay Down Arms, Surrender – European Parliament Tells LTTE," *The Colombo Times*, February 6, 2009; "U.N. Security Council Asks LTTE To Surrender," *RTT News*, April 22, 2009.

[83] For example, in January 2008, the Ugandan Amnesty Commission received funding of U.S. $10,055,278 from a World Bank Multi-Donor Trust Fund to support its work. The donors to this fund included state parties to the ICC such as Denmark, Norway, the Netherlands, Sweden, and the United Kingdom. See World Bank, Project Information Document: Uganda Emergency Demobilization and Reintegration Project (World Bank: January 23, 2008); "World Bank Offers over sh3 billion to Resettle Former ADF, LRA Rebels," *New Vision*, August 19, 2008.

[84] William A. Schabas, *An Introduction to the International Criminal Court*, 3rd ed. (Cambridge: Cambridge University Press, 2007), 87.

[85] Protocol Additional to the Geneva Conventions of August 12, 1949, and relating to the Protection of Victims of Non-International Armed Conflicts, June 8, 1977, 1125 U.N.T.S. 609, art. 6 (5).

[86] Claude Pilloud, Yves Sandoz, Christophe Swinarski, and Bruno Zimmerman, eds., *Commentary on the Additional Protocols of 8 June 1977 to the Geneva Conventions of 12 August 1949* (Geneva: International Committee of the Red Cross, 1987), para 4618.

legislation, but this does not automatically mean that these crimes will be prosecuted. In addition, even where a prosecution policy is adopted, it is generally restricted to trials of relatively small numbers of high-ranking or notorious offenders, while the middle and lower ranking offenders and their supporters escape legal accountability. This phenomenon was acknowledged by the UN secretary general in 2004 when he noted, "[i]n the end, in post-conflict countries, the vast majority of perpetrators of serious violations of human rights and international humanitarian law will never be tried, whether internationally or domestically."[87] The failure to prosecute could be due to multiple factors including a lack of evidence, a lack of judicial and penal capacity, limited financial resources, the ongoing political and military strength of the offenders, or a decision by the government to prioritize other policies such as development and security over the pursuit of justice. Governments facing these conditions may wish to prosecute past crimes and therefore decide to exclude international crimes from amnesty legislation to ensure that trials may be possible in the future where they cannot be held immediately. However, other states may exclude international crimes from amnesty legislation to conform to international pressure rather than in acceptance of a global accountability norm. This rhetorical adherence to the norm can be particularly apparent where exclusions for international crimes are not enforced during the implementation of amnesty legislation.[88]

The existence of a norm is not dependent on individuals or countries consistently adhering to it. Indeed, Lutz and Sikkink argue that "[j]ustifying norm breaking may … be a norm-affirming event, if in making the justification, the actor recognizes the existence of the norm and explains why it was not possible to abide by the norm in particular circumstances."[89] However, when states enact amnesty laws for serious human rights violations today, they rarely acknowledge the existence of a global accountability norm. Instead they argue that the amnesty is necessary to bring peace and promote reconciliation. These rationales are often echoed by international actors who support and fund amnesty processes. This therefore casts doubt on the extent to which a global accountability norm has emerged.

As the data cited previously illustrates, there are regional divergences in amnesty trends. In particular, the Americas region has undergone the steepest decline in the

---

[87] UN Security Council, *Report of the Secretary-General on the Rule of Law and Transitional Justice in Conflict and Post-Conflict Societies* (United Nations: 2004), para 46.

[88] For example, in the 1999 Algerian amnesty law, offenders who had committed crimes involving "the death or permanent disabling of a person, rape, or the use of explosives in public places" were excluded from the amnesty. However, victims' rights groups claimed that the probation committees, which administered the amnesty processes, tended to exonerate "repentis" after a cursory examination. As a result, suspected assassins were reportedly cleared to return home without punishment. See Amnesty International, *Algeria: Truth and Justice Obscured by the Shadow of Impunity* (London: Amnesty International, 2000).

[89] Lutz and Sikkink, "International Human Rights Law and Practice in Latin America," 655–6.

rate of amnesty law enactment and during the last decade, fewer amnesty laws were enacted in this region than elsewhere in the world. In addition, unlike amnesty laws enacted in the Americas during the 1970s and 1980s, amnesties in this region are now less likely to include serious human rights violations than to exclude them.[90] This data supports the conclusion that a justice cascade has developed in this region. Lutz and Sikkink have suggested that this may be due to the region's "tradition of commitment to international law and human rights norms." They further argue that "[b]ecause of this preexisting, well-established normative framework, international enforcement pressures resonated domestically as external pressures reinforced domestic values."[91] The data also indicates that similar trends have taken place in Europe and Central Asia due to the ongoing conflicts and political repression in the Newly Independent States and the Caucasus region of Russia. However, these trends are not yet as pronounced as in the Americas. In contrast, the existence of a justice cascade is less pronounced in Asia and sub-Saharan Africa, as in these regions the rate of amnesty laws has remained high and many of the amnesty laws enacted grant immunity to perpetrators of crimes under international law.

## CONCLUSION

Support for a global accountability norm among human rights activists and scholars has caused amnesty laws for serious human rights violations to become increasingly controversial in recent decades. However, much of the support for this norm has focused on the surge in the number of prosecutions for perpetrators of mass atrocity, but has failed to take into account global and regional trends in amnesty law enactment. Indeed, as this chapter has argued, until recent years, there have been surprisingly few large-N comparative studies of amnesty laws. Where these trends are explored using the Amnesty Law Database, they indicate that over the past thirty years amnesty law enactment has continued at a steady rate. In addition, throughout this period, although the number of new amnesty laws excluding international crimes has increased, so too has the number of amnesties including such crimes.

This chapter has argued that these trends cast doubt on the existence of the global accountability norm, particularly where the enactment of amnesty laws receives

---

[90]   In addition, the only amnesties in the Americas that have addressed serious human rights violations in the past decade have been the laws adopted in Colombia to reintegrate members of the Autodefensas Unidas de Colombia (AUC), a right-wing paramilitary organization. These laws are conditional on the offenders disarming and disclosing the truth about their criminal actions. However, the laws distinguish between offenses, with perpetrators of serious human rights violations receiving alternative punishments rather than amnesty. See Inter-American Commission on Human Rights, *Report on the Implementation of the Justice and Peace Law: Initial Stages in the Demobilization of the AUC and First Judicial Proceedings* (Washington, DC: Inter-American Commission on Human Rights, 2007).

[91]   Lutz and Sikkink, "International Human Rights Law and Practice in Latin America," 659.

diplomatic and financial support from international organizations and donor states. Although such support has yet to be systematically documented, it seems that it is particularly forthcoming where the amnesty is enacted in the midst of ongoing conflict to encourage combatants to surrender and disarm. This suggests that despite the development of international criminal law and transitional justice, a belief persists within states and the international community that in times of extreme violence, amnesty may be a necessary compromise to achieve peace.

# 4

## From Amnesty to Accountability

### The Ebb and Flow in the Search for Justice in Argentina

*Par Engstrom and Gabriel Pereira*

This chapter accounts for the political and judicial processes of accountability that led to the overturning of Argentina's amnesties and the reopening of trials for human rights violations committed by the military regime that ruled the country from 1976 to 1983.[1] It locates these processes in the broader context of transitional justice in Argentina and examines the role of the main actors involved. The chapter also identifies the key factors that explain the Argentine pathway to accountability and evaluates the extent of Argentina's uniqueness as the first country in Latin America to overturn domestic legislation shielding perpetrators of grave human rights crimes from prosecution. Looking beyond the region of Latin America, the Argentine transitional justice experience is important since the country has had to struggle with the moral and political dilemmas of justice and order in the context of rapid and uncertain political change, well before the establishment of transitional justice as a distinct academic discipline and field of policy expertise. Moreover, Argentina's processes have been viewed in the transitional justice literature as an example to be either emulated or avoided. As such, it is important to draw the appropriate conclusions on the basis of a sound understanding of the Argentine experience before evaluating the likelihood and appropriateness of other societies following a similar pathway to accountability.

The Argentine case shows that transitional justice is not a linear process. Political circumstances change as power balances shift and, consequently, the incentives facing relevant political actors change as well. Particularly, in relation to the search for justice, Argentina has gone through an "ebb and flow" process in which the initial opening to judicial accountability of human rights violations was gradually restricted

---

[1] In this chapter we understand the term *amnesty* in a broad sense as defined in the introduction by Francesca Lessa and Leigh A. Payne.

The authors are grateful to the editors, Francesca Lessa and Leigh A. Payne; Fernanda Doz Costa; and Leonardo Filippini for their constructive comments on earlier drafts.

and eventually foreclosed. However, unrestricted prosecution has been reopened almost twenty years after the beginning of the transition to democracy. These developments have occurred due to shifts in the balance of power and motivations of ruling governments, the military, and human rights organizations (HROs), together with broader shifts in the normative environment in which these actors operate, as Kathryn Sikkink points out in her chapter in this volume.

The chapter is divided into three parts. The first part recounts the initial efforts at and restrictions on prosecution under the Alfonsín administration. The second part examines the ways in which the subsequent Menem governments attempted to shift transitional justice politics away from prosecutions toward reconciliation and reparations and the response to that shift from HROs, primarily through increased judicial actions at home and abroad. The final part examines the process of overturning Argentina's amnesty laws by explaining the political context in which this process occurred and by accounting for the judicial process that led up to these historic events.

## FROM OVERTURNING THE MILITARY SELF-AMNESTY TO IMPUNITY (1983–1989)

Between 1983 and 1989, Argentina went through the first stage of a still ongoing transitional justice process characterized by variation in the extent of the prosecution of human rights crimes. The beginning and the end of this period are clearly marked. Initially, the government overturned the military self-amnesty law in December 1983, paving the way for prosecutions; the same government then enacted two amnesties in 1986 and 1987 that restricted the scope for justice. In essence, the balance of power between the civilian government and the military in the 1980s determined this outcome. The progress of the prosecution process was marked by the potential and then the actual military threat and the disagreement between the government and HROs regarding the extent of criminal prosecution. As a result, the government implemented a policy significantly restricting the scope of prosecution. However, this policy was even further constrained when the military threat to destabilize the democratic order was perceived as real by the government. Under these circumstances, the attempts of HROs to influence the government and to challenge the amnesties proved unsuccessful.[2]

---

[2]   The literature on the initial period of transitional justice in Argentina is very extensive. See in particular: Carlos S. Nino, *Radical Evil on Trial* (New Haven: Yale University Press, 1996); Jaime Malamud-Goti, *Game Without End: State Terror and the Politics of Justice* (Norman: University of Oklahoma Press, 1996); and Horacio Verbitsky, *Civiles y militares: Memoria secreta de la transición* (Buenos Aires: Sudamericana, 2003).

## Transition to Democracy and Annulment of the Military Self-amnesty

In 1983 the military regime responsible for massive human rights violations collapsed.[3] The victory of the United Kingdom in the Malvinas/Falklands war in 1982 severely undermined the military's position. However, even before the war, the military government and its civilian allies were criticized and weakened by strikes prompted by the mishandling of the economy and denunciations of acts of corruption. By 1982, Argentina experienced negative economic growth and inflation had reached 165 percent.[4] Economic and military incompetence[5] are clearly important factors in explaining the military's downfall, but the shift away from the general acquiescence among many sectors of the Argentine population over the alleged necessity for repressive policies to deal with subversion is also important in explaining the gradual erosion of the military's standing and support.

A month before the elections of October 30, 1983, a weak military government attempted to protect itself from prosecution by enacting a blanket self-amnesty law. The amnesty benefited any individual who had committed criminal acts with either subversive or antisubversive motives between 1973 and 1982.[6] The broad wording of the self-amnesty law sought to protect those involved in common political and criminal offenses including kidnappings, disappearances, murder, and rape and prohibited civil proceedings against amnesty beneficiaries.

However, HROs, the Alfonsín government, and the Argentine Supreme Court converged in the common goal of opening prosecutions for the human rights crimes perpetrated by the military. HROs reacted immediately against the self-amnesty and initiated a practice which has been salient throughout the transitional justice process in Argentina: the judicial challenge of amnesty laws and pardons. On September 26, 1983, the Center for Legal and Social Studies (CELS), a human rights NGO, issued a statement to the relatives of the disappeared, offering to help them fight the constitutionality of the self-amnesty.[7] Moreover, on September 27, 1983, the Buenos Aires Lawyers' Association filed a suit in a federal court, claiming that an unconstitutional government had no authority to declare an amnesty. The court declared that the self-amnesty was "a flagrant violation

---

3   For an account of the military regime's human rights record, see Alison Brysk, *The Politics of Human Rights in Argentina: Protest, Change, and Democratization* (Stanford: Stanford University Press, 1994).

4   *Inter-American Development Bank, Economics and Social Progress in Latin America: 1981 Report* (Washington, DC: John Hopkins University Press, 1981), 29.

5   Paul W. Zagorski, "Civil-Military Relations and Argentine Democracy: The Armed Forces under the Menem Government," *Armed Forces & Society* 20 (1994): 424.

6   Although the military ruled between 1976 and 1983, the amnesty also covered criminal actions committed during the government that ruled between 1973 and 1976.

7   Edward Schumacher, "Argentines Fight Amnesty for Army," *New York Times*, September 26, 1983.

of the law" and declared it "null and void."[8] Eventually, the Argentine Supreme Court declared the self-amnesty law unconstitutional, convicting some of the junta members in 1986.[9]

Elected in October 1983, Alfonsín was committed to the prosecution of those responsible for human rights violations during the military regime.[10] He successfully spearheaded the effort to annul the military's self-amnesty. As Alejandro Garro and Enrique Dahl point out, the self-amnesty was "a major legal obstacle to the prosecutions."[11] Under Argentine law, penal laws cannot be abrogated retroactively and if a law is modified after a criminal act, the judge should apply the law most beneficial to the defendant.[12] In December 1983, the National Congress passed a bill proposed by the executive presenting three arguments: statutes enacted by a de facto government possess only limited validity due to the illegitimate nature of the government that issued those norms; the self-amnesty violates article 29 of the constitution, which prohibits the concentration of all governmental power in one branch of the government; and the law violates article 16 of the constitution, which guarantees equal protection under the law.[13] In December 1983, the Argentine Congress adopted its first law in eight years, declaring the self-amnesty unconstitutional and "unequivocally null and void."[14] It should be noted that this bill went beyond the effects of a mere derogation, since it was necessary for the self-amnesty to be nullified *ex nihilo* to refute its binding force from inception.[15] The self-amnesty was treated as a "de facto imposed norm" that "did not carry the presumption of validity enjoyed by norms of democratic origin."[16] The norm would only be valid "if its content were just."[17] Bypassing the requirement that defendants benefit from the self-amnesty law as the most lenient law, the congress removed the obstacle to the prosecution of crimes committed during the military regime.[18]

---

[8]  Alejandro M. Garro and Enrique Dahl, "Legal Accountability for Human Rights Violations in Argentina: One Step Forward and Two Steps Backward," *Human Rights Law Journal* 8 (1987): 305.

[9]  Garro and Dahl, "Legal Accountability," 305–6.

[10]  During the electoral campaign, Alfonsín had promised to prosecute the human rights violations committed by the military during its seven-year regime. Unlike his rival, Peronist Ítalo Luder, Alfonsín had publicly challenged the validity of the military's self-amnesty.

[11]  Garro and Dahl, "Legal Accountability," 305–6.

[12]  Ibid.

[13]  Ibid.

[14]  Pablo F. Parenti, "The Prosecution of International Crimes in Argentina," *International Criminal Law Review* 10 (2010): 493.

[15]  Garro and Dahl, "Legal Accountability," 305–6.

[16]  Carlos S. Nino, "The Duty to Punish Past Abuses of Human Rights Put Into Context: The Case of Argentina," *Yale Law Journal* 100 (1991): 2624.

[17]  Nino, "Duty to Punish."

[18]  Nino, *Radical Evil*.

## The Military on Trial

The overturning of the self-amnesty law was part of a broader top-down human rights policy proposed by the Alfonsín government. For Alfonsín, the goal of this policy was to prevent any repetition of the "atrocious episodes" of the previous decade without endangering the stability of the democratic transition.[19] This policy included the prosecution of members of the armed forces guilty of serious human rights violations, the prosecution of members of guerrilla groups who committed criminal actions, the establishment of a truth commission, and the incorporation of international human rights treaties into the Argentine legal system. This policy was complemented with a series of official proposals aimed at institutional reform of the military and intended to secure the military's loyalty to the civilian government and reduce its political influence.[20] Thus, Alfonsín sought to distinguish between the armed forces as an institution in need of reform and the individual military officers who had committed serious crimes that required punishment.

In terms of the prosecution of members of the armed forces, the executive attempted to implement a cautious policy that limited the time period of the trials and the categories of persons considered responsible for criminal behavior.[21] The latter aspect of the original policy was eventually modified by the National Congress. In December 1983, the government sent a bill to the congress devising the legal structure of the prosecution. First, the bill determined that the Supreme Council of the Armed Forces (SCAAFF) would be in charge of the criminal prosecutions and that the civilian Supreme Court would review these judgments. The government expected the military to conduct a self-purging process and that the military's summary procedure would limit the duration of the trials.[22] Second, the bill restricted the number of prosecutions by adopting a presumption that unless the agent held decision-making authority, all those invoking the defense of due obedience either mistakenly believed that the orders were legitimate due to intense propaganda or, alternatively, were subject to an overall climate of threat of severe punishment

---

[19] Raúl Alfonsín, "Never Again in Argentina," *Journal of Democracy* 4 (1993): 17. From 1930 to 1983, no democratically elected president served out his term in office with the exception of Juan Perón in his first presidency (1946–55). Thus, government policies were significantly constrained by the omnipresent threat of the military. Emilio F. Mignone, Cynthia L. Estlund, and Samuel Issacharoff, "Dictatorship on Trial: Prosecution of Human Rights Violations in Argentina," *Yale Journal of International Law* 10 (1984): 125–6.

[20] Felipe Agüero, "Legacies of Transitions: Institutionalization, the Military, and Democracy in South America," *Mershon International Studies Review* 42 (1998): 393–4; and Zagorski, "Civil-Military Relations," 424.

[21] Alfonsín, "Never Again," 16.

[22] Nino, *Radical Evil*.

forcing them to commit crimes. This was a rebuttable presumption since it could be contradicted by evidence to the contrary.[23]

The congress passed Law No. 23,049 in February 1984. The law partially revised the official proposal by extending the review power of civil courts and by broadening the category of individuals subject to prosecutions. It accepted military jurisdiction but granted civilian courts the power to oversee and take control of prosecutions carried out by military courts. Additionally, the congress established that the due obedience presumption did not apply to the prosecution of atrocious or aberrant crimes. These revisions combined to significantly expand the scope of the limited prosecution policy initially proposed by Alfonsín.[24]

The initial accountability policies adopted in the early stages of Argentina's democratic transition were broadly controlled by the country's political elites. HROs strongly opposed the official prosecution policies, but they were unsuccessful in their attempts to challenge them in courts. They regarded them as too conciliatory toward the armed forces. But HROs also raised practical and constitutional concerns.[25] In particular, HROs claimed that the right to participate in the judicial process by victims and relatives' legal representatives was too narrow under military jurisdiction. They also pointed out that the military jurisdiction violated constitutional principles such as legal equality and due process, given that they constituted a special forum in which military officers would be treated. In relation to the due obedience presumption, they considered that all those responsible for human rights crimes should be punished according to their participation and pointed out that the Argentine penal code already included a form of due obedience presumption for unwilling participants in crimes.[26] HROs could not influence the parliamentary debate, however.[27] Later, they challenged Law No. 23,049 in courts to no avail.[28] Hence, despite their active mobilization, the influence of HROs proved fairly limited during this first phase.

The Argentine Supreme Court lent its support to the Alfonsín government's prosecution policy and demonstrated a generally cooperative attitude toward the executive branch, a role that would become a distinctive feature of the transitional

---

[23] Ibid.

[24] Carlos H. Acuña and Catalina Smulovitz, "Guarding the Guardians in Argentina: Some Lessons about the Risks and Benefits of Empowering the Courts," in *Transitional Justice and the Rule of Law in New Democracies*, ed. James McAdams (Notre Dame: University of Notre Dame Press, 1997), 97.

[25] Mignone, Estlund, and Issacharoff, "Dictatorship on Trial," 125–6.

[26] Juan E. Méndez, "Truth and Partial Justice in Argentina: An Update," Human Rights Watch, April 1991.

[27] Méndez, "Truth and Partial Justice."

[28] The human rights organizations pursued a legal strategy against the military jurisdiction. By mid-1984 more than 2,000 complaints were brought to court. More than 400 were filed by Centro de Estudios Legales y Sociales (CELS). See: Garro, and Dahl, "Legal Accountability," 306.

justice process not only during this stage but also later. Alfonsín's policy needed the Court to settle the constitutional controversies raised by human rights groups and the military.[29] It also needed a quick decision, which the Court duly provided. In the *Aramayo* and *Dufourq* cases, it affirmed that de facto laws were invalid if they were not ratified or if they were rejected by constitutional governments.[30] Although not related to the self-amnesty law, the rulings represented a clear signal to the executive that the military's self-amnesty would not pass the Court's constitutionality test. Also, against the legal challenges posed by relatives of the disappeared and the military, the Court validated the military and civilian jurisdictions.[31] In these cases the Court had to reverse its own jurisprudence in order to support the government's initiatives.[32] Additionally, the rulings were issued rapidly by Argentine standards.[33]

### Military Unrest and Government Reversal: The Full Stop and Due Obedience Laws

The military refused to cooperate with the government's prosecution policy. Despite its relative weakness in the early period of the transition, the military's ability to influence the government increased over time, in part due to its own actions and in part due to the government's gradual loss of popular support following bad economic performances. The SCAAFF delayed its decisions and no individuals were condemned for criminal acts. This meant that the self-purging process envisioned by the government never occurred.[34] The military's resistance to the government's human rights policy gradually turned into threats against the democratic regime toward the end of 1985. Violent attacks and acts of disobedience occurred as responses to the civilian court rulings that convicted some of the leaders of the military juntas and to the extended prosecution of a number of low-ranking officers.[35] After the historic conviction of five of the junta leaders by the federal appeals court, a coup plot against Alfonsín was discovered, witnesses were threatened and harassed, a bomb was found at the home of the president of the appeals court, and several bombs exploded in different areas of the city of Buenos Aires. Eventually, active armed forces officers

---

[29] Although the judges on the Supreme Court were appointed by Alfonsín it was generally regarded as an independent court. See Rebecca Bill Chavez, "The Evolution of Judicial Autonomy in Argentina: Establishing the Rule of Law in an Ultrapresidential System," *Journal of Latin American Studies* 36 (2004).

[30] Nino, *Radical Evil.*

[31] Mignone, Estlund, and Issacharoff, "Dictatorship on Trial," 127–30.

[32] For a detailed analysis of these rulings see Garro and Dahl, "Legal Accountability."

[33] Álvaro Herrero, "Court-Executive Relations in Unstable Democracies: Strategic Judicial Behaviour in Post-Authoritarian Argentina (1983–2005)" (DPhil dissertation, University of Oxford, 2008).

[34] Nino, *Radical Evil.*

[35] Ibid.

refused to obey judicial summons issued by civilian courts. These violent reactions were understood by the government as an indication of the scale of the unrest within the military and the likelihood of a successful military uprising against the democratic order.[36]

The Alfonsín government's response to the military unrest was to limit its prosecution policy by setting temporal boundaries. The most relevant measure in this respect was the Full Stop Law approved in December 1986. It was intended to expedite existing legal proceedings in order to limit the number of prosecutions of military personnel.[37] In fact, the law provided that only members of guerrilla groups and the armed forces, regardless of rank, who had been indicted within sixty days of the law's enactment could face prosecution. In cases not brought within the sixty-day limit, the suspects would no longer be liable for prosecution unless they were fugitives or in contempt of court. The law also permitted the civilian courts to assume control of cases pending before the SCAAF before the sixty-day limit expired, a safeguard in case the military courts delayed acting. The law did not apply to criminal prosecutions for the crimes of change of civil status and kidnapping and hiding of minors.

The implementation of the law did not provoke the effect intended because it backfired on the government. In spite of the relatively short time period for cases to be brought and the speed with which the legislation was passed, civilian courts exceeded expectations by working overtime to process the nearly 1,000 applications of murder, torture, and lesser abuse cases filed against military and police officials by lawyers working with victims and HROs. As a result, by March 1987, fifty-one military and police officers had been arrested on suspicion of human rights violations, of which twelve had been sentenced, along with the five convictions of the military junta confirmed by the Argentine Supreme Court. This meant that before Easter 1987 a large number of cases were still pending, with estimates ranging from 200 cases to 450 cases, one-third of which related to active duty officers.[38] In this context, the Full Stop Law did not achieve its goal of limiting the prosecutions of military officers. Rather, the tensions between the military and the government increased.

The subsequent reaction of the military marked its political resurgence after the period of institutional weakness in the early stage of the transition to democracy. An uprising led by middle- and low-ranking officers occurred on April 15, 1987.[39] The core group of rebels, based in the Campo de Mayo Infantry Base in Buenos

---

[36]  Ibid.

[37]  In that sense, the Punto Final Law is not a conventional amnesty as it does not forbid legal sanctions for specific categories of offenders. However, according to the definition of amnesties adopted in this volume, in this chapter we consider it an amnesty.

[38]  Nino, *Radical Evil*.

[39]  The rebellion started in the province of Córdoba and quickly spread to other provinces.

Aires, demanded the end of criminal prosecutions, which were seen as a systematic persecution of armed forces officers.[40] Although they argued that they did not wish to overthrow the constitutional government, the uprising was perceived as a coup attempt by the government and society at large. On April 21, Alfonsín visited the rebels and they surrendered. The president claimed that no negotiations took place.[41]

However, soon after, Alfonsín sent a bill to the congress establishing a due obedience clause to limit the scope of prosecutions. Although the president claimed that the law was an attempt to achieve reconciliation, it was generally perceived as part of a secret pact with the military aimed at preventing more destabilizing military actions.[42] The Due Obedience Law was passed on June 5, 1987. It foreclosed prosecutions of perpetrators who were lower-ranking officers and soldiers at the time they committed their crimes. The law established the presumption that they acted under duress, in subordination to a superior authority and following orders, without having the possibility of resisting or refusing to follow those orders or examining their lawfulness. This presumption was "irrebutable," and courts were not allowed to collect evidence to determine if the officer knew or should have known he was acting on illegal orders.[43] Additionally, this would apply to high-ranking officers unless the courts ruled within thirty days that they had acted on their own motivation or were involved in formulating the orders. The law did not apply to "crimes of rape, kidnapping, and hiding of minors, change of civil status, and appropriation of property through extortion." Both the irrebutable character of the presumption and the failure to exclude "atrocious and aberrant" crimes differentiated this law from that approved by the congress at the onset of the prosecutions in 1984.

The capacity of HROs to influence the government and the congress during this period was limited. They issued statements condemning the legislation passed limiting prosecutions and emphasized its negative impact on the reconstruction of the rule of law in the country. They staged widespread public demonstrations during the parliamentary debate of both bills.[44] However, they failed to prevent their enactment. HROs, thus, resorted eventually to judicial challenges.

As with the previous amnesty initiatives, the Argentine Supreme Court at the time supported the constitutionality of the Due Obedience Law. Only a month after its enactment, the Court issued a ruling in the *Camps* case, which had been in the docket for less than thirty days. The tribunal applied the due obedience notion to exculpate Camps, thus confirming the constitutionality of the Due Obedience

---

[40]  Nino, *Radical Evil.*
[41]  Ibid.
[42]  Verbitsky, *Civiles y militares.*
[43]  Ibid.
[44]  Méndez, "Truth and Partial Justice," 46–8.

Law.[45] Justice Petracchi's opinion in this case is particularly insightful. He began by explaining why due obedience laws are unconstitutional. Petracchi then appeared to reverse his opinion by describing the political circumstances that led to the approval of the Due Obedience Law. The justice argued that the interpretation of a law should incorporate a consideration of the context in which the law was passed and the impact that the invalidation of that law might provoke. In the midst of a tense political situation, Petracchi added that the Court did not have the appropriate authority to evaluate the laws as adopted by the legislature because it deemed that basic individual rights had not been breached, nor were the laws unreasonably out of proportion to the aims sought.[46] This decision is particularly significant given the Court's reversal of opinion in *Simón* almost two decades later.[47]

## Accountability Impasse

The failure of the government to impose its prosecution policies severely hampered its attempt at institutional reform of the military. Although some progress was achieved in terms of establishing a degree of civilian control and professionalization, the armed forces retained enough power to frustrate most of the government's reform efforts. The government on its part was unwilling to finance reforms until the armed forces showed loyalty to the democratic government.[48]

The enactment of the amnesty laws occurred in a period in which popular dissatisfaction with the government increased.[49] Apart from the military's destabilizing actions, the official economic program had deteriorated and a hyperinflationary spiral was in its very early stages. Social discontent against the socioeconomic performance of the government was manifest in the streets and the government lost the midterm election in 1987. Also, two additional military rebellions in 1988 and a failed attempt by an extreme left group to seize the La Tablada military regiment barracks in January 1989 occurred. All these factors led to the resignation of Alfonsín six months before the scheduled date for the transfer of power to the president-elect, Carlos Menem.

---

[45] The Court declared the constitutionality of the Due Obedience Law and turned over the sentences condemning General Ramón Camps and his former aides by a lower court. During the military regime, Camps was chief of the Police of Buenos Aires, a police force particularly known for its brutality throughout the military regime.

[46] Supreme Court of Argentina, Judgment in *Camps*, June 22, 1987. See also Eduardo Oteiza, *La Corte Suprema: Entre la justicia sin política y la política sin justicia* (La Plata: Librería Editora Platense, 1994), 150–1.

[47] See our discussion of the *Simón* case.

[48] Agüero, "Legacies of Transitions," 393–4; and Zagorski, "Civil-Military Relations," 424–6.

[49] Nino, *Radical Evil*, 99.

Hence, the first transitional justice stage in Argentina was marked by the balance of power between the different actors involved in this process and, particularly, by the capacity of the military to threaten the stability of the democratic order. In this context, the HROs' capacity to influence government policy was extremely limited. Despite their active mobilization, HROs needed a more sophisticated strategy to challenge impunity.

## CHALLENGING IMPUNITY: HUMAN RIGHTS MOBILIZATION AT HOME AND ABROAD (1989–2003)

In 1989, President Menem assumed power. Menem was not responsive to the HROs' agenda and he implemented a human rights policy that discursively emphasized "reconciliation"[50] and reparations over prosecutions, a preference maintained by the subsequent presidents, de La Rúa and Duhalde, until 2003. This period began with ending prosecutions against the military and granting impunity to those already punished. It finished with discrete but important developments toward the prosecution of human rights crimes nationally and internationally. Two relevant processes also occurred. First, the power of the military was substantively weakened and its capacity to influence politics was significantly constrained. Second, and more important, HROs increased their relative influence by developing a creative set of strategies to challenge impunity.

### *Impunity and the Political Weakening of the Military*

Because Alfonsín resigned six months before the end of his term, Menem took office in July 1989. Menem effectively implemented a policy to end the limited prosecution policy and grant impunity to those already condemned in court. Combined with the amnesty laws passed by Alfonsín, the new policy had the effect of a blanket amnesty for those responsible for human rights violations. Therefore, Menem achieved for the military the protection it had not been able to secure on its own.

Menem approached the issues pragmatically. The economic and social situation of the country was delicate and he needed stability to implement dramatic state reforms and socioeconomic policies. In this context, he developed a policy to contain the potential of the military to destabilize the government. In fact, in 1990 Menem faced another military rebellion, this time a bloody coup attempt by a group of noncommissioned and junior officers. He managed to defeat the mutiny through negotiations with the military leadership.[51]

---

[50] Menem was primarily concerned with the improvement of civil-military relations and as such reconciliation effectively meant the suppression of HROs' demands for prosecution of the military.

[51] Zagorski, "Civil-Military Relations," 425–6.

As a consequence, Menem's policy toward the armed forces included the removal of what the military perceived as a menace (i.e., prosecution) as well as reduction in government funding of the military, thereby limiting the potential of its political influence.[52] Ending the possibility of prosecution and granting full impunity were implemented through two types of presidential decrees. The first type benefited all military officials under investigation in civilian courts that had not already been exempted from prosecution by the Due Obedience and Full Stop Laws.[53] These were not pardons in a strict sense since under the Argentine constitution presidents have the power to pardon only convicted individuals. The second type of decree included *stricto sensu* pardons since they benefited all individuals already found responsible for human rights violations.[54] This included the former members of the military juntas and other armed forces officers, as well as members of the guerrilla groups.

The Supreme Court adopted a deferential role toward the official policy.[55] In the *Riveros* case, the Supreme Court upheld Menem's presidential pardons on a technicality.[56] The tribunal argued that the applicable procedural law did not give the claimants (i.e., victims of abuses by the pardoned military officers) the right to challenge the pardons. In other words, the tribunal did not even consider whether or not the pardons were constitutional. This ruling represented the constitutional validation of the closure of prosecutions and the granting of impunity for human rights violations.

By granting full immunity to the military, Menem gained a significant degree of freedom of action in order to reinitiate military reforms. By the end of Menem's second administration in 1999, the civilian control of the armed forces was fully achieved and a professionalization program was implemented.[57] These reforms led to the reduction of the armed forces' political influence.

### *Human Rights Mobilization: Circumventing Impunity and Challenging Amnesty*

The Menem government's policies on transitional justice were limited and emphasized reconciliation and reparations over prosecutions. However, since the

---

[52]  During the presidential campaign there had been rumors of a pact between Menem and factions of the military, suggesting he would get their support in exchange for pardons. Zagorski, "Civil-Military Relations," 425–7.

[53]  Parenti, "Prosecution of International Crimes."

[54]  Ibid.

[55]  Menem increased the number of Supreme Court judges and appointed a majority of judges who were loyal to him. See Jonathan Miller, "Evaluating the Argentine Supreme Court under Presidents Alfonsín and Menem (1983–1999)," *Southwestern Journal of Law and Trade in the Americas* 7 (2000).

[56]  Herrero, "Court-Executive Relations," 230.

[57]  Agüero, "Legacies of Transitions," 394.

government proved unwilling to meet and support their demands, human rights activists increasingly challenged government policies through the development of creative legal and judicial strategies at home and abroad. HROs pursued a number of different strategies that sought to circumvent the effects of Alfonsín's impunity laws and Menem's pardons or sought to directly challenge the validity of these measures, or some combination of the two. In what follows we highlight six distinct, yet partially overlapping, strategies.

First, on the domestic front, attempts were made to circumvent the impunity effects rendered by the amnesties and pardons by litigating cases that fell outside the scope of the impunity laws. In particular, cases of babies, born to mothers in clandestine detention, who had been stolen and then given to couples under false identities were brought to court. These kidnappings were not covered by the impunity laws.[58] The exemption meant that the courts could attempt to locate the missing children and prosecute military officers responsible for the abductions. Initially, military officials, including former junta members Videla and Massera, were charged individually for the stealing of children.[59] Not until 1999, when the courts started investigating the crime as a systematic plan put in place by the military regime, did a number of former high-ranking military officials face prosecution for their participation in this crime.[60] In doing so, Argentine courts also displayed an increasing willingness to draw on international human rights law in their judicial reasoning.[61]

It is important to note that the use of domestic courts by HROs was facilitated by the constitutional incorporation of international human rights treaties in 1994 that turned Argentine courts into key arenas for human rights politics. The 1994 constitutional reforms dramatically altered Argentina's constitutional order with regard to the substantive treatment of human rights, as well as the legal status of international human rights treaties. In particular, the constitutional reform incorporated international treaties on human rights into the Argentine constitution and gave some human rights treaties constitutional status and others legal superiority over national laws. The fact that international treaties were given legal superiority

---

[58] The Due Obedience Law explicitly excluded crimes of rape, kidnapping, hiding of children, change of civil status, and appropriation of property through extortion. Therefore, the trials advanced by HROs were allowed by the law. Thus, these legal actions are not the result of any loopholes in the law.

[59] Former officers could be prosecuted for crimes committed as a result of abducting children and altering their identities in order to give them away for adoption, yet were protected from prosecution for the murder of their parents or the killing of other children.

[60] Abuelas de Plaza de Mayo, *Niños desaparecidos, jóvenes localizados en Argentina desde 1976 a 1999* (Buenos Aires: Temas, 1999).

[61] For example, in *Videla* the Buenos Aires federal criminal court argued that the violations under the military regime constituted crimes against humanity and were therefore different from crimes covered by the Argentine criminal code. See María José Guembe, "Reopening of Trials for Crimes Committed by the Argentine Military Dictatorship," *Sur: International Journal on Human Rights* 3 (2005): 119–20.

over national laws provided legal activists with a stronger basis for circumventing the impunity laws.

Second, another judicial strategy adopted by HROs as part of attempts to challenge impunity consisted of pursuing so-called truth trials before domestic courts. The truth trials demonstrate the interaction between domestic judicial developments and international strategies pursued by Argentine HROs, particularly before the Inter-American Commission on Human Rights (IACHR). During the Menem period, a number of military officers came forward with confessions of responsibility for violations committed during the military regime.[62] As confessions continued, intense public pressure was generated for the reopening of human rights trials. A number of HROs called for truth trials in courts, arguing that victims had the right to know what happened to their relatives. Consequently, under considerable pressure from an increasing number of judicial cases submitted by HROs, particularly CELS, the courts – having the power to subpoena people suspected of crimes to appear and testify, yet without being able to charge or convict them – established the principle that even though laws may be passed to prevent the prosecutions of those responsible for crimes, judicial investigations could continue. Judicial action was therefore limited to investigation and documentation, and there was no possibility of prosecution or punishment. The truth trials operated under an uncertain mandate until 1999 when a friendly settlement agreement between the Argentine state and the petitioners who had initially brought the *Lapacó* case to the IACHR was signed.[63] In the settlement that followed from the *Lapacó* case, the Argentine state recognized victims' right to truth and committed itself to establishing appropriate procedures for the effective enforcement of this right. The Supreme Court recognized this right in 1998 but maintained that the way to establish the truth was not through criminal proceedings, but through *habeas data* petitions to Argentine courts.[64]

Third, HROs pursued opportunities in foreign courts to circumvent domestic impunity. Prosecutions conducted by foreign courts for abuses committed by state agents in Argentina increased during the 1990s. Countries such as Spain, Italy, Sweden,

---

[62] The character of confessions by perpetrators of atrocities ranged from the remorseful declaration of guilt in the case of Adolfo Scilingo to the "heroic confession" by Alfredo Astiz. See Horacio Verbitsky, *Confessions of an Argentine Dirty Warrior* (New York: The New Press, 2005); and Leigh A. Payne, *Unsettling Accounts: Neither Truth nor Reconciliation in Confessions of State Violence* (Durham: Duke University Press, 2008).

[63] Inter-American Court of Human Rights, Report 70/99 in *Carmen Aguiar de Lapacó* (Argentina), May 4, 1999. On the "right to truth" in Argentine courts: Alicia Oliveira and María José Guembe, "La verdad, derecho de la sociedad," in *La aplicación del derecho internacional de los derechos humanos por los tribunales locales*, ed. Martín Abregú and Christian Courtis (Buenos Aires: Editores del Puerto, 2004).

[64] Supreme Court of Argentina, Judgment in *Urteaga*, October 15, 1998.

France, and Germany demanded the extradition of various military personnel to be tried for the disappearances of their citizens, and trials *in absentia* were held in Italy and France.[65] Argentina's Supreme Court denied the legitimacy of these *in absentia* trials, stating that they violated due process guarantees in the Argentine constitution, particularly the right to a defense. The Menem government's response to these cases was somewhat mixed. While it initially appeared to offer some support to the litigants (financial support in the form of airfares, etc.), the government was less forthcoming with official support. In 1994, when Italian judges attempted to obtain evidence, Menem passed an executive decree against collaboration with foreign judges.[66] In 1996, as a result of the legal mobilization of Argentine exile communities in Europe, the Audiencia Nacional in Madrid requested the extradition of about 100 Argentine military and police officers. Menem, and subsequently the de la Rúa government, refused all extradition requests but external judicial pressures were building up with a range of convictions *in absentia* of such notorious figures of the military regime as Alfredo Astiz in Paris and Guillermo Suárez Mason in Rome. However, beyond a few isolated cases, Argentine judges were at this stage generally reluctant to directly challenge the impunity laws.

Fourth, HROs actively sought to leverage their domestic litigation efforts by challenging the validity of the impunity laws through the pursuit of international legal strategies, particularly through IACHR.[67] Almost immediately after the adoption of Alfonsín's impunity laws, several cases involving multiple petitioners were brought to the IACHR. In these cases it was alleged that the amnesty laws, and subsequently Menem's pardons, violated the rights of victims and their relatives to judicial protection, among other claims. In its report published in 1992 and throughout the subsequent process of monitoring compliance with the report's recommendations, the IACHR was strongly critical of Alfonsín's impunity laws and Menem's pardons and emphasized that they were incompatible with Argentina's international human rights obligations.[68] The response by the Menem government to the accumulation

---

[65]  CELS, *2001 Annual Report* (Buenos Aires, 2001), 46.

[66]  Ibid., 42–3.

[67]  The links between Argentine HROs and the IACHR date back to the fact-finding visit of the IACHR in 1979 that resulted in an authoritative and widely disseminated report on the military regime's human rights record. See further Par Engstrom, "Transnational Human Rights and Democratization: Argentina and the Inter-American Human Rights System (1976–2007)" (DPhil dissertation, University of Oxford, 2010). More generally on the Inter-American Human Rights System and democratization in Latin America, see Par Engstrom and Andrew Hurrell, "Why the Human Rights Regime in the Americas Matters," in *Human Rights Regimes in the Americas*, ed. Mónica Serrano and Vesselin Popovski (Tokyo: United Nations University Press, 2010).

[68]  The IACHR issued Report 28/92 in October 1992 with regards to ESMA (Escuela Mecánica de la Armada), in which it condemned Argentina for violation of human rights as a result of its blocking of judicial action following the impunity laws.

of cases before the IACHR was to pass a series of reparation laws.[69] Although the IACHR welcomed the reparation laws, it continued to press for fuller accountability measures including prosecution and punishment of perpetrators.

Fifth, in addition to their judicial strategies, HROs challenged the validity of the impunity laws by lobbying for their overturn through legislative measures. In 1998 a center-left coalition of parties, FREPASO, submitted a bill before the congress that sought to annul Alfonsín's impunity laws. An annulment would have effectively reopened the prosecution process since legislative annulments of laws have retroactive effects. This initiative failed due to the combined opposition of Menem's party and the Radical Party. Congress subsequently amended the original bill from annulment to derogation and passed the new law. But given that in the Argentine legal system derogation of laws has no retroactive effects, it could only be used in cases brought in the future. As a result, no cases could be reopened that had benefited from the earlier laws, and only new cases, never heard before, for human rights violations could be tried under this new law. Although potentially significant, at the time of the derogation it was generally regarded as merely symbolic due to the fact that most of the relevant legal cases had already been initiated and, thus, few new cases existed.

Finally, in March 2001, the Full Stop and Due Obedience Laws were directly challenged by Federal Judge Cavallo in the *Simón* case.[70] In his decision, Cavallo declared for the first time the unconstitutionality of these laws. He also ruled that the laws contradicted the provisions included in the international treaties to which Argentina was a party and that impose an obligation to investigate, prosecute, and punish serious violations of human rights. The immediate response of the military was to warn against the nullification of the impunity laws.[71] As a sign of military waning influence and the general preoccupation with the economic crisis of December 2001, these warnings had little effect.

Coincidentally, just a few days following Cavallo's ruling, the Inter-American Court of Human Rights (IACtHR) published its judgment in *Barrios Altos* declaring invalid, inter alia, the amnesty laws passed by the Fujimori government in Peru.[72] The sentence of the IACtHR was heavily referenced and quoted verbatim when Cavallo's decision was upheld in November 2001 by the Argentine Chamber

---

[69] For the development of reparation policies in Argentina, see María José Guembe, "Economic Reparations for Grave Human Rights Violations: The Argentinean Experience" in *The Handbook of Reparations*, ed. Pablo de Greiff (Oxford: Oxford University Press, 2006).

[70] Judge Cavallo was at the time in charge of the 4th Federal Court for Criminal and Correctional Matters of Buenos Aires. Julio Simón was a police officer during the military regime and indicted for his involvement in the detention of José Poblete Roa and Gertrudis Hlackzik de Poblete, as well as the appropriation of their child, Claudia, at a secret detention center (the "Olimpo").

[71] "Reacción militar ante posibles juicios," *La Nación*, March 3, 2001.

[72] Inter-American Court of Human Rights, Judgment in *Chumbipuma Aguirre and Others* (Peru), March 14, 2001.

of Appeals that declared the Full Stop and Due Obedience Laws null and void. According to the judges of the appeals court, given the Argentine state's international obligations it had a duty to prosecute and punish perpetrators of crimes against humanity. The appeals court judges also laid down a subtle challenge to the Supreme Court regarding the duty of the Argentine judiciary to ensure respect for the country's international obligations when it stated that:

> [T]here is no doubt that the Supreme Court is under a special obligation to impose respect for the fundamental human rights, since, within its sphere of competence, the Tribunal represents national sovereignty. [...] As such, it is the head of one of the branches of the Federal Government, competent, to settle issues that may involve international liability of the Argentine Republic, such as those that give rise to the intervention of [...] supranational organisms foreseen in the American Convention.[73]

These rulings quickly reverberated within the Argentine judicial system. For example, in July 2002, Federal Judge Claudio Bonadío ordered the arrests of ex-military President Galtieri and thirty-five retired military and police officers for the disappearance of Montoneros returning from exile in the early 1980s. Many of the accused had benefited from the impunity laws, which Bonadío had declared unconstitutional in a previous court case.[74]

The political impasse with regard to human rights under the Menem, de la Rúa, and Duhalde administrations, combined with the impunity laws and presidential pardons, effectively limited the possibilities of pursuing judicial action in domestic courts for violations committed during the military regime.[75] Yet, due to pressures from HROs – developing creative judicial strategies nationally and internationally – the question of accountability for human rights abuses was kept alive with some important developments such as reparations and truth trials during the 1990s, thereby reinforcing the trend toward an increasing judicialization of accountability politics for violations under the military regime.[76]

## OVERTURNING IMPUNITY LAWS AND REOPENING TRIALS
### (2003 TO THE PRESENT)

By the beginning of the 2000s, a significant momentum behind the HRO challenges of the impunity laws had built up in domestic courts and internationally. With the

---

[73] Judgment in *Simón, Julio*, November 9, 2001. As translated in Guembe, "Reopening of Trials," 124.
[74] "Ordenan la detención de 36 militares," *La Nación*, July 11, 2002.
[75] For an insider's account of the Menem government's human rights policies see Alicia Pierini, *1998–1999 – Diez años de derechos humanos* (Buenos Aires: Ministerio del Interior, 1999).
[76] Carlos Acuña and Catalina Smulovitz, "Guarding the Guardians"; Catalina Smulovitz, "The Discovery of Law: Political Consequences in the Argentine Experience," in *Global Prescriptions: The Production, Exportation, and Importation of a New Legal Orthodoxy*, ed. Yves Dezalay and Bryant Garth (Ann Arbor: University of Michigan Press, 2002).

dramatic weakening of the military as a political actor, the situation indeed seemed propitious for demands of accountability for abuses under the military regime. Yet, as in the earlier periods in the struggle for accountability, it was not until the executive gave its support to HRO demands and judicial proceedings that changes took place.

### Crisis and Reversal of Government Human Rights Policies

In 2001, the Argentine economy faced a meltdown that led to the resignation of President Fernando de la Rúa (Menem's immediate successor) and four subsequent presidents in a matter of two weeks.[77] By December 2001 much of the country was brought to an economic standstill as Argentina went into default on its foreign debt.[78] Widespread street protests and general unrest took place; popular demand to purge Argentina of the existing political elite rattled the country.[79] Néstor Kirchner came to power in May 2003 after a string of emergency interim presidents in the context of one of the most severe economic crises in modern Argentine history with more than half of the population falling below the poverty line. Yet, despite widespread and occasionally violent protests, the military remained in its barracks and Argentina's democratic institutions weathered the crisis.

Following the election of Kirchner, the expectations of advances on the human rights front were very low. Undeniably, this was partly due to the dire economic situation in the country. Moreover, as a former commercial lawyer and governor of the province of Santa Cruz, there was little in Kirchner's political background that would lead observers to expect human rights to be prioritized by the new government. Yet, shortly after his inauguration, Kirchner announced a number of measures that demonstrated his willingness to push the question of accountability for past human rights abuses.

In particular, Kirchner embraced the "Memory, Truth, and Justice" agenda of HROs, perceived as a source of legitimacy by the governing party. In May 2003, for example, Kirchner forced the military top leadership to retire.[80] In September 2003, in a speech to the UN General Assembly, Kirchner sought to connect his government with the human rights struggles of the past by claiming that all Argentineans are "the sons and daughters of the Mothers and Grandmothers of Plaza de Mayo."[81]

---

[77] Mariana Llanos and Ana Margheritis, "Why Do Presidents Fail? Political Leadership and the Argentine Crisis (1999–2001)," *Studies in Comparative International Development* 40 (2006).

[78] Manuel Pastor and Carol Wise, "From Poster Child to Basket Case," *Foreign Affairs* 80 (2001).

[79] Marcela Lopez Levy, *We Are Millions: Neo-Liberalism and New Forms of Political Action in Argentina* (London: Latin American Bureau, 2004).

[80] "Dura réplica de Kirchner a Brinzoni," *La Nación*, May 30, 2003.

[81] Speech by Néstor Kirchner to the fifty-eighth session of the UN General Assembly, September 25, 2003. On file with authors.

Kirchner reversed Argentina's policy on extradition, ordering cooperation with extradition requests for those not facing charges in Argentina. He also ratified the UN Convention on the Non-Applicability of Statutory Limitations to War Crimes and Crimes against Humanity, which prohibits statutes of limitations for crimes against humanity. He asked the congress to give the treaty provisions precedence over national law.[82] The Kirchner government also gave its support to memory projects promoted by some HROs, which has resulted in the construction of a number of memory sites to commemorate the disappeared.[83]

The unexpected advances on the human rights front need to be understood in the context of the precarious political circumstances in which Kirchner came to power.[84] With a weak political mandate entering the presidential office, Kirchner moved quickly and astutely to seize the opportunity to legitimize his rule through public support for accountability. Kirchner displayed a willingness to strategically push human rights in areas where there were few political obstacles, such as with the military, and sought to portray himself as a break with the Menemist past. Groups pursuing a human rights agenda found a willing interlocutor in the Kirchner government. The Kirchner administration gave these organizations legitimacy in terms of a public recognition of their role in recent Argentine history, and the administration broadly supported their agenda in relation to the annulment of the impunity laws, the reopening of human rights trials, and the establishment of numerous commemoration sites around the country.

In particular, Kirchner led the congress in August 2003 to vote in favor of nullifying the impunity laws.[85] This initiative was politically and legally significant because, although the congress had already repealed the Full Stop and Due Obedience Laws in 1998, this had had little legal effect; a proposal to annul the laws, potentially reopening prosecutions, had been defeated. The legal effect of the nullification allowed for the reopening of prosecutions since it meant that the amnesty laws had no validity when they were used to protect perpetrators from prosecution; they should be regarded as if they never existed. The annulment of the amnesty laws by

---

[82]  The Convention, passed by the UN in 1968 and approved by the Argentine Congress in 1995, states that there can be no statute of limitations for crimes against humanity, regardless of when they were committed. It also obliges ratifying states to bring their own laws into keeping with the provisions of the treaty and urges signatories to take steps toward extraditing those who commit such crimes according to international law.

[83]  In a symbolically resonant gesture Kirchner also changed the number of disappeared in the Nunca Más report from 9,000 to 30,000, and eliminated any references to the "theory of the two demons."

[84]  Kirchner won the presidential election with only about twenty-two percent of the votes after Menem withdrew his candidacy before the second round and after having gained about twenty-five percent of the votes in the first round. Menem was widely expected to lose the second round with a significant margin.

[85]  "Diputados aprobó la anulación de las leyes de perdón," *La Nación*, August 12, 2003.

legislative acts sparked a new legal debate regarding the power of the congress to annul laws. In general terms, it was argued that the congress had exceeded its own powers and the annulment was invalid. Therefore, the congressional nullifications required constitutional validation by the courts.

## Judicial Dismantling of Amnesty

By the beginning of the 2000s, the politics of accountability in Argentina had developed a significant momentum of its own, particularly in the courts. By the time Kirchner was elected the momentum built up by judicial proceedings, in Argentina and before foreign courts and international judicial instances including the IACHR, had begun to converge in a number of important ways.

Following the Cavallo ruling declaring the Full Stop and Due Obedience Laws unconstitutional, attention turned to the Supreme Court.[86] The Court gave a strong signal of intent regarding the development of its position on the constitutionality of the impunity laws in *Arancibia Clavel*.[87] In order to circumvent statutory limitations on the crimes committed by the military regime, in this case the Supreme Court relied on an expansive interpretation of international human rights law when arguing that the crimes were imprescriptible. Argentina had adopted the Convention on the Non-Applicability of Statutory Limitations to War Crimes and Crimes against Humanity in 1968 (the instrument entered into force in 1970) but had not ratified it until 2003 and after the human rights violations under consideration had been committed. The Supreme Court declared nevertheless that:

> the prohibition of the non-retroactivity of criminal law has not been infringed upon and a principle established by usage, already valid at the time the deeds were committed, is asserted. From this point of view, in the same way as it is possible to assert that international usage already deemed crimes against humanity as imprescriptible even before the convention, this usage was generalized in international law before the incorporation of the convention into domestic [i.e., Argentine] law.[88]

The Supreme Court's invocation of *jus cogens* principles enabled it to conclude that: "[...] the deeds for which Arancibia Clavel was convicted could not be declared

---

[86] The composition of the Supreme Court had, at this point, been partially changed after a reform initiated by the Kirchner government. The process of renewal of the court took place with unprecedented transparency and significant civil society input following a well-coordinated campaign by a coalition of NGOs, which resulted in a court widely recognized for its independence. See Alba M. Ruibal, "Self-Restraint in Search of Legitimacy: The Reform of the Argentine Supreme Court," *Latin American Politics and Society* 51 (2009).

[87] Enrique Arancibia Clavel was a Chilean secret agent involved in the assassination of Chilean General Carlos Prats in Buenos Aires in 1974.

[88] Supreme Court of Argentina, Resolution in *Arancibia Clavel*, August 24, 2004. As translated in Guembe, "Reopening of Trials," 120.

as invalid due to the passing of time according to international law on the day they were committed [...]." Hence, the rules of invalidity of criminal action as established in domestic laws are superseded by *jus cogens* and by the Convention on the Non-Applicability of Statutory Limitations to War Crimes and Crimes against Humanity.[89]

The Supreme Court thus played an important role in the dismantling of legal obstacles to prosecution. In June 2005, the Court declared the amnesty laws unconstitutional, in effect confirming Cavallo's original verdict in *Simón*.[90] In its decision upholding the declarations of unconstitutionality of the Full Stop and Due Obedience Laws of the lower courts, the Court also accepted the sentence of the IACtHR in *Barrios Altos*.[91] Moreover, in *Simón*, the Supreme Court reaffirmed the shifting balance of authority between the judiciary and the legislature with regard to human rights. While the Court had upheld the validity of the Full Stop and Due Obedience Laws in 1987, in 2005 the Court assumed authority in this matter and declared that the laws were against the constitution.[92]

Significantly, two of the Supreme Court judges in *Simón* had taken part in the Court's deliberations on the Due Obedience Law in 1987. One of the judges, Enrique Petracchi, justified his reversal on the grounds that, following the 1994 constitutional incorporation of a wide range of international human rights treaties, these laws had become unconstitutional. Carlos Fayt, however, maintained his original position reaffirming the constitutionality of the laws and reiterating the position that the laws were necessary at the time in order to uphold political stability.[93]

In addition to the overturn of the impunity laws, Menem's 1989 pardons of the members of the military juntas were declared unconstitutional by judges of the court of the first instance and subsequently ratified by courts of appeal. In July 2007 the Supreme Court upheld the decisions of the lower courts.

## Posttransitional Justice Trends

Overall, these shifts in the domestic legal framework and judicial thinking appear relatively secure. Moreover, similar decisions drawing on international human

---

[89] As translated in Guembe, "Reopening of Trials," 120–1.

[90] "El fallo de la Corte reavivó el debate por los indultos," *La Nación*, June 15, 2005. Mariano Fernández Valle, "La Corte Suprema Argentina frente al legado de la última dictadura militar: Reseña del fallo 'Simón,'" *Anuario de Derechos Humanos* (2006); Santiago Legarre, "Crimes against Humanity, Reasonableness and the Law: The Simon Case in the Supreme Court of Argentina," *Chinese Journal of International Law* 5 (2006).

[91] Luis Márquez Urtubey, "Non-Applicability of Statutes of Limitation for Crimes Committed in Argentina: *Barrios Altos*," *Southwestern Journal of Law and Trade in the Americas* 11 (2005).

[92] See, in particular, Supreme Court of Argentina, Judgment in *Simón, Julio Héctor and Others*, June 14, 2005, para. 16.

[93] Roberto Gargarella, "Human Rights, International Courts and Deliberative Democracy," in *Critical Perspectives in Transitional Justice*, ed. Oxford Transitional Justice Research (OTJR) (Antwerp: Intersentia, 2012).

rights law were taken in many cases in different parts of the country.[94] These judicial decisions declaring the Full Stop and Due Obedience Laws and pardons unconstitutional have given rise to the reopening of the trials concerning violations of human rights during the military regime in different courts around Argentina.[95]

Hence, actions by human rights activists through courts – both domestically and internationally – reinforced by the support of the Kirchner government drove the judicial and political process that led to the overturning of the impunity laws and pardons. The Supreme Court rulings opened the judicial floodgates, which has led to renewed human rights trials in Argentine courts.

Since the reopening of the trials, the prosecution of members of the military has gained significant momentum. In 2007 there were only forty-one individuals convicted, yet by December 2011 this number had increased to 267. The number of indicted individuals (*procesados*) also rose, from 349 to 843.[96] In addition to the quantitative expansion of prosecutions, there have been a number of significant developments in prosecutorial strategies, categories of crimes and individuals covered, and courts involved. For example, in some cases prosecutors have targeted the commission of sexual crimes. In 2010, a member of the armed forces was convicted for the rape of two women in the *Molina* case. The scope of investigations has expanded to include the alleged criminal responsibility of civilians. In the high-profile case of *Papel Prensa*, the managers and shareholders of a private company are under investigation for their alleged participation in the death and torture of former shareholders. In the *Ibáñez, Manuel Leandro y otros* case investigations have focused on how human rights violations were facilitated by the illegal relations between private companies and the military regime. The former minister of economy of the military regime, José Alfredo Martínez de Hoz, is being investigated for his participation in the kidnapping of an individual. Moreover, in the *Romero Niklinson* case former judge Manlio Martínez was accused of contributing to disappearances as he had unlawfully refused to initiate legal investigations between 1975 and 1983.[97] Finally, prosecutions for human rights crimes under the military regime

---

[94] Gabriel Chavez-Tafur, "Using International Law to By-pass Domestic Legal Hurdles: On the Applicability of the Statute of Limitations in the Menendez et al. Case," *Journal of International Criminal Justice* 6 (2008).

[95] For an extensive list of different court cases in various Argentine courts, see Guembe, "Reopening of Trials," 124.

[96] *Unidad Fiscal de Coordinación y Seguimiento de las causas por violaciones a los derechos humanos cometidas durante el terrorismo de Estado, Informe sobre el estado de las causas por violaciones a los derechos humanos cometidas durante el terrorismo de Estado* (Buenos Aires 2011), accessed February 22, 2012, http://www.mpf.gov.ar/Accesos/DDHH/Docs/Estado_Causas_dic_2011.pdf.

[97] "Un ex juez federal es acusado de colaborar con delitos de lesa humanidad," *El Diario*, 24, June 6, 2011.

have been federalized, with trials conducted in provinces where no trials had taken place before. Several provincial courts have issued their first rulings convicting individuals for human rights crimes.[98]

Given the scale and scope of the trials, progress on prosecution has depended on the degree of coordination among state prosecutors and judges, as well as coherence among the different trials in terms of litigation strategies (i.e., between state prosecutors and legal representatives), charges brought, and treatment of evidence, for example.[99] The Supreme Court has pointed out that the judiciary was initially not prepared adequately to administer the multitude and often complex judicial cases due to a lack of resources.[100] There is also some evidence of resistance to the trials – on ideological and practical grounds – among some sectors of the judiciary.[101] However, specialized agencies have been created by the Supreme Court and the General Prosecutor's Office respectively in order to address these concerns. Moreover, a committee comprised of members of the three branches of government was created in 2008. In addition, the initial executive policy on prosecutions has been expressly supported by the Supreme Court and the congress. In 2010, both institutions made official statements highlighting that prosecution has become a state policy and as such will not be reversed.[102]

The reopening of trials is a dramatic development that constitutes the culmination of a lengthy political and legal struggle. The significant weakening of the military as a political actor and the support of the Kirchner government were crucial in precipitating this most recent shift in Argentina's pathway to accountability. The process of judicial revision of Argentina's impunity laws and pardons also demonstrates the gradual yet significant changes in judicial thinking with regards to international human rights law and the human rights jurisprudence of the Inter-American Human Rights System in particular. Clearly influences external to the judiciary – including the Kirchner government and HROs – are important when accounting for these judicial changes. However, by giving human rights treaties constitutional status, the Argentine state has acknowledged special international obligations that limit the scope of political discretion and the autonomy of domestic laws in human rights matters. The significant evolution of international human rights jurisprudence in recent years has compelled Argentine judges to revise their

---

[98] A detailed analysis of these aspects, except the Romero Niklinson case, can be found in CELS, 2011 *Annual Report* (Buenos Aires, 2011). Details of the Romero Niklinson case were provided by staff of the Public Prosecutor Office in anonymous interview with the authors.

[99] See for example, CELS, 2011 *Annual Report*.

[100] *Supreme Court of Argentina: Delitos de lesa humanidad: Informe sobre la evolución de las causas actualizado al 16 de julio de 2010* (Centro de información judicial: 2010), accessed September 3, 2011, http://www.cij.gov.ar/lesa-humanidad.html.

[101] See Engstrom, "Transnational Human Rights and Democratization," chapter 5.

[102] CELS, 2011 *Annual Report*.

position on the prosecution of the crimes of the military regime. Yet without the sheer insistence and creativity of Argentina's highly mobilized HROs these developments would have been unlikely.

## CONCLUSION

This chapter has examined the key factors that explain the ebb and flow of transitional justice in Argentina. First, many different actors are involved in processes of transitional justice. Most clearly, the existence of highly mobilized, organized, and strategically creative HROs is crucial. Also, given the internationalized policy domain of transitional justice, robust connections with international institutions, such as the IACHR in the case of Argentina, and transnational networks can significantly strengthen the political position of domestic HROs.

Second, the Argentine experience demonstrates that HRO activism is not sufficient. In particular, in a country such as Argentina with a historical tradition of concentration of political power in the executive, presidential leadership has been crucial. The policies and motivations of Alfonsín, Menem, and Kirchner have fundamentally shaped the ups and downs of the transitional justice process, with the legislature and the judiciary largely accommodating their policies at key conjunctures.

Nonetheless, and third, the Argentine process of overturning amnesty also demonstrates the key role of courts as arenas of human rights politics. Shifts in judicial thinking tend to be slow and gradual and, of course, do not take place in a political vacuum. The Argentine judiciary, like other judiciaries in Latin America (and elsewhere), is often attuned to and generally accommodates political shifts. The law, however, and the interests and normative preferences of its practitioners, cannot be simply reduced to politics. As can be seen in the case of Argentina, developments in national and international law fundamentally shape the normative environment in which political actors operate.

Fourth, in addition to executive political leadership and judicial politics, the fate of prosecutions depends also on the institutional support and capacity of other state agencies. Clearly, the Argentine judiciary was not adequately prepared to deal with the reopening of prosecution. The political decision of the president and the dismantling of legal obstacles to prosecution might become merely symbolic if other agencies do not endorse the prosecution policy.

Finally, the Argentine transitional justice experience has clearly been shaped by the changing character of civil-military relations. The gradual, but steady, diminution of the Argentine military's political power since the democratic transition has provided a propitious context for ambitious attempts to hold military and police personnel accountable for their crimes. The contrast with other regional countries, such as Brazil for example, is striking in this regard.

Hence, the overturning of Argentina's amnesties and pardons, the reopening of human rights trials, and the ebb and flow of its path to justice can be explained by a highly propitious combination of factors: HRO mobilization and the remarkable perseverance of activists over time; fluctuations in the character of political leadership and support for human rights policies more generally; judicial responsiveness to human rights demands at key conjunctures and gradual but significant shifts in judicial thinking and responsiveness to the development of international human rights law particularly in the latter stages, institutional capacity; and a gradual strengthening of civilian control over the armed forces and the weakening of the military's political power.

In Latin America, a region that has in many ways been ahead of the curve when it comes to transitional justice innovations, the Argentine experience is in many ways unique. That said, there is a discernible regional trend of "post-transitional justice"[103] increasingly challenging the political bargains struck as part of the democratic transitions in the region. This trend is most clearly reflected in the rising number of human rights trials addressing human rights abuses under previous regimes in a number of Latin American countries. The persistence and resilience of democracy in the region, despite significant challenges, explains the opening of political spaces to challenge transitional bargains. Civil society activism, particularly by victims' organizations, has kept transitional justice on the political agenda, albeit with significant differences across the region. Increased civilian control over the military in many Latin American countries is also an important factor.

The short-term advantages of political pragmatism, which inevitably shapes approaches to transitional justice, have also been challenged by a regional accountability norm, discussed by Sikkink in this volume. The strength and penetration of the norm, however, is uneven. The norm has been fully internalized in Argentina; the Chilean response has to date at best been cautious; and in the case of Brazil the adoption is incipient if at all. Similarly, in the case of Peru accountability processes have been uneven following *Barrios Altos*, the publication of the Peruvian Truth and Reconciliation Commission report in 2003, and the conviction of Alberto Fujimori in April 2009.[104] And these countries differ significantly from the responses by the Mexican state whose reluctance to accept state responsibility for crimes committed during that country's period of repression in effect constitutes a de facto amnesty.

---

[103] Cath Collins, *Post-Transitional Justice: Human Rights Trials in Chile and El Salvador* (University Park: Pennsylvania State University Press, 2010).

[104] Jo-Marie Burt, "Accountability after Atrocity in Peru: The Trial of Former President Alberto Fujimori in Comparative Perspective," in OTJR, *Critical Perspectives in Transitional Justice*.

And yet transitional justice is quite clearly a moving target. Therefore, the Argentine experience can inform our understanding of processes of transitional justice generally and the appropriateness of amnesties in particular. Political circumstances change as power balances shift, consequently altering the incentives facing relevant political actors. But more subtle changes also occur over time in the normative environment in which actors operate. In other words, what is possible and desirable is prone to change over time. Hence, although accountability claims have a tendency to persist over time, timing is important, rendering what may seem a morally desirable sequencing of transitional justice mechanisms difficult to implement. It is often not a simple matter of choosing between different transitional justice mechanisms. A wide variety of mechanisms have been employed in the region in addition to amnesties, including investigations to establish the truth and identify perpetrators, reparations programs for victims of human rights violations (financial and symbolic in terms of memory sites), institutional measures to establish mechanisms to prevent recurrence of violations, and of course prosecutions and trials. The result of the region's decades long engagement with transitional justice and amnesties in particular is now a broad set of duties of states, rights of victims and families, and obligations to provide reparations that put pressure on governments to revise the political bargains of the past. Still, in many countries amnesty provisions are circumvented rather than overturned. Hence, a striking feature of regional trends consists of the persistence of amnesty laws despite significant challenges to impunity and pressures for accountability and for wide-ranging trials.

# 5

## Barriers to Justice

### The *Ley de Caducidad* and Impunity in Uruguay

*Francesca Lessa*

In 1974, Uruguayan senator Zelmar Michelini traveled to Rome to denounce the human rights abuses perpetrated by the Uruguayan dictatorship before the Russell Tribunal. Torture, incarceration, and terror had become commonplace in this tiny South American country – previously a land of relative peace, democracy, and freedom. Senator Michelini paid the ultimate price for exposing internationally the Uruguayan regime and its human rights repression when he was abducted and murdered in Buenos Aires in 1976. Three decades later, Zelmar's son, Felipe Michelini MP, deplored in a parliamentary address the impunity that still endured under democracy in Uruguay.

Impunity has for decades been the official policy regarding the human rights crimes committed during the Uruguayan dictatorship (1973–85). This chapter focuses on the legal and most visible face of impunity, its key symbol, namely Law No. 15,848 Caducidad de la Pretensión Punitiva del Estado (Expiry of the Punitive Claims of the State), or simply the Ley de Caducidad. Until October 2011, when the Ley de Caducidad was derogated, justice in Uruguay could only be achieved in the few occasions in which the amnesty was bypassed, that is, in cases involving crimes falling outside its scope. Over time, the strategy of circumventing the Ley de Caducidad had, however, become a double-edged sword. While it enabled the achievement of justice in some cases, it simultaneously reaffirmed and reinforced the impunity of crimes and individuals covered by the amnesty.[1] This approach

---

[1] Mirtha Guianze, "La Ley de Caducidad, las luchas por la justicia y la jurisdicción universal de los derechos humanos en el Uruguay," in *Luchas contra la impunidad: Uruguay 1985–2011*, ed. Gabriela

The author wishes to acknowledge the generous assistance received by the London School of Economics (Department of International Relations); the University of London Central Research Fund; and the Postgraduate Travel Grant of the Society for Latin American Studies (U.K.) that funded her fieldwork trips to Uruguay in 2007 and 2008. The author would also like to thank Diana Florez; Laura Balsamo and Madelon Aguerre from SERPAJ-Uruguay; Pablo Chargoñia; Pilar Elhordoy-Arregui; and Mirtha Guianze for their time, patience, and helpful advice.

further established a hierarchy of human rights abuses: some crimes (economic crimes or those perpetrated abroad) could be prosecuted, while others (torture and imprisonment) were amnestied. Consequently, impunity was the norm and justice remained arbitrary: particularly, the Ley de Caducidad deprived victims of past violations of unrestricted access to justice.

The chapter first provides a brief historical background on the Uruguayan dictatorship and its human rights violations; second, it discusses the origins and main provisions of the Ley de Caducidad; third, it recounts the various efforts undertaken to repeal the law from 1986 to 2011; finally, it suggests some tentative reasons behind the persistence of the Ley de Caducidad and impunity. The Uruguayan case reflects at different junctures the theoretical perspectives outlined in this volume. Elements of Kathryn Sikkink's justice cascade are witnessed in the unrelenting mobilization against impunity by Uruguayan activists who have resorted to regional and international bodies to attain accountability while also attempting to undermine the amnesty inside Uruguay.[2] Yet the amnesty has also been defended as "a necessary evil"[3] for peace and democracy, most notably by Presidents Sanguinetti and Lacalle in the 1980s and 1990s, but also more recently. Finally, between 2005 and 2011, elements of Tricia Olsen, Leigh Payne, and Andrew Reiter's justice balance[4] approach were present in Uruguay, since the Ley de Caducidad coexisted with notable trials and approximately 60 cases of past crimes pending judicial investigation.

## HUMAN RIGHTS VIOLATIONS IN THE "SWITZERLAND OF THE AMERICAS"

During the first half of the twentieth century, Uruguay was generally considered exceptional, referred to as the "Switzerland of the Americas," and its capital, Montevideo, was known as "the Athens of the River Plate."[5] National perception drew on expressions such as *"como el Uruguay no hay"* ("There is no place like Uruguay") and *"el Uruguay feliz"* ("Uruguay, the land of the merry").[6] These labels

---

Fried and Francesca Lessa (Montevideo: Trilce, 2011); Pablo Chargoñia, "Avances, retrocesos y desafíos en la lucha judicial contra la impunidad," in Fried and Lessa, *Luchas contra la impunidad.*

[2]   See Chapter 1 by Kathryn Sikkink in this volume.

[3]   See Chapter 2 by Mark Freeman and Max Pensky in this volume.

[4]   See conclusion in this volume.

[5]   Juan Rial, "The Social Imaginary: Utopian Political Myths in Uruguay (Change and Permanence during and after the Dictatorship)," in *Repression, Exile and Democracy: Uruguayan Culture,* ed. Saul Sosnowski and Louise B. Popkin (Durham and London: Duke University Press, 1993), 64; Luis E. González, *Political Structures and Democracy in Uruguay* (Notre Dame: University of Notre Dame Press, 1991), 3.

[6]   Rial, "The Social Imaginary," 64.

pointed to Uruguay's remarkable tradition of liberal and participatory democracy, its growing financial and economic markets, its rising urban middle class, and its population's high levels of education and political awareness.[7] All of these advances stood in stark comparison to the turbulence and authoritarianism that characterized neighboring countries.

However, by the late 1960s and early 1970s, Uruguay's exceptionalism was fading away. Against the backdrop of the Cold War, the country was beginning to resemble its neighbors more and more. The "Switzerland of the Americas" faced dire economic, social, and political crises; social and trade union polarization; repressive policies; and growing military intervention in political life. Further, leftist and right-wing armed groups emerged, namely the guerrilla Movimiento de Liberación Nacional-Tupamaros and the paramilitary Escuadrones de la Muerte, and political violence reached unprecedented levels.

The slow-motion coup initiated in February 1973 – when the armed forces were incorporated into government through the newly established National Security Council – culminated on June 27, 1973, when democratically elected President Juan María Bordaberry, backed by the armed forces, dissolved parliament and inaugurated a twelve-year reign of fear that combined economic mismanagement with political terror. Uruguay was no longer the exception of the region. By the late 1970s, it had been given a new and chilling label as the "Torture Chamber of Latin America," an appropriate tag underscoring the brutality of human rights violations.[8]

The Uruguayan dictatorship was "the closest approximation in South America of the Orwellian totalitarian state."[9] Uruguay's small size and population permitted infiltration into citizens' public and private lives. Military rule achieved unprecedented control of the country and permeated daily life through strict censorship of the press, the prohibition of political and trade union activities, the reshaping of the educational system and cultural foundations through the imposition of a rigid syllabus, censored textbooks, and the compulsory teaching of "moral and civic education" to encourage patriotism and traditional values.[10] Every citizen was attributed a letter of designation of democratic faith (A, B, or C), according to political reliability.[11] The regime created an oppressive atmosphere to paralyze society, instilling

---

7  Carlos Demasi, "La dictadura militar: Un tema pendiente," in *Uruguay cuentas pendientes: Dictadura, memorias y desmemorias*, ed. Hugo Achugar et al. (Montevideo: Trilce, 1995).

8  Jenny Pearce, *Uruguay: Generals Rule* (London: Latin America Bureau, 1980).

9  Mara Loveman, "High-Risk Collective Action: Defending Human Rights in Chile, Uruguay, and Argentina," *American Journal of Sociology* 104, no. 2 (1998): 503.

10  Cynthia Brown and Robert K. Goldman, "Torture, Memory and Justice," *The Nation*, March 27, 1989.

11  Charles Gillespie, *Negotiating Democracy: Politicians and Generals in Uruguay* (New York: Cambridge University Press, 1991).

passivity and compliant behavior and installing "a culture of fear characterized by *inxile*: a sullen wariness, self-censorship and longing to maintain anonymity against the brooding omnipresence of the state."[12]

The human rights repression took ideological inspiration from the National Security Doctrine; the defining features in Uruguay were the systematic use of torture and prolonged imprisonment. The human cost was extremely high. An estimated two hundred fifty thousand to five hundred thousand people left for exile for economic or political reasons, out of a population of approximately 2.5 million at the time.[13] Over sixty thousand people were arrested or detained. Indeed, between 1973 and 1977, Uruguay had the highest percentage of political detainees per capita in the world; further, there were around 6,000 long-term political prisoners. More than 160 people disappeared: 32 in Uruguay and over 130 in the region – mainly in Argentina through Plan Condor operations.[14] Finally, twenty-six people were executed extrajudicially, and children spent time in detention with their mothers, while others were disappeared or illegally appropriated.[15]

## THE DEFEAT OF HOPE: THE LEY DE CADUCIDAD

In August 1984, successful negotiations between the armed forces commanders and representatives of the Colorado, Civic Union, and Frente Amplio political parties culminated in the signing of the Navy Club Pact; national elections took place in November that year, paving the way for the return of democracy. In the early days, the main priority of the newly elected government of President Julio María Sanguinetti was the consolidation of democracy. The National Pacification Project of March 1985 provided for the amnesty and release of all political prisoners (except those condemned for homicide who would have their sentences reviewed, see Amnesty Law No. 15,737 of March 1985)[16]; the social reintegration of returning

---

[12] Paul C. Sondrol, "1984 Revisited? A Re-Examination of Uruguay's Military Dictatorship," *Bulletin of Latin America Research* 11, no. 2 (1992): 194; Carina Perelli, "Youth, Politics, and Dictatorship in Uruguay," in *Fear at the Edge: State Terror and Resistance in Latin America*, ed. Juan E. Corradi et al., (Berkeley: Unversity of California, 1992).

[13] Emilio Crenzel, "Present Pasts: Memory(ies) of State Terrorism in the Southern Cone of Latin America," in *The Memory of State Terrorism in the Southern Cone: Argentina, Chile, and Uruguay*, ed. Francesca Lessa and Vincent Druliolle (New York: Palgrave MacMillan, 2011).

[14] Plan Condor refers to the 1970s secret transnational network set up by the dictatorships of Argentina, Chile, Uruguay, Paraguay, Bolivia, and Brazil to target political opponents within the region through disappearances and assassinations.

[15] Alvaro Rico, "Detenidos-desaparecidos: Sistematización parcial de datos a partir de la investigación histórica de la Presidencia de la República Oriental del Uruguay," in *Historia reciente. Historia en discusión*, ed. Alvaro Rico (Montevideo: Tradinco, 2008).

[16] Article 5 of Law No. 15,737 explicitly excluded human rights violations perpetrated by members of the armed or security forces from the amnesty.

exiles; and the restoration of public jobs to employees unfairly dismissed during the dictatorship.[17] The executive had no plans to pursue accountability for past crimes; rather it opposed criminal prosecutions against members of the armed or security forces charged with human rights abuses. The administration's objective was the imposition of national amnesia, hiding the crimes of the recent past under a mantle of silence and oblivion.

However, in April 1985 – just one month into democracy – victims themselves or their relatives began bringing cases of human rights abuses suffered during state terrorism to the courts. By December 1986, 734 such cases were under judicial investigation.[18] As a result of increasing denunciations and judicial activity, the military became progressively restless and openly stated it would not comply with judicial summons to appear in court. Army Commander General Hugo Medina asserted that he was keeping summons in his personal safe, indicating that a "political solution" was required to prevent military "insubordination against the rule of law."[19] Simultaneously, the Sanguinetti administration portrayed the situation as an institutional crisis, underscoring the possibility of another military coup. In this context and, after previously failed attempts, parliament enacted the Ley de Caducidad on December 22, 1986 in a session that almost ended in a gunfight just hours before military officers were due to testify in court.[20] The passing of the law brought to an end the possibility of achieving justice and clarifying past crimes; it placed the question of accountability in the hands of the executive that, for decades, obstructed all attempts at elucidating the past.

## The Ley de Caducidad

For over two decades, the Ley de Caducidad defined the trajectory of transitional justice in Uruguay, constituting a real and a symbolic obstacle to advances in accountability.[21] The law dealt with the prosecution of military and police officers; the forced retirement of military personnel in 1974; and the role of civilian political institutions and armed forces in relation to the promotion of military officers. Its main purpose was to prevent judicial proceedings against military and police officers

---

[17] Alexandra Barahona de Brito, *Human Rights and Democratization in Latin America: Uruguay and Chile* (Oxford: Oxford University Press, 1997).

[18] Alexandra Barahona de Brito, "Truth, Justice, Memory, and Democratization in the Southern Cone," in *The Politics of Memory: Transitional Justice in Democratizing Societies,* ed. Alexandra Barahona de Brito et al., (Oxford: Oxford University Press, 2001).

[19] Ibid., 128.

[20] Ibid., 130.

[21] Personal interview, human rights activist, Partido por la Victoria del Pueblo, Montevideo, Uruguay, August 30, 2008.

accused of human rights violations. The law, with its long and convoluted name, was a hybrid and ambiguous legislative piece:

**Article 1** – It is recognized that, as a consequence of the logic of the events stemming from the agreement between the political parties and the Armed Forces signed in August 1984, and in order to complete the transition to full constitutional order, the State relinquishes the exercise of penal actions with respect to crimes committed until March 1, 1985, by military and police officials either for political reasons or in fulfilment of their functions and in obeying orders from superiors during the *de facto* period.

**Article 2** – The above article does not cover:

a) judicial proceedings in which indictments have been issued at the time this law goes into effect;

b) crimes that may have been committed for personal economic gain or to benefit a third party.

**Article 3** – For the purposes contemplated in the above articles, the court in pending cases will request the Executive branch to submit, within a period of thirty days of receiving such request, an opinion as to whether or not it considers the case to fall within the scope of Article 1 of this law.

If the Executive branch considers this law to be applicable, the court will dismiss the case. If, on the other hand, the Executive branch does not consider the case to fall under this law, the court will order judicial proceedings to continue.

From the time this law is promulgated until the date the court receives a response from the Executive branch, all pre-trial proceedings in cases described in the first paragraph of this article will be suspended.

**Article 4** – Notwithstanding the above, the court will remit to the Executive branch all testimony offered until the date this law is approved, regarding persons allegedly detained in military or police operations who later disappeared, including minors allegedly kidnapped in similar circumstances.

The Executive branch will immediately order the investigation of such incidents.

Within a 120-day period from the date of receipt of the judicial communication of the denunciation, the Executive Branch will inform the plaintiffs of the results of these investigations and place at their disposal all information gathered.[22]

---

[22] "Application to the Inter-American Court of Human Rights in the case of Juan Gelman, María Claudia García Iruretagoyena de Gelman y María Macarena Gelman García Iruretagoyena (Case 12.607) against the Oriental Republic of Uruguay," paragraph 49, accessed July 4, 2011 http://www.cidh.org/demandas/12.607%20Gelman%20Uruguay%2021ene10%20ENG.pdf.

Article 1 specified the temporal jurisdiction, covering crimes perpetrated during the "*de facto* period," that is, the years of the dictatorship: June 27, 1973 to March 1, 1985. The material jurisdiction was left imprecise; article 1 simply used the word "crimes," leaving ample room for interpretation. The vagueness of the wording was matched in practice by a broad reading of the law's scope as encompassing the whole range of abuses perpetrated during the dictatorship, including murder, torture, extrajudicial executions, prolonged imprisonment, and disappearances. In terms of its beneficiaries, article 1 defined its applicability to "military and police officials." The rapid discussion and enactment of the law, combined with specific pressures from the military to ensure that its own officers would not be put on trial, may have resulted in the way article 1 was formulated – a drafting that does not reflect the large complicity and active role played by civilians in the regime.[23] The latter half of the article, "in fulfilment of their functions and in obeying orders from superiors," further limited the law's application to officers in subordinate positions. Article 2 outlined two situations outside the amnesty's remit: judicial proceedings at the indictment stage by December 23, 1986, and economic crimes. Article 3 further established that courts had to transmit all denunciations of human rights violations to the executive; only the latter was in fact empowered to decide whether the law was applicable on a case-by-case basis. This article effectively weakened the independence of the judiciary because judges could not operate freely, but had to hand over cases to the executive and follow the latter's recommendation in each instance. Finally, article 4 entrusted the responsibility to investigate cases of disappeared adults and children to the executive. Here, too, the law forced judges to forgo their duties, transferring them onto the executive. Articles 3 and 4 were the most controversial provisions given that they undermined the separation of powers and rendered the judiciary dependent on the executive.

The Ley de Caducidad was contentious in at least three respects. Morally, it placed property and economic rights above physical integrity rights, permitting prosecutions for economic crimes, but not for violations of the right to life or prohibition of torture. Politically, it undermined the separation of powers and judicial independence, establishing a distorted system that granted the executive the exclusive power and competence to decide whether or not a case fell within the law's framework. This mechanism undermined judicial independence and citizens' access to justice and also established a form of arbitrary justice because some cases proceeded with investigations, while others did not, depending solely on the executive. Legally, investigations of disappearances, normally within the competence of judges, were placed in the hands of the executive. By allowing investigations into disappearances,

---

[23] Guianze, "La Ley de Caducidad."

the law offered in theory some form of redress to some of the victims; in practice, however, the government did very little. Furthermore, the majority of victims, who had suffered torture and imprisonment – crimes amnestied under the law – were completely excluded from truth and justice processes.

The Ley de Caducidad established a firm foundation for impunity, guaranteeing strong executive control and oversight over accountability. Indeed, between the late 1980s and 2005, the governments of Presidents Julio María Sanguinetti (1985–90; 1995–2000), Luis Alberto Lacalle (1990–5), and Jorge Batlle (2000–5) sponsored policies of silence and oblivion regarding past crimes, a situation well encapsulated in Sanguinetti's signature slogan *"no hay que tener los ojos en la nuca"* ("No need to have eyes at the back of your head"), calling for forgetting past divisions and building a bright democratic future.[24] Sanguinetti particularly believed that amnesty and forgetting were necessary to guarantee peace and stability, claiming that "either we're going to look to the future or to the past."[25] The desire for amnesia and impunity continued during subsequent administrations.

## AN UPHILL STRUGGLE: CHALLENGING THE LEY DE CADUCIDAD, 1986–2011

The Ley de Caducidad faced fierce opposition right after coming into existence. Since 1986, various legal and political tools have been employed to undermine the law inside and outside Uruguay. Uruguay's heterogeneous civil society, human rights lawyers, public prosecutors, intellectuals, and politicians continuously developed strategies to weaken the amnesty. This enduring mobilization shows how, in spite of a governmental policy of impunity, elements of the justice cascade trickled into Uruguay, catalyzing activism and maintaining awareness on accountability. The recent situation was well summarized in a 2010 debate between Uruguayan academic Gerardo Caetano and politician Felipe Michelini. Caetano contended that the Ley de Caducidad was "dead," and Michelini responded: "we now must ensure that it is buried."[26] This exchange underscored how the Ley de Caducidad had been "gravely" wounded over the years, but the fight against impunity was not over yet.

### The "Voto Verde" Campaign

On December 23, 1986, the day after the Ley de Caducidad was sanctioned, a group within civil society announced its intention to hold a referendum on the newly

[24] See Francesca Lessa, *"No hay que tener los ojos en la nuca*: The Memory of Violence in Uruguay, 1973–2010," in Lessa and Druliolle, *The Memory of State Terrorism in the Southern Cone.*
[25] Lawrence Weschler, *A Miracle, A Universe: Settling Accounts with Torturers* (Chicago and London: University of Chicago Press, 1998), 189.
[26] Roger Rodríguez, "Es la impunidad, idiota," in Fried and Lessa, *Luchas contra la impunidad*, 121.

enacted law.[27] A signature collection campaign was initially led by victims' groups, the widows of murdered Uruguayan politicians Zelmar Michelini and Héctor Gutiérrez Ruiz, and the grandmother of missing child Mariana Zaffaroni. Later, NGOs, intellectuals such as novelist Mario Benedetti, and politicians (mainly from the Frente Amplio Party that had opposed the law in parliament) joined the campaign. An umbrella organization, the National Commission for the Referendum, was created in January 1987 to lead the movement. While previously referenda had originated from the government and political parties, this initiative was the first initiated by civil society. The Commission decided to keep the issue of the referendum free from partisanship and political manipulation.[28] This is particularly significant for Uruguay, where most allegiances revolve around political parties. The Commission's message focused on ethics and morality, contending that only by bringing to justice those responsible for past crimes could legal redress be provided, such crimes prevented, and national reconciliation achieved.[29] The campaign aimed for society to freely express itself, exemplified by the slogans "I sign for the people to decide" and "All equal before the law."[30]

After months gathering signatures door to door throughout Uruguay, over 634,700 signatures were submitted to the Electoral Court in December 1987. Despite underhanded attempts to halt the process, such as the disqualification of thousands of signatures for dubious reasons, the referendum was scheduled for Sunday, April 16, 1989. On the day of the vote, 55.95 percent cast the yellow ballot (*voto amarillo*) to retain the Ley de Caducidad, while 41.30 percent cast the green (*voto verde*) to overturn it.[31] The referendum and preceding campaign produced wide social mobilization and were the focus of public debate for months: the policy of silence favored by Sanguinetti's government had been successfully challenged. Indeed, "the human rights issue, instead of remaining secluded in the private or sectarian realms, had dominated the public sphere."[32] Yet the referendum was perceived as sealing the problem from a political and legal point of view.[33] The vote had shown how the

[27] Luis Roniger and Mario Sznajder, "The Legacy of Human Rights Violations and the Collective Identity of Redemocratised Uruguay," *Human Rights Quarterly* 19, no. 1 (1997). Article 79 of Uruguay's constitution provides that the citizenry is entitled to hold a referendum to overturn a law if twenty-five percent of the electorate so requests within a year of the law's promulgation.

[28] Guillermo Waksman, "Uruguay: Consagración de la democracia tutelada," *Nueva Sociedad* 102 (julio–agosto 1989).

[29] *Americas Watch, Challenging Impunity: The Ley de Caducidad and the Referendum Campaign in Uruguay* (New York: Americas Watch, 1989).

[30] Carlos Demasi and Jaime Yaffé, *Vivos los llevaron...Historia de la lucha de Madres y Familiares de Uruguayos Detenidos Desaparecidos (1976–2005)* (Montevideo: Trilce, 2005), 67.

[31] Pablo Galain Palermo, "The Prosecution of International Crimes in Uruguay," *International Criminal Law Review* 10, no. 4 (2010): 604.

[32] Roniger and Sznajder, "The Legacy of Human Rights Violations," 74.

[33] Luis Roniger and Mario Sznajder, "La reconstrucción de la identidad colectiva del Uruguay tras las violaciones de los derechos humanos por la dictadura militar," *Araucaria* 9, no. 3 (2003).

majority was inclined, like the governing Colorado party, to take "the safer path." The vote, nevertheless, exposed the coexistence of "two incompatible logics," the "ethical logic" calling for the law's derogation and the "state logic" in favor of security and pragmatism.[34]

Concurrently to the *voto verde* campaign, an unconstitutionality appeal against the Ley de Caducidad had been launched by victims of human rights crimes in 1986; it contended that the law violated the principle of separation of powers, the right to due process, the independence of the judiciary, and equality before the law. In 1988, with a split three to two decision, the Supreme Court upheld the law's constitutionality, particularly acknowledging the "existence of a problematic social reality, which jeopardizes the attempt of institutionalizing democracy in peace."[35]

In the late 1980s, the failed unconstitutionality appeal and the unsuccessful referendum constituted significant blows to the human rights cause; for several years, accountability would be absent from the political agenda and public opinion in Uruguay. The referendum defeat, particularly, amounted to a proverbial bucket of cold water thrown on human rights activism, which only recovered in the mid-1990s.[36]

## Under International Scrutiny

In the early 1990s, challenges to the Ley de Caducidad and impunity shifted to the international sphere since domestic avenues for justice were completely closed off because of the referendum's result. The election of President Lacalle in November 1989 further guaranteed no change since he, like his predecessor, had no intention of championing accountability.

In the late 1980s, the Uruguayan Institute for Legal and Social Studies, with the support of Americas Watch, had filed eight petitions before the Inter-American Commission on Human Rights (IACHR). Uruguay was cited for grave violations of the right to life, liberty, and personal security and for violating the American Convention on Human Rights, since the Ley de Caducidad denied "judicial protection" and an "impartial investigation of the human rights violations" to victims.[37] In 1992, Uruguay's amnesty was declared incompatible with the American Declaration of the Rights and Duties of Man and the American Convention.[38] Uruguay, further,

---

[34]  Barahona de Brito, *Human Rights and Democratization*, 150.

[35]  Chargoñia, "Avances, retrocesos y desafíos," 163.

[36]  Personal interview, senator, Nuevo Espacio-Frente Amplio, Montevideo, Uruguay, September 3, 2008.

[37]  Inter-American Commission on Human Rights, Report N°29/92-Uruguay, accessed September 3, 2011, www.cidh.org/annualrep/92eng/Uruguay10.029.htm1992), paras. 8–10.

[38]  Ibid., para. 11.

had to pay compensation to the victims and investigate human rights violations of the de facto period. Uruguay's petition resulted in an unprecedented pronouncement: the IACHR was the first intergovernmental body to directly address the question of the compatibility of amnesty with a state's obligations under human rights law.[39] Yet the decision had little impact inside Uruguay, possibly because the IACHR had not expressly requested the law's repeal[40] and due to the minimal receptiveness of Uruguay's government on the matter.

The UN Human Rights Committee (UNHRC) had also received a complaint against Uruguay in 1988: Hugo Rodríguez denounced the torture suffered at the hands of state agents in 1983 and claimed that the Ley de Caducidad negated justice to victims.[41] In 1994, the UNHRC determined that the Ley de Caducidad was incompatible with Uruguay's obligations under the International Covenant on Civil and Political Rights, explicitly stressing how the law "contributed to an atmosphere of impunity which may undermine the democratic order and give rise to further grave human rights violations."[42] The UNHRC repeatedly reiterated this concern in its concluding observations on Uruguay's third and fourth periodic reports in 1993 and 1998, pointing to continued impunity and the failure to effectively investigate past abuses.[43] These decisions had no immediate effect, owing to the clear preference of Presidents Lacalle and Sanguinetti for impunity. Still, these critical pronouncements kept the question of accountability in Uruguay under the international spotlight and constituted important statements later cited by Uruguayan courts and the Supreme Court when the amnesty law was finally challenged at home.

## *Fighting Impunity "at Home"*

Between 1989 and 1996, the theme of accountability remained absent from the public agenda inside Uruguay, constituting "seven long years of the most absolute silence"[44]; at the time, the Ley de Caducidad faced principally international

[39]   Louise Mallinder, "Uruguay's Evolving Experience of Amnesty and Civil Society's Response," (working paper No. 4, "From Beyond Legalism: Amnesties, Transition And Conflict Transformation," Institute Of Criminology And Criminal Justice, Queen's University Belfast 2009), 59.

[40]   Ibid.

[41]   UNHRC, "Communication No. 322/1988: *Rodríguez v. Uruguay,*" (CCPR/C/51/D/322/1988: United Nations Human Rights Website – Treaty Bodies Database, 1994), para. 3.

[42]   Ibid., para. 12.4.

[43]   UNHRC, "Concluding Observations of the UN Human Rights Committee: Uruguay," (CCPR/C/79/Add.19: United Nations Human Rights Website – Treaty Bodies Database, 1993); UNHRC, "Concluding Observations of the Human Rights Committee: Uruguay," (CCPR/C/79/Add.90: United Nations Human Rights Website – Treaty Bodies Database, 1998).

[44]   Personal interview, human rights activist, Madres y Familiares NGO, Montevideo, Uruguay, August 29, 2008.

scrutiny. However, by the late 1990s, the struggle against impunity returned to Uruguay. What changed?

This shift reflected the existence of a different environment, where accountability could finally be championed owing to new local, regional, and international dynamics. First, the impact of Argentine navy captain Scilingo's confessions in 1995 of his involvement in the "death flights" reverberated in Uruguay, since most Uruguayans had in fact disappeared in Argentina. Second, the 1996 "March of Silence," initiated for the first time by Senator Rafael Michelini and the Mothers and Relatives NGO,[45] flooded Montevideo's main avenue with thousands of people demanding truth and justice. Third, the 1998 arrest of General Pinochet in London had a profound influence on the whole Southern Cone region. Finally, the recuperation of missing youngsters Macarena Gelman and Simón Riquelo, in 2000 in Montevideo and in 2002 in Buenos Aires respectively, resulted in a strong emotional impact on Uruguayan society.

In the late 1990s, three initiatives were proposed (a truth commission, mediation by the Catholic Church, and direct negotiations between the military and former Tupamaros) to uncover the fate of the disappeared.[46] None was accepted by the second Sanguinetti government, which still contended that amnesty made further investigation impossible, accused those seeking information of intolerance and of threatening democratic values, or simply ignored them.[47] Between 1995 and 2000, President Sanguinetti remained as strongly opposed to accountability as he had been during his first mandate in the 1980s, yet the first breakthrough in accountability was about to happen.

In December 1999, Tota Quinteros, the mother of disappeared teacher Elena Quinteros, and her lawyer, Pablo Chargoñia, had presented a *recurso de amparo* (appeal for legal protection) against the Uruguayan state to uphold Mrs. Quinteros' right of information regarding her daughter's fate.[48] In May 2000, Judge Estela Jubette endorsed Mrs. Quinteros' request, ordering for the first time that the executive had to carry out an investigation into Elena's disappearance.[49] The administrative investigation produced no significant findings and, in November 2000, Mrs. Quinteros and her lawyer requested that the criminal investigation

---

[45] Full name: Madres y Familiares de Uruguayos Detenidos Desaparecidos.

[46] Demasi and Yaffé, *Vivos los llevaron.*

[47] Barahona de Brito, "Truth, Justice, Memory."

[48] The *recurso de amparo*, originally from Mexico, is a remedy for the protection of rights and freedoms that exists in many Latin American countries, including Uruguay; "Almeida de Quinteros Maria del Carmen C/Poder Ejecutivo (Ministerio de Defensa Nacional) Amparo. Ficha 216/99. Sentence of May 10, 2000, accessed February 23, 2012, http://elenaquinterospresente.blogspot.com/2000/05/100500-fallo-de-la-jueza-stella-jubette.html.

[49] Elin Skaar, "Legal Development and Human Rights in Uruguay: 1985–2002," *Human Rights Review* 8, no. 2 (2007).

into Elena's disappearance – previously archived in 1995 – be reopened, emphasizing the inapplicability of the amnesty to civilians.[50] As a result, in October 2002, former foreign minister Juan Carlos Blanco was charged with Elena's unlawful imprisonment. It was a historic achievement for accountability: Blanco's trial and preventive imprisonment was the first to occur in Uruguay – seventeen years after the transition.[51]

At the beginning of the twenty-first century, challenges to impunity were multiplying and the new government of President Batlle was forced to respond to rising societal demands for accountability. Building on the idea of a truth commission initially proposed in the late 1990s, the executive established the Comisión para la Paz in August 2000 to receive and collate information on enforced disappearances occurred during the dictatorship.[52] Despite significant shortcomings, the April 2003 final report was important for constituting the first official acknowledgment by the executive that state terrorism crimes, especially torture, disappearances, and kidnapping of children, had been perpetrated. Nevertheless, many argue that the commission's establishment masked the executive's desire to really close the books on the past.[53] Instead, the commission generated important public discussion and attracted media attention.

Despite progress in shedding some light on disappearances, President Batlle's interest in accountability proved rather shallow, since no other significant initiative occurred; in particular, Batlle continued to apply the amnesty, including in the case of María Claudia Gelman in November 2003, resulting in it being shelved.

### The First Interpretative Law

Unlike the 1980s and 1990s, decades characterized by an official policy of silence on past crimes, the early years of the twenty-first century marked the return of

[50] An investigative commission within the senate had been established in June 1990 to determine whether Colorado Party senator Juan Carlos Blanco bore any responsibility for Elena's disappearance in 1976. Afterward, five Frente Amplio senators presented the case to the courts. Pablo Chargoñia, e-mail messages to author, September 16 and 17, 2011. For details on the Quinteros case, see Raúl Olivera and Sara Méndez. *Secuestro en la embajada: El caso de la maestra Elena Quinteros*, accessed February 23, 2012, http://descentralizacioncanaria.blogspot.com/.

[51] *Amnesty International Report 2003 – Uruguay* (Amnesty International: 2003), accessed February 23, 2012. http://www.unhcr.org/refworld/publisher,AMNESTY,ANNUALREPORT,URY,3edb47e216,0. html.

[52] Francesca Lessa, "Peace Commission (Uruguay)," in *Encyclopedia of Transitional Justice*, ed. Lavinia Stan and Nadya Nedelsky (New York: Cambridge University Press, forthcoming).

[53] Diego Sempol, "HIJOS Uruguay. Identidad, protesta social y memoria generacional," in *El pasado en el futuro: Los movimientos juveniles*, ed. Elizabeth Jelin and Diego Sempol (Madrid: Siglo XXI Editores, 2006).

accountability to the political and social agenda in Uruguay. The first ever left-wing government in Uruguay – led by President Tabaré Vázquez (2005–10) of the Frente Amplio Party – came to power in this new context. When compared to previous administrations, important developments happened, such as excavations at military sites and the identification of the remains of two disappeared in 2005 and 2006; the establishment of the legal category of "absent due to enforced disappearance" through Law 17,894 in 2005; the enactment of reparations laws in 2006 and 2009; and the adoption of a more progressive interpretation of the amnesty. Yet during Vázquez's administration the question of the past remained unresolved; the government's attitude on justice was ambivalent, possibly because – being the first leftist government ever in power – it sought to avoid direct confrontation with the armed forces on this issue.

At his 2005 inaugural speech, President Vázquez excluded from the Ley de Caducidad two emblematic cases of past crimes (Gelman; Michelini and Gutiérrez Ruiz).[54] The exclusion of only these cases, however, demonstrated that the executive considered the amnesty applicable to all other dictatorship crimes; moreover, it showed that the administration had no intention to derogate or to annul the law.[55] Nonetheless, victims, relatives, and their lawyers continued to present cases to the courts, following the successful precedent of the Blanco case.[56] Whenever consulted on the applicability of the amnesty for each case, the Vázquez administration allowed some prosecutions to take place. Since 2005, cases considered excluded from the amnesty's remit included: economic crimes; crimes committed by civilian leaders or high-ranking military/police officers during the dictatorship; crimes committed outside Uruguayan territory; and illegal appropriation of children.[57] A draft interpretative law, outlining these restrictions to the amnesty's scope, was presented to parliament in November 2005. The bill was strongly resisted by the armed forces and other political parties; the government decided not to force it through.[58] Nevertheless, while previous governments had systematically included all cases of

---

[54] "Discurso del Presidente de la República, Tabaré Vázquez, en el acto realizado en el Palacio Legislativo," March 1, 2005, accessed February 23, 2012, http://archivo.presidencia.gub.uy/_web/noticias/2005/03/2005030111.htm.

[55] Chargoñia, "Avances, retrocesos y desafíos," 166.

[56] Pablo Chargoñia, e-mail message to author, September 16, 2011.

[57] For the rationale behind the government's position see IACHR, "Application to the Inter-American Court of Human Rights," paragraph 55; and "Proyecto de ley interpretativa de la Ley de Caducidad," *Espectador.com*, November 14, 2005, accessed August 8, 2011. http://www.espectador.com/1v4_contenido.php?id=55990&sts=1.

[58] Mallinder, "Uruguay's Evolving Experience of Amnesty." The draft bill was also rejected by human rights groups, as the interpretation partially weakened the law but simultaneously legitimated it, allowing crimes against humanity to go unpunished. See Jorge Errandonea, "Justicia transicional en Uruguay," *Revista IIDH* 47 (enero–junio 2008): 29.

dictatorship crimes within the amnesty, the Vázquez administration adopted a more broadminded interpretation, permitting the start of judicial proceedings in approximately twenty-five cases, covering about sixty victims of human rights violations. The same approach was also pursued by President José Mujica (2010–15).

In recent years, thus, justice has been achieved in some of the most symbolic human rights crimes. In September 2006, a criminal judge in Montevideo ordered the trial of six military officers and two policemen for the kidnapping of Adalberto Soba, a member of the Partido por la Victoria del Pueblo disappeared in 1976 in Buenos Aires.[59] Afterward, another twenty-seven cases of Uruguayans disappeared in Argentina were added. The Soba case had initially been presented by his family with the support of the Human Rights Secretariat of the trade union Assembly of Inter-Union Workers (PIT-CNT) and lawyer Pablo Chargoñia.[60] The case was excluded from the amnesty because the events had occurred in Argentina and resulted in the first charges ever brought against military and police officials for dictatorship crimes.[61] In March 2009, the eight defendants received sentences ranging from twenty years to twenty-five years in prison for twenty-eight aggravated homicides, constituting the first judgment for state terrorism crimes handed down in Uruguay – twenty-four years after transition.[62] Other important verdicts occurred in cases of civilian and military leaders of the dictatorship, excluded from the amnesty's remit. In February 2010, former dictator Bordaberry was condemned to thirty years in prison for orchestrating two political murders and nine disappearances and attacking the constitution – an unprecedented verdict in Latin America relating to Bordaberry's role in the 1973 coup. In April 2010, Blanco was sentenced to twenty years for the aggravated homicide of Elena Quinteros. Finally, former dictator Gregorio Álvarez received a twenty-five-year imprisonment for thirty-seven aggravated murders – a sentence confirmed by the Supreme Court in September 2011.

In light of these developments, Uruguay is one of only a few countries to have condemned two former dictators for human rights violations. Progress in human rights trials was, however, accompanied for several years by the continued existence of the Ley de Caducidad. Until late in 2011, this state of affairs gave the false impression that justice could be obtained in spite of the amnesty. In the author's opinion, this was misleading since the achievement of justice was limited to a few exceptional instances, while impunity endured in relation to the vast majority of past crimes.

---

[59]  SERPAJ, *Derechos humanos en el Uruguay: informe 2006* (Servicio Paz y Justicia – Uruguay: Montevideo, 2006), 35–6.
[60]  Ibid., and SERPAJ, *Derechos humanos en el Uruguay: informe 2010* (Servicio Paz y Justicia—Uruguay: Montevideo, 2010).
[61]  Pablo Chargoñia, e-mail message to author, September 16, 2011.
[62]  SERPAJ, *Derechos humanos en el Uruguay: informe 2010*.

## The Ballot Box Again?

Although the government had adopted a more favorable posture toward account-ability since 2005, civil society groups and victim organizations nevertheless attempted to achieve the outright nullification of the amnesty. Twenty years after the 1989 referendum, another grassroots initiative occurred, led by the National Coordinating Committee for the Nullification of the Ley de Caducidad. It encompassed the trade union PIT-CNT, the students' federation, human rights NGOs, victims' groups, cultural and public figures, and Frente Amplio legislators. It promoted the law's nullification through the ballot box arguing that, despite substantial advances, many obstacles still stood in the way of justice.

The nullification was to be obtained through a constitutional reform project requiring the signatures of ten percent of the citizens eligible to vote (over two hundred and fifty thousand), as per article 331 of the constitution. Signatures were submitted to the Electoral Court in April 2009 and the plebiscite was scheduled for October 25, 2009 to coincide with national elections. The day of the plebiscite, the required quorum of 50 percent plus one vote was not reached, falling short by a few votes, with 47.98 percent voting for the nullification.[63] Unlike the 1989 referendum, which had inaugurated a long period of silence, the plebiscite instead reinvigorated mobilization against the Ley de Caducidad. It hailed the beginning of various activities and initiatives to widen the discussion on impunity, including the establishment of two new civil society groups, Todos y Todas contra la Impunidad (Everyone against Impunity) and Iguales y Punto (All Equal and Period), recalling the 1989 slogan "All equal before the law."

## The Sabalsagaray Case

Nibia Sabalsagaray was a literature professor and communist militant who died in military detention in 1974. In 2005, the Vázquez administration declared that military officials involved in the case benefited from the Ley de Caducidad, but that civilians did not.[64] In October 2008, public prosecutor Mirtha Guianze presented an unconstitutionality appeal against the amnesty to permit the prosecution of military officers in the *Sabalsagaray* case, since no civilians had been implicated. The prosecutor's action represented an astute and strategic approach to attacking impunity.[65] Indeed, Guianze – building on the dissenting opinion of Supreme Court judges Jacinta Balbela and García Otero in the 1988 constitutionality sentence[66] – argued

---

[63] "No a la anulación: lágrimas y desconsuelo," *La República*, October 26, 2009.
[64] Mirtha Guianze, e-mail message to author, July 15, 2011.
[65] Chargoñia, "Avances, retrocesos y desafíos."
[66] María del Pilar Elhordoy Arregui, "Denunciar la impunidad: Una obligación ética," in Fried and Lessa, *Luchas contra la impunidad.*

that the amnesty violated the principle of separation of powers and certain articles of the constitution. Further, Uruguay had failed to comply with the IACHR's 1992 decision, because it had not clarified the facts or identified those responsible for human rights violations.[67] Following the appeal, the executive branch and parliament proclaimed the unconstitutionality of the Ley de Caducidad in February 2009.[68] On October 19, 2009, the Supreme Court of Justice reached a historic decision: it declared articles 1, 3, and 4 of the amnesty unconstitutional and determined that the law violated the constitution (including the principle of the separation of powers) and various human rights agreements voluntarily ratified by Uruguay.[69] In reaching its decision, the Supreme Court significantly departed from previous jurisprudence and substantially incorporated international law by referring to IACHR and UNHRC reports on Uruguay, sentences by the IACtHR on amnesties for human rights violations, and the Argentine Supreme Court's 2005 *Simón* ruling.[70] The successful appeal enabled the prosecution of military officials involved in the Sabalsagaray case, previously obstructed by the amnesty. Judicial proceedings began in October 2010 against General (ret.) Chialanza and General Dalmao. The latter was the first active duty military official ever prosecuted in Uruguay for crimes of the dictatorship.[71]

According to article 259 of the Uruguayan constitution, the Supreme Court can declare a law's unconstitutionality only in relation to the case presented for consideration. Therefore, despite the importance of the pronouncement, the decision was only applicable in the *Sabalsagaray* case. Consequently, in December 2009, two further appeals were presented.[72] In November 2010, the Supreme Court declared the Ley de Caducidad unconstitutional in the *Human Rights Organizations* case, relating to nineteen murders committed in Uruguay between 1973 and 1976. Finally, in December 2010, a third sentence was handed down in the *García Hernández, Amaral and others* case, regarding the murders of five Tupamaros militants in 1974. The latter ruling is particularly important for allowing investigations on victims of the dictatorship, but also regarding survivors Amaral García (kidnapped minor whose identity was altered) and Julio Abreu (clandestinely transferred back to Uruguay from Argentina and tortured).[73] These unprecedented sentences not only produced

---

[67] "Guianze recurre contra la Ley de Caducidad por 'inconstitucional'," *La República*, October 29, 2008.

[68] "Poder Ejecutivo: La ley de impunidad es inconstitucional," *La República*, February 18, 2009; Julio Guillot and Marcelo Márquez, "Histórico: Parlamento se pronunció por la inconstitucionalidad de la Ley de Caducidad," *La República*, February 26, 2009.

[69] Supreme Court of Uruguay, Unconstitutionality Sentence no. 365, October 19, 2009.

[70] See Chapter 4 by Par Engstrom and Gabriel Pereira in this volume.

[71] Mauricio Pérez, "Fiscal solicitó el procesamiento de dos generales por crimen de Sabalsagaray," *La República*, October 14, 2010.

[72] Mauricio Pérez, "Nueva brecha a la Ley de Caducidad," *La República*, March 7, 2010.

[73] Mauricio Pérez, "Ley de Caducidad declarada inconstitucional por tercera vez," *La República*, February 10, 2011.

three declarations of unconstitutionality of Uruguay's amnesty, but demonstrated how prosecutors and judges were finally beginning to challenge the official wall of impunity surrounding past crimes.

## From Montevideo to San José de Costa Rica

For twenty-three years, Argentine poet Juan Gelman searched relentlessly for his missing granddaughter. Gelman's son, Marcelo, and daughter-in-law, María Claudia García Iruretagoyena, were kidnapped in Buenos Aires in 1976. María Claudia was pregnant at the time and gave birth in late 1976, after having been illegally transferred to Montevideo. There, in 2000, Gelman located his then twenty-three-year-old granddaughter, Macarena, who had been raised by a policeman and his family. In light of the denial of justice in Uruguay, Macarena and Juan Gelman, represented by the Center for Justice and International Law, lodged in 2006 a petition against Uruguay with the IACHR. The case related to María Claudia's forced disappearance and the suppression of Macarena's identity and nationality; it denounced the lack of access to justice and the suffering caused to the Gelmans, Macarena, and María Claudia's relatives because of Uruguay's decision, due to the Ley de Caducidad, not to investigate the facts and prosecute those responsible.[74] In 2010, the case was referred to the IACtHR, which later released its sentence in 2011. In line with previous jurisprudence (i.e., *Barrios Altos*, *La Cantuta*, *Almonacid Arellano*, and *Gomes Lund*), the IACtHR concluded that the Ley de Caducidad was invalid because of its incompatibility with the American Convention and the Inter-American Convention on Forced Disappearance of Persons and because it prevented and obstructed the investigation and eventual sanctioning of those responsible for grave human rights violations.[75] Furthermore, the IACtHR considered the amnesty inapplicable not only in the Gelman case, but in all other cases of human rights abuses that may have occurred in Uruguay.[76] According to the American Convention, the IACtHR's sentences are final and state parties must comply with them. As a consequence of the verdict, Uruguay had an international obligation to ensure that its amnesty would no longer constitute an obstacle in the investigation of the events in question and the identification and sanction of those responsible.

---

[74] Inter-American Commission on Human Rights, Report 30/07, March 9, 2007, OEA/Ser.L/V/II.130 Doc. 22, rev. 1.

[75] Inter-American Court of Human Rights, Caso *Gelman* vs. *Uruguay* – Sentencia de 24 de febrero de 2011 (Fondo y Reparaciones), February 24, 2011, paragraph 312.11, accessed June 20, 2011, http://corteidh.or.cr/docs/casos/articulos/seriec_221_esp1.pdf.

[76] Ibid., paragraph 232. Further, the IACtHR stressed how the Ley de Caducidad's approval in a democratic government and even its ratification or support by the citizens "on two occasions, [...] does not automatically or by itself grant legitimacy to the law under International Law"; Ibid., paragraph 238.

## A Second Interpretative Law

As Uruguay was facing the IACtHR for the first time, between August 2010 and September 2010 the governing Frente Amplio Party began considering the idea of another interpretative law to avoid international condemnation. This development was in line with the Frente Amplio program for 2010–15, since the amnesty's nullification had been included in the party's electoral platform for the 2009 presidential elections.[77]

The draft bill was presented to parliament in September 2010. It incorporated several human rights (i.e., right to life, right not to be disappeared or tortured, and access to justice for crimes against humanity) into the constitution, providing for their direct application by courts. It also established that the Ley de Caducidad violated the constitution and was therefore legally invalid. Moreover, it allowed for the reopening of all cases archived because of the law and created special provisions for crimes subjected to statutory limitations.[78] In October 2010, the Chamber of Deputies approved the bill.[79] The draft was then pending in the senate for six months because three Frente Amplio senators (Jorge Saravia, Rodolfo Nin Novoa, and Eleuterio Fernández Huidobro) opposed it, arguing that the bill disregarded the "will of the people" expressed in the 1989 referendum and the 2009 plebiscite.[80] After months of discussion, a modified version of the law was approved in April 2011.[81] Because of the revisions, the bill was sent back to the deputies for final endorsement. Just a few days before the vote, in May 2011, President Mujica met with Frente Amplio deputies, advising them that the interpretative law "was the wrong path" to eliminate the Ley de Caducidad, and fearing political costs to the party.[82] Although President Mujica changed his mind various times over the next several days, when the vote eventually happened in the early hours of May 20, 2011, the project failed to pass. By then, Uruguay had already been condemned by the IACtHR and the failure to adopt the interpretative law generated further international criticism, especially

---

[77] Federico Fasano-Mertens, "Por qué el multimedio plural quiere ahora que la ley del pánico, írrita y nula, se transforme en ley disuelta?" *La República*, March 15, 2009.

[78] Cámara de Representantes, anexo I al repartido N. 379, October 2010, page 4, accessed July 8, 2011, http://www0.parlamento.gub.uy/htmlstat/pl/pdfs/repartidos/camara/D2010100379-01.pdf.

[79] Ricardo Portela, "Tra 11,5 horas de discussión, diputados votó dejar sin efecto la Ley de Caducidad," *La República*, October 21, 2010.

[80] Daniel Isgleas and Valeria Gil, "Caducidad: Senado vota anulación bajo polémica," *El Pais*, April 12, 2011.

[81] The draft approved by senators added two provisions: a declaration on the independence of the Judicial Power and jurisdiction of the courts (article 2 revised); and new article 4a clarifying that cases archived under the Ley de Caducidad did not constitute *res judicata* (matter already judged upon). See Cámara anexo II al repartido N. 379, abril de 2011, accessed June 28, 2011, http://www0.parlamento.gub.uy/htmlstat/pl/pdfs/repartidos/camara/D2011040379-02.pdf.

[82] Valeria Gil, "Mujica: Esta ley para anular la Caducidad compromete al Frente," *El Pais*, May 5, 2011.

by Amnesty International, which underscored how Uruguay had missed a historic opportunity in the pursuit of justice.[83]

## IMPUNITY IN URUGUAY: SOME TENTATIVE EXPLANATIONS

From 2005 onward, the Ley de Caducidad no longer constituted a blanket amnesty, in light of the several exceptions restricting its application and the little legitimacy it had left as a result of the many challenges suffered. Yet it remained in force – despite various attempts to repeal it nationally and internationally – until October 27, 2011, when the Uruguayan parliament derogated it through law 18.831. Even though the amnesty has now been repealed, it is important to explore several possible explanations relating to the amnesty's persistence for over two decades.

### *The Framework of Transition*

In accounting for the endurance of the Ley de Caducidad and impunity, the mode of Uruguay's transition from authoritarian rule must be examined. As briefly mentioned earlier, the 1984 Navy Club Pact opened the way for national elections and redemocratization. This is the least controversial aspect of the transitional pact. What has never been established with some certainty is whether the issue of impunity for the armed forces was agreed upon in the pact. Many direct participants deny that the question of human rights violations was debated at the time, given this would have caused negotiations to fail.[84] Some suggest that an "informal gentlemen's agreement" was reached by Sanguinetti and General Medina to protect the military from prosecution.[85] Others recognize how the logic of negotiated transitions presupposes concessions and silences from both sides[86] and how it would be unlikely that the future government would break "the rules of the game and promote the trial of one of the parties involved in the pact."[87] This logic was further strengthened at the 1984 national elections when Sanguinetti, the architect of the Uruguayan transition, became president. The Colorado Party was the closest to the armed forces, and Sanguinetti's policy of *cambio en paz* (peaceful change) considered turning the page on the past as necessary to the consolidation of democracy; demanding truth

---

[83] "Uruguay Amnesty Vote a Missed Opportunity for Justice," May 20, 2011, Amnesty International, accessed January 10, 2012, http://www.amnesty.org/en/news-and-updates/uruguay-annuls-law-protecting-rights-abusers-trial-2011-05-19.

[84] Lilia Ferro Clérico, "Conjugando el pasado: El debate actual en Uruguay sobre los detenidos desaparecidos durante la dictadura" (paper presented at the XXI International Congress of the Latin American Studies Association, Chicago, Illinois, September 24–26, 1998).

[85] Barahona de Brito, *Human Rights and Democratization*.

[86] Personal interview, historian, Institute of Political Science, University of the Republic, Montevideo, Uruguay, August 26, 2008.

[87] Barahona de Brito, *Human Rights and Democratization*, 81.

and justice would only provoke the military, causing institutional destabilization.[88] It is clear that the scope for accountability was quite restricted during the first democratic government, a sort of "guarded democracy."[89] This situation was reinforced even further in 1987 when General Medina became defense minister, thus ensuring continued military oversight over the restored democracy. By 1989, the government's position was crystal clear. In the context of the referendum, Sanguinetti and Medina made no secret of their opposition to the campaign, accusing organizers of "looking backward."[90] In particular, Sanguinetti stated how signatures were "for rancour and revenge" and that citizens were "simply taking the country back to a period" better left in the past.[91] Medina went even further, issuing veiled threats such as "time would tell" and "it was difficult to know," when commenting on the possible reaction of the armed forces to an unfavorable outcome at the referendum.[92]

The balance of power inherited from the transition in Uruguay remained largely unchanged for decades, since traditional and conservative presidents remained in power until 2005. Because of the Ley de Caducidad, any progress in accountability was in the hands of the executive and was, thus, highly unlikely.

## The Ley de Caducidad and the Executive

A second reason for the endurance of impunity was the Ley de Caducidad itself. As outlined previously, the law endowed exclusive responsibility and power over accountability to the executive, undermining the separation of powers, dispossessing victims of access to justice and domestic remedies for the violations suffered, and stripping the judiciary of its functions and independence. Because of article 3, the executive was the ultimate interpreter of the Ley de Caducidad and the only one empowered to decide on the scope of accountability, often solely on the basis of political considerations, not judicial proofs or investigation. Article 4 especially constituted a "genius political move made to transfer investigative responsibility regarding the disappeared from the courts to the executive;" as a consequence, "where the executive has no will or interest to investigate these matters, the cases will stall in the presidential office."[93] Consequently, any progress on disappearances was dependent on the existence of political will in that respect.[94] The investigation of any human

---

[88] Demasi and Yaffé, *Vivos los llevaron.*

[89] Personal interview, academic, Centre for Inter-Disciplinary Studies, University of the Republic, Montevideo, Uruguay, August 28, 2008.

[90] Brown and Goldman, "Torture, Memory and Justice," 410.

[91] Barahona de Brito, *Human Rights and Democratization,* 148–9.

[92] Ibid., 149.

[93] Skaar, "Legal Development," 57.

[94] In May 1987, Defence Minister Medina entrusted investigations on disappearances to Military Prosecutor Sambucetti. Human rights groups immediately pointed to Sambucetti's lack of

rights violations in fact depended directly on the executive's resolve and willingness to elucidate the crimes and punish those responsible.

Complete lack of political will toward accountability for Uruguay's recent past characterized the governments of Sanguinetti (1985–90; 1995–2000), Lacalle (1990–5), and Batlle (2000–5). Indeed, the first charge for human rights crimes relating to the Quinteros case only took place in 2002, and related to a civilian official of the dictatorship. Until 2005, the executive consistently and systematically included all cases of human rights violations within the amnesty. Only President Vázquez adopted a new interpretation of the amnesty's scope, allowing justice to proceed in some cases. Indeed, the first charge against military and police officers occurred in 2006 – exactly twenty years after the Ley de Caducidad's enactment. This demonstrates how the will of the executive was the deciding factor in accountability and how an official policy of accountability in Uruguay remained lacking for many years. Until recently, the exclusion of cases from the amnesty was a good political solution for Frente Amplio governments in trying to strike a difficult balance between the competing demands of the human rights community and the possible political costs associated with the law's derogation or nullification.[95] Indeed, for many years, Frente Amplio administrations failed to adopt a straightforward policy on accountability; this could be partly explained with reference to the need to prevent radical confrontations with the armed forces and other political parties, especially the Colorado.

Political will is often a necessary condition for overcoming amnesties. Nevertheless, it is not enough on its own. In Uruguay, other factors, including civil society demands for accountability, limited power of potential spoilers (such as the armed forces), and receptivity of the accountability norm by the judiciary were necessary to achieve the derogation of the Ley de Caducidad.

### The Judiciary

A third reason for enduring impunity relates to some features of the judiciary. The Ley de Caducidad directly infringed upon the powers and remit of judges, substantially limiting their scope for action and undermining judicial independence regarding past human rights crimes. In Uruguay, "a political twist of the amnesty law effectively placed the courts in the pocket of the executive after the transition to democratic rule;" because of this, more than elsewhere in the region, "there was a

---

independence and impartiality; indeed, his investigations "concluded that the evidence did not substantiate allegations of security forces' involvement," see Mallinder, "Uruguay's Evolving Experience of Amnesty," 53.

95  Errandonea, "Justicia transicional en Uruguay."

close connection between official human rights policies and judicial (in)action …
in these matters."[96]

In addition to the system established by the amnesty, some specific characteristics of the judiciary, combined with the lack of training and reform, have hindered progress in accountability. The Uruguayan judiciary tends to be conservative, cautious, "resistant to change, and very orthodox in its interpretation of the laws."[97] Consequently, innovative notions, such as the domestic applicability of international human rights law or new interpretations of existing laws, have been resisted.[98] For instance, the consideration of enforced disappearances as permanent crimes – adopted in Argentina and Chile – has yet to be incorporated in Uruguayan jurisprudence.[99] Uruguay holds no tradition of applying international human rights law; although international law has the same standing as national law, in practice judges have traditionally invoked national law only.[100] National courts have particularly resisted applying international law – with the exception of the 2009 unconstitutionality sentence by the Supreme Court and a few other recent verdicts by judges Juan Carlos Fernández Lecchini and Mariana Mota who have directly employed international human rights law.[101]

Second, there is no institutional support for judges working on these complex cases and victims themselves commonly play a fundamental role in cases of past crimes, presenting denunciations to the courts and submitting relevant proof and documentation.[102] Furthermore, there has been limited training and debate on human rights issues, as well as exchanges with judges and prosecutors from nearby countries or internationally.[103] This lack of training and expertise in human rights questions was noted in the *Gelman* sentence by the IACtHR, which ordered Uruguay to implement a permanent program of human rights, targeting agents of the Public Ministry and judges. These factors, combined with the lack of reform to the court system after the transition,[104] the limited exposure to the international sphere (there was no equivalent of the Pinochet case), and little recourse to foreign courts, have allowed the judiciary to take a back seat on these questions. While it is true that,

---

[96] Elin Skaar, *Judicial Independence and Human Rights in Latin America: Violations, Politics, and Prosecution* (New York; Basingstoke: Palgrave Macmillan, 2011), 138.

[97] Daniel M. Brinks, *The Judicial Response to Police Killings in Latin America: Inequality and the Rule of Law* (Cambridge: Cambridge University Press, 2008), 199.

[98] Ibid.

[99] Guianze, "La Ley de Caducidad."

[100] Skaar, *Judicial Independence*.

[101] Errandonea, "Justicia transicional en Uruguay"; Guianze, "La Ley de Caducidad"; Walter Pernas, "La desaparición de Julio Castro es un delito de lesa humanidad," *Brecha*, October 7, 2011.

[102] Chargoñia, "Avances, retrocesos y desafíos"; Guianze, "La Ley de Caducidad."

[103] Guianze, "La Ley de Caducidad."

[104] Elin Skaar, "Un analisis de las reformas judiciales de Argentina, Chile y Uruguay," *America Latina Hoy* 34 (agosto 2003).

owing to the Ley de Caducidad, the judiciary had little independence and scope for action on human rights cases, nonetheless Uruguayan judges have been largely reactive to denunciations – only initiated by victims and their relatives – and there has been no sustained judicial effort to challenge dominant impunity.[105]

It should be noted, however, that attempts to defy the official policy of impunity came at a price. In 1997, Alberto Reyes, a criminal judge in Montevideo, lost his post and was compulsorily transferred to a civil court after ordering an investigation into the fate of 150 disappeared.[106] In 2000, Judge Jubette risked a similar sanction in the aftermath of her ruling in the Quinteros case; while the Supreme Court refused to oust her, the judge faced pressure and lack of cooperation from colleagues, eventually taking a lengthy sick leave.[107] In the same case, Prosecutor Guianze faced possible transfer to civil competence in 2003 (but this was later avoided).[108] Similarly, Judge Alejandro Recarey, who had made significant progress while covering for Judge Eduardo Cavalli in the Quinteros case, was suspended from the case in December 2003 when Judge Cavalli surprisingly resumed his duties before the end of his sick leave.[109] These examples highlight the legal and political pressures on the judiciary until 2005, which help understand why Uruguayan judges have been rather passive on the question of impunity.

### The "Voluntad Popular"

A final reason partially explaining the persistence of the Ley de Caducidad relates to the 1989 referendum and the 2009 plebiscite. These tools, employed initially with the purpose of overturning the law, have backfired, becoming unintentional seals of approval and guarantors of the law's legitimacy. The unsuccessful outcomes at the 1989 referendum and 2009 plebiscite have been used to argue that the Ley de Caducidad was one of the most popular and legitimate laws in Uruguay, having been ratified by the citizenry on two occasions. However, referenda to ratify laws do not exist in Uruguay, since there are no provisions for the citizenry to validate laws, only to repeal them.[110] Therefore, the only juridical effect of the 1989 referendum was that the amnesty remained in force: its confirmation "neither modified qualitatively its unlawful content, nor validated it."[111]

---

[105] Chargoñia, "Avances, retrocesos y desafíos."

[106] Skaar, *Judicial Independence.*

[107] Ibid.

[108] Guianze, "La Ley de Caducidad."

[109] Chargoñia, "Avances, retrocesos y desafíos"; "Cavalli reasumió investigación y suspendió citaciones a militares," *La República*, December 9, 2003.

[110] Guianze, "La Ley de Caducidad." Article 79 of the constitution states that referenda can be called upon "against laws."

[111] Errandonea, "Justicia transicional en Uruguay," 24; Oscar Lopez Goldaracena, *Derecho internacional y crímenes contra la humanidad* (Montevideo: SERPAJ 2006), 81.

The 2009 plebiscite asked the citizenry to vote for a constitutional reform project to nullify the Ley de Caducidad; the failure to achieve the required quorum was later presented as constituting a second seal of approval granted by the citizens. At the plebiscite, voters wishing to vote in favor of the constitutional reform had to include the pink ballot (*papeleta rosada*) together with ballots for the presidential and parliamentary candidates; those wishing to vote against the constitutional reform had to do nothing. Indeed, there was no inclusion of a ballot for those wishing to vote against the reform, those wanting to vote blank, or those wanting to annul their votes. There was no differentiation among these three different votes, generating a situation in which many people failed to take a stand. Eventually, all the votes that did not include the pink ballot were counted automatically as votes against the nullification.[112] Further, while the 1989 referendum took place in a context of fear and threats from the government and the military, the situation in 2009 was, while very different, again conducive to the law being retained. The plebiscite was initiated by civil society because the government was unwilling to repeal the amnesty. The project received little support from the political parties and presidential candidate Mujica only endorsed it in August 2008. During the electoral campaign and hundreds of public appearances, Mujica never mentioned the plebiscite.[113] The spotlight stayed on presidential and parliamentary elections, with scant consideration given to the pink ballot. While it is not possible to provide an exhaustive assessment of the result here, the voting system adopted and the lack of support for the amnesty's nullification by politicians and parties, among other factors, jeopardized the chances of its success.

In 2010 and 2011, references to complying with and respecting the *voluntad* or *soberania popular* (popular will or sovereignty) were employed by politicians across the board to justify the amnesty. These arguments gained renewed strength in debates surrounding the second interpretative law in 2011. Repeated mentions of *voluntad popular* came from members of several parties, the Colorados, the Blancos, the Frente Amplio (proponent of the draft bill), and the armed forces. Some examples are illustrative. The president of the Military Centre stated that "sovereign will was being destroyed," since legislators "were going against two plebiscites."[114] Similarly, Frente Amplio senator Saravia argued "the plebiscites that ratified the norm in the past must be respected."[115] The Blancos likewise argued that the will of the Uruguayans was being trampled upon. Finally, former president Sanguinetti highlighted that the government was twisting the "will of the citizens," that the two popular pronouncements "constituted the maximum authority in the institutional

---

[112]  Rodríguez, "Es la impunidad, idiota."
[113]  "Las idas y venidas del presidente," *El Pais*, May 20, 2011.
[114]  Santiago Sánchez, "Intérpretes," *La Diaria*, April 12, 2011.
[115]  Isgleas and Gil, "Caducidad: Senado vota anulación bajo polémica."

system," that the amnesty possessed "the highest degree of legitimacy possible," and could not be "touched."[116]

Without entering the debate over whether the ballot box was the appropriate mechanism to resolve the amnesty question, undoubtedly the results were turned into a seal of impunity and their effects are hard to eliminate; they constituted powerful rationalizations for the existence of the Ley de Caducidad.

## CONCLUSION

*La impunidad estimula al delincuente en todos los niveles, individual, personal y colectivo también. Y esta es una ley de impunidad, que además convirtió al Uruguay en el paraíso de la impunidad.*

Eduardo Galeano[117]

This chapter has argued that, until the derogation of the Ley de Caducidad in 2011, justice for past human rights violations in Uruguay had been limited to a few exceptional instances. Some important sentences were achieved – mainly owing to the continued mobilization of civil society and the relentless denunciations of past crimes by victims and human rights lawyers. The exclusion of some cases from the amnesty law's remit, however, constituted a double-edged sword, because it in turn implied "a reaffirmation of the validity of the law."[118] The chapter chronicled the challenges brought against the Ley de Caducidad between 1986 and 2011. Despite significant progress and a shift from complete impunity to partial justice, the amnesty remained in force for over two decades. Some tentative reasons for its longevity were also discussed, including the framework of transition, the law and the powers attributed to the executive, the judiciary, and the 1989 referendum and the 2009 plebiscite.

The case of Uruguay is frequently overlooked in the transitional justice literature, giving the impression that its processes matter little to comparative and global analysis. The discussion in this chapter has shown, in contrast, its significance and relevance to discussions on amnesties and justice. In particular, civil society, victim groups, and human rights defenders have continuously fought against the top-down imposed policy of impunity, resorting to international and regional human rights bodies, calling the citizenry to two public votes, and managing to break the wall of impunity through some judicial proceedings. Nonetheless, many politicians and presidents have defended the Ley de Caducidad as a necessary evil to guarantee

---

[116] Julio M. Sanguinetti, "Hay actitud revanchista o de frustración política," *El Pais*, May 10, 2011.

[117] "Impunity encourages the criminal at all levels, individual, personal, and collective as well. And this is a law of impunity, which moreover turned Uruguay into a paradise of impunity." "Contra el olvido obligatorio y contra la amnesia interesada," *La República*, August 12, 2008.

[118] Guianze, "La Ley de Caducidad," 191.

stability and peace and appease the armed forces in the aftermath of a negotiated transition. Last, the situation over the past few years exposed the coexistence of two conflicting logics as the referendum did back in 1989: the "ethical logic," with civil society pushing for accountability and justice, and the "state logic," with the government favoring electoral and political costs over ethical and moral commitments. These logics have dominated the Uruguayan politics of transitional justice for three decades. During the preparation of this chapter, significant developments occurred.

On June 30, 2011, the Uruguayan executive adopted Resolution CM/323 that retrospectively revoked all administrative acts enacted in compliance with the Ley de Caducidad from 1986 to 2011.[119] Such acts, which had archived judicial proceedings in many human rights cases, were rescinded owing to their legal incompatibility with treaties and sentences. The resolution, adopted to comply with the IACtHR's verdict, effectively reopened the possibility of justice in approximately eighty-eight previously archived cases.[120] Courts were to determine action in each, deciding whether or not investigations should be reopened.[121] This first development mirrored the argument presented here. The pursuit of justice in Uruguay continued to be characterized by contradictions and ambiguity from the executive. On the one hand, justice was within reach in these eighty-eight cases; on the other, the resolution neither derogated nor annulled the Ley de Caducidad. Because of this, most victims of human rights abuses (aside from those included in the eighty-eight cases) lacked access to justice. Indeed, until recently, any new case still had to go through the amnesty's mechanism. The resolution only partially complied with the IACtHR's sentence, permitting investigation in the eighty-eight cases, yet it failed to address broader questions regarding the lack of judicial independence, impunity, and unrestricted access to justice for victims. Finally, the resolution did not tackle the issue of the statute of limitations due to take effect on November 1, 2011. In Uruguay, most sentences for past human rights violations have typified these as common crimes, not crimes against humanity. Individuals responsible were mostly sentenced for the crime of aggravated homicide, even in cases of disappearances.[122] Indeed, only Judge Mariana Mota has accepted the categorization of "enforced disappearance" in her 2010 sentence relating to the disappearance of Gustavo Inzaurralde and Nelson Santana in 1977 in Paraguay, which was later endorsed by the Appellate Tribunal in 2011.[123] In Uruguay, homicide has a statutory limitation of twenty years; this has

---

[119] "Uruguay: President Mujica Backs Military Rule Inquiries," *BBC News*, June 28, 2011.

[120] Resolution CM/323, June 30, 2011, accessed July 1, 2011, http://medios.presidencia.gub.uy/jm_portal/2011/resoluciones/cons_min/cons_min_323.pdf.

[121] Pablo Meléndrez and Daniel Isgleas, "Caducidad: Ejecutivo revoca sus actos y prevén choque jurídico," *El Pais*, June 28, 2011.

[122] Guianze, "La Ley de Caducidad."

[123] "Bibliotecas: Tribunal de Apelaciones aceptó la figura de desaparición forzada en el caso Calcagno," *La Diaria*, July 28, 2011.

been increased by a third in light of the crimes' gravity, to twenty-six years and eight months. Thus, all crimes of homicide committed during the dictatorship would become prescribed on November 1, 2011. Independent of the Ley de Caducidad, unless these crimes are typified as crimes against humanity – thus not subject to statutory limitations – any possibility of justice for victims would be eliminated.[124]

As a result of rising pressure, both internationally because of the *Gelman* sentence and nationally in light of the statute of limitations due to set in, on October 27, 2011, the Uruguayan parliament adopted law 18,831 – later promulgated by President Mujica. The new law reestablishes the state's punitive capacity regarding the crimes of state terrorism committed until March 1, 1985, which had previously fallen under the remit of article 1 of the Ley de Caducidad; it prohibits the application of any statute of limitations or other legal tools; and it declares that the crimes of the dictatorship constitute crimes against humanity.[125] The Ley de Caducidad has obstructed justice in Uruguay for almost twenty-five years: its recent derogation opens the way for a new phase in transitional justice, one in which victims of past human rights abuses should be able to enjoy unrestricted access to justice remedies for the violations suffered. In the closing months of 2011, almost 200 new cases of torture (the characteristic crime of the Uruguayan dictatorship), rape, illegal detention, and kidnapping were presented to the courts.[126] While it is still too early to say what this new transitional justice scenario will look like and how different it will be, it is interesting to note that the new denunciations of human rights violations being presented to the courts are frequently grounded in international human rights law and the *Gelman* sentence. Owing to fears that Law 18,831 may be subjected to unconstitutionality appeals by the lawyers of military and police defendants, the victims' lawyers and public prosecutors often resort directly to international law to back up their judicial cases.[127]

Last, impunity in Uruguay went well beyond the Ley de Caducidad itself, having many faces: judicial, political, and factual. Indeed, other pending matters for Uruguay encompass the issue of complete and unrestricted reparations to victims;

---

[124] A possible solution has been advocated by Judge Fernández Lecchini, who suggested that the statutory limitation for the crimes of the dictatorship could not begin if the Ley de Caducidad is in place, owing to its incompatibility with the American Convention. "Tres tesis sobre la prescripción," *La República*, June 28, 2011.

[125] Ley N° 18.831 pretensión punitiva del estado restablecimiento para los delitos cometidos e aplicación del terrorismo de estado hasta el 1° de marzo de 1985, accessed January 9, 2012, http://wwwo.parlamento.gub.uy/leyes/AccesoTextoLey.asp?Ley=18831&Anchor=.

[126] "Denuncias masivas de delitos de la dictadura: 170 nuevos casos," *Subrayado*, accessed January 10, 2012, http://www.subrayado.com.uy/Site/News.aspx?Nid=5642.

[127] Mirtha Guianze, e-mail message to author, January 17, 2012. In Uruguay, only the Supreme Court of Justice is empowered to review the constitutionality of laws. See Roger Rodríguez, "2012, la profecía del 'calendario charrúa' Ministros de Suprema Corte con poder de sacerdotes mayas," *Caras & Caretas*, January 10, 2012.

the recuperation of former sites of detention; the lack of access to state archives; the location and identification of the bodies of the disappeared; unnecessary delays in judicial proceedings; and the lack of psychological support to victims and witnesses. These represent some of the challenges that Uruguay still has to reckon with in fully realizing the commitment of *Nunca Más* (Never Again).

# 6

## Resistance to Change

### Brazil's Persistent Amnesty and its Alternatives for Truth and Justice

*Paulo Abrão and Marcelo D. Torelly*

This chapter aims to analyze transitional justice in Brazil, particularly the developments in the fields of reparation and memory and the reasons behind the persistence of the 1979 amnesty law for perpetrators of grave human rights violations. In order to do so, the chapter is divided into three parts. It begins by analyzing the development of four main dimensions of transitional justice in Brazil, namely reparations, truth and memory processes, institutional reform, and the regularization of justice and reestablishment of equality before the law. It argues that the policy of reparations to victims is the lynchpin of the Brazilian transitional justice agenda, a mechanism that has fostered progress in the recovery of truth and memory, and more recently, in the pursuit of justice. Second, the chapter analyzes the political and judicial reasons behind the effectiveness of the 1979 amnesty law. Finally, it concludes by examining the ongoing pursuit of truth in Brazil as well as justice alternatives for addressing human rights violations.

The main argument is that Brazil has had an ambiguous amnesty process. The reparations policies adopted under the current democratic regimes emerged from a concept of "amnesty as freedom and reparations" substantially different from the concept of "amnesty as oblivion and impunity" imposed by the regime in 1979. In this sense, the reparations process has the potential to craft a democratic concept of amnesty. The reparatory policies contained in the 1988 constitution and developed during the governments of Fernando Henrique Cardoso and Luis Inácio Lula da Silva were carried out in a way that challenged the idea of a bilateral amnesty. The reparatory process connects amnesty and reparation, focusing on the politically persecuted and excluding the perpetrators. In this sense, progress with the policy of reparations legitimized amnesty for the victims and delegitimized amnesty for perpetrators. This allowed for the development of other transitional justice dimensions that would otherwise be blocked by the idea of "amnesty as impunity and oblivion." Therefore the reparations process opened up a national dialogue through which greater accountability might be possible in the future. This process involved an internal challenge to the culture of impunity in Brazil. Today, impunity faces additional external challenges, such as the IACtHR 2010 decision in the case of *Gomes Lund v. Brazil*. The Brazilian policy of reparations, coupled with international pressure, has fomented debate over the concept of amnesty without threatening democratic stability. The process has been slow, and often unsatisfying, but it is not over.

## TRANSITIONAL JUSTICE IN BRAZIL

The process of transitional justice after authoritarian rule is comprised of at least four key dimensions: reparations; truth and memory processes; institutional reform (particularly of the judiciary and police); and the regularization of justice and reestablishment of equality before the law (including the obligation to prosecute grave human rights violations).[1]

In Brazil, each of these components has been implemented with varying degrees of success and many measures have lagged behind those of other Latin American countries. In the following section, we present an overview of the development of each dimension followed by a contextual analysis of transitional justice in Brazil.

### Reparations

The genesis of the Brazilian reparation process developed gradually while the Brazilian military dictatorship (1964–85) was still in power. The reparations offered to those who were politically persecuted was a legal victory achieved through the promulgation of the amnesty law (Law No. 6,683/1979). The law formed the legal cornerstone of Brazil's political transition. It provided, in addition to amnesty for political and related crimes, reparation measures, including the restitution of political rights to the persecuted (i.e., the right to register in political parties and to participate in elections) and the right to job reinstatement for civil servants and military personnel who had been removed from their positions for political reasons.

It is important to emphasize that the amnesty law in Brazil was the result of popular demand, unlike the passage of other amnesty laws in the region.[2] For example, the Argentinean amnesty was imposed by the authoritarian regime and was an explicit self-amnesty designed to maintain impunity for the crimes perpetrated by the state. In Brazil, the amnesty was supported by civil society because it was originally intended to pardon crimes of resistance committed by the politically persecuted

---

[1] Teitel, *Transitional Justice*.
[2] Heloisa Amélia Greco, "Dimensões fundacionais da luta pela anistia" (Ph.D. dissertation, Minas Gerais Federal University, 2003), 2 volumes.

who had been banished, exiled, and imprisoned, thus promoting amnesty "as freedom and reparation." The fight for amnesty was so strong that Brazilian civil society viewed it as its first victory against the regime. Despite these claims of victory, the Brazilian civil society petition to parliament for a "broad, general and unrestricted" amnesty for the politically persecuted was denied. Instead, a partial victory was achieved when the legislature, controlled by the executive branch, approved a much more limited amnesty project. This amnesty was constructed by the regime and, though it did allow for some benefits to the politically persecuted, it also set the political basis for an extensive interpretation of bilateralism, including a dimension of "amnesty as oblivion and impunity" for the perpetrators. To this day the victory, albeit limited, achieved by the Brazilian Committees for Amnesty and supported by international pressure resonates throughout the country.

After the 1979 law's approval, Amendment No. 26/1985 was added to the 1969 constitution, which provided for the restitution of political rights to student leaders and added rights (mainly labor rights restitution) to amnesty law No. 6,683/1979. Furthermore, with the publication of the new constitution in 1988, the right to reparation and resistance for the politically persecuted was renewed as a constitutional guarantee and included in article 8 of the "Transitional Constitutional Act," sheltering broad sectors of society affected by the repression.

The reparation commissions were created under the government of Fernando Henrique Cardoso (1995–2002), more than two decades after the amnesty law and a decade after the Transitional Constitutional Act. The first commission, the Special Commission for Political Deaths and Disappearances, was restricted to the recognition of the state's responsibility for killings and disappearances (Law No. 9,140/1995). The second, the Amnesty Commission, aimed to offer reparation to those affected by acts of exception (such as the "institutional acts" that revoked fundamental rights), torture, arbitrary arrests, dismissals and transfers for political reasons, kidnapping, forced hiding and exile, banishment, student purges, and illegal monitoring (Law No. 10,559/2002).

The reparation program was not restricted to financial compensation. The laws included the declaration of political amnesty (a sort of official state apology) and provided other rights, such as the right to take time spent in exile and prison into account for retirement purposes, the right to resume education in public schools, and the right to recognize foreign university diplomas, among many others.

Furthermore, Law No. 10,559/2002 contained two procedural steps to comply with the 1988 constitutional reparation mandate: first, the declaration of political amnesty contingent on an examination of the facts and provisions in cases of persecution determined by the 1988 statute. The declaration of political amnesty is both an act of political recognition of the politically persecuted's right to resistance and an acknowledgment of the wrongdoing of the state against its citizens.[3] The second step was the granting of economic reparation.[4] It is possible for someone to be granted political amnesty without receiving economic compensation: because they have already been materially compensated by past legislation; because they are no longer eligible for compensation as a result of the victim's death, (such rights are not transferred to adult descendants, except for widows and dependents); or because they fall into specific categories excluded from Law No. 10,559/2002.

These legal findings highlight the substantial difference between being granted political amnesty and receiving economic reparation. To determine economic reparations, the constitution used criteria compatible with the most common repressive practice utilized by the authoritarian regime: the arbitrary termination of employment. Job loss only increased when the struggle against the dictatorship joined the strike movements in the 1980s and led to the final demise of authoritarian rule. In contrast to what occurred in other Latin American countries where the dictatorships were extremely violent, the military regime in Brazil was more legalistic; this led to a relatively smaller number of deaths (when compared to Argentina and Chile),[5] but also to a larger amount of institutionalized victimization, particularly through economic and social repression.[6] Thus, the Brazilian reparation model favors the restitution of lost employment or the return to education as a way to reestablish the

---

[3] The concept of the term *recognition* comes from Axel Honneth, *Luta por reconhecimento: A gramática moral dos conflitos sociais* (São Paulo: Ed. 34, 2003). It is also employed by Roberta Baggio, "Justiça de transição como reconhecimento: Limites e possibilidades do processo brasileiro," in *Repressão e memória política no contexto ibero-americano*, ed. Boaventura Santos et al. (Brasília/Coimbra: Department of Justice / Center for Social Studies of the University of Coimbra, 2010).

[4] Law No. 10,559/2002 provides, as a general rule of indemnity, the setting of a monthly payment of a permanent and continuing corresponding amount or remuneration pattern that the person would be receiving if he/she were on active duty, if he/she had not been removed from his/her employment status, or other arbitrary values based on market research. The other criterion set for the persecuted who did not lose their employment status is a single compensation of up to thirty minimum wages per year of political persecution with a legal ceiling of R$ 100,000 (±USD 58,000). Law 9,140/1995 also provides a single payment with a legal ceiling of R$ 152,000.00 (±USD 88,000) for the relatives of the dead and disappeared. This model is criticized because people affected by torture, disappearance, or death with no loss of employment status in their history of repression may eventually be compensated with lower values than people whose history includes the loss of employment status. For specific discussions on the asymmetries of economic reparations in Brazil and the severance payment special criterion, different from the classical division between material damage and moral damage in the Brazilian Civil Code, see Paulo Abrão and Marcelo D. Torelly, "Justiça de transição no Brasil: o papel da comissão de anistia do ministério da justiça," *Revista Anistia Política e Justiça de Transição* 1 (2009): 12–21.

[5] While estimates of the dead and disappeared in Brazil reach 400, in Argentina the number ranges from 9,000 to 30,000 and in Chile the number is estimated at about 3,000.

[6] Anthony Pereira, *Political (In)Justice – Authoritarianism and the Rule of Law in Brazil, Chile, and Argentina* (Pittsburgh: University of Pittsburgh Press, 2005).

previous status quo. If conditions make the recovery of jobs or education impossible, the reparation model allows for economic compensation.

Taking into account the full range of possible reparation measures (i.e., restitution, compensation, rehabilitation and satisfaction measures, and guarantees of nonrepetition)[7] the systematic achievements in Brazil are summarized in Table 6.1.

Lula's government (2003–10) broke new ground in Brazilian reparation policy by adding a range of symbolic reparation mechanisms. The government initiated the project "Right to Memory and Truth" (Direito à Memória e à Verdade), with an official record of deaths and disappearances, and the "Amnesty Caravans" (Caravanas da Anistia), with public concessions of amnesty and official apologies to the victims at the locations where the violations had occurred. The Lula government also created the project "Revealed Memories" (Memórias Reveladas), which made archives from the years of the military dictatorship available to the public. Bills to create a national truth commission (No. 7,376/2010) and to allow for the right to access public information (No. 41/2010) were also proposed. Since 2007, the Amnesty Commission has used the declaratory act of political amnesty to officially apologize for the wrongdoing committed by the state.

Table 6.2 lists the recent reparation measures taken by the Brazilian government under President Lula.

It is thus possible to draw conclusions regarding the reparations process carried out in democratic Brazil. The first important conclusion is that reparations are strictly connected to the amnesty process. The second is that article 8 of the Transitional Constitutional Act provided for the explicit recognition of the rights of resistance and reparation of the politically persecuted. Third, despite Law 6,683/1979, the constitution of 1988 and subsequent legislation granted amnesty to the persecuted, not the persecutors, promoting an idea of "amnesty as freedom and reparations" linked to civil society demands for amnesty in the 1970s. In other words, the 1988 constitutional amnesty rejected the notion of "amnesty as oblivion and impunity" imposed by the military's interpretation of the 1979 law. Finally, Brazil is also implementing a wide range of reparation measures, individual and collective, material and symbolic; on the other hand, rehabilitation measures for victims are almost nonexistent.

## Institutional Reform

In Brazil, institutional reform has been an ongoing task, carried out through the implementation of a set of measures adopted over twenty-five years of democratic governance: the extinction of the SNI (National Intelligence Service); the creation of

---

[7] Pablo de Greiff, "Justice and Reparations," in *The Handbook of Reparations*, ed. Pablo de Greiff (New York: Oxford University Press, 2006).

TABLE 6.1. *Legal reparation measures in Brazil*

| Exception and repression measures | Main fundamental rights violated | Modality of reparation | Provided rights | Legal provision |
|---|---|---|---|---|
| Politically persecuted and those affected by *lato sensu* exception acts | General fundamental rights and liberties | Public satisfaction and guarantee of nonrepetition | Declaration of the condition of those granted political amnesty* | Article 1, section I of Law 10,559/2002 |
| Political disappearances | Right to life project<br>Civil liberties and political rights<br>Civil, cultural, and religious rights | Compensation<br>and<br>Compensation and public satisfaction and guarantee of nonrepetition | Economic compensation in a single or monthly payment for political persecution of living persons ***<br>and<br>Right to find, identify, and delivery of remains | Article 11 of Law 9,140/1995 **<br>Article 1, section II, Civil Code<br>Article 9, single paragraph of Law 10,559/2002 ****<br>Article 4, section II of Law 9,140/1995 |
| Dead | Right to life<br>Civil liberties and political rights | Compensation<br>and<br>Compensation | Economic compensation in a single payment for death<br>and<br>Economic compensation in single or monthly ** payments for political persecution of living persons | Article 11 of Law 9,140/1995 **<br>Article 1, section II, Civil Code<br>Article 9, single paragraph of Law 10,559/2002 |
| Tortured | Right to physical and psychological integrity | Compensation | Compensation in a single payment | Article 1, section II, Civil Code<br>Article 2, section I of Law 10,559/2002 |
| Arbitrarily imprisoned | Right to liberty, right to due process | Compensation and restitution | Compensation in single or monthly payments and time count for pension purposes | Article 1, section II, Civil Code<br>Article 2, section I of Law 10,559/2002<br>Article 1, section III of Law 10,559/2002 |

*(continued)*

TABLE 6.1 *(continued)*

| Exception and repression measures | Main fundamental rights violated | Modality of reparation | Provided rights | Legal provision |
|---|---|---|---|---|
| Arbitrarily removed or compelled to leave employment in the public sector, with or without impediments to also pursuing one's specific professional activity in civilian life | Right to life project, right to work, right to freedom of thought, right to trade union association | Restitution or Compensation and restitution and rehabilitation | Ensured reintegration/ readmission, promotion if inactive or economic compensation of monthly payment Time count for pension purposes Indirect benefits maintained by the Public Administration to servers (insurance plans, medical, dental, and hospital care and housing finance) | Article 1, sections II, V, Civil Code Article 2, sections IV, V, IX, XI Article 1, section III of Law 10,559/2002 Article 14 of Law 10,559/2002 |
| Arbitrarily removed or compelled to leave employment in the private sector | Right to life project, right to work, right to freedom of thought, right to trade union association | Compensation and restitution | Economic compensation in a single or monthly payment and Time count for pension purposes | Article 1, section II, Civil Code Article 2, sections VI, XI Article 1, section III of Law 10,559/2002 |
| Punished with a work location transfer necessitating a change of residence location | Right to employment stability and to employment liberty, right to equality | Compensation | Economic compensation in a single or monthly payment | Article 1, section II, and Article 2, section II |
| Punished with loss of earnings or part of remuneration already built into the contract of employment related to an administrative career | Right to remuneration for their work and right to equality | Compensation and restitution | Economic compensation in monthly payment and time count for pension purposes | Article 1, section II and Article 2, sections III, XII Article 1, section III of Law 10,559/2002 |

| Human rights violation | Political rights affected | Reparation type | Economic compensation | Legal basis |
|---|---|---|---|---|
| Prevented from taking office after a valid tender | Political rights | Compensation and restitution | Economic compensation of monthly payment and time count for pension purposes | Article 1, section II and Article 2, section XVII<br>Article 1, section III of Law 10,559/2002 |
| Punished with forfeiture of already provided or inactive retirement benefits with pay loss | Right to equality, constitutional guarantees to employment | Compensation | Economic compensation in monthly payment | Article 1, section II, Article 2, sections X, XII of Law 10,559/2002 |
| Compulsorily retired from the public sector | Right to equality | Compensation | Economic compensation in monthly payment | Article 1, section II and Article 2, sections I, XII |
| Forced underground | Right to liberty, right to identity, right to life project | Compensation and restitution | Economic compensation in a single or monthly payment and Time count for pension purposes | Article 1, section II and Article 2, sections I, IV, VII |
| Banished | Right to a nationality, right to liberty, right to life project, right to family life | Compensation and Restitution | Economic compensation in a single or monthly payment and Time count for pension purposes and Recognition of foreign qualifications | Article 1, section II and Article 2, sections I, VII<br>Article 1, section III of Law 10,559/2002<br>Article 1, section IV of Law 10,559/2002 |
| Exiled | Right to liberty, right to life project, right to family life | Compensation and restitution | Economic compensation in a single or monthly payment and Time count for pension purposes and Recognition of foreign qualifications | Article 1, section II and Article 2, sections I, VII<br>Article 1, section III of Law 10,559/2002<br>Article 1, section IV of Law 10,559/2002 |

(continued)

TABLE 6.1 (continued)

| Exception and repression measures | Main fundamental rights violated | Modality of reparation | Provided rights | Legal provision |
|---|---|---|---|---|
| Politicians having their electoral mandates revoked | Political rights | Compensation and restitution | Economic compensation in a single payment and Time count for pension purposes | Article 1, section II and Article 2, sections VII, XIV Article 1, section IV of Law 10,559/2002 |
| Politicians having their remuneration revoked for the exercise of elective office | Right to equality and right to remuneration | Restitution | Economic compensation in a single payment | Article 2, section XIII |
| Sued by judicial and/ or administrative harassment inquiry, with or without disciplinary punishment | Right to liberty, right to due process | Compensation | Economic compensation in a single payment | Article 1, section II and Article 2, sections I, VII |
| Exiled children and grandchildren, illegal immigrants, imprisoned, tortured or affected by any exception acts | Right to life project, right to liberty, right to family life, right to physical and psychological integration | Compensation and restitution | Economic compensation in a single payment Time count for pension purposes, in some cases | Article 1, section II, Civil Code Article 2, section I of Law 10,559/2002 Article 1, section IV of Law 10,559/2002 |
| Illegally monitored***** | Right to privacy | Compensation | Economic compensation in a single payment | Article 1, section II, Civil Code Article 2, section I |

160

| Other exception acts, in a broad sense | General fundamental and political rights | Compensation | Economic compensation in a single payment | Article 1, sections I and II, Civil Code Article 2, section I |
|---|---|---|---|---|
| Students expelled from College | Right to education and right to a life project | Restitution and rehabilitation | College registration in public university | Article 1, section III |

\* The declaration of political amnesty is an act of recognition of the victims and the right to resistance. It is a condition for all other reparations of Law 10,559/2002. The victim or his successors or dependents must request it (Article 2, § 2 of Law 10,559/2002).

\*\* The indemnity provided in this act is granted to the following persons in the following order: spouse, partner, descendants, ascendants, collateral relatives up to the fourth degree (Article 10 of Law 9,140/1995).

\*\*\* In case of death of the person with political amnesty, the right to economic compensation is transferred to his or her dependents. This includes compensation in monthly payments in cases of proven loss of employment status because of persecution, in other cases compensation of a single payment. The compensation (economic reparations in single or monthly payments) of the Act 10,559/2002 cannot cumulate. The compensation can be cumulative with restitutions and rehabilitations, except the reparation in monthly compensation which cannot cumulate with work reintegration. The compensation of Law 10,559/2002 can cumulate with the compensations of Law 9,140/1995.

\*\*\*\* All economic indemnity reparations of Law 10,559/2002 provide the right to exemption from income tax.

\*\*\*\*\* The Amnesty Commission understands that the right to compensation only applies to cases in which monitoring made other repressive measures tangible.

TABLE 6.2. *Individual and collective reparation policies under the Lula government (2003–10)*

| Type of measure | Body | Governmental and state actions |
|---|---|---|
| Official apology requests | Amnesty Commission (AC) | Amnesty Caravans |
| Recognition of the victims | Death and Disappeared Commission (DDC) | Report "Right to Memory and Truth" (Direito à Memória e à Verdade) |
| | AC | Project "Record of Oral History" (Marcas de Memórias) |
| | National Archive | Project "Revealed Memories" (Memórias Reveladas) |
| Public tributes | AC | Memory sessions of the Amnesty Caravans |
| | AC | Act of homage to the thirty years of the former political prisoners' hunger strike |
| | AC | Public act commemorating the thirty-year fight for amnesty |
| Public hearings | AC | Thematic public hearings on the labor movement |
| | AC | Public statements on the amnesty caravans |
| | AC | Forum of representative bodies of politically amnestied |
| | Legislative Branch (LB) | Special amnesty commission of the House of Representatives |
| | AC | Public hearing on the scope of the Amnesty Law of 1979 |
| | AC | Public hearing on the legal rights of the politically persecuted |
| Memorials, Monuments, and Signs | AC | Amnesty Memorial Project |
| | DDC | Project "Indispensable People" (Pessoas Imprescindíveis) |
| Bills | LB | Law of reparation to the National Union of Students |
| | Civil House | Bill on access to public information |
| | Civil House | Bill to create the National Commission of Truth |
| Education and dissemination | AC/DDC | Photographic exhibition |
| | AC | Seminars and events about amnesty and transitional justice |
| | AC | Cultural amnesties |
| | AC/DDC | Publication of teaching material |
| | AC/DDC | Official publications of memory |
| | AC | Publication of the *Political Amnesty and Transitional Justice* magazine |

the Ministry of Defense, which subjected the military command to civilian control; the creation of the Public Ministry to protect democratic rule and guarantee collective and individual civil rights; the creation of the Public Defender of the Union; the creation of educational programs in human rights for the police, promoted by the Ministries of Education and Justice; the extinction of the repressive apparatus, specifically the dismantlement of DOI-CODI (Department of Information Operations – Centre for Internal Defense Operations) and DOPS (Department of Political and Social Order); the repeal of the dictatorship's censorship law; the elimination of the DSI (Division of Institutional Security) related to direct and indirect public administration agencies; the creation of the Special Secretariat for Human Rights; varied and comprehensive reforms to the authoritarian legislative framework; and the creation of independent electoral courts with functional and administrative autonomy. In addition, the country is continually expanding institutions that uphold the rule of law in order to deter future human rights violations.

Hence, there is an undeniable institutionalization of political participation and political competence maintained regardless of the political group in power. In addition to significant judicial reforms, control mechanisms designed to ensure bureaucratic transparency have also been implemented. Reforms to the military and public security systems are pending.

## Truth and Memory

Brazil has made considerable progress toward implementing truth and memory projects. Besides publishing the book *Right to Truth and Memory*, the Special Secretariat for Human Rights maintains a photographic exhibition called "Right to Memory and Truth – the dictatorship in Brazil 1964–1985" ("Direito à Memória e à Verdade – a Ditadura no Brasil 1964–1985"), and it has recently released two publications, "The History of Children Victimized by the Dictatorship" ("História de Meninas e Meninos Marcados pela Ditadura") and "Women's Memories" ("Memórias do Feminino").

The Reference Center of Political Struggles in Brazil (1964–1985) – Revealed Memories (Memórias Reveladas) was created on May 13, 2009 and is coordinated by the National Archive.[8] The Center was designed to be a space of convergence for the dissemination of documents and the production of studies and research on the political regime in power from April 1, 1964 to March 15, 1985. It brings together

---

[8]   The Revealed Memories database contains the descriptions of the documentary collection kept by participating institutions. In some cases, it is possible to see cartographic, iconographic, and text documents, among others. It is also possible to search for electronic publications, virtual exhibitions, videos, and interviews at the Centre's webpage: http://www.memoriasreveladas.gov.br.

public and private institutions and individuals who possess documents related to the political history of Brazil under military rule. Part of the "truth from the repression" – which allows access to a particular version of the truth produced by the regime – is recorded in official documents of the military regime, available in the Revealed Memories Reference Center. These documents are filled with authoritarian ideology, evident in records that misconstrue facts and attempt to justify the widespread acts of human rights violations.

It is important to mention that some of the richest collections of archives from the repressive period are currently in the possession of the reparatory commissions, which have contributed to the construction of historical truth through the eyes of the politically persecuted: the "truth from the resistors." Without the work of these commissions, created under Cardoso's government, much of the information available on the history of repression would not exist. However, there can be no doubt that the Lula government's initiative, which sent a draft law to the congress to create a national truth commission, will contribute to a new and crucial stage of revelation and knowledge of the recent history of the country, laying the groundwork for collective memories that will enrich our national identity.

Perhaps with the creation of the national truth commission, the right to truth through research may be fully realized along with the release of the locations of the intelligence and repression centers directly connected to the centers of military command structure – CISA (Air Force Information Centre), CIE (Army Information Centre), and CENIMAR (Navy Information Centre) – and the files these centers contain. Uncovering this information would identify and make public the state and private structures employed to perpetrate human rights violations, thus shedding some light on torture practices, forced disappearances, and the killing methods used, then transmitting this information to the competent justice bodies. The location and opening of missing armed forces files and the location of the remains of the politically disappeared are still debated and unresolved issues in Brazil.

## Justice and the Rule of Law

The greatest obstacles to transitional justice in Brazil fall under the category of justice and restoration of equality before the law, which involves the obligation to investigate, prosecute, and punish human rights crimes.

There have been no criminal trials in Brazil for individuals who perpetrated human rights violations during the military dictatorship and a culture of impunity impedes the recognition of victims' rights to judicial protection. Taking into consideration this lack of respect for these rights, the enormous amount of crimes reported by the victims and presented to the commission in order to obtain amnesty, and the obligations Brazil has under the international human rights treaties it has ratified, the Amnesty Commission of the Ministry of Justice hosted a public hearing, "Limits and Possibilities for the Judicial Accountability of Perpetrators of Human Rights Violations during the State of Siege in Brazil," on July 31, 2008.

This event marked the first time that the Brazilian government officially addressed the lack of accountability, almost thirty years after the enactment of the amnesty law. The public hearing was sponsored by the executive branch and tasked with encouraging the rearticulation of national pro-amnesty initiatives and integrating the various initiatives and perspectives of the Brazilian Bar Association; the Public Ministry of São Paulo; various civil organizations such as the Association of Judges for Democracy, the International Centre for Justice and International Law (CEJIL), the Brazilian Association of the Politically Amnestied (ABAP), and the Nationalist and Democratic Military Association (ADNAM).

The hearing resulted in a Supreme Court lawsuit brought under the Allegation of Breach of Fundamental Precept (Argüição de Descumprimento de Preceito Fundamental, ADPF No. 153).[9] It should be noted that the legal controversy debated by the Ministry of Justice and brought to the Supreme Court by the Brazilian Bar Association was not new and came about after several other tentative initiatives. These attempts at pursuing accountability include the work of the Federal Public Ministry of São Paulo to obtain court rulings in civil suits on the legal liability of torturers from the DOI-CODI and legal cases brought by relatives of dead and missing persons, such as the charges filed by the family of journalist Vladimir Herzog that, in 1978, resulted in a judgment stating that his death was the state's responsibility.[10]

In the trial conducted in April 2010 on the ADPF 153, the Supreme Court, by a margin of seven votes to two, decided in favor of the applicability of the 1979 amnesty law under the 1988 constitution in relation to perpetrators of human rights crimes during authoritarian rule. The Supreme Court declared that the interpretation of a bilateral amnesty in the law was valid. The Court stated that the amnesty was a political agreement that established the basis for the democratic constitution of 1988 and that only the legislative branch would be able to review it. The practical implication of the ruling was the denial of the right to judicial protection for victims, strengthening the idea of "amnesty as impunity and oblivion."

---

[9]  The Allegation of Breach of Fundamental Precept is the constitutional procedure established in the Brazilian federal constitution to be used against any act by public agents that might violate a fundamental principle of the 1988 constitution (even if the act took place before the constitution's promulgation but continued to have effects in the present).

[10]  For more information about the case, Marlon Alberto Weichert, "Responsabilidade internacional do estado brasileiro na promoção da justiça transicional," in *Memória e verdade – A justiça de transição no estado democrático brasileiro*, ed. Inês Virgínia Prado Soares and Sandra Akemi Shimada Kishi (Belo Horizonte: Editora Fórum, 2009), 153–68.

In the case of *Gomes Lund v. Brazil* in November 2010, the Inter-American Court stated that the Brazilian Supreme Court's April 2010 decision condoned impunity for human rights violations by interpreting Law 6,683 as a blanket self-amnesty for state crimes. This verdict challenged the Supreme Court's ruling. At the moment, it is unlikely that the IACtHR decision will change Brazil's attitude toward the amnesty law and its implied impunity provisions. We discuss this further later in this chapter.

### Assessing the Fundamental Characteristics of Transitional Justice in Brazil

The main conclusion to draw from this overview is that Brazil has experienced an ambiguous amnesty process. On one hand, the amnesty law allowed for the transition from authoritarian rule to democracy. In addition, it is considered a victory for the politically persecuted who mobilized under the dictatorship to promote it. On the other hand, Law 6,683/1979 has also been interpreted in such a way as to ensure impunity for grave human rights violations. The constitution and the laws that established the reparations process (9,140/1995 and 10.559/2002) have partially restored the earlier emancipatory and reconciliatory intentions of the original concept of amnesty supported by Brazilian civil society. Therefore, the reparations process for those politically persecuted and amnestied (as established in democratic legislation) has served as the lynchpin for the transitional justice agenda, allowing for some form of accountability through reparations, truth and memory, giving visibility to victims' claims, enabling the contestation of the idea of "amnesty as impunity and oblivion," and generating engagement between civil society actors and the state.

While reparations alone do not constitute full accountability, it is important to emphasize that the process of developing the reparations program triggered a shift in perceptions of what the Brazilian amnesty was about (focusing on the victims and not on the perpetrators). The reparations process also led to the public recognition of state crimes (which was nearly impossible to accomplish by legal means due to the ambiguity of the crimes covered in the 1979 amnesty law). Finally, the process integrated the victims' social movements with other sectors of civil society, expanding the original claim for reparations (mainly from the labor unions) to a broader demand for memory, truth, and justice supported by several politicians and civil society groups.

Transitional justice processes in Brazil are accelerating because the reparation commissions are increasingly adept at recognizing several types of civil and human rights violations that took place during authoritarian rule. Initiatives such as the 2008 Brazilian Bar Association lawsuit against amnesty for state crimes and the 2009 proposal for a truth commission took place right after the Commission on the Dead and Disappeared published its final report (August 2007) and the Amnesty

Commission organized a public hearing on accountability for state crimes (July 2008). The Amnesty Commission also started visiting all the regions of the country with the Amnesty Caravans (April 2008 to the present), bringing the commissions' reports on violations to the attention of the general public.

Even after the progress made after twenty-five years of democratic governments in Brazil, a recent public opinion poll showed that only forty percent of the population supported accountability for state crimes committed during authoritarian rule while forty-five percent opposed it. When questioned about political crimes perpetrated by regime opponents, forty-nine percent considered the amnesty valid in comparison to the thirty-seven percent who wanted criminal accountability despite the amnesty law (and knowing that most of the crimes from the opposition had actually been prosecuted by the regime before the amnesty law).[11] The poll showed a divided country, a division reflected in the composition of the Brazilian legislature. This polarization partially accounts for why almost all the transitional justice initiatives in Brazil have taken place through the executive branch. Recently, the executive branch, far more than the legislature or the judiciary, has been the greatest proponent of recognizing the state's international obligations to protect human rights. Unfortunately, the judicial system continues to interpret the laws in a way that maintains the culture of impunity in place under the dictatorship.

Indeed, international experiences have shown that it is not possible to formulate a distribution of benefits that establishes a particular order in which transitional actions should be adopted, considering the number of different, successful combinations.[12] Hence, the fact that the Brazilian transitional process has favored the reparatory dimension rather than the prosecutorial one is not a mark of inadequacy, but a characteristic feature of the transitional Brazilian model. It is not possible to understand the so-called late justice claim – after so many years of silence and impunity – from civil society for truth, memory, and justice without considering the role that the gradual implementation of the reparation process plays in revealing the truth regarding serious human rights violations. The reparations process has given visibility to victims' claims and has challenged the assumption that the 1979 amnesty was a bilateral amnesty that automatically led to impunity.

It is a fact that transitional justice measures in Brazil are well behind those adopted in other Latin American countries such as Argentina and Chile, but the Brazilian case has many peculiarities. It would be unlikely for a country that lived a transition by "transformation"[13] and that took nearly ten years to complete the first cycle of

---

[11]  Datafolha pool, *Folha de S. Paulo*, June 7, 2010.
[12]  According to: Javier Ciurlizza, "Entrevista: Para um panorama global sobre a justiça de transição: Javier Ciurlizza responde," *Revista Anistia Política e Justiça de Transição* 1 (2009): 26.
[13]  Samuel Huntington, *The Third Wave: Democratization in the Late Twentieth Century* (Norman and London: University of Oklahoma Press, 1991), 126.

political liberalization (1979–88) to adopt measures with the same impact as those implemented in Argentina, where the military collapsed in the wake of total defeat by the British in the Falklands War. The Brazilian approach to reparations allowed society to explore different means of accountability and, as we can see in current debates, actually stimulated the involvement of social movements in the transitional justice agenda, which in turn sparked a demand for a truth commission and for criminal accountability for perpetrators.

Facile claims that the reparation process alienates society by offering a payoff for nonaccountability ignore reality. The reparation process has helped unite civil society in the dispute over amnesty, has provided visibility to the human rights violations the regime denied took place, and has promoted the development of memory and archival projects designed to illuminate these violations. In addition, the establishment of the commissions to implement the reparation program created new governmental players that work from inside the state to expand the transitional justice dimensions of memory, truth, and justice. With the consolidation of the reparation process and the recognition of state crimes, human rights violations became more public, which led to stronger pressure for historical clarification and to increasing doubts about the legitimacy of the assumed bilateralism of the 1979 amnesty. The reparatory processes simultaneously legitimated the amnesty for the victims and delegitimized the amnesty for the perpetrators. This has led to a gradual (and still ongoing) erosion of society's support for the idea of bilateral amnesty or, at least, to the recognition of the necessity of other transitional justice measures related to truth and memory. In conclusion, we can state that, in Brazil, reparations created greater opportunities for further accountability despite social resistance to changing the scope of the amnesty law.

In this sense, it is possible to identify at least three positive outcomes of the reparations process in Brazil's transitional justice. First, the work of the reparation commissions has advanced the search for truth, revealing stories and deepening awareness of the need to make all violations public. Second, the official acts of recognition by the state of serious human rights violations and the evidence collected to prove that those violations really happened have served as the factual basis for legal initiatives within the Public Ministry, encouraging the pursuit of justice in a context where the evidence of the vast majority of crimes was destroyed by the old regime during the transition. Finally, the reparation process is making a significant contribution toward sustainable memory policies by publishing essential works like the book *The Right to Truth and Memory* that officially acknowledges state crimes, or by sponsoring programs such as the Amnesty Caravans and the Amnesty Memorial[14] that

---

[14]  The Political Amnesty Memorial includes a museum, an archive, a site of conscience, and a tribute to the victims. The Memorial is being built in the city of Belo Horizonte, Minas Gerais State (to be inaugurated in 2013), and will encompass a permanent exhibition about the dictatorship and

advance individual and collective memory building and challenge Brazil's tradition of oblivion. The reparation process has made public, for the first time, historical evidence of wrongdoing and has provided access to security force documents of repression as well as to recordings of oral testimonies of the politically persecuted. Transitional justice in Brazil is a dynamic and evolving process, with noticeable progress in some areas (reparations) and disappointing setbacks in others (justice). Despite notable progress in transitional justice, more could and should be done to bring accountability for past crimes. The next section analyzes the obstacles to carrying out criminal prosecutions against human rights violators.

## THE CONTINUED ABSENCE OF CRIMINAL ACCOUNTABILITY IN BRAZIL

Legal and political factors explain the limitations on justice for past political violence in Brazil. We examine how political context and judicial culture combine to form "empty legalities," or what Pereira refers to as "authoritarian legalities,"[15] where the dictatorship's impunity remains in place despite the new democracy and its rule of law system.

Analyzing the development of transitional justice in a particular case involves verifying the pro-justice mobilization strategies employed by a group of players and the success of these strategies, whether in the political or legal sphere, against the barriers put up by their opponents from the old regime. Members of the old regime intend to maintain, to some extent, popular support, and thus will attempt to impede judicial proceedings that may tarnish their reputations. It is in this sense that Leonardo Filippini and Lisa Margarrell state that "[...] the success of a proper transition depends on the right action planning, observing all the components of the process."[16]

The restoration of the rule of law can take place in a two-way manner: by the establishment of minimum legal guarantees for the future, and by reparations and justice for past violations. José Zalaquett highlights that "The ethical objectives and measures [...] must be fulfilled facing the political reality of different transitions. These transitions impose different degrees of restriction on the action of new

---

the social struggle for amnesty in Brazil; a public square with artistic tributes to the victims; and an annex with a center for research and documentation that will gather all of the Amnesty Commission files collected over more than a decade of investigation. For more information on the Memorial see: Paulo Abrão and Marcelo D. Torelly, "Dictatorship, Victims and Memorialization in Brazil," in *Museums and Difficult Heritage*, ed. Jari Harju and Elisa Sarpo (Helsinki: Helsinki City Museum, forthcoming).

15  Anthony Pereira, *Political (In) Justice*, 191.
16  Leonardo Filippini and Lisa Magarrell, "Instituciones de la justicia de transición y contexto político," in *Entre el perdón y el paredón*, ed. Angelika Rettberg (Bogotá: Universidad de los Andes, 2005), 151.

authorities."[17] In the Brazilian case, initiatives with retroactive temporal coverage, such as the investigation of past crimes, face severe political constraints from the old regime because these investigations would directly implicate former regime members in human rights abuses. Measures of reparation for the victims and guarantees of future rights are more successful at breaking through political obstacles since these measures do not directly affect the members of the old regime and the limitations the regime imposed over the transition while it was still in power.

## Political Reasons

We identify at least three political causes for the persistence of the amnesty law and impunity in Brazil: authoritarian legacy, judicial complicity, and fragmented social movements.

*Authoritarian legacy.* The Brazilian transitional process was strongly influenced by the outgoing regime. Samuel Huntington classifies the Brazilian transition, along with the Spanish one, as a "transition by transformation" and states that "[...] the genius of the Brazilian transformation is that it is virtually impossible to say at what point Brazil stopped being a dictatorship and became a democracy."[18] The former regime controlled the democratization process from its very beginning. Authoritarian influence is apparent in the wording of the 1979 amnesty law and extended at least until 1985, when political forces that supported the dictatorship, despite strong popular pressure, prevented the approval of the constitutional amendment in favor of direct presidential elections. In the indirect elections of 1985, the democratic opposition candidate, Tancredo Neves (Brazilian Democratic Movement-MDB), made an alliance with a leader of the regime's party, José Sarney (formerly National Renewal Alliance – ARENA and Social Democratic Party – PSD, who subsequently joined the Party of the Brazilian Democratic Movement – PMDB), to become his vice president. The result was a winning alliance in the indirect election which represented a moment of reconciliation between the institutionalized opposition and former political sectors that supported the regime.

In Brazil, the transition was labeled as controlled because the military would only accept a "slow, gradual and safe transition." Military officers delegated power to politicians and bureaucrats who defended the legitimacy of the allegedly pacted transition and advised reconciliation with the majority of the opposition. In this context the old regime was able to sustain a bureaucratic process of forgiveness in which the military would forgive opposition members who had fought against it during

---

[17]  José Zalaquett, "La reconstrucción de la unidad nacional y el legado de violaciones de los derechos humanos," *Revista Perspectivas* Special Issue 2 (1999): 395.

[18]  Huntington, *The Third Wave*, 124–6.

the dictatorship, trying to turn the amnesty into a process of forgetfulness ("amnesty as impunity and oblivion"). Victims rejected this concept of forgiveness because they did not consider their struggle against the authoritarian regime as criminal, but instead as resistance against tyranny.

The Brazilian dictatorship relied on two key mechanisms to ensure a sufficient level of legitimacy and control over the transition: the political dividends from the implementation of a national state developmentalist project (the so-called economic miracle) which, for a long period of time substantially strengthened the Brazilian economy; and the semantic construction of a discourse of fear, describing the members of the armed resistance as "terrorists," and the opposition in general as "subversives" and as "communists" in the Cold War context. Much of Brazilian society, fearing widespread chaos and remembering the days of economic growth, accepted this discourse. Fear tactics helped portray the opposition as enemies of the country and later depicted the amnesty as a necessary political pact for reciprocal reconciliation under the perceived threat of institutional instability or a return to authoritarianism.

During the fight for amnesty, Brazilian society was heavily mobilized in support of the approval of a "broad, general and unrestricted" amnesty law, that is: for all political prisoners, including those involved in armed conflict and violent political crimes (what this chapter defines as "amnesty as freedom and reparation").[19] The campaign for amnesty represented the return of public demonstrations, marches, and demands for rights, which fostered the awakening of an oppressed society and expanded citizen participation in the political sphere.

Despite protracted campaigning, the proposal for a broad amnesty was defeated in the congress, where the bill for a restricted amnesty from the military government was approved instead.[20] The regime's control over the transition played a large part in the decision since one-third of the national congress consisted of so-called bionic senators, parliamentarians appointed by the executive branch rather than popularly elected. It was just after this period of civil society awakening that the concept of bilateral amnesty started to take shape in a judicial system supervised by the executive branch. The amnesty law was enacted six years before the end of military rule, allowing for authoritarian control over the amnesty and transition process.

With the increasing disclosure that many disappearances and deaths were the result of state action, social pressure for criminal investigation increased, which led the judicial branch to systematically broaden the interpretive scope of the law.

---

[19] See Gilney Viana and Perly Cirpiano, *Fome de liberdade – A luta dos presos políticos pela anistia* (São Paulo: Fundação Perseu Abramo, 2009).

[20] Danyelle Nilin Gonçalves, "Os múltiplos sentidos da anistia," *Revista Anistia Política e Justiça de Transição* 1(2009): 280.

Courts began to consider the crimes of state agents as "related to political crimes" and also began to enforce the law even for crimes that occurred after 1979, outside the temporal scope of the law (such as those responsible for the *Rio Centro* case in 1980) in the name of "national pacification."

Over the years, the motto of "broad, general and unrestricted" amnesty for the politically persecuted, demanded by organized civil society and denied by the regime, became a "broad, general and unrestricted" amnesty to "both sides" displaying the strength of the regime's control. The regime was capable of manipulating popular support for the amnesty into a public guarantee of a supposed political agreement between the opposition and the existing regime that would initiate the transition to democracy. Challenging the assumption that the amnesty defended by civil society would cover crimes of state agents, Heloisa Greco asserts that:

> In the fight for a broad, general, and unrestricted amnesty, the political initiative lies with organized civil society, not with the government or its institutions. The subjects or main players are the militants of amnesty entities, the exiled and the political prisoners. The locus of this initiative, the place of action and discourse, or better yet, the place of history, is the seizing of the City as a political space. That is the rupture in the historical process in which [the regime] establishes that political space or institutional arena.[21]

The concept of a reciprocal amnesty, built by the military regime and strengthened by its power over the slow liberalization process, would be explicitly endorsed by the democratic judiciary in 2010 and implicitly by civil society before that. The following democratization years witnessed an increasingly fragmented network of political activists who did not successfully pressure the judiciary to investigate past crimes.[22]

*The judicial branch and the "legalized" dictatorship.* The Brazilian judiciary's interpretations of the 1979 amnesty law validated the notion that the political transition depended on forgiving or ignoring the regime's crimes and establishing a supposedly bilateral agreement. Law No 6,683 has been understood as bilateral, implicitly including state agents' crimes never mentioned in the text of the amnesty law. This interpretation reveals another important political institutional feature of the dictatorship and the Brazilian transition: the complicity of the judiciary in supporting the authoritarian regime's measures.

The table produced by Anthony Pereira for his comparative study of Brazil, Argentina, and Chile illustrates how each of the three regimes sought to "legalize" their dictatorship through illegitimate state actions (Table 6.3).

---

[21]   Greco, "*Dimensões fundacionais da luta pela anistia,*" 203.
[22]   It is worth pointing out that some persecuted families presented important initiatives, but these are isolated cases within the broad set of the persecuted people that could have sought justice and did not do it.

TABLE 6.3. *Features of authoritarian legality in Brazil, Chile, and Argentina*

| Features | Brazil (1964–85) | Chile (1973–90) | Argentina (1976–83) |
|---|---|---|---|
| Declaration of state of siege at the time of the coup | no | yes | yes |
| Suspension of parts of old constitution | yes | yes | yes |
| Eventual promulgation of new constitution | yes | yes | no |
| Military tribunals used to prosecute many civilian opponents and dissidents | yes | yes | no |
| Military courts wholly insulated from civilian judiciary | no | yes | yes |
| Habeas Corpus for political cases recognized in practice | 1964–8 1979–85 | no | no |
| Purges of Supreme Court | some removals and the increase in the number of judges | no | yes |
| Purges of rest of judiciary | limited | limited | yes |
| Judge's irremovability revoked | yes | yes | yes |

Source: Pereira, *Political (In)Justice*, 23.

In the table, it is evident that even though exceptional measures are very similar in the three countries, Brazil reflects the highest participation of civilians in the process, since one can verify their presence in military courts. The table also implicitly demonstrates judicial support of the military regime's legitimacy, evident in the smaller number of purges in the Brazilian judicial branch in comparison to those that took place in the Argentinean judicial branch.

Anthony Pereira highlights another important issue when comparing Brazil and Chile: while prosecutors were members of the armed forces in Chile, in Brazil they were civilians appointed by the regime. Civilian adherence to the Brazilian military regime (which qualifies as a civil-military dictatorship) was mostly directed toward the economic development project, but was also due to the ideology the military defended. This ideological agreement had a particular effect in the judicial branch, which could have been the last source of protection for society against oppression but was filled with legal practitioners who supported the dictatorship. It was very rare to see judges stand up to, much less oppose, the regime.

The absence of a lustration process in the postdictatorship judicial branch has allowed for the persistence of an elitist and authoritarian mentality. Judicial appointments occur slowly, with new members selected through public competitive examination, as stated in the new democratic constitution. To illustrate this point, the last judge of the Supreme Court appointed by the military dictatorship left office in 2003, eighteen years after the end of the dictatorship. In this case, he was not removed, but retired. This enabled the survival of a conservative mentality in the Brazilian legal system that has been maintained across generations.

As shown under the legal reasons behind the lack of investigation of state crimes, the judiciary's perception of the dictatorship, the 1979 amnesty, and how the two relate to the rule of law is fundamental to the Supreme Court's politicized decision to proceed with the nonimplementation of justice for crimes committed by the regime.

*Fragmented social movements.* The performance of civil society in the postdemocratization years is an important factor necessary to understanding the political roots of the state of impunity in Brazil. Civil society mobilized to push the government to grant amnesty for the politically persecuted, even if it did not achieve the desired outcome. Especially after the enactment of the 1988 constitution, the traditional agendas of human rights movements related to the fight for political freedom were replaced by "new kinds of social movements" characterized more by their criticism of the structural deficits of institutional arrangements than by their proposals for broad political alternatives.[23]

These social movements supported marginalized causes, such as land reform, gender rights, the right to nondiscrimination based on race and ethnicity, the rights of children and adolescents, the environmental movement, the rights of pensioners and the elderly, the rights of disabled people, and so forth. The civil society agenda after 1988 was largely fragmented in comparison to the days of dictatorship when all of the social movements had joined forces against the regime. The post-1988 social movements returned to their issue-specific agendas and began to realign their work with international players who shared their concerns, such as thematic international agencies and NGOs.

Therefore, the fight for transitional justice in Brazil was not a priority for these specialized social movements. Rather, the struggle was left in the hands of two specific groups: the relatives of the dead and disappeared, composed of a small number of families that continued to voice their demands for justice but had lost the capacity for widespread social mobilization; and the labor unions and lobbies, mainly composed of those who had been dismissed or prevented from working during the dictatorship for political reasons or because they had exercised their right of association. Sustained campaigning by victims' relatives resulted in the passage of Law 9,140/1995, which recognized the deaths and disappearance of opponents of the

---

[23]  Dieter Rucht, "Sociedade como projeto – Projetos na sociedade. Sobre o papel dos movimentos sociais," *Civitas – Revista de Ciências Sociais* 2 (2002): 19.

regime and compensated their families. The struggles of the labor unions resulted in the promulgation of Law 10,559/2002, which set up reparation measures for the other acts of exception (not only for union members but also for those who had been exiled, lived underground, etc.).

Undoubtedly, social pressure is the foundation for the implementation of transitional measures, especially in the Brazilian context where the democratic transition focused more on the establishment of free elections than on the pursuit of justice. Assessing this issue, Ruti Teitel states that "Civil society plays a large role in keeping this discussion [of transitional justice] alive, in pursuing what is necessary, more than just elections, for a transition to be completed."[24] In Brazil, due to the regime's control of the transition agenda and because of the limited success of the most affected victims to generate wider support from society, the issue of accountability was not considered as important as other social claims. Agencies and institutions such as the Public Ministry created several specialized groups focused on a variety of social issues. However, the creation of the first group dedicated to transitional justice only occurred in September 2010, with the establishment of a working group on truth and memory at the federal level.

The quest for accountability is often constrained by a practical desire to move forward, for as José Zalaquett points out, "after a gradual process of political opening, the worst violations have become part of a relatively distant past and there is a certain amount of popular forgiveness."[25] The addition of a time factor, in combination with the minimal support of civil society, generated another major political obstacle to the pursuit of criminal accountability in Brazil.

Catalina Smulovitz proposes a similar diagnosis; by comparing the Brazilian case to Argentina, she highlights at least three key distinctions that determine why the two countries diverged in their decisions on whether to conduct trials for human rights violations. These are: the fact that the Brazilian military regime had control over the transition agenda, unlike in Argentina where the intensification of internal unrest following the Argentinean defeat in the Falklands War crippled the military; the much larger amount of civil society campaigning for human rights trials in Argentina; and the larger time lapse between the most serious violations and the restoration of democracy in Brazil. Brazilian dictators managed to devise an exit strategy that guaranteed impunity by political means, in contrast to what occurred in Argentina:

[...] the intensification of intra-military conflicts, which took place as a consequence of the defeat in the Falkland Islands, imposed great difficulties on the

[24] Ruti G. Teitel, "Ruti Teitel responde (interview by Marcelo D. Torelly)," *Revista Anistia Política e Justiça de Transição* 3 (2010): 36.

[25] José Zalaquett, "La reconstrucción de la unidad nacional," 11.

Armed Forces to internally agree on a global exit plan. Nevertheless, the limitations encountered by the Executive Branch when attempting to impose its authority on society and the Armed Forces did not stop it from trying to politically administer the transition.[26]

Moreover, it is worth noting that even with the low levels of Brazilian civil society mobilization, the existing advances in accountability through the reparation commissions are the result of the continued efforts of the relatives of the dead and disappeared and those labor union workers dismissed for political reasons, even though such attempts have been disorganized and fragmented. This civil society mobilization for accountability reached such high levels that the armed forces were forced to abandon the position that Stanley Cohen describes as "literal denial," where perpetrators of a given violation defend themselves from the possibility of accountability using the laconic statement "nothing happened."[27]

More civil society interest in transitional justice began in 2002, with the approval of Law 10,559/2002, which held the state accountable for all repressive acts except "death or disappearance." With the passage of this law, new social movements following broad transitional justice agendas emerged. Groups devoted to advocacy for the right to reparation as well as those linked to labor unions of workers politically persecuted during the great strikes of the 1980s were among these movements. Recently, demands have expanded to include calls for accountability for torture, a truth commission, the right to memory, and the right to full reparation. Transitional justice issues are no longer exclusively the domain of those directly harmed by the dictatorship's repressive apparatus. Instead, these demands reflect a collective interest in strengthening the principles of democracy. With this newfound support for accountability coupled with important reports by the Commission on the Dead and Disappeared and the Amnesty Commission on grave human rights violations committed by state agents during the dictatorship, legal constraints on the prosecution of these violations have again come to the forefront of national debate.

### Legal Reasons

Currently, the main legal obstacle to accountability is the interpretation of the amnesty law. The dictatorship's judicial branch interpretation – recently reconfirmed by the democratic Supreme Court in the ADPF 153 case – reinforced the

---

[26] Carlos Acuña and Catalina Smulovitz, "Militares en la transición argentina: del gobierno a la subordinación constitucional," in *Historizar el pasado vivo en América Latina*, ed. Anne Pérotin-Dumon accessed July 31, 2011, http://www.historizarelpasadovivo.cl/downloads/acunasmulovitz.pdf, 83.

[27] Stanley Cohen, *Estado de negación – Ensayo sobre atrocidades y sufrimientos* (Buenos Aires: Buenos Aires University Law School/British Council Argentina, 2005), 124.

nondemocratic approach to rule of law in Brazil. The judicial branch also expanded the scope of the amnesty law. First it included a broader range of beneficiaries, adding members of the authoritarian regime. Then it extended the time frame to include events that occurred after 1979.

The Supreme Court's decision in ADPF 153 recognized the dictatorship as a legitimate rule of law regime and thus validated its interpretation of the 1979 amnesty law. It accepted the notion that a bilateral agreement between the regime and the institutionalized opposition initiated Brazil's democratization process. The Court recognized that essential elements of a democratic rule of law were put in place after the 1964 coup and were codified in the nondemocratic 1967 and 1969 constitutions. By legitimizing the alleged pact between two sides, the Court validated the use of political measures to justify the removal of a set of crimes from judicial review, thus denying in practice a citizen's right to redress for human rights violations committed by the authoritarian regime.

Eros Roberto Grau, the judge who presented the case to the Court, stated that "everyone who knows our history knows that the political agreement existed, resulting in the text of Law No. 6,683/1979," endorsing the belief in national pacification through oblivion and reiterating the authoritarian semantics of equating resistance with terrorism. Still, he continued: "What would be desired now in an attempt to, rather than rewrite, reconstruct the history? That the transition had been made, a day after the time of that agreement, with blood and tears? With violence?"[28]

A set of judges believed that the written law, though unpalatable because it amounted to concealing torture, was useful to national reconciliation and could not be changed because it had already achieved its intended results. In other words, the amnesty was given to both sides in 1979 and could not be removed only for one side in 2010. Only two judges of the Court, Ricardo Lewandowski and Carlos Ayres Britto, voted in favor of the lawsuit presented by the Brazilian Bar Association because they believed that amnesty, if applied to torture and crimes against humanity, would not only be unconstitutional but also contrary to international law; further, the notion of a bilateral amnesty would be meaningless. Granting amnesty to both sides in the same act would not nullify the fact that the regime was receiving a self-amnesty.

Nevertheless, the most important impact of the Supreme Court's decision was that the law of 1979 was deemed legally valid under the new democratic constitution, establishing a direct and objective continuity between the legal system of the dictatorship and the democratic one and preemptively prohibiting any investigation of criminal offenses that occurred between 1961 and 1979. Until the Court's decision in the 2010 ADPF 153 case, it was possible to treat the amnesty law as a legal obstacle

---

[28]  Grau, Eros Roberto. ADPF 153. Brasília: Supremo Tribunal Federal, voto do ministro relator, abril de 2010.

that could be circumvented to pursue criminal accountability for certain crimes. In the aftermath of that decision, this possibility was severely restricted. Today, the Supreme Court's decision is undoubtedly the most significant legal obstacle to the progress of criminal accountability in Brazil. The only legal challenge that the 1979 law currently faces is the recent decision of the IACtHR in the *Gomes Lund v. Brazil* case, discussed in the following section.

## CONCLUSIONS: THE PURSUIT OF TRUTH AND JUSTICE ALTERNATIVES IN BRAZIL

When outlining conclusions on transitional justice in Brazil we begin with the certainty that reparations constitute both the core of social mobilization to expand the transitional justice agenda and the most effective route to historical clarification of the crimes committed by the Brazilian dictatorship. The reparation process has enabled the uncovering of historical truth, access to documents, records of testimonies of the persecuted, and the holding of public hearings on the subject.

Nevertheless, it is clear that the two major challenges facing the Brazilian transition are truth and justice. From an ethical point of view, the disclosure of the past and the processing of crimes represent a commitment to nonrepetition. Meanwhile from a strategic point of view, applying amnesties to a certain set of crimes combined with selective trials for certain acts (i.e., crimes against humanity) deepens democracy and respect for human rights, prescriptively applying what Tricia Olsen et al. describe as the "justice balance" model.[29]

After the progress made by the reparation commissions, the principal means of breaking the silence surrounding past crimes involves the establishment of a truth commission. After a recent public debate on the creation of such a commission, which occurred at the National Conference on Human Rights and included delegates from all over the country, the proposal to create a truth commission was included in the Third National Plan for Human Rights. A working group, specially assigned to this task by the president of the republic, formulated the bill detailing the structure of the new truth commission. Bill No. 7,376/2010 was approved by congress as Law No. 12,528 on November 18, 2011, creating a commission with the following characteristics (Table 6.4).

Justice alternatives today focus on three main possibilities: international courts, domestic civil suits, and domestic criminal cases outside the reach of the amnesty law. International justice is likely to involve filing claims with the IACHR for adjudication in the Inter-American Court. The IACtHR, however, has no means of enforcing its rulings and can only recommend that the state investigate and punish

[29] Olsen, Payne, and Reiter, *Transitional Justice in Balance*.

TABLE 6.4. *Truth Commission (Law No. 12,528/2011)*

| Truth Commission (Law No. 12,528/2011) | |
| --- | --- |
| Commission objectives | – Examine and clarify the severe human rights violations committed between 1946 and 1988;<br>– Produce the final report |
| Number of members | Seven, appointed by the president |
| Duration of members' mandate | For the entire process which ends with the publication of the report |
| Commission's mandate | – Clarify the facts and circumstances of severe cases of human rights violations that occurred in Brazil between 1946 and 1988;<br>– Promote detailed awareness of cases of torture, deaths, forced disappearances, concealed corpses, and the perpetrators of such crimes, even if they took place abroad;<br>– Identify and make public the structures, venues, institutions, and the circumstances related to the practice of human rights violations and their possible connections to several different state institutions and society;<br>– Send all information that might help locate and identify bodies and remains of missing people to public agencies;<br>– Cooperate with all governmental agencies in order to investigate human rights violations;<br>– Recommend the adoption of public policies and measures to ensure the nonrecurrence of human rights violations and to promote effective national reconciliation; and<br>– Based on evidence in the final report, promote the reconstruction of the case histories of severe human rights violations and recommend full state cooperation so that assistance to victims of such violations is provided. |
| Commission's powers | – Receive testimony, information, data, and documents that have been sent voluntarily, ensuring the nonidentification of the owner or witness when asked;<br>– Request information, data and documents from governmental bodies and entities, even when classified;<br>– Call in people for interviews or testimony who are not directly related to the facts and circumstances of a case;<br>– Monitor the state's diligence in collecting or retrieving information, documents, and data;<br>– Promote public hearings;<br>– Request protection from public bodies for anyone in a threatening situation because of his/her collaboration with the National Commission of Truth;<br>– Promote partnerships with national or international, public or private agencies and entities to exchange information, data, and documents; and<br>– Request the assistance of public bodies and entities. |
| Commission's duration | Two years |

human rights violators and compensate the victims. Because the IACtHR depends on Brazilian courts to implement its decisions, IACtHR judgments may not be enforced due to the rampant culture of impunity in the Brazilian judiciary. However, international court rulings, like the IACtHR's decision in the *Gomes Lund v. Brazil* case, play a key role in mobilizing society and exerting pressure on the national judiciary. Also, some progress may be possible in the political arena since international condemnation calls into question the authoritarian reading of the amnesty law as "amnesty as oblivion and impunity" and reinforces the idea that amnesties are possible for freedom.

The IACtHR does not limit its jurisdiction to legal remedy; it has also recommended complementary reparation and truth efforts. Specifically, in addition to demonstrating that the Supreme Court's interpretation of amnesty for state crimes is incompatible with the American Convention on Human Rights (hereinafter American Convention), the IACtHR also demanded that the state locate the remains of guerrilla members killed during the massacres in Araguaia that took place between 1972 and 1974. The Brazilian government has partially complied. It formed a working group that has begun excavation in the Araguaia region to locate the remains.

The main obstacle to implementing the current IACtHR decision is the Supreme Court's interpretation of the 1979 amnesty law. Some conservative legal scholars have stated that Brazil should not accept the IACtHR jurisdiction for events that occurred before the country recognized the jurisdiction of the Inter-American Court in 1998. This position violates the IACtHR precedent that permanent crimes (such as forced disappearance) are considered ongoing until the victims' remains are located, as discussed by Par Engstrom and Gabriel Pereira in this volume.

However, the positions taken by the Supreme Court and the IACtHR may not be as incompatible as they seem. The Supreme Court states that under the 1988 Brazilian constitution, the 1979 amnesty is valid for all crimes. The IACtHR states that amnesty for certain crimes (e.g., human rights violations) violates the American Convention. The Supreme Court ruling is based on the Brazilian constitution and the IACtHR ruling is based on international agreements. Thus, it is possible to see the IACtHR position as complementary to the Supreme Court's decision. International law, and more specifically the American Convention, does not expressly prohibit amnesty. It does, however, limit its application as Mark Freeman and Max Pensky discuss in their chapter in this volume. Without repealing the 1979 amnesty law, the judiciary could exclude some crimes from it, thereby adapting the original scope of the law to Brazil's international obligations under the American Convention. This strategy has been used in Chile. Chilean domestic criminal courts try cases of human rights violations while continuing to grant amnesty for less grave crimes committed by the regime. For this to occur in Brazil, however, the Supreme Court would have to recognize the IACtHR's jurisdiction over events prior to 1998.

Brazil remains divided over accountability for human rights violations. Unlike their counterparts in other Latin American countries, Brazilian social movements have not consistently used the judiciary to challenge and weaken the amnesty law. By questioning the Brazilian Supreme Court's 2010 decision to uphold a bilateral interpretation of the 1979 amnesty law, the IACtHR's judgement in the *Gomes Lund v. Brazil* case may galvanize public opposition to the law, building pressure for change. This pressure could increase with factual revelations from the proposed truth commission. Moreover, many victims might see the IACtHR decision as an opportunity to circumvent the Supreme Court's ruling and file more lawsuits in local courts.

Domestic courts also play a key role. The following legal openings exist for prosecution despite the persistence of the amnesty law: the investigation of torture, disappearances, and deaths that occurred after August 1979 and are therefore not covered by the amnesty law; accountability in civil courts for severe human rights violations, particularly through declaratory actions in which the state is deemed responsible for crimes that cannot be punished under criminal law; the implementation of Argentine-style truth trials with the involvement of the judiciary in revealing concealed evidence; and the prosecution of forced disappearances as permanent and ongoing crimes until the victim's body or remains appear, which removes these crimes from the scope of the 1979 amnesty law.

In all cases, mobilization on the part of civil society is key. It feeds the transitional justice agenda, particularly in contexts of transition by transformation where authoritarian enclaves retain control. The strategies identified to circumvent the amnesty law depend on human rights and prodemocracy movements that actively engage state institutions. Even individuals can challenge impunity by demanding justice. The progress on reparations and its capacity to spread to other transitional justice mechanisms illustrates the importance of social movements that create institutional opportunities to advance a democratic agenda despite the political and legal obstacles that still exist.

# 7

# De Facto and De Jure Amnesty Laws

## The Central American Case

### Emily Braid and Naomi Roht-Arriaza

At the beginning of this volume, Kathryn Sikkink argues that the justice cascade is the product of separate streams that converge to form an international norm of accountability. She points out that there is a particularly "strong accountability stream" coming from Latin America, focused on domestic prosecutions for past human rights violations. While there is undeniable evidence of numerous criminal prosecutions in the Southern Cone of Latin America, particularly in Chile and Argentina (see Par Engstrom and Gabriel Pereira's chapter on Argentina in this volume), the case of Central America is not so clear cut. It represents an example within the region where accountability streams have not yet succeeded in cascading or washing away persistent cultures of impunity. Central America thus points to the limitations of the justice cascade.

To examine the limited ability of the international accountability norm embodied in the justice cascade to permeate domestic legal systems, this chapter considers the cases of Guatemala and El Salvador. Despite significant anti-impunity rulings, recommendations of official investigatory commissions, and decisions issued by UN human rights bodies, the IACHR, and the IACtHR, amnesty laws in both countries remain on the books, although they are applied in different ways. However, it is not the existence of an amnesty law per se that perpetuates impunity, but rather the lack of political will to prosecute and the existence of threats, corruption, and a climate of fear that have made it difficult to hold the powerful accountable for past (or present) violations. The international cascade toward individual criminal prosecutions has been more of an inconsistent trickle within the political and legal spheres of El Salvador and Guatemala. Only in 2011, almost thirty years after the worst of the human rights violations, did the trickle toward accountability accelerate in Guatemala, although it is not clear if this will dry up before it becomes a consolidated cascade. In El Salvador, impunity still seems impervious to trickles, streams, and cascades, although some evidence of change may be seen.

The persistence of impunity in Central America can be attributed to a number of factors. First, while these countries have in fact signed and ratified many of the international treaties that contain prosecutorial obligations to investigate and try perpetrators of human rights abuses, such treaties have limited enforceability at the domestic level unless and until their provisions are incorporated into national criminal law[1] and despite repeated orders from the Inter-American Court to investigate and prosecute violations there is not much the Court can do besides nagging when governments ignore its decisions. Second, powerful military and civilian figures – including former security forces and former insurgents – responsible for ordering human rights crimes are singularly uninterested in criminal investigations into the past.[2] Civil society in El Salvador and Guatemala is weak and few civil society actors focus on the crimes of the past given the magnitude of more recent challenges. These include a marked lack of citizen security due to the actions of gangs and drug cartels, some of which evolved from, and still have ties to, the former security forces. Even if the political will to prosecute is present, shaky, corruption-ridden prosecutorial and judicial systems in both countries do not reliably meet the minimum requirements of objectivity, effectiveness, and impartiality.[3] The prosecutors' offices have had a particularly bad reputation for corruption and ineptitude (which is now changing at least at the time of writing in Guatemala), and the courts have proven uneven and inconsistent in their rulings despite significant reform.

These systems are a product of decades of authoritarian rule during which economic, military, and political elites failed to protect human rights and to prosecute those responsible for their violation.[4] Both El Salvador and Guatemala experienced military-dominated counterinsurgency wars that reached their violent peaks during the 1980s. The twelve-year Salvadoran civil war, beginning in 1979, killed an estimated seventy-five thousand people.[5] Meanwhile, the thirty-six-year Guatemalan

---

[1]  These treaties include the Geneva Conventions of 1949, the 1948 Genocide Convention, the 1984 Convention against Torture and Other Cruel, Inhuman or Degrading Treatment or Punishment, and the 1994 Inter-American Convention on Forced Disappearance of Persons.

[2]  See Naomi Roht-Arriaza, "Making the State do Justice: Transnational Prosecutions and International Support for Criminal Investigations in Post-Armed Conflict Guatemala," *Chicago Journal of International Law* 81 (2008):79–106.

[3]  UN Security Council, Annex, *From Madness to Hope: The 12-year War in El Salvador: Report of the Commission on the Truth for El Salvador*, S/25500 (United States Institute of Peace, 1993), part V, "Recommendations."

[4]  Margaret Popkin, "El Salvador: A Negotiated End to Impunity?" in *Impunity and Human Rights in International Law and Practice*, ed. Naomi Roht-Arriaza (Oxford: Oxford University Press, 1995), 199.

[5]  UN Security Council Annex, *From Madness to Hope: The 12-year War in El Salvador*, S/25500 (United States Institute of Peace, 1993), 18–25. Sieder gives the figure as fifty thousand. Rachel Sieder, "War, Peace and Memory Politics in Central America," in Barahona de Brito Enríquez, and Aguilar, *The Politics of Memory*, 164–5.

conflict originating in 1960 resulted in approximately two hundred thousand deaths, including tens of thousands of disappeared and "acts of genocide" against groups of Mayan origin.[6] The conflicts in El Salvador and Guatemala ended with the signing of peace accords and transitions to elected government. The new governments continued to face constraints on democracy due to weak checks and balances and the persistent power of the military and economic elites over the political system.[7] A culture of impunity prevailed, which included one or more amnesty laws that accompanied each country's peace processes. These amnesty laws remain in force today.

Some evidence, nonetheless, supports the justice cascade claims regarding the accountability norm's diffusion at the national level. Guatemala's 1996 amnesty law, for example, explicitly excludes most serious human rights violations and has generally not been the major impediment to prosecutions. The El Salvador Supreme Court's 2000 decision to uphold the 1993 blanket amnesty left room for case-by-case evaluation of the applicability of amnesty.[8] These changes in law and legal culture result from the streams Sikkink identifies in her chapter in this volume: victims' relatives and human rights organizations and activists within and outside the countries, the influence of the United Nations in drafting peace accords, domestic courts, and regional and foreign courts. These accountability efforts are noteworthy because they have come about in a highly adverse set of circumstances. Unlike the killings, torture, and disappearances in the Southern Cone, which largely affected a vocal and educated middle class able to lobby nationally and internationally, the crimes committed in these Central American countries largely targeted poor peasants (who in Guatemala were mostly indigenous Maya) less able to mobilize such resources during and immediately after the conflicts. The political parties and social forces that governed during the height of the violations remained in place in El Salvador until recently; in Guatemala, such forces continue to hold a large quota of power. Drugs and other smuggling, private security forces, and shadowy "parallel powers" created a far greater degree of continuing insecurity than elsewhere in the Americas.

This chapter explores the mixed results of the efforts at accountability in Central America. El Salvador's 1993 blanket amnesty continues to impede quests for justice, although some progress was made in 2011 through foreign courts. The more

---

[6] Commission for Historical Clarification, "Conclusions: The Tragedy of the Armed Confrontation," *Guatemala: Memory of Silence*, (Guatemala City: Guatemalan Commission for Historical Clarification, 1999), http://shr.aaas.org/guatemala/ceh/report/english/conc1.html.

[7] Each country's particular history of conflict and subsequent amnesty laws will be discussed in depth in the country case sections.

[8] Naomi Roht-Arriaza, "Impunity in Latin America: National Courts and Continuing Challenges" (paper presented at the "Amnesty in the Age of Accountability: Brazil in Comparative and International Perspective" Conference, University of Oxford, United Kingdom, October 22–23, 2010).

partial, limited nature of the amnesty passed in Guatemala has at least improved the chances of cases finding some traction within the country's domestic legal system. Ultimately, once the cases manage, despite significant obstacles, to come to trial, lower courts have for the most part interpreted the amnesty laws so as not to preclude prosecution. Even the highest courts have often upheld decisions to prosecute, although they have been ambivalent on related issues and at times have bent over backward to protect powerful defendants; these decisions have not turned on the existence or validity of an amnesty.

The following sections of this chapter examine the various struggles to apply or circumvent amnesty laws in Guatemala and El Salvador, first outlining the history of both countries' armed conflict and then presenting the challenges to amnesty and impunity at the international, regional, and national levels. The chapter will conclude with some final thoughts on the degree to which these challenges provide evidence of a justice cascade in Central America.

## GUATEMALA

The end of Guatemala's armed conflict was less a pacted transition than an unspoken victory for the army, mediated by UN supervision of the peace accords signed December 12, 1996. The Guatemalan umbrella guerrilla group, the National Guatemalan Revolutionary Unity (UNRG) was all but destroyed. For much of the early 1990s, the political elite remained subordinate to the military.[9] In this climate, the 1996 National Reconciliation Law (NRL) was passed six days after the signing of the peace accords. While the immediate justification for the law was to construct the legal basis for the reincorporation of members of the URNG into Guatemala society, the NRL also established provisions for "extinguishing criminal responsibility" for crimes committed by members of the military, civil patrollers, and politicians between the start of the armed conflict and the date of the law's passage.[10] Various articles of the law apply to members of the armed insurgency and state actors. Article 2 authorizes amnesty for political crimes against the state committed by the insurgency during the internal armed conflict, while article 3 establishes the common crimes related to those political crimes that are also eligible for amnesty. Article 5 of the law authorizes the courts to grant amnesty to state actors (or members of any other force established by law such as civil patrols) for common crimes perpetrated in the armed conflict with the objective of preventing, impeding, pursuing, or repressing the political and related common crimes committed by the insurgents.[11]

[9]  Sieder, "War, Peace and Memory Politics in Central America," 167–8.
[10]  Margaret Popkin, "Guatemala's National Reconciliation Law: Combating Impunity or Continuing it?" *Revista* 24 (1996): 174.
[11]  Ibid.

The relationship between the crimes committed and the preventive goal must be "rational and objective," and the crimes must not have been committed for personal motives. Article 6 establishes that the amnesty provisions apply to state actors for actions that were ordered, carried out, or not carried out to avoid a greater harm, as well as to acts related to the peace negotiations, all of which are considered of a political nature.[12]

Two other articles of the 1996 NRL explicitly recognize international law limitations to its scope. Article 8 states that "exemption from criminal responsibility will not apply to crimes of genocide, torture and forced disappearance" in conformity with internal legislation and international treaties ratified by Guatemala.[13] However, the article leaves cases of extrajudicial execution by the security forces and deliberate and arbitrary killings by the armed opposition open to the interpretation of the courts regarding the application of amnesty.[14] Whether the NRL is applicable is decided on a case-by-case basis: Article 11 states that "crimes that are outside the scope of the present law … or that do not allow for the extinction of criminal liability [that is, that are not subject to a statute of limitations] according to the international treaties adopted or ratified by Guatemala, will be processed in accordance with the proceedings established in the Guatemalan Code of Criminal Procedure."[15] How these articles shape challenges to the 1996 NRL at international, regional, and domestic levels are discussed in the following section.

### Applicability of International Human Rights Treaty Law

During the late 1980s and early 1990s, several amnesty laws were passed as part of the Esquipulas peace process, but these had little impact and were subsumed into the 1996 NRL. Immediately after the law's passage, human rights groups brought a challenge to its constitutionality, on grounds, inter alia, that it violated international human rights law. In October 1997, the Guatemalan courts rejected the challenge on grounds that the law could be interpreted and applied in a way consistent with international law, and that it was therefore not unlawful prima facie.[16] Since then, international human rights bodies have not demanded the repeal but, rather, the effective interpretation and *enforcement* of the NRL. These demands stem from article 8 of the

[12]  Ibid.
[13]  Decreto No. 145–96, *Diario de Centro America*, Numero 54, December 27, 1996, accessed July 11, 2011, http://www.unhcr.org/refworld/docid/3dbe6a606.html.
[14]  Amnesty International, *Guatemala: State of impunity*, AMR 34/002/1997 (Amnesty International, April 24,1997), 3, accessed July 11, 2011, http://www.unhcr.org/refworld/docid/45bf71642.html.
[15]  Decreto No. 145–96, *Diario de Centro America*, Numero 54.
[16]  Popkin, "Combating Impunity," 179. See also Guatemalan Constitutional Court Opinion on Amnesty, No. 8–97, 20–97, October 7, 1997.

NRL, which highlights the law's conformity with international obligations (see Mark Freeman and Max Pensky in this volume). For example, in the summary of the 2008 Universal Periodic Review from the UN Human Rights Council, the International Commission of Jurists (ICJ) noted that the state has not adequately enforced the NRL and that the remedy of *amparo* – the ability to challenge government actions in violation of constitutional rights – was being used unlawfully or abusively to obstruct the trials of persons accused of committing serious human rights violations.[17] The ICJ recommended that the state strictly enforce the NRL.

Demands for enforcement rather than repeal have made it easier for the Guatemalan government to use article 8 as a kind of rhetorical shield against international scrutiny. In 2008, the UN Committee against Torture (CAT) issued a series of recommendations and conclusions expressing the committee's concern for the impunity that persisted regarding most of the human rights violations committed during the internal armed conflict, with over 600 massacres documented by the Historical Clarification Commission still to be investigated:

> The Committee notes with concern that in practice the 1996 National Reconciliation Act has become an obstacle to the effective investigation of the 1982 case of the Las Dos Erres massacre, which is making no headway due to procedural delays without any legal justification.[18]

In response to these concerns, the Guatemalan state pointed out that article 8 of the NRL would be applied effectively, in the sense that this law does not relieve perpetrators of crimes against humanity such as genocide, torture, or forced disappearance from criminal responsibility.[19] Such international pressure has only recently had an effect on the national judicial system, mainly due to the appointment of Claudia Paz y Paz to the position of attorney general in early 2011. Paz y Paz and her human rights legal team have rigorously pursued the investigation of ex-members of the Guatemalan army and security forces, resulting in a flurry of recent criminal prosecutions (see "Guatemalan national courts: self-defined jurisdiction" section later in this chapter). These changes in the public prosecutors' office in combination

---

[17]  Allan R. Brewer-Carias, "Some Aspects of the 'Amparo' Proceeding in Latin America as a Constitutional Judicial Mean Specifically Established for the Protection of Human Rights," accessed July 8, 2011, http://www.allanbrewercarias.com. See also UN Human Rights Council, "Summary prepared by the Office of the High Commissioner for Human Rights, in accordance with paragraph 15(c) of the Annex to Human Rights Council Resolution 5/1 – Guatemala, April 2, 2008," A/HRC/WG.6/2/GTM/3, 7, accessed August 15, 2011, http://www.unhcr.org/refworld/docid/4859f5c0.html.

[18]  UN Committee against Torture (CAT), "Comments by the Government of Guatemala concerning the conclusions and recommendations of the Committee against Torture (CAT/C/GTM/CO/4)," January 30, 2008, CAT/C/GTM/CO/4/Add.1, accessed July 8, 2011, para 58, page 9, http://www.unhcr.org/refworld/docid/47be90b92.html.

[19]  Ibid.

with international pressure, particularly in the form of transnational prosecutions, have made headway in the battle against impunity in Guatemala (See Freeman and Pensky in this volume).

### Transnational Prosecution: The Guatemala Genocide Case

The difficulties in getting the Guatemalan courts to act despite the fact that the amnesty law did not provide a legal impediment led human rights activists to pursue domestic and transnational justice on parallel tracks. In Guatemala, this strategy has involved simultaneous national and transnational prosecutions of several former military commanders, which involved extensive debates on the propriety of universal jurisdiction within Guatemala's constitutional order. In December 1999, the Menchú Foundation brought a complaint to the Spanish Audiencia Nacional[20] alleging that the country's ex-Presidents Efraín Ríos Montt and Óscar Humberto Mejía Victores, former defense minister Anibal Guevara, former army chief of staff Benedicto Lucas García, ex-police chief Germin Chupina, and former head of the secret police Pedro Arredondo were responsible for genocide, torture, enforced disappearances, arbitrary detention, and terrorism, all acts for which the perpetrators remain liable under the NRL. The defendants were among those most implicated in the conceptualization and execution of the repressive state strategy that resulted in the deaths of two hundred thousand Guatemalans and the destruction of over 400 villages.[21] On July 7, 2006, Judge Pedraz of Spain's Audiencia Nacional issued arrest warrants for four of these men followed by formal extradition requests on charges of genocide, state terrorism, torture, and forced disappearance. Pedraz based Spanish jurisdiction over crimes committed by Guatemalans in Guatemala on article 23.4 of the Organic Law of the Judicial Branch (LOPJ), a Spanish law that allows for universal jurisdiction over certain crimes committed by non-Spaniards outside Spain, including genocide, terrorism, and other crimes recognized in international treaties ratified by Spain.[22] Universal jurisdiction is based in part on the legal principle of *aut dedere aut judicare* – extradite or prosecute – and is designed to ensure that those who have committed crimes under international law can be tried wherever they are found.[23] Because such individuals are considered *hostis humani generis* – enemies of all mankind – any state, including their own, can punish them through its domestic courts.[24]

---

[20] The audiencia nacional acts as Spain's federal-type court, hearing cases involving, among others, international crimes.

[21] Roht-Arriaza, "Making the State do Justice," 79.

[22] Ibid., 84–5.

[23] Ibid.

[24] Ibid. In contrast, the concept of universal jurisdiction in customary law is generally considered permissive but not mandatory.

In November 2006, Guatemala's Fifth Tribunal for Crime, Drug Trafficking and Environmental Offenses executed four of the six arrest warrants. The men were held in a military hospital or went into hiding to escape arrest. The defendants delayed the proceedings considerably by filing numerous writs of *amparo*, complaining that their constitutional rights had been violated by the local court's execution of the arrest warrants.[25] The Guatemalan trial court rejected these arguments and found Spanish jurisdiction was proper.[26] The decision was appealed but the appeals court sent the case back to the lower trial court, which again found jurisdiction. The appeals court, in October 2007, agreed.[27] However, on December 12, 2007, the Guatemala Constitutional Court (GCC) ruled that the Spanish arrest warrants were invalid and the defendants could not be extradited. Ultimately the GCC concluded that universal jurisdiction could not be maintained against Guatemalans for crimes committed in Guatemala because it affronted Guatemalan sovereignty and the GCC would not recognize the extraterritorial jurisdiction of another national court. The GCC also found that the crimes alleged were common crimes connected to political crimes, signaling that these crimes were not subject to extradition and suggesting that any domestic prosecution would fall under the NRL.[28] Amnesty International condemned the ruling, stating that the GCC's decision was yet another example of the endemic impunity for grave violations of human rights in Guatemala.[29] The GCC did however recognize the obligations of the Guatemalan courts to investigate and prosecute under the rule of *aut dedere aut judicare*:

> While the jurisdiction of the Guatemalan State cannot recognize as viable the request for extradition of citizens of this country [to the Kingdom of Spain, which requests the extradition based on the principle of universal jurisdiction in Spanish law], the interested party would still have the power to submit a complaint to the Public Ministry for the prosecution of any crimes as may be identified, and based on the State receiving such a request [that is, Guatemala,] would be bound to fulfill its essential function of imparting justice.[30]

This ruling simply glossed over the underlying fact that the charges for these crimes had been on file with the public prosecutors' office for years and had gone nowhere.

---

[25] Roht-Arriaza, "Making the State do Justice," 86.

[26] Resolución, Tribunal Quinto, No 2–2006 (March 28, 2007).

[27] Roht-Arriaza, "Making the State do Justice," 92.

[28] For a discussion of the legal arguments in the GCC decision, see Roht-Arriaza, "Making the State do Justice," 95.

[29] Amnesty International Public Statement, "Guatemala: Inconsistent Ruling by the Constitutional Court Rejects Extraditions Sought by Spain," December 21, 2007, AI Index: AMR 34/026/2007, 2, accessed September 2, 2011, http://www.amnesty.org/en/library/asset/AMR34/026/2007/en/da903391-c9d6–11dc-928b-93fa24316dd4/amr340262007eng.pdf.

[30] Due Process of Law Foundation (DPLF), *Digest of Latin American Jurisprudence on International Crimes* (Washington, DC: Due Process of Law Foundation, 2010), 220.

Ultimately, the GCC's decision to invalidate the arrest warrants indicates the limits of transnational courts in actually gaining custody over defendants if the state of custody does not agree. On January 9, 2008, Judge Pedraz issued his own ruling condemning the GCC's decision, calling on anyone who had information about the case to bring it directly to him through the proper channels.[31] In February 2008, witnesses began to come forward and testify in Spain, and a Guatemalan trial court judge, José Eduardo Cojulún, began to conduct witness interviews in Guatemala with the intent of sending the results to the Spanish court. Among the witnesses were experts who explained why what had happened in Guatemala constituted genocide and who presented military documents that the army itself had denied existed. These contributions to breaking the wall of impunity around the genocide are now having domestic implications.

### *IACtHR Rulings: Bridging the Gap between International Norms and State Practice*

Guatemala has had a contentious relationship with the IACHR and the IACtHR. For years Guatemala ignored the IACHR and attempted to minimize on-site visits from the commission. In many of Guatemala's emblematic cases, the Commission and the Court have found the Guatemalan state responsible for violations and have ordered reparations, often including substantial monetary awards in addition to recommendations or orders to investigate and prosecute the crimes. From 2000 onward, however, the Portillo government's decision to admit state responsibility in a large number of cases before the Commission and the Court marked a substantial shift in the relationship between the Guatemalan executive branch and the Inter-American system. While the government from then on was happy to pay compensation, it had a harder time effectively investigating and prosecuting as the Court required.

The Las Dos Erres massacre, for example, was a high-profile case for which the state recognized responsibility, signing a friendly settlement agreement on April 1, 2000:

> The Government of Guatemala recognizes the institutional responsibility of the State for the events that occurred December 6 to 8, 1982, in the place known as the *parcelamiento* Las Dos Erres, village of Las Cruces.... The Government of Guatemala also recognizes the institutional responsibility of the Guatemalan State for the delay in justice in terms of investigating the facts related to the massacre,

---

[31] Auto dejando sin efecto las comisiones rogatorias a la republica Guatemala (January 16, 2008), juzgado central de instrucción No. 1, Audiencia Nacional, Diligencias Previas 331/1999–10, accessed July 13, 2011, http://www.derechos.org/nizkor/espana/doc/pedrazl.html.

identifying the direct perpetrators and masterminds, and applying the respective punishment.[32]

However, in April 2001 the Constitutional Court held that the NRL applied to the officers responsible for ordering and carrying out the massacre. A week before the decision, one of the Constitutional Court judges was threatened and chose to leave the country; human rights groups charged that former military officers had intimidated the Court.[33] Again, in 2005, the Constitutional Court granted *amparos* (appeals for legal protection) in favor of other military officers, sending their cases to be decided under the NRL as well. On February 26, 2006, the petitioners decided to discontinue the friendly settlement process due to the lack of credible prosecution.[34] On November 24, 2009, the IACtHR concluded that the events of the Las Dos Erres massacre, recognized by the state, constituted grave human rights violations.[35] The Court determined that the application of amnesty under the NRL in this case contradicted the obligations derived from the American Convention, particularly articles 8.1 and 25.1. Because of this, the Court ruled that the Guatemalan state must continue the investigation, judgment, and eventual sanction of those responsible for the multiple offenses generated by the events of the massacre.[36] The ruling (similar ones have been issued in the *Mack*, *Plan de Sánchez*, and *Carpio* cases) required the state to remove de facto and legal mechanisms and obstacles that maintain impunity. Any attempts to delay the investigation further were deemed unacceptable.

The IACtHR's ruling was not unexpected.[37] More surprising, on February 8, 2010, the Penal Chamber of the Guatemalan Supreme Court found the amnesty inapplicable in the Las Dos Erres case and ordered the lower court to immediately and effectively proceed against anyone with outstanding arrest warrants. The Guatemalan court cited the need to follow the IACtHR's mandate in its reasoning.[38]

---

[32]  Inter-American Commission on Human Rights, Case 11.681, Application to the IACtHR in the Case of *Las Dos Erres v. The Republic of Guatemala*, para 56, accessed July 12, 2011, http://www.cidh.oas.org/demandas/11.681%20Masacre%20de%20las%20Dos%20Erres%20Guatemala%2030%20julio%20 2008%20ENG.pdf.

[33]  Communiqué from Special Affairs Office, Menchú Foundation, April 23, 2001, accessed August 31, 2011, http://www.abogarte.com.ar/guatemala.html.

[34]  Inter-American Court of Human Rights, Case of *Las Dos Erres v. The Republic of Guatemala*, Judgment of November 24, 2009 (Preliminary Objection, Merits, Reparations, and Costs), para 1, accessed July 12, 2011, http://cja.org/downloads/IACtHR_Dos_Erres_Judgment_2009.pdf.

[35]  Ibid., para 130–1.

[36]  Ibid.

[37]  The court has issued similar orders in a number of high-profile cases. Naomi Roht-Arriaza and Marcie Mersky, "Guatemala," in *Victims Unsilenced: The Inter-American Human Rights System and Transitional Justice in Latin America*, ed. Due Process of Law Foundation (DPLF) (Washington, DC: Due Process of Law Foundation, 2007), 23, accessed July 14, 2011, http://www.dplf.org/uploads/1190403828.pdf.

[38]  Roht-Arriaza, "Impunity in Latin America."

On July 25, 2011, the trial of four ex-Kaibiles (Guatemalan Special Forces) implicated in the massacre began, and four days later the four were convicted and sentenced to long prison terms.[39] On December 15, 2011, possibly as a response to the recent convictions, President Alvaro Colom issued an official state apology for the 201 villagers who died in the massacre.[40]

Las Dos Erres is slated to be merely the first in a series of high-profile cases that will be pursued by the public prosecutor, and the convictions in the Las Dos Erres case were followed rapidly by the arrests of four ex-military officers involved in the 1982 Plan de Sánchez massacre. The arrests came seven years after the 2004 IACtHR ruling in the *Plan de Sánchez* case, which recommended prosecutions and provided reparations to the massacre survivors and victims' families.[41]

The Guatemalan government did pay reparations but did not progress with an investigation into the perpetrators of the massacre until the arrests on August 12, 2011 of former military commissioner Lucas Tecú and former members of civilian self-defense patrols (PAC) Mario Julián Acoj, Eusebio Grave Galeano, and Santos Rosales García.[42] Judge Patricia Flores has determined that the four will stand trial for the deaths of 256 inhabitants of Plan de Sánchez.[43] These recent arrests and convictions demonstrate the increasing domestic impact of IACtHR rulings but they cannot yet demonstrate the effective internalization of an accountability norm. The IACtHR's jurisprudence, as well as the human rights emphasis in the Inter-American system, is still unevenly understood, and sometimes ignored, by Guatemalan national courts.

## *Guatemalan National Courts: Self-defined Jurisdiction*

On October 7, 1997, as noted previously, the Constitutional Court upheld the amnesty law on the grounds that "there is no flagrant unconstitutionality, nor is any permanent injury likely to be caused."[44] The Court did, however, offer a narrow interpretation of several of the terms defining the crimes covered by the amnesty.

---

[39] "Guatemala Las Dos Erres Civil War Massacre Trial Begins," *BBC News*, July 25, 2011, accessed July 26, 2011, http://www.bbc.co.uk/news/world-latin-america-14285665.

[40] "Guatemalan President Colom Apologises for 1982 Massacre," *BBC News*, December 15, 2011, accessed January 5, 2012, http://www.bbc.co.uk/news/world-latin-america-16210930.

[41] Inter-American Court of Human Rights, Case of *Plan de Sánchez Massacre v. Guatemala*, Judgment of April 29, 2004 (Merits), para 49 and 52, accessed August 15, 2011, http://www.lawschool.cornell.edu/womenandjustice/legalresources/upload/IACtHR-20Plan-20de-20Sanchez-20Massacre-20v-20Guatemala.pdf.

[42] "Guatemala Arrests Four Suspects of 1982 Civil War Massacre," *Channel 6 News*, August 12, 2011, accessed August 14, 2011, http://channel6newsonline.com/2011/08/guatemala-arrests-four-suspects-of-1982-civil-war-massacre/.

[43] "Militar y cuatro más van a juicio por massacre," *elPeriodico*, December 15, 2011, accessed January 5, 2012, http://www.elperiodico.com.gt/es/20111215/pais/205132/.

[44] Popkin, "Combating Impunity," 179.

For example, the Court emphasized that crimes that qualified for amnesty under article 5 of the NRL (applicable to state agents) had to meet every single requirement delineated in that article.[45] While the GCC's 1997 ruling upholding the NRL is still in place, the law's applicability has been consistently evaluated on a case-by-case inquiry into the facts. For example, while article 11 of the NRL explicitly states that any cases involving crimes covered by articles 4 and 5 of the NRL must be transferred to the appeals chamber for a determination of the applicability of the amnesty, Judge Delgado of the Juzgado Primero de Primera Instancia Penal de Sentencia (first instance criminal trial court) refused to transfer the *Mack* case involving the killing of well-known anthropologist Myrna Mack by state agents.[46] Judge Delgado reasoned that murder was not one of the crimes listed as a common crime related to a political crime and thus did not fall under the amnesty law.[47] This ruling followed Judge Delgado's earlier ruling in the *Carpio* case, which he also declined to transfer to the appellate court.

Guatemala's case-by-case approach to the 1996 NRL has yielded an inconsistent body of appellate jurisprudence, with the Constitutional Court in particular zigzagging back and forth with little coherence in its arguments. Nonetheless, despite innumerable *amparo* motions and continuing intimidation of judges, lawyers, and witnesses, the pace of convictions has clearly accelerated. In September 2009, a trial court in Chimaltenango sentenced Felipe Cusanero, an ex-paramilitary chief, to 150 years in prison for the disappearance of six indigenous Mayan farmers.[48] The sentence issued in the *Cusanero* case was the first ever for the crime of forced disappearance.[49] On December 3, 2009, in another landmark case involving forced disappearances, the Chiquimula Sentencing Tribunal sentenced army officer Marco Antonio Sánchez Samayoa and three other military commissioners to forty years in prison for the crime of forced disappearance of five civilians, and thirteen years and four months for the crime of the illegal detention of eight members of

---

[45]  Roht-Arriaza and Gibson, "The Developing Jurisprudence on Amnesty," 882. See also Guatemalan Constitutional Court Opinion on Amnesty, No. 8–97, 20–97, part IV, October 7, 1997. Such requirements were: 1) that they had been committed in the armed internal conflict; 2) that such crimes were committed with the objective of preventing, impeding, pursuing, or suppressing crimes committed by insurgents; 3) a rational and objective relationship between the crime and the objectives listed in 2).

[46]  Roht-Arriaza and Gibson, "The Developing Jurisprudence on Amensty," 882.

[47]  Popkin, "Combating Impunity," 181. Article 4, which relates to the insurgent's crimes, lists the crimes that can be considered "related common crimes," and does not include murder. Article 5, which refers to crimes by state actors, includes no list.

[48]  "Guatemala Sees Landmark Sentence," *BBC News*, September 1, 2009, accessed July 13, 2011, http://news.bbc.co.uk/1/hi/world/americas/8231142.stm.

[49]  "Historic First Sentence Against Former Member of Guatemalan Military for Crime of Forced Disappearance," *Guatemala Solidarity Network*, December 6, 2009, accessed August 10, 2011, http://www.guatemalasolidarity.org.uk/?q=content/historic-first-sentence-against-former-member-guatemalan-military-crime-forced-disappearance.

the community of El Jute in the department of Chiquimula in 1981.[50] In 2008, the GCC had rejected Sanchez's appeal for amnesty under the 1996 NRL.[51] The GCC ruled that, although the law was applicable in this case, the Supreme Court judges had failed to take into account its exclusion of "certain crimes [including forced disappearances] related to human rights violations from the ambit of permissible amnesties."[52]

As mentioned previously, the slowly increasing quantity of criminal prosecution is in part due to the new investigative rigor of the public prosecutors' office under Claudia Paz y Paz. Paz y Paz faces several significant obstacles to her pursuit of human rights violators, mainly a reduced budget (cut by 200 million quetzals in 2010) and the recent election of former General Otto Pérez Molina, a conservative with a questionable human rights record, to the presidency on November 6, 2011.[53] Pérez Molina has expressed reserved support for Paz y Paz, confirming that she will continue in her current position. He has also stated that one of the priorities of his government will be to obtain the necessary funds to strengthen the investigations of the public prosecutor's office, though it remains to be seen how such promises will play out after his recent assumption to the presidency in January.[54] Paz y Paz continues to proceed as rapidly as possible with investigations and prosecutions related to human rights abuses during the armed conflict.

In June 2011, two high-profile arrests were made; the first was Héctor Bol de la Cruz, the former director of the national police implicated in the 1984 disappearance of student and labor leader Edgar Fernando García. Héctor Bol de la Cruz awaits trial for the crime of forced disappearance and, as of October 2010, two other ex-agents of the national police, Hector Roderico Ramírez Ríos and Abraham Lancerio Gómez, have been sentenced to forty years in prison for their roles in Edgar Fernando García's disappearance.[55] The second landmark arrest was that of

---

[50] Ibid.

[51] "Guatemalan Constitutional Court Decision Paves the Way for El Jute Trial," *Impunity Watch News Archive*, April 3, 2009, accessed July 10, 2011, http://www.impunitywatch.org/en/publication/36.

[52] Ibid.

[53] Rosario Calderón, "Aumento de presupuesto al MP es necesario para evitar despidos, asegura Claudia Paz y Paz," *Noticias de Guatemala*, May 3, 2011, accessed January 5, 2012, http://noticias.com.gt/nacionales/20110503-aumento-de-presupuesto-al-mp-es-necesario-para-evitar-despidos-asegura-claudia-paz-y-paz.html.

[54] "Reunión de diplomáticos con candidate presidencial del PP," *Comisión Internacional contra la Impunidad en Guatemala (CICG)*, October 18, 2011, accessed January 5, 2012, http://cicig.org/index.php?mact=News,cntnt01,detail,0&cntnt01articleid=123&cntnt01returnid=67; "Pulling Guatemala Back from the Brink," *LatIntelligence Analysis on Latin America*, August 2, 2011, accessed August 10, 2011, http://www.latintelligence.com/tag/claudia-paz-y-paz/.

[55] Emily Willard, "Former Senior Guatemalan Officials Arrested for Genocide and Forced Disappearance," *National Security Archives*, June 30, 2011, accessed August 10, 2011, http://nsarchive.wordpress.com/2011/06/30/former-senior-guatemalan-officials-arrested-for-genocide-and-forced-disappearance/.

Héctor Mario López Fuentes, an ex-armed forces chief connected to the deaths of 317 villagers during massacres that took place in 1983 in the Maya Ixil Triangle.[56] The arrest comes ten years after the Centre for Human Rights and Legal Action (CALDH), representing massacre survivors from eleven different villages, filed a criminal case in 2001 against López Fuentes and other military officials, including former President Efraín Ríos Montt, accusing them of genocide.[57] However, no arrest warrants were issued and little progress was made on the case until nearly ten years later when, on June 20, 2011, Judge Patricia Flores of the Juzgado Primero de Alto Riesgo ordered López Fuentes to stand trial for charges of genocide and crimes against humanity in a detention center on a military base. Flores denied López Fuentes's lawyers' petition to transfer him to a private health clinic due to his delicate physical condition.[58] In October 2011, former general Mauricio Rodríguez Sánchez, head of Guatemala's G-2 military intelligence force in 1982 during Lopez Fuentes's tenure as army general staff head, was arrested and will face charges of genocide and crimes against humanity committed in the El Quiche department between 1978 and 1985.[59]

Meanwhile, Pedro Pimentel Ríos, a former member of the Kaibiles implicated in the Las Dos Erres massacre, was deported from the United States on July 13, 2011 and turned over to the Guatemalan authorities.[60] Edgar Pérez, a lawyer representing the petitioners in the case, has stated that more than 100 witnesses are willing to testify.[61] Considering the IACtHR and Guatemalan Supreme Court decisions ordering investigation and prosecution in the Las Dos Erres case, as well as the recent sentencing of the four other ex-Kaibiles members implicated in the massacre, it is very likely Pimentel Ríos will shortly stand trial.[62] The most high-profile arrest to date was made in October 2011 when former defense minister and ex-general Mejía Victores was declared a fugitive from the law and arraigned on October 17, 2011 for crimes against humanity committed in the Ixil Triangle from 1982 to 1984. Unfortunately,

[56] "Guatemala Disappearance: Former Police Chief Arrested," *BBC News*, June 9, 2011, accessed July 19, 2011, http://www.bbc.co.uk/news/world-latin-america-13722568. See also "Guatemala, Ex-armed Forces Chief Lopez Fuentes Arrested," *BBC News*, June 18, 2011, accessed July 19, 2011, http://www.bbc.co.uk/news/world-latin-america-13819853.

[57] Centre for Human Rights and Legal Action (CALDH) and the Association for Justice and Reconciliation (AJR), "A Historic Opportunity for Justice in Guatemala," June 21, 2011, accessed August 15, 2011, http://nisgua.blogspot.com/2011/06/historic-opportunity-for-justice-in.html.

[58] "Envían a prisión preventiva al general guatemalteco acusado de genocidio," *El Mundo*, June 20, 2011, accessed August 10, 2011, http://www.elmundo.es/america/2011/06/21/noticias/1308617873.html.

[59] "Capturan a ex militar vinculado en masacre del Triangulo Ixil," *Prensa Libre*, October 12, 2011, accessed January 17, 2012, http://www.prensalibre.com/noticias/justicia/Guatemala-masacres-Triangulo_Ixil-capturado-militares_0_571143009.html.

[60] "AP News Break: US Deports Guatemala Massacre Suspect," *The Associated Press and Local Wire*, July 13, 2011, Nexis U.K.

[61] Ibid.

[62] Ibid.

as of October 31, 2011 he is unable to stand trial according to a medical evaluation performed by the National Institute of Forensic Science and the prosecutors' office has now withdrawn the indictment.[63]

Guatemalan national court decisions have shown an increasing willingness to demand accountability in individual cases. The limited but growing number of prosecutions can be attributed to a combination of external and internal pressures: decisions issued by international human rights bodies (specifically the UN Human Rights Council and CAT), the IACHR, especially the IACtHR, insist on the effective enforcement of the 1996 NRL, while at the domestic level Guatemalan civil society continues to demand justice, resulting in significant shifts toward pursuing criminal accountability in the public prosecutors' office. While the amnesty law has not been the fundamental factor impeding prosecution, it has been one of the legal arguments raised and considered by domestic courts, with varying results. In the lower courts, it has rarely been applied to cases involving grave rights violations, but the higher courts have been much more indecisive.

## EL SALVADOR

Twelve years of armed conflict, brought on by a combination of severe political and economic exclusion and unbridled repression by security forces, ended in a military stalemate between a guerrilla organization, Farabundo Martí Front for National Liberation (FMLN), and the Salvadoran military.[64] Two years of UN-mediated peace negotiations culminated in the signing of the Chapultepec Accords on January 16, 1992. The peace accords established two specific mechanisms for dealing with the past: the Ad Hoc Commission and the Truth Commission. The Ad Hoc Commission, designed to purge the military of perpetrators of human rights abuses, recommended the removal or transfer of 103 officers, including virtually the entire high command.[65] After much delay and protest, the Cristiani government carried out most of the Ad Hoc Commission's recommendations, which contributed to military reform. However, many officers who worked in intelligence units, heavily involved in death squad activities and torture, remained in their posts.[66]

The Salvadoran Truth Commission received the broader task of investigating and revealing the most serious acts of violence during the civil conflict. Article 5 of

---

[63] "Guatemala: General Mejia Victores Arrested for Genocide Declared Unfit to Stand Trial," *The Guatemala Times*, October 31, 2011, accessed January 5, 2012, http://www.guatemala-times.com/news/guatemala/2605-guatemala-general-mejia-victores-arrested-for-genocide-declared-unfit-to-stand-trial.html.

[64] Sieder, "War, Peace, and Memory Politics in Central America," 166.

[65] Popkin, "El Salvador: A Negotiated End to Impunity," 200.

[66] Ibid., 204.

the peace agreement required the Truth Commission to clarify and stop impunity, emphasizing that "acts of the nature, regardless of the sector to which their perpetrators belong, must be the object of exemplary action by the law courts so that the punishment prescribed by law is meted out to those found responsible."[67] Thus, far from sanctioning an amnesty, the Chapultepec Accords contemplated a process of eventual investigation and prosecution. The state and the opposition parties acknowledged the vital role the Truth Commission would play in rehabilitating society.

The Truth Commission gathered testimony from over 2,000 people about violations involving more than 7,000 victims. It examined thirty-three cases in detail, and when there was sufficient proof, the commission named the individuals involved, an unprecedented decision not repeated in Guatemala.[68] The Truth Commission also called for the dismissal of persons found responsible for human rights violations from the armed forces and civil service and recommended extensive judicial reform, including the voluntary resignation of the current Supreme Court justices.[69] Despite UN endorsement, funding, and staffing, the Truth Commission's findings and recommendations were widely rejected as biased, incomplete, and unjust by government officials and high-ranking military commanders.[70]

Five days after the release of the Truth Commission's final report, *From Madness to Hope: The 12-year War in El Salvador*, President Cristiani pushed through a sweeping amnesty that extinguished civil and criminal responsibility for political crimes committed by the FMLN and the government.[71] The 1993 General Amnesty Law for the Consolidation of Peace (Decree 486) prompted outrage over El Salvador's approach to addressing human rights abuses through "rampant impunity" and "bury[ing] the past."[72] Unlike Guatemala's 1996 NRL, Decree 486 included no exclusion of human rights violations. Article 1 of Decree 486 granted "broad, absolute, unconditional amnesty for anyone that in whatever form had participated in the commission of political crimes, common crimes connected to political crimes and common crimes in which more than twenty persons took part, before

[67]  *Chapultepec Peace Agreement*, ch.1, Armed Forces, article 5, January 16, 1992, accessed August 9, 2011, http://www.votb.org/elsalvador/Reports/peaceaccords.pdf.

[68]  Mike Kaye, "The Role of Truth Commissions in the Search for Justice, Reconciliation and Democratisation: The Salvadoran and Honduran Cases," *Journal of Latin American Studies* 29 (1997): 700.

[69]  Popkin, "El Salvador: A Negotiated End to Impunity," 209.

[70]  Salvadoran defense minister Ponce, in a nationally televised appearance during which he was flanked by other military commanders, denounced the report as "unjust, incomplete, illegal, unethical, partisan and insolent." "Posición de la fuerza armada de El Salvador ante el informe de la comisión de la verdad, March 23, 1993," *El Diario de Hoy* (San Salvador), March 24, 1993.

[71]  Legislative Decree No. 486, art. 4, *Diario Oficial*, 318 (56), March 22, 1993.

[72]  Popkin, "El Salvador: A Negotiated End to Impunity," 199. See also Margaret Popkin and Nehal Bhuta, "Latin American Amnesties in Comparative Perspective: Can the Past be Buried?" *Ethics and International Affairs* 13 (1999): 103.

January 1, 1992."[73] Article 4 extinguished all civil liability. In addition, the 1993 General Amnesty Law repealed article 6 of the 1992 National Reconciliation Law, passed at the time of the peace accords, which had excluded certain crimes from amnesty: 1) persons convicted by juries, aimed at preventing the release of the two officers convicted for the 1989 killing of six Jesuit priests, their housekeeper, and housekeeper's daughter (the Jesuit or Central American University [UCA] case); and 2) persons named in the Truth Commission's report as having committed serious human rights violations, aimed at allowing the completion of the Truth Commission's investigations. President Cristiani explained the decision to overrule these exceptions with the 1993 General Amnesty Law as imperative for "turn[ing] that painful page and seek[ing] a better future for our country."[74] The Salvadoran government's political will regarding accountability did not waver in successive Nationalist Republican Alliance (ARENA) administrations. Cristiani's successor, President Francisco Flores, responded to the IACHR report on the merits of the Jesuit case in 2000 by stating: "The declaration of this organization [the IACHR] is a recommendation to the government and we receive it as such, just as we have received many other recommendations.... To heed the suggestions in the document would jeopardize peace in the country."[75] He repeated this position at an October 18, 2002 press conference. When asked about a possible repeal of the amnesty law, Flores responded:

> [T]e amnesty law is the cornerstone of the peace accords, it's what enables us to grant ourselves forgiveness.... The prosecution of war crimes would have led to another war; it would have closed the doors to the possibility of reconciliation among us.... It seems to me that those who want to remove that cornerstone of the peace accords are capable of immersing us in another serious conflict.[76]

This political climate, in combination with a judiciary system described in the Truth Commission's report as lacking "the minimum requirements of objectivity," has created a definitive gap between international condemnation of the 1993 General Amnesty Law and domestic attempts at investigating and prosecuting those responsible for human rights violations.[77]

---

[73] Popkin, "El-Salvador: A Negotiated End to Impunity," 211. See also Legislative Decree 486, art. 1, *Diario Oficial* 318 (56), March 22, 1993.

[74] Popkin, "El-Salvador: A Negotiated End to Impunity," 211. See also excerpts from "Address to the Nation by His Excellency the President of the Republic," Alfredo Cristiani, March 18, 1993."

[75] *El Diario de Hoy*, January 7, 2000, quoted in Benjamín Cuéllar Martínez, "El Salvador," in DPLF, *Victims Unsilenced*, 68 n. 32.

[76] Press conference, October 18, 2002, quoted in Benjamín Cuéllar Martínez, "Los dos rostros de la sociedad salvadorena," in *Verdad, justicia y reparación: Desafíos para la democracia y la convivencia social*, ed. Gilda Pacheco Oreamuno, Lorena Acevedo Narea, and Guido Galli (San Jose: IDEA/IIDH, 2005), 170.

[77] UN Security Council Annex, *From Madness to Hope: The 12-Year War in El Salvador*, part V, "Recommendations."

## Salvadoran National Courts: Judicial Inertia

In the Salvadoran court system, the general approach to the application of the amnesty law has been on a case-by-case basis. While upholding the power of the legislature to pass an amnesty law, the Supreme Court has held that whether or not its provisions apply cannot be determined a priori where fundamental rights are involved. In a first decision, the Criminal Chamber of the Salvadoran Supreme Court in the *Guevara Portillo* case upheld the constitutionality of the 1993 amnesty law. The decision not only deemed the law constitutional, but described it as a manifestation of sovereignty granted by the constitution, which prevails over all treaties and ordinary laws.[78]

The 1993 amnesty law was again upheld by the Supreme Court in 2000. However, possibly in response to criticism of the earlier ruling, the Court left room for a case-by-case consideration of cases in which the amnesty might not apply: those in which fundamental rights are at issue.[79] The Court held:

> From this perspective, it is clear that [constitutional] Article 2(1) – which is a basic provision in the context of the Constitution in that it lays the groundwork for the effective enjoyment of fundamental rights – also constitutes a restriction on the powers conferred on the Legislative Assembly pursuant to [constitutional] Article 131(26), insofar as any interpretation of the latter must be consistent with those restrictions. This means that the Legislative Assembly may grant amnesty for political crimes or for common crimes related to them, or for common crimes committed by a number of persons that shall not be fewer than 20, as long as that amnesty does not get in the way of safeguards to preserve and defend – through criminal prosecution – the fundamental rights of the human person.[80]

In 2003 the same Court held, considering the lack of prosecution in the Jesuit case, that it was up to trial court judges to decide if the amnesty applied in a particular case.[81]

However, local prosecutors and courts have never utilized this approach to find that the amnesty law was inapplicable. For example, in the case of the assassination of Archbishop Romero by a military death squad, the judicial case file was archived in 1984 but reactivated the following year with minimal further investigation. On

---

[78] *Guevara Portillo Case* Sala de lo Penal de la Corte Suprema de Justicia, San Salvador (August 16, 1995).

[79] Roht-Arriaza, "Impunity in Latin America."

[80] Acción de inconstitucionalidad contra los artículos 1 y 4 del Decreto Legislativo No. 486, Sala de lo Constitucional, Corte Suprema de Justicia, September 27, 2000. The court reiterated this case-by-case approach in 2003. Proceso de Amparo promovido por Juan Antonio Ellacuría Beascoechea y otros, Sala de lo Constitucional, Corte Suprema de Justicia, December 23, 2003.

[81] Roht-Arriaza, "Impunity in Latin America."

March 31, 1993, Judge Luis Antonio Villeda Figueroa applied the 1993 General Amnesty Law "for the purpose of dismissing, with prejudice, charges against Captain Alvaro Saravia, the only one of the accused against whom an order for provisional detention had been issued."[82] During an IACHR November 2001 hearing on the *Romero* case, government representatives failed to explain why the persons allegedly responsible for this most high-profile of murders were never investigated or prosecuted.[83]

The same result was reached in another emblematic case. In the hamlet of El Mozote, over 765 people were extrajudicially executed by members of the military in December 1981.[84] The Salvadoran Truth Commission in its final report included the massacre and determined the liability of members of the armed forces. The victims' families tried to bring the case before the domestic courts. The Salvadoran government argued that the amnesty law was enacted for the good of Salvadoran society as a whole, as an essential part of the groundwork for the long-sought peace. With that overriding concern in mind, the judge hearing the case applied the amnesty law, finding in addition that it was consistent with the lack of identification of the perpetrators of the massacre during the legal proceedings.[85]

### Applicability of International Human Rights Treaty Law

Within the realm of international jurisprudence, various international human rights bodies have repeatedly challenged the legality of the 1993 General Amnesty Law. International human rights committees have primarily cited the amnesty law's violations of the right to remedy provisions set forth in various international treaties, broadly understood as state obligations to ensure the rights of victims of human rights violations to reparation, including compensation, through judicial or possibly nonjudicial proceedings.[86] In 1994, in its consideration of reports submitted by state parties, the UNHRC expressed "grave concern over the adoption of the [Salvadoran] Amnesty Law, which prevents relevant investigation and punishment of perpetrators of past human rights violations and consequently precludes relevant compensation."[87]

---

[82] Inter-American Commission on Human Rights, Case 11.481, *Monsignor Oscar Arnulfo Romero y Galdámez v. El Salvador*, April 13, 2000, accessed July 12, 2011, http://www.cidh.org/annualrep/99eng/merits/elsalvador11.481.htm.

[83] Benjamín Cuéllar Martínez, "El Salvador," in DPLF, *Victims Unsilenced*, 49.

[84] Inter-American Commission on Human Rights, Report 24/06, "Admissibility Petition: Massacre El Mozote," March 2, 2006, accessed July 12, 2011, http://www.cidh.oas.org/annualrep/2006eng/ELSALVADOR.10720eng.htm.

[85] Ibid., para 27.

[86] Freeman, *Necessary Evils*, 21.

[87] UN Human Rights Committee, "Consideration of Reports Submitted by States Parties under Article 40 of the Covenant," CCPR/c/79/Add.34, April 18, 1994, para 3, accessed June 21, 2011, http://www.unhcr.org/refworld/pdfid/3ae6b011c.pdf.

The committee urged the government to fulfill its obligation to ensure that victims of human rights violations had an effective remedy, recommending that the state "review the effect of the Amnesty Law and amend or repeal it as necessary."[88] In its 1995 report, the UN Committee on the Elimination of Racial Discrimination (CERD) expressed similar concern "over the adoption of the Amnesty Law and the failure to exclude those who had violated human rights from serving in the military, the national police, the judiciary or other branches of Government."[89] It also urged the government to provide information on the implementation of the right to effective remedy as provided for in article 6 of the Convention on the Elimination of All Forms of Racial Discrimination.[90]

International committees, such as the CAT, have also cited "nonderogable state obligations" as justification for opposing the 1993 General Amnesty Law (see Freeman and Pensky in this volume). In 2009, the CAT urged the Salvadoran government to repeal the law on the basis that "amnesties or other impediments which preclude or indicate unwillingness to provide prompt and fair prosecution and punishment of perpetrators of torture or ill-treatment violate the principle of non-derogability."[91] While Guatemala's 1996 NRL excludes torture from its coverage, El Salvador's 1993 blanket amnesty has no such saving graces; without any restrictions or exclusion of human rights abuses, it simply condones impunity.

## Repeated Condemnation by the Inter-American System

For the most part, El Salvador has ignored the recommendations just discussed, becoming the Latin American country least compliant with IACHR decisions. Despite the commission's visits, approved case reports, and the petitions brought before it by national and international civil society organizations, it has been difficult to achieve a sustained dialogue with the Salvadoran government on compliance with recommendations concerning the amnesty laws.[92]

In its 1994 report on the situation of human rights in El Salvador, the IACHR revisited the 1993 amnesty law, criticizing it for the inclusion of crimes that impeded judicial proceedings, such as perjury and false expert opinions and reports.[93]

---

[88] Ibid., para 12.

[89] Committee on the Elimination of Racial Discrimination, "Official Records of the General Assembly, Fiftieth Session, Supplement No. 18 (A/50/18)," September 22, 1995, para 471, accessed June 20, 2011, http://www.unhcr.org/refworld/pdfid/453779970.pdf.

[90] Ibid.

[91] Committee against Torture, "Concluding Observations," CAT/C/SLV/CO/2, December 9, 2009, para 15, accessed June 28, 2011, http://www2.ohchr.org/english/bodies/cat/docs/CAT.C.SLV.CO.2_en.doc.

[92] Santiago Canton, "Amnesty Laws," in DPLF, *Victims Unsilenced*, 172.

[93] The commission argued that "there was no justification for including in an amnesty law intended to 'promote and achieve national reconciliation,' crimes committed by officers of the court and by

Furthermore, the commission found that the law would "do nothing to further reconciliation and … [was] certainly not consistent with the provisions of Articles 1, 2, 8 and 25 of the American Convention."[94] It stated that, even with the argument of the need for peace negotiations, the General Amnesty Law violated the international obligations of El Salvador "because it makes possible a 'reciprocal amnesty' without first acknowledging responsibility (despite the recommendations of the Truth Commission); because it applies to crimes against humanity; and because it eliminates any possibility of obtaining adequate pecuniary compensation, primarily for victims."[95]

In December 1999, on the basis of its preceding considerations (Case 10.480 – *Lucio Parada Cea et al.*), the IACHR reiterated that Decree 486 violated the international obligations of El Salvador since it covered crimes against humanity, made it impossible to investigate human rights violations, and eliminated any possibility of obtaining adequate reparations.[96] The IACHR stated that the 1993 amnesty law "eliminated the possibility of undertaking any further judicial investigations through the courts to establish the truth and it denied the right of the victims, their relatives and society as a whole to know the truth."[97] For the second time the commission called on the government to nullify the General Amnesty Law; conduct a full, impartial, and effective investigation; and prosecute those responsible.[98]

In the *Serrano-Cruz* case, submitted to the IACtHR on June 14, 2003, the Inter-American Court also condemned the amnesty law.[99] The Serrano-Cruz sisters were seven and three years old respectively when they were "[allegedly] captured and abducted by soldiers, members of the Atlacatl Battalion of the Salvadoran Army, during a [military] operation known as 'Operación Limpieza,' which took place in

---

litigants in court proceedings, especially in a country where many criminal acts – including grave and systematic violations of basic human rights – went unpunished because that country had no trustworthy, independent and effective judiciary." *Inter-American Commission on Human Rights, Report on the Situation of Human Rights in El Salvador*, OEA/Ser.L-II.85,(IACHR, February 11 1994), accessed July 20, 2011, http://www.cidh.oas.org/countryrep/ElSalvador94eng/II.4.htm.

94  Ibid.
95  Ibid.
96  Inter-American Commission on Human Rights, Case 10.480, *Lucio Parada Cea and others v. El Salvador*, January 27, 1999, accessed July 12, 2011, http://www.cidh.org/annualrep/98eng/merits/elsalvador%2010480.htm. On August 25, 1989, the IACHR received a complaint against the Republic of El Salvador concerning the detention of farm worker Lucio Parada Cea and others by units of the Salvadoran army. According to the complaint, these farmers were tortured and two of them died as a result of the torture they suffered.
97  Ibid.
98  Ibid.
99  Inter-American Court of Human Rights, Case of the *Serrano-Cruz Sisters v. El Salvador*, Judgement of November 23, 2004, (Preliminary Objections), para 171–2, accessed August 4, 2011, http://www.corteidh.or.cr/docs/casos/articulos/seriec_118_ing.pdf.

the municipality of San Antonio de la Cruz, Chalatenango Department, from May 27 to June 9, 1982."[100] Although the amnesty law was in force, the court ordered El Salvador to prosecute and punish the individuals responsible for the forced disappearance of the Serrano-Cruz sisters because a failure to investigate the disappearances and take appropriate action against those responsible violated articles 1, 8, and 25 of the American Convention.[101] Specifically, the Inter-American Court stated:

> The Court observes that [El Salvador] must ensure that the domestic proceedings to investigate what happened to [the girls] and, if appropriate, punish those responsible, has the desired effect. The State must abstain from using figures such as amnesty and prescription or the establishment of measures designed to eliminate responsibility, or measures intended to prevent criminal prosecution or suppress the effects of a conviction.[102]

Both the Inter-American Court and the Commission have continued to follow up on their previous recommendations to the Salvadoran state to pursue thorough domestic investigations and prosecutions of past human rights violations. A number of cases are now pending before the Court. On March 2, 2006, the IACHR admitted a petition filed by victims and their relatives in the El Mozote massacre. In March 2011, the IACHR sent the *El Mozote* case to the IACtHR due to the failure of the Salvadoran government to investigate and prosecute those responsible for the massacre.[103] The Court will rule on whether the application of amnesty for the accused was in fact valid or was a violation of Articles 1.1, 2, 4, 5, 7, 8, 11, 19, 21, and 25 of the American Convention.[104]

Unfortunately, unlike in other places where the recommendations and decisions of the Inter-American system have proven effective in spurring changes, the Salvadoran government did not move to change the amnesty law or to precipitate prosecutions in light of pressure from the regional human rights system. It took a complaint brought in the Spanish courts to move the case forward.

---

[100]   Ibid., para 2.

[101]   Ibid., para 107, 218.

[102]   Ibid., para 172. The Court reiterated this in a subsequent case involving a former FMLN commander who was assassinated. See also Inter-American Court of Human Rights, Case of *García Prieto et al. v. El Salvador*, Judgment of November 20, 2007 (Preliminary Objections, Merits, Reparations and Costs), para 215, accessed August 8, 2011, http://www.corteidh.or.cr/docs/casos/articulos/seriec_168_ing.pdf. A third case, involving the El Mozote massacre, is now before the Court.

[103]   Xeily Alfaro, "Caso El Mozote pasa a la corte interamericana," *La Prensa Gráfica*, March 25, 2011, accessed August 10, 2011, http://www.laprensagrafica.com/el-salvador/judicial/180447-caso-el-mozote-pasa-a-la-corte-interamericana.html.

[104]   Inter-American Commission on Human Rights, "Admissibility Petition: Massacre El Mozote," March 2, 2006, para 31, accessed September 1, 2011, http://www.cidh.org/annualrep/2006eng/elsalvador.10720eng.htm#_ftn1.

## Spanish Jurisdiction in the Jesuit Case

On November 13, 2008, the Center for Justice and Accountability (CJA) filed charges with the Spanish Audiencia Nacional against former Salvadoran president and commander in chief of the armed forces, Alfredo Cristiani Burkard, and fourteen former officers and soldiers of the Salvadoran army for their role in the Jesuit killings.[105] Like in the Guatemala genocide case, the Spanish court found jurisdiction based on the Spanish LOPJ, since the defendants were accused of "crimes against humanity, state terrorism and the separate crime of the concealment of crimes against humanity."[106] All of these crimes are now covered under the LOPJ. On January 13, 2009, the Spanish National Court charged the fourteen Salvadoran ex-officers with crimes against humanity and state terrorism.[107] After the CJA presented evidence in Madrid in 2009 and 2010, the Court added six additional defendants and on May 30, 2011, three years after the initial complaint was filed with the Audiencia Nacional, Spanish Judge Eloy Velasco issued a seventy-seven-page indictment and arrest warrants for the twenty Salvadoran former officers accused of participating in the Jesuit murders.[108] The defendants were all members of the Salvadoran military, including Rafael Humberto Larios, the minister of defense at the time of the massacre; former general Rafael Bustillo; Colonel Orlando Zepeda, vice minister of defense; and Colonel Inocente Orlando Montano, vice minister of public safety. Cristiani, the civilian former president, was not indicted at this stage.

The indictment described the conspiracy to kill the Jesuit priests and its conceptualization as a military operation at the highest levels of the Salvadoran army and military intelligence.[109] In explaining the basis for the issuance of the indictment and the arrest warrants, the judge stated that any claim of double jeopardy should fail because the 1991 trial held in El Salvador, in which nine military officers and soldiers stood trial for murder, acts of terrorism, and acts preparatory to terrorism related to the Jesuit killings, was a "sham trial."[110] The 1991 proceedings were plagued by intimidation tactics by high-ranking military officials and the reluctance

---

[105] Center for Justice and Accountability (CJA), "Case Summary CJA's Human Rights Prosecution: the Jesuits Massacre," November 13, 2008, 1, accessed August 8, 2011, http://cja.org/downloads/jesuits_summary.pdf.

[106] Ibid.

[107] Center for Justice and Accountability (CJA), "Jesuits Massacre Case: In Brief," November 13, 2008, accessed August 10, 2011, http://www.cja.org/article.php?list=type&type=84.

[108] Bruce Zagaris, "Spanish Judge Issues Indictments in 1989 Jesuits Massacre Case in El Salvador," *International Enforcement Law Reporter*, August 2011, Nexis U.K. See also Centre for Justice and Accountability (CJA), "Spanish Judge Issues Indictments and Arrest Warrants in Jesuits Massacre Case," May 31, 2011, accessed August 8, 2011, http://cja.org/article.php?id=1004.

[109] Zagaris, "Spanish Judge Issues Indictments in Jesuits Massacre Case."

[110] CJA, "Spanish Judge Issues Indictments and Arrest Warrants in Jesuits Massacre Case."

of the Salvadoran government and armed forces to provide evidence and witnesses. Ultimately, only two officers were convicted of murder, and the conviction was overturned in 1993 when President Cristiani passed the blanket amnesty law.[111] On August 8, 2011, nine of the twenty former officers indicted by Judge Velasco in May turned themselves in at a military base as Salvadoran police were preparing to arrest them on an order from Interpol based on Judge Velasco's warrants.[112] Another officer, Innocente Montano, was arrested at his home in the United States on charges of visa fraud; though he was released on bail on August 24, 2011, it is not clear how the United States will respond to an extradition request on the more serious Spanish charges.[113] On that same day, the Salvadoran Supreme Court decided that it would not formally order the arrest of the nine military officers because it had not received a formal extradition request from Spain. The Court stated that the "red notice" it had received from Interpol required only that the nine suspects be located, not arrested.[114] Spanish Judge Velasco responded that the Spanish Audiencia Nacional could not issue such a request until it had been officially informed of the arrest. The Salvadoran Supreme Court's decision mirrors the 2005 Guatemalan Constitutional Court ruling in the Guatemala genocide case, illustrating yet again the limits of transnational courts in gaining custody over defendants if the state of custody does not agree. The Salvadoran Supreme Court has said it will consider an extradition request if it receives one, although the recusal of three of its most progressive members, Belarmino Jaime (president of the Supreme Court), Florentín Meléndez, and Sidney Blanco, puts a positive outcome in doubt.[115] Jaime recused himself in order to analyze a habeas corpus petition submitted by the nine military officers' lawyers.[116] At the same time, Meléndez recused himself because he disagreed with the Salvadoran Supreme Court's 2010 decision to refuse to provide the Spanish Audiencia Nacional with particular documentation related to the Jesuit case. Finally, Blanco removed himself from the case because he had been the prosecutor in the 1991 trial in which

---

[111]　CJA, "Case Summary CJA's Human Rights Prosecution: the Jesuits Massacre," 11.

[112]　Gabriel Labrador and Ricardo Vaquerano, "Militares reclamados por España pasan a manos de corte suprema," *El Faro*, August 8, 2011, accessed August 8, 2011, http://www.elfaro.net/es/201108/noticias/5186/.

[113]　"Jesuit Death's Suspect Out on Immigration Charge," *Boston Herald*, August 24, 2011, accessed September 1, 2011, http://www.bostonherald.com/news/regional/view/20110824jesuit_deaths_suspect_out_on_immigration_charge/. See also Centre for Justice and Accountability (CJA), "U.S. Arrests Former Salvadoran Official and Massachusetts Resident for Immigration Fraud Related to 1989 Jesuits Massacre," August 23, 2011, accessed September 1, 2011, http://www.cja.org/article.php?id=1027.

[114]　"Salvadoran Court Blocks Arrests for Priest Murders," *Reuters*, August 24, 2011, accessed September 1, 2011, http://www.reuters.com/article/2011/08/25/us-elsalvador-spain-jesuits-idUSTRE77O0P520110825.

[115]　"Spain Pushes El Salvador Jesuit Murders Case," *BBC News*, August 25, 2011, accessed September 1, 2011, http://www.bbc.co.uk/news/world-latin-america-14672692.

[116]　Iván Pérez, "CSJ retoma este viernes caso Jesuitas," *La Pagina*, August 19, 2011, accessed September 8, 2011, http://www.lapagina.com.sv/nacionales/55005/2011/08/19/CSJ-retoma-este-viernes-caso-Jesuitas.

nine military officers were accused of participating in the Jesuit killings.[117] If extradition is denied, the focus will shift to the Salvadoran government's international obligation to extradite or prosecute war crimes and/or crimes against humanity.

Ultimately, despite the small opening afforded by the 2000 Supreme Court decision that explicitly allowed for case-by-case consideration of the applicability of the 1993 amnesty law, there have not been any "as-applied" rulings denying amnesty. Only the recent arrests of the former military officers involved in the Jesuit killings provide for the possibility of trial and conviction notwithstanding the amnesty, if the nine officers are in fact extradited to Spain. At the domestic level, the decision of whether to characterize the charges in a given case as violations of fundamental rights is in the first instance one for the prosecutor, and to date the prosecutors' office has not seen fit to find even the most egregious violations of rights during the civil war as constituting the kind of fundamental human rights violations needed to overcome the amnesty law.[118] This decision has been maintained both through the several governments headed by ARENA (the government in power when many of the violations were committed), but also since the government has been in the hands of the center left FMLN. The explanation may lie in fear of the FMLN as well as of right-wing forces that could potentially face charges based on war crimes committed during the conflict. Meanwhile, the fact that the network of Salvadoran human rights groups is weak and has little popular support has also slowed any progression toward criminal accountability.

Nonetheless, the current Funes government has changed its tone, if not the actions of its prosecutors or legislators. Approximately six months after assuming office, the new president, on the eighteenth anniversary of the end of the conflict, offered an apology for abuses committed by state agents, recognizing the responsibility of the state for human rights violations committed between 1980 and 1992. This announcement marked the first time a Salvadoran president had formally and publicly recognized state responsibility for human rights abuses.[119] This apology has been followed by others, notably Funes's request for forgiveness for the Salvadoran state's involvement in the El Mozote Massacre, calling it "the worst massacre of civilians in contemporary Latin American history."[120] Funes has also broken with preceding administrations' persistent avoidance of investigation into Archbishop Romero's murder and has apologized for the crime, stating that the archbishop was a victim of right-wing death squads "who unfortunately acted with the protection,

[117]  Ibid.
[118]  Roht-Arriaza, "Impunity in Latin America."
[119]  Christian Volkel, "President Offers Apology for Civil War Crimes in El Salvador," *Global Insight*, January 18, 2010, Nexis U.K.
[120]  "El Salvador Head Apologises for 1981 El Mozote Massacre" *BBC News*, January 17, 2012, accessed January 17, 2012, http://www.bbc.co.uk/news/world-latin-america-16589757.

collaboration, or participation of state agents."[121] Funes indicated that it was up to the courts to bring cases of past violations forward, since the Supreme Court has already found that the amnesty law cannot apply to grave human rights violations.[122] The new president has also taken the first step in complying with the 2005 IACtHR decision in the *Serrano-Cruz* case by signing an executive decree that created a new National Search Commission for Disappeared Children to look for children forcibly disappeared during the armed conflict.[123] However, the commission still has inadequate resources and support for its task.[124] In the Jesuit case, the Funes government accepted the Spanish arrest warrants and ordered police to arrest the suspects for possible extradition to Spain. While the government may see this case, involving Spanish citizens, as best gotten rid of rather than as a precedent for cases involving only Salvadorans, it does at least begin a conversation about the role of the domestic prosecutor and courts. And the Salvadoran courts, at least, have changed. Upon assuming office, Funes appointed four reform-minded judges to the Supreme Court, one of whom was a prosecutor in the initial proceedings in the Jesuit case. Once appointed, the four judges immediately began investigating a backload of cases, institutional nepotism, and pilferage of public funds.[125] However, the contingent of reformists faces stiff opposition from the nine conservative judges that also sit on the Salvadoran Supreme Court. Their actions in the upcoming extradition proceedings will provide a barometer for how much has actually changed in the judiciary.

## CONCLUSION

Legal outcomes in Guatemala and El Salvador indicate that, as in Chile, attempts to interpret the existing amnesty laws to allow investigation have fared better than direct challenges to the constitutionality of amnesty laws.[126] In Guatemala, the amnesty laws have been intermittently and inconsistently applied to preclude prosecution, but for the most part have been interpreted as not applying to the most

[121]  Oscar Batres, "Funes pide perdón por asesinato de arzobispo Romero," *La Prensa*, March 24, 2010, accessed August 9, 2011, http://www.laprensa.com.ni/2010/03/24/internacionales/20095.

[122]  Ibid.

[123]  Amnesty International, *Annual Report: El Salvador 2011* (Amnesty International, May 28, 2011), accessed August 9, 2011, http://www.amnestyusa.org/research/reports/annual-report-el-salvador-2011?page=show.

[124]  Centre for Justice and International Law (CEJIL), "United Nations Recommends El Salvador to Investigate the Whereabouts of the Serrano-Cruz Sisters," February 5, 2010, accessed August 9, 2011, http://cejil.org/en/categoria/pais/el-salvador-0.

[125]  Linda Garret, "El Salvador Update-2011," Centre for Democracy in the Americas, August 3, 2011, accessed August 10, 2011, http://www.democracyinamericas.org/around-the-region-blog/el-salvador-update-july-2011/.

[126]  Roht-Arriaza and Gibson, "The Developing Jurisprudence on Amnesty," 884.

serious crimes. To the extent the Guatemalan Constitutional Court has addressed the amnesty issue, it is impossible to pull out a consistent line of reasoning from the cases, which seem to depend more on the particulars of court composition and political moment than on principled legal argument. Allegations of constitutional violations due to the failure to apply the amnesty seem aimed more at delay than at well-reasoned legal challenges. It remains to be seen how the higher courts will react to the latest burst of trial court convictions.

In El Salvador, there are few judicial decisions on amnesty because the prosecutor has refused to bring forward cases that would raise the issue. The amnesty law seems to still enjoy broad support from political elites across the spectrum, but the Supreme Court's decision on extradition of the suspects in the Jesuit case may provide clues as to how it might rule in future domestic cases. Or not; the recusal of the Court's most progressive judges may make the extradition case a particularly difficult one. The Court's refusal to uphold the Spanish arrest warrant does not bode well for future efforts. The Jesuit case, even if unsuccessful in the Salvadoran courts, may reopen public discussion of the issue in a way that influences the prosecutors' office.

Equal or more important than the legal obstacles to overcoming impunity are more general or systemic barriers, including rampant crime, corruption, and intimidation of judicial actors, lawyers, and witnesses as well as limited police and prosecutorial resources.[127] Many clandestine security forces responsible for human rights violations during the armed conflict are rumored to have strong ties to drug trafficking activities as well as to organized crime in general. Many assume a certain amount of overlap between those responsible for past human rights violations and present common crime.[128] These factors have overwhelmed a fragile judiciary, maintaining a pervasive sense of insecurity. Drug traffickers and other powerful people – far beyond the military and paramilitary involved in the internal armed conflicts – have a vested interest in maintaining an ineffective judicial system.[129] While everyone is affected by crime, elites are better able to isolate themselves behind private security forces and gated communities; the poor, female victims of an epidemic of femicide,

---

[127] Roht-Arriaza, "Impunity in Latin America."

[128] To deal with the broader problem of impunity, Guatemala created the International Commission against Impunity in Guatemala (CICG), designed as an independent investigatory commission under joint UN/Guatemalan government auspices intended to "determine the existence of illegal security groups and clandestine organizations"; collaborate with the state in the dismantling of these groups; promote the investigation, criminal prosecution, and punishment of those crimes committed by their members. See Roht-Arriaza, "Making the State do Justice," 102. See also Andrew Hudson and Alexandra Taylor, "The International Commission Against Impunity in Guatemala," *Journal of International Criminal Justice* 8 (2010): 56–7.

[129] Roht-Arriaza, "Making the State do Justice," 102.

and land and rights activists bear the brunt of a culture of impunity.[130] Courts incapable of enforcing an everyday level of justice will inevitably struggle to pursue accountability for human rights violations committed decades ago. This overlap, and the manner in which it colors the politics of impunity in the region, may be the biggest single factor in limiting a potential justice cascade.

---

[130] According to the 2011 World Development Report issued by the U.S. Department of Justice, Guatemala's murder rate is forty-six per one hundred thousand people, while El Salvador's is over sixty per one hundred thousand. Whole sections of Guatemala's northern department Petén are under control of the Mexican Zetas drug cartel, responsible for massacring twenty-seven people on a ranch located near the Guatemalan-Mexican border. See "The Tormented Isthmus," *The Economist*, April 14, 2011, accessed July 11, 2011, http://www.economist.com/node/18558254. See also Nicholas Casey, "Mexican Gang Moves into Guatemala," *The Wall Street Journal*, June 22, 2011, accessed July 13, 2011, http://online.wsj.com/article/SB10001424052702304887904576398292265171806.html.

# 8

## Creeks of Justice

### Debating Post-Atrocity Accountability and Amnesty in Rwanda and Uganda

*Phil Clark*

For the last twenty years, Rwanda and Uganda have experienced some of the most violent and destructive conflicts in the world. The overlapping nature and the scale of these conflicts – involving tens of thousands of civilian perpetrators and victims – inevitably shape the international and domestic justice processes designed to address mass crimes. Since 1986, the civil war in northern Uganda between the Ugandan government and the Lord's Resistance Army (LRA), a rebel force infamous for its abduction and enlistment of children, has killed tens of thousands of civilians. In response, a government "protection" policy of forced displacement has driven an estimated 1.7 million people, nearly ninety percent of the total northern Ugandan population, into 200 squalid camps for internally displaced persons (IDPs).[1] In 1994 in Rwanda, between five hundred thousand and one million Tutsi and their perceived Hutu and Twa sympathizers were systematically murdered in a genocide that lasted a little over three months.[2] The *génocidaires*, many of whom knew their victims personally, killed intimately, with basic weapons such as machetes, hoes, and spiked clubs known as *panga*, and usually near victims' homes.[3]

This chapter focuses on the accountability measures adopted in response to atrocities in Rwanda and Uganda and situates them specifically in ongoing debates about

[1] United Nations, *Consolidated Appeal for Uganda 2006* (United Nations Office for the Coordination of Humanitarian Affairs, November 30, 2005), accessed January 19, 2012, http://ochaonline.un.org/HUMANITARIANAPPEAL/webpage.asp?Page=1373.
[2] Most writers estimate the number of Tutsi deaths during the genocide to be in the range of five hundred thousand to one million. In her comprehensive analysis of the Rwandan genocide, Alison Des Forges estimates that five hundred thousand Tutsi were murdered: Alison Des Forges, *Leave None to Tell the Story: Genocide in Rwanda* (New York: Human Rights Watch, 1999), 15–16. Historian Gérard Prunier, however, calculates "the least bad possible" number of deaths to be eight hundred fifty thousand; Gérard Prunier, *The Rwanda Crisis: History of a Genocide* (London: Hurst and Co., 1998), 265.
[3] See Des Forges, *Leave None to Tell the Story*, 209–12; African Rights, *Rwanda: Death, Despair and Defiance* (Revised edition) (London: African Rights, 1995), chapter 9; Romeo Dallaire, *Shake Hands with the Devil: The Failure of Humanity in Rwanda* (Toronto: Random House Canada, 2003), chapter 11.

the appropriateness and legality of amnesty for perpetrators of serious human rights violations. In particular, this chapter examines accountability trends in these countries in light of Kathryn Sikkink and Ellen Lutz's theory of the justice cascade, represented by "the dramatic shift in the legitimacy of the norms of individual criminal accountability for human rights violations and an increase in actions (prosecutions) on behalf of those norms."[4] In her chapter in this volume, Sikkink emphasizes the importance of international and domestic norm entrepreneurs, including international human rights organizations, activists, and scholars, in fostering the "international diffusion" of norms of individual criminal accountability that culminated in the adoption of the Rome Statute in 1998 and the commencement of the ICC's work in 2002.

The basis for this research is nearly 700 interviews that I conducted in Rwanda, Uganda, Tanzania, and the Netherlands between 2003 and 2011 with international, national, and community-level political and judicial officials, lawyers, civil society representatives, and the general population and firsthand observations of international, national, and community court hearings into serious crimes. The analysis in this chapter focuses on the involvement of international and national policymakers and affected populations in policy decisions about how best to address mass atrocity and in the practical implementation of those decisions.

This chapter argues that the justice cascade interpretation of global norm diffusion does not adequately explain why Rwanda and Uganda have developed innovative strategies to deliver accountability to atrocity perpetrators over the last twenty years. The justice cascade concept implies a linear, even teleological, trajectory of diffusion in which states move inexorably – because of the convergence of domestic and international normative streams – from employing amnesties to individual criminal accountability through prosecutions of high-ranking suspects. The experiences of Rwanda and Uganda run counter to the justice cascade interpretation in three key respects. First, domestic policy decisions regarding accountability have fluctuated greatly, with amnesty processes being accepted, modified, rejected, and reinstated at different times depending on prevailing political, legal, and social circumstances. Second, international norm entrepreneurs have wielded minimal influence over domestic accountability decisions, which have often been made in explicit opposition to the narrow prescriptions of advocates of individual criminal accountability. Rather than converging, international and domestic streams have tended to oppose one another. Finally, the advocacy and critique by international norm entrepreneurs have often served to stymie innovative and context-specific domestic attempts at accountability. In this regard, the specific form of individual criminal accountability proposed by the justice cascade model – namely prosecutions of senior political and officials deemed most

---

4    Sikkink's "The Age of Accountability: The Rise of Individual Criminal Accountability," 19.

responsible for human rights violations – has harmed domestic justice endeavors that
have had to contend with broader forms of criminal culpability.

In short, justice has not cascaded in Rwanda and Uganda in the ways described
by Sikkink and Lutz, but rather ebbed, flowed, sometimes dried up completely and
quickly restarted – and usually emanated from domestic or regional sources in direct
opposition to external trends. Justice in these countries has manifested as a series of
winding creeks and tributaries rather than a predictable and harmonious cascade.
Within this context, amnesty – in various forms – has persisted as an important
domestic response to conflict, despite the protestations of external actors. This chapter contends that, despite this uneven justice process, Rwanda and Uganda have
often pursued domestic accountability strategies that are more appropriate to local
settings and likely to yield greater long-term benefits than the modes of accountability proposed by international norm entrepreneurs. This finding is relevant for
our understanding of the ways in which norms develop domestically and of how
accountability policies evolve within conflict-affected countries. It also underscores
that well-intentioned international advocates may sometimes do a great disser-
vice to the cause of justice when they hew to a narrow view of individual criminal
accountability.

This chapter is structured as follows. Part I provides a brief background to the conflict situations in Rwanda and Uganda, highlighting important regional overlaps of
violence. Parts II and III analyze the transitional justice responses to conflict in both
countries, focusing on debates over amnesty and modes of accountability. Part IV
then draws together the analyses from these sections to highlight regional trends in
terms of transitional justice decision making and the relevance of these findings for
broader theoretical debates about international norm diffusion and the appropriateness of amnesty as a postconflict remedy.

## BACKGROUND TO GREAT LAKES CONFLICTS

This section provides a brief overview of the conflicts in the countries under examination, laying a foundation for the discussion of transitional justice processes in the
subsequent sections.

### Rwanda

Between April 1994 and July 1994, Rwanda experienced one of the most devas-
tating waves of mass killing in modern history. In around 100 days, nearly three-
quarters of the total Tutsi population (which constituted around eleven percent of
the overall population of Rwanda in 1994, while Hutu constituted nearly eighty-four
percent) were murdered and hundreds of thousands more exiled to neighboring

countries.[5] What distinguishes the Rwandan genocide from other cases of mass murder in the twentieth century, and in particular from the genocide of Jews during the Second World War, is the use of low-technology weaponry, the mass involvement of the Hutu population in the killings, the social and cultural similarities of the perpetrators and victims, and the astonishing speed of the genocide.

The broader civil war context of the early 1990s is critical in explaining why the genocide occurred.[6] On October 1, 1990, the Rwandan Patriotic Front (RPF), comprising mainly descendants of Tutsi refugees who fled Hutu violence in the 1960s, invaded Rwanda from Uganda.[7] Government forces repelled the RPF and a guerrilla war broke out in the northeast of the country. After nearly three years of fighting, the government and the RPF signed the UN-brokered Arusha Peace Accords in August 1993.

On the night of April 6, 1994, Rwandan President Juvénal Habyarimana and Burundian President Cyprien Ntaryamira were returning from regional talks in Tanzania. At around 8:30 P.M., as their plane neared Kayibanda Airport in Kigali, two missiles fired from near the airport's perimeter struck the aircraft, which crashed into the garden of the presidential palace, killing everyone on board. Within an hour of the crash, government roadblocks were set up across Kigali, and troops and militias known as *interahamwe* began stopping vehicles and checking identity papers. Shots rang out across the city as killings began at the roadblocks and presidential guards and militiamen went house to house, killing Tutsi and Hutu accused of collaborating with Tutsi.[8] The killing spree spread rapidly beyond Kigali into towns and villages across Rwanda. In the following weeks, government leaders fanned out from the capital to incite the entire Hutu population to murder Tutsi, backed by messages of hate on Radio-Télévision Libres de Mille Collines (RTLM). By most estimates, around two hundred fifty thousand Tutsi were killed in the first two weeks of the genocide.[9]

## Uganda

Since 1986, northern Uganda has experienced one of Africa's longest and most destructive civil wars. The civilian population has suffered widespread murder, rape, torture, abduction, looting, and mass displacement into IDP camps, resulting in immense social and cultural fragmentation among northern communities,

---

[5]  Prunier, *The Rwanda Crisis*, 264–8.
[6]  For a useful account of the flurry of key events in 1990, see Peter Uvin, *Aiding Violence: The Development Enterprise in Rwanda* (West Hartford, CT: Kumarian Press, 1998), 60–5.
[7]  Prunier, *The Rwanda Crisis*, 72 and chapter 3.
[8]  Dallaire, *Shake Hands with the Devil*, chapter 10.
[9]  African Rights, *Death, Despair and Defiance*, 258; Des Forges, *Leave None to Tell the Story*, 770; Alan Kuperman, *The Limits of Humanitarian Intervention: Genocide in Rwanda* (Washington: Brookings Institution Press, 2001), 16.

especially in the Acholiland region. A 2007 UN study of perceptions among northern Ugandans shows that the majority of the affected population considers both the
government and the LRA responsible for the harm it has suffered.[10] Recent peace
talks between the government and rebels in Juba, southern Sudan, which led to
the signing of a cessation of hostilities agreement in August 2006 but ultimately collapsed in April 2008, represented one of the best opportunities of securing lasting
peace in northern Uganda.

Crucial to the motivations and tactics of the LRA has been the personality of
its leader, Joseph Kony, whom Douglas Johnson and David Anderson describe as
"mantic,"[11] belonging to *manti*, diviners or healers who often openly oppose main-
stream social and political structures. Kony, proclaiming himself a messenger from
God and a mediator between the population and the spirit world, has continually
claimed that the Acholi require purification because of their failure to directly
counter President Yoweri Museveni's forces in northern Uganda. There is much
debate over Kony's and the LRA's precise political and military objectives.[12] Some
authors dismiss the LRA as a collection of spiritual cranks with no coherent political
agenda.[13] However, at the heart of many of Kony and other LRA leaders' public pronouncements is a consistent political message regarding the need to recognize long-
standing Acholi grievances, greater integration of Acholi into Ugandan national life,
the dismantling of the IDP camps, as well as more spiritual claims concerning the
need for cleansing and purification of the Acholi.[14] Complicating interpretations of
the LRA's objectives is that, in seeking the greater integration of Acholi into national
life, the LRA has used violence against the Acholi population as a military tactic and
has abducted thousands of children from Acholi and other northern communities,
thus weakening its ability to win popular support.

## RWANDA: POST-GENOCIDE TRANSITIONAL JUSTICE

This section on transitional justice processes in Rwanda follows a structure that is
replicated in the subsequent section on Uganda. First, it describes briefly the nature

---

[10] OHCHR, *Making Peace Our Own: Victims' Perceptions of Accountability, Transitional Justice and
Reconciliation in Northern Uganda* (Geneva: OHCHR, 2007), 3, accessed September 3, 2011, http://
www.ohchr.org/english/docs/northern_Uganda_august2007.pdf.

[11] Douglas Johnson and David Anderson, "Revealing Prophets," in *Revealing Prophets: Prophecy in
Eastern African Studies*, ed. David Anderson and Douglas Johnson (London: James Currey, 1995), 14.

[12] For a thorough overview of various commentators' interpretations of the LRA's political agenda, see
Adam Branch, "Neither Peace nor Justice: Political Violence and the Peasantry in Northern Uganda,
1986–1998," *African Studies Quarterly* 8 (2005): 4–9.

[13] See, for example, "Girls Escape Ugandan Rebels," *British Broadcasting Corporation*, June 25, 2003,
accessed September 5, 2011, http://news.bbc.co.uk/2/hi/africa/3018810.stm.

[14] Sverker Finnström, "In and Out of Culture: Fieldwork in War-Torn Uganda," *Critique of Anthropology*
21 (2001): 247–8.

of the challenges that shape the adoption of transitional justice measures. Second, it outlines the trajectory of transitional justice policymaking in the country, focusing on issues of amnesty and accountability. Third, it explores the responses of international norm entrepreneurs to domestic transitional justice policymaking. Fourth, it analyzes the country's transitional justice experience in light of the theoretical questions identified at the outset of this chapter.

## Post-Genocide Challenges

The principal elements determining transitional justice decisions in Rwanda are the enormity of the genocide in terms of the number of victims and perpetrators, and the severe resource limitations of an impoverished nation further weakened by mass violence. In the months following the genocide in Rwanda, around one hundred twenty thousand genocide suspects, mostly Hutu, were rounded up and transported to jails around the country built to hold only forty-five thousand inmates.[15] Most detainees were never formally charged with any crime and were forced to live in hellish conditions: underfed, drinking dirty water, and crammed into tiny rooms where they were often made to sleep in latticework formations for lack of space.[16]

During the genocide, the Rwandan judicial system – which showed signs of breakdown before 1994 – was nearly completely destroyed, as the infrastructure of the national courts was decimated and many judges and lawyers were killed or fled the country.[17] With the existing judicial system incapable of dealing with massive numbers of suspects, the government sought new mechanisms to hear tens of thousands of genocide cases. Furthermore, the scale of the genocide – which affected every Rwandan directly in some way – necessitated a range of nonlegal responses, including processes designed for truth recovery and reconciliation.

## Trajectory of Transitional Justice Policymaking in Rwanda

It took the Rwandan government nearly seven years to settle on the three-pronged approach to justice that has since been used to address genocide crimes, comprising the ICTR, established in November 1994; the Rwandan national courts; and the *gacaca* community-level jurisdictions. At an international conference in Kigali in October 1995, the government considered both a general amnesty and the traditional version of *gacaca* (used for centuries as a dispute resolution tool) as possible methods for dealing with genocide suspects. Amnesty was rejected on the grounds

---

[15] International Centre for Prison Studies (King's College), *Prison Brief for Rwanda* (London: ICPS, 2002), accessed August 26, 2011, www.kcl.ac.uk/depsta/rel/icps/worldbrief/africa_records.php?code=39.

[16] Author's field notes, Butare Central Prison, February 4, 2003.

[17] Amnesty International, *Rwanda – Gacaca: A Question of Justice*, AI Doc. AFR 47/007/2002 (Amnesty International, December 2002), 12–13.

that it would inflame many genocide survivors' perceived desire for vengeance. Prosecutor General Martin Ngoga argues that the RPF-dominated government opposed amnesty because it had been used extensively by the Habyarimana regime to shield perpetrators of serious violations during periods of mass violence, for example through the August 1962, May 1963, February 1979, and November 1991 amnesty laws.[18] The government dismissed traditional *gacaca* on the grounds that it violated existing Rwandan law regarding the need to formally prosecute serious crimes, particularly murder.[19]

In 1996 and 1997, the government, with major assistance from international NGOs such as the Belgian organization Avocats Sans Frontières (ASF) and the Danish Centre for Human Rights (DCHR), began a major overhaul of the national courts. The dire state of the post-genocide judicial system forced the government and international donors to embark on a nationwide campaign of training new judges and lawyers. The national court system also suffered from a lengthy history of corruption and repression, since before the genocide the courts were highly politicized and invariably a tool of an authoritarian executive. These factors necessitated the post-genocide vetting and training of judicial personnel. In an attempt to speed the prosecution of genocide cases in the national courts, the government passed the Organic Law of August 1996, which divided genocide suspects into four categories according to the severity of their crimes, and established a plea bargaining scheme that offered decreased sentences in exchange for suspects' confessions.[20]

The national courts were initially slow in hearing the cases of genocide suspects. By 2000 the courts had heard only 2,500 cases, less than three percent of the genocide backlog. Of those cases, around 500 accused were acquitted and 400 received the death penalty. Plea bargaining in these cases was extremely rare, with fewer than twenty percent of defendants pleading guilty. It was clear that, at this rate, the vast majority of genocide cases would never be heard, necessitating the search for alternative mechanisms to process the backlog.[21]

Policy discussions turned to the possibility of employing a South Africa-style truth commission. As Jeremy Sarkin points out, there is a precedent of employing such an

---

[18] Martin Ngoga, "The Institutionalisation of Impunity: A Judicial Perspective of the Rwandan Genocide" in *After Genocide: Transitional Justice, Post-Conflict Reconstruction and Reconciliation in Rwanda and Beyond*, ed. Phil Clark and Zachary D. Kaufman (London: Hurst and Co. Publishers, 2008), 321–32.

[19] Republic of Rwanda, "Minutes of the Symposium on Gacaca," Hotel Umubano, Kigali, March 6–7, 2000, 13.

[20] Republic of Rwanda, "Loi Organique No. 8196 du 30/8/96 sur l, organisation des poursuites des infractions constitutives du crime de genocide ou de crimes contre l'humanité, commises à partir de 1er octobre 1990," *Official Gazette of the Republic of Rwanda*, September 1, 1996, Articles 2–9. (From here on referred to as the "Organic Law.")

[21] Amnesty International, *Rwanda: The Troubled Course of Justice*, AI Index: AFR 47/10/00 (Amnesty International, April 2000), 2–3.

institution in Rwanda. After the signing of the Arusha Accords in 1993, a truth commission was established in Rwanda to investigate human rights abuses committed between 1990 and 1993. Its work was severely undermined by ongoing violence in Rwanda in late 1993, but it still produced a final report that detailed crimes against humanity committed during the civil war period.[22] In 1997, the government considered, then rejected, the idea of using a truth commission to address genocide crimes on the grounds that it would not adequately punish *génocidaires*.[23]

The year 1998 marked the reemergence in public discourse of the potential use of *gacaca* for hearing and prosecuting genocide cases. Between May 1998 and March 1999, President Pasteur Bizimungu held "reflection meetings" each Saturday at Urugwiro Village in Kigali.[24] The purpose of these meetings was to gather political, social, legal, and religious authorities to discuss the most pressing issues concerning national reconstruction.[25] Questions of justice and reconciliation featured heavily in the talks and in June 1998 the possibility of revitalizing *gacaca* was again raised, primarily by a group of provincial prefects including Protais Musoni, then prefect of Kibungo and now minister of local government; Good Governance; Community Development; and Social Affairs. Fatuma Ndangiza, former executive secretary of the National Unity and Reconciliation Commission (NURC), describes Musoni as the "father of gacaca"[26] and the individual chiefly responsible for convincing the government to reform *gacaca* to deal with genocide cases.

On October 17, 1998, Bizimungu established a commission to investigate the possibility of restructuring *gacaca* into a system appropriate for handling genocide cases.[27] Musoni describes the debates at Urugwiro during this period as protracted and often heated, a fact not readily expressed by many state sources that tend to characterize the government's decision to transform the traditional practice of *gacaca* as rapid and almost inevitable.[28] My interviews with President Kagame, Musoni, and

---

[22] Jeremy Sarkin, "The Necessity and Challenges of Establishing a Truth and Reconciliation Commission in Rwanda," *Human Rights Quarterly* 21 (1999): 777–8.

[23] For analyses of these debates regarding a truth commission in Rwanda, see, Sarkin, Ibid., and Mark Drumbl, "Sclerosis: Retributive Justice and the Rwandan Genocide," *Punishment and Society* 2 (2000): 296.

[24] For a detailed synthesis of these meetings, see, Republic of Rwanda, *Report on the Reflection Meetings Held in the Office of the President of the Republic from May 1998 to March 1999,* (Kigali: Office of the President of the Republic, August 1999).

[25] For an overview of these meetings, see Charles Murigande, "Report on Urugwiro Talks from May 1998 to March 1999," *Report on the National Summit of Unity and Reconciliation,* (Kigali: NURC, October 18–20, 2000), 22–34.

[26] Author's government interview, Fatuma Ndangiza, Executive Secretary, National Unity and Reconciliation Commission, Kigali, June 10, 2006.

[27] Republic of Rwanda, *Report on the Reflection Meetings,* 9.

[28] Author's government interview, Protais Musoni, Rwandan Minister of Local Government, Good Governance, Community Development and Social Affairs, Kigali, June 13, 2006.

other government officials indicate that four main divisions were apparent during
the Urugwiro talks: between lawyers and nonlawyers; urban and rural elites; the
RPF military and political hierarchy; and members of the RPF who had fought
or been present in Uganda or Rwanda during the civil war and the genocide and
diasporic figures who had returned to Rwanda after the genocide.

Lawyers, urban elites, and RPF (especially military) leaders who had lived through
the conflict generally favored stronger forms of justice for genocide suspects than
they perceived in the proposed use of *gacaca*. These groups opposed *gacaca* for
slightly different reasons. Lawyers favored more conventional judicial responses to
genocide crimes that reflected their own legal training. Urban elites favored similar
legal measures because they would centralize accountability processes in Kigali,
while lawyers and urban leaders converged in their depictions of *gacaca* as a primi-
tive, rural practice appropriate only for low-level community infractions and in
their distrust of the population's capacity to address serious crimes so soon after the
genocide.[29] RPF leaders, particularly in the military, with firsthand experience of
the genocide advocated strict justice for the crimes they had witnessed directly and
invoked survivors' demands in the community for such measures.

On the other side, nonlawyers, rural elites, RPF political officials, and returned
diasporic figures argued that conventional court processes for genocide crimes
would prove inadequate in the face of hundreds of thousands of suspects still in
prison and would fail to address crucial social issues of healing and reconciliation
in the countryside. Some RPF political leaders advocated the use of *gacaca* by
invoking principles of popular justice from their days in Uganda supporting Yoweri
Museveni's National Resistance Movement (NRM) and Uganda's history of using
Local Councils (LCs) to address crimes in the community. Designed initially as fora
for collective decision making on day-to-day community issues, the LCs evolved
into the primary local-level political and judicial institution throughout Uganda.
The LCs, as they became known after Museveni's election victory in 1996, grew out
of Resistance Councils (RCs) established by his forces during the Ugandan bush
war to maintain law and order in rebel-held regions and to gather intelligence and
mobilize recruitment in areas held by Milton Obote's army. Soon after the NRM's
rise to power, Museveni proclaimed that "popular justice" could help overcome
the rampant corruption of political and judicial structures inherited from Amin
and Obote and reinvigorate Ugandan community life.[30] In 1987, the Resistance
Councils and Committees Statute afforded the RCs the role of hearing low-level
civil cases as a means to overcoming the congestion of the magistrates' courts and to

---

[29]  See also, Republic of Rwanda, *Report on the Reflection Meetings*, 60.
[30]  Yoweri Museveni, *Sowing the Mustard Seed: The Struggle for Freedom and Democracy in Uganda*
      (London: MacMillan, 1997), 30.

making justice more accessible – physically and culturally – to local populations.[31] At Urugwiro, several RPF political leaders argued that *gacaca* could similarly aid Rwanda's attempts to decongest the national courts of their genocide caseload while also pursuing healing and reconciliation at the community level.[32]

Meanwhile, diasporic elites, particularly Tutsi who had returned from Europe and the United States, argued that the state needed to consider international opinion of Rwanda's post-genocide policies because foreign aid and diplomatic support were essential to the reconstruction process.[33] A government official who had been at the Urugwiro meetings and spoke to me on the grounds of anonymity highlighted a key area of international disquiet:

> There was major pressure on the government because of the public executions of *génocidaires* like the ones in the Amahoro [Stadium]. There was anger from survivors because of the lack of justice and anger from the international community because of how we were [initially] going about justice, so it was very difficult. The world was sympathetic to us after the genocide because of what we'd been through but some people [at Urugwiro] were saying we needed to take a softer line. We had to act calmly and reasonably. We couldn't afford to lose international support because that would mean losing aid and being isolated again.[34]

This official stated that the key element that eventually convinced Kagame and others of the virtues of *gacaca* was concern over international perceptions of Rwanda's approach to post-genocide accountability.[35] The timing of the Urugwiro talks was especially important in this sense, commencing in May 1998, several weeks after a number of widely reported public executions of convicted *génocidaires* in stadia around Rwanda during the official genocide commemorations in April.[36] The parties at Urugwiro decided eventually that international apprehension over public executions of *génocidaires* outweighed any disquiet over reviving *gacaca*. The latter concerns could be addressed by instilling sufficient safeguards for due process as *gacaca* was reformed to handle genocide cases. These descriptions of the Urugwiro

---

[31]   Bruce Baker, "Popular Justice and Policing from Bush War to Democracy: Uganda, 1981–2004," *International Journal of the Sociology of Law* 32 (2004): 336.

[32]   Republic of Rwanda, *Report on the Reflection Meetings*, 60.

[33]   On this theme, see also, Barbara Oomen, "Donor-Driven Justice and its Discontents: The Case of Rwanda," *Development and Change* 36 (2005): 887–910. In 2002, Richard Sezibera, the Rwandan ambassador to the United States, said, "We have modified the [traditional *gacaca*] process to meet international standards as much as possible and placed the gacaca courts under the control of our supreme court." (Richard Sezibera, "The Only Way to Bring Justice to Rwanda," *The Washington Post*, April 7, 2002.)

[34]   Author's government interview, Anonymous Rwandan Official, Kigali, June 14, 2006.

[35]   Ibid.

[36]   See, for example, "From Butchery to Executions in Rwanda," *British Broadcasting Corporation*, April 27, 1998, accessed September 5, 2011, news.bbc.co.uk/1/hi/programmes/from_our_own_correspondent/84120.stm.

meetings highlight the major divisions within the Rwandan government and the manifold concerns raised during debates over appropriate justice and reconciliation measures.

In February 1999, after the UN Office of the High Commissioner for Human Rights (OHCHR) assisted a post-Urugwiro study of *gacaca*, the UN special rapporteur stated, "gacaca is not competent to hear crimes against humanity, but it could be utilized for purposes of testifying in connection with reconciliation."[37] Ignoring the UN's advice, Bizimungu's commission produced a draft proposal in June 1999 detailing how *gacaca* jurisdictions might be divided among the various levels of local administration – cell, sector, district, province – with each level hearing and prosecuting cases according to the categories of crime outlined in the Organic Law.[38] Following debate of this draft, the Gacaca Law was passed in January 2001.[39]

For nine years, *gacaca* jurisdictions overseen by locally elected judges have prosecuted around four hundred thousand genocide suspects in more than one million trials. These trials have had a marked but highly variable impact on the Rwandan population, as I have explored in detail elsewhere.[40] Nevertheless, *gacaca* has proven remarkably successful at prosecuting such an enormous backlog of genocide cases, individualizing culpability by connecting specific crimes to specific perpetrators and unearthing microlevel truths about genocide events while costing the Rwandan state only around $40 million.

Over time, however, sections of the government, including the President's Office, have grown frustrated with the slow pace of *gacaca*, believing that it consumes valuable resources and distracts from attempts to pursue national development. Such were the government's concerns that in 2006 it again considered an amnesty for some genocide perpetrators in order to hasten the justice process. President Kagame said:

> We have faced many difficulties in trying to speed up gacaca.... We need to stress that gacaca is not open-ended because, as a nation, we have other aims, such as developing our economy and building the country's skills base. Today the genocide caseload is still massive, so with gacaca we may have to think of new ways to address

[37] OHCHR, *Report on the Situation of Human Rights in Rwanda*, UN Doc. E/CN.4/1999/33 (OHCHR, February 8, 1999), 12. A member of the OHCHR team responsible for the 1999 report later published a longer critique of the proposed *gacaca* process. See Leah Werchick, "Prospects for Justice in Rwanda's Citizen Tribunals," *Human Rights Brief* 8 (2001): 15–18.

[38] Stef Vandeginste, "Justice, Reconciliation and Reparation after Genocide and Crimes against Humanity: The Proposed Establishment of Popular Gacaca Tribunals in Rwanda" (paper presented at the All-Africa Conference on African Principles of Conflict Resolution and Reconciliation, Addis Ababa, November 8–12, 1999), 17–20.

[39] Republic of Rwanda, "Organic Law 40/2000 of 26/01/2001 Setting Up Gacaca Jurisdictions and Organising Prosecutions for Offences Constituting the Crime of Genocide or Crimes against Humanity Committed Between October 1, 1993 and December 31, 1994," *Official Gazette of the Republic of Rwanda*, October 2000, Article 13.

[40] Phil Clark, *The Gacaca Courts, Post-Genocide Justice and Reconciliation in Rwanda: Justice without Lawyers* (Cambridge: Cambridge University Press, 2010).

this.... Even an amnesty is possible, especially for low-level perpetrators. Anything is possible, even for more serious cases. What we have attempted here is justice on a massive scale but the costs have also been immense.[41]

The government eventually rejected the amnesty option and chose instead to streamline aspects of the *gacaca* procedure to hasten genocide trials. It also revised the Gacaca Law to decrease the sentences of most convicted *génocidaires* and promoted the use of community service as punishment rather than prison terms. It is expected that *gacaca* will complete its work by the middle of 2012, after which further prosecutions of genocide suspects will be handled by the national courts.

### Domestic and International Norm Entrepreneurs' Responses to Transitional Justice in Rwanda

From the outset, international norm entrepreneurs – principally human rights organizations such as Amnesty International (AI) and Human Rights Watch (HRW), which Sikkink identifies as among the most important actors in ushering in the global "age of accountability" (as discussed in her chapter in this volume) – have opposed Rwanda's domestic approaches to post-genocide accountability while broadly supporting the efforts of the ICTR. A small group of international actors such as ASF, DCHR, and Penal Reform International (PRI) have adopted a quieter, more technical role, critiquing Rwanda's methods behind closed doors and collaborating with the government in remedying perceived problems. The most vocal human rights groups, however, have vehemently opposed the use of *gacaca* to prosecute genocide suspects, echoing some of the concerns expressed by OHCHR in its 1999 study into *gacaca*.

In a report published in December 2002, AI argues:

[T]he legislation establishing the Gacaca Jurisdictions fails to guarantee minimum fair trial standards that are guaranteed in international treaties ratified by the Rwandese government.... [G]acaca trials need to conform to international standards of fairness so that the government's efforts to end impunity ... are effective. If justice is not seen to be done, public confidence in the judiciary will not be restored and the government will have lost an opportunity to show its determination to respect human rights.[42]

Elsewhere, AI argues that it is

principally concerned with the extrajudicial nature of the gacaca tribunals. The gacaca legislation does not incorporate international standards of fair trial. Defendants appearing before the tribunals are not afforded applicable judicial

---

[41] Author's government interviews, President Paul Kagame, June 13, 2006.

[42] Amnesty International, *Gacaca: A Question of Justice*, 2.

guarantees so as to ensure that the proceedings are fair, even though some could face maximum sentences of life imprisonment.[43]

Five years later, AI repeated similar criticisms of *gacaca*, namely that it "fails to meet international standards for fair trial and lacks independence, impartiality and transparency."[44] HRW echoed this view in 2009, equating *gacaca* with the U.S. government's military commissions in Guantanamo Bay: "Human Rights Watch knows of no criminal justice system other than Rwanda's highly discredited gacaca courts in which hearsay is admitted before a jury of non-lawyers, as would be the case with the revised military commissions."[45]

International norm entrepreneurs such as AI and HRW have also increasingly criticized the work of the Rwandan national courts, especially in light of the possible transfer and extradition of genocide suspects from the ICTR or third party states to Rwanda. An HRW *amicus curiae* brief was particularly influential in the recent decisions by the ICTR and the U.K. High Court not to transfer high-level suspects to Rwanda, stating that defendants would not receive a fair trial in Rwanda.[46]

As I argue elsewhere, these international critiques of Rwandan domestic approaches to transitional justice are inadequate for numerous reasons.[47] Regarding *gacaca*, international actors such as AI and HRW fail to take *gacaca* on its own terms; they critique it on the basis of a conception of formal, deterrent justice for which it was never intended. These commentators – who base their arguments on little empirical evidence from *gacaca* hearings – ignore *gacaca*'s many nonretributive benefits in terms of truth recovery and widespread popular involvement in trials. Thus, international critics adopt a narrow legal framework and, by insisting on a strict form of due process, fail to recognize the substantial challenges (especially the enormous genocide caseload and Rwanda's severe resource limitations) that necessitated *gacaca* in the first place.

Regarding the national courts, critiques by AI and HRW constitute generalizations about the nature of political space under the RPF's rule, rather than the

---

[43]  Amnesty International, "Rwanda: Gacaca – Gambling with Justice," press release, AI Index: AFR 47/003/2002, June 19, 2002, 1. For a detailed exploration of AI's approach to *gacaca* and how, for example it differs from PRI's, see Ariel Meyerstein, "Between Law and Culture: Rwanda's Gacaca and Postcolonial Legacy," *Law and Social Inquiry* 32 (Spring 2007): 467–508.

[44]  Amnesty International, "Rwanda: Fear for Safety/Legal Concern: François-Xavier Byuma," AI Index: AFR 47/007/2007(Amnesty International, May 9, 2007), 1.

[45]  Human Rights Watch, "U.S.: Revival of Guantanamo Military Commissions a Blow to Justice," Human Rights Watch, May 15, 2009.

[46]  Human Rights Watch, "Brief of Human Rights Watch as Amicus Curiae in Opposition to Rule 11bis Transer," in *The Prosecutor v. Fulgence* Kayishema (Kigali: International Criminal Tribunal for Rwanda, January 3, 2008).

[47]  Clark, *Justice without Lawyers*; Phil Clark and Nicola Palmer, "The International Community Fails Rwanda Again," (Oxford Transitional Justice Research Working Paper, Oxford, May 5, 2009).

specificities of the judicial process. These groups' opposition to the transfer of geno-cide suspects to Rwanda has denied the Rwandan judiciary – which at the national and community levels has already conducted hundreds of thousands of genocide trials – the opportunity to prosecute high-ranking suspects at home. In the case of the U.K. High Court proceedings, international norm entrepreneurs have preferred that genocide suspects be released within the United Kingdom rather than face pros-ecution in Rwanda.

*Analysis: Rwanda's Relevance for Amnesty and Accountability Debates*

The Rwandan example is important for the theoretical debates about amnesty and accountability outlined at the beginning of this chapter. First, Rwanda's policymak-ing on transitional justice issues has been far from linear or predictable. Immediate and changing political circumstances matter enormously, as does the relative strength of political actors and factions with varying views on what transitional justice should entail. As the Urugwiro negotiations highlight, the Rwandan gov-ernment was deeply divided over the question of how to address genocide crimes. *Gacaca* as the centerpiece of Rwanda's transitional justice strategy was the result of a political compromise between influential factions within the RPF.

On the question of amnesty, Rwanda has adopted a changeable position. Rwandan decision makers initially rejected amnesty for genocide perpetrators, only to recon-sider it several years later when the full burden of delivering justice for so many perpetrators became apparent, before eventually choosing more lenient forms of accountability (especially through community service). Whereas the RPF's and genocide survivors' anger and motives of revenge drove policymaking directly after the genocide and explain why amnesty was initially rejected, judicial pragmatism constituted a stronger motivation many years later when amnesty was reconsidered.

Second, international advocates of accountability have played a fluctuating role in Rwanda's transitional policymaking. Overall, debates about accountability for genocide crimes have been profoundly domestic, with international actors play-ing a peripheral (and often entirely ignored) role. Regional elements have also proven crucial, particularly Rwanda's borrowing principles and practices of local justice from Uganda (which, as we will see, has come full circle in Uganda's use of *gacaca* as a touchstone for debates about local accountability in northern Uganda). International concerns over Rwanda's use of capital punishment directly after the genocide motivated some policymakers to pursue more moderate justice measures, highlighting some international influence over the eventual creation of the *gacaca* jurisdictions. However, this element emerged late in the government discussions about transitional justice and represented the final factor that convinced some prin-cipal actors such as Kagame to adopt *gacaca*.

Once *gacaca* was functional, it attracted sustained criticism from international commentators – who in the main were ignored domestically because their critiques were deemed unrealistic and ideologically driven and failed to chime with pressing local legal and political concerns. The only international actors that have substantially influenced transitional processes in Rwanda have been those such as DCHR, ASF, and PRI, which have adopted a technical assistance role. This highlights that international norm entrepreneurs themselves can be deeply divided regarding how accountability should be delivered and how they should position themselves vis à vis the state mandated to oversee transition.

In contrast to Sikkink's depiction of groups such as AI and HRW (drawing mainly on the Latin American experience), these organizations, if anything, have undermined attempts at accountability for Rwandan genocide crimes. AI and HRW have critiqued *gacaca* and the Rwandan national courts – which have sought to prosecute all genocide cases – but they have been less clear regarding feasible alternatives for delivering justice. While these norm entrepreneurs have supported broadly the work of the ICTR, mandated to prosecute only a handful of the most senior perpetrators of the genocide, they have neglected the pressing question of what to do with the hundreds of thousands of everyday citizens who participated in the genocide. Thus, international actors have had only minimal influence over accountability debates in Rwanda, and domestic justice has often been pursued in direct opposition to the prescriptions of international advocates of criminal justice. Contrary to the justice cascade model, international and domestic streams of justice have not converged in the Rwandan case and a narrow conception of individual criminal accountability only for elite suspects has proven inadequate in the face of massive popular participation in the genocide.

## UGANDA AND TRANSITIONAL JUSTICE

Similar to Rwanda, the Ugandan case highlights critical challenges for processes designed to address mass atrocity. The next sections set out the context and the evolution of those processes to deal with past atrocity.

### Post-Atrocity Challenges

Tens of thousands of everyday Ugandan civilians have perpetrated violence against other civilians, often their own neighbors and family members. Further complicating transitional justice questions, many perpetrators are children abducted and coerced into rebel ranks to commit crimes against their own communities. Meanwhile the Ugandan government is heavily implicated in massive human rights violations, including torture and forced displacement.

Transitional processes in Uganda must therefore address the scale of the conflict in terms of the numbers of victims and perpetrators, as well as the intimate relations among the parties involved and the culpability of the same government mandated to oversee key transitional institutions. Furthermore, the twenty-four year civil war in northern Uganda arguably is still not over, which means that transitional justice occurs in a context of ongoing conflict and instability.[48] While the LRA has ceased military operations in northern Uganda, it continues similar patterns of violence elsewhere in the region from bases in Garamba National Park in northeastern DRC.

### *Trajectory of Transitional Justice Policymaking in Uganda*

Uganda's transitional justice landscape has been defined by peace talks, amnesty processes aimed at encouraging the disarmament and reintegration of rebel groups, and a wide range of accountability measures. Uganda has employed amnesty in a much more sustained and systematic manner than Rwanda. The Ugandan amnesty process that persists today began with lobbying by an umbrella civil society group, the Acholi Religious Leaders Peace Initiative (ARLPI), during the 1999 peace talks between the government and the LRA. Following President Museveni's statement in July 1998 that he would accept a ceasefire with the LRA, the ARLPI – along with the Acholi Parliamentary Group and Acholi in the diaspora – campaigned for amnesty for all rebels in northern Uganda to permanently halt the violence. The ARLPI conducted widespread consultations with northern victims' groups and found a strong desire among the population for personal and collective healing and reconciliation with the rebels.[49]

There are several precedents for employing amnesties in Uganda. In 1987, the NRM offered an amnesty to the Uganda People's Democratic Army (UPDA) and the Uganda People's Army (UPA) in exchange for a cessation of their insurgencies against the government.[50] Thereafter, several army commanders, working with traditional and cultural leaders, used unofficial amnesties to help end conflict. Beginning in 1996, Maj. Gen. Katumba Wamala successfully encouraged large numbers of rebels

---

[48] See, for example, Nicholas Waddell and Phil Clark, eds., *Courting Conflict? Peace, Justice and the ICC in Africa* (London: Royal African Society, 2008).

[49] Gilbert Khadiagala, "The Role of the Acholi Religious Leaders Peace Initiative (ARLPI) in Peace Building in Northern Uganda," Appendix in USAID/Management Systems International, *The Effectiveness of Civil Society Initiatives in Controlling Violent Conflicts and Building Peace: A Study of Three Approaches in the Greater Horn of Africa* (Washington DC: USAID/MSI, March 2001), 4–6.

[50] Barney Afako, "Reconciliation and Justice: 'Mato Oput' and the Amnesty Act" in *Protracted Conflict, Elusive Peace: Initiatives to End the Violence in Northern Uganda*, ed. Okello Lucima (London: Conciliation Resources/Accord, 2002), 65.

from the West Nile Bank Front (WNBF), which had regularly attacked western Uganda from bases in southern Sudan and eastern Zaire, to lay down their arms and return from the bush. Assuring the rebels that no returnees would face retribution and the army would facilitate their reintegration into their home communities, Wamala succeeded in ending the WNBF's insurgency in 1998.[51]

Following the ARLPI's public consultations, the government began its own public surveys and debated the best transitional options. Like the Rwandan government, the Ugandan government explored the virtues of adopting a South Africa-style TRC but eventually rejected such an approach (largely on technical grounds that Uganda lacked the resources to run a nationwide truth process like South Africa's). In contrast to Rwanda, the Ugandan government concluded that an amnesty for perpetrators of mass crimes was preferable to punishment, arguing that it would more effectively reintegrate former combatants and foster reconciliation.[52]

In January 2000, the Ugandan parliament passed the Amnesty Act. Rare among amnesty legislation around the world, it was explicitly conceived as an expression of the broader population's and especially victims' concerns. The preamble to the Amnesty Act claims that the legislation reflects "the expressed desire of the people of Uganda to end armed hostilities, reconcile with those who have caused suffering and rebuild their communities."[53] The Act establishes the Amnesty Commission to oversee the amnesty process, affording it two primary responsibilities that highlight the importance of reintegration and reconciliation: first, "to persuade [rebels] to take advantage of the amnesty and to encourage communities to reconcile with those who have committed the offences;" and second, "to consolidate the progress so far made in amnesty implementation and ensure that more insurgents respond to the amnesty and that the community is ready to receive them."[54] The Amnesty Commission is a temporary institution, with its mandate renewed every six months until parliament deems it has succeeded or ceased to be useful in helping end conflict.[55] The Act also establishes a Demobilisation and Resettlement Team (DRT) to decommission the arms of combatants seeking amnesty and to demobilize, resettle, and reintegrate them into their home communities.[56]

The Amnesty Act is at once broader and more limited than that proposed by the ARLPI. Whereas the ARLPI's lobbying for an amnesty concerned only rebels in

---

[51]  Refugee Law Project, "Negotiating Peace: Resolution of Conflicts in Uganda's West Nile Region" (Working Paper No. 12, Kampala. RLP, June 2004, 18–21).

[52]  Author's interview, Onega.

[53]  Amnesty Act, Preamble.

[54]  Uganda Amnesty Commission, *A Handbook for Implementation of the Amnesty Act 2000: Procedures and Principles of Operation*, 2001, Section 3.11.

[55]  Author's interview, Lucian Tibarahu, Attorney General, Republic of Uganda, Kampala, March 2, 2006.

[56]  Amnesty Act, Section 12.

northern Uganda, the Act relates to combatants nationwide. This provision followed the government's national consultations – building on the ARLPI's more focused surveys in the north – which showed countrywide support for some form of amnesty to help end conflict. Meanwhile, the Amnesty Act does not afford the sort of blanket amnesty which the ARLPI proposed but rather an individualized amnesty in which each rebel wanting to benefit from the provision must voluntarily return from the bush, register with a designated government official (usually an army or police officer or a local magistrate), sign a declaration renouncing conflict, and surrender any weapons in his or her possession. The reporter (as a returned combatant seeking amnesty is known) does not have to admit to committing any particular crime, only to "renounce or abandon involvement in the war or rebellion."[57] After these steps, the reporter's file is transferred to the Amnesty Commission. The commission cannot cross-check information through direct investigation but may request further information from the reporter. Once satisfied with a reporter's case, the commission issues an amnesty certificate, which entitles him or her to a resettlement package containing two hundred sixty-three thousand Ugandan shillings in cash, a mattress, blankets, saucepans, plates, cups, maize seeds, and flour.[58] Most of the funding for the packages has come from a $4.2 million (U.S. million) World Bank Multi-country Demobilisation and Reintegration Program (MDRP) grant issued in March 2005.[59]

The government amended the Amnesty Act in May 2006 to exclude the LRA commanders indicted by the ICC. However, Amnesty Commission chairman Justice Peter Onega argued that the commanders may still gain amnesty through a loophole in the law. "The amendment only gives the Internal Affairs minister powers to forward to Parliament names of people who should be excluded from benefiting from Amnesty," Justice Onega said. "As far as I know, it went as far as that [but] no name has up to today been produced."[60]

To date, between seventeen thousand and twenty thousand rebels have come in from the bush under the amnesty provision, though fewer than half of these have received their resettlement packages.[61] Around half of the returnees are LRA combatants – including senior LRA commanders such as Brig. Kenneth Banya and Brig. Sam Kolo – most of whom have resettled in Gulu and Kitgum districts. Several thousand returnees are from various rebel groups in West Nile, where Justice Onega

---

[57]  Ibid., Section 4.1.c.

[58]  Author's interview, Onega. The cash amount provided is equivalent to three months' salary for a policeman or teacher, at the passing of the Amnesty Act, plus twenty thousand Ugandan shillings for transport costs.

[59]  Ibid.

[60]  "Uganda News Summary," *Radio Rhino International Afrika*, July 5, 2006, accessed September 5, 2011, http://www.radiorhino.org/htm_material/archiv/text/press/monitor/Rria%20060706%20ICC%20 Reacts%20to%20Amnesty%20for%20JK.htm.

[61]  Author's interview, Onega.

was a principal mediator among the government and several rebel groups. In Gulu district, Banya, whom the Uganda People's Defence Force (UPDF) considers "the main military and technical brain behind the [LRA] rebellion,"[62] now oversees a government farm at Labora, where around 600 LRA returnees work as part of their repatriation. Established jointly in 2004 by the government, UPDF and Gulu District LC5, Labora Farm was designed to facilitate the former rebels' "economic empowerment and reintegration into society."[63]

Over time, the northern Ugandan population has increasingly expressed discontent with the amnesty process. A 2007 study by OHCHR showed that much of the population today views the Amnesty Act as lacking in two key respects: an inability to convince returnees to tell the truth about their crimes and a lack of compensation for victims of violence.[64] Many victims question why those responsible for committing mass atrocities have been rewarded with reintegration packages while those who have suffered most during the conflict continue to live in abject poverty. "We see what these people get," said an elderly woman in Gulu town, "and it makes us angry. These people have killed others – killed women and children. And now they get food and money from the government, while the government ignores us."[65] A senior UN worker in Gulu said, "The reintegration packages are often more trouble than they're worth. They might provide some incentive to rebels to come home but they mostly produce huge jealousies, especially for those in the IDP camps who rely on small food handouts and feel ignored by the government and international agencies."[66]

Similar problems surround the establishment of Labora Farm, a central component of the amnesty and reintegration process in Gulu district. Some victims argue that the farm provides returnees with the sort of agricultural training and access to land and farm produce that are denied the IDPs. "We have waited twenty years to return to our land," said one man in the Bobi IDP camp:

> When the LRA and the government started fighting, we all fled our land. In this camp, we are all farmers but no one farms now. Our food comes from the WFP. Our men can't farm. Our children don't know how to live on the land. Yet, Banya and these others are given that farm [at Labora] and all those benefits.[67]

[62] "Uganda: Senior LRA Commander Captured by the Army," *IRIN News*, July 15, 2004, accessed September 5, 2011, http://www.irinnews.org/report.aspx?reportid=50811.

[63] Internal UN Document, on file with author. Those responsible for the establishment of Labora Farm were Grace Akello, minister of state for northern Uganda, Walter Ochora, LC5 chairman of Gulu district, Max Omeda, Gulu resident district commissioner, and Brig. Nathan Mugisha, commander of the 4th Division of the UPDF.

[64] OHCHR, *Making Peace Our Own*.

[65] Author's interview, General Population, Gulu, March 9, 2006.

[66] Author's interview, UN Official, Gulu, March 8, 2006.

[67] Author's interview, General Population, Bobi, March 13, 2006.

Much of the population sees Labora Farm as a means by which returned combatants benefit materially while avoiding direct engagement with their victims and the wider population. "A sense of community can't be re-established with those LRA [fighters] coming back and working on a government-run farm," said Norbert Mao, the Gulu district LC5 chairman. "They have to be accepted back by those they have wronged. This will take a long time and the process must be based on direct contact. What kind of genuine connection is possible between those on the farm and those in the [IDP] camps?"[68]

Further weakening the use of Labora Farm in the post-amnesty reintegration process are allegations by several UN and NGO workers in Gulu that Banya and other former LRA leaders have used the farm to recreate LRA power structures, supervising young returnees whose abduction and drafting into the LRA they originally ordered. "Banya is a known rapist and torturer of abducted children who are forcibly recruited to the LRA," said one UN worker. "That he is now in charge of the same children at Labora, in the name of reintegration and reconciliation, is just a scandal."[69]

Alongside debates about amnesty in northern Uganda, sections of the northern civil society and population have advocated the use of local rituals to cleanse and reintegrate former combatants into their communities. The increased interest in the use of the rituals to deal with aspects of the current conflict coincides with attempts to revitalize the traditional leadership. A crucial international dimension impinges on considerations of local rituals in the Ugandan conflict. Several Western NGOs, principally the Northern Ugandan Peace Initiative (NUPI), an interagency U.S. government initiative, have actively supported the reinvigoration of local rituals, particularly in Gulu district. This has led some observers to claim that an industry has emerged in which the rituals carry more meaning for their foreign proponents and donor agencies than for the local communities from which they supposedly derive.[70]

Between the start of the nineteenth century and the beginning of the British colonial era, around seventy chiefdoms comprising more than 350 clans existed in the central and northern regions of Uganda today affected by the war.[71] Colonial policy weakened the chieftancies, in particular by installing proxy chiefs and setting them against each other politically. The regimes of Milton Obote and Idi Amin almost destroyed customary structures entirely. In 1995, the new Ugandan constitution

---

[68] Author's interview, Mao.

[69] Author's interview, UN Official, Gulu, March 8, 2006.

[70] Author's interviews, UN Official, Kampala, March 3, 2006; International Humanitarian Worker, Gulu, March 13, 2006.

[71] Ronald Atkinson, *The Roots of Ethnicity: The Origins of the Acholi of Uganda* (Kampala: Fountain Publishers, 1999), 261.

reinstated the Acholi traditional leadership known as Ker Kwaro Acholi (KKA). An influential 1997 report by Dennis Pain, titled *The Bending of the Spears*, called for a community-based approach to resolving conflict in northern Uganda.[72] Spurred by the findings of the report, the Belgian government in 1999 funded research conducted by the Gulu-based organization ACORD into Acholi traditional leadership. Subsequently, in 2000, Acholi traditional chiefs known as *rwodi* were elected and the Rwot of Payira in Gulu district was named the Acholi Paramount Chief, leader of the KKA, a position that Tim Allen claims had never before existed.[73] NUPI and other NGOs have helped identify traditional leaders and run programs "introducing" them to the population, mainly to Acholi youth groups and IDP communities.[74]

Soon traditional leaders, most notably Acholi Paramount Chief Elect Rwot David Acana II, began advocating the use of local rituals, particularly *mato oput*, to hold Joseph Kony and other LRA commanders accountable for their crimes and to help reconcile them with affected communities.[75] Members of the ARLPI, founded the year before ACORD's research into traditional leadership, also strongly supported the use of local rituals, emphasizing the importance of their embedded notions of forgiveness, atonement, and mercy. The concurrent emergence of organized traditional and religious leadership in northern Uganda and support for this process from foreign governments and NGOs are crucial to any analysis of the legitimate and effective use of local rituals.

Debates over these rituals took on new forms as a result of two key transitional justice developments in Uganda: the intervention of the ICC and the Juba peace talks between the government and the LRA. As I have reported elsewhere, for nearly a year before President Museveni referred the situation in Uganda to the ICC prosecutor, there were substantial negotiations between The Hague and Kampala over the nature and ramifications of a state referral.[76] My interviews with Ugandan

---

[72] Dennis Pain, *The Bending of the Spears: Producing Consensus for Peace and Development in Northern Uganda* (London: International Alert and Kacoke Madit, 1997). For detailed critiques of this report, see Chris Dolan, "Inventing Traditional Leadership? A Critical Assessment of Dennis Pain's 'The Bending of the Spears'" (COPE working paper 31, April 2000); and Mark Bradbury, *An Overview of Initiatives for Peace in Acholi, Northern Uganda,* October 1999, accessed September 3, 2011, www.cdainc.com/publications/rpp/casestudies/rppCase02 Uganda.pdf.

[73] Tim Allen, *Trial Justice: The International Criminal Court and the Lord's Resistance Army* (London: Zed Books, 2006), 149. See also, Tim Allen, "Ritual (Ab)use? Problems with Traditional Justice in Northern Uganda," in Waddell and Clark, *Courting Conflict? Justice, Peace and the ICC in Africa,* 47–54.

[74] Ker Kwaro Acholi and the Northern Uganda Peace Initiative, *Report on Acholi Youth and Chiefs Addressing Practices of the Acholi Culture of Reconciliation* (USAID, June 2005), accessed September 4, 2011, http://www.nupi.or.ug/pdf/Youth_ChiefConferenceReport15–6-05.pdf.

[75] Author's interview, Rwot David Acana II, Acholi Paramount Chief, Gulu, February 27, 2007.

[76] Phil Clark, "Law, Politics and Pragmatism: The ICC and Case Selection in the Democratic Republic of Congo and Uganda," in Waddell and Clark, *Courting Conflict? Justice, Peace and the ICC in*

government officials indicate that Prosecutor Ocampo approached President Museveni in 2003 and, despite the president's initial reluctance, persuaded him to refer the northern Uganda situation to the ICC. The referral suited both parties, providing the ICC with its first state referral of a case and the Ugandan government with another political and legal tool to wield against the LRA.[77]

President Museveni referred the situation in Uganda to the ICC prosecutor in December 2003.[78] In its communication, the Ugandan government underscored crimes committed by the LRA, but the prosecutor notified President Museveni that the ICC would interpret the referral as concerning all crimes under the Rome Statute committed in northern Uganda, leaving open the possibility of investigating atrocities by government forces. The ICC's decision to open investigations in the Uganda situation was based on the gravity of the crimes reported and the inability of Ugandan authorities to capture and arrest LRA commanders considered responsible for mass atrocities in northern Uganda, who at that stage were located in southern Sudan. Highlighting the volatile environment in which the ICC would operate in Uganda, one week after the ICC announced its opening of investigations, the LRA attacked an IDP camp at Abia in Lira district, killing fifty civilians. In August 2004, the prosecutor stated that he expected to commence the trial of LRA suspects within six months and that this would help bring about a swift end to the conflict in northern Uganda.[79]

In October 2005, the ICC issued arrest warrants for five LRA commanders: Joseph Kony, Vincent Otti, Raska Lukwiya, Okot Odhiambo, and Dominic Ongwen. The indictments against the five commanders comprised a range of alleged war crimes and crimes against humanity during LRA attacks between July 2002 and July 2004. The warrant for Kony's arrest accused him of thirty-three separate counts (twelve for crimes against humanity and twenty-one for war crimes) deriving from six separate attacks, during which he is alleged to have been responsible for murder, rape, enslavement, sexual enslavement, and the forced enlistment of children.

Announcing the issuance of the arrest warrants, the prosecutor justified the selection of LRA rather than Ugandan government cases on the basis of their relative gravity, though he did not rule out the possibility of investigating government crimes in the future. At a workshop in London in March 2007, the prosecutor said, "LRA

*Africa*, 37–45; Phil Clark, "Grappling in the Great Lakes: The Challenges of International Justice in Rwanda, the Democratic Republic of Congo and Uganda," in *The Role of International in Rebuilding Societies after Conflict: Great Expectations*, ed. Brett Bowden, Hilary Charlesworth, and Jeremy Farrall (Cambridge: Cambridge University Press, 2009), 244–69.

77  Author's Interviews, Ugandan Government Officials, Kampala, March 2–4, 2006.
78  Office of the Prosecutor, "Press Release: President of Uganda Refers Situation Concerning the Lord's Resistance Army (LRA) to the ICC," January 29, 2004.
79  Peter Apps, "ICC Hopes for Uganda Trial in 6 Months, Then Congo," *Reuters*, January 26, 2005, accessed September 5, 2011, http://www.globalpolicy.org/intljustice/icc/2005/0126ugandatrial.htm.

killings were 100 times worse than those by the UPDF. There's no question we had to start by investigating LRA crimes."[80] Since the issuance of the arrest warrants, however, some indicted LRA commanders have died, while the others remain at large.[81] During and after the Juba peace negotiations, the LRA has repeatedly stated that it will not sign the remaining sections of the peace agreement with the government, nor countenance laying down its arms and demobilizing its forces, until the ICC indictments are withdrawn.[82]

Further complicating transitional justice discussions in Uganda, questions of accountability and reconciliation became central to the Juba peace talks. The LRA delegation to the Juba talks, along with various northern Ugandan civil society leaders, for example, advocated the use of local practices to address crimes committed during the conflict. These parties argued that local (especially Acholi) rituals constituted a vital alternative to prosecutions of atrocity perpetrators by the ICC, which they characterized as a neo-colonialist imposition by external actors and a form of punitive justice that would deter the LRA from further negotiations and ultimately jeopardize peace.[83]

In an attempt to keep the LRA at the negotiating table, the government considered whether northern Ugandan rituals could be codified to produce a system capable of addressing LRA crimes. A cyclical genealogy of ideas emerged, as the Ugandan government considered the post-genocide version of *gacaca* (partly inspired by the transfer of concepts from RPF leaders' experiences fighting with the NRM in Uganda) as a model for its own considerations of community-based processes. In 2006, a Ugandan parliamentary committee was established to consider whether local (particularly Acholi) rituals could be codified and nationalized, similar to Rwanda's reform and formalization of the *gacaca* courts. "We are considering whether something like gacaca in Rwanda provides a model for us here in Uganda," a government official said. "There are pros and cons to the use of traditional practices and we have to weigh up what the best approach is. But certainly we believe traditional methods can teach us a lot about dealing with the current situation."[84] The language of *gacaca* has also gained significant currency in Ugandan public discussions. In an article in the Ugandan state-owned *New Vision* newspaper, one

---

[80] Luis Moreno Ocampo, "The Lord's Resistance Army: War, Peace and Reconciliation workshop," London School of Economics, March 3, 2007, notes on file with author.

[81] Lukwiya was shot dead near Kitgum in August 2006 during fighting between the LRA and Ugandan government forces. In October 2007 Otti was killed by LRA elements close to Kony after major disagreements between the two leaders, principally over LRA strategy at the Juba peace talks.

[82] "LRA Leader Kony Reportedly Willing to Face Trial in Uganda, Not The Hague," *Daily Monitor*, December 20, 2006, accessed September 5, 2011, http://www.ugandacan.org/archive/1/2006-12.

[83] LRA Delegation to the Juba Talks, "LRA Position Paper on Accountability and Reconciliation in the Context of Alternative Justice System for Resolving the Northern Ugandan and Southern Sudan Conflicts," Juba, August 2006, 1.

[84] Author's interview, Ugandan Government Official, Kampala, March 3, 2006.

commentator characterized the "free and fair" elections in Uganda in 1989, which he described as exhibiting little executive interference, as a "gacaca (community) exercise devoid of vertical civic ... discourse."[85]

### *Polarized Debates: Domestic and International Norm Entrepreneurs' Responses to Transitional Justice in Uganda*

Before and during the Juba process, the linkage of local Ugandan rituals with notions of amnesty and forgiveness proved highly controversial, since some critics claimed the rituals would not deliver the sort of punishment of perpetrators that the Ugandan population expects and justice requires.[86] A polarized debate subsequently emerged between commentators supporting peace, which they claimed could only be achieved through enticing combatants from the bush with an amnesty and local reintegration ceremonies, and those supporting justice through the ICC or some other formal punitive mechanism. A corollary to the peace versus justice debate in the Ugandan context has been an argument over traditional/informal/restorative versus Western/formal/retributive justice.[87]

The consideration of local rituals to address mass crimes in northern Uganda is a coherent development in Uganda's long history of reforming customary practices to address present-day needs, as exemplified by the earlier discussion of the LCs and RCs. Nevertheless, we must also recognize that the highly politicized context of the Juba negotiations shaped debates over local rituals. In particular, different parties supported or opposed the turn toward local practices for very different reasons. Greater unity of opinion manifested among opponents of this development, principally human rights groups such as AI and HRW and legal commentators who stated that community-based rituals could not deliver the degree of accountability necessary for perpetrators of egregious crimes; a task, they argued, that should be the sole purview of the ICC or another form of conventional court.[88]

---

[85] Asuman Bisika, "Otunnu is Not Obama Because Uganda is Not USA," *The New Vision*, September 2, 2009, accessed September 5, 2011, http://www.newvision.co.ug/D/8/22/693156.

[86] See, for example, Amnesty International, "Uganda: Proposed National Framework to Address Impunity Does Not Remove Government's Obligation to Arrest and Surrender LRA Leaders to the International Criminal Court," AI Index: AFR 59/002/2007, August 15 2007.

[87] See, for example, Tristan McConnell, "Uganda: Peace versus Justice?" *openDemocracy*, September 13, 2006, accessed September 3, 2011, http://www.opendemocracy.net/democracy-africa_democracy/uganda_peace_3903.jsp; Louise Parrott, "The Role of the International Criminal Court in Uganda: Ensuring that the Pursuit of Justice Does Not Come at the Price of Peace," *Australian Journal of Peace Studies* 1 (2006): 8–29; "Hunting Uganda's Child-Killers: Justice versus Reconciliation," *The Economist*, May 7, 2007, 57. Adam Branch, "Uganda's Civil War and the Politics of ICC Intervention," *Ethics and International Affairs* 21 (2007): 179–98.

[88] See, for example, Amnesty International, "Proposed National Framework"; Human Rights Watch, "Trading Justice for Peace Won't Work," Human Rights Watch, May 2, 2007.

On the other hand, the widespread support for the use of local rituals among the LRA delegation in Juba, much of Acholi civil society, and other Ugandan actors stemmed from a confluence of factors. As underscored in the previous section, there had already been substantial discussion of rituals such as *mato oput* and *gomo tong* in Acholiland nearly a decade before the Juba talks. For actors such as the ARLPI, local rituals were seen as a crucial support for the nationwide amnesty process (which had commenced with the passing of the Amnesty Act in 2000) and a means to the reintegration and reconciliation of a wide range of rebel groups. The commencement of ICC investigations in northern Uganda in 2004 catalysed the domestic championing of local rituals. ARLPI and other northern civil society groups criticized the ICC as an illegitimate international actor that risked scuppering the fragile Betty Bigombe-led peace process (which preceded the Juba talks), in which amnesty for LRA combatants was a fundamental component. Northern Ugandan civil society – along with the reports of several international NGOs[89] – was instrumental in fostering the polarized discourse of peace versus justice and Western versus traditional justice, seeing the ICC as a direct threat to the amnesty and local ritual agenda that had gained such momentum since the late 1990s.

Some northern Ugandan actors also viewed support for local rituals as an important riposte to the perceived overly cozy relationship between President Museveni and the ICC. In this view, the ICC was doing the government's bidding by indicting only LRA suspects and continuing Museveni's subjugation of northern ethnic groups, principally the Acholi. Some Acholi politicians in Kampala echoed this view, including one member of parliament who said, "the ICC has become Museveni's political tool."[90]

Finally, when the Juba negotiations got under way, the LRA – as highlighted in its position papers quoted earlier – pressed claims for local rituals to be central features of any agreement on accountability and reconciliation. The LRA viewed local rituals as "alternative mechanisms" to the ICC, whose arrest warrants against their commanders they wanted removed.[91] This again furthered the binary discourse of international versus local justice. Thus, as all of these different arguments highlight, a broad spectrum of actors advocated the centrality of local rituals for manifold reasons, ranging from philosophical statements regarding northern Ugandan sovereignty and the need for domestic ownership of any transitional justice processes designed to address the conflict to self-interested concerns about the

---

[89] See, for example, Liu Institute for Global Issues, "Pursuing Peace and Justice: International and Local Initiatives," May 2005; *The Justice and Reconciliation Project, 'Abomination': Local Belief Systems and International Justice*, Liu Institute for Global Issues and the Gulu District NGO Forum, Field Notes No. 5, September 2007.

[90] Author's interview with Ugandan member of parliament, Kampala, March 2, 2006.

[91] LRA, "Position Paper on Accountability and Reconciliation."

threat of ICC prosecution and a desire to safeguard the national amnesty process and pursue peace.

### Analysis: Uganda's Relevance for Amnesty and Accountability Debates

As with Rwanda, the Uganda case is important for the theoretical debates regarding amnesty and accountability raised by Sikkink, Lutz, and others. First, similar to Rwanda, transitional justice debates and policymaking in Uganda have been highly variable, reflecting changing political and popular concerns. In the late 1980s and 1990s, there was considerable support for amnesty processes because of the success of such measures in disarming and reintegrating the WNBF, UPA, and other armed groups. This track record of successful amnesties largely explains why the population supported the adoption of the Amnesty Act in 2000. Furthermore, it must be recognized – as the OHCHR report in 2007 found – that considerable support for processes of amnesty, forgiveness, and reconciliation (which most respondents defined discretely) emerges because many Ugandans view the perpetrators of violence as their own children who must be treated leniently.[92] Support for amnesty therefore is based not only on the positive use of such measures in the past but also the intimacy of relations between victims and perpetrators.

The Uganda case therefore poses a major challenge for opponents of amnesty, who often argue that the use of amnesty hampers a long-term transition toward democracy. Uganda represents an example of a democratic amnesty with widespread popular consultations conducted by Ugandan government and civil society indicating nationwide support for amnesty, for the reasons outlined previously. Arguably, international opposition to democratic amnesty may undermine democracy in the long term.

Over time, however, northern Ugandans' disquiet with the use of amnesty has grown. This has had little to do with opposition to amnesty provisions by international norm entrepreneurs such as AI and HRW but reflects instead more localized concerns such as frustration with a lack of truth telling and compensation through the amnesty process, practical problems with the delivery of reintegration packages, and the use of Labora Farm as a tool for reintegrating returned combatants. These frustrations partly explain support for local rituals among many northern Ugandans, since practices such as *mato oput* and *gomo tong* in Acholiland require returnees to confess to their crimes before they can be reintegrated and require perpetrators' clans to compensate victims' clans.

The critique of local rituals by groups such as AI and HRW – equating them with amnesty and impunity – has overlooked the local context, namely that popular

---

[92] OHCHR, *Making Peace Our Own.*

concerns over amnesty were one of the key factors in motivating popular support for the rituals. Furthermore, studies by OHCHR and the International Center for Transitional Justice[93] show that the population holds highly nuanced views on transitional justice, which allow for a combination of international and national trials, as well as local rituals. In viewing the ICC as the sole legitimate transitional justice response to the Ugandan conflict, AI and HRW ignored these more complex debates occurring within Ugandan society. Crucially, they have ignored the fact that much of the impetus for local rituals comes from a desire for greater – not less – accountability than the previous amnesty process. Similarly problematic has been the ardent support for local rituals and opposition to the ICC by international norm entrepreneurs such as NUPI and the Liu Institute. In viewing community-level accountability as the singular response to the northern Ugandan conflict, these organizations have also misinterpreted the motivations behind domestic accountability debates and consequently skewed these discussions. As in the Rwanda case, international norm entrepreneurs' influence over domestic transitional justice discussions has been generally negligible but, where it has had any impact, it has tended to be negative and highly detached from local concerns.

## CONCLUDING REMARKS

Important similarities emerge from debates over amnesty and accountability in Rwanda and Uganda and raise important questions for more general theoretical discussions of these issues. First, in both countries, transitional justice policymaking has been an organic process often involving a reversion to previously rejected approaches (including various forms of amnesty). This highlights the importance of particular political leaders and changing political, legal, and social conditions for determining transitional justice decisions. Political circumstances and national needs change in dynamic conflict and postconflict environments, and transitional justice tends to follow – rather than shape – these local dimensions. In the experience of Rwanda and Uganda, transitional justice has not been teleological or even linear but rather highly contingent and variable, sometimes even circular. Amnesty, for example, has proven politically useful at some times and not at others; it has encouraged disarmament and a cessation of hostilities in some periods and sometimes had little effect on conflict; it has generated popular support in some moments and widespread discontent in others. In this region, justice has not cascaded, but constantly twisted and turned.

---

[93] International Center for Transitional Justice/Human Rights Center Berkeley, *Forgotten Voices; A Population-Based Survey on Attitudes about Peace and Justice in Northern Uganda*, July 2005.

Second, international norm entrepreneurs (themselves not a monolithic group) have had little impact on domestic transitional justice policymaking and often found themselves in marked opposition to a wide range of local actors. Regional "borrowing" of transitional principles and practices, especially regarding localized accountability mechanisms, has proven more influential than international perspectives in shaping local transitional justice trajectories. International organizations such as AI and HRW have interpreted criminal accountability solely as the purview of the ICTR, ICC, and other international mechanisms. This narrow perspective has led to a form of ideological barracking, rather than nuanced analysis of local conditions and limitations, which domestic actors have tended to ignore. Whereas Sikkink and others suggest that AI and HRW have played an important role in promoting accountability in Latin America, the impact of human rights organizations in central Africa is significantly smaller. This may stem from international actors' greater willingness to engage with domestic actors in Latin America and greater scope for coalition building. In Rwanda and Uganda, these norm entrepreneurs have tended to isolate themselves, developing few alliances with local actors, and thus have dampened their impact.

Finally, international actors' opposition to innovative domestic accountability measures – such as *gacaca* in Rwanda or local rituals in northern Uganda – risks undermining the broader cause of justice for atrocity. Organizations such as AI and HRW have appeared concerned primarily with promoting a particular conception of international criminal justice, which may be appropriate for prosecuting a small group of senior suspects but is ill-equipped to address the culpability of large swathes of everyday citizens who participated in crimes. Thus, international norm entrepreneurs have wrestled insufficiently with the key question of how to address mass participation in mass atrocity. Rather than promoting the diffusion of norms of accountability, these actors have opposed domestically driven attempts to deliver a form of justice even more comprehensive than the internationally preferred model. In Rwanda and Uganda, the impulse for accountability has come from within, often in unpredictable ways and often in opposition to international advocacy.

# 9

## Accountability through Conditional Amnesty

### The Case of South Africa

*Antje du Bois-Pedain*

At a time when amnesty appears well on its way toward pariah status among transitional policy options, South Africa's bold attempt, in the mid-to-late 1990s, to incorporate a generous domestic amnesty arrangement into an accountability process for politically motivated crimes deserves our attention. This chapter reviews the history and implementation of South Africa's conditional amnesty law and its longer term domestic impact. It also offers an assessment of this policy option as a blueprint for an accountability mechanism to be employed in other political transitions.

## A REVIEW OF SOUTH AFRICA'S CONDITIONAL AMNESTY SCHEME

South Africa's amnesty scheme for politically motivated offenders is sometimes presented as a restrictive one in which amnesty is confined to perpetrators who acted in a morally defensible way. Such benign perceptions of the scheme are put into question by the generosity and ease with which amnesty was granted by the Amnesty Committee for atrocious deeds. In this section, I draw on the results of my empirical study of the Amnesty Committee's decisions[1] to argue that the practical scope of the scheme was in fact much broader than many international observers believe it to have been, and address the implications of these findings.

### History and Legal Framework

In 1995, the first democratically elected South African parliament created the South African Truth and Reconciliation Commission (TRC) to investigate the human rights abuses committed, by whichever side of the political conflict, between

---

[1] Antje du Bois-Pedain, *Transitional Amnesty in South Africa* (Cambridge: Cambridge University Press, 2007).

March 1, 1960 and May 10, 1994.[2] In fulfillment of the negotiated promise – enshrined in the epilogue of the interim constitution of 1993 – that amnesty be granted "in respect of acts, omissions and offences associated with a political objective and committed in the course of the conflicts of the past,"[3] the legislation also vested in the commission the authority to grant, through the Amnesty Committee as one of the commission's constituent committees, amnesty to certain persons involved in these conflicts.[4] In order to receive amnesty, eligible individuals had to apply within a specified timeframe in respect of an offense or delict[5] classified as political[6] and to make full disclosure thereof.

The legislation set out a two-stage test for determining whether an offense qualified as political for this purpose. The first step in establishing the political character of the applicant's deed was to show its connection with the policies of the organization or institution of which the applicant had been a part: the applicant had to have acted in the exercise of his or her functions as a member or supporter of a liberation movement, a political party, or a state institution or in the performance

---

[2]  Act 34 of 1995 (hereafter referred to as the TRC Act), as amended by the Promotion of National Unity and Reconciliation Amendment Act 87 of 1995, the Judicial Matters Amendment Act 104 of 1996, the Promotion of National Unity and Reconciliation Amendment Act 18 of 1997, the Promotion of National Unity and Reconciliation Second Amendment Act 84 of 1997, and the Promotion of National Unity and Reconciliation Amendment Act 33 of 1998. The provisions relating to the mandate period are to be found in s 18(1) and s 20(2) of the TRC Act. Originally the mandate period ended on December 5, 1993. It was extended, however, by the Constitution of the Republic of South Africa Amendment Act 35 of 1997 to acts, omissions, or offenses committed "before 11 May 1994." Thus it ends at midnight on May 10, 1994.

[3]  Constitution of the Republic of South Africa Act 200 of 1993. The provision retains its validity under the final constitution (Constitution of the Republic of South Africa Act 108 of 1996) in terms of s 22 thereof.

[4]  A constitutional challenge brought against the amnesty provisions failed in 1996: *AZAPO and others v. Truth and Reconciliation Commission and others* 1996 (4) SA 671 (CC). For analysis and discussion, see Du Bois-Pedain, *Transitional Amnesty*, chapter 1 and the chapter by Mark Freeman and Max Pensky in this volume.

[5]  An "offense" here means a crime under South African law, while the expression "delict" refers to torts, acts that give rise to civil liability for negligent or intentional injury. The category of delicts eventually had no independent significance for the amnesty process. Applicants applied for amnesty in respect of criminal offenses that were sometimes (when individual victims had been harmed) also torts, but they did not apply in respect of any torts that were not also criminal offenses.

[6]  In restricting amnesty to acts which were offenses or delicts under South African law, the scope of the amnesty under the TRC Act is possibly narrower than the amnesty clause in the epilogue of the interim constitution, whose wide and unspecific reference to "acts, omissions and offences committed in the course of the conflict of the past" arguably covers both offenses under South African law and "legalised apartheid crimes" like forced removals. Compare also Amnesty Decision No AC/1999/176 (Applicant Maropeng Matthews Sehlwana and thirteen others) where counsel unsuccessfully tried to convince the committee that the amnesty provisions in the TRC Act were in conflict with the interim constitution to the extent that they required acts for which amnesty is granted to constitute any offense or delict at all.

of a coup d'état. Persons who had on reasonable grounds believed that they were acting in the course and scope of their duties and within the scope of their express or implied authority could also receive amnesty.[7] In respect of applicants who passed this threshold, the committee was instructed to consider the overall political nature of their conduct by having regard to certain criteria based on a set of principles originally formulated in 1989 for the release of political prisoners in Namibia.[8] This guidance included purely factual, descriptive criteria (such as motive, context, objective, direction, order, or approval of the deed) and normatively restrictive, evaluative concepts (such as the gravity of the offense, its legal nature, and its proportionality in relation to the objective pursued).[9] Persons who had acted out of personal malice, ill will, or spite directed against the victim or solely for personal gain were disqualified from amnesty, even if they acted within a political context.[10]

Eligibility for amnesty was thus based on the dual requirements of individuation and full disclosure of politically motivated crimes. Amnesty could be granted only to individual applicants and in relation to their personal involvement in a specified act associated with a political objective (this is what individuation refers to), provided that the applicant had made a full disclosure of the relevant facts. Furthermore, the definition of an "act associated with a political objective" placed all political conduct in an organized setting. Applicants had to have acted in their capacity as employees, members or supporters of a political group, movement, or state institution. They had to have – or believed themselves to have – a mandate for what they did: not from "the people," but from the group or organization on whose behalf they had acted. Their deed was considered part of a collective political endeavor.

The granting of amnesty extinguished any criminal or civil liability in respect of the act for which amnesty had been granted, to the benefit of the applicant and any person or organization (including the state) that might otherwise have been

---

[7]  See s 20 (2) TRC Act.

[8]  The application of the Norgaard principles in Namibia is discussed by Gerhard Erasmus, "Namibian Independence and the Release of Political Prisoners," *South African Yearbook of International Law* 14 (1988–89): 137 and by Johan Rautenbach, "Namibia – The Release of Political Prisoners Revisited," *South African Yearbook of International Law* 15 (1989–90): 148. Raylene Keightley, "Political Offences and Indemnity in South Africa," *South African Journal on Human Rights* 9 (1993): 347, observes that some of the criteria in Norgaard's catalog were slightly reformulated so as to enable their wording to be applied to agents and supporters of the government as well as members of the liberation movements.

[9]  See s 20(3)(a) to (f) of the TRC Act. The criteria contained in the pretransitional indemnity laws of 1990 and 1992 (Indemnity Act 35 of 1990, Indemnity Amendment Act 124 of 1992 and Further Indemnity Act 151 of 1992) were also to be taken into account. The main beneficiaries of these earlier Acts were members and supporters of the liberation movements. For details see Keightley, "Political Offences and Indemnity," and Florian Kutz, *Amnestie für politische Straftäter in Südafrika: Von der Sharpeville-Amnestie bis zu den Verfahren der Wahrheits- und Versöhnungskommission* (Berlin: Berlin Verlag Arno Spitz GmbH, 2001), 39–62.

[10]  See s 20(3)(i) and (ii) TRC Act.

vicariously liable for the applicant's act.[11] Any criminal conviction based on the act was effectively expunged from all official documents and records.[12] If amnesty was refused, the applicant remained liable to prosecution and civil claims in ordinary legal proceedings.[13] However, any incriminating answer or evidence obtained by the commission in the course of its proceedings was inadmissible in a criminal or civil case against the applicant.[14] Where an amnesty application related to more than one incident, applicants could receive amnesty for their participation in some of these incidents but not in others. With relation to a particular incident, they could be given amnesty for some rather than all of the offenses they committed. When applications submitted by more than one perpetrator related to the same incident, some of them could be successful while others were not, since each perpetrator's application was assessed on its own merits. The full names of every person granted amnesty, together with sufficient information to identify the act, omission, or offense in respect of which amnesty had been granted, were published in the *Government Gazette*.[15]

## The Work of the Amnesty Committee

The committee became operational in April 1996. Originally composed of five members, the committee's membership eventually grew to nineteen, and the committee sat in panels of three to deal more efficiently with the workload. Committee members had some legal training, and active or retired judges chaired the panels. When the committee was officially dissolved on May 31, 2001, it had held more than 250 public hearings and made 1,100 formal amnesty decisions.[16] A report of its work was published in volume 6 of the *TRC Report* in 2003.[17]

---

[11] See TRC Act, s 20 (7) (a) and (b). Section 20 (7) (c) further removes any vicarious liability for acts in regard to which amnesty could have been granted were it not for the fact that the direct perpetrator is deceased.

[12] TRC Act, s 20 (10).

[13] TRC Act, s 21.

[14] This follows from s 31 (3) of the TRC Act, which applies to "any person … questioned by the Commission in the exercise of its powers in terms of this Act" and any person "subpoenaed to give evidence or to produce any article at a hearing of the Commission," and from the confidentiality of amnesty applications prior to any hearing (s 19 (8) of the TRC Act). One might query whether the wording in s 31 of the TRC Act necessarily covers amnesty applicants, since they submit their applications voluntarily. However, it is hardly likely that the South African parliament meant to penalize unsuccessful applicants doubly by making their self-incriminating evidence available in future criminal proceedings against them. The prosecution authorities now view such evidence as inadmissible.

[15] TRC Act, s 20 (6).

[16] All but twenty-one of the committee's decisions are accessible on the commission's homepage at http://www.doj.gov.za/trc/. Nineteen of the missing decisions are on file with the author. In this chapter, decision numbers of amnesty decisions are given with the full year ("AC/1998/124" instead of "AC/98/124") and with a three-digit decision number after the year. The committee's practice is uneven.

[17] Truth and Reconciliation Commission of South Africa, *TRC Report*, vol. 6 (Cape Town: Juta, 2003). Volumes 1 to 5 of the report were already published in 1998.

Most amnesty applications were submitted during two extensions of the original application period, first to May 10, 1997 and then to September 30, 1997.[18] According to the committee, sixty-five percent of the applications came from persons in custody.[19] In the event, the high volume of applications – well over seven thousand in the committee's count[20] – was not a cause for joy. It quickly emerged that the amnesty process was infested with improper applications brought by persons serving prison sentences for clearly nonpolitical crimes.[21] In order to identify and remove applications by common criminals, the committee subjected all applications to a preliminary screening process. When applicants had been investigated or had stood trial for incidents to which their application referred, the committee obtained court records and police dockets, as well as prison records in the case of convicted applicants.[22] The committee also contacted the organization on behalf of which the applicant professed to have acted and asked it to confirm the applicant's membership and mandate. When these early inquiries suggested that an application had been made by a common criminal, the committee would communicate its prima facie impression that the application did not relate to any political offenses and afford the applicant an opportunity to make further submissions to explain gaps or clarify discrepancies which the investigation had revealed. If no satisfactory explanation was forthcoming, the application would be rejected administratively.[23]

Prima facie political applications were divided into hearable and chamber matters. Hearable matters were applications which related to acts, omissions, or offenses that may have involved the commission of a gross human rights violation (defined in section 1 (1) of the TRC Act as the killing, abduction, torture, or severe ill treatment

---

[18] The original application period ended on December 14, 1996. The first extension attracted so many further applications that the TRC on May 6, 1997 announced that it had opened special "amnesty hotlines" to handle calls from people wishing to apply for amnesty. According to the same press statement, the TRC had at this point registered five thousand five hundred applications in its database. More were awaiting registration. The second extension of the deadline followed the extension of the mandate period of the commission to the date of the first democratic elections, but the committee also accepted applications by anyone who had been unaware of the earlier extension, "either because they were out of the country, in prison or did not see the Government Gazette." (Statement by the TRC's Vice-Chairman, Dr Alex Boraine, on July 17, 1997). De facto this amounted to an extension of the deadline for everyone.

[19] *TRC Report*, vol. 6, 34.

[20] Ibid., 36.

[21] Former TRC staff member Madeleine Fullard estimates that all in all about four thousand to five thousand applications came from common criminals. See Madeleine Fullard and Nicky Rousseau, "Truth, Evidence and History. A Critical Review of Aspects of the Amnesty Process," in *The Provocations of Amnesty: Memory, Justice and Impunity*, ed. Charles Villa-Vicencio and Erik Doxtader (Claremont: David Philip, 2003), 198.

[22] *TRC Report*, vol. 6, 26.

[23] See Martin Coetzee, "An Overview of the TRC Amnesty Process," in Villa-Vicencio and Doxtader, *The Provocations of Amnesty*, 187.

of the victim or any attempt, conspiracy, incitement, instigation, command, or pro-
curement to commit such an act during the mandate period of the commission by
a person acting with a political motive). The committee could only grant amnesty
in relation to such matters after holding a public hearing of which any traceable
victims had been notified. By contrast, applications related to conduct that did not
constitute any such gross human rights violations could be disposed of in chambers
without holding a hearing.[24]

According to its own count of applications from bona fide amnesty applicants,[25]
the committee received applications from 293 applicants who belonged to the
state security forces[26]; 998 applicants from the African National Congress (ANC)[27]
or ANC-related organizations such as the United Democratic Front (UDF)[28]; 109
applicants connected to the Inkatha Freedom Party (IFP)[29]; 138 applicants linked
to the Pan-Africanist Congress (PAC) and its armed wing, the Azanian People's
Liberation Army (APLA)[30]; and 107 applicants who were members or supporters of

---

[24]  Section 19 (3) (a) and (b) of the TRC Act. For details see *TRC Report*, vol. 6, 36–3, 47–50.

[25]  The expression "bona fide amnesty applicant" refers to an applicant connected to one of the political
parties or state institutions engaged in the conflict and whose activities appear to have had a political
background in the broadest sense – in other words, not a common criminal.

[26]  *TRC Report*, vol. 6,182.

[27]  The ANC was created in 1912 by educated black South Africans in order to strive for equality and
to defend the disadvantaged's civil and political rights. In the 1960s, the ANC was driven into exile
after police opened fire at demonstrators in Sharpeville, killing and injuring many unarmed people.
A state of emergency was imposed and most opposition groups and previously lawful forms of civil
disobedience were outlawed, blocking off traditional avenues for nonviolent political resistance. The
Sharpeville massacre also triggered the creation of an "armed wing" of the ANC, called "Umkhonto
we Sizwe" or "MK." See generally Saul Dubow, *The African National Congress* (Johannesburg:
Jonathan Ball, 2000) and Stephen Ellis and Tsepo Sechaba, *Comrades Against Apartheid: The ANC
and the South African Communist Party in Exile* (London: James Currey, 1992). On the history of MK,
see Howard Barrell, *MK: The ANC's Armed Struggle* (Harmondsworth: Penguin, 1990).

[28]  *TRC Report*, vol. 6, 265. The United Democratic Front (UDF) was formed in 1983 as a loose coalition
of nearly 700 organizations, including civil rights organizations, trade unions, student groups, youth
groups, women's organizations, religious groups, and the like, in order to help coordinate resistance
campaigns against apartheid. See Thomas G. Karis, "Black Politics: The Road to Revolution," in
*Apartheid in Crisis*, ed. Mark A. Uhlig (New York: Vintage Books, 1986). For the connections between
the ANC in exile and the UDF, see Dubow, *African National Congress*, esp. chapters 8 and 9.

[29]  *TRC Report*, vol. 6, 340. Inkatha was founded in 1975 by Mangosuthu Buthelezi, a Zulu leader and
erstwhile "chief minister" of the KwaZulu "homeland." It was presented as a cultural movement but
from its inception possessed strong political undertones. In its early years, Inkatha "played up the idea
that it represented a reincarnation of the banned [ANC]" (Adrian Guelke, *South Africa in Transition.
The Misunderstood Miracle* (London: I.B. Tauris, 1999), 93). But its ambiguity on the issue of ethnicity
prevented it from gaining the full backing of the ANC in exile. Inkatha reconstituted itself as a political party after restrictions for political activity were lifted in early 1990 and quickly became the ANC's
main competitor for political support among the Zulu-speaking black population.

[30]  *TRC Report*, vol. 6, 375. The PAC was a more distinctly Africanist grouping which broke away from
the ANC in 1959 under the leadership of Robert Sobukwe. On the PAC, see especially Benjamin
Pogrund, *How Can Man Die Better: Sobukwe and Apartheid* (London: Halban, 1990). The figure

white right-wing organizations.[31] Only a tiny proportion of applicants were female.[32] One applicant, who professed to have acted for a smaller black liberation group, was viewed as a common criminal whose claims of a political background to his actions were found to be untrue.[33]

This means that in total, the committee registered 1,645 applicants as affiliated to one of the larger qualifying state institutions, liberation movements, or political organizations. At first blush, this figure may appear quite low. However, it must be borne in mind that most applicants applied for amnesty for their involvement in more than one incident of political violence. It is also clear that (with the possible exception of some ANC members who may have seen their amnesty applications as a form of support for the TRC's appeal to reveal the truth about apartheid-era violence) most amnesty applicants were either still serving sentences for their crimes, were currently subject to prosecutions, or had concrete reasons to fear exposure and investigation in the future.[34] And many potential applicants did not have to fear the arm of the law. The perpetrators of countless acts of police brutality which victims reported to the TRC, as well as many of the activities of the South African defense force, were shielded from prosecution and from civil claims by indemnities provided for in the Indemnity Acts of 1961 and 1977, which had followed on the heels of the Sharpeville massacre in 1961 and the 1976 Soweto riots; section 103 of the Defence Act of 1955 which protected members of the military from liability

---

given in the text includes members of the PAC's armed wing, the Azanian People's Liberation Army (APLA), which in the early 1990s conducted attacks on white South Africans as part of an aggressive policy of "repossession."

[31] *TRC Report*, vol. 6, 452. The white right-wing organizations with the largest political support base among white South Africans were: (1) the Conservative Party (CP), formed in 1982 and headed by Andries Treurnicht, (2) the Afrikaner Weerstandsbeweging (AWB) under Eugene Terre'Blanche, and (3) the Freedom Front, a conglomerate of right-wing parties headed by General Viljoen which emerged during the negotiations period.

[32] The *TRC Report* lists all applicants connected to the IFP and the PAC/APLA as male (*TRC Report*, vol. 6, 340, 375). Of the 998 applicants from the ANC or ANC-related organizations, only 26 were female (*TRC Report*, vol. 6, 265). While the report does not mention the gender of applicants from the security forces and the white right-wing, applicants from these groups subsequently referred to by name in the report are clearly all male.

[33] *TRC Report*, vol. 6, 442.

[34] See Du Bois-Pedain, *Transitional Amnesty*, chapter 2. Investigations and trials of members of the state security forces connected to a clandestine police hit squad based at a disused farm near Pretoria, Vlakplaas, under the leadership of Eugene de Kock, were particularly significant in making state perpetrators come forward. De Kock was convicted in 1996 of (inter alia) various murders committed by him and his unit and is still in prison, his amnesty application in respect of some of his crimes having failed. The committee points out that "the number of applicants in De Kock-related incidents accounts for 48% of all Security Branch applications" (*TRC Report*, vol. 6, 184). Volker Nerlich, in his review of the trials conducted prior to and during the amnesty phase, describes amnesty and prosecution as "parallel processes" (Volker Nerlich, "The Contribution of Criminal Justice," in *Justice and Reconciliation in Post-Apartheid South Africa*, ed. François du Bois and Antje du Bois-Pedain (Cambridge: Cambridge University Press, 2008), 96–104).

for their activities within and outside South Africa; and various regulations passed during the successive states of emergency between 1986 and 1990.[35] Moreover, large numbers of persons – former opponents of the apartheid government as well as some right-wing political extremists – benefited from a range of indemnities granted by the last apartheid government during the negotiations with the political opposition in the early 1990s.[36] The negotiations process was also accompanied by an agreed early release of prisoners convicted for political crimes and by various general early release programs.[37] Political offenders who were released early may have had a certain interest to apply for amnesty under the TRC Act despite their release in order to clear their criminal record, but few of them seem to have bothered to do so.

## The Amnesty Applicants and their Deeds

A study of the 1,100 decisions rendered by the committee – which are, in the committee's own words, "the sole repository of the Committee's views on all the substantive issues that were relevant to its activities in relation to the matter of amnesty in general and to the specific amnesty applications it considered"[38] – reveals the following about the applicants and their deeds.[39]

[35] Although it might have been possible to challenge the posttransitional validity of these provisions designed to shield apartheid's agents from liability in court, this was not done. This may explain why the amnesty applications did not cover most or even all gross human rights violations committed during the mandate period of the commission. Nearly thirty-seven thousand gross human rights violations were reported by victims to the commission (for a detailed breakdown, see *TRC Report*, vol. 3 at 3 and 7ff.). In a discussion of a subcommittee of the parliamentary Ad Hoc Committee on Reparations on June 23, 2003, Ms. M. Smuts, a member of parliament for the Democratic Alliance (DP), put the overlap at 2,975 cases of human rights violations reported to the TRC for which amnesty applications were also received.

[36] The 1990 and 1992 Indemnity Acts which accompanied the negotiations for peace, have been repealed by section 48 of the TRC Act, but the validity of any indemnity granted under these Acts is expressly preserved notwithstanding their repeal. The Office for Indemnity, Immunity and Release received 14,002 applications for indemnity, of which 207 were refused, 650 were inadmissible, and 3,481 were completed in such a way that indemnity was not acquired. Close to ten thousand individuals thus appear to have benefited from these indemnities, which were, however, not granted for offenses that had caused serious injury to other persons. See Du Bois-Pedain, *Transitional Amnesty*, chapter 1.

[37] By April 30, 1991, 933 liberation movement fighters had been released pursuant to an agreement reached in the negotiations process. The Further Indemnity Act 151 of 1992 governed the release of 262 prisoners serving sentences for politically motivated offenses. Those released early included two prisoners from a group which came to be referred to as the "Sharpeville Six," convicted for a mob killing, MK cadre Robert McBride who had put a bomb into a busy Durban bar, killing three young women and injuring many others, and Barend Strydom, a militant right-winger who had gunned down nine black pedestrians in a Pretoria square. Estimates of the numbers of prisoners released under schemes not aimed specifically at political offenders range from ten thousand to sixty thousand. See Du Bois-Pedain, *Transitional Amnesty*, chapter 1 and Kutz, *Amnestie für politische Straftäter*, 62–3 for details.

[38] *TRC Report*, vol. 6, 2.

[39] The information given in this subsection summarizes the detailed findings and graphs presented in Du Bois-Pedain, *Transitional Amnesty*, chapter 2.

The committee's formal decisions concern 1,701 named applicants. Of the 857 applicants affiliated to ANC, 237 were members of the ANC's military wing, MK[40] and 105 were high-ranking ANC officials who offered to take collective responsibility for the politically motivated deeds committed by ordinary ANC members and supporters on behalf of the ANC.[41] Two-hundred eighty-nine applicants came from the state security forces and were predominantly employed by the security branch of the police. Hardly any members of the military applied.[42] Of the 116 applicants associated with the PAC, 85 belonged to the PAC's military wing, APLA. In addition, the committee was also approached by 130 anonymous PAC applicants, who merely gave their code names in their applications, and by a further unidentified number of applicants from APLA's high command.[43] Since the true identity of these applicants was not disclosed to the committee, their applications could not be taken into account for the purposes of this study. Seventy-seven applicants were members of white right-wing organizations. Eighty-five were members of the IFP. A further 277 applicants were part of political splinter groups or common criminals, or their organizational affiliation could not be determined on the basis of the information contained in the committee's decisions.

Only 1,499 applicants submitted amnesty applications that concerned activities within the temporal and material jurisdiction of the committee – that is, acts or omissions amounting to the commission of an offense or delict which emanated from "the conflicts of the past," were associated with a political objective, and were committed inside or outside the Republic of South Africa between March 1, 1960 and May 10, 1994.[44] Of the 202 applicants who did not, 97 applicants submitted applications which related entirely to deeds outside the jurisdiction of the committee. Thirty of these were bona fide liberation movement fighters who had become

[40] This figure includes MK members who were active in so-called self-defense units (SDUs) in townships after 1990; hence, it is larger than the committee's count of 180 MK cadres who applied for acts committed between 1960 and 1989 in *TRC Report*, vol. 6, 273. After the townships had become largely ungovernable by agents of the apartheid state during the 1980s, self-defense units composed of local residents emerged in the early 1990s when attacks on residents and violent clashes between supporters and perceived supporters of different political parties, particularly between IFP and ANC members, became frequent occurrences. To what extent this violence was actively fomented by apartheid state agents is disputed. It is beyond doubt, however, that the apartheid state initially supplied both weaponry and military training (for supposedly defensive purposes) to persons associated with the IFP.

[41] See Decision No AC/1999/046 and Decisions No AC/1999/086 – No AC/1999/164 (ANC leadership).

[42] Not included in the figure of 289 security force applicants are 37 applicants from the security forces of the so-called independent homelands, over whose activities the South African government had no direct control.

[43] The applications from the 130 unidentified individuals who claimed to have been members of the PAC were declared invalid by the committee on July 3, 1998 (see TRC press release of July 3, 1998; no formal decision is available in respect of them). The collective amnesty application of the APLA high command was ruled inadmissible in Decision AC/2000/101. See also *TRC Report*, vol. 6, 432.

[44] TRC Act, s 20 (1) read in conjunction with s 1 (1) (b).

involved in common crime, while the remaining sixty-seven were common criminals or members of political splinter groups. One hundred five high-ranking ANC applicants failed to specify any personal involvement in the commission of politically motivated crimes.[45]

Many applications were made by different perpetrators for their participation in the same incident. Applications concern in total 2,208 different incidents of political violence, of which 1,081 involved the commission of human rights violations. This latter figure includes 616 incidents in which at least one victim was killed.

Counted in participation acts (one participation act being one applicant's personal contribution to an incident which forms the subject matter of an amnesty application), amnesty was sought for 4,052 participation acts in prima facie politically motivated incidents, 2,338 of which related to deeds involving the commission of gross human rights violations (1,389 of these included killings). One thousand four hundred twenty-six participation acts affected only politically active victims, while 912 also harmed victims who were not themselves politically active persons. The vast majority of participation acts were performed between 1990 and 1994 (1,669) and between 1985 and 1989 (1,497). By contrast, only 127 participation acts were committed between 1960 and 1979, and only 418 between 1980 and 1984. For the 341 remaining participation acts, no year of commission could be determined from the committee's published decisions.

Most applicants applied for amnesty for at least one participation act that involved the commission of a human rights violation. This is the case for 572 of the 857 applicants connected to the ANC (including 160 of 237 MK members, but none of the 105 applicants from the ANC leadership, since their applications failed to specify any deeds in which these high-ranking applicants were personally and directly involved). Human rights violations were also committed by 95 of the 116 applicants linked to the PAC (including 80 of 85 APLA cadres), 75 of the 85 applicants who belonged to the IFP, 248 of the 289 members of the state security forces, and 53 of the 77 applicants involved in white right-wing organizations.

The overwhelming majority of applicants who applied for amnesty for their participation in specified incidents of political violence were ordinary rank and file members of their organization, relatively low in their organization's internal hierarchy, and with little personal authority (1,045). Such applicants could be police officers who were not permanently heading a particular local police branch or unit, MK cadres and APLA soldiers, SDU members, and the like. Quite a small number of applicants (eighty-eight) had permanent commanding functions, and only a handful (twenty-nine) can be classified as true leaders who were part of the top

---

[45] See Du Bois-Pedain, *Transitional Amnesty*, chapter 1, text at notes 137–43 for further details on the ANC leadership case.

structures within the organizational hierarchy.[46] The generals and politicians indeed stayed away from the amnesty process.

At the other end of the scale was a number of applicants of very low hierarchical status (173) who were effectively on the fringes of the organization or institution on whose behalf they endeavored to act. At this level, we find police *askaris*[47] and mere supporters of political organizations, whose involvement was not based on proper, formalized membership and was in fact marginal. This pattern of distribution holds true for all perpetrator groups.

Interesting, the fact that most applicants were ordinary rank and file members of their organizations does not mean that they predominantly acted on orders. When looking at applications for participation in incidents involving the commission of human rights violations,[48] we find that a large number of applicants had in fact no clear orders (or at least direct instructions) to perform the deed for which they applied for amnesty. Altogether, 30.1 percent of applicants acted on their own initiative and discretion compared to 21.5 percent who had direct instructions and to 29.4 percent who acted on orders in the presence of an operational commander while performing the deed. A small minority acted spontaneously and unthinkingly in reaction to some situation they found themselves confronted with (3.2 percent), while 7.2 percent of applicants acted on the basis of a collective decision (often one in which they themselves had taken part).

### How did the Committee Apply the Preconditions for Amnesty?

The Amnesty Committee rarely explains why it views the applicants' conduct as an "act associated with a political objective" as defined by the TRC Act. It is likewise highly unusual for the committee to engage in a discussion of different possible interpretations of legal concepts featuring in the list of criteria for its consideration contained in the legislation, or even to clarify its own understanding of these terms. In order to get a grip on the committee's interpretation of the political offense requirement, one therefore has to take one's clues from trends revealed by a comparison of the success rates of amnesty applications in relation to different factual

---

[46] Since only applications in which applicants specified their participation in particular incidents are taken into account at this stage, the 105 applicants from the ANC leadership who failed to provide such specifications do not appear in these figures.

[47] The term *askari* refers to a former liberation movement fighter who, usually under pressure and in exchange for money, was forced to work for the former security branch. Many *askaris* were housed at the Vlakplaas farm, which formed the secret base of operations for the C1-Unit of the security branch. See *TRC Report*, vol. 6, 217–18.

[48] In regard to those which did not, the information contained in the committee's amnesty decisions is often too scanty for one to determine what instructions, if any, the applicant had received from his organization.

features of the case that might, in the light of the criteria that served the committee as guidelines, have had an impact on the outcome of the application.[49]

It is crucial for the defensibility of this approach that it measures the outcome of amnesty applications in an analytically convincing manner. One of the fundamental problems with the committee's own data is that the committee never settled on an appropriate basic unit for this sort of exercise in the *TRC Report*. With regard to some perpetrator groups, the committee stated the outcome of their amnesty applications in relation to "applications." In other cases, the outcomes were stated in relation to "incidents." Neither unit is appropriate. Statistics based on "applications" accord an application that relates to a multitude of serious political crimes the same weight as one that deals with one, relatively minor, incident.[50] Statistics based on "incidents" accord equal weight to an incident in which ten applicants participated and an incident in which only one applicant was involved. What is more, in any case where there is more than one applicant in relation to an incident, the outcome of their applications may differ. It is unclear whether the incident should, in such a situation, be counted once, twice, or not at all.

The approach I opted for in my study was to count the incident as many times as amnesty has been granted or refused to an applicant in relation to it. In effect, this means that I did not count "incidents" as such, but something different: the outcome of applications as they relate to an applicant's *participation* in a particular incident. One participation act is constituted by one applicant's personal contribution to an incident that forms the subject matter of an amnesty application. This has the added advantage that the basic statistical unit – the participation act – is aligned with the reference point for the investigation whether the applicant's deed was "political." This is also to be judged in relation to participation in an incident and not in relation to the event as such.

The most important result of my analysis of the outcome of amnesty applications is that the overall success rate of admissible amnesty applications – measured by the outcomes of applications for individual acts of participation in prima facie political incidents – is extremely high. It stands at 88.3 percent and hardly drops for applications relating to participation in incidents involving gross human rights violations as defined in the TRC Act (84.3 percent). Even when such applications concern events in which the death of at least one victim was caused, the success rate is still high at 80.1 percent. The success rates are higher when the victim of a gross human

---

[49] For a detailed description of the methodology, see Du Bois-Pedain, *Transitional Amnesty*, chapter 2.

[50] The *TRC Report*, for instance, gives the outcome of the applications by seven members of an alleged IFP hit squad, which covered between five and fifty-one separate incidents each, as "six applications granted, one 'other.'" Had the outcome of these applications (recorded in Decision AC/1999/332) been expressed in incidents, it would have read: fifty granted, one refused.

rights violation was politically active (87.2 percent), and lower when at least one victim was not a political opponent of the applicant (79.7 percent).

With regard to the hierarchical position of amnesty applicants within their organizations, one finds that the success rate of applications from persons at leadership level (for applications relating to specified acts of participation in political crimes)[51] stands at 95.4 percent. Applicants with permanent commanding functions received amnesty in 95.1 percent of all cases, whereas ordinary rank and file members were granted amnesty in 88.0 percent of cases. For applicants at the bottom end of their organizations' internal hierarchy, the success rate drops to 69.9 percent.

At all hierarchical levels, applicants who acted on orders in the presence of an operational commander received amnesty in 89.2 percent of cases. The success rate of those who had direct instructions to perform the acts in question stands at 83.9 percent, which is more or less the same as the success rate of applications from applicants who acted on their own initiative and discretion (83.6 percent). Success rates drop to 72.6 percent in the case of applicants who relied on a collective decision as authorization for their deeds, and further to 62.2 percent when applicants reacted spontaneously and unthinkingly to a situation they were suddenly confronted with.

When one looks more closely at the reasons given by the committee why amnesty had been refused to an applicant, one finds that lack of full disclosure plays a significant role.[52] This is particularly so for applicants from the ranks of the security police. Applicants from the liberation movements also frequently stumble over the full disclosure requirement. By contrast, it rarely plays a role in the decisions to refuse amnesty to right-wing applicants (one notable exception is the decision concerning the killers of Chris Hani, Conservative Party members Janusz Walus and Clive Derby-Lewis).[53] However, other reasons feature alongside the full disclosure requirement. Many applications are refused for what one might describe as a motive-related reason, encompassing cases in which the applicant acted for personal gain or out of personal animosity against the victim, but also (and more frequently) cases in which the applicant was aware that, in acting as he did, he overstepped the bounds of his internal organizational mandate or competence.[54] Finally, there are instances

---

[51] Since this study is based on the outcomes of admissible applications only, the applications by 105 members from the ANC leadership based on their collective political responsibility for the implementation of ANC strategies by the organization's members and supporters are not included in this figure. See text at note 46.

[52] Forty-one point one percent of the rejected amnesty applications failed because of the insufficiency of information with which the applicant supplied the committee. Significant, in 24.5 percent of cases, this is the only reason why the application is rejected. For figures regarding applicants from different perpetrator groups, see Du Bois-Pedain, *Transitional Amnesty*, chapter 2.

[53] Decision No AC/1999/172.

[54] This occurs in 36.9 percent of participation acts for which the amnesty application is rejected, and is given as the only reason in 14.2 percent of rejected applications.

when amnesty applications are refused because the deed as such could not qualify for amnesty (for instance, because it was disproportionate, or in the case of security force agents not directed against a political opponent).[55] That said, given the range of crimes committed during the South African political conflicts, some of which – such as torture in police cells[56] or the PAC's "repossession policy"[57] – are arguably international crimes, whereas others – for instance, the killing of alleged witches for political reasons[58] and many of the loyalty-based crimes in KwaZulu-Natal[59] – fall on the borderlines of modern notions of political conduct even in a broad and factual sense, it is surprising that the character of the deed is not cited more often as a reason for refusing amnesty.

## Explaining the Committee's Policy of Generosity

The committee accepted every strategy adopted by a political organization or institution during the conflict as political irrespective of the repulsiveness of that strategy in moral terms. It refused to pass any kind of judgment on the objective itself and to treat certain objectives as insufficiently weighty to justify the use of some means in their pursuit.[60] An analysis of the very few cases in which the committee judged a politically motivated action to have been disproportionate shows that the only kind of act the committee frowned upon as disproportionate was the politically senseless act. It castigated as disproportionate deeds whose alleged political objective (to render the victim incapable of running the affairs of the local community) had already been achieved (the victim had fled the area and almost all her fellow councilors had resigned), deeds committed with needless cruelty, or deeds devoid of any discernible

---

55  In 29.1 percent of rejected applications, this reason is relied on by the committee and given as the only reason why the application fails in 7.8 percent of cases. As for other grounds of rejection, common criminality is rare for bona fide political offenders who passed the initial screening process and mentioned in only 15.6 percent of rejected applications (in 11.2 percent of them as the only reason). Similarly infrequent are applications for lawful conduct: This reason for turning down an application is relied on in 13.1 percent of rejected applications (in 11.1 percent as the only reason).

56  See Decision No AC/1999/027.

57  See Decision No AC/2001/106.

58  See the Amnesty Committee's discussion of these cases, *TRC Report*, vol. 6, 39–41, 332–7.

59  The committee comments: "Historical fiefdoms and allegiances in KwaZulu and Natal made it impossible for residents to remain neutral. People's identities were tied to where they lived, their families, their clans and to local authority figures such as *indunas* (local headmen) and chiefs.... The conflict also threw up old rivalries. In some cases, the roots of the conflict were found in clashes between extended families. Traditional structures featured prominently in incidents described by amnesty applicants" (*TRC Report*, vol. 6, 322–3).

60  The consistent application of this approach also means that some applicants will qualify for amnesty for graver crimes than others, depending on the strategies their political masters promoted and endorsed. This goes a long way toward explaining apparent inconsistencies between the handling of individual applications by applicants from different perpetrator groups.

rational relation whatsoever between what was done to the victim in question and the applicant's stated political aim. But violence which served a function and did not exceed the degree necessary to secure its particular aim in the circumstances was seen as proportionate to its objective, even if the aim was, for instance, to strike terror among a particular section of the population and an increased level of violence served to achieve that aim.[61] That international law might condemn the applicant's actions as a crime was likewise considered unimportant, so long as it was clear that the TRC Act meant to make amnesty available for this kind of conduct to the extent that it also constituted an offense or delict under South African law.[62]

The committee thus took a purely pragmatic, matter of fact approach to the political offense requirement. Its reluctance to evaluate the legitimacy and importance of the applicant's political objective when applying the proportionality test means that the proportionality requirement no longer operated as a normative constraint on the kinds of deeds which could, as a matter of principle, be accepted as political in nature. Instead, it became part of the factual test whether an applicant stayed within, or whether he or she strayed beyond, his or her organizational mandate. In its determinations, the committee was prepared to accept as political any act objectively, or in the estimation of the offender, connected to the struggle for power within a particular community, and shunned the application of morally restrictive criteria which ultimately would involve a determination on whether the conduct in question amounted to legitimate political activity. In doing so, the committee aimed to ensure that every applicant who did in fact perform an "act associated with a political objective … in the course of the conflicts of the past" and made full disclosure thereof could qualify for amnesty irrespective of the gravity of his or her deed. The committee was unhappy about occasions when, because of factually restrictive legislative requirements for amnesty, it could not extend the benefit of amnesty to each and every politically motivated offender.[63] Consequently, eligibility for amnesty within the legislative framework created by the TRC Act did not necessarily correlate to moral deservedness. What makes an applicant "morally deserving" of amnesty was not what he or she did – it was (if anything) his or her willingness to make full disclosure. This means that the moral justification of the amnesty scheme

---

[61]  See Du Bois-Pedain, *Transitional Amnesty*, chapter 3, notes 95–100 and accompanying text.

[62]  In Decision No AC/1999/027 on the application by former police officer Jeffrey Theodore Benzien in respect of torture of political suspects, the committee brushes aside the argument that Benzien's conduct "amounted to an international crime … and for that reason his application for amnesty should not be entertained" with the laconic observation that "[t]orture or severe ill treatment are included in the definition of 'gross violation of human rights in terms of … the [TRC] Act,'" for which amnesty can be granted – perhaps in recognition of the argument put to the committee by other security force applicants that international law concepts should not be brought to bear on the amnesty process because in doing so, the committee would "introduce factors which treat different parties unequally other than that permitted by the Act". See further Du Bois-Pedain, *Transitional Amnesty*, chapter 3.

[63]  See *TRC Report*, vol. 6, 89.

rested more heavily on the requirement for full disclosure than it would have done if eligibility for amnesty had already been restricted to perpetrators of political deeds that were morally legitimate all things considered.

Arguably, the very breadth of the Amnesty Committee's interpretation of the political offense requirement was a prerequisite of the scheme's practical success. Only a broad and factual interpretation gave potential applicants the reassurance they needed to come forward and expose their past deeds to the committee. What is more, a broad and factual interpretation of the political offense requirement encouraged applicants to disclose the more unsavory aspects of their deeds. This served the TRC's primary task of establishing as complete a picture as possible of the "causes, nature and extent" of the human rights violations committed in the course of the conflict.[64] In one particularly crass example, an applicant who had participated in one of the violent attacks that engulfed the Vaal townships in the early 1990s answered the question of why a nine-month-old baby was deliberately killed with "a snake gives birth to another snake."[65] This explanation is as repulsive as the deed. But it is important to learn that this *was* the true explanation for this particular act of brutality. No one's understanding of past events would be furthered if applicants like this one told fictitious stories of accidental killings in order to receive amnesty. In owning up to the true motivation behind their deeds, such perpetrators' testimonies made a key contribution to exposing the wider truth that politically motivated violence is often ugly, frequently irrational, and corrupts those caught up in it with its own dynamics that flow from the dehumanization of the enemy in the minds of the perpetrators. The commission would not have gotten to that truth if it had not signaled to applicants that it was prepared to take their past understandings of a political deed on board.[66]

Furthermore, a factual conception of political offenses prevailed in public preconceptions of the amnesty scheme. People expected that amnesty would be available to anyone who had done anything that "in those days" was readily understood and

---

[64] See s 3 (1) (a) TRC Act.

[65] Testimony of amnesty applicant Victor Mthembu, cited in *TRC Report*, vol. 5, 289. The applicant was granted amnesty for his participation in the attack. See Decision No AC/2000/209 (Boipatong Massacre).

[66] This is not to deny that some temptation to underplay the atrocious nature of past events, rationalize personal motivations, and leave acts of gratuitous violence unacknowledged will always be there. Piers Pigou, a former member of the TRC's investigation unit, deplores the tendency of applicants to present "neat and seemingly sanitised versions of events" and observes that "many applications ... studiously avoided mention of excessive abusive behaviour or personal (financial or material) gain." (Piers Pigou, "Degrees of Truth: Amnesty and Limitations in the Truth Recovery Project," in Villa-Vicencio and Doxtader, *The Provocations of Amnesty*, 221). Nagy has expressed a similar concern that, by forcing applicants to explain their racist motivations as political (directed against "oppressors") as opposed to private (simply an opinion which they held), "[m]any 'private' acts of ethno-racism and revenge were ... excluded from the transformative message about breaking the continuum of violence" (Rosemary Nagy, "Violence, Amnesty and Transitional Law: 'Private' Acts and 'Public' Truth in South Africa," *African Journal of Legal Studies* 1, no. 1 (2004): 22).

recognized as political. Rejections of amnesty applications based on an argument that some applicants' actions, despite having been political in this factual sense, could not qualify for amnesty before the TRC, would have been notoriously hard to communicate. A critical application of concepts such as proportionality would also have involved the committee in an evaluation of the political strategies endorsed by the different parties during the conflict. But any finding that an applicant could not qualify for amnesty because the policies that his or her organization had formulated and endorsed were inherently disproportionate or (as was argued in the case of state torture) amounted to an international crime, would have put an end to the inclusiveness of the scheme and jeopardized the achievement of its transitional policy objectives. Acceptance of the conditional amnesty by potential applicants and the general public depended on the Amnesty Committee's plumping for a nondivisive, nearly all-encompassing notion of the political offense.

### Developments after the Amnesty Phase

The public disclosure requirement connected to the offer of amnesty, and uncertainty regarding the willingness of former ministers of state and of some political parties to stand by those who had used violence on their behalf, meant that it was unrealistic to expect that everyone who had committed crimes in supporting or resisting apartheid would come forward and apply. And, as pointed out earlier, many potential applicants indeed stayed away while others failed to obtain amnesty. In respect of all these, it was widely assumed that investigations and prosecutions would be continued with vigor alongside and beyond the completion of the Amnesty Committee's work. But the prosecutorial record since 1998 is thin and in many respects disappointing.[67] The main trial against a high-ranking military officer who had been an outspoken opponent of the TRC, Wouter Basson, ended in a debacle for the prosecution.[68] Some trials that were resumed against accused persons who had failed to get amnesty resulted in convictions,[69] others in acquittals.[70] Only a

---

[67] For details on post-TRC prosecutions, see Antje du Bois-Pedain, "Post-conflict Accountability and the Demands of Justice: Can Conditional Amnesties Take the Place of Criminal Prosecutions?" (University of Cambridge Faculty of Law Research Paper 32/2011), also in Oxford Transitional Justice Research (OTJR), *Critical Perspectives in Transitional Justice.*

[68] Basson was charged early in 1998 with a multitude of offenses relating to a clandestine South African Defence Force (SADF) project entitled "Project Coast." Some of the charges were thrown out by the trial court on grounds of lack of jurisdiction (*S v. Basson* 2001 (1) SACR 235 (T)). Basson was acquitted on all remaining charges in April 2002. The state later successfully challenged the trial judge's ruling on the jurisdictional issue in the constitutional court. However, the case was not reopened by the prosecution.

[69] Convicted of murder were, in 2004, homeland policemen Tyani and Gumengu. The trial against police officers Nieuwoudt, Van Zyl, and Koole for their alleged murder of anti-apartheid activists is on hold since 2004; one of the defendants, Nieuwoudt, died of cancer in 2005.

[70] Acquitted of murder were, in 2002, former police officer Michael Luff and, also in 2002, homeland police officers Mkosana and Gonya.

handful of fresh cases were brought.[71] With the exception of a trial which ended with a plea bargain in 2007,[72] where the accused included a former minister of law and order, Adriaan Vlok, and a former police general, Johann van der Merwe, no high-ranking former apartheid state agents were charged or convicted. A review by experienced prosecutors of more than 450 cases handed over by the TRC to the prosecution service identified only sixteen cases in which a successful prosecution seemed feasible.[73] In 2005, prosecutorial guidelines later found unlawful sought to enable prosecutors to close all cases in which the suspect's crime could have qualified for amnesty under the TRC Act.[74] The political will to conduct further criminal trials seems to have seeped away quickly among perceptions that such trials were costly and difficult and might prove politically divisive. What is more, a special pardons process has been under way since 2007 for prisoners and other convicted persons who did not apply for amnesty despite having acted in a political context.[75] It is in these developments that concerns over impunity for apartheid-era violence are rooted. Unlike successful amnesty applicants who had to stand up in public and confess to their crimes, others who played for time and avoided making any damaging admissions may now really be getting away with murder.

## CONDITIONAL AMNESTY: FACILITATOR OR IRRITANT ON THE PATH TO JUSTICE AND THE RULE OF LAW?

Whatever one may think of the wisdom and justification of making promises of amnesty during the process of negotiations for peace, a post-transitional government sets out on a risky path – both morally and politically – when it tries to renege on promises made and agreements reached during the transition. At the very least, it will make a set of diehard political enemies: those who, by the post-transitional

---

[71] In 2003, right-winger Eugene Terre'Blanche pled guilty to five counts of terrorism in return for a six-year suspended sentence of imprisonment. A former ANC activist, Blani, was convicted of murder in 2005. Four APLA members charged with having attacked the Willowvale police station also pled guilty in return for a noncustodial sentence. Five defendants were charged with the attempted murder of apartheid critic Frank Chikane; their trial ended with a plea bargain as detailed in the next footnote.

[72] *S v. Johannes Velde van der Merwe, Adriaan Johannes Vlok, Christoffel Lodewikus Smith, Gert Jacobus Louis Hosea Otto and Hermanus Johannes van Staden*, Plea and Sentencing Agreement in Terms of Section 105A of Act 51 of 1977 (as amended), August 17, 2007.

[73] See Ole Bubenzer, *Post-TRC Prosecutions in South Africa. Accountability for Political Crimes after the Truth and Reconciliation Commission's Amnesty Process* (Leiden: Martinus Nijhoff, 2009), 29.

[74] National Prosecution Authority, *Prosecution Policy* (Revision Date: December 1, 2005), Appendix A "Prosecution Policy and Directives Relating to the Prosecution of Offences Emanating from Conflicts of the Past and Which Were Committed on or Before May 11, 1994," held unlawful in *Nkadimeng and others v. The National Director of Public Prosecutions and others*, Case no. 32709/07, High Court of South Africa (Transvaal Provincial Division), unreported judgment of December 12, 2008. For discussion, see Du Bois-Pedain, "Post-conflict Accountability."

[75] These developments are reviewed in Du Bois-Pedain, "Post-conflict Accountability."

government's choice not to honor the promise to grant them amnesty, are effectively excluded from the benefits of peace. At worst, such a government will undermine its own credibility by being perceived as a two-faced political actor whose word, given by those of its members involved in the negotiations for peace, cannot be trusted. Responsibility for backtracking on a negotiated amnesty agreement cannot always be shirked effectively by pointing out that conduct for which amnesty was first promised but later refused was "an international crime." When such a reassessment is not based on the discovery of new facts or on proof of facts previously denied, the unqualified earlier promise of amnesty for all politically motivated acts must be understood as meant to cover such conduct, too. It is therefore a significant argument in favor of the South African amnesty scheme, as well as one of the potential reasons for the adoption of similar schemes in the future, that it was agreed between the negotiating parties that *all* conduct associated with a political objective should be subject to amnesty, and only the precise shape of that amnesty was left for the post-transitional government to design and implement.[76]

I cannot, for reasons of space, discuss the – disputed – legality of amnesties for conduct that international law directly marks out as a criminal act. As Mark Freeman and Max Pensky bring out in their chapter in this volume, in the absence of any explicit prohibition on amnesty in any of the treaty sources, the permissibility of amnesty for international crimes depends on one's interpretation of the particular treaty provisions said to imply such a restriction and on one's views of the current and constantly evolving content of customary norms in this area.[77] I have argued elsewhere that South Africa's amnesty law was not in conflict with international law binding on South Africa at the time.[78] Other countries, depending on the type of conflict they were engaged in and on the range of international treaties ratified by them, may well find themselves in a stricter legal corset – in their case, the legal permissibility of a conditional amnesty along South African lines may truly stand or fall with the argument that this model constitutes not so much a breach of prosecutorial obligations

---

[76] For the terms of the amnesty agreement enshrined in South Africa's negotiated interim constitution of 1993, see text at note 3.

[77] Freeman and Pensky, Chapter 2 in this volume.

[78] During the apartheid era, South Africa had not signed or ratified any human rights treaties. While it was bound by the 1949 Geneva Conventions, these impose prosecutorial obligations for "grave breaches" of the laws of war only in international conflicts. Customary humanitarian law at the time when South Africa passed its amnesty law did not extend this obligation to grave breaches committed in noninternational armed conflicts – and it was moreover debatable on the facts whether the violence that surged through South Africa did in fact constitute an "armed conflict" between sufficiently organized opponents (the international law definition excludes civil unrest and sporadic uprisings as insufficient). While acts of torture and extralegal killings violated customary human rights law even then, the obligation to prosecute these misdeeds was not part of customary law but derived from human rights treaties not binding on South Africa as a nonsignatory state. For detailed analysis and argument, see Du Bois-Pedain, *Transitional Amnesty*, chapter 8.

as a legitimate modification of the manner in which human rights violators are held to account.[79] It is likewise unclear whether a conditional amnesty, accompanied by a credible domestic prosecution policy against those who do not seek amnesty or whose applications are denied, would be taken to trigger or block the prosecutorial competence of the ICC under the Rome Statute.[80] Since the ICC prosecutor in this event would have to form a view, not about a state's disposal of each and every case taken in isolation, but of the state's overall policy that stands behind the resolution of individual cases, it appears likely that a state that restricts the availability of amnesty in the way South Africa's amnesty law has done, while making genuine efforts to prosecute those who avoid or fail to receive amnesty, would not be judged "unwilling" to prosecute the perpetrators of international crimes.

Some would say, however, that in honoring an amnesty promise for very serious acts of interpersonal violence, for state crimes, and for acts that could be classified as crimes under international law, a post-transitional government undermines its legitimacy in a different direction: it exposes itself as morally bankrupt from its inception. This is a serious objection and one that can only be met by showing that it is possible to justify amnesty as a morally defensible political choice – and here, the element of conditionality and the grounds of conditionality in the South African model are of the utmost importance. They provide the factual foundation for a moral defense of this type of amnesty that rests on the argument that it holds those who receive amnesty on its terms sufficiently to account for their past acts and constitutes a valuable and defensible component in a wider accountability process.

To see this, one has to attend, first, to the (limited) degree to which individual perpetrators who participate in the amnesty process are held to account. Second, one has to appreciate how the very limitations of conditional amnesty as a form of individual accountability can increase the value of this amnesty as a component of a broader social quest for accountability.

## Conditional Amnesty as an Individual Accountability Process

The full and public disclosure of their political crimes sets amnesty applicants apart from other perpetrators of such deeds who are not prepared to come forward. The

---

[79]  Such an argument has been put forward by Ronald C. Slye, "The Legitimacy of Amnesties Under International Law and General Principles of Anglo-American Law: Is a Legitimate Amnesty Possible?" *Virginia Journal of International Law* 43 (2002–3): 173.

[80]  What amounts to a credible prosecution policy is, of course, also open to debate. It is certainly interesting to note that (given the duration over many years of many of these court cases), the relatively few trials held in South Africa since 1998 nevertheless mean that, in terms of Kathryn Sikkink's charting of the justice cascade (see Chapter 1, Figure 1.1 in this volume), each year between 1994 and 2007 has, for the South African courts exercising their domestic jurisdiction over apartheid-era violence, been a "prosecution year."

conditional offer of amnesty encapsulates a call to account for politically motivated wrongdoing that requires applicants to respond by providing an explanation of their past conduct in a public forum where they can be confronted with an evaluation of their conduct as wrong. This limited yet meaningful demonstration of their acceptance of the victims' and the political community's moral and legal right to call them to account for their actions[81] justifies treating amnesty applicants differently from, and more leniently than, politically motivated perpetrators who do not apply for amnesty.

But the conditional amnesty process cannot – despite the very real burdens for applicants of full, public confessions and the extent to which such a process serves some of the needs of victims[82] – be considered a response that holds successful amnesty applicants fully to account for their past acts. This is so because given the serious nature of the deeds for which amnesty was made available, it cannot be maintained that the perpetrators of such deeds deserve no sanction. Assessed from the perspective of the victims of such acts, amnesty remains an unjust response to a politically motivated crime. Moreover, an amnesty that offenders are *entitled* to receive simply upon making full disclosure of a politically motivated crime is not able to provide a framework in which restorative justice objectives can be met.[83] At most it can be argued that the public disclosure that the scheme requires, and the emphasis it places on the communal and organized dimension of the political violence it deals with, make it possible to regard the amnesty process as an exceptional "'rite of passage' into citizenship unencumbered by the past for those who are willing to commit themselves to the new political order, in which any resort to violence as a means of (domestic) politics is characterized as wrong."[84] The requirement of full disclosure turns a conditional amnesty scheme into a tool for accountability, not impunity.[85] But this accountability, qua individual accountability, remains only partial.[86]

### Conditional Amnesty as a Component in a Collective Accountability Process

The justice deficit at the heart of amnesty can, however, prove beneficial for the newly constituted polity. To see why this is so, recall the element in respect of which the definition of a political offense in the South African case was still restrictive: it required the applicant's acts to have been embedded in a wider organizational

---

[81]  Du Bois-Pedain, *Transitional Amnesty*, 297–9.
[82]  Ibid., chapter 6.
[83]  Ibid., chapter 7.
[84]  Ibid., 298.
[85]  Ibid., chapter 4.
[86]  Ibid., chapter 7.

context and to have emanated from his institutional role. What amnesty applicants were thus asked to account for were their personal – criminal – contributions to collective political endeavors. Amnesty is made available because the perpetrators' choices and deliberations at the time took place in a framework provided by the objectives and strategies of the political party or cause to which they had aligned themselves. The granting of amnesty thus responds to the fact that the organizations and institutions behind the applicants, as well as their leaders and arguably their members, brought that legitimating framework into being and for this reason bear *political responsibility* for the applicants' acts.

The internationally preferred accountability model for politically motivated crimes embodied in the justice cascade described by Kathryn Sikkink in this volume – specifically the attribution of individual criminal responsibility in criminal trials and the imposition of punishment commensurate with the seriousness of the individual acts – reinforces and marks the individual's responsibility for his or her actions.[87] By the same token, however, it fails to respond adequately to the collective dimension of the kinds of deeds for which amnesty was made available in the South African context. In the criminal trial, this dimension features usually as a background against which the defendant's actions are judged and may lead to less serious punishment being imposed than in otherwise comparable cases of nonpolitical crimes. But it is not addressed as something for which responsibility can be ascribed to a suitable entity and responded to as shared. This evaporation of the element of noncriminal collective responsibility in criminal trials has potentially serious long-term consequences for a transitional polity seeking to overcome a legacy of political violence. It facilitates denials of responsibility by members of the collectives from which the individual criminal perpetrators drew guidance, sustenance, reassurance, and inspiration at the time of their deeds. This hidden cost of an accountability process that – qua accountability – relies only on prosecutions of individual agents can be avoided through an accountability process that combines (as in South Africa) broader attributions of responsibility contained in the pronouncements of an investigative commission with a conditional, prosecutions-flanked amnesty.[88]

But it is only when the criteria for amnesty, and the moral communication of the body applying these criteria, breaks through the simple equation, "I did what I did for politics, therefore I am entitled to amnesty," that applicants begin to account for their deeds in an ethically appropriate and socially meaningful way. When a conditional amnesty scheme is, as in South Africa, accompanied by a truth and reconciliation process that imposes on the amnestied deeds a concurrent legal

---

[87] See Sikkink, Chapter 1 in this volume.

[88] For the full argument, see Antje du Bois-Pedain, "Communicating Criminal and Political Responsibility in the TRC Process," in du Bois and du Bois-Pedain, *Justice and Reconciliation in Post-Apartheid South Africa*, 62–89.

evaluation as "serious human rights violations," this creates the communicative space to break through the simple equation of a political motivation with an entitlement to amnesty. Through the requirement of full disclosure the amnesty process is directly tied into this communication and promotes its achievement. The classification of many amnestied acts as serious human rights violations reminds us that amnesty does not, and cannot, mean that the morality subscribed to by one or more parties to the conflict provides a full justification for the wounds inflicted on others. Political violence is denounced as conduct that results in unwarranted suffering by fellow citizens.

The TRC process as a whole, in my view, succeeded in a fair and effective ascription of responsibility for politically motivated crimes, and it did so by breaking through the criminal law responsibility paradigm that can so easily ground denials of responsibility by anyone beyond the reach of *this* paradigm. In this context, the very injustice of amnesty served an important communicative function. Amnesty reminded people of the fact that the human rights violations committed by the amnesty applicants took place in a social context that legitimated these acts of violence; that they were done in (many of) their names. They were therefore injustices in which others were powerfully – politically, though not criminally – implicated. And while the political backdrop to these crimes was not, to paraphrase Antjie Krog, a "good enough reason to have committed murder,"[89] it was a good enough reason to be granted amnesty for them. Through amnesty, the conventional view of the comparative seriousness of criminal and political responsibility was turned on its head. Criminal responsibility could be waived; political responsibility could not.

## CONCLUSION

Conditional amnesty's defensibility ultimately depends on the requirements for a successful transition. Stability is fostered, not undermined, when (even unpopular) negotiated agreements are kept. Accountability is ensured, not denied, when noncriminal, political responsibility for past violence is not swept under the carpet, but exposed and made salient in a polity's response to past violence. Justice, which allows us to afford special treatment to political offenders to the extent that their conduct then was indeed recognizably part of a collective political endeavor, provided that their conduct now – in making full disclosure – credibly signals their willingness to account for these acts as wrongful harms to their victims, is demonstrated, not violated, through such a scheme.

South Africa's conditional amnesty arguably offers an enduring example of an ethically justifiable and politically effective transitional amnesty law that can serve

[89] Antjie Krog, *Country of My Skull* (Johannesburg: Random House, 2002), 104.

as a blueprint for a credible accountability process in other political transitions. Its various interrelated political objectives – to facilitate the TRC's investigation of the causes and effects of past political violence, to help South Africa reconstitute itself as a stable polity free of political violence and committed to the rule of law, to make those formerly engaged in that violence account for their acts while at the same time offering them an avenue for social reintegration – are undoubtedly valuable, and proved achievable. But a conditional amnesty process is not an easy way out for a polity incapable or unwilling to conduct successful prosecutions. In order to reap the benefits, it needs to be embedded in a broader truth finding effort and supported by a real threat of prosecution against those who fail to participate.[90] One must also remain conscious of the fact that conditional amnesty "always involves a shift away from the standard justice script involving prosecution and the possibility of punishment – a shift which must be publicly justified, politically managed and in its future implications contained within the transitional moment."[91]

Arguably, conditional amnesty has created a problematic legacy for the perceived legitimacy of South Africa's present-day criminal justice system.[92] But this is a result, not of the justice deficit that was an undeniable feature of the conditional amnesty, but of the attempts to justify conditional amnesty fully as an instantiation of an allegedly superior ideal of justice: restorative as opposed to retributive. As the follow-up pardons for offenders who did not avail themselves of the amnesty offer made through the TRC suggest,[93] the linking of conditional amnesty to supposedly superior conceptions of justice, intended to shore up the legitimacy of the TRC, made it difficult to confine amnesty to the transitional phase.

At the same time, South Africa today is surprisingly free of political violence, and not just the country's elites but also ordinary people are committed to the inclusive sociopolitical vision so memorably captured in the self-description as a "Rainbow Nation." What prevented the "miracle" of South Africa's transition to democracy from dissolving like a mirage in the heat of divisive political agendas was the foregrounding of reconciliation as the "regulative ideal"[94] of the transitional phase. The redrawing of lines of interaction practiced and made visible in the TRC's public hearings – no longer, as during apartheid rule, between oppressor and oppressed, but between co-citizens with equal rights and equal value – gave credibility to the

---

[90] In South Africa, this threat was palpable and effective prior and during the application period for conditional amnesty. Prosecutions of those who did or could not avail themselves of the amnesty offer were, by contrast, few and only occasionally successful. See already note 34 and text at notes 68 to 75.

[91] Du Bois-Pedain, *Transitional Amnesty*, 298.

[92] For a full discussion, see Du Bois-Pedain, "Post-conflict Accountability."

[93] The problems connected to the drawn out and acrimonious pardons process that followed the conditional amnesty scheme are described in Du Bois-Pedain, "Post-conflict Accountability."

[94] The phrase is taken from Andrew Schaap, "Assuming Responsibility in the Hope of Reconciliation," *Borderlands e-journal* 3 (2004), accessed September 3, 2011, www.borderlandsejournal.adelaide.edu.au.

newly constituted democracy's claim to pursue "justice through reconciliation."[95] Wrongdoing was addressed by a mechanism designed to reintegrate victims and offenders into the same political community. Conditional amnesty contributed to this goal by generating a public accounting for political actions in which rationalizations for the use of violence for political ends turned stale as those who paid the price for these choices became visible in their personal suffering.

While the truth finding efforts of truth commissions are universally supported, many commentators deplore the fact that truth commissions often in practice come to function as "substitutes," rather than complementary mechanisms, for criminal justice.[96] This is indeed a problematic feature of transitional processes in which the steps taken to document past atrocities, important as they are in preserving the social memory of these events, are not accompanied by a credible process to hold those responsible for these human rights violations to account. But as this study of the South African model of a conditional amnesty reveals, it is possible to mold an amnesty arrangement into a building block for an accountability process capable of reaching the fundamental objectives of truth, justice, and social healing that any given set of transitional policies seeks to achieve. This form of amnesty does not undermine justice and ought not to be outlawed.

---

[95] For a full discussion, see François du Bois and Antje du Bois-Pedain, "Post-conflict Justice and the Reconciliatory Paradigm," in du Bois and du Bois-Pedain, *Justice and Reconciliation in Post-Apartheid South Africa*, 289–311.

[96] This view is often taken by human rights activists and NGOs. For the views of academics, see Charles Harper, *Impunity: An Ethical Perspective. Six Case Studies from Latin America* (Geneva: WCC Publications, 1996); Barahona de Brito, *Human Rights and Democratization in Latin America: Uruguay and Chile*, and Luis Roninger and Mario Sznajder, *The Legacy of Human-Rights Violations in the Southern Cone: Argentina, Chile and Uruguay* (Oxford: Oxford University Press, 1999).

# 10

# De Facto Amnesty?

## The Example of Post-Soeharto Indonesia

### Patrick Burgess

In Indonesia, unlike the other cases discussed in this volume, efforts to introduce formal amnesties for perpetrators of gross human rights violations have not succeeded. But the purpose that such amnesties have served elsewhere – to protect those responsible for mass human rights violations and suppress the truth about the past – has been achieved. Despite failing to adopt an official amnesty law, Indonesia does not represent a case of "doing nothing." On the contrary, in response to a long list of cases of mass violations of human rights, successive Indonesian governments have passed a plethora of laws, established specialized human rights courts and other mechanisms, created commissions of inquiry, undertaken a range of investigations, and completed trials.

A cumulative analysis of these various attempts to achieve a level of truth and justice, however, provides a striking pattern of failure. Not one senior officer or official has been held accountable despite scores of events in which the national security forces have been implicated in serious violations, including at least seven separate cases of systematic violence in which more than 1,000 civilians lost their lives, over a dozen commissions of inquiry, and the trial of thirty-four individuals before the human rights courts. Although progressive forces in Indonesia can claim significant victories in advancing human rights, reports of serious violations persist and little progress has been made in the areas of truth and accountability.

In the absence of a specific term that accurately describes this phenomenon, it is useful to use the imperfect term of a *de facto amnesty*. One might argue that *amnesty* refers to a legal designation and therefore cannot be described as *de facto*. However, the term *de facto amnesty* is increasingly used by international human rights organizations,[1]

---

[1] For example, Amnesty International, Human Rights Watch, and the International Commission of Jurists, "Joint Open Letter to Prime Minister Khanal of Nepal on Persistent Impunity," May 24, 2011, accessed September 12, 2011, http://www.hrw.org/news/2011/05/24/joint-open-letter-prime-minister-khanal-nepal-persistent-impunity; Richard Dicker, "Handing Qaddafi a Get-Out-Of-Jail-Free Card," *The International Herald Tribune*, accessed September 14, 2011, www.nytimes.com/2011/08/01/opinion/01iht-eddicker01.html.

academics, and the United Nations.[2] The UN Office of the High Commissioner for Human Rights, for example, provides the following definition:

> *De facto* amnesties [...] describe legal measures such as State laws, decrees or regulations that effectively foreclose prosecutions. While not explicitly ruling out criminal prosecution or civil remedies, they have the same effect as an explicit amnesty law. Such amnesties are impermissible if they prevent the prosecution of offences that may not lawfully be subject to an explicit amnesty.[3]

This chapter will present an overview of how such a de facto amnesty has served to protect perpetrators responsible for mass crimes in Indonesia. After providing a brief historical background and an outline of the relevant legal framework, the chapter looks at impunity for those responsible for mass crimes committed in seven different contexts, which resulted in a combined death toll of more than 1,000. These include violence following the transition to power of Major General Soeharto in 1965; the May 1998 events in Jakarta; and particular events in Maluku, Poso, Timor Leste, Aceh, and Papua. The patterns revealed in this analysis are reinforced through a brief examination of two emblematic cases: the murder of human rights activist Munir in 2004 and the shooting of hundreds of civilians at Tanjung Priok, Jakarta in 1984. In addition, the chapter considers the amnesty, which did not cover serious human rights violations and led to the 2004 peace accord in Aceh as well as two attempts to create de jure amnesty mechanisms: the law creating a national Truth and Reconciliation Commission (TRC) and the binational Commission for Truth and Friendship (CTF).

## HISTORICAL BACKGROUND

The birth of the Indonesian state took place in the aftermath of mass human rights violations including killings, torture, and sexual slavery during Japan's World War II occupation. Nationalists declared independence at the end of the war, which was disputed by the former Dutch colonial power, leading to a war of independence. Following victory by the nationalists, the territories formerly known as the Dutch East Indies were formally handed over in 1949, with the exception of Dutch New Guinea (later known as Papua). The modern state of Indonesia comprises seventeen thousand islands (six thousand inhabited), the fourth most populous country in the world (240 million citizens), the largest Islamic population in any country in the world, and hundreds of ethnic groups.

The first Indonesian president, Sukarno, was, in effect, a dictator who ruled through "guided democracy" and declared himself president for life in 1963. The

---

[2]  For example, the UN Committee Against Torture, "Committee against Torture, Conclusions and recommendations of the Committee against Torture – Nepal," April 13, 2007, CAT/C/NPL/CO/2, para. 24.
[3]  OHCHR, *Rule-of-Law Tools*, 43.

transition to the military dictatorship of Soeharto in 1965 was the darkest period in Indonesia's modern history, resulting in the killing of an estimated five hundred thousand to one million civilians in an anti-communist fervor that many commentators claim was manipulated as part of an attempted coup and counter coup.[4]

During Soeharto's three decades of dictatorship, the army operated according to the policy of *dwifungsi* (literally "two functions," providing security and sociopolitical development), which allowed the army to participate in all aspects of politics, economics, and the sociocultural field.[5] Military posts were established at the village level across the country and military actors became involved in all civilian affairs. A guaranteed proportion of seats in the parliament and senior civil service positions was reserved for the armed forces. Over seventy-five percent of the budget of the security forces was raised by their own legally operated businesses, which included ownership of five-star hotels and massive timber, oil, and natural resources holdings.

Human rights organizations' reports during this period repeatedly raised allegations that conflicts were manipulated in order to justify a significant military presence and the control of military actors in conflict areas, enabling members of the armed forces to reap significant financial rewards from the natural resources available in those areas.[6]

In such a context, a culture of impunity developed for members of the security forces involved in human rights violations, including commanders allegedly responsible for systematic and widespread crimes committed against civilians. This protection was facilitated by the fact that the police and military were part of the same organization until 1999. The judicial system was seriously compromised during the Soeharto dictatorship; it was routinely used as a tool to punish political opponents. The legacy of such manipulation endures; the Indonesian judicial system is still regarded as one of the most deeply flawed in the world.[7]

## LEGAL FRAMEWORK FOR MASS CRIMES

As a result of international pressure following the 1999 violence in East Timor, the Indonesian parliament passed Law No. 26 of 2000 (Law 26), which provides for the

---

4  Benedict Anderson and Ruth McVey, A *Preliminary Analysis of the October 1, 1965 Coup in Indonesia* (Cornell: Cornell Modern Indonesia Project, 1966).

5  Nugroho Notosusanto, *The Dual Function of the Indonesian Armed Forces, especially since 1966* (Jakarta: Department for Defence and Security, Centre for Armed Forces History, 1970).

6  Human Rights Watch, *Too High a Price: The Human Rights Cost of the Indonesian Military's Economic Activities*, C1805 (Human Rights Watch, June 21, 2006), accessed September 30, 2011, http://www.unhcr.org/refworld/docid/44c75e154.html.

7  Lilian Budianto, "Indonesia's Judicial System Rated the Worst in Asia: Survey," *The Jakarta Post*, September 15, 2008, accessed August 22, 2011, http://www.thejakartapost.com/news/2008/09/15/indonesia039s-judicial-system-rated-worst-asia-survey.html.

investigation and prosecution of gross human rights violations, defined as crimes against humanity and genocide.

According to Law 26, allegations of crimes against humanity or genocide are to be first examined through a "pro-justicia inquiry" of the national human rights commission (NHRC).[8] If the commission finds "sufficient preliminary evidence that a gross violation of human rights has occurred,"[9] it forwards the case file to the Attorney General's Office (AGO), which must commence formal investigation and prosecution within ninety days of receiving a completed file from the commission.

Law 26 legally also established four regional human rights courts in the country to deal with cases of gross human rights violations that occurred after the passage of the law in October 2000. At the time of this writing, only one (in Makassar) had actually begun hearing cases. For acts committed prior to its passage, Law 26 set up ad hoc courts for each specific case, requiring a presidential decree based on a recommendation from the lower house of parliament (DPR). Two such courts have been established, for the cases of Tanjung Priok and East Timor. As of September 2011 the permanent and ad hoc courts had completed trials in the cases of thirty-four individuals (all eventually acquitted).

In six other cases of mass human rights violations,[10] the NHRC completed its investigation, found that crimes against humanity had occurred, and recommended prosecution. However, the AGO has not commenced any investigation into these crimes, leaving progress on accountability stagnant.

The NHRI and the AGO hold differing views on the obligation to move forward with formal investigation and prosecution of these cases. The view of the NHRI is that the AGO is legally obligated to commence formal investigations and that inaction is due to a lack of political will to prosecute. The AGO claims that for cases which occurred prior to the passage of Law 26 of 2000 it may not commence investigation until parliament recommends that an ad hoc court for the specific case be established by presidential decree.[11] The Constitutional Court has stated that the parliament may only make such a recommendation if it is grounded in the previous findings of the organizations legally mandated to conduct inquiries and investigations: the NHRC and the AGO, producing a catch-22 situation.[12] Perhaps

---

[8]  The Indonesian NHRC's Indonesian title is Komnas HAM.

[9]  Law 26/2000 of the Republic of Indonesia Concerning Human Rights Courts, Article 18, accessed September 30, 2011, http://hrli.alrc.net/mainfile.php/indonleg/132/.

[10] These six cases are: Talangsari, Wamena and Wasior, Trisakti, Semangi I and Semanggi II, and the May 1998 riots.

[11] International Center for Transitional Justice and KontraS (the Commission for the Disappeared and Victims of Violence), *Derailed Transitional Justice in Indonesia Since the Fall of Soeharto* (New York: International Centre for Transitional Justice /KontraS, April 7, 2011), 42, accessed September 30, 2011, http://ictj.org/publication/derailed-transitional-justice-indonesia-fall-soeharto-report.

[12] Decision of the National Constitutional Court of Indonesia in the case of Eurico Guterres, accessed September 5, 2011, http://www.mahkamahkonstitusi.go.id/index.php?page=sidang_eng.

the most striking aspect of this standoff is that no productive step has been taken by the president, the parliament, or any government department to solve the practical gridlock or to clarify the legislative obligations. For more than ten years the block has continued, preventing the prosecution of extremely serious cases in which the NHRC has completed comprehensive inquires and found that crimes against humanity were committed.

In one significant matter, concerning the disappearance of thirteen prodemocracy activists in 1998, the parliament did in fact make a recommendation for the establishment of an ad hoc court to prosecute those responsible, relying on the NHRC findings, without an investigation by the AGO. Even in this case, however, military commanders named by the NHRC as bearing responsibility for the disappearances have avoided prosecution. More than two years after the parliamentary recommendation, the president still has not issued a formal decree establishing the ad hoc court and the AGO has not commenced an investigation into the case.

The situation just described provides an example of how a de facto amnesty operates. Considerable effort has been taken to create new laws and structures. Commissioners and staff serving with the NHRC have expended significant amounts of state resources and a great deal of time and energy completing these inquiries but the efforts have been blocked by resistance on the part of the AGO to carry the process forward in the case of the disappearances, and a failure of the president to follow the parliamentary recommendation and establish the court. Moreover, senior government officials have taken no effective steps to unblock the process involving the NHRC and the AGO, which has continued for more than ten years.

## SEVEN CONTEXTS OF MASS HUMAN RIGHTS VIOLATIONS

A long series of cases of serious human rights violations occurred after Soeharto came to power in 1965. The following analysis briefly deals with how the de facto amnesty has protected state agents responsible for human rights violations in seven contexts in which the estimated civilian death toll was greater than 1,000.

### 1965

The truth behind the mass murder of those perceived to be supportive of the Indonesian Communist Party (PKI) in 1965 is still unknown and strongly suppressed, particularly regarding the role that the security forces and Islamic religious groups may have played. The International Crisis Group provides the following brief summary of how the killing began:

> A group of revolutionary junior officers backed by some members of PKI, murdered six generals and announced they had taken power to forestall an army coup.

Major-General Suharto, who some claim had prior knowledge of the coup attempt, rallied the army. Over the next six months, Suharto engineered the transfer of power from Sukarno to himself and encouraged a purge of PKI leaving as many as half a million dead.... The worst killings took place in East Java, where the army encouraged local Muslim youth groups to take revenge for PKI's efforts to unilaterally seize and redistribute land, and in Bali and Aceh.[13]

Tens of thousands of members of leftist organizations, including cooperatives, youth groups, women's networks, as well as thousands of artists, writers, and intellectuals were labeled procommunist and imprisoned for a decade or longer.[14]

Controversy surrounds attempts to examine the events of 1965. Some contend that the factors that triggered this incident and its legacy must be understood because of their profound influence over the country's present and future. Others strongly disagree and actively oppose any attempt to uncover the truth. A Truth and Reconciliation Commission (TRC) law including an investigation into these and other mass violations was passed by the national parliament in 2004. The list of recommended commissioners was forwarded to the president for approval, but no action was taken for over a year, until the Constitutional Court overturned the law establishing the TRC in 2006. As a result, nobody has been investigated or prosecuted for their role in leading the systematic and widespread killings, torture, and other crimes in 1965.

## May 1998

The Asian economic crisis of 1998 led to dramatic price increases for food and other staples in Indonesia, catalyzing discontent with the military dictatorship. At the same time, the killing of four Trisakti university students by members of the army generated massive public demonstrations with over 1,000 people killed, the systematic rape of women, large-scale beatings, and destruction of property.[15]

---

[13] International Crisis Group, "Indonesia Conflict History," accessed September 3, 2011, http://www. crisisgroup.org/en/key-issues/research-resources/%7e/link.aspx?_id=d61f8aed3ff0470aacf6bbcob4df52 2f&_z=z.

[14] Government-controlled newspapers reported that the generals had been sexually tortured to death and that the murders involved members of the Indonesian women's movement aligned to the PKI. This has been disputed by academics such as Professor Benedict Anderson of Cornell, who cites post mortem reports that include no such injuries. Ben Anderson, "How did the Generals Die," *Indonesia* 43 (April 1987): 109–34, accessed September 30, 2011, http://www.antenna.nl/~fwillems/eng/ic/pki/ anderson.html.

[15] Indonesian National Commission on Violence Against Women (Komnas Perempuan), Special Rapporteur Report: *Time To Settle the Sense of Security* (Jakarta: Komnas Perempuan,2008), accessed October 2, 2011, http://www.komnasperempuan.or.id/publikasi/English/Komnas%20Publish/july2011/ MEI%201998%20(14–12–10).pdf.

A fact-finding team led by the head of the NHRC found that the violence was largely the result of the political elite's struggle to retain power. It named a number of high-ranking military personnel as responsible for orchestrating the violence and found that some of the violence had been initiated and directed by provocateurs, whose actions indicated they were well-trained and had the use of communications equipment and access to transport. In some cases, military personnel were found to have provoked the violence.[16] The team recommended immediate follow-up, including prosecution of implicated civilians and high-ranking military officials. The recommendations also included compensation and rehabilitation for victims.[17] The report recommended that the chief operational commander be held accountable and that named senior officers be brought to trial before a military court for their role in the abductions.[18] Despite these recommendations, none of the senior officials implicated have been prosecuted; instead, the chief operational commander named in the report was promoted, eventually becoming the deputy minister of defense.

### Maluku

Instability surrounding the fall of Soeharto in 1998 led to inter-religious violence between Christian and Islamic groups that increased during 1999. Witnesses and victims have provided repeated descriptions of the instigation of violence by provocateurs unknown to the local population. It is interesting to note the striking similarity of allegations of accounts of witnesses in relation to the roles played by provocateurs suspected of being linked to the security forces, and inaction by the police in the face of serious crimes being committed in the 1998 incidents in Jakarta and the Poso inter-religious violence examined later in this chapter. The conflict produced displacement of over seven hundred thousand people, or one-third of the population of the region, with a death toll of more than five thousand by the time the Malino peace agreement was reached in 2002.[19]

A fact-finding team was established by the president. After one year's work, the planned launch of its report was canceled and none of the findings have been made public or shared with the parties to the Malino agreement. It is clear that the results

---

[16] *Report of the Joint Fact-finding Team on the Events of 13–15 May 1998: Executive Summary* (KontraS: Jakarta October 23, 1998), 10.

[17] Ibid.

[18] Indonesian National Human Rights Commission Investigation findings of the Ad Hoc Team of Inquiry on Gross Human Rights Violations in the Enforced Disappearances of 1997–1998: Executive Summary (Jakarta: Komnas HAM the Indonesian National Human Rights Commission, October 30, 2006), 24.

[19] The Moluccas Agreement in Malino (Malino II), February 12, 2002, item 6.

of the investigation were suppressed; indeed, no information has been made public and no prosecutions of implicated state actors have followed.

## *Poso*

Christian-Muslim tensions broke out in the area around Poso, Sulawesi, during the instability around the fall of Soeharto in 1998. By 2002, an estimated 1,000 victims had been killed. Witnesses reported that incidents involving the provocateurs in areas of high tension led to an escalation involving local religious communities caught up in a cycle of increasing payback attacks. The security forces were implicated in the violence itself and in failing to prevent or stop the escalation of violence once it had begun.[20]

A fact-finding team made up mostly of military, police, and government officials also included some religious leaders. Its report was presented to the coordinating minister but it was never made public.[21] As in previous cases, there were no prosecutions for senior commanders of the security forces involved in the Poso violence.

## *East Timor (Timor Leste)*

When the state of Indonesia was created following World War II, its borders included the western half of the island of Timor that had been under Dutch colonial rule, but not the territory of East Timor, which was controlled by Portugal. Following a decision by Portugal to release its colonies in 1974, a short civil war led to a declaration of independence by the victorious Fretilin party. Ten days later, after receiving a green light from U.S. President Gerald Ford, Indonesia launched a massive military invasion.[22]

The following twenty-four-year period of military occupation was characterized by serious human rights violations on a massive scale, resulting in the death of up to one-third of the population.[23] In 1999, following the fall of Soeharto, a UN-sponsored ballot was conducted in which 78.5 percent of participants voted for independence from Indonesia.

---

[20] Human Rights Watch, *Breakdown: Four Years of Communal Violence in Central Sulawesi* (New York: Human Rights Watch, December 2002). International Center for Transitional Justice, *Derailed*, 99; Shanty, "Penyelidikan TPF Poo Selesai 20 November," *Media Indonesia Online*, November 16, 2006, accessed September 5, 2011, http://www.comm.or.id/cmm-ind_more.php? Id=A3229_0_3_0_M.

[21] International Center for Transitional Justice, *Derailed*, 99.

[22] East Timor Commission on Reception, Truth and Reconciliation (CAVR), *CHEGA!* (Jakarta: CAVR, 2005), chapter 7.1 Self Determination, 53–8.

[23] A comprehensive statistical survey carried out by the CAVR on the basis of four data sets produced an estimate of at least one hundred thousand conflict-related deaths which could be as high as two hundred thousand. Ibid., chapter 6.1.1, 3.

The period surrounding the vote was marred by widespread violent intimidation by Indonesian security forces and their Timorese proxies, aimed at pressuring East Timorese to cast their ballots to remain part of Indonesia, and then punishing them for not doing so. More than twelve hundred individuals were killed, four hundred thousand people were displaced, and seventy percent of all buildings in the territory were burned or destroyed in three weeks.[24]

The violence was halted by the arrival of international peacekeepers, the withdrawal of the Indonesian security forces and Timorese militias across the border into Indonesian West Timor, and the establishment of the UN Transitional Administration in East Timor (UNTAET) with a UN Security Council mandate to administer the territory and prepare it for independence, which was achieved in May 2002.

Following the violence, a mission by UN special rapporteurs, a commission of inquiry mandated by the UN Security Council, and the NHRC found that the Indonesian military forces and their proxy militias had been primarily responsible for the violence, considered crimes against humanity.[25] The East Timor Commission for Reception, Truth and Reconciliation (CAVR) later collected and analyzed more than eighty thousand reported violations and found that in eighty-four percent of cases victims reported that those responsible were members of the Indonesian security forces and the militia groups they controlled.[26] A multisample statistical analysis found that a minimum of one hundred two thousand East Timorese, out of a population of less than seven hundred thousand, had died as a result of the conflict.[27]

The UN Commission of Inquiry recommended to the UN Secretary General that an international criminal tribunal be established. However, UN Secretary General Kofi Annan accepted Indonesia's assurances that those responsible would be brought to justice in its national courts, and stated that he would "closely monitor progress towards a credible response in accordance with international human rights principles."[28]

In response, a special human rights court was established in Jakarta for the East Timor case and eighteen senior Indonesian officials, including the former governor of East Timor, several generals, the senior commander of the Indonesian police in Timor during the ballot period, and Timorese militia leaders, were indicted for

---

[24] Geoffrey Robinson, "East Timor 1999 Crimes Against Humanity," in *CHEGA!*, CAVR (Jakarta: CAVR, 2005), Annex 1, 40–4.

[25] UN General Assembly, 54th Session, *Report of the International Commission of Inquiry on East Timor to the Secretary-General* (A/54/726, S/2000/59) (UN General Assembly, January 31, 2000).

[26] CAVR, *CHEGA!*, chapter 8, table 2, 13.

[27] Ibid., chapter 6.

[28] UN General Assembly, *Report of the International Commission of Inquiry on East Timor to the Secretary-General*.

crimes against humanity committed in East Timor in 1999. Following a series of trials, six of those charged were convicted, but all were gradually acquitted following appeals.

David Cohen describes the trial process as "intended to fail."[29] As he states, "The trials as a whole were not based on an impartial evaluation of the available evidence, because the most important available evidence was not produced in court and the prosecution too often seemed to be working in the service of the defense."[30]

In Timor Leste, the UN administration had established a serious crimes process including a hybrid court presided over by international and national judges. At the time of the formal closure of the serious crimes process in 2005, a total of eighty-eight East Timorese militiamen had been convicted and sentenced to imprisonment for periods of up to thirty-three years. Investigations resulted in the indictment of an additional 300 individuals believed to have fled to Indonesia, including General Wiranto, the supreme commander of the Indonesian armed forces in 1999, and a number of senior generals.

Despite the undertakings provided by the government of Indonesia to the UN and significant steps taken to pass progressive new laws and establish new human rights courts to deal with the Timor mass violations, the result after more than five years of investigations, prosecutions, and appeals is zero convictions. This stands in stark contrast to the efforts of the hybrid special panels of the Timorese courts, which completed fifty-five trials resulting in eighty-four convictions of offenders for crimes committed in the same context.[31] The government of Indonesia has refused to hand over any of the 300 indicted individuals believed to be in Indonesia, and has not taken steps to investigate or prosecute them in Indonesian courts. This case provides a striking example of how the de facto amnesty has protected those most responsible for the mass violations in Indonesia, while lower level perpetrators acting under their command and control have been successfully tried on the same or similar evidence in newly independent Timor Leste.

## Aceh

Aceh is a region with a population of around four million situated at the northern end of the island of Sumatra. After the territory chose to become part of Indonesia,

---

[29] David Cohen, *Intended to Fail: The Trials Before the Ad hoc Human Rights Court in Jakarta* (International Center for Transitional Justice, Occasional Paper series, August 1, 2003), 63, accessed October 2, 2011, http://ictj.org/sites/default/files/ICTJ-Indonesia-Rights-Court-2003-English.pdf.

[30] Ibid., 63.

[31] Caitlin Reiger and Marieke Wierda, The Serious Crimes Process in Timor Leste: In Retrospect (ICTJ Prosecution Case Studies Series: March 1, 2006), accessed October 2, 2011, http://ictj.org/sites/default/files/ICTJ-TimorLeste-Criminal-Process-2006-English.pdf..

it was promised special autonomy status by President Sukarno. During the Soeharto dictatorship, this autonomy was withdrawn and local resentment of the movement of the profits from some of the world's largest oil and gas fields in Aceh to Jakarta with relatively little investment in the region increased support for independence in the 1970s.[32]

The period from 1976 until 2004 was characterized by large-scale human rights violations, which included attacks by the Free Aceh Movement (GAM) forces and periods of intense suppression by security forces, resulting in an estimated twelve thousand to fifty thousand deaths.[33]

A fact-finding team on crimes committed in Aceh, established by presidential decree following the transition to democracy in 1999, found that "The acts of violence conducted by the military constituted a form of state violence. This means the violence was strongly perceived by the people as 'cultivated' by the state to ensure the exploitation of natural resources from Aceh for the benefit of the central government and of national and local elites."[34] The report included detailed descriptions of the kinds of crimes committed, including rape and sexual violations, severe torture, and killings.

A contentious role of the security forces was to guard the oil and gas installations, particularly those run by Exxon Mobil. At the time of writing, a case based on a claim by a number of Acehnese victims was ongoing in U.S. courts. The victims' legal action is based on the claim that Exxon Mobil was responsible for the murder, rape, and torture carried out by Indonesian military actors acting as their agents in Aceh. In August 2011, a press statement released by Exxon Mobil stated that it was in the process of selling off its operation in Aceh.[35]

Despite the scale of the crimes, no senior military officer has been prosecuted for the crimes in the Aceh. Prosecutions of low-level military personnel have begun in military courts. In 2003, Human Rights Watch reported that "the light sentences, selective prosecution, and the low rank of those charged demonstrate a lack of seriousness in punishing or deterring crimes by members of the armed forces."[36]

---

[32] Tim Kell, *The Roots of Acehnese Rebellion, 1989–1992* (Ithaca: Cornell Modern Indonesia Project, Southeast Asia Program, Cornell University, 1995), 14–18, and International Crisis Group, *Aceh: Can Autonomy Stem the Conflict*, ICG Asia Report No. 18 (International Crisis Group, June 27, 2001), accessed October 2, 2011, http://www.crisisgroup.org/en/regions/asia/south-east-asia/indonesia/018-aceh-can-autonomy-stem-the-conflict.aspx.

[33] Katri Merikallio, *Making Peace: Ahtisaari and Aceh* (Juva: WS Bookwell Oy, 2006), 223–4.

[34] Presidential Decree 88/1999 on the Independent Commission for the Investigation of the Violence in Aceh. *Report of the Commission: DOM dan Tragedi Kemanusiaan di Aceh* (Bahasa/Jakarta: KontraS, January 27, 2000), quoted in International Center for Transitional Justice, *Derailed*, 2n.

[35] Linda Yulisman, "Pertamina Says it is not Interested in Exxon Assets," *Jakarta Post*, August 10, 2011.

[36] Human Rights Watch, *Aceh Under Martial Law: Inside the Secret War* (New York: Human Rights Watch, December 2003), Vol. 15, No. 10 (C), 44.

## The 2004 Tsunami

In December 2004, a massive tsunami in the Indian Ocean transformed events in Aceh. The tsunami killed an estimated one hundred sixty-seven thousand people in Aceh, most of them in the space of one day, and left five hundred thousand more homeless.[37] In the words of newly elected President Yudhoyono, "the tsunami produced an overwhelming moral, political, economic, social imperative to end the conflict."[38] Peace talks led by former Finnish president Marti Attishari led to the signing of a peace accord, formalized in the Helsinki Memorandum of Understanding (MOU) of August 15, 2005. The European Union established the Aceh Monitoring Mission (AMM) to monitor various aspects of the accord. The MOU included an agreement to establish a human rights court and a TRC for Aceh, provision of an amnesty to GAM members, and support to ex-combatants and civilians affected by the conflict. To date, neither the human rights court nor the TRC have been established.

The MOU included a commitment that the government of Indonesia: "Will, in accordance with constitutional procedures, grant amnesty to all persons who have participated in GAM activities as soon as possible and not later than within 15 days of the signature of this MoU."[39]

The amnesty was incorporated into national law by presidential decree on August 30, 2005.[40] At a press conference, the secretary of state commented that "The amnesty is applied to all persons involved in activities of the Free Aceh Movement in Indonesia and overseas," but the amnesty would not cover members of GAM who had committed criminal acts or those who continued to carry out acts of rebellion after the date of the signing of the Helsinki accord.[41]

In July 2006 the Law on Governing Aceh, or LOGA, was passed to provide national legal implementation to most of the other provisions of the Helsinki MOU.

---

[37] Jennifer Hyndman, "Siting Conflict and Peace in Post-tsunami Sri Lanka and Aceh, Indonesia, Norwegian Journal of Geography" 63, no.1 (2009): 89–96. See also an estimate of the Indonesian Dept. of Social Affairs in June 2005 in Asian Development Bank Institute, "Aceh-Nias Reconstruction and Rehabilitation: Progress and Challenges at the End of 2006: The Impacts" (discussion paper No.7, Asian Development Bank Institute, June 29, 2007), accessed October 2, 2011, http://www.adbi.org/discussion-paper/2007/06/29/2288.acehnias.reconstruction.rehabilitation/the.impacts/.

[38] President Yudhoyono, "Building Permanent Peace in Aceh: One Year after the Helsinki Accord," (opening speech, conference held in Jakarta, August 14, 2006).

[39] "Memorandum of Understanding between the Government of the Republic of Indonesia and the Free Aceh Movement," point 3.1.1, accessed October 2, 2011, https://peaceaccords.nd.edu/matrix/status/18/human_rights.

[40] "Regarding the Granting of Amnesty and Abolition to Every Person Involved in the Free Aceh Movement, Indonesian Presidential Decree," Perpu No 22/2005 August 30, 2005.

[41] "LEAD: Indonesia Grants Amnesty to Aceh Rebels," *Asia Political News*, September 5, 2005, accessed October 2, 2011, http://www.thefreelibrary.com/LEAD%3A+Indonesia+grants+amnesty+to+Aceh+rebels.-a0136080451.

This law provided an increased level of autonomy for Aceh along with a larger share of revenue from local resources. In late 2006, regional elections brought the surprise result of a majority of former GAM cadres to the regional parliament, led by Irwandi Yusuf as governor.

The provisions relating to amnesty agreed on in Helsinki began to be implemented even before they had been included in national laws. Two days after the signing of the MOU, on Indonesia's national independence day of August 17, 298 members of GAM were released.[42] Following the presidential decree on August 31, 2006, a further 1,424 persons were released. Upon release, they were given clothes and some basic goods, a payment of $200, and transport to their home districts. Each person released as part of the amnesty received two further payments of $150 during the following months. In addition, each released prisoner was eligible for a payment of $1000 per family upon registration with the government reintegration project in 2007.[43]

Over 100 cases could not be immediately decided due to disagreement among the parties over the beneficiaries of the amnesty. Government officials interpreted the terms of the amnesty to include only those who had been charged with treason. However, GAM representatives explained that this charge had only been used since 2003 and before that GAM supporters had been imprisoned on trumped up criminal charges such as robbery or assault.

The Helsinki MOU included a provision that the head of the AMM had the power to rule on disputed cases of amnesty. However, in order to provide a more objective approach to this contentious issue, the AMM contracted Swedish judge Christer Karphammar to decide on the remaining cases. In the absence of guiding or binding legal principles, Judge Karphammar used two criteria to decide which cases deserved amnesty: the level of gravity of the crime, and whether the acts had been carried out in furtherance of GAM's goals. That is, if acts were committed by members of GAM for other purposes such as gaining money for themselves, or were criminal acts not connected to GAM's political goals, they would not qualify. Eventually his decisions led to an additional sixty-four disputed cases being covered by the amnesty.

An additional 366 individuals were released not as part of the amnesty but through a process of remission of their sentences. In total more than 2,000 former members of GAM were released under the amnesties and remissions programs.

---

[42] Kirsten E. Schulze, *Mission Not So Impossible: The AMM and the Transition from Conflict to Peace in Aceh, 2005–2006*, Case study for the Madrid Report of the Human Security Study Group (Centre for the Study of Global Governance, 2005–2006), accessed October 2, 2011, http://www.lse.ac.uk/Depts//global/PDFs/HS2007AMM.pdf.

[43] International Crisis Group, *Aceh: Post-conflict Complications*, Asia Report No 139 (International Crisis Group, October 4, 2007), accessed September 3, 2011, http://www.crisisgroup.org/~/media/Files/asia/south-east-asia/indonesia/139_aceh_post_conflict_complications.pdf.

Those who applied for amnesty but were excluded after consideration by the AMM scheme remained in prison. Gradually these individuals have been released, but two former GAM activists convicted and sentenced to twenty years imprisonment for bombing the national stock exchange in 2001 remain in prison in Jakarta.

The Aceh case provides an example of how amnesty can serve as a powerful tool for the resolution of conflict if certain conditions are met. The factors contributing to the success of the amnesty were the following. The amnesty did not provide protection to those implicated in serious human rights violations. It did not have to deal with serious objections from the parties to the conflict, victims' groups, or human rights organizations. In addition, it did not seriously reduce the potential to establish respect for the rule of law in post conflict Aceh. The promise to release the prisoners, moreover, was carried out quickly, with hundreds released within weeks. A mechanism was also established in which an independent actor, a Swedish judge contracted by the AMM, had responsibility for resolving disputed cases. Finally, provision was made for practical assistance for those released in accordance with the amnesty, significantly increasing the potential for its benefits to be sustainable in the long term.

The contribution to a sustainable peace provided by the amnesty for GAM members has been undermined by a failure to respect other promises made in return for GAM's promise to demobilize and surrender weapons. In particular, the commitment of the government of Indonesia to establish a human rights court and a TRC for Aceh has not been implemented seven years after the end of the conflict. Once again, significant steps were taken toward the goals of truth and justice but they were neutralized by a failure to implement fully.

### Papua

In 1949, the Dutch agreed to formally surrender the territories under their control to Indonesian nationalists, with the exception of West Papua, which they believed should be prepared for independence. Under the New York agreement of May 1962, the UN would administer the territory for one year before handing authority to the government of Indonesia, with the provision that at some unspecified time Papuans would be given the opportunity to decide on the issue of independence.

The highly contentious "Act of Free Choice" was carried out in 1969 under UN auspices, resulting in a vote for integration into Indonesia. Rather than providing each person with one vote the methodology chosen was "consensus of elders" (*musyawarah*) involving the votes of 1,054 specifically selected representatives. Allegations that these individuals were selected to ensure a particular outcome and that rewards, threats, violence, and coercion were used to ensure that those involved chose to remain part of Indonesia have led to claims that the process did not allow for a free and fair choice.[44]

Opposition to the large-scale military presence in Papua and support for the right to self-determination have continued since that time, including attacks on Indonesian military posts by the relatively small Free Papua Movement (OPM). In a number of cases, this has been followed by heavy retaliation including attacks on civilians in surrounding areas. There has been no objective process of determining the truth of the scale of violations in the region but many observers believe the conflict has caused tens of thousands of deaths. The 2006 World Report of Human Rights Watch stated that "military operations in Papua and Aceh are characterized by undisciplined and unaccountable troops committing widespread abuses against civilians, including extrajudicial executions, torture, forced disappearances, beatings, arbitrary arrests and detentions, and drastic limits on freedom of movement."[45]

In the past few years, the scale of serious violations reported in Papua has significantly diminished. However, there are continuing reports of violations including killing and torture involving security forces personnel, and the deep resentment associated with the manner in which the Act of Free Choice was conducted has not been resolved.[46]

In December 2000, in the context of opposition to the heavy presence of security forces in Papua, unknown individuals attacked a police station at Abepura, killing two police officers and a security guard. The reaction by the police included a process known as "sweeping," whereby they violently swept through student dormitories in this case, taking more than 100 students into custody. During and after this operation hundreds were beaten, a number of those detained severely tortured, and three were summarily executed.

An investigation by the NHRC recommended the prosecution of four senior officers for command responsibility and twenty-one for their role in the operation. Two years later, two officers were tried before the permanent human rights court in the region of Makassar. Both of these police officers were acquitted.

In 2001 the national parliament passed a law establishing the province of Papua and providing it with special autonomy status. The law also created an obligation on the part of the government to establish a TRC for Papua, a mandate that included "clarifying the history of Papua in order to stabilize the integrity of the nation within the Unitary State of Indonesia" and "to formulate and determine reconciliation

---

44  Neles Tebay, "Human Rights in Papua: An Overview" (Paper presented at "Autonomy for Papua – Opportunity or Illusion?" Berlin, Germany, June 4–5, 2003).

45  Human Rights Watch, *World Report 2006-Indonesia* (Human Rights Watch, January 18, 2006), accessed September 5, 2011, http://www.unhcr.org/refworld/docid/43cfaea111.html.

46  Human Rights Watch, "Indonesia: Investigate Torture Video from Papua," October 20, 2010, accessed October 2, 2011, www.hrw.org/news/2010/1020/indonesia-investigate-torture-video-papua.

measures."[47] Ten years later, the statutory obligation to establish a TRC in Papua has not been fulfilled.

On November 10, 2010, a Papuan indigenous leader and vocal supporter of the right to self-determination of the Papuan people, Theys Eluay, was killed on his way home from an event at the regional headquarters of the Indonesian Special Forces (Kopassus). His driver, who went to report the killing to the Kopassus post, disappeared.

Following intense pressure, an investigative commission was established. Despite the nature of the allegations involving members of the security forces, President Megawati Sukarnoputri appointed a retired police official as chair and a serving army major general as another member. A military tribunal subsequently found seven members of Kopassus guilty of mistreatment and battery, but not murder, and sentenced them to relatively light sentences of two and a half and three years of imprisonment. Those sentenced for this extremely serious crime continued to serve in the military. Following the verdict, the army chief of staff stated: "The law says they are guilty OK, they're punished. But for me they are heroes."[48]

As a result, no senior officers have been investigated or tried for the mass violations in Papua with the exception of the Abepura case. In that case, only two members of the police force were charged despite the Komnas HAM report naming more than twenty allegedly involved, and both of those indicted were acquitted. Nobody was found responsible for the killing of Theys Eluay and the disappearance of his driver, despite the fact that seven lower level military personnel were tried and given relatively light sentences for assault committed during this incident.

## EMBLEMATIC CASES

Although the analysis provided in this chapter focuses on situations of mass violations involving more than 1,000 victims, the cases of the murder of human rights activist Munir in 2004 and the attack on the Islamic community in Tanjung Priok in 1984 provide particularly relevant evidence in relation to the operation of the de facto amnesty.

### Munir

Munir Said Thalib, known as Munir, was a leading human rights activist who worked to promote accountability and help families of victims whose loved ones had disappeared. In 1998, Munir led the advocacy surrounding the kidnapping and

---

[47] Republic of Indonesia Law No 21 of 2001, s 45 and s 46, accessed September 30, 2011, http://www. papuaweb.org/goi/otsus/files/otsus-en.html.

[48] General Ryamizard, "Theys Hiyo Eluay's Murderer is a Hero," *TEMPO Interactif*, April 23, 2003, accessed October 2, 2011, http://www. Tempointeractif.com/share.

disappearance of prodemocracy activists in which members of the Kopassus special forces were implicated.

In 2004, Munir died from the results of an overdose of arsenic poison while traveling on the Indonesian government-owned airline Garuda en route to begin postgraduate studies in Holland. Following national and international outrage, the president issued a decree appointing a fact-finding team. The team provided a report that implicated senior personnel in the National Intelligence Agency (BIN) in the poisoning. This report was never made public despite the fact that its publication was required by presidential decree.

During his trial, Pollycarpus Priyanto, an off-duty Garuda pilot suspected of acting as an agent of BIN, was found to have arranged to be on Munir's flight and provided him with his own business class seat before administering a massive dose of arsenic in a cup of tea while on a stopover en route, causing Munir's death. Pollycarpus was convicted of the murder and given a twenty-year prison sentence. The deputy commander of BIN was also indicted and tried. Prosecutors alleged that the BIN deputy commander had ordered the murder, motivated by revenge for being removed from his position in 1998 through Munir's work on the disappearances cases. At the trial major witnesses withdrew testimonies they had earlier given to police. The BIN deputy commander argued that the records of forty-one telephone calls he made to Pollycarpus prior to the killing were irrelevant since the phone had been stolen. He was acquitted of the murder.

Munir's case provides a representative example of the pattern of establishing fact-finding teams but then suppressing the facts found. In this case the formal legal obligation to publish the findings under the terms of the presidential decree was not respected. A civilian allegedly acting as an agent of the national intelligence service was convicted of the murder. However, the facts relating to who had ordered the killing and why remain unsubstantiated and the trial of a senior official for ordering the murder resulted in an acquittal that has been accompanied by significant controversy.

### Tanjung Priok

Indonesian state ideology includes recognition of only one god but five official religions. In 1984, near the Jakarta port of Tanjung, a crowd of several thousand gathered around the local military headquarters calling for the release of four representatives of their mosque detained for delivering a sermon in which the state ideology was questioned. The military opened fire on this crowd, killing an unknown number (estimated in the thousands) and wounding many others.[49] The incident

---

[49] Ulma Haryanto, "Death Toll from 1984 Massacre at Tanjung Priok Still Uncertain," *Jakarta Globe*, April 15, 2010, accessed September 30, 2011, http://www.thejakartaglobe.com/city/death-toll-from-1984-massacre-at-tanjung-priok-still-uncertain/369555.

was followed by military operations in that area and other regions, in which many more were detained, tortured, and eventually subjected to unfair judicial proceedings that resulted in convictions on charges of subversion and resisting arrest.[50]

Victims demanded an inquiry but no action was taken for fourteen years. In 1998, following the fall of Soeharto, a NHRC "pro-justicia inquiry" into the case concluded that gross human rights violations had been committed and recommended prosecution of those military officers responsible.

An ad hoc human rights court for this case was established in 2001. Fourteen representatives of the military forces were indicted and tried, resulting in twelve convictions. The former district military commander was found responsible and sentenced to ten years of imprisonment, while lower ranking personnel received lesser sentences. On appeal, the Court of Appeal and the Supreme Court overturned all the convictions. Thus, all fourteen persons who stood trial were eventually acquitted, resulting in a zero conviction rate. Similar to the East Timor case, appellate court decisions annulled the effect of all trial convictions earlier hailed as historic reversals of the long-standing impunity and protection of members of the security forces allegedly involved in mass violations. In the East Timor and Tanjung Priok cases the total number of convictions overturned by the Court of Appeal and Supreme Court was eighteen out of eighteen, a 100 percent success rate for the appeals.

## DE JURE AMNESTY FOR HUMAN RIGHTS VIOLATIONS IN INDONESIA

Article 14 of the Constitution of the Republic of Indonesia provides that:

(1) The President may grant clemency and restoration of rights and shall in so doing have regard to the opinion of the Supreme Court.
(2) The President may grant amnesty and the dropping of charges and shall in so doing have regard to the opinion of the DPR.[51]

Two separate attempts have been made to create institutions with powers to recommend formal amnesties for perpetrators of human rights violations: the draft law establishing a national TRC and the mandate of the binational Indonesia-Timor Leste Truth and Friendship Commission. As discussed later in this chapter, the national TRC has not yet been established and the Truth and Friendship Commission decided not to use the amnesty powers in its mandate.

---

[50] International Centre for Transitional Justice, *Derailed*, 48.
[51] The 1945 Constitution of the Republic of Indonesia, as amended in 1999, 2000, 2001, and 2002, accessed 30 September 2011, http://ww7w.embassyofindonesia.org/about/pdf/IndonesianConstitution.pdf.

Since the transition from the Soeharto military dictatorship, a coalition of Indonesian national human rights organizations had worked toward the establishment of a national truth and reconciliation commission that would investigate the background, causes, and nature of the human rights violations committed in 1965 and a range of other conflicts. In 2004, the Indonesian national parliament passed a law that required the government to formally establish a national truth and reconciliation commission within six months.[52]

The law on the TRC provided that compensation could only be provided to victims if they and the perpetrator of the crimes committed against them had "forgiven one another," and as a result of this "forgiveness," the perpetrator received amnesty.[53] The use of this terminology is striking because it implies that somehow victims of violations need to be forgiven by the perpetrator. This reflects a failure to accept that state actors are fully responsible for crimes and assumes instead that violence involves "two demons" who share equal responsibility.

The provisions of the TRC law gave the plenary of the TRC power to decide on individual requests for amnesty and established an amnesty committee to produce criteria and procedures for processing applications.[54] Amnesties recommended by the TRC needed to be considered by the lower house of parliament which could forward a recommendation to the president.[55]

In March 2005, the president signed a presidential decree establishing a panel whose duty was to select the commissioners for the TRC. The panel recommended forty-two individuals and forwarded their names to the president for approval. More than one year later the president had not approved any of these names. In the meantime national human rights organizations challenged the amnesty provisions of the law before the national Constitutional Court.

In December 2006, the Constitutional Court ruled that the state's obligation to protect citizens from gross human rights violations and to provide them with reparations was a duty enshrined in the national constitution and should be interpreted as taking into account "the universal practice and custom as stated in the UN Basic Principles and Guidelines on the Right to Remedy and Reparations."[56] The Court held that this duty to protect and provide reparations to victims could

---

[52] Republic of Indonesia Law 27/ 2004 on the Truth and Reconciliation Commission, accessed September 30, 2011, http://hrli.alrc.net/mainfile.php/indonleg/131/.

[53] Ibid., s 19 and s 2.

[54] Ibid., s 10 and s 23.

[55] Ibid., ch. VI, s 25.

[56] The court noted that the customary international law provisions should be taken into account in interpreting Articles 28A, 28D(1), 28I(1), (4) and (5) of the national constitution on this issue. See OHCHR, *Updated Set of Principles for the Protection and Promotion of Human Rights through Action to Combat Impunity*, UN Doc. E/CN.4/2005/Add.1 (OHCHR, February 2, 2005), especially principles 19 and 24.

not be diminished by making its implementation conditional on the granting of amnesty, and therefore the provisions relating to amnesty in the TRC law were unconstitutional.

The legal challenge in this case was restricted to the claim that article 27 of the law, which related to amnesties, was unconstitutional. However the Court's decision, which agreed with the claims of the human rights groups that had brought the appeal, then went on to crush their hopes of finally achieving the goal of the establishment of a credible national TRC by quashing the entire law:

> Whereas although the petition granted relates only to Article 27 of the KKR (TRC)[57] Law, as the overall implementation of the KKR Law depends on and must pass by way of the aforementioned article, the declaration that Article 27 of the KKR Law is inconsistent with the 1945 Constitution and does not have binding force renders all the provisions of the KKR Law unenforceable.[58]

The Court's reasoning in throwing out the entire law is difficult to follow since the mandate of the TRC to investigate human rights violations and to recommend that reparations be provided to victims could have been achieved if the provisions relating to amnesty had merely been severed. Critics in the national media launched allegations that the result was part of an informal agreement designed to ensure that the truth relating to the past mass violations remained hidden. An article in the *Jakarta Post* declared that:

> The timing could not have been worse. On the eve of the International Human Rights Day, the Constitutional Court last week annulled the legislation establishing the Truth and Reconciliation Commission, thus dashing the hopes of the many victims of human rights abuses for justice and some form of compensation.... This commission would have given the final seal of approval to Indonesia's democratic credentials, for it would have put an end [to] the culture of impunity, especially for human rights violators.... Was there a conspiracy involving the court and the President? One could certainly be forgiven for thinking so.[59]

The law establishing the TRC has been redrafted and tabled before parliament, but at the time of writing, it had not yet been provided with priority for consideration.

---

[57] Komisi Kebenarandan Rekonsiliasi or KKR is the Bahasa Indonesian translation for Truth and Reconciliation Commission (TRC.)

[58] Decision of the Indonesian National Constitutional Court. No. 006/PUU-IV/2006 (2006), 24, accessed September 30, 2011, http://www.mahkamahkonstitusi.go.id/putusan/putusan_sidang_eng_Verdict%20No.%20006-PUU-IV-2006.pdf.

[59] "Evaporating Truth, Justice," *Jakarta Post Editorial*, December 13, 2006, accessed January 18, 2012, http://www.asia-pacific-solidarity.net/southeastasia/indonesia/netnews/2006/ind46v10.htm#Evaporating%20truth,%20justice.

Human rights advocates were pessimistic about its chances of being passed by parliament.

The Constitutional Court's decision seriously diminished the chances of the establishment of a national TRC and indirectly blocked the establishment of a TRC for Aceh, agreed to under the terms of the Helsinki peace agreement. Although the Helsinki agreement made no reference to a national TRC, the national law drafted to implement the agreement changed the original terms, adding the provision that the Aceh TRC "shall not be separated from" the national TRC. Some Indonesian lawyers argue that, since the Constitutional Court nullified the law establishing the national TRC, the law establishing the Aceh Commission cannot be implemented. An alternate view is that the provision linking the two TRCs was intended only to refer to the manner of administration and not to create a conditional relationship. Despite the difference of opinion, the questionable decision of the Constitutional Court has blocked both TRCs.

The second example of attempts to create de jure amnesties involves the mandate of the Indonesia-Timor Leste Truth and Friendship Commission. Following the formal act of independence of Timor Leste in 2002, the Indonesian government clearly stated its opposition to ongoing calls for justice for Indonesian perpetrators of crimes in Timor, and the Timorese government, representing a tiny, vulnerable new nation surrounded by much more powerful neighbors, agreed.

In September 2004, Timor Leste's foreign minister, Jose Ramos Horta, called for the establishment of an "international Truth and Reconciliation Panel" that would include the involvement of highly respected international experts as commissioners. Negotiations with Indonesia over issues of accountability and reconciliation led to a change in this approach. The involvement of objective international experts was jettisoned, and a binational TRC, the Indonesia-Timor Leste Commission for Truth and Friendship (CTF), was established. This body consisted of commissioners and staff from Indonesia and Timor Leste. Its mandate included establishing and reporting the truth on the nature, causes, and extent of the human rights violations committed in 1999. It was not provided with the power to conduct its own investigations, but to consider and issue findings based on the information available from four previous mechanisms: the ad hoc human rights court trials in Jakarta, the serious crimes process and trials in Dili, the CAVR in Timor Leste, and the investigation conducted by the Indonesian NHRC. Despite the absence of specific powers to collect additional information and conduct public hearings, the CTF did in fact interview actors involved in the conflict and conducted a number of problematic public hearings.

It seems clear that the CTF was established with the goal of avoiding rather than contributing to accountability and justice for the 1999 crimes. The preamble to the commission's mandate, set out in an MOU between the governments of the two countries, included the following provision:

> Indonesia and Timor-Leste have opted to seek truth and promote friendship as a new and unique approach rather than the prosecutorial process. True justice can be served with truth and acknowledgement of responsibility. The prosecutorial system of justice can certainly achieve one objective, which is to punish the perpetrators; but it might not necessarily lead to the truth and promote reconciliation.[60]

Article 13(c) of the MOU added, "Based on the spirit of a forward looking and reconciliatory approach, the CTF process will not lead to prosecution and will emphasize institutional responsibilities" and the CTF may not "recommend the establishment of any other judicial body."[61]

Article 14(c)(I) provided the CTF with the power to "recommend amnesty for those involved in human rights violations who cooperate fully in revealing the truth."[62]

The provision of this amnesty clause led to strong criticism of the CTF by many who saw it as a vehicle through which the Indonesian government hoped to achieve officially sanctioned impunity for officials and military officers responsible for violations in Timor. The mandate did not include any clear criteria for determining who should receive amnesty.

The role of United Nations personnel who had been present throughout East Timor while the mass violations were committed during the ballot period was obviously an important issue for the CTF to consider. However, the inclusion of the amnesty clause in violation of international legal norms led to a decision by the UN that its staff should not appear to give evidence before the CTF.[63]

Article 14(c) paragraphs (I)–(IV) provided examples of the measures the commission might recommend. It could:

1) Recommend amnesty for those involved in human rights violations who cooperate fully in revealing the truth;
2) Recommend rehabilitation measures for those wrongly accused of human rights violations;
3) Recommend ways to promote reconciliation between peoples based on customs and religious values.

---

[60] Megan Hirst, *Too Much Friendship, Too Little Truth* (International Center for Transitional Justice, Occasional Paper series, January 18, 2000), accessed September 30, 2011, http://ictj.org/sites/default/files/ICTJ-Indonesia-Commission-Monitoring-2008-English.pdf.

[61] Ibid., art. 10.

[62] Ibid., art 14.

[63] See Leonie von Braun, "Trading Justice for Friendship: An Analysis of the Terms of Reference of the Commission of Truth and Friendship for Indonesia and East Timor," *Watch Indonesia!* March 29, 2005, accessed September 30, 2011, http://home.snafu.de/watchin/CTF.htm.

The final report of the CTF surprised many critics. It included findings that the main perpetrators of crimes against humanity were militia groups who opposed independence and had acted with the involvement and systematic support, including money and weapons, of Indonesian civilian, military, and police officials who knew that the militias were committing human rights violations. Indonesian military actors controlled the militias but had not used that control to stop the crimes.[64] The fact that the report was jointly accepted by the presidents of both countries at a public event marked a significant change of attitude by the Indonesian government which had, up to that time, repeatedly denied the role of the security forces in the violence.

Human rights groups welcomed the report and called for it to be followed up by prosecutions and reparations for victims. However, it appears that official acceptance of the report signified not the opening of the door to justice and reparations but rather an informal agreement involving both governments to close the issue of these past violations.[65] Timor Leste's President Jose Ramos Horta has said that the government of Timor Leste is bound by the agreement signed with Indonesia at the time the CTF was established not to pursue prosecutorial solutions to the 1999 violations. He has also stated that he supports a blanket amnesty for crimes committed in Timor Leste during the entire twenty-four-year Indonesian occupation.[66]

The commission chose not to exercise its powers to recommend amnesties. The rationale for this decision was expressed in the final report: "[A]mnesty would not be in accordance with its goals of restoring human dignity, creating the foundation for reconciliation between the two countries, and ensuring the non-recurrence of violence within a framework guaranteed by the rule of law."[67]

Other factors the commission found relevant to its decision not to use the amnesty powers included the fact that the CTF had not established a fair, open process for the receipt and processing of amnesty applications or for the investigation and determination of individual cases. In addition, the commission found that a number of alleged perpetrators who had testified before the commission at public hearings had not provided the requisite "full cooperation," because they had "failed to testify truthfully, or had not shown any remorse."[68]

---

[64] The Commission of Truth and Friendship, *Report of the Indonesia-Timor Leste Commission of Truth and Friendship* (The Commission of Truth and Friendship, 2008), 232, accessed September 30, 2011, http://violet.berkeley.edu/~warcrime/East_Timor_and_Indonesia/Reports/PER%20MEMORIAM%20AD%20SPEM%20Eng_ver.pdf.

[65] International Center for Transitional Justice, *Derailed*, 27.

[66] Hirst, *Too Much Friendship, Too Little Truth*; Simon Roughneen, "Seven Questions: José Ramos-Horta. East Timor's Nobel Prize-winning President Asks, Just Who is the Failed State Here?" *Foreign Policy*, July 2007, accessed 30 September 2011, www.foreignpolicy.com/articles/2009/07/09/seven_questions_jose_ramos_horta.

[67] The Commission of Truth and Friendship, *Report of the Indonesia-Timor Leste Commission of Truth and Friendship*, 297.

[68] Hirst, *Too Much Friendship, Too Little Truth*, 32–5.

The case of Maternus Bere provides an interesting follow-up to the series of steps taken in relation to truth and justice for the crimes committed in East Timor and how these issues continue to affect the relationship between the governments of Indonesia and Timor Leste, which contributes to de facto amnesty. Bere was an East Timorese militia leader indicted for his role in crimes committed in 1999 who then fled across the border to Indonesian West Timor with the arrival of international peacekeepers. Ten years later, in 2009, he was arrested while attempting to cross the border back into East Timor. The ceremony for the tenth anniversary of the UN ballot in Timor on August 30, 2009, attended by many dignitaries, was interrupted since the Indonesian delegation required a guarantee that Bere, now an Indonesian citizen, would be released before their plane would land. Prime Minister Xanana Gusmão agreed to this step even though the legal authority to release a prisoner charged with a serious crime rests solely with the judiciary.

On the order of the prime minister, Bere was released and transferred to the Indonesian embassy in Dili where he remained until he was transferred to Indonesia several weeks later. In response to severe criticism by national civil society and political representatives that these acts were illegal, Prime Minister Gusmão stated that his action was a political decision justified by the national interest.[69] The unilateral steps taken by a political leader to release a prisoner arrested on charges of murder and crimes against humanity according to the due process of law raise serious issues of the separation of powers, violations of the constitution, and the criminal nature of the act of releasing the prisoner without due process. As of the time of this writing, Bere remained free in Indonesia and no steps have been taken to prosecute him.

## ANALYSIS AND CONCLUSIONS

The age of amnesty, while still present in Indonesia, has evolved significantly since the reign of Soeharto. International pressure and a national movement for accountability and respect for human rights, two of the streams described by Kathryn Sikkink in this volume, have led to significant legal reforms and the establishment of a range of mechanisms designed to provide truth and justice in relation to mass human rights violations. These include constitutional amendments; security sector reforms such as the removal of a guaranteed quota of seats in parliament and a gradual diminishing of the business interests of the military; inclusion in the national legal system of gross human rights violations, defined as crimes against humanity and genocide; the establishment of a separate court structure with jurisdiction to try

---

[69]  International Center for Transitional Justice, *Impunity in Timor Leste: Can the Serious Crimes Investigation Team Make a Difference?* (New York: International Center for Transitional Justice, June 2010), 108, 110, accessed September 14, 2011, http://ictj.org/sites/default/files/ICTJ-TimorLeste-Investigation-Team-2010-English.pdf.

those responsible for these crimes; and a series of commissions of inquiry mandated to inquire into allegations of violations.

These hard-won successes resulting from active human rights and democratization movements and progressive government factions have not, however, uncovered the truth behind mass violations or brought those responsible to justice. In some cases junior, and in a few cases mid-level, military officers have been tried by military courts and have received relatively lenient sentences. The scale of the crimes in which members of the security forces are implicated in a variety of settings over a number of years leads to the inescapable conclusion that senior commanders must bear responsibility in many of these contexts.

The startling juxtaposition of a long list of legal and informal mechanisms, expenses allocated, trials, appeals, commissions of inquiries, and draft laws for truth and reconciliation commissions cast against a net result of zero convictions of senior officials or commanders for cases of mass violence illustrates the concept of a de facto amnesty. This is evident in the lack of prosecutions for the alleged involvement of members of the security forces in at least thirteen different cases of mass human rights violations in various parts of the country at different times, with a death toll estimated at somewhere between six hundred fifty thousand and two million people.[70] It is also evident in the lack of follow-through on the NHRC recommended investigation and prosecution of 137 named individuals. While thirty-four faced indictment, only eighteen were found guilty at trial, and all eighteen were acquitted on appeal. No investigation into that appeals process in the Court of Appeals and Supreme Court that overturned all of the convictions has occurred. The NHRC has made findings that crimes against humanity occurred and recommended formal investigation and prosecution in six additional major cases which remain blocked. Despite the failure of AGO to respond to these recommendations over the last ten years, neither the executive nor the legislature has intervened.[71] A parliamentary recommendation to establish an ad hoc court to try those responsible for the disappearances of thirteen prodemocracy advocates has not been followed by the required presidential decree needed to establish the court more than two years after the recommendation. Seven years after the 2005 Helsinki agreement to provide a TRC and human rights court for Aceh, neither has been established. The Papua Special Autonomy Law included the establishment of a TRC for Papua without any progress to date. The Constitutional Court annulled the entire law establishing a national TRC due to disputes over the amnesty provision. Finally, repeated

---

[70] These cases are the mass violations surrounding Soeharto's rise to power in 1965, the 1998 riots, East Timor, Aceh, Papua (including Abepura), the disappearance of the prodemocracy activists in 1998, Maluku, Poso, Talangsari, Wamena and Wasior, Trisakti, Semangi I and Semanggi II.

[71] These cases are Talangsari, Wamena and Wasior, Trisakti, Semangi I and Semanggi II, and the May 1998 riots.

fact-finding teams or commissions of inquiry have failed to make their reports public, even when ordered to do so by presidential decree.

What explains the widespread impunity in Indonesia despite the streams rushing toward a justice cascade? Some assume conspiracy. Yet the range of actors and the long period of time render such a premise illogical. Instead, the cultural legacy of the more than thirty years of dictatorship and the *dwifungs* doctrine of the New Order regime provides a more likely explanation. In this system, police, prosecutors, judges, government officials, and members of the security forces were part of a strictly enforced structure that diverted massive amounts of state revenue to the personal accounts of officials and senior security forces personnel through institutionalized corruption. In such a culture, senior members of the security forces were beyond the reach of criminal laws.

Little research into the link between corruption and impunity for human rights violations exists. Indonesia may provide the emblematic case, because Soeharto, for example, occupied the number one position on the list the UN and World Bank report prepared for the Stolen Assets Recovery (StAR) Initiative to recover monies stolen by dictators. The StAR report estimated that Soeharto had stolen between $15 billion and $35 billion (U.S. billion), three times the estimate stolen by the dictator in the second place on the list, former President Marcos of the Philippines, $5 billion to $10 billion (U.S. billion).[72]

The New Order regime has left a legacy of unwillingness to reveal the lessons of the past and hold those responsible accountable. The breadth of the network created by the web of corruption, nepotism, and impunity and the fact that the police, military, and judiciary were so closely linked during the Soeharto period means that any investigation of serious crimes by the police of AGO may in some way involve the very individuals tasked to investigate members of their families, colleagues, and superiors.

We can detect a less than enthusiastic approach to uncovering the truth of the past through the appointment of commissioners who would not be expected to bring an objective approach to commissions of inquiry, keeping the results of many extensive commissions secret, investigators' failure to interview the most relevant witnesses, and prosecutors not providing strong evidence in their possession to the court. In one of the few cases in which a senior general in the armed forces was charged with crimes against humanity in the ad hoc human rights court for East Timor the prosecutors argued in favor of acquittal. Career judges of the Court of Appeal and Supreme Court, who were all judges during the Soeharto years, have overturned

---

[72] United Nations Office on Drugs and Crime, *Stolen Assets Recovery Initiative Launch (The International Bank for Reconstruction and Development* (Washington DC: The International Bank for Reconstruction and Development/The World Bank, September 17, 2007), accessed September 30, 2011, www.unodc.org/documents/corruption/StAR-Sept07-full.pdf.

every single conviction (eighteen in total) handed down by panels involving new, noncareer judges in the national human rights court. In all of these instances, we see the indications of the ongoing battle between the new, progressive forces which have been successful in passing the laws, establishing the courts and commissions, and launching the investigations, only to be outfoxed by the old forces of the elite who still hold the key positions of power.

An interesting contextual anecdote is revealed by comparing the results of two specialized courts established during the period following the transition from the rule of Soeharto. As of September 2011, the system of human rights courts, which have tried mostly members of the security forces, had achieved a 100 percent acquittal rate. In contrast, the Anti-Corruption Court, which has tried mostly civilian officials, has achieved a 100 percent conviction rate.[73]

The culture in which the de facto amnesty continues will not last forever. Worms are eating away at the foundations. There are ghosts in the machine. Human rights activists and progressive members of the government and parliament continue to struggle forward and have been responsible for many advances, but the strength of the denial culture has been maintained. In the meantime, Indonesians are unable to avail themselves of the opportunity to learn lessons drawn from their past or to study an accurate history of major events.

Many individuals responsible for committing the most serious crimes possible against Indonesian law are not only free but continue to play a major role in shaping Indonesia's future. However, recent history indicates that the international trend toward justice and accountability will gradually also extend to Indonesia. In Asia, we see trials for mass crimes committed in Bangladesh in 1971 taking place forty years later. In Cambodia, former Khmer Rouge leaders are being tried for actions committed more than thirty-five years ago. Across the globe we see examples of old men being tried for mass crimes they committed as young men when they believed they were untouchable and invincible.

Political change is taking place rapidly in Indonesia. The human rights record of the nation is also dramatically improving, but has not yet produced an improvement in terms of accountability or a willingness to learn from an analysis of past violations.

The efforts underway in Argentina and Uruguay, represented in the chapters by Par Engstrom and Gabriel Pereira, and Francesca Lessa in this volume, to challenge legal amnesties and allow for accountability, are very different situations than the situation faced in Indonesia. The de facto amnesty in Indonesia is also under attack from lawyers, activists, and progressive government actors; whether undermining a de facto system is easier than weakening a formal amnesty is not clear.

---

[73] Norimitsu Onishi, "Corruption Fighters Rouse Resistance in Indonesia," *New York Times*, July 25, 2009, accessed September 30, 2011, www.nytimes.com/2009/07/26/world/asia/26indo.html.

On one hand it may appear that a formal amnesty is stronger, supported by the force of law, requiring formal legal steps to reverse it. Although extremely challenging, the approach and strategy required to achieve these changes are often relatively clear. Indonesian human rights advocates argue that a complex web of relationships, inertia, questionable appointments, and failure to energetically fulfill mandates that extends across a range of institutions and structures to produce a de facto amnesty may be more difficult to combat.[74]

The target is not visible, it is hidden and always moving, denied, transformed, often not clearly identified but still successful in achieving the goals of an amnesty – protection of perpetrators and suppression of the truth. Even the existence of what has been described in this chapter as a de facto amnesty is hidden, not apparent on examination of any single case, and only emerging clearly when the totality of cases of mass violations is combined and analyzed. Combating the de facto amnesty therefore requires deep systemic change, an increase in the accountability mechanisms of all of the institutions that play a role in maintaining the protection of the elites: police, prosecutors, the judiciary, government officials, even the office of the president.

In years to come Indonesia will also be welcomed into the community of nations that has accepted the principle that in order to build an open and prosperous future, the factors that allowed many thousands of innocent civilians to be killed, raped, and tortured must be uncovered and studied and those responsible brought to justice. The message of the global march toward justice is clear; no longer is any leader safe to attack or condone attacks on his or her own people. Formal amnesties provide only temporary protection. De facto amnesties are, hopefully, even more fragile. The coming years in Indonesia will provide a valuable insight into whether this optimistic view is true.

---

[74] Discussion between the author and representatives of six national human rights organizations, Jakarta, March 15, 2011.

# 11

# A Limited Amnesty?

## Insights from Cambodia

*Ronald C. Slye*

The Cambodian government passed two successive amnesties in the 1990s in answer to the lingering question of how to respond to the legacy of the Khmer Rouge. That legacy began in 1975 when Pol Pot and his Party of the Democratic Kampuchea, also known as the Khmer Rouge, seized power from the U.S.-backed Cambodian regime led by Lon Nol. In 1975, Cambodia was recovering from a recent civil war, had endured invasion by various neighbors, and been blanketed with over two hundred fifty thousand tons of bombs dropped by the United States in an effort to disrupt the Ho Chi Minh Trail during the Vietnam War. Pol Pot entered Phnom Penh on April 17, 1975, declaring the start of "year zero," and initiated a brutal campaign to remake Cambodian society. Hundreds of thousands of people were tortured and murdered, and millions more perished as a result of starvation and disease. By the time the Vietnamese invaded and overthrew the Khmer Rouge in 1979, over two million people had died.

While international criminal trials for gross violations of human rights gained popularity in the 1990s as the preferred method for addressing such atrocities (see Kathryn Sikkink's chapter in this volume), negotiations between the United Nations and the Cambodian government to create a judicial mechanism for holding individuals accountable for similar crimes committed two decades earlier by the Khmer Rouge stalled repeatedly. Until recently, the Cambodian government's primary official response to those responsible for one of the worst regimes of violence in human history has been the passage of two amnesties. The result has been a consistent official policy of impunity and amnesia. It was only in 2003 (almost thirty years after the removal of the Khmer Rouge) that the government entered into an agreement with the United Nations to establish the Extraordinary Chambers in the Courts of Cambodia (the ECCC, or Tribunal)[1] to prosecute those most responsible for

---

[1] Agreement Between the United Nations and the Royal Government of Cambodia Concerning the Prosecution under Cambodian Law of Crimes Committed During the Period of Democratic Kampuchea (June 6, 2003), Art. 11(1).

atrocities committed during the Khmer Rouge period. It took another four and a half years for the Tribunal to be established and to adopt its rules of procedure.[2] The Tribunal has been marred with controversy since its inception, including allegations of corruption, political interference, and fundamental disagreements between international and Cambodian prosecutors and other Tribunal personnel.[3] Yet the Tribunal has also convicted Kaing Guek Eav ("Duch"), the commander of the notorious S-21 torture prison,[4] in a trial many observers conclude was fair.

The Cambodia government is not alone in preferring amnesty to trials in response to a legacy of discrimination and violence. Most countries emerging from a history of widespread violations of the fundamental rights of their peoples have preferred amnesty to prosecutions and other forms of accountability, as the studies by Louise Mallinder and Tricia Olsen et al. have shown.[5] While state preference for amnesty is common, there is a large variation among states with respect to the type of amnesty promulgated. The self-amnesty passed by Chilean military dictator Pinochet in 1978 is fundamentally different from the amnesty administered by the Truth and Reconciliation Commission in South Africa from 1996 to 2001. The Chilean amnesty was a blanket one, promulgated by the government to shield its members from any form of accountability.[6] The South African amnesty, as Antje du Bois-Pedain's chapter in this volume shows, was much more sophisticated, promulgated by a newly elected and democratic parliament for the purpose of providing a minimal level of truth and accountability for crimes committed during the apartheid era. South Africa required full disclosure as a condition for amnesty, thus transforming amnesty from a truth-hiding to a truth-revealing mechanism. Along the continuum represented by the Chilean and South African amnesties, the Cambodian amnesties fall closer to the Chilean end of the spectrum; they are designed to entrench impunity and discourage even the most minimally required investigation and accountability. Thus they discourage rather than further justice.

---

[2]   See Robert Petit and Anees Ahmed, "A Review of the Jurisprudence of the Khmer Rouge Tribunal," *Northwestern University Journal of International Human Rights* 8 (2009): 165.

[3]   See Petit and Ahmed, "A Review of the Jurisprudence of the Khmer Rouge Tribunal," and Open Society Justice Initiative, *Recent Developments at the Extraordinary Chambers in the Courts of Cambodia: June 2011 Update*, accessed August 23, 2011, http://www.soros.org/initiatives/justice/articles_publications/publications/cambodia-eccc-20110614/cambodia-eccc-20110614.pdf.

[4]   S-21, or Tuol Sleng, was an infamous torture camp established by the Khmer Rouge in a former girls' school. An estimated twenty thousand people were processed through Tuol Sleng; only seven people survived the experience. Today Tuol Sleng has been converted into a museum dedicated to the memory of the victims of the Khmer Rouge. See http://www.TuolSlengmuseum.com/index.htm.

[5]   Mallinder, *Amnesty, Human Rights and Political Transitions*, Olsen, Payne, and Reiter, *Transitional Justice in Balance.*

[6]   Amnesty International and the International Commission of Jurists produced a legal brief arguing how the Chilean amnesty violates international law. See http://www.amnesty.org/en/library/info/AMR22/002/2001/en.

What makes the Cambodian amnesties unjust? Typically an amnesty has two consequences: it prevents the criminal prosecution and punishment of perpetrators, and it prevents victims from seeking reparations, truth, and other forms of accountability from those responsible for the violation of their rights. There is some debate over whether international law obliges, or should oblige, the prosecution and punishment of those responsible for gross violations of human rights, as Mark Freeman and Max Pensky discuss in Chapter 2 of this volume. There is general agreement, however, that international law requires something more than blanket amnesties provide. At a minimum, international law requires some form of accountability and some form of recognition of the harm suffered by victims. The Cambodian amnesties provide neither.

Rather than discussing what international law and morality require with respect to accountability for gross atrocities,[7] I will use the example of the Cambodian amnesties to discuss two important choices facing drafters that affect an amnesty's legitimacy: *who* should be protected by an amnesty; and *how long* such an amnesty should last. The first question concerns amnesty beneficiaries, and is a relatively common one raised by those who draft and study amnesties. The second question concerns the temporal nature of the amnesty. The temporal nature of an amnesty is rarely, if ever, raised by drafters or observers because drafters invariably intend their amnesties to be immediate and permanent. The beneficiary question is directly raised by the content of the Cambodian amnesties; the temporal question is raised by the history of amnesty and accountability in Cambodia and other transitional societies.

Recognizing the temporal nature of amnesties – and in particular emerging state practice with respect to the effective life of amnesties – suggests a new mechanism for addressing historical injustices: a "limited amnesty." A limited amnesty is restricted by time. It provides protection from prosecution and other formal legal processes for a set period of time. After that period of protection, a limited amnesty is converted into a permanent amnesty, is removed completely (thus allowing prosecutions or other mechanisms of legal accountability), or is replaced with another amnesty that is conditional on acts of accountability, reconciliation, or reparation.

## THE CAMBODIAN AMNESTIES

In 1994, the Cambodian government issued a proclamation that banned the Khmer Rouge, reaffirmed criminal liability for members of the Khmer Rouge for certain offenses, and provided amnesty for such crimes to Khmer Rouge guerrillas who

---

[7] For that discussion, see the Freeman and Pensky chapter in this volume; Roht-Arriaza and Gibson, "The Developing Jurisprudence of Amnesty," 843; Orentlicher, "Settling Accounts," 2537; and Roht-Arriaza, "State Responsibility," 449.

defected to the government during a six-month window (July 7, 1994 to January 7, 1995).[8] The amnesty provision states:

> This law shall grant a stay of six months after coming into effect to permit the people who are members of the political organization or military forces of the "Democratic Kampuchea" group [i.e., the Khmer Rouge] to return to live under the control of the Royal Government of the Kingdom of Cambodia, without facing punishment for crimes which they have committed.[9]

The 1994 proclamation states that the amnesty does not apply to leaders of the Khmer Rouge.[10] It also provides that, pursuant to the Cambodian constitution, the king may give partial or complete amnesty or pardon, presumably for the crimes mentioned in the legislation.[11] The 1994 proclamation also states in article 3 that any individual (with a specific reference to members of the Khmer Rouge) who commits the crimes of murder, rape, robbery of people's property, or the destruction of public and private property "shall be sentenced according to existing criminal law."[12] It also provides in article 4 that any person who commits secession, destruction of the royal government, destruction against organs of public authority, or incitement or forcing the taking up of arms against public authority "shall be charged as criminals against the internal security of the country and sentenced to jail for 20 to 30 years or for life."[13] In addition to providing amnesty for any crimes they may have committed, members of the Khmer Rouge are subjected to new liabilities based solely on their membership in the Khmer Rouge – in other words the proclamation criminalizes membership in the Khmer Rouge.[14]

Two years after this first amnesty, on September 14, 1996, the king issued a royal decree granting amnesty to the former deputy prime minister of the Khmer Rouge government, Ieng Sary. The two prime ministers, Norodom Ranaridh (the king's son) and Hun Sen (a former official in the Khmer Rouge government), requested

---

[8]  Anette Marcher, "Rin Verdict Leads to KR Tribunal Doubts," *Phnom Penh Post*, July 21–August 3, 2000, 9. An estimated sixty-six hundred members of the Khmer Rouge took advantage of the amnesty provision and defected to the government.

[9]  The Law on the Outlawing of the "Democratic Kampuchea" Group, Article 5 (July 7, 1994), reprinted in the *Phnom Penh Post* (July 21–28, 1994) (hereinafter "1994 proclamation"). For most of the text of the 1994 proclamation, see Decision on Appeal Against Provisional Detention Order of Ieng Sary, ECCC, Pre Trial Chamber, October 17, 2008, C22/I/74 (hereinafter "Decision on Appeal"), para. 26.

[10] 1994 Proclamation, article 6 ("For leaders of the 'Democratic Kampuchea' group the amnesty described above does not apply.")

[11] Ibid., article 7 ("The King shall have the right to give partial or complete amnesty as stated in Article 27 of the Constitution.")

[12] Ibid., article 3.

[13] Ibid., article 4.

[14] Ibid., article 2 ("From the time this Law comes into effect, all people who are members of the political organization or military forces of the 'Democratic Kampuchea' group shall be considered as offenders against the Constitution and offenders against the laws of the Kingdom of Cambodia.")

the Sary amnesty. The amnesty was granted in return for Sary's defection from the Khmer Rouge. The relevant passage of the decree reads as follows:

> An amnesty to Mr. Ieng Sary, former Deputy Prime Minister in charge of Foreign Affairs in the Government of Democratic Kampuchea, for the sentence of death and confiscation of all his property imposed by order of the People's Revolutionary Court of Phnom Penh dated 19 August 1979; and an amnesty for prosecution under the Law to Outlaw the Democratic Kampuchea Group, promulgated by Reach Kram No. 1, NS 94, dated 14 July 1994.[15]

The amnesty appears to protect Sary from his conviction *in absentia* for gross violations of human rights committed while he was deputy prime minister for foreign affairs from 1975 to 1979; his membership in the Democratic Kampuchea Group, which had been criminalized by the 1994 proclamation; and prosecution pursuant to the 1994 proclamation. Although the royal decree speaks of an amnesty, it appears to grant both an amnesty and a pardon; the decree *pardons* Sary for his conviction by the Vietnamese-backed tribunal in 1979 and provides him with an *amnesty* for his liability arising from membership in the outlawed Democratic Kampuchea Group – liability created by the 1994 proclamation – and for any liability he might otherwise have for the crimes specifically listed in the 1994 proclamation.

Amnesty for prosecution of the specific crimes under the 1994 proclamation can be interpreted in three different ways. First, the amnesty could apply only to the crime of being a member of the Khmer Rouge. Even if the 1994 proclamation is interpreted to apply the amnesty to the other crimes listed, this position would argue that it is limited to those acts made criminal by the 1994 law itself and does not protect the recipient from any liability separately created by virtue of the Cambodian criminal code. The 1994 proclamation, under this interpretation, does not provide for liability for the crimes listed in article 3, but rather states that an individual "shall be sentenced according to existing criminal law" for such crimes. Article 3 then directs the government to prosecute and sentence but does not itself create criminal liability. Similarly, although less persuasively, this position would argue that with respect to the four crimes listed in article 4 the proclamation provides an interpretation that such acts satisfy the requirement of "crime against the internal security of the country." Article 4 then provides an interpretation but does not itself create criminal liability. Thus, the amnesty provided to Sary is limited to those acts that are themselves criminalized by the 1994 proclamation, and does not reach those acts for which the proclamation only provides for sentencing or charging.

---

[15] For most of the text of the decree, see Decision on Appeal, para. 27; see also an unofficial translation, accessed August 5, 2011, http://www.unakrt-online.org/Docs/Other/1996-09-14_pardon_for_ieng_sary. pdf.

The second interpretation would argue that the amnesty applies to membership in the criminalized group as well as the crimes listed in article 4. The amnesty would apply to this second set of crimes because the proclamation itself makes those acts criminal. This position would interpret the "shall be charged as criminals" language as providing for the criminalization of acts that up until the issuance of the proclamation were not criminal; in other words, the 1994 proclamation created these four new crimes. Under this second interpretation the amnesty would not apply to the offenses of inter alia murder, rape, and robbery found in article 3 since such acts are already criminalized under Cambodian law and thus derive their criminality separate from the proclamation.

The third interpretation argues that the amnesty applies to all of the crimes listed in the 1994 law, including crimes such as murder, rape, and robbery separately listed in the criminal code. This position argues that Sary's amnesty reaches those acts already criminalized under Cambodian law because they are referred to in, rather than criminalized by, the 1994 proclamation. In other words the amnesty "for prosecution under" the 1994 proclamation provides protection from prosecution for all of the crimes referred to in the proclamation regardless of whether they are criminalized by the proclamation. This would seem to be the better interpretation, and is, in fact, the interpretation adopted by Sary before the ECCC.[16]

The agreement between the United Nations and the government of Cambodia for the establishment of the ECCC makes an oblique reference to the Cambodian amnesties. While the UN historically had been agnostic about, or even encouraged, amnesties in the context of peace agreements, with the revival of international criminal law accountability in the 1990s the UN has consistently adopted the position that international law prohibits amnesties for war crimes, crimes against humanity, and genocide. Consistent with Sikkink's notion of the justice cascade outlined in Chapter 1 of this volume, the agreement states that the Cambodian government "shall not request an amnesty or pardon for any persons who may be investigated for or convicted of crimes referred to in the present Agreement."[17] This provision prevents the Cambodian government from granting new pardons or amnesties. The amnesty provided to Sary is referred to in a separate provision, though the reference is only to the pardon for the 1979 conviction (thus making no reference to the amnesty for the 1994 proclamation). In that provision, the agreement states that the "scope" of the pardon is to be left to the ECCC. The law creating the

---

[16] See "Ieng Sary's Submissions Pursuant to the Decision on Expedited Request of Co-Lawyers for a Reasonable Extension of Time to File Challenges to Jurisdictional Issues," ECCC Pre Trial Chamber, C22/I/26, (hereinafter "Sary Appeal"), para. 31.

[17] Agreement Between the United Nations and the Royal Government of Cambodia Concerning the Prosecution under Cambodian Law of Crimes Committed During the Period of Democratic Kampuchea, article 11(1).

ECCC incorporated these provisions and removed the ambiguity by stating that the government shall not request an amnesty or pardon for any crime within the jurisdiction of the tribunal and that "[t]he scope of any amnesty or pardon that may have been granted prior to the enactment of this Law is a matter to be decided by the Extraordinary Chambers."[18]

Both the 1994 proclamation and the 1996 decree have been discussed by the ECCC. The co-investigating judges introduced the 1996 decree in their initial decision ordering the provisional detention of Sary, the former deputy prime minister of the Khmer Rouge, and thus one of those alleged to be "most responsible" for its crimes.[19] The Provisional Detention Order held that the 1979 conviction did not preclude, under the general principle of *ne bis in idem*,[20] Sary's prosecution before the ECCC, and that the 1996 decree also did not prevent Sary's trial. In finding the principle of *ne bis in idem* inapplicable, the co-investigating judges noted that the 1979 conviction was for genocide, an offense for which Sary did not face prosecution before the ECCC. Since the ECCC was not prosecuting Sary for the same offense, the principle of *ne bis in idem* did not apply.[21] With respect to the amnesty provided in the 1996 decree, the co-investigating judges concluded that it was not applicable as it only applied to domestic crimes under Cambodian law and the ECCC was prosecuting Sary for international crimes not covered by the amnesty.[22]

Sary challenged both of these holdings in an appeal to the pretrial chamber. Specifically, he argued that the principle of *ne bis in idem* applied because he had already been prosecuted and convicted by the 1979 tribunal for the same conduct at issue before the ECCC, and that even if the same conduct test did not apply, the 1996 decree provided amnesty from ECCC prosecution because it covered all of the crimes listed in the 1994 proclamation in addition to the 1979 conviction.

The prosecution defended the provisional detention order of the co-investigating judges. However, the reasoning of the prosecution differed from that of the co-investigating judges. First, the prosecution argued that *ne bis in idem* did not apply because the 1979 trial did not conform to international standards of fair trials, and

---

[18] Law on the Establishment of the Extraordinary Chambers in the Courts of Cambodia for the Prosecution of Crimes Committed During the Period of Democratic Kampuchea (NS/RKM/1004/006), (October 27, 2004) (hereinafter "ECCC statute"), Art. 40new.

[19] Provisional Detention Order, No. 0002/14–0802006.

[20] The principle of *ne bis in idem*, also referred to as the prohibition against double jeopardy, is found in Article 14 (7) of the International Covenant on Civil and Political Rights (which is in turn incorporated into the ECCC statute), and reads, "No one shall be liable to be tried or punished again for an offence for which he has already been finally convicted or acquitted in accordance with the law and penal procedure of each country."

[21] See Provisional Detention Order, para. 8–10.

[22] Ibid., article 13.

thus was not a judgment that could be used in defense of a subsequent trial.[23] This argument, which was alluded to by the co-investigating judges but which does not form the basis of their decision, is based in part on the principle codified in the Rome Statute of the ICC that an individual cannot claim the protection of a previous conviction if that previous conviction was intended to shield the individual from criminal responsibility or was conducted in a manner inconsistent with an intent to bring the individual to justice.[24] This is a curious argument to make because there is no indication that the Vietnamese-backed prosecution of Sary, Pol Pot, and others was designed to protect any of the members of the Khmer Rouge from accountability; in fact, the more common criticism of the 1979 trial is that it was a show trial conducted with the predetermined result of conviction and thus violated the due process rights of the defendants.[25] The prosecution also argued here that, because the 1979 trial did not conform to fair trial standards, it did not qualify as a final conviction, and thus the current prosecution before the ECCC was not in conflict with a previous conviction. Second, the prosecution argued that the trial for different offenses based upon the same criminal acts does not violate *ne bis in idem* so long as any multiple convictions are taken into account in sentencing.[26]

With respect to the 1996 decree, the prosecution argued that the amnesty did not apply to the crimes before the ECCC. The prosecution did not adopt the reasoning of the co-investigating judges (that the ECCC has jurisdiction over international crimes and the 1994 proclamation that is the object of the amnesty only applies to domestic crimes), but instead argued that the 1994 proclamation only refers to crimes committed after its promulgation and thus does not apply to prior acts, including those within the 1975 to 1979 temporal jurisdiction of the ECCC.[27] The prosecution argued in the alternative that even if the amnesty was interpreted to apply to acts committed prior to the enactment of the 1994 proclamation, it is a clear principle of international law that amnesty cannot be granted for the interna-

[23] Prosecution Response to Ieng Sary's Submission on Jurisdiction, Case No. 002/19/-09–2007-ECCC/OCIJ (PTC 03) (May 16, 2008) (hereinafter "Prosecutor's Response"), paras. 8–9.

[24] See Rome Statute, article 20.

[25] For an excellent discussion and defense of the 1979 trial, see John Quigley, "Introduction," in *Genocide in Cambodia: Documents from the Trial of Pol Pot and Ieng Sary*, ed. Howard J. De Nike, John Quigley, and Kenneth J. Robinson (Philadelphia: University of Pennsylvania Press, 2000), 19.

[26] Prosecutor's Response, para. 10.

[27] Ibid., para. 33. The prosecution's argument here is based on the fact that the 1994 proclamation refers to sentencing and charging for crimes that an individual "commits," without referring to those that may have "been committed" in the past. The problem with this argument is that although articles 3 and 4 use the present tense "commit" (and thus support the prosecutor's interpretation), article 5 provides that members of the Khmer Rouge may return to live under the control of the government "without facing punishment for crimes which they have committed." The language of the proclamation, therefore, is at best ambiguous.

tional crimes within the jurisdiction of the ECCC (i.e., war crimes, crimes against humanity, and genocide).[28]

The prosecution also argued that the pardon provided for in the 1996 decree only applied to the nonexecution of the sentence of the 1979 conviction and that the pardon, as an act of domestic law, was not binding on the ECCC since it was ultimately governed by international law.[29] These arguments with respect to the applicability of the pardon are curious because the effectiveness of the pardon would itself seem to have no bearing on the real issue at hand, which is the alleged violation of the principle of *ne bis in idem.*

The pretrial chamber ruled against Sary on a number of grounds. First, it dismissed Mr. Sary's *nebis in idem* claim. The pretrial chamber reasoned that the 1979 conviction was for the crime of genocide, a crime for which Sary did not face charges before the ECCC.[30] In other words the prosecution before the ECCC for war crimes and crimes against humanity did not trigger the principle of *ne bis in idem* because it was premised on a different set of offenses than the 1979 conviction. In so ruling, the pretrial chamber seemed to adopt the internationally accepted definition of *ne bis in idem* as prohibiting subsequent prosecutions for the same offense, rather than subsequent prosecution for the same acts. The pretrial chamber muddied these waters, however, by stating that it was leaving open the possibility that a claim under *ne bis in idem* might be applicable later in the proceedings when it would be clearer whether the specific *acts* (as opposed to offenses) for which Mr. Sary was charged before the ECCC were the same as those for which he was charged before the 1979 tribunal. In so ruling the chamber shifted its reasoning to embrace the Cambodian definition of *ne bis in idem*, which prohibits subsequent prosecutions for the same *acts* rather than *offenses*. This is misplaced as the agreement between the government of Cambodia and the United Nations to establish the ECCC clearly refers to the principle of *ne bis in idem* as found under international law, rather than as found in Cambodian law, thus suggesting that the applicable test should focus on the same *offenses* and not the same *acts.*[31]

Second, the chamber held that although the amnesty provided in the 1996 decree did protect Mr. Sary from prosecution under the 1994 law, the offenses prosecutable by the 1994 law were not within the jurisdiction of the ECCC (because they were domestic crimes) and thus the amnesty was irrelevant.[32] The pretrial chamber's

---

[28] Ibid., para. 23.
[29] Ibid., For the prosecutor's argument that the ECCC is not bound by national law, see para. 39.
[30] Decision on Appeal, para. 51.
[31] Agreement between the United Nations and the Royal Government of Cambodia Concerning the Prosecution under Cambodian Law of Crimes Committed During the Period of Democratic Kampuchea, Art. 13 (1) (incorporating article 14 of the International Covenant on Civil and Political Rights which refers to offenses and not acts).
[32] Decision on Appeal, para. 61.

reasoning here is similar to that of the co-investigating judges, but instead of resting its argument on the actual indictment of Sary, the pretrial chamber opines more broadly concerning the general jurisdiction of the ECCC. In doing so, the pretrial chamber paints with too broad a brush, as the ECCC statute makes clear that the Tribunal has jurisdiction over some domestic crimes provided for in the Cambodian penal code, including homicide.[33] The chamber may have meant to adopt the more narrow reasoning of the co-investigating judges – the ECCC also has jurisdiction over international crimes not found in the Cambodian penal code, and the crimes for which Sary was indicted were in fact those international, and not domestic, crimes – but the language of the pretrial chamber suggests something broader. In coming to the conclusion that none of the crimes prosecutable under the 1994 proclamation are within the jurisdiction of the ECCC, the pretrial chamber also failed to make clear what offenses in its view are in fact prosecutable under the 1994 law.[34] In other words, the pretrial chamber did not make clear its choice among the three different interpretations of the 1996 decree discussed previously in this chapter, and thus does not make clear if it interprets the amnesty to apply to those crimes listed in articles 3 and 4 of the 1994 proclamation, or whether the amnesty only applies to the crime of being a member of the Khmer Rouge. The pretrial chamber erroneously and unnecessarily concluded that there was no overlap between the crimes provided for under the 1994 proclamation and the ECCC without indicating what crimes were in fact at issue.

## LEGITIMACY AND THE CAMBODIAN AMNESTIES

The amnesties created by the 1994 proclamation and 1996 decree were designed to entice defections from, and thus weaken, an insurgent army, in this case the Khmer Rouge.[35] Such use of amnesties is common historically.[36] The broad use of amnesties during an armed conflict is often justified as a necessary condition for bringing about peace and preventing additional gross violations of human rights, as

---

[33] See ECCC statute, article 3 (providing for jurisdiction for certain crimes in the 1956 Penal Code). In fact the pretrial chamber made reference to the ECCC's jurisdiction over these domestic crimes earlier in its opinion. Decision on Appeal, para. 50.

[34] This is somewhat ironic, as the pretrial chamber in its summary of the arguments of the parties noted that the prosecutors had identified as a key question "the scope of prosecutable offences under the 1994 Law." Decision on Appeal, para. 38.

[35] See Sary Appeal, note 15 (*Asia Week* quoting Hun Sen to the effect that the defection of Sary would lead to widespread defections from and weakening of the Khmer Rouge). Press reports indicate that sixty-six hundred members of the Khmer Rouge took advantage of the amnesty provided in the 1994 proclamation to defect to the government.

[36] See Jonathan Truman Dorris, *Pardon and Amnesty under Lincoln and Johnson* (Chapel Hill: University of North Carolina Press, 1953).

Freeman and Pensky discuss in their chapter in this volume. While such amnesties may facilitate the cessation of conflict and contribute to short-term peace, they do not necessarily promote human rights protections and in fact may further impunity. Certain amnesties provide a measure of accountability, and thus contribute to the creation of a peaceful and just society. Other amnesties purposefully hinder accountability and entrench a culture of impunity, thus leading to a superficially peaceful order precariously built on a foundation of injustice. The Cambodian amnesties as drafted are of the latter type.

The creation of the ECCC, the general disfavor for amnesties found in international law, and the indications so far that the ECCC will use its interpretive power to nullify the effect of the Cambodian amnesties provides an opportunity for the de facto creation of what I call a limited amnesty. A limited amnesty combines elements that address the immediate impetus for peace and social stability often cited by defenders of amnesties with elements of accountability that address the requirements of justice and international law.

## LEADERS AND FOLLOWERS: THE CHOICE OF BENEFICIARIES

One of the most important decisions facing an amnesty drafter is the choice of beneficiaries. There exists a continuum of choices, ranging from an amnesty that applies to every individual for all acts to an amnesty that applies to one individual for one specific event. The first end of this continuum provides no collective system for holding individuals accountable for their acts. Near this end of the continuum is an amnesty that applies to all individuals for all acts committed prior to a certain date. A number of amnesties have taken this approach. Moving further along this continuum are amnesties limited not only by the acts they cover or the time period to which they apply, but also by beneficiary qualifications. Thus, some amnesties protect a *class* of individuals for any act committed prior to a cut-off date – for example all members of a military force, all members of a government, or all individuals involved in a particular conflict. Some amnesties protect all individuals for a limited set of acts – thus all those who committed a politically motivated act, or all those who tortured or killed. The focus in this section is on the choice of amnesty beneficiaries, and specifically whether there is a difference between granting amnesty to political or military *leaders*, and granting amnesty to *followers* or *foot soldiers*. In particular, what are the consequences of such a choice on the effectiveness and justice of an amnesty?

International law provides some basis for distinguishing between leaders and followers (superiors and subordinates) in a chain of command. As a general rule, superiors cannot evade responsibility for violations of international law committed by their subordinates by arguing that they did not "commit" the act, and subordinates cannot evade responsibility for their own violations by arguing they were just following the orders of a superior. Superiors can be held responsible for the wrongful acts of their subordinates,[37] echoing the general agency principle of *respondeat superior*. The easy case is when the superior orders a wrongful act; the superior is then held liable for the resulting unlawful acts committed by the implementation of that order. A superior may also be held liable for a wrongful act committed by a subordinate without such an order if the superior knew or should have known about the commission of the act and did nothing to prevent it.[38] At the same time, subordinates ordered to commit an illegal act will not be liable unless it can be shown that the subordinate knew the act was unlawful or the order or act was manifestly unlawful.[39] Even in those cases in which the subordinate did not know the act was unlawful – or the act was not manifestly unlawful – following orders does not provide an absolute defense; instead it may be used in mitigation with respect to sentencing. Strict liability thus does not apply to either superiors or subordinates. For the superior one needs to show actual knowledge or objective facts (the "should have known" prong of the test) and a failure to attempt to prevent; for the subordinate subject to an order one needs to show that the order was to commit an act that was manifestly unlawful (with orders to commit war crimes, crimes against humanity, and genocide considered in all circumstances to be manifestly unlawful), or that the subordinate actually knew the act was unlawful.

As Par Engstrom and Gabriel Pereira document in their chapter in this volume, Argentina passed one of the few amnesties that distinguishes superiors from subordinates. The Argentine Due Obedience Law establishes an irrefutable presumption that a subordinate who committed a violation acted under orders without any ability to resist or to assess the orders' lawfulness.[40] The presumption in the Argentine law removes liability from subordinates who commit wrongful acts, even if clearly unlawful, but holds the most senior military officials culpable for ordering those acts.[41]

---

[37] See Protocol I to the Geneva Conventions reprinted in Diplomatic Conference on Reaffirmation and Development of International Humanitarian Law Applicable in Armed Conflict, Protocols I & II to the Geneva Conventions, 16 I.L.M. 1391 (1977); See also Rome Statute, article 28.

[38] See Rome Statute, article 28; Statute of the International Tribunal for the Former Yugoslavia, S. C. Res. 827, UN SCOR, 48th Sess. 3217th mtg., at 1–2, UN Doc. S/Res/827 (1993), reprinted in 32 I.L.M. 1159, 1175, Art. 7(3); Statute of the International Tribunal of Rwanda, S.C. Res. 955, UN SCOR, 49th Sess., 3453d mtg., at 1, UN Doc. S/Res/955 (1994), reprinted in 33 I.L.M. 1598, 1604–5, Art. 6 (3).

[39] The statute of the ICC provides that following orders is a valid defense only if (1) the person was under a legal obligation to obey, *and* (2) the person did not know the order was unlawful, *and* (3) the order was not to commit genocide, crimes against humanity, or other manifestly unlawful acts. Rome Statute, article 33.

[40] Law No. 23,521 (June 4, 1987) (the Due Obedience Law), reproduced in Neil Kritz ed., *Transitional Justice: How Emerging Democracies Reckon With Former Regimes* (Washington, DC: United States Institute of Peace, 1995), 507.

[41] Fewer than fifty officers were left unprotected by the law. See Roht-Arriaza, "State Responsibility," 451.

Similarly, the 1994 Cambodian amnesty excludes "leaders," thus nominally making a distinction between superiors and subordinates.[42] (The 1994 amnesty does not, however, define "leaders.") The 1996 amnesty, on the other hand, is limited to one superior as its beneficiary, Sary.

Does it matter whether an amnesty focuses on subordinates or superiors? To answer this question we must refer to two different approaches to the legitimacy of amnesties: a rights-based approach and a social order approach. The rights-based approach draws upon our collective sense of justice and morality. The social order approach, while certainly not unconcerned with justice and morality, draws much more than the first upon empirical arguments concerning peace and social stability. The rights-based approach focuses on the rights of individual victims and asserts that there are certain fundamental rights that must be protected by the state, including the right to truth, accountability, acknowledgment, participation, and reparations. The rights-based approach focuses on an amnesty's contribution to the fulfillment (or violation) of these rights. The social order approach focuses on the empirical question of whether an amnesty results in a substantial lessening of violence and violations and the creation of a peaceful social order. The social order approach assumes that peace is defined relatively thinly as an absence of overt conflict, and not an absence of conflict combined with or resulting from some minimal attainment of social justice.

Defenders of the rights-based approach argue that states have a primary obligation to protect and further the fundamental rights of individuals, and that peace and stability will only be achieved in any meaningful sense if the rights of victims are recognized, vindicated, and protected. Defenders of the social order approach argue that too great a focus on the rights of victims – in particular seeking accountability of perpetrators – will undermine efforts to create a stable social order, and the absence of such order will lead to more violence and thus more violations of fundamental rights. This is reflected in the proponents approach and obstinate amnesties pathway outlined by Tricia Olsen, Leigh Payne, and Andrew Reiter in this volume. Whether truth, accountability, acknowledgment, participation, and reparations contribute to a more meaningful social peace as argued by the rights-based camp presents an empirical question, and the evidence we have so far is inconclusive. This inquiry is a subset of the more general question of whether the rule of law and individual accountability more generally contribute to a just and stable society – the overwhelming consensus, reflected in Sikkink's chapter in this volume, is that they do.

The case of amnesties for human rights abuses presents a narrower question than either of the two just posited: whether holding an individual accountable is necessary

---

[42] The ECCC statute adopts a similar position, limiting its jurisdiction to "senior leaders" and "those most responsible" for the Khmer Rouge atrocities, and thus mirrors international law's heightened focus on superiors over subordinates. ECCC Statute, article 1.

for, compatible with, or detrimental to a stable and just society. The example most cited to support the assertion that forced amnesia, whether through a formal amnesty or an informal system of impunity, provides a stable peace is that of post-Franco Spain, described in this volume by Paloma Aguilar. Spain did not respond to the death of Franco by engaging in inquiries and prosecutions for clear violations that occurred under the dictator; rather, the government and the overwhelming majority of the population refused to even acknowledge that violations had occurred. Spain did not descend into civil conflict, but instead has developed into a relatively stable and peaceful democracy. Post-Khmer Rouge Cambodia also provides an example of impunity coupled with relative peace and security.[43]

The rights-based and social order approaches may be distinguished by the value they place on deterrence. The effectiveness of accountability in deterring future violations is an important consideration for defenders of the rights-based approach. Conversely, defenders of the social order approach place less faith in the effectiveness of deterrence. This analysis of the importance of deterrence to the two approaches is somewhat simplified; a full understanding of the role and importance of deterrence must take into account the different effects of immunizing subordinates or superiors.

*Followers.* An amnesty that focuses on subordinates, or foot soldiers, provides a benefit to those most immediately responsible for a violation – the torturer, for example. Such an amnesty, if coupled with a truth requirement like the South African amnesty, provides detailed forensic information about specific violations: who did what to whom; how, where, and when a victim died; where a victim's body might be found. While most victims are interested in these sorts of details, they are also interested in *why* certain violations were committed and why they or their loved ones were the targets of such acts. Subordinates can provide some answers to these questions. At the most basic level, they might be able to provide information about why an individual was chosen as a target and who chose the target. Subordinates may also be able to point the finger across and up the chain of command, and thus increase the number of people publicly identified with a particular atrocity and reveal the system of repression – the formal policies and orders – that resulted in such violations.

Limiting an amnesty to subordinates may further justice in an important way: it may facilitate the prosecution and accountability of superiors and leaders, those most responsible for creating the conditions – including those who directly issued

---

[43] I say relative peace and security since violence continues in Cambodia and may be related to the failure to hold individuals accountable for gross violations of human rights, as Anders Themner has argued in the cases of the Republic of Congo and Sierra Leone, Anders Themner, *Violence in Post-Conflict Societies: Remarginalization, Remobilizers and Relationships* (Abingdon and New York: Routledge, 2011).

the orders – that resulted in gross violations of human rights. An amnesty for subordinates may facilitate such accountability in two ways. First, by pointedly omitting superiors, it focuses public attention on responsible individuals left unprotected by the amnesty. Second, such an amnesty may result in testimony and other information from subordinates that can be used to hold superiors accountable. With the threat of prosecution removed, subordinates may be more willing to come forward and testify.

On the other hand, such an amnesty will result in those who were most immediately responsible for torture and other atrocities walking free with minimal accountability and no punishment. This offends the collective sense of justice and morality embodied in the rights-based approach. A system of impunity for subordinates has two important consequences. First, it means that individual torturers may mingle among their victims – for example by shopping in the same market – leading to the possibility of victims experiencing additional trauma and fear and tempting them to exact personal retribution. Second, providing amnesty to torturers undercuts specific and general deterrence. With respect to specific deterrence, immunizing torturers allows an individual who has demonstrated the capacity to inflict the most horrendous pain on another human being to continue to operate freely in society. Such an individual may be prone to other acts of violence and may be susceptible to playing a similarly violent role on behalf of another political movement or even for nonpolitical ends. With respect to general deterrence, immunizing torturers as part of a political compromise sends a message that acts of extreme violence will result in accountability only if they are not part of a successful political movement, thus creating an incentive for wrongdoers to lessen the prospect of punishment by causing the most amount of disruption possible in the hopes of striking a similar political compromise. The person who tortures alone will rarely if ever be the subject of amnesty, while the torturer who acts on behalf of a political movement that successfully challenges or supplants the government may benefit from a negotiated amnesty.

*Leaders.* Holding superiors accountable provides important benefits to a transitional society. Superiors are closely identified with the reign of terror they created or oversaw: they are the Pinochets, the Hitlers, the Pol Pots, and those just below them, the Contrerases, the Eichmanns, and the Sarys. They are thus highly symbolic figures whose prosecution and accountability act as an important proxy for holding their governments and associates accountable for their collective acts of wrongdoing. Moreover, holding superiors accountable furthers in an important way specific and general deterrence. Accountability for superiors furthers specific deterrence by decreasing the possibility that they and their associates will regain power and oversee a similar reign of terror and violations. Accountability for superiors furthers general deterrence by discouraging others with political ambitions from pursuing policies that may result in gross violations of human rights for fear of being later held accountable.

In addition to furthering these instrumental deterrence-based goals, holding superiors and leaders accountable also corresponds to our collective moral sense that those most responsible for systematic violations should be held accountable. Agnes Heller famously distinguished "evil" from "bad" individuals.[44] "Evil" individuals promote, order, and create the environment that results in or encourages gross violations of human rights. They are the proper object of our moral judgment for they exercise the most choice. "Bad" individuals carry out the policies of evil individuals, but do not themselves formulate those policies. They have less, although certainly still some, choice with respect to their actions. They agree to commit atrocities because they are so ordered, because they are seduced by political ideology, because they want to increase their standard of living, because they want to feed their family, because they want to avoid harm to their family or themselves. They are thus appropriately subjected to a lesser degree of moral judgment than evil individuals. Holding leaders accountable therefore satisfies a basic idea of justice – that of just deserts. That is, those who are most culpable, and who commit the most heinous acts, are most deserving of being brought to justice.

International law reflects this heightened sense of superiors' responsibility for their own acts and certain subordinates' acts. The legal doctrine of command responsibility in both military and civilian contexts supports the general idea that leaders are more culpable and blameworthy than followers. We do not hold subordinates responsible for the acts, including the orders, of superiors. We do, however, hold superiors responsible for the acts of subordinates *even when* superiors did not have actual knowledge of subordinates' acts if, given all the circumstances, superiors had effective authority or control over subordinates and objective evidence exists that superiors *should have known* of the abuses.

There are, however, strong arguments against shielding subordinates from accountability through an amnesty if superiors are pursued. Even without the protection of an amnesty, superiors are not always the defendant of choice for state prosecutors bringing criminal claims and victims bringing private civil claims. Other issues besides moral culpability affect the decision of whom to pursue, including the availability of evidence, the obscenity of the wrongful acts performed by the immediate violator, and the legal and political resistance an individual can mount to deflect accountability. Ironically, sensitivity to such considerations usually results in an accountability strategy that focuses on subordinates and not leaders. This is because evidence regarding the culpability of the immediate perpetrator is more

---

[44] Agnes Heller, "The Natural Limits to Natural Law and the Paradox of Evil," in *On Human Rights: The Oxford Amnesty Lectures*, ed. Stephen Shute and Susan Hurley (New York: Basic Books, 1993), 149.

easily discovered than evidence linking someone higher up the chain of command. A torture victim, for example, is more likely to be able to identify the torturer than the individual who ordered or encouraged the violation. The horrendous acts committed by the immediate perpetrator are more likely to stir the passions of the public and result in a demand for justice than the more distant, although crucial, role of their superiors. Such sentiments argue for an amnesty limited to superiors and allowing for the use of prosecution and other forms of accountability against individual torturers and killers. By allowing victims to hold subordinates accountable, amnesties limited to superiors satisfy the important goals of justice and morality frustrated by a subordinate-only amnesty. By the same token, superior-only amnesties frustrate other equally important justice goals that would be furthered by holding superiors accountable – the sense that we should ultimately hold Agnes Heller's "evil" people more accountable than the merely "bad." The Cambodian amnesties illustrate the distinction between granting amnesty for subordinates and superiors. The 1994 amnesty explicitly excludes leaders of the Khmer Rouge, thus limiting itself to subordinates. All of the benefits identified earlier with respect to such amnesties are thus available to support the work of the ECCC and other mechanisms to pursue accountability for the crimes of the Khmer Rouge. Subordinates who were important eyewitnesses to the violations that occurred as well as to the chain of command that resulted in such violations should be available to provide evidence given the protection provided by the 1994 amnesty. This evidence may facilitate the successful prosecution of those high-profile leaders most associated with the crimes of the Khmer Rouge.

The singling out of Sary by the 1996 amnesty provides the only possible exception to this window of opportunity to hold leaders accountable. As noted earlier, amnesties to superiors are often cited by defenders of the social order approach as crucial to preventing future violations. The Cambodian government defended the amnesty provided to Sary with such an argument, noting that it was necessary to weaken and eventually eliminate the military threat and the danger to human rights posed by the insurgent Khmer Rouge. Today, with the benefit of hindsight, it is not clear this concession to Sary was necessary to defend against the threat posed by the Khmer Rouge. Even if one questions the wisdom of the Cambodian government in granting such an amnesty, it is limited to only one individual, and thus does not, and in fact so far has not, prevented the prosecution of a number of other senior Khmer Rouge leaders.

Despite the 1996 amnesty and pardon, Sary has in fact been indicted by the ECCC. What effect, if any, will the two amnesties and the pardon have on the prosecution of Sary? While many argue that international law and state practice make clear that amnesties cannot be granted for international crimes, the case of Cambodia illustrates the hesitancy with which the international community and transitional societies embrace this position. The United Nations and the govern-ment of Cambodia avoided pronouncing on the legality of the amnesties, expressly leaving that question to the ECCC. The statute of the ECCC prohibits the gov-ernment from granting any amnesty beyond that granted to Sary, and leaves it to the discretion of the chambers to determine whether to recognize and give effect to any amnesty granted prior to the creation of the ECCC.[45] The Tribunal has so far sidestepped the legal effect of the amnesty and pardon granted to Sary. The Tribunal will eventually have to pronounce on the legality of the amnesty granted to him. If the Tribunal follows the global trend with respect to such amnesties, it will affirm what many claim is already a well-settled principle of international law: amnesty cannot be granted for acts that constitute a war crime, a crime against humanity, or genocide. If the Tribunal were to declare Sary's 1996 amnesty illegal, it would reaffirm the importance of holding those most responsible for gross violations of human rights accountable, a principle embodied in the very statute that governs the ECCC.

## PEACE AND JUSTICE: THE DEVELOPMENT OF THE "LIMITED AMNESTY"

The possible erosion of Sary's amnesty by the ECCC, occurring after the dissipation of the threat posed by the Khmer Rouge, provides another opportunity to underscore the difference between the rights-based and social order approaches to amnesty, and an opportunity to consider a new form of amnesty that may address the concerns of both schools of thought: the limited amnesty.

The decision whether to grant an amnesty to superiors such as Sary, is often viewed as a choice between providing accountability for existing victims of violations and preventing further violations, and is often articulated as a choice between peace and justice or, as discussed previously, a choice between the social order and rights-based approaches to amnesty. Peace and justice, however, are not unrelated; each is dependent on the other. Injustice undermines peace, and conflict hinders account-ability. Efforts to further the development and protection of rights must involve both justice and conflict resolution. In other words, the rights-based and social order approaches are more intimately intertwined than many commentators are willing to admit. How, then, to further the goals of both rather than pitting the one against the other? A brief examination of the recent history of amnesty and accountability in

---

[45] Article 40*new* of the ECCC statute states in full: "The Royal Government of Cambodia shall not request an amnesty or pardon for any persons who may be investigated for or convicted of crimes referred to in Articles 3, 4, 5, 6, 7 and 8 of this law. The scope of any amnesty or pardon that may have been granted prior to the enactment of this Law is a matter to be decided by the Extraordinary Chambers."

transitional societies suggests an answer. This leads to the second issue concerning amnesties: how long should such an amnesty last?

Amnesties are not meant to be temporary. A small minority of amnesties is only available for a limited period of time; most, once granted, are intended to provide permanent protection to their recipients. Recently, however, governments that inherited amnesties clearly meant to be permanent have been placed under increasing pressure to restrict or annul such amnesties. Initially, such challenges were brought before the domestic courts of the country promulgating the amnesty and, until recently, all such challenges have failed. By contrast, the few international courts that have addressed amnesties granted for gross violations of human rights have all held that such amnesties are illegal. Domestic pressure by victims and human rights advocates, along with the advent of Pinochet-style transnational prosecutions that refuse to defer to foreign amnesties and the increased activity of the ICC, have recently emboldened domestic courts to question the legitimacy of their own governments' amnesties. Argentinean judges, for example, began to challenge that country's amnesty laws, as Par Engstrom and Gabriel Pereira discuss in their chapter in this volume, culminating in the formal repeal of those laws by the Argentinean Congress. Similar moves have been made by Chilean judges to hold individuals accountable for gross violations of human rights committed during the Pinochet dictatorship.[46]

At the same time that courts have begun to challenge amnesties both foreign and domestic, de facto grants of impunity resulting from the failure to prosecute or otherwise address historical crimes have also come under challenge. The large number of cases arising out of human rights violations committed during and in connection with World War II – including claims arising from Nazi gold and art seizures, from Italian and German insurance policies that were never paid, and from the use of slave labor by the Japanese and German governments – illustrates a newfound zeal to pursue violations that have lain dormant in the public imagination for decades. The ECCC, established close to three decades after the overthrow of the Khmer Rouge, is a more recent example of a revived determination to address such historical crimes, along with post-Franco Spain, post-Vichy France, and the post-Civil War United States.

---

[46] The Chilean Supreme Court in July 1999, for example, declared that the country's 1978 amnesty law did not apply to cases of disappearances. See Gustavo Gonzalez, "Rights-Chile: 'Caravan of Death' Trial to Proceed Says High Court," *Inter Press Service*, July 20, 1999, accessed September 3, 2011, http://www.oneworld.org/ips2/july99/00_14_001.html. In 2006, the Inter-American Court of Human Rights also held that the amnesty was incompatible with the American Convention on Human Rights as it purported to provide amnesty for crimes against humanity. Case of *Almonacid-Arellano et al. v. Chile*, Judgment of September 26, 2006, accessed September 4, 2011, http://www.corteidh.or.cr/docs/casos/articulos/seriec_154_ing.pdf/.

These are examples of delayed accountability. They illustrate a trend in state practice of granting immediate impunity only to be followed, sometimes decades later, by accountability.

These examples illustrate how the passage of time decreases a society's hesitation to, or perhaps even fear of, holding individuals accountable for past atrocities. This should not come as a surprise, for the passage of time has always affected our sense of what justice requires. The most obvious manifestation of the effect of time on justice is limitations periods, sometimes referred to as statutes of limitation.[47] Another manifestation of the relationship between the passage of time and accountability is official immunities. The effect of statutes of limitation is the opposite of the evolving state practice of amnesties in that limitations periods initially allow claims to be brought and then bar such claims after the passage of the statutory amount of time. Immunities are more like the recent practice of amnesties in that they usually bar claims immediately upon the occurrence of a wrongful act, only later to provide an opening for accountability. The policies underlying statutes of limitation, head of state and diplomatic immunities, and current trends in the law with respect to all three, provide a basis for revisiting the contemporary treatment and legitimacy of amnesties.

Statutes of limitation attempt to establish the temporal point at which the pursuit of accountability risks injustice. Claims for wrongs committed in the distant past are viewed with trepidation for two major reasons: they present high evidentiary barriers and they disrupt reasonable expectations of social stability and certainty. The ability to establish and corroborate evidence becomes more difficult with the passage of time – witnesses die, move, or become less sure in their recollections, and documents deteriorate or disappear. Statutes of limitation are thus designed to make sure that matters are raised and adjudicated before the onset of such evidentiary concerns. In addition, statutes of limitation protect reasonable expectations of stability and certainty by requiring that defendants be given timely notice of any claim against them. By establishing a time after which a claim may not be brought, statutes of limitations provide closure and certainty with respect to liability. In fact this latter justification concerning notice to potential defendants is probably stronger than the evidentiary concern, since legal systems regularly tolerate the passage of a fair amount of time between the filing of a complaint and the testing of evidence through the evidentiary rigors of a trial.

Concerns raised by stale evidence and the desire for closure are given less weight in cases involving the most extreme violations. The more serious a violation, the longer the period in which a claim may be brought. The crime of murder, for

---

[47] There are others as well, including the equitable doctrine of laches, similar to the doctrine of statute of limitations. The laches doctrine precludes the assertion of a claim if the delay in asserting that right works a disadvantage on another. Most of the observations I make concerning statutes of limitations also apply to other similar legal mechanisms.

example, is not subject to any period of limitations in most U.S. states. Under international treaty law, war crimes and crimes against humanity are not subject to any period of limitations. In addition, limitations periods may be tolled if the delay in bringing a claim is caused by forces outside of the control of the claimant. Examples of such delay include the fraudulent concealment by a suspect of a cause of action; the plaintiff is subject to a legal disability, such as infancy, insanity, or imprisonment; or the plaintiff is prevented from filing suit by force of law.

The policies underlying an extended or null statute of limitation for the most serious crimes, and for tolling the limitations period in cases involving fraud and other similar circumstances, provide the basis for a serious challenge to many amnesties. First, we can discern a general principle that the most serious crimes should not be subject to any limitations period. This would support the idea of making amnesties for the worst international crimes prohibited or at least temporary. Second, even in cases of lesser crimes we extend the period in which a claim can be brought out of a sense of fairness to the claimant – in other words fairness to the claimant outweighs concerns about evidence or settled expectations. This suggests that claims for justice – the claims espoused by the rights-based approach to amnesties – should eventually outweigh the claims of those defending the social order approach.

Diplomatic and head of state immunities, like amnesties, bar claims for accountability immediately upon the commission of a violation. After the passage of some period of time, however, such immunities usually fall away and open the door to accountability. The effective life of an immunity is not tied to the passage of time, but to the change in the official status of the individual. Immunities generally attach to an office, and only derivatively to the individual who holds that office. With official immunities we see a pattern of immediate immunity with, after an individual leaves office, the opening of a window of accountability. This pattern is similar to the emerging trend of amnesties in practice: they usually delay, rather than prohibit, accountability. The ICJ has made clear that such immunities are not a bar to prosecuting an official before an international criminal court[48]; the indictment of Slobodan Milošević, a sitting president, by the ICTY further supports this position.

Defenders of head of state immunity justify the doctrine by claiming that it protects the nature and dignity of the office, comity, mutual respect among nations, and the stability of international relations and diplomacy. Similarly, defenders of the more general practice of granting diplomatic immunity to state officials cite the importance of preserving relations among states and facilitating the official actions of state representatives. These pragmatic arguments defending such immunities are not unlike those employed by the defenders of the social order approach to amnesties.

---

[48] See Case Concerning the Arrest Warrant of April 11, 2000 (*Democratic Republic of the Congo v. Belgium*) 41 ILM 536 (2002).

Statutes of limitations and immunities, therefore, allow accountability long after the occurrence of the underlying crime, through tolling in the case of the former and the removal of a person from his official position in the case of the latter. The evolving practice of amnesties, whereby immunity attaches immediately and then is later lifted, is similar in effect to diplomatic and head of state immunity and the tolling of limitations periods. In each of these cases accountability is delayed, but not foreclosed. The principles and policies that support limitations periods and their tolling and that support immunities for those holding office but not for those who have left office, also support an approach to amnesties that first provides immunity but then opens the window of accountability.

The evolving practice of states with respect to amnesties, and the principles used to justify exceptions to limitations periods and lifting of official immunities, suggests a new form of amnesty that may continue to be attractive to its beneficiaries while at the same time providing some possibility of accountability. State practice with respect to amnesties approximates something like a reverse statute of limitations: a period of time during which accountability is initially barred and then lifted after some period of time so that some form of accountability – sometimes as much as a criminal trial – can take place. We could thus posit a formal rule of international law permitting the granting of a limited amnesty – an amnesty that would provide immunity for a maximum period of time, for example ten years, after which it might be lifted. Such an amnesty could be made conditional on the recipient not engaging in any criminal or related activity during this period of protection. A breach of such condition could then result in the lifting of the amnesty immediately. At the end of the amnesty period, an evaluation could be made to determine if the beneficiary should be entitled to a permanent amnesty or something less. Such a determination could be based upon the actions of the beneficiary during the "probationary" amnesty period. This would create an incentive for beneficiaries: to show through their words and deeds that they no longer pose a threat to society; to provide personal reparations not only to their immediate victims but to the larger society; and to model human rights positive behavior to similarly situated individuals who might otherwise commit or sponsor gross violations of human rights. For such a rule to be effective the life span of the initial amnesty would need to be more than a token amount, to provide a sweet enough "carrot" to induce its recipient to give up power, as well as to provide enough time for the beneficiary to demonstrate more than a superficial commitment to human rights and the rule of law. A permanent amnesty at the end of the probationary period might be rare, and could be conditioned on further demonstrations of support, such as participating in a truth commission, testifying at the trial of others, or otherwise assisting in investigations. If a permanent amnesty is not granted, the actions during the probationary period that were found not to be sufficient could be used in mitigation during any subsequent criminal or civil action.

This proposed limited amnesty should appeal to the defenders of both the social order approach and the rights-based approach to amnesties. The rights-based defenders may be concerned that the amnesty provides impunity, at least for a period of time. In return for that small period of impunity, however, are two benefits – first, a mechanism for neutralizing those who would threaten peace and social order; second, a process that creates an incentive for the beneficiaries to contribute in a positive way to the creation of a human rights protective society. Both of these effects should appeal to the underlying values and goal of the rights-based defenders: a peaceful society that respects human rights and the rule of law.

The social order defenders may be concerned about the limited time period and conditions of the limited amnesty. They may be concerned that providing "only" five or ten years of protection *and* requiring good behavior and good deeds may not be attractive enough to induce the intended beneficiaries to give up power. The alternative, however, is either no amnesty at all, or the promise of a permanent amnesty that, as we have seen, is later reversed. The limited amnesty is designed to appeal to the legitimate concerns of both schools of thought and to provide a compromise that ultimately achieves the aspirations of both.

Finally, a limited amnesty could be applied to both leaders and followers. Given the power they wield in society, leaders may create the most disruption if not provided with some protection, and also have the ability to contribute the most to creating an atmosphere of peace and human rights. Followers may be less able to disrupt at the larger societal level, but given their numbers and the likelihood that they will continue to be in contact with their victims, providing an incentive for them to contribute in a positive way to building a more protective society may have a more immediate effect on victims – through the absence of violence as well as through contributions to reconciliation through reparations.

## CONCLUSION

The answer to the "who" and "how long" questions influence the legitimacy of an amnesty but are not in themselves decisive of that question. While some argue that all amnesties by their nature are illegitimate, I have argued elsewhere that some types of amnesties can qualify as legitimate. I have divided amnesties into three broad categories: amnesic, compromise, and accountable.[49] I am here proposing

[49] An amnesty is "accountable" if it imposes some form of accountability on wrongdoers and provides some relief or reparations to victims. The 1995 South African amnesty is the only amnesty that currently qualifies as an accountable amnesty. Compromise amnesties fall between accountable and amnesic amnesties, and partially reveal and partially conceal. Amnesties passed in Guatemala and Honduras are good examples of compromise amnesties. I have discussed in more detail these three categories of amnesties in Slye, "The Legitimacy of Amnesties," 173. There is a fourth category, corrective amnesties, that is not applicable to this discussion.

a particular form of what I would call an accountable amnesty: a limited amnesty. Such an amnesty would be limited in time and would provide an incentive for its beneficiaries to contribute in a meaningful way to truth, accountability, and reconciliation. The Cambodian amnesties as promulgated are amnesic. Their primary purpose is to conceal and forget, rather than to reveal and account. They provide no accountability, no benefits to victims, and no revelations concerning the violations of the amnesty's beneficiaries. If allowed to survive in their present form through enforcement before the ECCC, they will continue to be illegitimate.

The creation of the ECCC and its power to revisit any previously granted amnesty illustrates the contemporary ambiguity with respect to amnesties for such serious crimes and the contemporary pressure to limit the reach and strength of such amnesties. The work of the ECCC to hold members of the Khmer Rouge accountable is welcome. It would be a shame to mar such a development by recognizing and giving legitimacy to the illegitimate Cambodian amnesties, particularly the 1996 amnesty granted to Sary. Empowering the ECCC to revisit the 1996 amnesty opens the possibility that Sary could effectively be the recipient of a limited amnesty as described above. Sary benefited from the protection of the 1996 amnesty for eleven years until he was arrested in 2007. If he were to be tried and convicted by the tribunal, his sentence could be mitigated if he has demonstrated adequate remorse and rehabilitation through acts of reconciliation and personal reparation. He would then be the first recipient of what I am here calling a limited amnesty. If they have the courage to do so, the chamber judges might piece together a limited amnesty that contributes to both truth and justice, and thus make an important contribution to the creation of a rule of international law that recognizes the important political realities facing transitional societies without ignoring the importance of accountability for gross violations of human rights.

# 12

# The Spanish Amnesty Law of 1977 in Comparative Perspective

## From a Law for Democracy to a Law for Impunity

*Paloma Aguilar*

Without trying to be exhaustive, this chapter presents some of the main arguments found in the literature regarding the pursuit or avoidance of accountability for past political violence by transitional governments. After assessing the extent to which the Spanish case fits these arguments, I analyze the political process that led to the final approval of the 1977 Amnesty Law. The Spanish experience is then compared to those in Argentina and Chile to provide a deeper understanding of the limitations that characterize Spain's transitional justice choice. Briefly, I argue that the role played by a very conservative judiciary, together with the absence of strong social demand for accountability and the lack of resolute political will on the part of the executive and most of the legislature, explain Spain's adherence to amnesty over the pursuit of truth and justice.

## SETTLING ACCOUNTS WITH THE PAST

The dilemma of how to settle accounts with the past without jeopardizing the transition to democracy was probably first addressed by Guillermo O'Donnell and Phillipe Schmitter[1] and, subsequently, by Samuel Huntington.[2] Guillermo O'Donnell and Phillipe Schmitter emphasized that, to understand democratization processes, it was necessary to consider the repressive role played by the armed forces, the extent of such repression and the form it had taken, as well as the length of time elapsed since the worst violations of human rights had occurred. They also identified a paradox: where situations in countries make it easy to bury the past, those same situations make it unnecessary to do so. They concluded moreover that "consensus among

[1] Guillermo O'Donnell and Philippe Schmitter, *Transitions from Authoritarian Rule: Tentative Conclusions About Uncertain Democracies* (Baltimore: The Johns Hopkins University Press, 1986).
[2] Huntington, *The Third Wave*.

I am very grateful to Francesca Lessa and Leigh A. Payne, the editors of this book, for having undertaken such a wise and careful revision of my chapter.

leaders about burying the past," however useful it might be, "may prove ethically unacceptable to most of the population."[3]

Samuel Huntington drew a conclusion regarding the problem of "how to treat authoritarian officials who had blatantly violated human rights." In most of the transitions that had taken place up until then, "[j]ustice was a function of political power. Officials of strong authoritarian regimes that voluntarily ended themselves were not prosecuted; officials of weak authoritarian regimes that collapsed were punished, if they were promptly prosecuted by the new democratic government."[4]

The capacity of authoritarian leaders to avoid these purging processes was also underlined by Stephen Haggard and Robert Kaufman,[5] who maintained that transitions occurring in good economic times allow leaders to negotiate terms of impunity for themselves before relinquishing power (as in the case of Chile). However, in processes of political change that take place during crises, it is easier to exploit the weakness of authoritarian elites in order to subject their actions to judicial review (as in Argentina).

More recently, Monika Nalepa has attempted to tackle the problems of "credible commitments" that arise during democratization processes.[6] In order to offer an explanation as to why transitional justice measures are adopted or avoided, she focuses on events in Eastern Europe and argues that authoritarian leaders will not negotiate the holding of free elections in exchange for amnesty for themselves unless it can be guaranteed that the opposition will uphold its commitment to respect such an agreement once in power. The cases she analyzes in depth (Poland, Hungary, and Czechoslovakia) allow her to affirm that opposition groups will only uphold their commitment when they believe that, under the dictatorship, they were heavily infiltrated by the communist regime and that "lustration laws," should they be passed, could be detrimental to many members of the opposition who, during the dictatorship, collaborated with the regime as secret informers.[7]

The Spanish case has a number of specific features that set it apart from the cases analyzed by the aforementioned authors. First, many of the worst human rights violations were not carried out by a military junta and the Francoist regime

---

[3]   O'Donnell and Schmitter, *Transitions from Authoritarian Rule*, 30.

[4]   Huntington, *The Third Wave*, 209; 228.

[5]   Stephen Haggard and Robert Kaufman, "The Political Economy of Democratic Transitions," *Comparative Politics* 29 (1997): 263–83.

[6]   Monika Nalepa, "Captured Commitments: An Analytic Narrative of Transitions with Transitional Justice," *World Politics* 62, no.2 (2010): 341–80.

[7]   The logic that explains why lustration measures were adopted from the outset in Czechoslovakia and why this was not the case in Poland and Hungary is as follows: "If an opposition party was not highly infiltrated, it would benefit from lustration that disproportionately affected successor parties to the communist regime. However, if the opposition party underestimated the degree to which it had been infiltrated, then lustration could damage the opposition party itself." Ibid., 342, 348–9.

cannot be considered a military dictatorship. Furthermore, the armed forces and the militarized police were not the only actors involved in political repression; the (civilian) judicial system, through its direct and long-lasting participation in the military courts and in the special jurisdictions devoted to the repression of the enemies of the regime, also played a key role.

Second, in contrast to Stephen Haggard and Robert Kaufman's hypothesis, the fact that the Spanish transition took place during a period of economic crisis neither undermined the negotiating power of the elites as the country moved from Francoism to democracy nor allowed for the possibility of judicial accountability for human rights violations.

Third, Francoism did not manage to infiltrate opposition groups, and informers were few and far between. Nonetheless, and unlike several Eastern European countries, the Francoist reformers agreed to negotiate with the opposition and made no attempt, prior to the first democratic general election, to guarantee impunity. Indeed, they felt so secure that it never occurred to them that anyone would attempt to try them. The attempted coups in the early years of the transition testify to the residual power of the dictatorship. It should be emphasized that these failed attempts took place without any threat or mention of investigating the dictatorship's human rights violations, let alone the possibility of bringing the chief perpetrators to trial.

Fourth, unlike the cases of the countries of the Southern Cone or Eastern Europe, the worst human rights violations in Spain took place during the late 1930s and early 1940s, over thirty years before the beginning of the democratization process. According to Jon Elster: "When the predemocratic regime has been of short duration, memories of wrongdoing and suffering tend to be vivid and (other things being equal) emotions correspondingly strong. If it has been of long duration, the intensity of emotion and of the demand for retribution will depend (other things being equal) on when the worst atrocities took place."[8]

Finally, throughout the Spanish Civil War, the two opposing sides, despite different repressive machinery, power, and philosophies, committed atrocities. This created a need for mutual and reciprocal forgiveness in Spanish society that proved far more intense than the demand for justice for the dictatorship's excesses. Indeed, the demand for justice was entirely absent throughout the transition.[9] The traumatic memory that continued to haunt Spaniards on both sides of the civil war explains the consensus to avoid justice measures against human rights violators not only among political elites, but also within Spanish society during the transition.

---

[8]   Jon Elster, *Closing the Books*, 75.

[9]   Paloma Aguilar, "Justice, Politics and Memory in the Spanish Transition," in Barahona de Brito, Enríquez, and Aguilar, *The Politics of Memory*; Mercedes García Arán, "Repercusiones penales de la Ley de Amnistía de 1977," in *30 años de la Ley de Amnistía (1977–2007)*, ed. Jesús Espuny and Olga Paz (Madrid: Dykinson S.L., 2009), 191.

Besides the lack of a very strong social demand in terms of truth and justice after Franco's death, another factor usually overlooked in the literature should be considered: the crucial role that the judiciary may play in transitional justice processes. As it will be shown, whereas a very committed judiciary against impunity can manage to obtain changes in the legislation (Argentina), or at least get around its formal limits (Chile), a conservative judiciary, totally unwilling to investigate the dictatorial past, plays a key role in explaining the shortcomings of the Spanish case in terms of truth and justice.[10]

## THE POLITICAL PROCESS LEADING TO THE PASSAGE OF THE LAW

The presence of traumatic memory from the civil war and the obsessive desire to avoid its repetition encouraged the main political actors and the majority of Spanish citizens to look to the future.[11] It was firmly believed that only in this way would it be possible to ensure a peaceful transition to democracy. It is true that, given the existing correlation of political forces, clearly favorable to the Francoist reformists, it would have been extremely difficult to try those responsible for the most serious human rights violations, even if the Amnesty Law had not been passed. Yet it is equally true that neither the political actors nor the social organizations with significant social backing even considered the possibility of promoting punitive measures against such crimes. In this respect, the efforts of politicians and the demands of certain associations went no further in the first years of democracy than material reparations (indemnity payments and pensions) for the victims of Francoism and their relatives.

The political change in Spain was characterized by a process in which the most important rules of the new democratic game were adopted by consensus between the Francoist reformists and the moderates of the democratic opposition. In addition, there was a tacit agreement regarding certain "gag rules,"[12] which made the bellicose and dictatorial past a forbidden topic of political debate, and a piece of legislation, the Amnesty Law, that shielded this past against any judicial proceedings. All of this, together with the measures of material reparation for the benefit of the vanquished, became known as the "national reconciliation policy."

[10]   I have developed this argument in "Authoritarian Repression, Judicial System and Transitional Justice: The Spanish Case in Comparative Perspective," Centro de Estudios Avanzados en Ciencias Sociales, *Instituto Juan March de Estudios e Investigaciones*, Working Paper n° 263, Madrid, 2011.

[11]   Paloma Aguilar, *Memory and Amnesia* (Oxford: Berghahn Books, 2002); Paloma Aguilar, *Políticas de la memoria y memorias de la política* (Madrid: Alianza Editorial, 2008).

[12]   Stephen Holmes, "Gag Rules or the Politics of Omission," in *Constitutionalism and Democracy*, eds. Jon Elster and Rune Slagstad (New: Maison des Sciences Press, [1988] 1993).

One of the principal founding agreements of Spanish democracy is based on a premise of "never again" which, unlike what we find in other countries, refers neither to the dictatorship nor its crimes, but to the civil war. This difference is crucial. The widespread agreement among citizens does not center on a rejection of the dictatorship, but instead relates to the notion of ending a political conflict in which both sides committed atrocities. Society as a whole aimed to guarantee that war would never happen again. Prior to Franco's death, the opposition's most insistently repeated demand was for amnesty. Once the dictator passed away (on November 20, 1975), the pressure for amnesty intensified.

The government inherited from the dictatorship succumbed to this pressure to some extent, approving partial pardons, for example on November 25, 1975, the day of King Juan Carlos I's coronation. In July 1976, the monarchy's first government – still a nondemocratic one – passed the Amnesty Decree Law, which included crimes involving acts of political intent, but with the following proviso: "as long as they have not endangered or infringed on the life or integrity of individuals."[13]

This clause was interpreted in a very restrictive sense by extremely conservative judges, which explains why the already multitudinous pro-amnesty demonstrations continued. The Basque region provides an important focal point for this set of events. Intense social pressure in the region for amnesty resulted from the high concentration of Basque political prisoners in Spanish prisons at the time. The desire to ensure Basque nationalist participation in the first democratic election (June 15, 1977), moreover, led the Suárez government to approve two amnesty decrees in March 1977. The decrees released most of the political prisoners. Some activists, particularly members of the terrorist group Euskadi Ta Azkatasuna (Basque Homeland and Freedom, ETA),[14] however, remained in prison.[15] Eventually, on May 20, 1977, the cabinet approved the release of most of the Basque prisoners accused of terrorist crimes, who remained in jail. Neither of these measures mentioned the possibility of amnestying the crimes of the dictatorship.

From then on, although the number of demonstrators dwindled and the protests were virtually confined to the Basque region, mobilizations in favor of total amnesty for political prisoners continued. The law eventually adopted reflected public opinion: in September 1977, just one month before the Amnesty Law was passed, thirty-three percent of Spaniards felt the scope of the amnesty should be extended, and

---

[13] Real Decreto-Ley 10/1976, de 30 de julio, sobre amnistía, accessed August 8, 2011, http://noticias.juridicas.com/base_datos/Admin/rdl10–1976.html.

[14] ETA is a terrorist, nationalist, and Marxist-Leninist organization that aims at the independence of the Basque region. It was born during the Francoist regime, but its bloodiest actions took place during the Spanish transition to democracy.

[15] Ignacio Sánchez-Cuenca and Paloma Aguilar, "Terrorist Violence and Popular Mobilization: The Case of the Spanish Transition to Democracy," *Politics & Society* 37, no. 3 (2009): 437.

thirty-one percent felt it should cover "all political crimes without distinction," including violent crimes and terrorism.[16]

The amnesty of October 15, 1977 was the first law passed by the recently inaugurated democratic parliament, a result of the election held just four months earlier. This fundamental piece of legislation, which affects political crimes and offenses, also led to the release of the few remaining political prisoners (most of whom had been sentenced for terrorism-related crimes), the recovery of active rights (job reinstatement, except in the case of the military) and passive rights (pensions) of the convicted, as well as the expunging of their criminal records. The most groundbreaking aspect of this law is that it covered crimes involving bloodshed up until December 15, 1976 (the date of approval, by referendum, of the Political Reform Law), and from then until June 15, 1977 (the date of the first democratic general election), provided that a connection could be established between the crime and the intention to "restore public freedoms" or to demand autonomy. The latter enabled imprisoned members of the ETA terrorist organization to avail themselves of this law, a matter of particular concern to the political class. Although those who had suffered imprisonment as a consequence of the civil war had already benefited from a number of pardons, the Amnesty Law of 1977 entitled them to collect a pension and ensured that their criminal record would, at long last, be expunged.

The first drafts of the law were presented by opposition parties without any specific references to impunity for the Francoist authorities. When the center right governing party Unión de Centro Democrático (UCD) presented its own draft, however, two articles provided for this impunity. Through these proposals and the parliamentary discussion of them, the UCD managed to secure impunity for Francoist authorities in exchange for the liberation of political prisoners accused of crimes involving bloodshed, including ETA members.[17]

The law was eventually approved by the vast majority of the congress (296 votes in favor, 18 abstentions, 2 votes opposed, and 1 invalid vote). All eighteen abstentions came from Alianza Popular (AP), the right-wing party consisting largely of people who had held important posts during the dictatorship, due to the objection to an amnesty for violent crimes committed by anti-Francoist forces. A radical Basque MP voted against the law because its temporal restrictions meant that a number of ETA prisoners who had continued to attack democracy after the first democratic elections would remain in prison. The other vote against the law came from socialist Julio Busquets, one of the founders of the Democratic Military Union

[16]  CIS no. 1139, September 1977.
[17]  Paradoxically, the 1977 amnesty did not stop ETA from killing (in fact, 1979–80 would prove to be the terrorist organization's most deadly period), nor did it prevent attempted coups d'état despite having established the impunity of the dictatorship.

(UMD, Unión Militar Democrática), on the grounds that the law did not allow for the reinstatement of UMD members in the army.[18]

In spite of the blanket amnesty provided by this law, it should not be confused with other amnesty laws in which the leaders of a dictatorship negotiate a peaceful handover of power and guarantee the holding of free elections in exchange for their own impunity. What should be kept in mind is the fact that the heirs of the dictatorship, some of whom held significant roles in key democratic institutions (such as the army, the police, and the judiciary), accepted, albeit with many reservations, the release of terrorists convicted of violent crimes. Such a compromise rendered unthinkable the possibility of prosecuting the former officials of the dictatorship for human rights violations. The Spanish transition in general and the Amnesty Law in particular cannot be understood without considering the context of political violence at the time, particularly the fact that ETA terrorism often targeted the army and the police. The existence of crimes committed by radical sectors of the opposition and the violent climate in which the transition unfolded explain why democratic stability took precedence over all other objectives. Prevailing traumatic memory of the political violence of the 1930s and the desire to avoid its repetition at all costs further reinforced the goal of political stability over accountability.

Stephen Holmes has defended the adoption of "gag rules" for particularly divisive and controversial issues, especially at such delicate and uncertain times as transitions to democracy. He cites amnesty laws as "classic examples of democracy-stabilizing gag rules."[19] According to Stephen Holmes, "by closing the books on the past, keeping retribution for former crimes off the political agenda, the organizers of a new democracy can secure the compliance of strategically located elites – cooperation which may be indispensable for a successful transition from dictatorship to self-government."[20] However, he also acknowledges the provisional nature of such "gag rules:" a legislative body – such as the congress – may decide to adopt them, "but it could not effectively gag the public or the press."[21] He also points out that gag rules "are seldom neutral; they implicitly support one policy and undermine alternatives."[22] Finally, "To prevent overload, all individuals and groups must sup-

---

[18] The UMD was a clandestine organization set up in 1974 to spread democratic ideas among the Francoist armed forces from which it had emerged. Some of the officers who belonged to this organization were tried, imprisoned, and dismissed from the army. The army emphatically refused to permit the reinstatement of UMD members, a form of redress that the Amnesty Law of 1977 made available to all other Spaniards who had been dismissed from their jobs for political reasons.

[19] Holmes, "Gag Rules or the Politics of Omission," 27.

[20] Ibid., 27.

[21] Ibid., 43.

[22] Ibid., 56.

press *some* controversial problems. [...] But issue-avoidance, however attractive, will always be one-sided and potentially dangerous."[23]

This dangerous and one-sided outcome is precisely what happened in the Spanish case. The ideological heirs of the dictatorship ended up benefiting far more from the agreement not to stir up the past than those who had suffered reprisals at the hands of the former regime. It was true that both sides had committed intolerable atrocities during the war (although most of the defeated had already been tried for these crimes during the subsequent period, whereas none of the winners had been tried). However, on the vast majority of occasions throughout the dictatorship, victims and executioners were clearly differentiated. Therefore, the veil drawn over the past in the political sphere principally benefited those who had held public office under Francoism, as well as those who had actively collaborated with the dictatorship's repressive activities.[24]

Finally, the fact that the Amnesty Law left important issues unresolved is demonstrated by all the complementary legislation that followed. For example, an important void in the Amnesty Law involved the status of the prodemocratic clandestine military organization UMD. Until December 1986 those convicted of political offenses did not have the right to rejoin the military. The new complementary legislation restored their right to do so. In fact, the preamble to the 1986 law acknowledges that the amnesty of 1977 "offered unequal treatment to those who, falling within its scope of application, held professional serviceman or civil servant status. Such unequal treatment manifested itself in the lack of provision for the full rehabilitation of the former, since they were not granted the opportunity to rejoin the Forces, Corps or Institutions from which they were discharged."[25]

## THE SPANISH CASE IN COMPARATIVE PERSPECTIVE

According to Jon Elster, in any democratization process the new political elites "have had to decide whether leaders of, collaborators with or agents of the former regime should be brought to court or otherwise penalized, and whether and how

---

[23] Ibid., 58.
[24] The amnesty mutually and reciprocally granted by the heirs of the dictatorship and the democratic opposition was not symmetrical, "neither in legal terms, nor in political terms." On the one hand, "most of the crimes for which the democrats were amnestied ceased to be criminal offences, and many of them came to constitute a straightforward exercise of political rights. [...] On the other hand, the actions of 'authorities, civil servants and law enforcement agents' carried out against the exercise of fundamental rights [...] continued to constitute crimes according to the new laws. [...] Therefore, the amnesty was more generous to the servants of Francoism: they could have been prosecuted, but they were not." Arán, "Repercusiones penales de la Ley de Amnistía de 1977," 189.
[25] Ley 24/1986, de 24 de diciembre, de rehabilitación de militares profesionales, accessed September 8, 2011, http://www.boe.es/boe/dias/1986/12/30/pdfs/A42370–42371.pdf.

the victims of the regimes should be rehabilitated and compensated."[26] Reparation measures are usually considered more innocuous than those aimed at providing justice, which is why they have been resorted to more frequently. Furthermore, in their eagerness to appease the human rights abusers of the preceding regime so as to ensure that they will not conspire against the incipient democratic regime, new democratic governments have tended to resort to clemency, particularly through amnesty processes.

As described by Par Engstrom and Gabriel Pereira in their chapter in this volume, Argentina's first democratic government after the dictatorship made a surprising decision *not* to favor amnesty over accountability. The adoption of amnesty measures and pardons in the late 1980s and early 1990s in Argentina did not prevent the onset in the late 1990s of trials for the illegal appropriation of children, the truth trials, or the ongoing human rights trials in Argentina today. While it may be true that "gag rules" can play a fundamental role in political change processes and remain in force for many years, they are far from irrevocable and are always subject to the fluctuating political context. One explanation for the difference between Argentina, Chile, and Spain may be political leadership and judicial will. Presidents Raúl Alfonsín of Argentina and Michelle Bachelet in Chile a few years later worked with human rights organizations and associations of victims' relatives. They demonstrated a commitment to accountability and against impunity that reflected in no small part their own position as opponents of the former authoritarian regime, victims of the repressive apparatus, or human rights defenders during the dictatorship. None of the prime ministers in Spain possessed an equivalent background, nor did they demonstrate a resolute political will to promote accountability.

Chile provides another interesting comparison to explain the process in Spain. Unlike the amnesty law in Spain passed after the end of the dictatorship, Chile's Decree Law 2191 of April 1978 is a self-amnesty adopted by the military dictatorship of General Pinochet that society accepted as part of the terms of the transition. The Amnesty Law was rigorously enforced until General Pinochet's arrest in London. This fortuitous event, together with the revelation of the financial scandals of the dictator (the Riggs Bank affair), forced Chileans to review some of the agreements upon which their political change process relied. The subsequent resurrection of the past was not, therefore, the result of an "intentional remembrance," but rather, "[t]his time, as never before in the transition, memory [imposed] itself."[27] From then on, judges began to reinterpret this law and some even considered that

---

[26]　Jon Elster, "Coming to Terms with the Past: A Framework for the Study of Justice in the Transition to Democracy," *European Journal of Sociology* 39 (1998): 7–48.

[27]　Norbert Lechner and Pedro Güell, "Construcción social de las memorias en la transición chilena," in *La caja de pandora. El retorno de la transición chilena*, ed. Amparo Menéndez-Carrión and Alfredo Joignant (Santiago de Chile: Planeta/Ariel, 1999), 194.

the cases of the disappeared constituted, in accordance with international legislation, "non-prescriptible crimes," which allowed them to reopen cases prior to 1978. Chile's Amnesty Law remains in force to this day, despite the IACtHR's sentence in the 2006 *Almonacid-Arellano* case, in which it considered Decree 2191 as incompatible with the American Convention and thus lacking any legal effects.[28] Although the self-amnesty's removal from the statute books has been the subject of parliamentary debate, congress has yet to reach a definitive decision on the matter. In fact, in August 1990 the Constitutional Court ratified the constitutionality of this law. In spite of the declarations of former President Bachelet indicating that the amnesty could be abrogated, she left office without having carried this measure out.

During its first fifteen years in force, the Amnesty Decree Law of 1978 was applied, barring exceptions, without any investigation whatsoever being conducted. However, the law itself provides that "the judge needs to carry out an investigation before granting amnesty," in order to establish the type of participation of the individuals on trial, distinguishing between criminals, accomplices, and obstructers of justice.[29] In spite of this provision, the Chilean Supreme Court decided to interpret the law differently, granting amnesty without conducting any inquiries. In contrast, Judge Carlos Cerda opted to carry out all the necessary investigations before granting amnesty. In the 1990s, "Judge Cerda's lines of argument prevailed: amnesty could only be applied if the requirements laid down in Decree-Law 2191 were fulfilled, that is, if an investigation were carried out and if, through the latter, it were confirmed that a homicide had occurred and that the participation of those responsible could be established."[30] This is what came to be known as the "Aylwin doctrine." There is a notable difference between the Chilean amnesty and its Spanish counterpart. In Chile, judges have helped to clarify the facts without undermining the amnesty law. Moreover, in some cases they have decided to investigate crimes regarded as non-prescriptible according to international law. Finally, the Chilean amnesty only covers the period prior to 1978, whereas the Spanish amnesty covers the entire period of Franco's dictatorship. Therefore, accountability in Chile is legally possible for crimes committed during the dictatorship between 1978 and the election of the democratic government presided over by Patricio Aylwin in 1990. The political will, political leadership, and the legal and creative processes used to circumvent the amnesty law in Chile have no parallel in the Spanish case.

---

[28] Case of *Almonacid-Arellano et al. v. Chile*. Preliminary Objections, Merits, Reparations and Costs. Judgment of September 26, 2006. Series C No. 154.

[29] Decreto-Ley 2.191, 18 de abril de 1978 (Ley de Amnistía), accessed September 3, 2011, http://www.derechos.org/nizkor/chile/doc/amnistia.html.

[30] Lira, "The Reparations Policy for Human Rights Violations in Chile," in de Greiff, *The Handbook of Reparations*, 86.

In Chile, the main trials and imprisonments for human rights violations began in 1995.[31] In spite of the fact that Eduardo Frei's government, under pressure from the right and the military, tried to put limits on justice – albeit while continuing to support the search for the disappeared – a reform in the Supreme Court and the appointment of new judges meant that this judicial body, between 1997 and 1998, started changing its decisions, holding that "international law was superior to the amnesty law and that a disappearance is an ongoing crime until the body is found, which means that it cannot be subject to amnesty until it is resolved."[32] As has already been mentioned, Pinochet's arrest also acted as a catalyst, and since then, "Chilean courts have prosecuted more than 300 military officers for human rights violations."[33] As of June 2011, over 700 had been tried and sentenced in Chile.[34]

The fact that in Spain, unlike the other two countries analyzed, the military saw no need to approve a self-amnesty prior to the change of regime is probably due to three factors. First, the context in which the Spanish transition took place was not as sensitive to the international climate of opposition to impunity that would eventually come to prevail; this would explain why those who occupied positions of power under the dictatorship felt less apprehensive.[35] Second, however, it may also highlight how confident the Francoist elites were in their ability to keep the process of change under control. Finally, it should be emphasized that the power of the Francoist dictatorship and the responsibility for past violations, unlike the Southern Cone dictatorships, did not lie only with the military security apparatus.

In Spain, none of the cases involving human rights violations recorded during the civil war or the dictatorship has been reviewed. It should be highlighted that the type of repression carried out by the Francoist authorities was far less clandestine and considerably more protected by the regime's legislation than in the other two cases discussed; still, both during and immediately after the war there were extrajudicial executions and disappearances, and, throughout the entire regime, tortures

[31] The most important trial that took place prior to this date was that concerning the "Letelier case," as a result of which Manuel Contreras and Pedro Espinosa were sentenced to prison.

[32] Barahona de Brito, "Truth, Justice, Memory," 148.

[33] Katherine Hite, "The Politics of Memory, The Languages of Human Rights," in *Latin America After Neoliberalism: Turning the Tide in the 21st Century*, ed. Eric Hershberg and Fred Rosen (New York: The New Press, 2006), 205.

[34] Observatorio de Derechos Humanos of the Diego Portales University (Santiago, Chile), accessed September 2, 2011, http://www.icso.cl/observatorio-derechos-humanos/.

[35] What Kathryn Sikkink has named the "justice cascade" was still far into the future (see her chapter in this volume). However, despite this later trend toward accountability, amnesty has remained an attractive option to many transitioning countries (see Louise Mallinder's chapter and the concluding chapter by Tricia D. Olsen, Leigh A. Payne, and Andrew G. Reiter in this volume). For more detailed studies on the application of amnesty in the world, see Olsen, Reiter, and Payne, *Transitional Justice in Balance*; Freeman, *Necessary Evils*; and Mallinder, *Amnesty, Human Rights and Political Transitions*.

and trials without due process. Repression in the Southern Cone was essentially "clandestine and illegal, even according to the laws of the dictatorships."[36] In fact, surprising enough, although the death penalty had been reestablished during the Argentinean dictatorship, it was never enforced. And under Pinochet's dictatorship, after the first three years of harsh repression, the death penalty was only applied in four cases, all entirely unrelated to political issues. In Spain, meanwhile, although it is not known exactly how many death sentences were enforced by the dictatorship during the postwar period, it is believed they amount to as many as fifty thousand.[37] Between 1947 and 1975 there were forty-one civilian court-ordered executions by garrotte[38] (for nonpolitical crimes) and, between 1958 and 1975, thirteen executions (four by garrotte and the rest by firing squad) imposed by military courts (many of them for political crimes).[39]

In the seventh term of Spanish democracy (2000–4), with the main conservative party (Partido Popular, PP) in power, various parliamentary groups requested the invalidation of the verdicts passed by the Francoist military courts.[40] In 2003, the socialist group presented an initiative along these lines[41] and, one year later, with the Partido Socialista Obrero Español (PSOE) in power, decided that the tasks carried out by the Inter-Ministerial Commission responsible for writing the draft of the so-called Law of Historical Memory should include "a juridical study on the annulment of unjust judgments delivered in the summary trials conducted under Francoist legislation." The report that was eventually submitted by the commission expressed strong objections to this measure. Consequently, the Reparation Law of 2007, passed during José Luis Rodríguez Zapatero's first term in office (2004–8), does not provide for the invalidation of summary trials.[42] Instead, it merely declares

---

[36] Barahona de Brito, "Truth, Justice, Memory," in Barahona de Brito, Enríquez, and Aguilar, *The Politics of Memory*, 119.

[37] In Spain, the death penalty was abolished for common crimes in 1978 and for all types of crimes in 1995. In Chile and in Argentina it has only been abolished for common crimes, in 2001 and 1984 respectively.

[38] "A method of execution formerly practiced in Spain, in which a tightened iron collar is used to strangle or break the neck of a condemned person," www.thefreedictionary.com.

[39] *Comentario Sociológico* 12–13 (October 1975–March 1976): 1014.

[40] "Compensation may also take more symbolic forms, notably the invalidation of verdicts passed on regime opponents." See Elster, *Closing the Books*, 129. This is what has been done in Germany, a case which could constitute an interesting precedent for many other countries, in particular Spain. Consult the "Law to Annul Unjust National-Socialist Sentences in the Administration of Criminal Justice" (August 25, 1998, reformed by the Law of July 23, 2002).

[41] *Official Parliament Gazette*, September 8, 2003, 7th Term, Series D, issue 580.

[42] In spite of all its limitations, this is probably the most important law for the victims of Francoism that has been passed since the democratization period, and, without any doubt, the most controversial of all. For more details about this norm and the political tensions that arose during this term, see Paloma Aguilar, "Transitional or Post-transitional Justice? Recent Developments in the Spanish Case," *South European Society & Politics* 13 (2008): 417–33.

certain tribunals and judgments illegitimate – as opposed to illegal – and offers the possibility of obtaining a "declaration of reparation and personal recognition" to those who suffered certain court rulings under the protection of laws issued on grounds of ideology or religious belief. Although Amnesty International (2007) has criticized this law for not guaranteeing those concerned effective recourse to secure the annulment or revocation of sentences,[43] the legal consequences of this declaration remain to be seen. In fact, the second additional provision of the aforementioned law states that the provisions contained therein "are compatible with the prosecution of actions and access to the ordinary and extraordinary judicial proceedings provided for in domestic laws or in the international treaties and conventions signed by Spain," which implies a tacit adherence to the dictates of international legislation.[44]

The possibility of summary judgments rendered by Francoist military tribunals (which included members of the ordinary jurisdiction) being declared void has stirred up controversy in political, social, and legal circles. The government's position, supported by various Supreme Court rulings[45] and the opinion of the Constitutional Court[46] has been challenged by others who have spoken out in favor of going beyond the arguments used hitherto. Cándido Conde Pumpido, the state public prosecutor at the end of the 2004–8 parliamentary term, has shown his willingness to promote the review of Francoism's ideological rulings, including those by military courts. It is important to remember that hardly anybody in Spain is calling for the prosecution of those who issued tens of thousands of death sentences in unjust trials without due process of law, or of those who subsequently caused the death of detainees or, later during the transition, demonstrators and strikers. Instead, the comparatively modest aim is to review and, when appropriate, revoke or annul the sentences with marked political or ideological overtones in order to demonstrate that they were unjust, which would contribute to the moral reparation of the victims. Prior to the passage of the Reparation Law, Joan Queralt, a professor of criminal law, argued in favor of annulling these sentences as opposed to merely revoking them,

---

[43]  Equipo Nizkor argues that the UN declared Francoism illegitimate in 1946 and that, therefore, all its actions should, sooner or later, be declared void. It also complains that all the summary trials held under the dictatorship are still not even listed in an official inventory. "La excepción española," *El País*, May 7, 2006, 24.

[44]  However, as will be seen, the only initiative in this respect has provoked an offensive reaction from the far right and an extremely obstructive attitude on the part of the judiciary.

[45]  The Military Division of the Supreme Court has repeatedly refused to review the sentences handed out by Francoist tribunals. Marc Carrillo has disagreed with the Supreme Court's actions and has argued that "before dismissing the appeal, it should exhaust the probative procedure if there is a scintilla of evidence, and not reject the appeal on the grounds that the evidence submitted is insufficient." See Alicia Gil, *La justicia de transición en España* (Barcelona: Atelier, 2009).

[46]  "Our Constitutional Court has already confirmed the impossibility of applying the Constitution to rulings prior to its entry into force that have ceased to have effect." Ibid.

in accordance with the German precedent.[47] Carlos Jiménez Villarejo, former chief prosecutor of the Anti-Corruption Office, has asked the judiciary to be courageous when applying the law and even to initiate judicial proceedings with a view to revoking Francoist sentences.[48]

Regardless of what eventually happens as a result of the application of the Reparation Law, the fact is that the Spanish legislature has decided not to undertake legislative reforms similar to those implemented in countries such as Germany. Likewise, and also in contrast to other cases, only one judge has given precedence to international legislation in order to overcome the restrictions of the Amnesty Law (see conclusions). Virtually no effort has been made to follow Chile's lead, that is, to investigate certain cases for as long as it takes to establish the truth, even if it is known beforehand that amnesty will have to be granted to the guilty parties. The only (unsuccessful) attempt to do this was with the Ruano case.[49] The trial concerning his death demonstrates that if the judicial proceedings had been initiated earlier (and, of course, in this particular case, if the crucial evidence had not been deliberately withheld), it would have been possible to clear up certain political crimes without this having had to entail any conviction whatsoever because the Amnesty Law would have prevented it. José Manuel Gómez Benítez, the Ruano family's lawyer, maintained that "there would have been no objection to amnesty being granted had the defendants admitted to having committed the crime and to having acted for political reasons, as stipulated by the prerequisites for application of the 1977 Law."[50]

As Alicia Gil shrewdly points out, on the basis of the strategy deployed by Gómez Benítez, "amnesty does not preclude investigation and verification of the facts and the political motive [...], whereas, on the contrary, the court's verification of these circumstances is a condition for its application. This interpretation would bring our Amnesty Law more in line with a truth-finding mechanism."[51] However, as the same author maintains, barring the exception of the Ruano family, those affected did not initiate any prosecution whatsoever. "The victims themselves thought that the amnesty covered untried cases and that there was no need for the alleged perpetrators to prove or acknowledge anything."[52] In view of this case, one cannot help but be struck once

---

[47] "Desmemoria histórica," *El País*, January 5, 2007, 26.

[48] "Jiménez Villarejo pide a la justicia que aplique 'con valentía' la ley y anule de oficio juicios franquistas," *Diario Siglo XXI*, October 18, 2007.

[49] Enrique Ruano, a twenty-year-old law student, was detained in 1969 by the police for distributing political propaganda. He died three days after his detention. According to the police he committed suicide by jumping out of a window from a seventh floor while in custody. The official version contained many contradictions and crucial forensic evidence eventually disappeared. Most opposition parties considered the Ruano case a political murder and promoted a series of mobilizations. For more details about this case, see Ana Domínguez, ed., *Enrique Ruano. Memoria viva de la impunidad del franquismo* (Madrid: UCM, 2011).

[50] Gil, *La justicia de transición en España*, 86.

[51] Ibid., 86.

[52] Ibid., 101.

again by the lack of initiative of judges, lawyers, and prosecutors in Spain, given that, as opposed to what has occurred in other countries, very few advised the families of the victims about the ins and outs of the law in order to secure, if not justice, at least the truth and, thereby, moral reparation. Also remarkable, in comparison with the Chilean and Argentine cases, is the low level of civil society activism in Spain around victims and survivors or human rights to promote accountability at the local and international level. As regards the institutional reforms which often serve to profoundly democratize new regimes without needing to bring anyone to trial, it is worth pointing out that the legacies of the dictatorship in Chile were far more significant, and far more of a hindrance to the democratic process, than in either of the other two cases. The well-established constraints range from the 1980 constitution to the presence of Pinochet as commander in chief of the army and, from March 1998 onward, as senator for life, while other examples include a set of laws that placed severe restrictions on freedom of expression. Several of the measures approved by the Chilean dictatorship before handing over power aimed not only to guarantee the impunity of the repressors, but also to grant control of certain key institutions to the right and to the military. It took many years to introduce reforms designed to democratize their functioning, and a number of other important measures have yet to be approved at the time of this writing. In spite of the many changes made to the constitution, legal continuity has been very important in Chile: "the death penalty is still in force for crimes related to national security, military tribunals have jurisdiction over certain offences committed by civilians, and the military regime's verdicts remain valid."[53]

In Spain, the continuity in the legal system,[54] the armed forces,[55] and the police inherited from the dictatorship was overwhelming. The most far-reaching

---

[53] Carlos H. Acuña, "Transitional Justice in Argentina and Chile," in *Retribution and Reparation in the Transition to Democracy*, ed. Jon Elster (New York: Cambridge University Press, 2006), 225.

[54] It is worth pointing out that all the judges belonging to the Court of Public Order (Tribunal de Orden Público), with the exception of its president, who was murdered by ETA, came to form part of the National High Court (Francisco Gor, "De la justicia franquista a la constitucional," in *Memoria de la transición*, ed. Santos Juliá, Javier Pradera, and Joaquín Prieto (Madrid: Taurus-El País, 1996), 222 quoted in Gil, *La justicia de transición en España*, 55), the same institution to which Baltasar Garzón belongs. And the Court of Public Order was created under Francoism precisely to prosecute political crimes. Thousands of persons were charged and condemned until its dismantling in 1977 (see Juan José del Águila, *El TOP. La represión de la libertad* [Barcelona: Planeta, 2001]). As some authors have pointed out, "the pacted and consensual nature of the transition process precluded any sort of prosecution of former officials of the authoritarian regime [...]; there was a high degree of continuity from the authoritarian to the democratic regimes [in this second sentence, the authors are dealing simultaneously with Spain, Greece, Portugal, and Italy] in organization and personnel." Pedro C. Magalhães, Carlo Guarnieri, and Yorgos Kaminis, "Democratic Consolidation, Judicial Reform, and the Judicialization of Politics in Southern Europe," in *Democracy and the State in the New Southern Europe*, ed. Richard Gunther, Nikiforos P. Diamandouros, and Dimitri A. Sotiropoulos (Cambridge: Cambridge University Press, 2006),147–8.

[55] The Spanish case, unlike those of Argentina, Greece and Portugal, is characterized by the complete lack of purging of the armed forces. See Felipe Agüero, *Militares, civiles y democracia* (Madrid: Alianza Editorial, 1995), 22–3.

institutional reforms in these spheres did not begin until the PSOE came to power, although they never led to a serious purging of personnel. Continuity in all three realms was the general trend to which transfers and early retirements were more the exception than the rule. In Argentina, unlike the other two country cases, "the purging of the Supreme Court and the modification of military jurisdiction" were determining factors that explain why judges refused to halt legal proceedings after the Full Stop and Due Obedience Laws and Menem's pardons.[56] As has already been stressed, the negotiating capacity of outgoing dictatorial elites is decisive in explaining the survival of authoritarian enclaves from which resistance to reforms can be organized and assurances of impunity obtained, although room for maneuvering is usually reduced once democracy is consolidated. Moreover, politicians tend to underestimate the strength and influence that other powers, such as the judiciary, or other actors, such as social organizations, can wield in order to oppose the measures they approve. In other words, they overestimate their capacity to offer long-lasting guarantees of impunity or of limited justice to the leaders of the previous regime.

Although Jon Elster does not go so far as to expound a general theory of transitional justice,[57] he does observe, as we have already mentioned, that the temporal remoteness of the worst atrocities helps to attenuate the pressure in favor of justice measures. For instance, the fact that the worst crimes of the Argentinean and Chilean dictatorships were more recent made them more difficult to address, but also more difficult to ignore. In Chile and, particularly, in Argentina, although some of the policies relating to the past got off to a flying start, circumstances caused the official reparation process to reach an impasse.[58] However, certain sectors of society rallied in response to this standstill by continuing to mobilize against impunity,[59] a combative stance also assumed by some judges. In recent years, this social, judicial, and political impetus has brought about notable advances in both countries in the spheres of justice, truth, and memory.

---

[56] Barahona de Brito, "Truth, Justice, Memory," 137.

[57] According to his own words: "I do not aim at presenting a 'theory of transitional justice.' [...] I have found the context-dependence of the phenomena to be an insuperable obstacle to generalizations." Elster, *Closing the Books*, 77.

[58] In both cases, the justice and truth policies undertaken provoked disturbing military reactions which succeeded in altering, at least in part, the political agenda. Four military uprisings took place (one in 1987, two in 1988, and the last in 1990) in Argentina alone. In Spain, however, the attempted coup in 1981 was not caused by the military having anticipated the possibility of their acts coming under the scrutiny of judicial review. On the one hand, the Amnesty of 1977 made that impossible, and on the other, the army had not played the same exclusive role in the political repression as in the other two cases.

[59] The pardon decrees approved by Menem were widely rejected by the citizenry. From then on, it was the human right organizations that kept the flame of memory alive and persisted in demanding justice. International bodies also played a fundamental role. Patricia Tappatá de Valdez, "El pasado, un tema central del presente. La búsqueda de verdad y justicia como construcción de una lógica democrática," in Oreamuno, Narea, and Galli, *Verdad, justicia y reparación*, 94, 97.

Furthermore, the fact that repression in the Southern Cone was essentially clandestine explains why these demands have been raised with much greater insistence than in Spain, where the trials that resulted in tens of thousands of executions during the early years of the dictatorship were of an official nature. Nevertheless, it remains surprising that, despite the time elapsed, an official inventory of these trials has yet to be drawn up, which explains why their exact number is still not known. Furthermore, there is still much we do not know about the extrajudicial killings perpetrated by the winning side in the war and during the first stage of Francoism. Though these killings were neither carried out as systematically nor had the same significance as in the other two countries examined, they did take place. The existence of a very conservative judiciary in Spain is crucial to understanding a key obstacle to truth and justice.

Argentina and Chile have gone further than Spain in terms of publicly and officially revealing the truth. Both have managed to try and imprison some of the perpetrators of the worst human rights violations and, when faced with restrictions imposed by the prevailing laws (the Amnesty Law in Chile and the Full Stop and Due Obedience Laws in Argentina), have even been able to bypass them more effectively than in Spain, owing to the pressure exerted by society, the attitude of certain judges who have not hesitated to resort to international law or to alert victims to the complexities of the relevant legislation in force, and a resolute political will. Finally, the symbolic reparations afforded to victims in both countries have been far more convincing and visible than in Spain.[60]

It is obvious that the Spanish Amnesty Law was closely linked to the memory of the civil war. As has been repeatedly highlighted, the idea of national reconciliation, then regarded as the foundation stone on which the new democratic regime had to be built, was inextricably bound up with the terms "forgetting," "burying," "erasing," and "overcoming." At the same time, one of the obsessions of the left was to demonstrate its conciliatory disposition and that it harbored neither ill feeling nor a desire for revenge. Finally, the civil and military right retained power that although would eventually be revealed to have been more limited than was assumed at that time, was far from negligible. In any case, political actors make their decisions according to what they perceive, either rightly or wrongly, at any given time. As things stood, a political – let alone judicial – review of the repressive actions of the dictatorship was barely conceivable in the democratization period. Even after democracy was resting comfortably on firm foundations, military power was subordinate to civil power, and the lack of political backing for extreme right-wing parties was plainly evident, parliamentary elites continued to demonstrate a lack of political and judicial will to allow truth or justice.[61]

---

[60] See Aguilar, *Políticas de la memoria y memorias de la política*.
[61] Ibid.; Aguilar, "Transitional or Post-transitional Justice? Recent Developments in the Spanish Case."

However, it is also true that in Spain, in spite of the fact that amnesty has not been used in conjunction with trials or with truth commissions – combinations which, according to research carried out by Tricia Olsen, Leigh Payne, and Andrew Reiter[62] increase the likelihood of improving respect for human rights and the functioning of democracy – there does exist a consolidated democracy that functions reasonably well. In fact, the statistics relating to respect for human rights are no worse than in the other two countries analyzed. Nevertheless, the lack of public initiatives to clarify the truth and to exhume the thousands of remains whose whereabouts are still unknown, has enabled the right to consolidate a culture of impunity for the past, for which they have no guilty feelings whatsoever, and has allowed fundamentally conservative values to remain prevalent among the judiciary. This culture accounts for the refusal to invalidate the unjust trials of Francoism and to carry out judicial truth-finding investigations, irrespective of the obligation to grant amnesty once such proceedings come to an end.

## MEMORY IRRUPTION AND JUDICIAL REACTION

For many years, the Spanish Amnesty Law went unnoticed. The vast majority of citizens are unaware that it contains two articles that make it equivalent to a blanket amnesty for Francoist perpetrators, and unlike what happened in other countries, judges never made any attempt to challenge or bypass this law. Moreover, given the lack of a substantial social demand in favor of bringing proceedings against the dictatorship, the only occasions on which this law had come to the fore have been confined to the political sphere, since practically all the reparation measures aimed at the victims of the civil war and of Francoism approved during the democratic era have stemmed from the provisions contained in the Amnesty Law of 1977.

In recent years, however, this law has taken on major importance. The creation, in 2000, of the Association for the Recovery of Historical Memory, responsible for many of the exhumation processes that have taken place over the last decade in Spain, soon gave rise to the first formal complaints concerning the restrictions imposed by the 1977 Amnesty Law on the scope for reviewing the past and redressing victims. Some argue that the law is preconstitutional, since the Spanish constitution dates from December 1978, and that, therefore, it should undergo review. Although this law was passed by the first democratically elected parliament, some consider that the two articles that firmly establish the impunity of Francoist crimes were introduced as a result of the considerable pressure and influence that the heirs of the dictatorship were able to wield at that time.

---

[62]  Olsen, Payne, and Reiter, *The Justice Balance*.

But what finally thrust this law into the limelight was the initiative of the ruling issued by Judge Baltasar Garzón on October 16, 2008. Until then, an ongoing paradoxical situation had meant that while some Spanish judges played a fundamental role in prosecuting individuals who had committed crimes regarded as nonprescriptible by international law, in Spain there was not even a debate about the non-prescriptibility of certain crimes, or about the obligation, according to the United Nations and various international treaties ratified by Spain, to offer reparation or moral redress to all the victims of violence during the civil war and the dictatorship. The problem, according to some experts in criminal law – though this is a hotly debated issue – is that the worst atrocities in Spain were committed before the creation of the Universal Declaration of Human Rights (1948) and the International Covenant on Civil and Political Rights (1966). This means, according to the more rigid interpretation of the law, that the obligation to prosecute civil war and immediate postwar crimes is less clear in the Spanish case. However, experts in international criminal law tend to point either to previous international legal precedents, including natural law or to the post-1948 human rights violations that took place in Spain (e.g., torture, extrajudicial executions, and forced disappearances) to claim that Spain has an obligation to prosecute past abuses.[63]

The recent proliferation of associations determined to carry out the exhumation of numerous common graves has been extraordinary. These associations, in December 2006, filed various formal complaints with the National High Court (these were just the first; many more would follow)[64] regarding the "illegal detentions" and "forced disappearances" – both considered crimes against humanity – that occurred as a result of the coup d'état of June 18, 1936 led by General Francisco Franco against the legitimate government of the Second Republic. Judge Garzón declared his competence to investigate the complaints in October 2008. Although he subsequently declared himself incompetent once it was proved that the main perpetrators of the aforementioned crimes were no longer alive, and for this reason transferred the complaints to the regional courts, the National High Court also held that Garzón lacked jurisdiction over this matter. Months later, two private criminal lawsuits were filed against Judge Garzón, in which it was claimed that the decisions he made to declare himself competent initially could be classified as a "perversion of the course of justice." It is particularly significant that the plaintiffs are organizations linked to the extreme right; one of them is Falange Española de las JONS (the fascist-inspired party whose protagonist role in the political repression during and after the Spanish

---

[63] Aguilar, *Políticas de la memoria y memorias de la política*, 481–93.
[64] See Javier Chinchón, "La actuación de la Audiencia Nacional en la investigación y juicio de los crímenes contra la humanidad cometidos en la Guerra Civil y el franquismo," *La Ley* 1 (2009): 1415–24.

Civil War is well known).[65] The action is still in progress at the moment of writing this text. On May 14, 2010, following the formal order for commencement of trial, Garzón was temporarily suspended from his duties on the alleged grounds that there was sufficient evidence to claim that he had committed the crime of "prevarication"[66] by attempting to open investigations into the crimes of Francoism, knowing full well that the Amnesty Law did not allow such an action. This decision sparked a massive controversy both at home and abroad. A few days later, the General Council of the Judiciary gave him permission to leave the country and take up a post as an external advisor to the chief prosecutor of the ICC in The Hague.

Those who believe that Judge Garzón was not guilty of prevaricating, in general terms, argue that a number of international agreements signed by Spain oblige, or at least enable, this country to investigate crimes regarded as nonprescriptible, and that the Amnesty Law should not be applied to crimes against humanity.[67] Moreover, in order for the law to be applied, the facts must be investigated and the offenders identified beforehand; only after such actions have been carried out can the law be applied. In addition, many experts point out that it is one thing to disagree with Judge Garzón's interpretations of the law, but quite another to consider his acts illegal, warranting his expulsion from the legal profession.

## CONCLUSIONS

As has been stated by a criminal law expert, who is otherwise opposed to Judge Garzón's initiative (because she considers that international obligations do not apply in this case), "amnesty does not preclude investigation and verification of the facts [...], whereas, on the contrary, the court's verification of these circumstances is a condition for its application. This interpretation would bring our Amnesty Law more in line with a truth-finding mechanism and not one of complete forgetting."[68] As we have seen in the Chilean case, this is precisely what was done under the "Aylwin doctrine," whereas in Spain, such efforts were only made – and with many limitations, as mentioned earlier – in connection with the investigation of the Ruano case.

---

[65] In April 2010 the first demonstration against the impunity of Francoism took place in Spain. The judicial initiatives against Garzón triggered this demonstration and many of the participants exhibited banners supporting him.

[66] Prevarication is a crime committed by a public servant or a judge when he/she enacts an order knowing in advance that this is unjust. This crime was attributed to Garzón by those who thought that he began the judicial process knowing in advance that he did not possess judicial competence to prosecute or investigate this crime.

[67] See Javier Chinchón and Lydia Vicente, "La investigación de los crímenes cometidos en la guerra civil y el franquismo como delito de prevaricación," *Revista Electrónica de Estudios Internacionales* 19 (2010): 1–43.

[68] Gil, *La justicia de transición en España*, 86.

There are at least three striking aspects in the Spanish case. First, the fact that Garzón's initiative was so late in coming. This accounts for the paucity of social demands in this respect[69]; in sharp contrast with cases of the Southern Cone, in Spain the human rights associations did not play any important mobilization role – beyond the fight for the amnesty – nor did they pose any serious challenge to the different governments. Very particular to the Spanish case is the judges' lack of will to undertake such initiatives (again, in sharp contrast with cases in the Southern Cone), together with the absence of a resolute political will by the executive and the majority of the parliament. The boost provided by the 2007 reparation law as it was being passed by parliament most clearly explains why the previously mentioned associations filed their complaints with the National High Court and why Garzón was willing to take charge of them.

Second, it is highly indicative of the patently conservative ideological bias of the governing bodies of the judiciary that the only judge intent on undertaking a judicial review of the past in Spain has been temporarily suspended and could be barred from the bench for up to twenty years, when the fact that the crimes to be tried fell under the umbrella of the Amnesty Law is, at the very least, a subject of major legal controversy. A decision as serious and exceptional as a disqualification from public office should at least elicit agreement among experts, especially if we are talking about perverting the course of justice, but such consensus is still a long way off in this case. The Garzón case probably exemplifies better than any other case the limits that, even today, the Amnesty Law poses to any potential judicial review of Spain's past.

Finally, the contrast between Spain and other cases, such as Argentina and Chile, which also had to deal with legal limits to prosecute perpetrators of human rights violations, is very indicative of the crucial (and even somewhat autonomous) impact that the judiciary has had in the reparation policies finally adopted in the three countries. There is an evident lack of will by Spanish judges to follow the pathways opened up in Latin America by their colleagues.

---

[69] "The example of the Ruano case would have allowed [...] all the victims of Francoism to put their tormentors and torturers in the dock and force them to acknowledge the facts and the political motive as a prerequisite for the application of amnesty. Unfortunately, this was only done in the Ruano case. A prosecution was not even initiated in the remaining cases." Ibid., 101.

# Conclusion

## Amnesty in the Age of Accountability

*Tricia D. Olsen, Leigh A. Payne, and Andrew G. Reiter*

Is amnesty an appropriate response to past human rights atrocities? This is the question that motivates this volume. That seemingly simple inquiry provokes many more questions. For those who answer "yes," for example, we would probe "under what conditions?" For those who answer "no," we might ask, "why have amnesties persisted despite the age of accountability?" The authors in this volume, however, do not give simple "yes" or "no" answers to the underlying question. They instead thoughtfully reflect on the conditions, relationships, patterns, and outcomes they observe in their research on amnesties and accountability in the contemporary era.

In this conclusion, we aim to summarize the main points that emerge from this set of historical, philosophical, cross-national, statistical, and qualitative case study analyses of amnesties. We begin by situating the arguments made in the previous chapters within the broader context of the transitional justice literature regarding amnesty. We then empirically examine the persistence of amnesty in the age of accountability. The third section of the chapter explores the multiple ways in which states have combined amnesty and accountability. In the last section of the chapter, we consider the future of amnesties and accountability based on the analysis provided in this volume. In all of these sections we draw not only on the theoretical and empirical analyses offered in this volume, but also on the broader transitional justice literature and empirical experiences.

## AMNESTIES AND TRANSITIONAL JUSTICE

The academic literature on transitional justice tends to overlook or condemn amnesties for past human rights violations, considering them anathema to international norms of accountability following past atrocity. Kathryn Sikkink's chapter on "The Age of Accountability" in this volume and her book-length treatment of the "justice cascade" illustrate this prevailing emphasis in the literature on the welcome arrival of trials that hold perpetrators criminally responsible for past human rights abuses.[1] International and domestic nongovernmental organizations, international governmental organizations, and states themselves have converged, forming accountability streams that challenge amnesty laws. While these efforts do not always succeed – indeed, Sikkink herself concurs with the empirical finding from Louise Mallinder's chapter in this volume that the threat of prosecution may even lead to new amnesty laws – the "challenger" approach recognizes and commends the global processes that have promoted retributive and restorative justice against amnesty and impunity.

By promoting justice to replace impunity, the "challenger" approach questions a "proponent" approach, or the view that amnesties can play a role in shielding transitional democracies from instability, ongoing conflict, and additional human rights abuses. Some existing scholarship suggests that prosecutions may jeopardize transitions from authoritarian rule and civil conflict, bringing negative outcomes rather than the positive ones they intend. Mark Freeman and Max Pensky's chapter in this volume questions whether "challengers" have adequately understood the ambiguity in international law surrounding amnesty. They suggest that international law is sometimes silent on amnesties or sometimes supportive of them, but it is not clear on the legitimacy of particular types, contexts, or content of amnesty provisions. Indeed, the authors note that the persistent adoption of amnesty across states and the ambiguities in that body of law in terms of what is left unsaid or unspecified, brings into question the "crystallization" of norm-barring amnesty practices. Those states seeking to justify amnesties may find international law less resolved and more malleable than "challengers" assume it to be.

Yet even while staking out arguments in favor of challenging amnesty laws or arguments that recognize their legitimacy in law, policy, and practice, the authors of the theoretical framing chapters join the authors of the empirical chapters in developing a more nuanced – "contingent" – approach to amnesty laws and processes. They show that in certain contexts amnesties may serve a purpose, particularly during early phases of transitions from authoritarian rule or civil conflict. Moreover, because of the wide variety of amnesties and their uses, they do not necessarily block trials, human rights, and democracy goals. Some authors in this volume suggest that amnesty laws and processes may even advance those goals under certain conditions. In the next section, we summarize the three broad approaches to amnesty in the field and situate the authors in this volume within those approaches.

### Challenger Approach

The challenger approach views amnesty as a barrier to improvements in human rights, and, therefore, an inappropriate mechanism for addressing past human rights

---

[1] Sikkink, *The Justice Cascade*.

abuses. This approach stems from the moral, political, and legal imperative to prosecute perpetrators of past human rights violations.

The challenger approach contends that states have a moral obligation to bring
justice to victims and survivors of past state crimes.[2] As Juan Méndez argues, "victims have a right to a process that fully restores them in the enjoyment of their
rights and in the dignity and worth that society owes to each of its members."[3] States
should also pursue accountability to separate individual guilt from collective guilt.
In other words, states have a duty to hold individual perpetrators accountable to
remove the stigma of guilt from innocent members of organizations that society
blames collectively for past atrocities. Amnesties potentially produce the opposite
result by perpetuating a culture of impunity that fails to end the cycle of human
rights violations.

Moreover, political and strategic considerations cannot justify states' decisions
to grant amnesties. On the contrary, a political obligation requires states to bring
former authoritarian forces and violent actors under control and lay the foundation
for the rule of law.[4] The challenger approach argues that, by adopting amnesties
and failing to deal with the past through trials, a state will encourage retributive
violence[5] or vigilante justice[6] and work against the promotion of human rights.

International law, moreover, imposes a duty to prosecute perpetrators of past
atrocities as the only effective remedy for victims of past human rights violations.[7]
The Convention on the Prevention and Punishment of the Crime of Genocide
(CPPCG); the Convention Against Torture and Other Cruel, Inhuman or
Degrading Treatment or Punishment (CAT); and customary international law
establish responsibilities for states to provide legal remedy for particular abuses.
The CPPCG explicitly states the duty of countries to enact domestic legislation
to punish perpetrators of genocide and their responsibility to provide effective

[2]   Kathleen D. Moore, *Pardons: Justice, Mercy, and the Public Interest* (New York: Oxford University
      Press, 1989); John J. Moore Jr., "Problems with Forgiveness: Granting Amnesty under the Arias Plan
      in Nicaragua and El Salvador," *Stanford Law Review* 43, no. 3 (1991).
[3]   Juan E. Méndez, "Accountability for Past Abuses," *Human Rights Quarterly* 19, no. 2 (1997), 277.
[4]   Payam Akhaven, "Justice in The Hague, Peace in the Former Yugoslavia? A Commentary on the
      United Nations War Crimes Tribunal," *Human Rights Quarterly* 20, no. 4 (1998).
[5]   John Borneman, *Settling Accounts: Violence, Justice, and Accountability in Postsocialist Europe*
      (Princeton: Princeton University Press, 1997); Richard J. Goldstone, "Exposing Human Rights
      Abuses – A Help or Hindrance to Reconciliation?" *Hastings Constitutional Law Quarterly* 22, no. 3
      (1995).
[6]   Bass, *Stay the Hand of Vengeance*.
[7]   Orentlicher, "Settling Accounts"; Roht-Arriaza, "State Responsibility"; Naomi Roht-Arriaza, ed.,
      *Impunity and Human Rights in International Law and Practice* (New York: Oxford University Press,
      1995); M. Cherif Bassiouni, "International Crimes: Jus Cogens and Obligatio Erga Omnes," *Law and
      Contemporary Problems* 59, no. 4 (1996); Scharf, "The Letter of the Law."

penalties for those found guilty. Likewise, the CAT compels countries to make all acts of torture offenses under their laws, and it requires state parties either to prosecute or to extradite alleged torturers. In addition, other international agreements that outlaw and punish hijacking, aircraft sabotage, the taking of hostages, and terrorism all include explicit extradition or punishment provisions.[8] These accountability provisions exist not only to punish, but also to deter future human rights violations.

Legal interpretations of other international treaties – including the International Covenant on Civil and Political Rights (ICCPR), the European Convention for the Protection of Human Rights and Fundamental Freedoms (ECPHR), and the American Convention on Human Rights (ACHR) – also consider prosecutions and punishments the only effective means of ensuring protection of the rights enumerated within the treaties. The European Court of Human Rights (ECtHR) and the IACtHR have ruled that criminal accountability is the only effective remedy for violations of the European and American Conventions and the only means to reduce human rights violations in member countries.[9]

The challenger approach thus argues that amnesty processes, particularly "blanket amnesties," block human rights goals by perpetuating a culture of impunity. This approach advocates human rights trials to raise the cost of committing future atrocities, establish effective judicial institutions, and meet states' obligations to victims and survivors. The specific features associated with human rights trials – costs to individual perpetrators, a normative shift from impunity, and institution building – deter human rights violations and strengthen democratic mechanisms. The challenger approach thus advocates invalidating those amnesty laws, or at least weakening them, to allow for accountability.

Several chapters in this book, besides Sikkink's, document the process by which international and domestic governmental and nongovernmental strategies have weakened amnesties and promoted accountability. The most dramatic example is perhaps Argentina's process of annulling its amnesty law, recounted in Par Engstrom and Gabriel Pereira's chapter. Yet Francesca Lessa's chapter on Uruguay also shows the dramatic shift from endorsing to rejecting amnesty laws. Other chapters lament the limited success of similar challenges, particularly Emily Braid and Naomi Roht-Arriaza's chapter on Guatemala and El Salvador. Similarly, Patrick Burgess considers the conundrum of the persistence of de facto amnesties and the absence of individual criminal accountability in Indonesia, despite impressive international and domestic efforts to bring perpetrators to justice.

---

[8]  Roht-Arriaza, "State Responsibility," 464–5.
[9]  Ibid., 471–2; Orentlicher, "Settling Accounts," 2580.

## *Proponent Approach*

In contrast to the challenger approach, the proponent approach focuses on the value of amnesty and its persistence. Amnesty provides a mechanism to defuse the threat from former authoritarian regime forces, establish peace, safeguard democracy, and allow human rights protections to flourish. Failure to promote amnesties may jeopardize the transition process, possibly even provoking an authoritarian reversal with grave consequences for human rights and the stability of new democracies.

The proponent approach views amnesty as essential to striking the political bargains that facilitate institution building and strengthen the rule of law.[10] Though many may consider amnesties unjust for victims of human rights violations, they may justify their use in terms of their long-term capacity to reduce future injustices or deflect other grave social harms. Amnesties provide "a far stronger base for democracy than efforts to prosecute one side or the other or both," some proponents contend.[11]

Historically, countries have employed amnesties in conflict scenarios as an incentive to gain a tentative peace before the transition process begins.[12] Outgoing regimes have also initiated amnesties to secure their withdrawal from power. Amnesties further reassure former regime forces and their supporters that they may continue to play a role within the new political system and need not overthrow it.[13] For example, in the Argentine case, some scholars contend that amnesties successfully professionalized and depoliticized the armed forces.[14]

In addition, according to Jon Elster, hard and soft constraints limit states' ability to pursue justice in new democracies.[15] Hard constraints, originating in the dynamics of the transition itself, make some options "absolutely unfeasible."[16] There may be a tradeoff between justice and the very survival of the new regime. Soft constraints, such as the need for economic reconstruction or the transition to a market economy, limit the feasibility of prosecutions and reparations in the eyes of the new regime. The proponent approach thus views amnesty as the most effective means of dealing

---

[10] Tonya Putnam, "Human Rights and Sustainable Peace," in *Ending Civil Wars: The Implementation of Peace Agreements*, ed. Stephen J. Stedman, Donald Rothchild, and Elizabeth M. Cousens (Boulder, CO: Lynne Rienner, 2002).

[11] Huntington, *The Third Wave.*

[12] For a historical discussion of the use of amnesties, see O'Shea, *Amnesty for Crime in International Law and Practice.*

[13] Snyder and Vinjamuri, "Trials and Errors."

[14] Zagorski, "Civil-Military Relations and Argentine Democracy."

[15] Jon Elster, *Retribution and Reparation in the Transition to Democracy* (Cambridge, U.K.: Cambridge University Press, 2006), 188–215.

[16] Ibid., 188.

with the past, by reducing violence, protecting the transition process, and concentrating on forward-looking issues for the new regime's success.

Those advocating the proponent approach do not view amnesties as amnesia or impunity. On the contrary, they suggest that amnesties inherently acknowledge past crimes and advance justice. An official amnesty law identifies certain acts as criminal, and thus, as Mallinder contends, it is not necessarily associated with amnesia.[17] Freeman further states, "Rather than be cast as the antithesis of transitional justice, amnesty becomes its enabler by potentially helping to pave the way at the national level for increased truth, reparation, and reform with respect to past violations, and for increased democracy, peace, and justice in the long term."[18]

The vulnerability of transitions from authoritarian rule creates an imperative for protecting human rights with amnesties. In some cases, amnesties provide the tools new democratic governments require to acknowledge past violations as crimes, appease potential spoilers to avoid jeopardizing the democratic process, and safeguard that process to allow for human rights protections. The proponent approach, therefore, contends that amnesty can improve human rights, while human rights improvements often deteriorate in transitions that eschew amnesties.

The proponent view is not limited to the practical solutions amnesties provide. Freeman and Pensky also argue in this volume that challengers have exaggerated the international consensus on norms regarding accountability and the use of amnesties. They show that legal doctrine does not specifically define the legitimacy or validity of amnesties. The international community lacks consensus in its pressure to weaken amnesties. The Geneva Convention, for example, suggests that in certain contexts international law promotes the use of amnesty. Amnesties persist, in other words, not only because of the failure of the international community to act, but also because the international community and domestic actors justify them as good practice in particular contexts.

Such a view is somewhat evident in this volume. In addition to the discussion by Freeman and Pensky on the ambiguities in international law regarding amnesties, some of the empirical chapters highlight potential justifications for them. The Brazilian case, discussed by Paulo Abrão and Marcelo Torelly, and the Spanish case, examined by Paloma Aguilar, show that some amnesty processes receive widespread support within civil society. This support emerges not only from those associated with the former authoritarian regime, but also from its opposition. In these contexts, amnesties achieve a form of legitimacy by providing the means to end conflict, restore citizenship, consolidate democracy, and look to the future. Trials, amnesty proponents argue, could plunge the country anew into polarized divisions,

---

[17] Mallinder, *Amnesty, Human Rights and Political Transitions*, 14.
[18] Freeman, *Necessary Evils*, 19.

threatening peace and democracy. The increase in amnesty laws, documented in Mallinder's cross-national study, confirms that amnesties continue to have some legitimacy and appeal even in the age of accountability.

## Contingent Approach

Another view of amnesties, the contingent approach, accepts that amnesties may, under certain conditions, advance positive outcomes and, more important, do not necessarily block accountability. Most of the authors in this volume, and in the broad transitional justice literature, would fall into the contingent approach. Even scholars concerned about the difficulty of pursuing accountability when amnesties persist might recognize the importance of accepting amnesty as the cost of ending conflict and facilitating transitions from authoritarian rule. These scholars, however, might defend the moral, legal, and political duties to hold perpetrators of human rights violations accountable, but judge certain political moments inauspicious for pursuing such goals, advocating instead a more gradual process of delayed justice. Other scholars may view amnesties as acceptable, and perhaps even instrumental, as long as they form part of a set of transitional justice mechanisms that includes restorative or retributive justice mechanisms. The contingent approach may also consider certain accountability mechanisms, such as truth commissions, reparations, or lustration, less risky than trials and therefore more compatible with amnesty processes.[19] Decisions regarding amnesty therefore do not evolve in a void, but rather are contingent, "dictated, in most instances, by the mode and politics of the particular situation."[20] Those on board with the contingent approach recognize that a new democracy's bold and blind promotion of prosecutions might jeopardize the survival of the regime. Some concessions to actors who threaten the transition process may be necessary to secure the transition, but such concessions do not necessarily take accountability off the table forever.[21] The contingent approach further recognizes

[19] Neil J. Kritz, "Coming to Terms with Atrocities: A Review of Accountability Mechanisms for Mass Violations of Human Rights," *Law and Contemporary Problems* 59, no. 4 (1996); Martha Minow, *Between Vengeance and Forgiveness: Facing History after Genocide and Mass Violence* (Boston: Beacon Press, 1998); Ruti G. Teitel, "How Are the New Democracies of the Southern Cone Dealing with the Legacy of Past Human Rights Abuses?" (paper presented to Council on Foreign Relations, May 17, 1990), excerpted and reprinted in *Transitional Justice: How Emerging Democracies Reckon with Former Regimes,* ed. Neil Kritz (Washington, DC: United States Institute of Peace, 1995).

[20] Alexander L. Boraine, "South Africa's Amnesty Revisited," in Villa-Vicencio and Doxtader, *The Provocations of Amnesty.*

[21] Jaime Malamud-Goti, "Trying Violators of Human Rights: The Dilemma of Transitional Governments," in *State Crimes: Punishment or Pardon,* ed. Aspen Institute Justice and Society Program (Wye Center, MD: Aspen Institute, 1989); Jamie Malamud-Goti, "Transitional Governments in the Breach: Why Punish State Criminals?" *Human Rights Quarterly* 12, no. 1 (1990); Aryeh Neier, "What Should Be Done about the Guilty?" *New York Review of Books,* February 1, 1990; Nino, "The Duty to Punish"; Nino, *Radical Evil.*

that putting all perpetrators on trial is probably neither possible nor desirable, given the pressing political and economic context in which newly elected leaders must operate. Thus, the contingent approach promotes a middle ground between full judicial accountability and impunity.

To achieve this middle ground, the contingent approach outlines a number of potential pathways. Some contingent approach scholars might advance truth commissions, for example, to establish accountability through the public exposure and condemnation of perpetrators for their past violence. Truth commissions potentially restore the dignity of citizens victimized by the violence by publicly confirming their accounts of past criminal acts. Indeed, according to their advocates, truth commissions acknowledge, condemn, and deter violence more effectively than trials, and they do so without jeopardizing democracy and rule of law. They provide a victim-centered process of accountability that balances political constraints with justice demands. Victim-centered processes might also include financial, medical, or symbolic restoration for survivors of past violence. While supporters of the old regime often dislike these mechanisms, they are unlikely to threaten the new democratic regime because of them, particularly if states simultaneously amnesty those associated with the previous regime.

The South African Truth and Reconciliation Commission (TRC), as described by Antje du Bois-Pedain in this volume, predicated amnesty on perpetrators' public confessions of past political atrocities. The amnesty encouraged perpetrators to come forward and, in some cases, to communicate directly with their victims and ask for forgiveness. Far from a culture of impunity, therefore, these processes can hold perpetrators individually accountable for past crimes without jeopardizing the political transition. The South African TRC threatened prosecutions for perpetrators who failed to participate in the process or who failed to receive amnesty due to incomplete confessions. The success of amnesty in promoting truth and reconciliation was, thus, contingent on perpetrators' confessions and the threat of prosecution.

Writing on Rwanda and Uganda, Phil Clark examines another possible contingent approach. In both cases, international actors have pressed for individual criminal accountability – at the UN ad hoc International Criminal Tribunal for Rwanda and, for Uganda, at the ICC. Clark suggests, however, that innovative amnesty processes in which perpetrators participate in community justice mechanisms may deliver a greater sense and scope of justice to most victims of past violence. He suggests, therefore, that amnesty may provide more room for these innovative mechanisms that deliver more, not less, justice. This is particularly true, he argues, in contexts of massive and intimate violence, where most victims reside far from the adjudicating courts, and where local justice mechanisms have some legitimacy. In his view, meaningful justice is contingent on restorative local processes that often involve amnesties.

The success of amnesty laws in improving human rights and democracy may also prove contingent on the content of those laws. Ronald Slye points this out in his description of limited amnesty in Cambodia that specified a six-month window for application and explicitly excluded the leadership of the Khmer Rouge. The notion of limited amnesty assumes that such processes will allow for some accountability, thereby strengthening rule of law, democracy, and human rights. Amnesties' success in promoting justice is thus contingent on accompanying retributive or restorative justice processes.

The notion of amnesty in combination with accountability to bring human rights improvements extends beyond the volume's cases analyzed here. Our previous analysis of the Transitional Justice Data Base, a cross-national study of transitional justice mechanisms, illustrates the use and effectiveness of this combination.[22] We examine ninety-one transitions in seventy-four countries and find that statistically neither trials alone (challenger approach) nor amnesties alone (proponent approach) correlate with improvements in human rights and democracy. The combination of amnesties and trials, with or without truth commissions, however, has a positive, statistically significant effect on changes in human rights and democracy measures. We find, in other words, that amnesties' success in promoting human rights and democracy is likely contingent upon their coexistence with trials.

To explain our findings, we developed a "justice balance" argument to capture the combination of accountability and amnesty mechanisms. The argument hinges on both amnesty and accountability playing a role in bringing improvements in human rights and democracy. We contend that amnesties provide the necessary stability to advance democracy and human rights goals and institutions. We further argue that trials develop judicial institutions to improve democracy and deter human rights violations. Each of these mechanisms, in other words, is contingent on the other to improve human rights and democracy.[23]

In terms of the stability function of amnesties, we examine economic and political concerns. In terms of economic stability, we found that countries with stagnating economies were more likely to adopt amnesties than countries with higher levels of economic growth. This provides some evidence to support our conclusion that democratic leaders may choose to use amnesties to enhance stability during periods of low economic growth and when costly trials could jeopardize the democratic transition. This evidence further suggests that countries emerging from widespread authoritarian state violence and civil conflict may not have yet achieved the level of economic development associated with strong judicial institutions, professional personnel, legal capacity, or funds to promote human rights trials. The economic or

---

[22]  Olsen, Payne, and Reiter, *The Justice Balance*.
[23]  Ibid.

developmental concerns that exist in transitional states do not necessarily endure, allowing for the possibility of holding perpetrators criminally accountable over time. In addition, countries may opt to grant amnesties to protect some perpetrators from justice while holding others accountable. These models provide both sequential and simultaneous combinations of amnesties and trials.

Political instability may also constrain governments' transitional justice decisions. Vulnerable democracies may choose amnesty to appease supporters of the former regime, thereby fortifying the new democracy against potential spoilers. We find, for example, that governments use trials most often in democratic transitions in which the former authoritarian regime collapses. In situations in which the former authoritarian regime negotiates its way out of power – where spoilers would likely be present – new democracies tend to avoid trials. We also find that the longer an authoritarian regime holds power and the worse its repression, the more likely the new democracy is to grant an amnesty. States are thus most likely to adopt amnesty in situations where authoritarian actors are deeply institutionalized and where more individuals are complicit in human rights violations. Stated bluntly, new regimes tend to use amnesty in situations in which former authoritarian actors are most likely to resist attempts to pursue a path of accountability. Over time, however, these spoilers may no longer represent a threat, opening up the possibility of holding perpetrators accountable. In addition, accountability may take the form of finding justice for certain abuses or abusers, while granting amnesty for others. Again, amnesty and accountability can follow sequential or simultaneous patterns of adoption.

The justice balance, and other contingent approaches, thus helps us explain the persistence of amnesty in the age of accountability. It suggests that transitional countries adopt amnesties and trials, rather than choosing between these mechanisms. It further suggests that with a balanced use of both amnesties and trials countries are likely to improve human rights and democracy outcomes. The theoretical approaches that advocate one mechanism instead of a specific combination, therefore, reflect neither contemporary transitional justice decisions nor effective outcomes.

## THE AGE OF ACCOUNTABILITY OR THE AGE OF AMNESTY?

Empirical evidence suggests that states are increasingly adopting the contingent approach to address past human rights violations. Mallinder demonstrates that amnesty laws have increased, rather than declined, perhaps in response to the threat of trials. She does not dispute the global spread of the accountability norm and the creation of institutions to promote it, but she suggests that, paradoxically, the norm might bring more, not fewer, amnesty protections for perpetrators of past violence.

While operationalizing amnesties differently from Mallinder,[24] in our previous work we also find that the level of amnesties has not dropped off despite the increase in trials during the age of accountability. We see a steady rate of amnesties that does not increase or decrease dramatically over time or with the rising threat of prosecutions. We take this to mean that amnesties have always had appeal as a mechanism to deal with past violence and they will likely retain that appeal. What is different, therefore, is the rise in the number of trials. Regardless of whether the number of trials goes up or down, however, amnesties have remained, and will likely to continue to remain, steady.

In addition to noting the persistence of amnesties, therefore, we also can confirm the age of accountability. While measuring trials differently than Sikkink does, we still find a dramatic increase in trials over time.[25] In addition, when we account for the number of transitions in recent decades, and thus establish a rate of trials, we still find an increase in human rights trial verdicts during this era. Because amnesties remain consistent over the period in which trials increase, our findings cannot confirm that trials replace amnesties in the age of accountability. The age of accountability thus refers to an era in which the use of trials increases, but not an era in which amnesties decline. We see the persistence of amnesties even in the age of accountability. Trials and amnesties are compatible, not tradeoffs. Countries may opt for amnesties and trials, rather than selecting one mechanism or the other.

Examining recent transitions enables us to further explore trends in the use of amnesty during the age of accountability. If we use General Augusto Pinochet's arrest in London in 1998 as a starting point for the global threat of prosecution, we see the negligible impact of the Pinochet effect on domestic prosecutions. Only two countries transitioning after 1998 adopted trials without amnesties (Serbia and Montenegro and Sierra Leone). In contrast, four adopted amnesties without trials (Algeria, Guinea-Bissau, Niger, and Nigeria). Six countries used neither trials nor amnesties, suggesting the use of de facto amnesties (Armenia, Cote d'Ivoire, Croatia, Kenya, Lesotho, and Senegal).[26] These results further show the persistent use of de facto and de jure amnesties despite the age of accountability.

---

[24] As described in Mallinder's chapter in this volume, the Amnesty Law Database defines amnesties more broadly as any amnesty that is a de jure measure, enacted by the state through laws, peace agreements, or executive policies and is related to political sanctions. Amnesties must also be formally implemented.

[25] Sikkink, as she explains in her chapter, defines trials as the full range of prosecutorial activity, while we look only at verdicts. This means Sikkink's Human Rights Prosecution Data Base notes the prosecutorial activity each year, and our research notes only those cases that end in a verdict and only the year in which the verdict was rendered. See http://www.tc.umn.edu/~kimx0759/thrp.website/home. html.

[26] Tricia D. Olsen, Leigh A. Payne, and Andrew G. Reiter, "Amnesty Laws in the Age of Accountability" (paper presented at the Law and Society Association Annual Meeting, San Francisco, June 2–5, 2011).

Rather than viewing amnesties as a response to the threat of trials in the age of accountability, or the age of accountability as the end of the age of amnesty, our cross-national data confirms what the authors in this volume have written about: multiple amnesty and trial scenarios in the age of accountability. While we found in the justice balance that combinations of trials and amnesties are likely to produce positive changes in human rights and democracy outcomes, these combinations are not always guaranteed to unfold nor will they always bring positive results. Drawing on the empirical case studies in this volume, we can begin to explore what factors likely lead to positive combinations of trials and amnesties, and what factors may block those positive outcomes.

## AMNESTY AND ACCOUNTABILITY SCENARIOS

From the challenger (trials only), to the contingent (trials and amnesty), to the proponent (amnesty only) approaches to amnesty in the age of accountability, transitional justice choices are assumed to affect outcomes for human rights and democracy. The chapters in this book allow us to further develop those arguments and attempt to explain when certain mechanisms or combinations are likely to produce positive political outcomes, when they are not, and why.

The chapters in this book allow us to develop a set of scenarios in which transitional countries have combined amnesties and accountability. On one end of that continuum is the scenario in which amnesty is democratically displaced, allowing for accountability without the constraint of the amnesty process. Close to that end of the continuum, some counties have not achieved legal annulment of amnesty laws, but have still found ways to challenge them legally, or to creatively circumvent them. These two categories, we argue, offer the greatest likelihood of improvements in democracy and human rights. Consistent with the justice balance argument, the amnesty law allowed sufficient stability to advance democracy in the early transition years. Democratic stability then allowed for challenges to the amnesty law to allow for trials, building stronger judiciaries and rights-based democracies.

If the first set of amnesty-accountability scenarios shifts toward accountability and away from amnesty, the second set moves in the other direction, toward amnesty and away from accountability. In some situations, human rights organizations, victim-survivor groups, lawyers, and judges prove incapable of sufficiently weakening amnesty laws. Due to direct or indirect domestic and international pressure, however, some trials occur. These trials in some cases may be the exceptions that confirm the culture of impunity. Thus, although amnesty and accountability coexist, the few trials that have occurred have not succeeded in building strong and independent judiciaries, provided judicial access to citizens, or made it clear that human rights abuses will be legally sanctioned. This creates an accountability impasse in

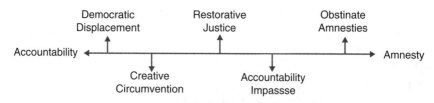

FIGURE C.1. Amnesty-accountability continuum.

which trials occur, but without significantly undermining the amnesty law. On the other end of the continuum, amnesty is obstinately preserved, with very little, if any, room for trials. States may pursue other types of transitional justice mechanisms, but the strong presence of amnesties blocks trials from taking place. In this scenario, the outcome of strong judiciaries to independently pursue human rights cases, the access to justice for victims-survivors of past human rights abuses, and the deterrence function of trials do not emerge.

Somewhere in the middle of this continuum is a combination of amnesties and accountability that involves a range of different accountability measures, including trials. In this scenario, the limitations of individual criminal accountability, specifically the failure to hold all perpetrators accountable in a court of law, may be addressed by instituting restorative justice mechanisms. These restorative justice mechanisms supplement accountability, while simultaneously reinforcing amnesties and pardons (Figure C.1).

The authors in this volume, and the transitional justice literature and practices more generally, identify factors that might explain the placement of particular countries along this continuum. These include: sequencing mechanisms, the level of threat from spoilers, the strength of proaccountability actors and governments, support or resistance from the international community, and the political and economic costs of trials or amnesties. We discuss each scenario in more detail later, using the eleven country case studies included in this volume as illustration.

### *Democratic Displacement*

This pathway describes those processes in which democratic governments that initially accept blanket amnesties subsequently overturn them, removing the amnesty obstacle to prosecuting perpetrators of past human rights abuses. In this case, amnesties provide much needed stability through the initial period of the transition. Once the country firmly establishes the democratic rules of the game, trials follow. These trials end the culture of impunity, restore or create sufficiently powerful courts to initiate individual criminal prosecutions, and provide judicial access to victims-survivors of human rights abuses.

Argentina, as Engstrom and Pereira describe in their chapter, could represent any of the scenarios developed in this chapter at different transitional justice phases. The authoritarian regime adopted a self-amnesty (1983) before relinquishing power. In 1984, however, trials began, and by July 1984, approximately 250 members of the armed services had been convicted. This was followed by the well-known trial of the juntas (1985). Responding to military threats, democratic governments initiated amnesty laws and presidential pardons following these trials (1986, 1987, 1989, and 1990). The Supreme Court, however, ruled against the amnesty laws, allowing trials to recommence in 2006. To date, over 700 individuals face trial for past human rights violations and 187 human rights violators have been convicted and are behind bars in Argentina.[27] Argentina thus appears to embody the global accountability norm and its capacity to erode old amnesty provisions in favor of justice. It represents the democratic displacement of amnesty with accountability.

Few other countries had the same factors in place that would allow them to repeal amnesty laws. In that sense, Argentina is unique due to: the collapse of the authoritarian regime; the persistence, energy, and strength of the victim-survivor, human rights, and legal communities; and foreign courts and the IACtHR engagement with past domestic and international human rights violations. Even during the various amnesty periods, justice entrepreneurs found loopholes to hold perpetrators accountable, most notably around the kidnapping of children and in the truth trials. Political will also played a key role with the initiation of trials in the first democratic government after the dictatorship under former President Raúl Alfonsín and the emphasis former President Néstor Kirchner placed on human rights trials two decades later. Certain judges also actively pursued cases brought by legal representatives of human rights and victim-survivor groups. The combination of high demand for justice in society and government, responsive courts, an engaged international human rights community, and little support for spoilers, allowed the Kirchner government and Argentina to move farther to displace the amnesty law than in any other case.

Lessa shows a similar example of democratic displacement of the amnesty law in Uruguay. Since 2005, the executive has adopted a more progressive interpretation of the amnesty law, allowing some prosecutions of past human rights violations to take place. In 2009, Uruguay's Supreme Court ruled the amnesty law unconstitutional. That ruling did not strike down the amnesty law, but rendered it inapplicable in a particular case. This decision opened up the possibility of individual criminal accountability in the Sabalsagaray case within the confines of a valid amnesty law. Lessa writes about the perception of the law within Uruguayan society, and focuses

---

[27] CELS, "Crímenes del terrorismo de estado – Weblogs de las causas," accessed August 4, 2011, http://www.cels.org.ar/wpblogs/.

particularly on the two plebiscites held in 1989 and 2009. She contrasts the earlier narrow defeat of the referendum (fifty-six percent) to a strong perception within Uruguay that trials could jeopardize the democratic process[28] with a more subtle interpretation of the recent 2009 plebiscite. The peculiarities of the ballot format and the lack of political party support at key moments may better explain the outcome than strong societal support for amnesty.

Even before the derogation of the amnesty provisions in October 2011, former President Bordaberry faced house arrest and imprisonment for forced disappearance and homicide before he died in 2011. In other cases, Presidents Vázquez (2005–10) and Mujica (2010–15) have used the discretion provided by the law to put other perpetrators on trial. These presidents' decisions receive support from a mobilized human rights and legal community, which nearly defeated the amnesty law in both public votes.[29]

In sum, Argentina and Uruguay show that countries might move along the amnesty-accountability continuum from one end to the other. The exceptional set of propitious factors, however, shows that most countries are unlikely to replicate this process and may become stuck along the way, either on the amnesty or accountability ends of the continuum.

## Creative Circumvention

Efforts by particular groups in society can find ways around amnesty laws to promote trials. They may not succeed in displacing those laws; rather trials coexist with them. Engstrom and Pereira discuss the differences between the outcome of the ebb and flow of the Argentine process that eventually led to annulling the amnesty law and the Chilean process in which the amnesty remains in place. Trials have occurred nonetheless in Chile. Indeed, in one recent assessment, Chile has outpaced Argentina in trying perpetrators despite the continued legality of the Chilean amnesty law and the annulment of the Argentine one.[30] Chile thus provides an example of creative circumvention.

Chile shows that trials and amnesties can coexist without forgoing accountability. By retaining amnesties, rather than displacing them, their value of appeasing potential spoilers and their supporters continues even if only symbolically. On the other hand, creative uses of the amnesty provisions and the opportunities presented by challenges to the law have allowed for individual criminal accountability. Many of

---

[28] Barahona de Brito, "Truth, Justice, Memory."

[29] For a detailed discussion of the Uruguayan case see Gabriela Fried and Francesca Lessa, eds., *Luchas contra la impunidad: Uruguay 1985–2011* (Montevideo: Trilce, 2011).

[30] Human Rights Observatory, "Human Rights in Chile," Universidad Diego Portales, Santiago, Chile Bulletin No. 4, March 2010.

the factors present in the democratic displacement scenario have allowed for progress along the amnesty-accountability continuum (e.g., the persistence, energy, and strength of the victim-survivor, human rights, and legal communities; foreign courts and the IACtHR engagement with past domestic and international human rights violations; legal loopholes and the efforts by justice entrepreneurs to pursue them; political will at key moments). Chile also represents an example of a negotiated transition in which supporters of the original amnesty law continue to successfully defend its legality even after it has lost much of its power to protect perpetrators.

## Restorative Justice

As some of the authors in this volume point out, and as the transitional justice literature as a whole emphasizes, individual criminal accountability may not be the only, or even the best, measure of accountability. The decision to adopt other forms of accountability may sometimes result from the lack of confidence in the judiciary's capacity or fairness or from political and economic impediments blocking individual criminal court cases. Indeed, in some cases restorative justice mechanisms coexist with individual criminal trials. Restorative justice advocates, however, tend to perceive other forms of accountability not only as practical alternatives, but also preferable alternatives to individual criminal accountability. Restorative justice tends to coexist comfortably, and may even directly involve amnesty or pardon processes. When amnesties and pardons form part of the restorative justice process, they tend to enhance the stability of the new government, particularly by incorporating former perpetrators into democratic civil society. The search for restorative justice alternatives or supplements to the individual criminal accountability model seems to emerge in contexts of massive human rights abuses that would otherwise overwhelm the number and capacity of domestic courts. Another factor that explains the emergence of this model is the prior politicization of ethnic or racial division in society that could threaten to reerupt with the perception of trials as political, ethnic, or racial vendettas.

Three countries explored in this volume – South Africa, Rwanda, and Uganda – fit this category of restorative justice. Some trials have occurred in each of these countries. But each country has also explored alternative restorative justice mechanisms to individual criminal accountability. These alternatives combine amnesties and pardons with noncriminal forms of accountability.

In the case of South Africa, the use of reputational costs to perpetrators by inducing them to make public confessions of their past political crimes is documented in du Bois-Pedain's chapter. The threat of trials for those who failed to apply for amnesty, or who did not receive it, no doubt encouraged perpetrators to participate in the process and provide information on their past political crimes. It is quite clear that without this process, and relying solely on individual criminal prosecutions, South Africans would know less about past clandestine activities of the apartheid security forces. Several of the high-level trials that did occur ended in innocent, rather than guilty, verdicts, increasingly showing the limits of the individual criminal accountability model. The South African process therefore questions whether individual criminal accountability is the only, or the best, form of addressing past atrocities. The South African model further suggests that combining amnesty with criminal and noncriminal forms of accountability may offer an innovative way of enhancing transitional justice objectives.

Clark's discussion of Uganda and Rwanda further suggests that individual criminal accountability for high-ranking officials, in the context of massive violations and weak judicial systems, may backfire and render a sense of less, rather than more, justice. Top leaders are held accountable for past abuses in international courts far from the places where the atrocities occurred. At the same time, local-level initiatives have combined criminal as well as noncriminal accountability mechanisms with amnesty processes to bring justice to victims and survivors. These local initiatives face significant challenges but they are more finely attuned to the particularities of the conflicts in question than international criminal court processes. Clark suggests, moreover, that the focus on individual criminal accountability for senior officials as the only valid response to past atrocity tends to invalidate innovative forms of justice. He further suggests that by incorporating victims and perpetrators directly into community justice processes, local mechanisms may better achieve the goals of democratic citizenship, human rights norms, peace, and stability.

In all three cases, amnesties play a crucial role in limiting trials and facilitating alternative forms of accountability. Restorative justice, particularly in situations in which the number of perpetrators is great and state capacity to prosecute is low, can be a crucial tool in bringing some sense of accountability to victims and society, while at the same time developing democracy and human rights objectives.

## Accountability Impasse

Various chapters in this volume expose how the path toward individual criminal accountability has seemed to have begun, trials have taken place, but without producing justice. These might be considered "hijacked" justice processes in which governments pay lip service to the accountability norm without implementing any serious costs to committing past atrocity. They might do so for cynical reasons, only superficially complying with an international accountability norm to receive reputational or aid benefits and distorting the norm in the process.[31] Those searching

---

[31] Jelena Subotic, *Hijacked Justice: Dealing with the Past in the Balkans* (Ithaca: Cornell University Press, 2009).

for evidence of individual criminal accountability may mistake the shallow gestures toward accountability as justice and ignore the severe constraints that continue to block justice efforts.

The chapter on Cambodia by Slye and the chapter on Guatemala and El Salvador by Braid and Roht-Arriaza provide an illustration. All three countries have adopted amnesties as part of an internationalized peace process. They have also had some prosecutorial activity. As the authors of these case studies show, however, it remains to be seen whether the initiation of prosecutions will firmly establish independent and capable judiciaries to pursue individual criminal accountability and to provide judicial remedy to victims and survivors. Both chapters raise some doubt about such an outcome and, instead, perceive the few trials as exceptions to the accountability impasse. This impasse seems to emerge from the lack of political will to pursue criminal accountability, complicity of political leaders in past violence, corruption, and weak and compromised judicial institutions.

El Salvador makes clear that neither party to the peace agreement – the government of El Salvador or the Farabundi Marti Liberation Front – would have accepted a ceasefire without the amnesty for both sides that participated in the armed conflict. However, the 1993 amnesty law, which superseded the 1992 National Reconciliation Law passed at the time of the peace accords, was unconditional and broad, extinguishing any criminal and civil liability for human rights violations. The chapter by Braid and Roht-Arriaza shows that the recent efforts at initiating accountability processes have continued to meet great institutional resistance owing to the persistent control over politics of those complicit in past atrocity and the likelihood that those individuals remain involved in ongoing violence in the country.

The Guatemalan case resembles El Salvador in adopting a peacemaking amnesty and then later initiating trials. The Guatemalan amnesty, however, is remarkable in excluding human rights violators from its beneficiaries. This should have opened up the possibility of trials for past human rights violations. As Braid and Roht-Arriaza show, progress has been extremely slow on that front. Guatemalan courts only recently convicted and imprisoned several military officers, including those involved in the murder of Bishop Juan José Gerardi Conedera, the author of the Catholic Church's truth commission report (REMHI). The even more recent August 2011 decision to sentence the four soldiers in the 1982 killings in the Las Dos Erres case to 6,060 years of imprisonment each suggests that Guatemala has begun to chip away at the impunity fortress.[32] Braid and Roht-Arriaza, however, question whether these important judicial decisions indicate a meaningful shift away from impunity, and do not instead serve as mere exceptions that confirm the impunity rule in Central America.

[32] "Guatemala Dos Erres Massacre Soldiers Sentenced," *BBC News*, August 3, 2011, accessed September 14, 2011, http://www.bbc.co.uk/news/world-latin-america-14383071.

The Cambodian government, Slye shows us, has applied and ignored amnesties for the Khmer Rouge perpetrators of the Cambodian genocide at different political moments. The creation, under some international pressure, of the hybrid Extraordinary Chambers lowered the economic and political cost of prosecuting a few top Khmer Rouge officials. But it may have also signaled a shift toward the individual criminal accountability model. Such a model might implicate those at the top of the current government in past atrocities, as well as current abuses, thereby reducing the appeal of trials among current government officials. The hybrid trial model, while seeming to overcome the important constraints on individual criminal accountability in the form of judicial capacity and high costs, suggests that these – and other – models may continue to face constraints due to the lack of domestic political will.

The persistence of beneficiaries of amnesty processes in positions of political power will likely bring an accountability impasse. This does not mean that trials will not occur. On the contrary, we have seen in Cambodia, El Salvador, and Guatemala that they will. It does cast doubt on whether these trials will achieve the goal of shifting domestic norms toward accountability and away from amnesty. Such an impasse, moreover, will likely constrain the processes of building independent judiciaries and providing access to justice for victims and survivors. Improvements in human rights and democracy may still occur from a very low initial baseline; but progress may falter like the accountability process itself. On the other hand, these examples of prosecutions may awaken a dormant human rights community capable of using the opportunities opened up by trials to push for more, thus moving along the continuum toward accountability.

### Obstinate Amnesties

Finally, in this scenario, de facto or de jure amnesties block accountability efforts. In some cases, trials begin and are subsequently reversed with amnesties due to threats of violence. In other cases, trials occur, but only long after the end of violence to avoid any threats to the system. In most cases of obstinate amnesties, these amnesties persist unchallenged. Governments use the perceived or real threat of violence as evidence that the country cannot pursue trials. Trials would jeopardize the democratic and human rights gains of the transitional governments and beyond. Retrospective justice would accomplish little, and the costs – rancor, revenge, and instability – would undermine national peace and the pact upon which it is based.

The chapters on Spain by Aguilar, Indonesia by Burgess, and Brazil by Abrão and Torelly illustrate the obstinate amnesty scenario. Not all of these countries resemble each other. Brazil and Spain may look more similar because both have deflected any challenges to their amnesty laws. Indonesia, on the other hand, never established an amnesty law for perpetrators and convicted perpetrators (subsequently exonerated). Brazil, however, has diverged from the Spanish obstinate amnesty model by initiating truth processes, and eventually an official truth commission. In terms of determining key explanatory factors behind obstinate amnesties, the strongest similarities seem to be weak accountability proponents in comparison with opponents, and the capacity on the part of political leaders to draw on cultural and historical understandings of past violence to offset challenges to the amnesty law from civil society, the legislature, and the judiciary.

In Spain, the defense of the amnesty law as a necessary mechanism to maintain peace has lasted for over forty years. While civil war has ended, many fear that opening up a debate over prosecutions would necessarily involve revisiting the civil war and the violence that tore apart the country, communities, and families. Although the violence occurred long ago, the persistent terrorist violence from Basque separatists reminds Spaniards of the precariousness of peace. Accountability, therefore, seems to take the form of responsibility to protect the country from renewed conflict; it is not about holding individuals criminally responsible for past violence. In such a context, as Aguilar suggests, justice entrepreneurs advancing the individual criminal accountability model may not find resonance, and instead face sanctions. Paradoxically, the role that Spain played in catalyzing human rights trials in Chile and Latin America, through its use of universal jurisdiction, has been blocked in initiating investigations of its own past human rights atrocities.

As in Spain, Brazil's amnesty law dates back to the late 1970s. Paralleling Spain's experience, Brazil has faced no successful challenges to its amnesty law. The challenges Brazil has faced, however, suggest that the country might move toward accountability on the continuum. Specifically, Brazil has been forced to confront condemnation of its amnesty law by the IACtHR. Various domestic courts have also reconsidered the amnesty law. The government's own documents and truth gathering processes have further revealed the names of perpetrators, victims, and the atrocities committed. An official truth commission approved by the lower house in September 2011 may increase the demand for justice for these atrocities. Abrão and Torelly suggest that the reparations and ongoing truth processes represent restorative justice, but these processes themselves seem to substitute, rather than complement, the individual criminal accountability processes in the rest of the region. Thus, even in the age of accountability – where domestic and international human rights and justice entrepreneurs, as well as political will exist – amnesty laws may still possess historic legitimacy that will block trials.

In Indonesia, an official amnesty law does not exist. Nonetheless, Burgess shows the patterns by which a de facto amnesty blocks accountability and shields perpetrators from individual criminal responsibility. On one hand, the de facto amnesty seems to protect a fragile peace; challenging it with trials might return the country to the decades-long violence perpetrated by the Indonesian armed and security forces in Aceh and East Timor. Yet distrust of trials matches the distrust of peace. For many, trials in the current context would merely perpetuate political manipulation, not justice. While human rights and justice entrepreneurs promote individual criminal accountability models, as well as restorative justice alternatives, the lack of political will and widespread corruption is not likely to produce positive results on either score.

These five scenarios show the variety of combinations of amnesty and accountability. The combination does not automatically lead to greater or fewer gains for democracy and human rights. Instead, particular factors are associated with a country's placement on the continuum and how those factors block or promote democratizing or rights-enhancing outcomes. The continuum is not meant to assume that the progress along it is linear and always moving in a positive direction. In some cases, as Argentina and Uruguay show, countries may move along the continuum. In other cases, however, they may get stuck at an impasse and fail to move very far along it. Even in these cases, unpredictable catalysts may occur that could move countries closer to accountability or closer to amnesty, in more or less democratic and rights-enhancing directions. In all of these cases, amnesties have persisted, and in many of these cases they will continue to exist, despite the age of accountability.

## THE FUTURE OF AMNESTY

The encouraging news this volume offers is that accountability has increased around the world. It further illustrates that the persistence of amnesty during this age of accountability has not prevented justice. The bad news is that the struggle for justice will not always be won; the pathway to accountability is not easy, linear, or inexorable. It takes a lot of work, and even then it may face setbacks and reversals.

The scenarios identified here, drawing from the rich empirical and theoretical work in the volume, include those most likely to bring justice, but also ones in which justice remains elusive. Combining accountability and amnesty has been shown to be the most likely path to bring about improvements in human rights and democracy, but such an outcome is not guaranteed. Just as human rights advocates and victims groups have designed innovative techniques to circumvent and even undermine amnesties, so too have governments and courts thwarted those efforts. We have also observed that even if the statistically significant combination of amnesty and accountability provides the most likely scenario for improving democracy and human rights scores, exceptions exist.

"Politics is the art of the possible," some contend,[33] and we could extend that view to the politics of accountability. The achievements in accountability cannot be attributed to a particular era like the age of accountability, to a particular type (e.g., individual criminal accountability), or to a particular scenario such as democratic displacement. No set of factors, scenarios, or processes leads inexorably to more justice and less impunity. Neither the era nor the models do the work. Victims, human rights advocates, lawyers and judges, and politicians must, and certainly will, try to advance the accountability goal, sometimes against all odds. They may find ways, when faced with an accountability impasse, to creatively circumvent obstacles, or to find innovative restorative justice mechanisms to enhance accountability by other means. These creative accountability proponents have not assumed that justice is impossible; they have tirelessly assumed the opposite. Such creative thinking may not end obstinate amnesties. On the other hand, the rich set of theoretical and empirical case studies included in this volume shows that the intuition behind the creative struggle for accountability is correct: amnesties do not render accountability impossible. It takes hard work and artistry to produce the accountability outcome. Contextual factors make some amnesties more difficult than others to overcome. But in all cases accountability is achievable even when amnesties persist.

---

[33] This quote is attributed to a number of political and scholarly figures including Albert O. Hirschman and Otto von Bismarck.

# Bibliography

Abrão, Paulo, and Marcelo D. Torelly. "Justiça de transição no Brasil: O papel da Comissão de Anistia do Ministério da Justiça." *Revista Anistia Política e Justiça de Transição* 1 (2009): 12–21.

"Dictatorship, Victims and Memorialization in Brazil." In *Museums and Difficult Heritage*, edited by Jari Harju and Elisa Sarpo. Helsinki: Helsinki City Museum, forthcoming.

Abrão, Paulo, Marcelo D. Torelly, and Leigh A. Payne, eds. *A anistia na era da responsabilização: O Brasil em perspectiva internacional e comparada*. Brazilian Ministry of Justice, 2011.

Abuelas de Plaza de Mayo. *Niños desaparecidos, jóvenes localizados en Argentina desde 1976 a 1999*. Buenos Aires: Temas, 1999.

Acuña, Carlos H. "Transitional Justice in Argentina and Chile." In *Retribution and Reparation in the Transition to Democracy*, edited by Jon Elster, 206–38. New York: Cambridge University Press, 2006.

Acuña, Carlos H., and Catalina Smulovitz. "Guarding the Guardians in Argentina: Some Lessons about the Risks and Benefits of Empowering the Courts." In *Transitional Justice and the Rule of Law in New Democracies*, edited by James McAdams, 93–122. Notre Dame: University of Notre Dame Press, 1997.

"Militares en la transición argentina: del gobierno a la subordinación constitucional." In *Historizar el pasado vivo en América Latina*, edited by Anne Pérotin-Dumon, 1–94. Accessed July 31, 2011. http://www.historizarelpasadovivo.cl/downloads/acunasmulovitz.pdf.

Afako, Barney. "Reconciliation and Justice: 'Mato Oput' and the Amnesty Act." In *Protracted Conflict, Elusive Peace: Initiatives to End the Violence in Northern Uganda*, edited by Okello Lucima. London: Conciliation Resources/Accord, London 2002. Accessed September 1, 2011. www.c-r.org/our-work/accord/northern-uganda-update/negotiating_justice.php.

Afghanistan Independent Human Rights Commission. "The Legality of Amnesties." Discussion paper, International Centre for Transitional Justice, Afghanistan Human Rights Commission, February 21, 2010. Accessed September 14, 2011. http://www.aihrc.org.af/2010_eng/Eng_pages/Reports/Thematic/Amnesties_paper_23_Feb_2010.pdf.

African Rights. *Rwanda: Death, Despair and Defiance*, Revised edition. London: African Rights, 1995.

Agüero, Felipe. "Legacies of Transitions: Institutionalization, the Military, and Democracy in South America." *Mershon International Studies Review* 42 (1998): 383–404.

*Militares, civiles y democracia*. Madrid: Alianza Editorial, 1995.

Águila, Juan José del. *El TOP. La represión de la libertad*. Barcelona: Planeta, 2001.

Aguilar, Paloma. "Justice, Politics and Memory in the Spanish Transition." In *The Politics of Memory: Transitional Justice in Democratizing Societies*, edited by Alxandra Barahona de Brito, Carmen González Enríquez, and Paloma Aguilar, 92–118. Oxford: Oxford University Press.

"Transitional or Post-transitional Justice? Recent Developments in the Spanish Case." *South European Society & Politics* 13 (2008): 417–33.

*Memory and Amnesia: The Role of the Spanish Civil War in the Transition to Democracy*. Oxford: Berghahn Books, 2002.

*Políticas de la memoria y memorias de la política*. Madrid: Alianza Editorial, 2008.

Akhavan, Payam. "Justice and Reconciliation in the Great Lakes Region of Africa: The Contribution of the International Criminal Tribunal for Rwanda." *Duke Journal of Comparative and International Law* 7 (1997): 325–48.

"Justice in The Hague, Peace in the Former Yugoslavia? A Commentary on the United Nations War Crimes Tribunal." *Human Rights Quarterly* 20 (1998): 737–816.

Alfonsín, Raúl. "Never Again in Argentina." *Journal of Democracy* 4 (1993): 15–19.

Allen, Tim. "Ritual (Ab)use? Problems with Traditional Justice in Northern Uganda." In *Courting Conflict? Peace, Justice and the ICC in Africa*, edited by Nicholas Waddell and Phil Clark, 47–54. London: Royal African Society, 2008.

*Trial Justice: The International Criminal Court and the Lord's Resistance Army*. London: Zed Books, 2006.

Amnesty International Public Statement. "Guatemala: Inconsistent Ruling by the Constitutional Court Rejects Extraditions Sought by Spain," December 21, 2007. AI Index: AMR 34/026/2007. Accessed September 2, 2011. http://www.amnesty. org/en/library/asset/AMR34/026/2007/en/da903391-c9d6–11dc-928b-93fa24316dd4/ amr340262007eng.pdf.

Amnesty International, Human Rights Watch, and the International Commission of Jurists. "Joint Open Letter to Prime Minister Khanal of Nepal on Persistent Impunity." May 24, 2011. Accessed September 12, 2011. http://www.hrw.org/news/2011/05/24/joint-open-letter-prime-minister-khanal-nepal-persistent-impunity.

Amnesty International. *Amnesty International Report 2003 – Uruguay*. Amnesty International, 2003. Accessed September 16, 2011. http://www.unhcr.org/refworld/country,,AMNESTY,, URY,4562d94e2,3edb47e216,0.html.

*Kenya: Concerns about the Truth, Justice and Reconciliation Commission Bill*. London: Amnesty International, 2008.

"Rwanda: Fear for Safety/Legal Concern: François-Xavier Byuma". AI Index: AFR 47/007/2007. Amnesty International, May 9, 2007.

"Rwanda: Gacaca – Gambling with Justice." press release, AI Index: AFR 47/003/2002, June 19, 2002.

"Uganda: Proposed National Framework to Address Impunity Does Not Remove Government's Obligation to Arrest and Surrender LRA Leaders to the International Criminal Court." AI Index: AFR 59/002/2007, August 15, 2007.

*Algeria: Truth and Justice Obscured by the Shadow of Impunity*. London: Amnesty International, 2000.

*Annual Report: El Salvador 2011*. Amnesty International, May 28, 2011. Accessed August 9, 2011. http://www.amnestyusa.org/research/reports/annual-report-el-salvador-2011?page=show.

*Guatemala: State of Impunity*, AMR 34/002/1997. Amnesty International, April 24, 1997. Accessed July 11, 2011. http://www.unhcr.org/refworld/docid/45bf71642.html.

*Rwanda – Gacaca: A Question of Justice, AI Doc. AFR 47/007/2002*. Amnesty International, December 2002.

*Rwanda: The Troubled Course of Justice, AI Index: AFR 47/10/00*. Amnesty International, April 2000.

*Uganda: Agreement and Annex on Accountability and Reconciliation Falls Short of a Comprehensive Plan to End Impunity*. London: Amnesty International, 2008.

Americas Watch. *Challenging Impunity: The Ley De Caducidad and the Referendum Campaign in Uruguay*. New York: Americas Watch, 1989.

Anderson, Ben. "How did the Generals Die." *Indonesia* 43 (April 1987): 109–34. Accessed September 30, 2011. http://www.antenna.nl/~fwillems/eng/ic/pki/anderson.html.

Anderson, Benedict, and Ruth McVey. *A Preliminary Analysis of the October 1, 1965, Coup in Indonesia*. Cornell: Cornell Modern Indonesia Project, 1966.

Arán, Mercedes García. "Repercusiones penales de la ley de amnistía de 1977." In *30 años de la Ley de Amnistía* (1977–2007), edited by Jesús Espuny and Olga Paz, 187–91. Madrid: Dykinson S.L., 2009.

Asian Development Bank Institute. "Aceh-Nias Reconstruction and Rehabilitation: Progress and Challenges at the End of 2006: The Impacts." Discussion paper No.7, Asian Development Bank Institute, June 29, 2007. Accessed October 2, 2011. http://www.adbi.org/discussion-paper/2007/06/29/2288.acehnias.reconstruction.rehabilitation/the.impacts/.

Atkinson, Ronald. *The Roots of Ethnicity: The Origins of the Acholi of Uganda*. Kampala: Fountain Publishers, 1999.

Aukerman, Miriam J. "Extraordinary Evil, Ordinary Crime: A Framework for Understanding Transitional Justice." *Harvard Human Rights Journal* 15 (2002): 39–97.

Baggio, Roberta. "Justiça de transição como reconhecimento: Limites e possibilidades do processo brasileiro." In *Repressão e memória política no contexto Ibero-Americano*, edited by Boaventura Santos, Paulo Abrão, Cecília MacDowell Dos Santos, and Marcelo D. Torrelly, 260–85. Brasília/Coimbra: Department of Justice/Center for Social Studies of the University of Coimbra, 2010.

Baker, Bruce. "Popular Justice and Policing from Bush War to Democracy: Uganda, 1981–2004." *International Journal of the Sociology of Law* 32 (2004): 333–48.

Barahona De Brito, Alexandra. *Human Rights and Democratization in Latin America: Uruguay and Chile*. Oxford: Oxford University Press, 1997.

"Truth, Justice, Memory, and Democratization in the Southern Cone." In *The Politics of Memory: Transitional Justice in Democratizing Societies*, edited by Alexandra Barahona de Brito, Carmen González Enríquez, and Paloma Aguilar, 119–60. Oxford: Oxford University Press, 2001.

Barahona De Brito, Alexandra, Carmen González Enríquez, and Paloma Aguilar, eds. *The Politics of Memory: Transitional Justice in Democratizing Societies*. Oxford: Oxford University Press, 2001.

Barrell, Howard. *MK: The ANC's Armed Struggle*. Harmondsworth: Penguin, 1990.

Bass, Gary. *Stay the Hand of Vengeance: The Politics of War Crimes Tribunals*. Princeton: Princeton University Press, 2000.

Bassiouni, M. Cherif. "Combating Impunity for International Crimes." *University of Colorado Law Review* 71 (2000): 409–22.

"Searching for Peace and Achieving Justice: The Need for Accountability." *Law and Contemporary Problems* 59 (1996): 9–28.

"International Crimes: Jus Cogens and Obligatio Erga Omnes." *Law and Contemporary Problems* 59 (1996): 63–74.

Bassu, Giovanni. "Law Overruled: Strengthening the Rule of Law in Postconflict States." *Global Governance* 14 (2008): 22–38.

Bell, Christine. *On the Law of Peace: Peace Agreements and the Lex Pacificatoria*. Oxford: Oxford University Press, 2008.

Binningsbø, Helga Malmin, Jon Elster, and Scott Gates. "Civil War and Transitional Justice, 1946–2003: A Dataset." Paper presented at the "Transitional Justice and Civil War Settlements" workshop in Bogotá, Colombia, October 18–19, 2005.

Boraine, Alexander L. "South Africa's Amnesty Revisited." In *The Provocations of Amnesty: Memory, Justice and Impunity*, edited by Charles Villa-Vicencio and Erik Doxtader, 165–81. South Africa: David Philip, 2003.

Borneman, John. *Settling Accounts: Violence, Justice, and Accountability in Postsocialist Europe*. Princeton: Princeton University Press, 1997.

Bradbury, Mark. *An Overview of Initiatives for Peace in Acholi, Northern Uganda*. Cambridge: The Collaborative for Development Action, Inc., October 1999. Accessed September 3, 2011. www.cdainc.com/publications/rpp/casestudies/rppCase02Uganda.pdf.

Branch, Adam. "Neither Peace nor Justice: Political Violence and the Peasantry in Northern Uganda, 1986–1998." *African Studies Quarterly* 8 (2005): 1–31.

"Uganda's Civil War and the Politics of ICC Intervention." *Ethics and International Affairs* 21 (2007): 179–98.

Brewer-Carias, Allan R. "Some Aspects of the 'Amparo' Proceeding in Latin America as a Constitutional Judicial Mean Specifically Established for the Protection of Human Rights." Accessed July 8, 2011. http://www.allanbrewercarias.com.

Brinks, Daniel M. *The Judicial Response to Police Killings in Latin America: Inequality and the Rule of Law*. Cambridge: Cambridge University Press, 2008.

Broomhall, Bruce. *International Justice and the International Criminal Court: Between Sovereignty and the Rule of Law*. Oxford: Oxford University Press, 2003.

Brysk, Alison. *The Politics of Human Rights in Argentina: Protest, Change, and Democratization*. Stanford: Stanford University Press, 1994.

Bubenzer, Ole. *Post-TRC Prosecutions in South Africa: Accountability for Political Crimes after the Truth and Reconciliation Commission's Amnesty Process*. Leiden: Martinus Nijhoff, 2009.

Burgers, Herman J., and Hans Danelius. *The United Nations Convention Against Torture: A Handbook on the Convention against Torture and Other Cruel, Inhuman or Degrading Treatment or Punishment*. Dordrecht, Netherlands: Martinus Nijhoff, 1988.

Burt, Jo-Marie. "Guilty as Charged: The Trial of Former Peruvian President Alberto Fujimori for Human Rights Violations." *International Journal of Transitional Justice* 3 (2009): 384–405.

"Accountability After Atrocity in Peru: The Trial of Former President Alberto Fujimori in Comparative Perspective." In *Critical Perspectives in Transitional Justice*, edited by Oxford Transitional Justice Research (OTJR), 119-46. Antwerp: Intersentia, 2012.

Canton, Santiago. "Amnesty Laws." In *Victims Unsilenced: The Inter-American Human Rights System and Transitional Justice in Latin America*, edited by Due Process of Law Foundation, 167–93. Washington, DC, 2007. Accessed July 14, 2011. http://www.dplf.org/uploads/1190403828.pdf.

Cassel, Douglass. "Lessons from the Americas: Guidelines for International Response to Amnesties for Atrocities." *Law and Contemporary Problems* 59 (1996): 197–230.

Cassese, Antonio. *International Law*. 2nd ed. New York, Oxford: Oxford University Press, 2005.

Cassese, Antonio, Albin Eser, Giorgio Gaja, Philip Kirsch, Alain Pellet, and Bert Swart, eds. *The Rome Statute for an International Criminal Court: A Commentary*. Oxford: Oxford University Press, 2002.

Center for Justice and Accountability (CJA). "Case Summary CJA's Human Rights Prosecution: the Jesuits Massacre," November 13, 2008. Accessed August 8, 2011. http://cja.org/downloads/jesuits_summary.pdf.

"Jesuits Massacre Case: In Brief," November 13, 2008. Accessed August 10, 2011. http://www.cja.org/article.php?list=type&type=84.

"Spanish Judge Issues Indictments and Arrest Warrants in Jesuits Massacre Case," May 31, 2011. Accessed August 8, 2011. http://cja.org/article.php?id=1004.

"U.S. Arrests Former Salvadoran Official and Massachusetts Resident For Immigration Fraud Related to 1989 Jesuits Massacre," August 23, 2011. Accessed September 1, 2011. http://www.cja.org/article.php?id=1027.

Centre for Human Rights and Legal Action (CALDH) and the Association for Justice and Reconciliation (AJR). "A Historic Opportunity for Justice in Guatemala," June 21, 2011. Accessed August 15, 2011. http://nisgua.blogspot.com/2011/06/historic-opportunity-for-justice-in.html.

Centre for Humanitarian Dialogue. "Charting the Roads to Peace: Facts, Figures and Trends in Conflict Resolution." *Mediation Data Trends Report*. Geneva: Centre for Humanitarian Dialogue, 2007.

Centre for Justice and International Law (CEJIL). "United Nations Recommends El Salvador to Investigate the Whereabouts of the Serrano-Cruz Sisters." February 5, 2010. Accessed August 9, 2011. http://cejil.org/en/categoria/pais/el-salvador-0.

Centro de Estudios Legales y Sociales (CELS). *Crímenes del terrorismo de estado – weblogs de las causas*. Accessed August 4, 2011. http://www.cels.org.ar/wpblogs/.

*Annual Report*. Buenos Aires: CELS, 2001.

*Annual Report*. Buenos Aires: CELS, 2011.

Chargoñia, Pablo. "Avances, retrocesos y desafíos en la lucha judicial contra la impunidad." In *Luchas contra la impunidad: Uruguay 1985–2011*, edited by Gabriela Fried and Francesca Lessa, 163–88. Montevideo: Trilce, 2011.

Chavez, Rebecca Bill. "The Evolution of Judicial Autonomy in Argentina: Establishing the Rule of Law in an Ultrapresidential System." *Journal of Latin American Studies* 36 (2004): 451–78.

Chavez-Tafur, Gabriel. "Using International Law to By-pass Domestic Legal Hurdles: On the Applicability of the Statute of Limitations in the Menendez et al. Case." *Journal of International Criminal Justice* 6 (2008):1061–75.

Chinchón, Javier. "La actuación de la Audiencia Nacional en la investigación y juicio de los crímenes contra la humanidad cometidos en la Guerra Civil y el franquismo." *La Ley* 1 (2009): 1415–24.

Chinchón, Javier, and Lydia Vicente. "La investigación de los crímenes cometidos en la guerra civil y el franquismo como delito de prevaricación." *Revista Electrónica de Estudios Internacionales* 19 (2010): 1–43.

Ciurlizza, Javier. "Entrevista: Para um panorama global sobre a justiça de transição: Javier Ciurlizza responde." *Revista Anistia Política e Justiça de Transição* 1 (2009): 23–9.

Clark, Ann Marie. *Diplomacy of Conscience: Amnesty International and Changing Human Rights Norms*. Princeton: Princeton University Press, 2001.

Clark, Phil. *The Gacaca Courts, Post-Genocide Justice and Reconciliation in Rwanda: Justice without Lawyers*. Cambridge: Cambridge University Press, 2010.

"Grappling in the Great Lakes: The Challenges of International Justice in Rwanda, the Democratic Republic of Congo and Uganda." In *The Role of International in Rebuilding Societies after Conflict: Great Expectations*, edited by Brett Bowden, Hilary Charlesworth, and Jeremy Farrall, 244–69. Cambridge: Cambridge University Press, 2009.

"Law, Politics and Pragmatism: The ICC and Case Selection in the Democratic Republic of Congo and Uganda." In *Courting Conflict? Peace, Justice and the ICC in Africa*, edited by Nicholas Waddell and Phil Clark, 37–45. London: Royal African Society, 2008.

Clark, Phil, and Nicola Palmer. "The International Community Fails Rwanda Again." Oxford Transitional Justice Research Working Paper, Oxford, May 5, 2009.

Cobban, Helena. *Amnesty After Atrocity? Healing Nations After Genocide and War Crimes*. Boulder, CO: Paradigm Publishers, 2007.

Coetzee, Martin. "An Overview of the TRC Amnesty Process." In *The Provocations of Amnesty: Memory, Justice and Impunity*, edited by Charles Villa-Vicencio and Erik Doxtader, 181–94. South Africa: David Philip, 2003.

Cohen, David. *Intended to Fail: The Trials Before the Ad hoc Human Rights Court in Jakarta*. International Center for Transitional Justice, Occasional Paper series, August 1, 2003. Accessed October 2, 2011. http://ictj.org/sites/default/files/ICTJ-Indonesia-Rights-Court-2003-English.pdf.

Cohen, Stanley. *Estado de negación – Ensayo sobre atrocidades y sufrimientos*. Buenos Aires: Buenos Aires University Law School/British Council Argentina, 2005.

Collins, Cath. *Post-Transitional Justice: Human Rights Trials in Chile and El Salvador*. University Park: Pennsylvania State University Press, 2010.

Commission for Historical Clarification. *Guatemala: Memory of Silence*. Guatemala City: Guatemalan Commission for Historical Clarification, 1999. Accessed September 4, 2011. http://shr.aaas.org/guatemala/ceh/report/english/conc1.html.

Commission of Truth and Friendship. "Terms of Reference." March 9, 2005. Accessed September 3, 2011. http://www.kbri-canberra.org.au/special/TOR_CTF.pdf.

*Report of the Indonesia Timor Leste Commission of Truth and Friendship*. Commission of Truth and Friendship, 2008. Accessed September 30, 2011. http://violet.berkeley.edu/~warcrime/East_Timor_and_Indonesia/Reports/PER%20MEMORIAM%20AD%20SPEM%20Eng_ver.pdf.

Committee of Experts on Torture. "Committee of Experts on Torture, Syracuse, Italy, 16–17 December 1977." *Revue Internationale de Droit Pénal* 48, nos. 3/4 (1977).

Crenzel, Emilio. "Present Pasts: Memory(ies) of State Terrorism in the Southern Cone of Latin America." In *The Memory of State Terrorism in the Southern Cone: Argentina, Chile, and Uruguay*, edited by Francesca Lessa and Vincent Druliolle, 1–13. New York: Palgrave MacMillan, 2011.

Dallaire, Romeo. *Shake Hands with the Devil: The Failure of Humanity in Rwanda*. Toronto: Random House Canada, 2003.

Dancy, Geoff, Hunjoon Kim, and Eric Wiebelhaus. "The Turn to Truth: Trends in Truth Commission Experimentation." *Journal of Human Rights* 9 (2010): 45–64.

Darehshori, Sara. *Selling Justice Short: Why Accountability Matters for Peace*. New York, NY: Human Rights Watch, 2009.

de Greiff, Pablo, ed. *The Handbook of Reparations*. Oxford: Oxford University Press, 2006.

"Justice and Reparations." In *The Handbook of Reparations*, edited by Pablo de Greiff, 451–77. Oxford: Oxford University Press, 2006.

Demasi, Carlos. "La dictadura militar: Un tema pendiente." In *Uruguay cuentas pendientes: Dictadura, memorias y desmemorias*, edited by Hugo Achugar, Carlos Demasi, Roger Mirza, Alvaro Rico, and Marcelo Viñar, 29–50. Montevideo: Trilce, 1995.

Demasi, Carlos, and Jaime Yaffé. *Vivos los llevaron … Historia de la lucha de Madres y Familiares de Uruguayos Detenidos Desaparecidos (1976–2005)*. Montevideo: Trilce, 2005.

Des Forges, Alison. *Leave None to Tell the Story: Genocide in Rwanda*. New York: Human Rights Watch, 1999.

Dolan, Chris. "Inventing Traditional Leadership? A Critical Assessment of Dennis Pain's 'The Bending of the Spears.'" COPE Working Paper 31, April 2000.

Domínguez, Ana, ed. *Enrique Ruano. Memoria viva de la impunidad del franquismo*. Madrid: UCM, 2011.

Dorris, Jonathan Truman. *Pardon and Amnesty under Lincoln and Johnson*. Chapel Hill: University of North Carolina Press, 1953.

Drumbl, Mark. "Sclerosis: Retributive Justice and the Rwandan Genocide." *Punishment and Society* 2 (2000): 287–307.

du Bois, François and Antje du Bois-Pedain, eds. *Justice and Reconciliation in Post-Apartheid South Africa*. Cambridge: Cambridge University Press, 2008.

"Post-conflict Justice and the Reconciliatory Paradigm: The South African Experience." In *Justice and Reconciliation in Post-Apartheid South Africa*, edited by François du Bois and Antje du Bois-Pedain, 289–311.Cambridge: Cambridge University Press, 2008.

du Bois-Pedain, Antje. "Post-conflict Accountability and the Demands of Justice: Can Conditional Amnesties Take the Place of Criminal Prosecutions?" University of Cambridge Faculty of Law Research Paper 32/2011.

*Transitional Amnesty in South Africa*. Cambridge: Cambridge University Press, 2007.

"Communicating Criminal and Political Responsibility in the TRC Process." In *Justice and Reconciliation in Post-Apartheid South Africa*, edited by François du Bois and Antje du Bois-Pedain, 62–89. Cambridge: Cambridge University Press, 2008.

Dubow, Saul. *The African National Congress*. Johannesburg: Jonathan Ball, 2000.

Due Process of Law Foundation (DPLF). *Digest of Latin American Jurisprudence on International Crimes*. Washington, DC: Due Process of Law Foundation, 2010.

*Victims Unsilenced: The Inter-American Human Rights System and Transitional Justice in Latin America*. Washington, DC: Due Process of Law Foundation, 2007. Accessed July 14, 2011. http://www.dplf.org/uploads/1190403828.pdf.

Dugard, John. "Dealing with Crimes of a Past Regime. Is Amnesty Still an Option?" *Leiden Journal of International Law* 12 (1999): 1001–15.

"Reconciliation and Justice: The South African Experience." *Transnational Law and Contemporary Problems* 8 (Fall 1998): 277–312.

Dunbar, N. C. H. "The Myth of Customary International Law." *Austin Yearbook for International Law* 1 (1983): 1–19.

East Timor Commission on Reception, Truth and Reconciliation (CAVR). *CHEGA!* Jakarta: CAVR, 2005.

Elhordoy Arregui, María del Pilar. "Denunciar la impunidad: una obligación ética." In *Luchas contra la impunidad: Uruguay 1985–2011*, edited by Gabriela Fried and Francesca Lessa, 155–61. Montevideo: Trilce, 2011.

Ellis, Stephen, and Tsepo Sechaba. *Comrades Against Apartheid: The ANC and the South African Communist Party in Exile.* London: James Currey, 1992.

Elster, Jon. "Coming to Terms with the Past. A Framework for the Study of Justice in the Transition to Democracy," *European Journal of Sociology* 39 (1998): 7–48.

*Closing the Books: Transitional Justice in Historical Perspective.* Cambridge, New York: Cambridge University Press, 2004.

*Retribution and Reparation in the Transition to Democracy.* Cambridge, UK: Cambridge University Press, 2006.

Engstrom, Par. "Transnational Human Rights and Democratization: Argentina and the Inter-American Human Rights System (1976–2007)." DPhil diss., University of Oxford, 2010.

Engstrom, Par, and Andrew Hurrell. "Why the Human Rights Regime in the Americas Matters." In *Human Rights Regimes in the Americas*, edited by Mónica Serrano and Vesselin Popovski, 29–55. Tokyo: United Nations University Press, 2010.

Erasmus, Gerhard. "Namibian Independence and the Release of Political Prisoners." *South African Yearbook of International Law* 14 (1988–89): 137–43.

Errandonea, Jorge. "Justicia transicional en Uruguay." *Revista IIDH* 47 (enero–junio 2008): 13–69.

Ferro Clérico, Lilia. "Conjugando el pasado: El debate actual en Uruguay sobre los detenidos desaparecidos durante la dictadura." Paper presented at the XXI International Congress of the Latin American Studies Association, Chicago, Illinois, September 24–26, 1998.

Filippini, Leonardo, and Lisa Magarrell. "Instituciones de la justicia de transición y contexto político." In *Entre el perdón y el paredón*, edited by Angelika Rettberg, 143–70. Bogotá: Universidad de los Andes, 2005.

Finnemore, Martha, and Kathryn Sikkink. "International Norm Dynamics and Political Change." *International Organizations* 52 (1998): 887–917.

Finnström, Sverker. "In and Out of Culture: Fieldwork in War-Torn Uganda." *Critique of Anthropology* 21 (2001): 247–58.

Freedom House. "Freedom in the World Country Ratings." Accessed July 11, 2011. http://www.freedomhouse.org/uploads/fiw09/CompHistData/CountryStatus&RatingsOvervie w1973–2009.pdf.

Freeman, Mark. *Necessary Evils: Amnesties and the Search for Justice.* Cambridge: Cambridge University Press, 2009.

Fried, Gabriela, and Francesca Lessa, eds. *Luchas contra la impunidad: Uruguay 1985–2011.* Montevideo: Trilce, 2011.

Fullard, Madeleine, and Nicky Rousseau. "Truth, Evidence and History. A Critical Review of Aspects of the Amnesty Process." In *The Provocations of Amnesty: Memory, Justice and Impunity*, edited by Charles Villa-Vicencio and Erik Doxtader, 195–216. South Africa: David Philip, 2003.

Galain Palermo, Pablo. "The Prosecution of International Crimes in Uruguay." *International Criminal Law Review* 10 (2010): 601–18.

Gargarella, Roberto. "Human Rights, International Courts and Deliberative Democracy." In *Critical Perspectives in Transitional Justice*, edited by Oxford Transitional Justice Research (OTJR), 101–18. Antwerp: Intersentia, 2012.

Garret, Linda. "El Salvador Update-2011." Centre for Democracy in the Americas, August 3, 2011. Accessed August 10, 2011. http://www.democracyinamericas.org/around-the-region-blog/el-salvador-update-july-2011/.

Garro, Alejandro M., and Enrique Dahl. "Legal Accountability for Human Rights Violations in Argentina: One Step Forward and Two Steps Backward." *Human Rights Law Journal* 8 (1987): 283–344.

Gavron, Jessica. "Amnesties in the Light of Developments in International Law and the Establishment of the International Criminal Court." *International and Comparative Law Quarterly* 51 (2002): 91–117.

Gil, Alicia. *La justicia de transición en España*. Barcelona: Atelier, 2009.

Gillespie, Charles. *Negotiating Democracy: Politicians and Generals in Uruguay*. New York: Cambridge University Press, 1991.

Goldstone, Richard J. "Exposing Human Rights Abuses – A Help or Hindrance to Reconciliation?" *Hastings Constitutional Law Quarterly* 22 (1995): 607–22.

*For Humanity: Reflections of a War Crimes Investigator*. New Haven: Yale University Press, 2000.

Gonçalves, Danyelle Nilin. "Os múltiplos sentidos da anistia." *Revista Anistia Política e Justiça de Transição* 1(2009): 272–95.

González, Luis E. *Political Structures and Democracy in Uruguay*. Notre Dame, IN: University of Notre Dame Press, 1991.

Gor, Francisco. "De la justicia franquista a la constitucional." In *Memoria de la transición*, edited by Juliá Santos, Javier Pradera, and Joaquín Prieto, 332–5. Madrid: Taurus-El País, 1996.

Gowlland-Debbas, Vera, and Vassilis Pergantis. "Rule of Law." In *Post-Conflict Peacebuilding: A Lexicon*, edited by Vincent Chetail, 320–36. Oxford: Oxford University Press, 2009.

Grant, Ruth, and Robert O. Keohane. "Accountability and Abuses of Power in World Politics." *American Political Science Review* 99 (February 2005): 29–43.

Greco, Heloisa Amélia. "Dimensões fundacionais da luta pela anistia." Ph.D. diss., Minas Gerais Federal University, 2003.

Guelke, Adrian. *South Africa in Transition. The Misunderstood Miracle*. London: I.B. Tauris, 1999.

Guembe, María José. "Economic Reparations for Grave Human Rights Violations: The Argentinean Experience." In *The Handbook of Reparations*, edited by Pablo de Greiff, 21–55. Oxford: Oxford University Press, 2006.

"Reopening of Trials for Crimes Committed by the Argentine Military Dictatorship." *Sur: International Journal on Human Rights* 3 (2005): 120–37.

Guianze, Mirtha. "La Ley de Caducidad, las luchas por la justicia y la jurisdicción universal de los derechos humanos en el Uruguay." In *Luchas contra la impunidad: Uruguay 1985–2011*, edited by Gabriela Fried and Francesca Lessa, 189–202. Montevideo: Trilce, 2011.

Haggard, Stephen, and Robert Kaufman. "The Political Economy of Democratic Transitions." *Comparative Politics* 29 (1997): 263–83.

Harper, Charles. *Impunity: An Ethical Perspective: Six Case Studies from Latin America*. Geneva: WCC Publications, 1996.

Hayner, Priscilla. *Negotiating Peace in Sierra Leone: Confronting the Justice Challenge*. Geneva: Centre for Humanitarian Dialogue, 2007.

Heller, Agnes. "The Natural Limits to Natural Law and the Paradox of Evil." In *On Human Rights: The Oxford Amnesty Lectures*, edited by Stephen Shute and Susan Hurley, 149–74. New York: Basic Books, 1993.

Herrero, Álvaro. "Court-Executive Relations in Unstable Democracies: Strategic Judicial Behavior in Post-Authoritarian Argentina (1983–2005)." DPhil diss., University of Oxford, 2008.

Hirst, Megan. *Too Much Friendship, Too Little Truth*. International Center for Transitional Justice, Occasional Paper series, January 18, 2000.

Hite, Katherine. "The Politics of Memory, The Languages of Human Rights." In *Latin America After Neoliberalism: Turning the Tide in the 21st Century*, edited by Eric Hershberg and Fred Rosen, 193–212. New York: The New Press, 2006.

Holmes, Stephen. "Gag Rules or the Politics of Omission." In *Constitutionalism and Democracy*, edited by Jon Elster and Rune Slagstad, 19–58. New York: Maison des Sciences Press, [1988] 1993.

Honneth, Axel. *Luta por reconhecimento: A gramática moral dos conflitos sociais*. São Paulo: Ed. 34, 2003.

Hudson, Andrew, and Alexandra Taylor. "The International Commission against Impunity in Guatemala." *Journal of International Criminal Justice* 8 (2010): 53–74.

Human Rights Observatory. "Human Rights in Chile." Universidad Diego Portales, Santiago, Chile Bulletin No. 4, March 2010.

Human Rights Watch. *Aceh Under Martial Law: Inside the Secret War*. New York: Human Rights Watch, December 2003.

——— "Brief of Human Rights Watch as Amicus Curiae in Opposition to Rule 11bis Transer." In *The Prosecutor v. Fulgence Kayishema*, Kigali: International Criminal Tribunal for Rwanda, January 3, 2008.

——— "Indonesia: Investigate Torture Video from Papua." October 20, 2010. Accessed October 2, 2011. www.hrw.org/news/2010/1020/indonesia-investigate-torture-video-papua.

——— "Trading Justice for Peace Won't Work." Human Rights Watch, May 2, 2007.

——— "US: Revival of Guantanamo Military Commissions a Blow to Justice." Human Rights Watch, May 15, 2009.

——— *Breakdown: Four Years of Communal Violence in Central Sulawesi*. New York: Human Rights Watch. December 2002.

——— *Too High a Price: The Human Rights Cost of the Indonesian Military's Economic Activities*. Human Rights Watch, June 21, 2006. Accessed September 30, 2011. http://www.unhcr.org/refworld/docid/44c75e154.html.

——— *World Report 2006-Indonesia*. Human Rights Watch, January 18, 2006. Accessed September 5, 2011. http://www.unhcr.org/refworld/docid/43cfaea111.html.

Humphreys, Stephen. *Theatre of the Rule of Law: Transnational Legal Intervention in Theory and Practice*. Cambridge: Cambridge University Press, 2010.

Huntington, Samuel. *The Third Wave: Democratization in the Late Twentieth Century*. Norman and London: University of Oklahoma Press, 1991.

Huyse, Luc and Mark Salter, eds. *Traditional Justice and Reconciliation After Violent Conflict: Learning from African Experiences*. Stockholm: International IDEA, 2008.

Hyndman, Jennifer. "Siting Conflict and Peace in Post-tsunami Sri Lanka and Aceh, Indonesia." *Norwegian Journal of Geography* 63 (2009): 89–96.

Independent Commission for the Investigation of the Violence in Aceh. *Report of the Commission: DOM dan Tragedi Kemanusiaan di Aceh.* Bahasa/Jakarta: KontraS, Bahasa/Jakarta, January 27, 2000.

Indonesian National Commission on Violence Against Women (Komnas Perempuan). *Special Rapporteur Report Time: To Settle the Sense of Security.* Jakarta: Komnas Perempuan, 2008. Accessed October 2, 2011. http://www.komnasperempuan.or.id/publikasi/English/Komnas%20Publish/july2011/MEI%201998%20(14–12–10).pdf.

Indonesian National Human Rights Commission. *Investigation findings of the Ad Hoc Team of Inquiry on Gross Human Rights Violations in the Enforced Disappearances of 1997–1998: executive summary.* Jakarta: Komnas HAM the Indonesian National Human Rights Commission, October 30, 2006.

Ingelse, Chris. *The U.N. Committee Against Torture: An Assessment.* The Hague: Martinus Nijhoff Publishers, 2001.

Inter-American Commission on Human Rights. *Report on the Implementation of the Justice and Peace Law: Initial Stages in the Demobilization of the AUC and First Judicial Proceedings.* Washington D.C: Inter-American Commission on Human Rights, 2007.

*Report on the Situation of Human Rights in El Salvador.* OEA/Ser.L-II.85. IACHR, February 11, 1994. Accessed July 20, 2011. http://www.cidh.oas.org/countryrep/ElSalvador94eng/II.4.htm.

Inter-American Development Bank. *Economics and Social Progress in Latin America: 1981 Report.* Washington D.C: John Hopkins University Press, 1981.

International Center for Transitional Justice and KontraS (the Commission for the Disappeared and Victims of Violence). *Derailed Transitional Justice in Indonesia since the Fall of Soeharto.* New York: International Centre for Transitional Justice/KontraS, April 7, 2011. Accessed September 30, 2011. http://ictj.org/publication/derailed-transitional-justice-indonesia-fall-soeharto-report.

"What is Transitional Justice?" The International Center for Transitional Justice. Accessed September 11, 2011. http://ictj.org/about/transitional-justice.

*Impunity in Timor Leste: Can the Serious Crimes Investigation Team Make a Difference?* New York: International Center for Transitional Justice, June 2010. Accessed September 14, 2011. http://ictj.org/sites/default/files/ICTJ-TimorLeste-Investigation-Team-2010-English.pdf.

International Center for Transitional Justice/Human Rights Center Berkeley. *Forgotten Voices: A Population-Based Survey on Attitudes about Peace and Justice in Northern Uganda.* New York: International Center for Transitional Justice, July 2005.

International Centre for Prison Studies (King's College). *Prison Brief for Rwanda.* London: ICPS, 2002. Accessed August 26, 2011. www.kcl.ac.uk/depsta/rel/icps/worldbrief/africa_records.php?code=39.

International Criminal Court. "Paper on Some Policy Issues before the Office of the Prosecutor." International Criminal Court. Accessed September 25, 2011. http://www.icc-cpi.int/NR/rdonlyres/1FA7C4C6-DE5F-42B7-8B25-60AA962ED8B6/143594/030905_Policy_Paper.pdf.

International Crisis Group. *Aceh: Post-conflict Complications, Asia Report No 139.* International Crisis Group, October 4, 2007. Accessed September 3, 2011. http://www.crisisgroup.org/~/media/Files/asia/south-east-asia/indonesia/139_aceh_post_conflict_complications.pdf.

"Indonesia Conflict History." Accessed September 3, 2011. http://www.crisisgroup.org/ en/key-issues/research-resources/%7e/link.aspx?_id=d61f8aed3ff0470aacf6bbc0b4df522 f&_z=z.

*Aceh: Can Autonomy Stem the Conflict, ICG Asia Report No. 18.* International Crisis Group, June 27, 2001. Accessed October 2, 2011. http://www.crisisgroup.org/en/regions/ asia/south-east-asia/indonesia/018-aceh-can-autonomy-stem-the-conflict.aspx.

Jelin, Elizabeth. *State Repression and the Labors of Memory.* Minneapolis: University of Minnesota Press, 2003.

Johnson, Douglas, and David Anderson. "Revealing Prophets." In *Revealing Prophets: Prophecy in Eastern African Studies,* edited by David Anderson and Douglas Johnson, 1–26. London: James Currey, 1995.

Joinet, Louis. *Study on Amnesty Laws and their Role in the Safeguard and Promotion of Human Rights.* June 21, 1985. ECOSOC, E/CN.4/Sub.2/1985/16.

Karis, Thomas G. "Black Politics: The Road to Revolution." In *Apartheid in Crisis,* edited by Mark A. Uhlig, 113–129. New York: Vintage Books, 1986.

Kaye, Mike. "The Role of Truth Commissions in the Search for Justice, Reconciliation and Democratization: The Salvadoran and Honduran Cases." *Journal of Latin American Studies* 29 (1997): 693–716.

Keightley, Raylene. "Political Offences and Indemnity in South Africa." *South African Journal on Human Rights* 9 (1993): 334–57.

Kell, Tim. *The Roots of Acehnese Rebellion, 1989–1992.* Ithaca: Cornell Modern Indonesia Project, Southeast Asia Program, Cornell University, 1995.

Kelly, Patrick J. "The Twilight of Customary International Law." *Virginia Journal of International Law* 40 (2000): 449–544.

Ker Kwaro Acholi and the Northern Uganda Peace Initiative. *Report on Acholi Youth and Chiefs Addressing Practices of the Acholi Culture of Reconciliation.* USAID, June 2005. Accessed September 4, 2011. http://www.nupi.or.ug/pdf/Youth_ChiefConferenceReport15–6–05. pdf.

Khadiagala, Gilbert. "The Role of the Acholi Religious Leaders Peace Initiative (ARLPI) in Peace Building in Northern Uganda." Appendix in USAID/Management Systems International. *The Effectiveness of Civil Society Initiatives in Controlling Violent Conflicts and Building Peace: A Study of Three Approaches in the Greater Horn of Africa.* Washington DC: USAID/MSI, March 2001.

Kim, Hunjoon, and Kathryn Sikkink. "Explaining the Deterrence Effect of Human Rights Prosecutions for Transitional Countries." *International Studies Quarterly* 54 (2010): 939–63.

Kritz, Neil J., ed. *Transitional Justice: How Emerging Democracies Reckon With Former Regimes.* Washington, DC: United States Institute of Peace, 1995.

"Coming to Terms with Atrocities: A Review of Accountability Mechanisms for Mass Violations of Human Rights." *Law and Contemporary Problems* 59 (1996): 127–52.

Krog, Antjie. *Country of My Skull.* Johannesburg: Random House, 2002.

Kuperman, Alan. *The Limits of Humanitarian Intervention: Genocide in Rwanda.* Washington: Brookings Institution Press, 2001.

Kutz, Florian. *Amnestie für politische Straftäter in Südafrika: Von der Sharpeville-Amnestie bis zu den Verfahren der Wahrheits- und Versöhnungskommission.* Berlin: Berlin Verlag Arno Spitz GmbH, 2001.

Laplante, Lisa J. "Outlawing Amnesty: The Return of Criminal Justice in Transitional Justice Schemes." *Virginia Journal of International Law* 49, no. 4 (2009): 915–84.

Lechner, Norbert, and Pedro Güell. "Construcción social de las memorias en la transición chilena." In *La caja de Pandora. El retorno de la transición chilena*, edited by Amparo Menéndez-Carrión and Alfredo Joignant, 185–210. Santiago de Chile: Planeta/Ariel, 1999.

Legarre, Santiago. "Crimes against Humanity, Reasonableness and the Law: The Simon Case in the Supreme Court of Argentina." *Chinese Journal of International Law* 5 (2006):723–32.

Legro, Jeffrey. *Rethinking the World: Great Power Strategies and International Order*. Ithaca: Cornell University Press, 2005.

Lessa, Francesca. "*No hay que tener los ojos en la nuca*: The Memory of Violence in Uruguay, 1973–2010." In *The Memory of State Terrorism in the Southern Cone: Argentina, Chile, and Uruguay*, edited by Francesca Lessa and Vincent Druliolle, 179–208. New York: Palgrave MacMillan, 2011.

"Peace Commission (Uruguay)." In *Encyclopedia of Transitional Justice*, edited by Lavinia Stan and Nadya Nedelsky. New York: Cambridge University Press, forthcoming.

Lessa, Francesca, and Vincent Druliolle, eds. *The Memory of State Terrorism in the Southern Cone: Argentina, Chile, and Uruguay*. New York: Palgrave MacMillan, 2011.

Levy, Marcela Lopez. *We Are Millions: Neo-Liberalism and New Forms of Political Action in Argentina*. London: Latin American Bureau, 2004.

Lévy, René. "Pardons and Amnesties as Policy Instruments in Contemporary France." *Crime and Justice* 36 (2007): 551–90.

Lira, Elizabeth. "The Reparations Policy for Human Rights Violations in Chile." In *The Handbook of Reparations*, edited by Pablo de Greiff, 55–101. Oxford: Oxford University Press, 2006.

Liu Institute for Global Issues. *Pursuing Peace and Justice: International and Local Initiatives*. May 2005. Accessed February 21, 2012. http://www.ligi.ubc.ca/sites/liu/files/Publications/HSUpdate-Northern_UgandaMay05.pdf.

Llanos, Mariana, and Ana Margheritis. "Why Do Presidents Fail? Political Leadership and the Argentine Crisis (1999–2001)." *Studies in Comparative International Development* 40 (2006): 77–103.

Lopez Goldaracena, Oscar. *Derecho internacional y crímenes contra la humanidad*. Montevideo: SERPAJ, 2006.

Loveman, Mara. "High-Risk Collective Action: Defending Human Rights in Chile, Uruguay, and Argentina." *American Journal of Sociology* 104 (1998): 477–525.

LRA Delegation to the Juba Talks. "LRA Position Paper on Accountability and Reconciliation in the Context of Alternative Justice System for Resolving the Northern Ugandan and Southern Sudan Conflicts." Juba, August 2006.

Lutz, Ellen L., and Caitlin Reiger, eds. *Prosecuting Heads of State*. Cambridge: Cambridge University Press, 2009.

Lutz, Ellen L., and Kathryn Sikkink. "The Justice Cascade: The Evolution and Impact of Foreign Human Rights Trials in Latin America." *Chicago Journal of International Law* 2 (2001): 1–33.

"International Human Rights Law and Practice in Latin America." *International Organizations* 54 (Summer 2000, 2000): 633–59.

Magalhães, Pedro C., Carlo Guarnieri, and Yorgos Kaminis. "Democratic Consolidation, Judicial Reform, and the Judicialization of Politics in Southern Europe." In *Democracy and the State in the New Southern Europe*, edited by Richard Gunther, Nikiforos P. Diamandouros, and Dimitri A. Sotiropoulos, 138–96. Cambridge: Cambridge University Press, 2006.

Malamud-Goti, Jaime. "Trying Violators of Human Rights: The Dilemma of Transitional Governments." In *State Crimes: Punishment or Pardon*, edited by Aspen Institute Justice and Society Program. Wye Center, MD: Aspen Institute, 1989.

*Game Without End: State Terror and the Politics of Justice.* Norman: University of Oklahoma Press, 1996.

"Transitional Governments in the Breach: Why Punish State Criminals?" *Human Rights Quarterly* 12 (1990): 1–16.

Mallinder, Louise. "Uruguay's Evolving Experience of Amnesty and Civil Society's Response." Working Paper No. 4 from Beyond Legalism: Amnesties, Transition and Conflict Transformation: Institute Of Criminology and Criminal Justice, Queen's University Belfast 2009.

"Cross-National Perspectives on Amnesties." Paper presented at the "Amnesty in the Age of Accountability: Brazil in Comparative and International Perspective" conference, University of Oxford, October 22–23, 2010.

"Can Amnesties and International Justice be Reconciled?" *International Journal of Transitional Justice* 1 (2007): 208–30.

"Peacebuilding, the Rule of Law and the Duty to Prosecute: What Role Remains for Amnesties?" In *Building Peace in Post-Conflict States*, edited by Faria Medjouba. London: British Institute of International and Comparative Law, 2012.

"Uganda at the Crossroads: Narrowing the Amnesty?" Working Paper No. 1 from Beyond Legalism: Amnesties, Transition and Conflict Transformation, Institute of Criminology and Criminal Justice, Queen's University Belfast, March 2009.

*Amnesty, Human Rights and Political Transitions: Bridging the Peace and Justice Divide.* Oxford: Hart, 2008.

Martínez, Benjamín Cuéllar. "El Salvador." In *Victims Unsilenced: The Inter-American Human Rights System and Transitional Justice in Latin America*, edited by Due Process of Law Foundation, 33–70. Washington, DC, 2007. Accessed July 14, 2011. http://www.dplf.org/uploads/1190403828.pdf.

"Los dos rostros de la sociedad salvadorena." In *Verdad, justicia y reparación: Desafíos para la democracia y la convivencia social*, edited by Gilda Pacheco Oreamuno, Lorena Acevedo Narea, and Guido Galli, 145–74. San José: IDEA/IIDH, 2005.

McConnell, Tristan. "Uganda: Peace versus Justice?" *openDemocracy*, September 13, 2006. Accessed September 3, 2011. http://www.opendemocracy.net/democracy-africa_democracy/uganda_peace_3903.jsp.

Meintjes, Garth, and Juan E. Méndez. "Reconciling Amnesties with Universal Jurisdiction – A Reply to Mr. Phenyo Keiseng Rakate." *International Law FORUM Du Droit International* 3 (2001): 47–9.

"Reconciling Amnesties with Universal Jurisdiction." *International Law FORUM Du Droit International* 2 (2000): 76–97.

Méndez, Juan E. "Accountability for Past Abuses." *Human Rights Quarterly* 19 (1997): 255–82.

"Truth and Partial Justice in Argentina: An Update." Human Rights Watch, April 1991.

Merikallio, Katri. *Making Peace: Ahtisaari and Aceh.* Juva: WS Bookwell Oy, 2006.

Meyerstein, Ariel. "Between Law and Culture: Rwanda's Gacaca and Postcolonial Legacy." *Law and Social Inquiry* 32 (Spring 2007): 467–508.

Mignone, Emilio F., Cynthia L. Estlund, and Samuel Issacharoff. "Dictatorship on Trial: Prosecution of Human Rights Violations in Argentina." *Yale Journal of International Law* 10 (1984): 118–50.

Miller, Jonathan. "Evaluating the Argentine Supreme Court under Presidents Alfonsín and Menem (1983–1999)." *Southwestern Journal of Law and Trade in the Americas* 7(2000): 369–434.

Minow, Martha. *Between Vengeance and Forgiveness: Facing History after Genocide and Mass Violence*. Boston: Beacon Press, 1998.

Moore Jr., John J. "Problems with Forgiveness: Granting Amnesty under the Arias Plan in Nicaragua and El Salvador." *Stanford Law Review* 43 (1991): 733–77.

Moore, Kathleen D. *Pardons: Justice, Mercy, and the Public Interest*. New York: Oxford University Press, 1989.

Murigande, Charles. "Report on Urugwiro Talks from May 1998 to March 1999." *Report on the National Summit of Unity and Reconciliation*. Kigali: NURC, October 18–20, 2000.

Museveni, Yoweri. *Sowing the Mustard Seed: The Struggle for Freedom and Democracy in Uganda*. London: MacMillan Education Ltd., 1997.

Nagy, Rosemary. "Violence, Amnesty and Transitional Law: 'Private' Acts and 'Public' Truth in South Africa." *African Journal of Legal Studies* 1 (2004): 1–28.

Nalepa, Monika. "Captured Commitments: An Analytic Narrative of Transitions with Transitional Justice." *World Politics* 62 (2010): 341–80.

Neier, Aryeh. *Taking Liberties: Four Decades in the Struggle for Rights*. New York: Public Affairs, 2003.

*War Crimes: Brutality, Genocide, Terror, and the Struggle for Justice*. New York: Times Books: 1998.

Nerlich, Volker. "The Contribution of Criminal Justice." In *Justice and Reconciliation in Post-Apartheid South Africa*, edited by François du Bois and Antje du Bois-Pedain, 96–104. Cambridge: Cambridge University Press, 2008.

Ngoga, Martin. "The Institutionalisation of Impunity: A Judicial Perspective of the Rwandan Genocide." In *After Genocide: Transitional Justice, Post-Conflict Reconstruction and Reconciliation in Rwanda and Beyond*, edited by Phil Clark and Zachary D. Kaufman, 321–32. London: Hurst and Co. Publishers, 2008.

Ní Aoláin, Fionnuala, and Colm Campbell. "The Paradox of Transition in Conflicted Democracies." *Human Rights Quarterly* 27, 1 (2005): 172–213.

Nino, Carlos S. "The Duty to Punish Past Abuses of Human Rights Put Into Context: The Case of Argentina." *Yale Law Journal* 100 (1991): 2619–40.

*Radical Evil on Trial*. New Haven: Yale University Press, 1996.

Notosusanto, Nugroho. *The Dual Function of the Indonesian Armed Forces, especially since 1966*. Jakarta: Department for Defence and Security, Centre for Armed Forces History, 1970.

Ntoubandi, Faustin Z. *Amnesty for Crimes Against Humanity Under International Law*. Leiden: Brill, 2007.

O'Donnell, Guillermo, and Philippe Schmitter. *Transitions from Authoritarian Rule. Tentative Conclusions about Uncertain Democracies*. Baltimore: The Johns Hopkins University Press, 1986.

O'Shea, Andreas. *Amnesty for Crime in International Law and Practice*. The Hague: Kluwer Law International, 2002.

Office of the Prosecutor. *Report on Prosecutorial Strategy*. Office of the Prosecutor, September 14, 2006. Accessed September 3, 2011. http://www.icc-cpi.int/library/organs/otp/OTP Prosecutorial-Strategy-20060914 English.pdf.

"Press Release: President of Uganda Refers Situation Concerning the Lord's Resistance Army (LRA) to the ICC." January 29, 2004.

Oliveira, Alicia, and María José Guembe. "La verdad, derecho de la sociedad." In *La aplicación del derecho internacional de los derechos humanos por los tribunales locales*, edited by Martín Abregú and Christian Courtis, 541–58. Buenos Aires: Editores del Puerto, 2004.

Olivera, Raúl, and Sara Méndez. *Secuestro en la embajada: El caso de la maestra Elena Quinteros*. Accessed September 20, 2011. http://descentralizacioncanaria.blogspot.com/.

Olsen, Tricia D., Leigh A. Payne, and Andrew G. Reiter. "The Justice Balance: When Transitional Justice Improves Human Rights and Democracy." *Human Rights Quarterly* 32 (2010): 980–1007.

"Amnesty Laws in the Age of Accountability." Paper presented at the Annual Meeting of the Law and Society Association, San Francisco, June 2–5, 2011.

"Amnesty in the Age of Accountability." Paper presented at the Annual Meeting of the Law and Society Association, Chicago, 2010.

*Transitional Justice in Balance: Comparing Processes, Weighing Efficacy*. Washington, DC: United States Institute of Peace, 2010.

Oomen, Barbara. "Donor-Driven Justice and its Discontents: The Case of Rwanda." *Development and Change* 36 (2005): 887–910.

Open Society Justice Initiative. *Recent Developments at the Extraordinary Chambers in the Courts of Cambodia: June 2011 Update*. Accessed August 23, 2011. http://www.soros.org/ initiatives/justice/articles_publications/publications/cambodia-eccc-20110614/cambodia-eccc-20110614.pdf.

Orentlicher, Diane F. "Settling Accounts: The Duty to Prosecute Human Rights Violations of a Prior Regime." *The Yale Law Journal* 100 (1991): 2537–614.

Oreamuno, Gilda Pacheco, Lorena Acevedo Narea, and Guido Galli eds. *Verdad, justicia y reparación: Desafíos para la democracia y la convivencia social*. San José: IDEA/IIDH, 2005.

Oteiza, Eduardo. *La Corte Suprema: Entre la justicia sin política y la política sin justicia*. La Plata: Librería Editora Platense, 1994.

Oxford Transitional Justice Research (OTJR), ed. *Critical Perspectives in Transitional Justice*. Antwerp: Intersentia, 2012.

Pain, Dennis. *The Bending of the Spears: Producing Consensus for Peace and Development in Northern Uganda*. London: International Alert and Kacoke Madit, 1997.

Parenti, Pablo F. "The Prosecution of International Crimes in Argentina." *International Criminal Law Review* 10 (2010): 491–507.

Parker, Robert. "Fighting the Siren's Song: The Problem of Amnesty in Historical and Contemporary Perspective." *Acta Juridica Hungaria* 42 (2001): 69–89.

Parrott, Louise. "The Role of the International Criminal Court in Uganda: Ensuring that the Pursuit of Justice Does Not Come at the Price of Peace." *Australian Journal of Peace Studies* 1 (2006): 8–29.

Pastor, Manuel, and Carol Wise. "From Poster Child to Basket Case." *Foreign Affairs* 80 (2001):60–72.

Payne, Leigh A. *Unsettling Accounts: Neither Truth nor Reconciliation in Confessions of State Violence*. Durham: Duke University Press, 2008.

Pearce, Jenny. *Uruguay: Generals Rule*. London: Latin America Bureau, 1980.

Pensky, Max. "Amnesty on Trial: Impunity, Accountability, and the Norms of International Law." *Ethics and Global Politics* 1 (2008).

"The Status of Domestic Amnesties for International Crimes in International Law: Beyond the Crystallization Thesis." Paper presented at the "Amnesty in the Age of Accountability: Brazil in Comparative and International Perspective" Conference, University of Oxford, United Kingdom, October 22–23, 2010.

Pereira, Anthony. *Political (In)Justice – Authoritarianism and the Rule of Law in Brazil, Chile, and Argentina*. Pittsburgh: University of Pittsburgh Press, 2005.

Perelli, Carina. "Youth, Politics, and Dictatorship in Uruguay." In *Fear at the Edge: State Terror and Resistance in Latin America*, edited by Juan E. Corradi, Patricia W. Fagen, and Manuel A. Garretón-Merino, 212–32. Berkeley: University of California, 1992.

Petit, Robert, and Anees Ahmed. "A Review of the Jurisprudence of the Khmer Rouge Tribunal." *Northwestern University Journal of International Human Rights* 8 (2009): 165–89.

Pierini, Alicia. *1998–1999 – Diez años de derechos humanos*. Buenos Aires: Ministerio del Interior, 1999.

Pigou, Piers. "Degrees of Truth: Amnesty and Limitations in the Truth Recovery Project." In *The Provocations of Amnesty: Memory, Justice and Impunity*, edited by Charles Villa-Vicencio and Erik Doxtader, 217–36. South Africa: David Philip, 2003.

Pilloud, Claude, Yves Sandoz, Christophe Swinarski, and Bruno Zimmerman, eds. *Commentary on the Additional Protocols of 8 June 1977 to the Geneva Conventions of 12 August 1949*. Geneva: International Committee of the Red Cross, 1987.

Pion-Berlin, David. "The Pinochet Case and Human Rights Progress in Chile: Was Europe a Catalyst, Cause or Inconsequential?" *Journal of Latin American Studies* 36 (2004): 479–505.

Pogrund, Benjamin. *How Can Man Die Better: Sobukwe and Apartheid*. London: Halban, 1990.

Popkin, Margaret. "El Salvador: A Negotiated End to Impunity?" in *Impunity and Human Rights in International Law and Practice*, edited by Naomi Roht-Arriaza, 198–217. Oxford: Oxford University Press, 1995.

"Guatemala's National Reconciliation Law: Combating Impunity or Continuing it?" *Revista* 24 (1996): 173–84.

Popkin, Margaret, and Nehal Bhuta. "Latin American Amnesties in Comparative Perspective: Can the Past be Buried?" *Ethics and International Affairs* 13 (1999): 99–122.

Power, Samantha. *A Problem from Hell: America and the Age of Genocide*. New York: Basic Books, 2002.

Prunier, Gérard. *The Rwanda Crisis: History of a Genocide*. London: Hurst and Co., 1998.

Putnam, Tonya. "Human Rights and Sustainable Peace." In *Ending Civil Wars: The Implementation of Peace Agreements*, edited by Stephen J. Stedman, Donald Rothchild, and Elizabeth M. Cousens, 237–72. Boulder, CO: Lynne Rienner, 2002.

Quigley, John. "Introduction." In *Genocide in Cambodia: Documents from the Trial of Pol Pot and Ieng Sary*, edited by Howard J. De Nike, John Quigley, and Kenneth J. Robinson, 1–18, Philadelphia: University of Pennsylvania Press, 2000.

Ratner, Steven, and Jason Abrams. *Accountability for Human Rights Atrocities in International Law: Beyond the Nuremberg Legacy*. Oxford: Oxford University Press, 2001.

Rautenbach, Johan. "Namibia – The Release of Political Prisoners Revisited." *South African Yearbook of International Law* 15 (1989–90): 148–58.

Refugee Law Project. "Negotiating Peace: Resolution of Conflicts in Uganda's West Nile Region." Working Paper No. 12, Kampala, RLP, June 2004.

Reiger, Caitlin, and Marieke Wierda. *The Serious Crimes Process in Timor Leste: In Retrospect.* ICTJ Prosecution Case Studies Series, March 1, 2006. Accessed October 2, 2011. http:// ictj.org/publication/serious-crimes-process-timor-leste-retrospect.

Republic of Rwanda. *Report on the Reflection Meetings Held in the Office of the President of the Republic from May 1998 to March 1999.* Kigali: Office of the President of the Republic, August 1999.

Reydams, Luc. "The Rise and Fall of Universal Jurisdiction." Unpublished paper. Leuven Center for Global Governance Studies. Accessed September 4, 2011. http://ghum. kuleuven.be/ggs/publications/opinions/opinions3_luc_reydams.pdf P. 3.

Rial, Juan. "The Social Imaginary: Utopian Political Myths in Uruguay (Change and Permanence During and after the Dictatorship)." In *Repression, Exile and Democracy: Uruguayan Culture,* edited by Saul Sosnowski and Louise B. Popkin, 59–79. Durham and London: Duke University Press, 1993.

Rico, Alvaro. "Detenidos-desaparecidos: sistematización parcial de datos a partir de la investigación histórica de la Presidencia de la República Oriental del Uruguay." In *Historia reciente. Historia en discusión,* edited by Alvaro Rico, 227–311. Montevideo: Tradinco, 2008.

Robinson, Darryl. "Serving the Interests of Justice: Amnesties, Truth Commissions and the International Criminal Court." *European Journal of International Law* 14 (2003): 481–505.

Robinson, Geoffrey. "East Timor 1999 Crimes Against Humanity." In *CHEGA!* Annex 1. Jakarta: CAVR, 2005.

Rodley, Nigel, and Jayne Huckerby. "Outlawing Torture: The Story of Amnesty International's Efforts to Shape the UN Convention against Torture." In *Human Rights Advocacy Stories,* edited by Deena Hurwitz, Margaret L. Satterthwaite, and Douglas B. Ford, 15–41. New York, NY: Foundation Press, Thomson/West, 2009.

Rodley, Nigel. *The Treatment of Prisoners Under International Law.* Oxford: Clarendon Press, 1999.

Rodríguez, Roger. "Es la impunidad, idiota." In *Luchas contra la impunidad: Uruguay 1985–2011,* edited by Gabriela Fried and Francesca Lessa, 119–23. Montevideo: Trilce, 2011.

Roht-Arriaza, Naomi, ed. *Impunity and Human Rights in International Law and Practice.* New York: Oxford University Press, 1995.

"Impunity in Latin America: National Courts and Continuing Challenges." Paper presented at the "Amnesty in the Age of Accountability: Brazil in Comparative and International Perspective" Conference, University of Oxford, United Kingdom, October 22–23, 2010.

"Making the State do Justice: Transnational Prosecutions and International Support for Criminal Investigations in Post-Armed Conflict Guatemala," *Chicago Journal of International Law* 81 (2008): 79–106.

"State Responsibility to Investigate and Prosecute Grave Human Rights Violations in International Law." *California Law Review* 78 (1990): 449–513.

*The Pinochet Effect: Transnational Justice in the Age of Human Rights.* Philadelphia: University of Pennsylvania Press, 2005.

Roht-Arriaza, Naomi, and Lauren Gibson. "The Developing Jurisprudence on Amnesty." *Human Rights Quarterly* 20 (1998): 843–85.

Roht-Arriaza, Naomi and Marcie Mersky. "Guatemala." In *Victims Unsilenced: The Inter-American Human Rights System and Transitional Justice in Latin America*, edited by Due Process of Law Foundation, 7–32. Washington, DC, 2007. Accessed July 14, 2011. http://www.dplf.org/uploads/1190403828.pdf.

Roniger, Luis, and Mario Sznajder. "La reconstrucción de la identidad colectiva del Uruguay tras las violaciones de los derechos humanos por la dictadura militar." *Araucaria* 9 (2003): 45–69.

"The Legacy of Human Rights Violations and the Collective Identity of Redemocratized Uruguay." *Human Rights Quarterly* 19 (1997): 55–77.

*The Legacy of Human-Rights Violations in the Southern Cone: Argentina, Chile and Uruguay*. Oxford: Oxford University Press, 1999.

Rucht, Dieter. "Sociedade como projeto – Projetos na sociedade. Sobre o papel dos movimentos sociais." *Civitas – Revista de Ciências Sociais* 2 (2002): 13–28.

Ruibal, Alba M. "Self-Restraint in Search of Legitimacy: The Reform of the Argentine Supreme Court." *Latin American Politics and Society* 51 (2009): 59–86.

Sánchez-Cuenca, Ignacio, and Paloma Aguilar. "Terrorist Violence and Popular Mobilization: The Case of the Spanish Transition to Democracy." *Politics & Society* 37 (2009): 428–53.

Sarkin, Jeremy. "The Necessity and Challenges of Establishing a Truth and Reconciliation Commission in Rwanda." *Human Rights Quarterly* 21 (1999): 767–823.

*Carrots and Sticks: The TRC and the South African Amnesty Process*. Antwerp: Intersentia, 2004.

Schaap, Andrew. "Assuming Responsibility in the Hope of Reconciliation," *Borderlands e-journal* 3 (2004). Accessed March 2, 2012. http://www.borderlands.net.au/vol3no1_2004/schaap_hope.htm.

Schabas, William A. *An Introduction to the International Criminal Court*, 3rd ed. Cambridge: Cambridge University Press, 2007.

"Amnesty, the Sierra Leone Truth and Reconciliation Commission and the Special Court for Sierra Leone." *U.C. Davis Journal of International Law & Policy* 11 (2004): 145–69.

Scharf, Michael. "From the eXile Files: An Essay on Trading Justice for Peace." *Washington & Lee Review* 63 (2006): 339–78.

"The Letter of the Law: The Scope of the International Legal Obligation to Prosecute Human Rights Crimes." *Law and Contemporary Problems* 59 (1996): 41–62.

"Getting Serious about an International Criminal Court." *Pace International Law Review* 6 (1994): 103–19.

Schiff, Benjamin. *Building the International Criminal Court*. Cambridge: Cambridge University Press, 2008.

Schulze, Kirsten E. *Mission Not So Impossible: The AMM and the Transition from Conflict to Peace in Aceh, 2005–2006*, Case study for the Madrid Report of the Human Security Study Group. Centre for the Study of Global Governance, 2005–2006. Accessed October 2, 2011. http://www.lse.ac.uk/Depts//global/PDFs/HS2007AMM.pdf.

Sempol, Diego. "Hijos Uruguay. Identidad, protesta social y memoria generacional." In *El pasado en el futuro: Los movimientos juveniles*, edited by Elizabeth Jelin and Diego Sempol, 185–220. Madrid: Siglo XXI Editores, 2006.

Servicio Paz y Justicia (SERPAJ). *Derechos humanos en el Uruguay: Informe 2006*. Montevideo: Servicio Paz y Justicia, 2006.

*Derechos humanos en el Uruguay: Informe* 2010. Montevideo: Servicio Paz y Justicia, 2010.

Shaw, Rosalind and Lars Waldorf, eds. *Localizing Transitional Justice: Interventions and Priorities After Mass Violence*. Palo Alto: Stanford University Press, 2010.

Sieder, Rachel. "War, Peace and Memory Politics in Central America." In *The Politics of Memory: Transitional Justice in Democratizing Societies*, edited by Alexandra Barahona de Brito, Carmen González Enríquez, and Paloma Aguilar, 161–89. Oxford: Oxford University Press, 2001.

Sikkink, Kathryn. The *Justice Cascade: How Human Rights Prosecutions are Changing World Politics*. New York: W.W. Norton, 2011.

Sikkink, Kathryn, and Carrie Booth Walling. "The Impact of Human Rights Trials in Latin America." *Journal of Peace Research* 44 (2007): 427–45.

Skaar, Elin. "Legal Development and Human Rights in Uruguay: 1985–2002." *Human Rights Review* 8 (2007): 52–70.

"Un analisis de las reformas judiciales de Argentina, Chile y Uruguay." *America Latina Hoy* 34 (agosto 2003): 147–86.

*Judicial Independence and Human Rights in Latin America: Violations, Politics, and Prosecution*. New York; Basingstoke: Palgrave Macmillan, 2011.

Slye, Ronald C. "The Legitimacy of Amnesties under International Law and General Principles of Anglo-American Law: Is a Legitimate Amnesty Possible?" *Virginia Journal of International Law Association* 43 (2002): 173–247.

Smulovitz, Catalina. "The Discovery of Law: Political Consequences in the Argentine Experience." In *Global Prescriptions: The Production, Exportation, and Importation of a New Legal Orthodoxy*, edited by Yves Dezalay and Bryant Garth, 249–75. Ann Arbor: University of Michigan Press, 2002.

Snyder, Jack, and Leslie Vinjamuri. "Trials and Errors." *International Security* 28 (2003/2004): 5–44.

Sondrol, Paul C. "1984 Revisited? A Re-Examination of Uruguay's Military Dictatorship." *Bulletin of Latin America Research* 11 (1992): 187–203.

Sriram, Chandra Lekha. "Revolutions in Accountability: New Approaches to Past Abuses." *American University International Law Review* 19 (2003): 301–429.

*Globalizing Justice for Mass Atrocities: A Revolution in Accountability*. London: Routledge, 2005.

Struett, Michael. *The Politics of Constructing the International Criminal Court*. New York: Palgrave Macmillan, 2008.

Subotic, Jelena. *Hijacked Justice: Dealing with the Past in the Balkans*. Ithaca: Cornell University Press, 2009.

Sunstein, Cass R. *Free Markets and Social Justice*. Oxford: Oxford University Press, 1997.

Supreme Court of Argentina. *Delitos de, lesa humanidad: Informe sobre la evolución de las causas Actualizado al 16 de julio de 2010*. Centro de información judicial, 2010. Accessed September 3, 2011. http://www.cij.gov.ar/lesa-humanidad.html.

Tebay, Neles. "Human Rights in Papua: An Overview." Paper presented at "Autonomy for Papua – Opportunity or Illusion?" Berlin, Germany, June 4–5, 2003.

Teitel, Ruti G. *Transitional Justice*. New York; Oxford: Oxford University Press, 2000.

"How Are the New Democracies of the Southern Cone Dealing with the Legacy of Past Human Rights Abuses?" Paper presented to Council on Foreign Relations, May 17, 1990.

"Ruti Teitel responde (interview by Marcelo D. Torelly)." *Revista Anistia Política e Justiça de Transição* 3 (2010): 28–38.

"Transitional Justice Genealogy." *Harvard Human Rights Journal* 16 (2003): 69–94.

The Justice and Reconciliation Project. *'Abomination': Local Belief Systems and International Justice.* Liu Institute for Global Issues and the Gulu District NGO Forum. Field Notes No. 5, September 2007.

Themner, Anders. *Violence in Post-Conflict Societies: Remarginalization, Remobilizers and Relationships.* Abingdon and New York: Routledge, 2011.

Thoms, Oskar N. T., James Ron, and Roland Paris. "State-Level Effects of Transitional Justice: What do we Know?" *International Journal of Transitional Justice* 4 (2010): 329–54.

Tove Grete Lie, Helga Malmin Binningsbø, and Scott Gates. *Post-Conflict Justice and Sustainable Peace.* Oslo: PRIO, 2007.

Trumbull, Charles. "Giving Amnesties a Second Chance." *Berkeley Journal of International Law* 25 (2007): 283–345.

Truth and Reconciliation Commission of South Africa. *TRC Report, vol. 6.*Cape Town: Juta, 2003.

UN General Assembly. *54th Session, Report of the International Commission of Inquiry on East Timor to the Secretary-General, (A/54/726, S/2000/59).* UN General Assembly, January 31, 2000

UN Security Council Annex, *From Madness to Hope: The 12-year War in El Salvador: Report of the Commission on the Truth for El Salvador.* S/25500 United States Institute of Peace, 1993.

*Report of the Secretary-General on the Rule of Law and Transitional Justice in Conflict and Post-Conflict Societies.* United Nations, 2004.

Unidad fiscal de coordinación y seguimiento de las causas por violaciones a los derechos humanos cometidas durante el terrorismo de estado. *Informe sobre el estado de las causas por violaciones a los derechos humanos cometidas durante el terrorismo de Estado.* Buenos Aires, 2011. Accessed February 22, 2012. http://www.mpf.gov.ar/Accesos/DDHH/Docs/Estado_Causas_dic_2011.pdf.

United Nations Office of the High Commissioner for Human Rights (OHCHR). *Making Peace Our Own: Victims' Perceptions of Accountability, Transitional Justice and Reconciliation in Northern Uganda.* Geneva: OHCHR, 2007. Accessed September 3, 2011. http://www.ohchr.org/english/docs/northern_Uganda_august2007.pdf.

*Report from OHCHR Fact-finding Mission to Kenya.* Geneva: OHCHR, February 6–28, 2008.

*Report on the Situation of Human Rights in Rwanda,* UN Doc. E/CN.4/1999/33. OHCHR, February 8, 1999.

*Report of the Working Group on the Universal Periodic Review –Algeria,* UN Doc. A/HRC/8/29. OHCHR, May 23, 2008. Accessed September 14, 2011. http://www.ohchr.org/en/hrbodies/upr/pages/dzsession1.aspx.

Rights of the Child, U.N. H.C.H.R. *Report on mission to assess the situation on the ground with regard to the abduction of children from northern Uganda,* UN Doc. E/CN.4/2002/86. OHCHR, November 9, 2001.

*Rule-of-Law Tools for Post-Conflict States, Amnesties,* HR/PUB/09/1. New York and Geneva: OHCHR, 2009. Accessed September 8, 2011. http://www.ohchr.org/Documents/Publications/Amnesties_en.pdf.

*Updated Set of Principles for the Protection and Promotion of Human Rights through Action to Combat Impunity*, UN Doc. E/CN.4/2005/Add.1.OHCHR: February 2, 2005.

United Nations Office on Drugs and Crime. *Stolen Assets Recovery Initiative Launch.* Washington DC: The International Bank for Reconstruction and Development/The World Bank, September 17, 2007. Accessed September 30, 2011. www.unodc.org/documents/corruption/StAR-Sept07-full.pdf.

United Nations. *Consolidated Appeal for Uganda 2006.* United Nations Office for the Coordination of Humanitarian Affairs, November 30, 2005. Accessed January 19, 2012. http://ochaonline.un.org/HUMANITARIANAPPEAL/webpage.asp?Page=1373.

Uppsala Conflict Data Program. "Active Conflicts by Region." Accessed July 26, 2011. http://www.pcr.uu.se/research/UCDP/graphs/conflict_region_2008.pdf.

Urtubey, Luis Márquez. "Non-Applicability of Statutes of Limitation for Crimes Committed in Argentina: Barrios Altos." *Southwestern Journal of Law and Trade in the Americas* 11 (2005):109–32.

Uvin, Peter. *Aiding Violence: The Development Enterprise in Rwanda.* West Hartford, CT: Kumarian Press, 1998.

Valdez, Patricia Tappatá. "El pasado, un tema central del presente. La búsqueda de verdad y justicia como construcción de una lógica democrática." In *Verdad, justicia y reparación: Desafíos para la democracia y la convivencia social*, edited by Gilda Pacheco Oreamuno, Lorena Acevedo Narea, and Guido Galli, 85–113. San José: IDEA/IIDH, 2005.

Valle, Mariano Fernández. "La Corte Suprema Argentina frente al legado de la última dictadura militar: reseña del fallo 'Simón.'" *Anuario de Derechos Humanos*, (2006): 165–74.

Van Dyke, Jon M., and Gerald W. Berkley. "Redressing Human Rights Abuses." *Denver Journal of International Law and Policy* 20 (1992): 243–67.

Vandeginste, Stef. "Justice, Reconciliation and Reparation after Genocide and Crimes against Humanity: The Proposed Establishment of Popular Gacaca Tribunals in Rwanda." Paper presented at the All-Africa Conference on African Principles of Conflict Resolution and Reconciliation, Addis Ababa, November 8–12, 1999.

Verbitsky, Horacio. *Civiles y militares: Memoria secreta de la transición.* Buenos Aires: Sudamericana, 2003.

*Confessions of an Argentine Dirty Warrior.* New York: The New Press, 2005.

Viana, Gilney, and Perly Cirpiano. *Fome de liberdade – A luta dos presos políticos pela anistia.* São Paulo: Fundação Perseu Abramo, 2009.

Villa-Vicencio, Charles and Erik Doxtader, eds. *The Provocations of Amnesty: Memory, Justice and Impunity.* South Africa: David Philip, 2003.

Vinjamuri, Leslie and Aaron Boesenecker. *Accountability and Peace Agreements: Mapping Trends from 1980 to 2006.* Geneva: Centre for Humanitarian Dialogue, 2007.

Waddell, Nicholas and Phil Clark, eds. *Courting Conflict? Peace, Justice and the ICC in Africa.* London: Royal African Society, 2008.

Waksman, Guillermo. "Uruguay: Consagración de la democracia tutelada." *Nueva Sociedad* 102 (julio–agosto 1989): 13–19.

Weichert, Marlon Alberto. "Responsabilidade internacional do estado brasileiro na promoção da justiça transicional." In *Memória e verdade – A Justiça de transição no estado democrático brasileiro*, edited by Inês Virgínia Prado Soares and Sandra Akemi Shimada Kishi, 153–168. Belo Horizonte: Editora Fórum, 2009.

Werchick, Leah. "Prospects for Justice in Rwanda's Citizen Tribunals," *Human Rights Brief* 8 (2001): 15–18.

Weschler, Lawrence. *A Miracle, A Universe: Settling Accounts with Torturers.* Chicago and London: University of Chicago Press, 1998.

Williams, Sarah. "Amnesties in International Law: The Experience of the Special Court of Sierra Leone." *Human Rights Law Review* 5 (2005): 271–309.

*Hybrid and Internationalised Criminal Tribunals.* Oxford: Hart Publishing, 2011.

Wing, John and Peter King. *Genocide in West Papua? The Role of the Indonesian State Apparatus and a Current Needs Assessment of the Papuan People.* Jayapura: West Papua Project at the Centre for Peace and Conflict Studies, University of Sydney, August 2005. Accessed October 2, 2011. http://sydney.edu.au/arts/peace_conflict/docs/WestPapuaGenocideRpt05.pdf.

World Bank. *Project Information Document: Uganda Emergency Demobilization and Reintegration Project.* World Bank, January 23, 2008.

Zagorski, Paul W. "Civil-Military Relations and Argentine Democracy: The Armed Forces under the Menem Government." *Armed Forces & Society* 20 (1994): 423–37.

Zalaquett, José. "La reconstrucción de la unidad nacional y el legado de violaciones de los derechos humanos." *Revista Perspectivas* Special Issue 2 (1999): 385–405.

# Index